Human-Centric Interfaces for Ambient Intelligence

Human-Centric Interfaces for Ambient Intelligence

Edited by

Hamid Aghajan
Stanford University, USA

Ramón López-Cózar Delgado
Universidad de Granada, Spain

Juan Carlos Augusto
University of Ulster, UK

AMSTERDAM • BOSTON • HEIDELBERG • LONDON
NEW YORK • OXFORD • PARIS • SAN DIEGO
SAN FRANCISCO • SINGAPORE • SYDNEY • TOKYO
Academic Press is an imprint of Elsevier

Academic Press is an imprint of Elsevier
30 Corporate Drive, Suite 400, Burlington, MA 01803, USA
525 B Street, Suite 1900, San Diego, California 92101-4495, USA
84 Theobald's Road, London WC1X 8RR, UK

Library of Congress Cataloging-in-Publication Data
Application submitted

British Library Cataloguing-in-Publication Data
A catalogue record for this book is available from the British Library.

ISBN: 978-0-12-374708-2

For information on all Academic Press publications
visit our Web site at www.elsevierdirect.com

Printed in the United States of America
09   10   11   12   6   5   4   3   2   1

Contents

PART 2 SPEECH PROCESSING AND DIALOGUE MANAGEMENT

PART 3 MULTIMODAL INTERFACES

PART 4   SMART ENVIRONMENT APPLICATIONS

Foreword

In the early days of cinema, its inventors produced simple film clips. Because little was known about people's perceptions, behaviors, expectations, and reactions, the field did not go far. The maturation of film as a medium occurred only when engineers and scientists began to work hand in hand with designers and artists to achieve a balance between science, engineering, and art.

Like early film, today's many new technologies do not exist in a vacuum. Rather, they powerfully affect people at work, at home, and on the street both individually and socially, impacting the way we interact with each other, the way we design and construct our buildings and cities, and the way we conduct daily life. However, many of these technologies are not well designed for the masses and many are implemented without fully taking into account the way people perceive and interact with information, and how their use may influence social behavior. This renders them much less effective than they could be.

Because of the pervasive nature and encompassing character of technologies that interface with people in different daily life environments, those who design, develop, and implement them have an important—and unprecedented—responsibility to incorporate user concerns and behavior norms in their design, development, and implementation efforts. Technologists are good in their respective areas, such as writing code and designing systems, but they generally do not have the necessary understanding of or experience in how people perceive information, interact socially, and use and interact with technology.

Human-centered computing (HCC) has emerged from the convergence of multiple disciplines and research areas that concern understanding human behavior, human communication, and the design of computational devices and interfaces. These areas include computer science, sociology, psychology, cognitive science, engineering, the arts, and graphic and industrial design.

Human-Centric Interfaces for Ambient Intelligence addresses these broad areas within the framework of Ambient Intelligence (AmI). Its fundamental message is twofold:

- Serving the user should be the central aim of an AmI application.
- A system should not demand specific training or technical knowledge on the part of the user if the intention is to achieve natural and efficient interaction.

Presented here is a snapshot of the state of the art in human-centric interface (HCI) design for ambient intelligence that lays out the fundamental concepts and introduces recent advances in practical application. The editors and contributors are well-known experts in signal and speech processing, computer vision, multimodal analysis, interface design, human–computer interaction, and related fields. The book is an excellent resource for researchers, students, and practitioners in human-centered computing in general and in ambient intelligence and multimodal human-centric interfaces in particular.

Nicu Sebe

University of Trento, Italy and University of Amsterdam, The Netherlands

May 2009

Preface

Ambient intelligence (AmI) is a fast-growing multidisciplinary field that is ushering in new opportunities for many areas of research to have a significant impact on society. Its foundation is the enrichment of the environment, through sensing and processing technologies, to understand, analyze, anticipate, and adapt to events and to users and their activities, preferences, intentions, and behaviors. Basically, AmI gathers real-time information from the environment and combines it with historical data accumulated over time, or a knowledge base, to provide user services.

Interfacing with the user is a major aspect of any AmI application. While interfaces may employ different technologies, the underlying notion of user centricity dominates their design. In AmI, the traditional paradigm of human–computer interfaces, in which users must adapt to computers by learning how to use them, is replaced by a new one, in which computers adapt to users and learn how to interact with them in the most natural way. The monopolar emphasis on the user in the new terminology (human-centric) reflects the shift from the bipolar phrase (human–computer) used in the traditional terminology.

Considering that serving the user is the central aim of the AmI application and that AmI systems should not demand special training and technical knowledge on the user's part, user interface design is of paramount importance. This book offers a description of the state of the art in human-centric interface design for AmI applications, focusing not only on fundamental concepts but also on recent advances in practical applications. The different parts of the book provide a perspective on the research potentials in the field through studies on visual, audio, and multi-modal interfaces and applications in smart environments.

AMBIENT INTELLIGENCE

AmI has been presented not just as another step toward embedding technological advances in society but also as a new computing paradigm that will revolutionize the way we conceive the relationship between computing systems and users. At present, in order to benefit from traditional computing devices, users must have some degree of knowledge and experience. This restricts the groups of people that can benefit from computing power and in some cases has resulted in the creation of the so-called "digital divide."

Integration of multiple sensors in a distributed human-centric interface embodies new research and development opportunities in algorithm design based on collaborative sensing and processing, data fusion, event interpretation, context extraction, and behavior modeling. The development of proper algorithmic interfaces between quantitative information units (in charge of sensing and processing) and high-level qualitative information units (in charge of context and behavior models) is another area of growing interdisciplinary interest within the field of ambient intelligence. Figure 1 is an example of the multiple layers of processing and reasoning leading to the accumulation of knowledge from user observations and the deduction of a user behavior model based on activities and events observed.

HUMAN-CENTRIC DESIGN

Human-centric design has been interpreted in a few different ways depending on the application or technology context. For example, in vision-based reasoning, where employment of cameras may have implications for user privacy, "smart cameras" can abstract information by local processing and then delete the images captured. Another interpretation of human-centric design is systems that are easy or intuitive to use without the need for training. This has paramount implications for adoption of the technology by the masses and for reaching segments of the

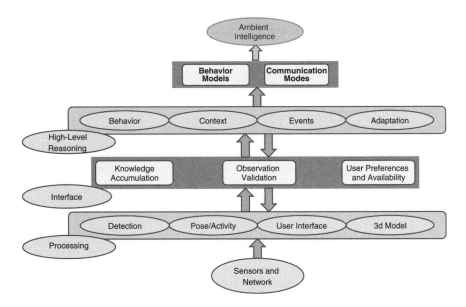

FIGURE 1

Multilayer data processing and reasoning for modeling user behavior and preferences in an AmI application.

community on the other side of the "digital divide." A final example of human centricity relates to smart environments that sense and interpret user-based events and attribute without requiring wearable sensors.

Yet, in the context of applications that are designed to assist users with physical disabilities, human-centric design may take on a totally different meaning, one in which, for example, a system may provide assistance to its user, employing the same interfaces developed for security or biometric systems such as iris detection, eye tracking, or fingerprint identification (biometric systems are often regarded as intrusive as they are mostly used in network-centric surveillance applications). In such applications, both the system and the user will go through a training phase to learn each other's behavior and response mechanisms over time.

An important consideration in introducing new technologies into daily life is the social implications created, which can potentially promote, inhibit, or in different ways reshape the way a technology is adopted and utilized by various user segments. The pace of technology development often limits a developer's timely access to usage models obtained from observations in the field. However, such information may offer vital design paradigm clues at the early stages of technology development. For example, privacy concerns of users of a camera-based assisted-living application can guide the developer in designing a system based on smart cameras employing local processing in such a way that no image data is sent out. This decision will in turn have implications for the types of vision-processing algorithms needed, as well as the communication bandwidth and latency factors to be considered.

Thus, while the notion of human centricity finds many interpretations, its true meaning goes beyond any of the individual aspects that have been discussed in the literature. It truly refers to a new paradigm in the development and use of technology to serve the user in whatever form and flavor best offer the intended experience of the application of interest. In the new paradigm, privacy management, ease of use, unobtrusive design, and customization can each be part of the definition of a human-centric interface.

These factors are not regarded as rigid requirements when the essence of human centricity is considered, meaning that different levels of each factor and relative priorities among them must be derived from the context and objective of the application. For example, the same vision-sensing mechanism that may be perceived as intrusive when used in surveillance applications can be employed in a human-centric paradigm to improve the quality of life of patients and the elderly by timely detection of abnormal events or accidents.

Figure 2 illustrates the new application design space based on novel concepts and methods in user-centric smart environments, ambient intelligence, and social networks. Many applications can be enabled in this space, through proper interfacing of a sensing system, a processing and reasoning engine, a networking infrastructure, and an interactive response system, when a user-centric framework is adopted for technology development.

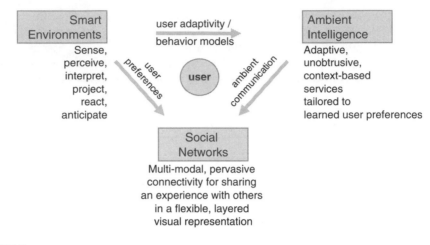

FIGURE 2

User-centric design space enabling novel application domains.

VISION AND VISUAL INTERFACES

Along with other sensing modalities, cameras embedded in a smart environment offer much potential for a variety of novel human-centric interfaces through the provisioning of rich information. Vision-based sensing fits well with pervasive sensing and computing environments, enabling novel interactive user-based applications that do not require wearable sensors. Access to interpretations of human pose and gesture obtained from visual data over time enables higher-level reasoning modules to deduce the user's actions, context, and behavior, and to decide on suitable actions or responses to a given situation. Local processing of acquired video at the source camera facilitates operation of scalable vision networks by avoiding transfer of raw images. Additional motivation for distributed processing stems from an effort to preserve the user's privacy by processing the data near the source.

Vision networks offer access to quantitative knowledge about events of interest such as the user's location and other attributes. Such quantitative knowledge can either complement or provide specific qualitative distinctions for AmI-based functions. In turn, qualitative representations can provide clues on which features would be of interest to derive from the visual data, allowing the vision network to adjust its processing operation according to the interpretation state. In this way the interaction between the vision-processing module and the reasoning module in principle enables both sides to function more effectively.

For example, in a human gesture analysis application, the observed elements of gesture extracted by the vision module can assist the AmI-based high-level reasoning module in its interpretative tasks, while the deductions made by the reasoning system can provide feedback to the vision system from the available contextual or

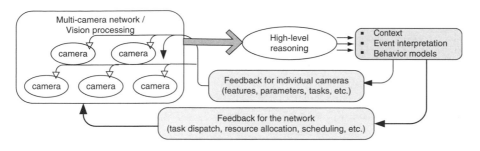

FIGURE 3

Example interactions between vision-processing and high-level reasoning modules.

behavior model knowledge to direct its processing toward the more interesting features and attributes. Figure 3 illustrates these interactions.

Various technologies have been explored for receiving explicit or implicit user input. Many applications interact with the user through the presentation of information on displays. Supporting remote collaboration among users is a growing area of development. In collaborative applications the participants may use gestures or a touch screen to communicate data or expressions (see Chapter 1, Face-to-Face Collaborative Interfaces).

The availability of inexpensive sensing and processing hardware and powerful software tools has created unprecedented opportunities in applications for interactive art, offering new visual interfaces, driving experimentation based on the combination of art and technology, and enabling a new domain for expressiveness in both audience-interactive and performance art (see Chapter 2, Computer Vision Interfaces for Interactive Art).

Many interactive applications obtain valuable information from the user's facial analytics. Gaze, with its various behavioral elements, plays an important role in social interaction. A person's area of interest, duration of attention, facial expressions accompanying a gaze, and even mental state can be inferred by studying gaze through a vision-based interface. Such inference can often provide a situation-aware response or facilitate acquisition of the user's behavior model within the prevailing application context (see Chapter 3, Ubiquitous Gaze: Using Gaze at the Interface).

Vision-based processing normally leads to the measurement of a set of quantitative parameters from the environment under observation. As applications in ambient intelligence start to demand a higher level of cognition, they call for the abstraction of acquired information, which is often obtained under uncertainty, to a semantic level, and even possibly its description using a natural language (see Chapter 4, Exploiting Natural Language Generation in Scene Interpretation).

Description of visual interpretation results in human-centric interfaces can also be symbolically represented through a language whose elements reflect human actions to a fine granularity. Such a language can offer a universal platform for describing human activities in a variety of applications (see Chapter 5, The Language of Action: A New Tool for Human-Centric Interfaces).

SPEECH PROCESSING AND DIALOGUE MANAGEMENT

Speech processing involves a number of technologies to enable speech-based interaction between computers and humans. These include automatic speech recognition, speaker recognition, spoken language understanding, and speech synthesis. Dialogue management aims to provide a speech-based interaction that is as natural, comfortable, and friendly as possible, especially taking into account the state-of-the-art limitations of automatic speech recognition. Interfaces supporting speech processing technologies are appealing in human-centric applications, as they enable, for example, turning lights on or off by talking directly into a microphone or ambiently to speech sensors embedded in the environment.

Automatic speech recognition (ASR) is the basis of a speech-based interface. However, in spite of advances made in recent years, the performance of ASR systems degrades drastically when there is mismatch between system training and testing conditions. Hence, it is necessary to employ techniques to increase the robustness of these systems so that they can be usable in a diversity of acoustic environments, considering different speakers, task domains, and speaking styles (see Chapter 6, Robust Speech Recognition Under Noisy Ambient Conditions).

Speaker recognition is the process of the identification of the current user by the system through speech signals. This is important in human-centric AmI interfaces in order to adapt the interface to the preferences and/or needs of the current user and to optimize its performance (see Chapter 7, Speaker Recognition in Smart Environments).

The goal of spoken language understanding is to infer a speaker's intentions in order to build intelligent interfaces. This is a challenging topic not only because of the inherent difficulties of natural language processing but also because of the possible existence of recognition errors in the sentences to be analyzed (see Chapter 8, Machine Learning Approaches to Spoken Language Understanding).

Dialogue management techniques are fundamental in speech-based interfaces given the current limitations of state-of-the-art ASR systems. These techniques enable the interface to decide whether it must ask the user to confirm recognized words, clarify the intended message, or provide additional information. For example, the user may say "Turn on the light" in a room where there are several lamps, requiring the interface to ask for clarification (see Chapter 9, The Role of Spoken Dialogue in User–Environment Interaction).

The goal of speech synthesis is to enable the speech-based interface to "talk" to the user. However, even though significant advances have been made in recent years, current speech synthesis systems are far from offering the same flexibility that humans have. They can produce speech that is arguably pleasant to human ears, but they are limited in a number of aspects, such as their affective processing capabilities and their adaptation of synthesized output to different environments and user needs (see Chapter 10, Speech Synthesis Systems in Ambient Intelligence Environments).

MULTIMODAL INTERFACES

Ambient intelligence systems must deliver interaction in the best possible way for users. The infrastructure thus needs a combination of sensing and actuating capabilities to determine how the system is structured and how it operates. Multimodal interfaces, which have a place of their own in human-centric interface design, represent a strategic area of development in ambient intelligence as well. Modern technology is continuously offering new opportunities for interaction with the user through a diversity of modalities.

Ambient augmented reality provides ways to make invisible information visible to the user of an AmI system. Augmented reality interfaces enhance the user's real environment with a virtual information overlay. Combining this technology with ambient intelligence offers the user visualized access to relevant data in the system via a tangible and seamless interface, and hence provides the user with ways to make better decisions and to better understand the outputs and behavior of the system or the decisions it makes on the user's behalf (see Chapter 11, Tangible Interfaces for Ambient Augmented Reality Applications).

Computing devices and interfaces supporting an ambient intelligence system are embedded in the physical environment so that users can interact with them naturally, as they do with the physical environment. The various devices and interfaces are interconnected and must work together even though they have different input and output capabilities depending on their purpose. Together they provide services that may go beyond their separate capabilities. Interaction in such an environment, where the physical and digital worlds intertwine, calls for new design paradigms (see Chapter 12, Physical Browsing and Selection—Easy Interaction with Ambient Services).

Richer ways to analyze context are being investigated given the tremendous potential for understanding users through nonverbal cues. One such line of research focuses on exploiting the richness of gestures, both intentional and unintentional, as a means of communication. Qualitative analysis of gestures can facilitate understanding of a user's intended message and at the same time pick up subtler clues about the mood, habits, or background of the user (see Chapter 13, Nonsymbolic Gestural Interaction for Ambient Intelligence).

Coupled with the development of richer interaction between humans and artificial systems through a diversity of modalities is the need to evaluate the performance of and differences between interaction systems. Both quantitative and qualitative parameters can be used to measure a system's dimensions, including performance, usability, acceptability, and quality of experience. A challenging aspect of assessing the adequacy of such systems is the variety of domains and user preferences to be accommodated and measured in serving a specific individual (see Chapter 14, Evaluation of Multimodal Interfaces for Ambient Intelligence).

SMART ENVIRONMENT APPLICATIONS

Underpinning the promise of smart environments that sense, perceive, interpret, anticipate, and react to events and activities is a confluence of advances in sensing, processing, and networking solutions. Hence, research and development in smart environments offer opportunities in a multitude of disciplines involving sensor fusion, human-centric interfaces, networking, pervasive computing, and responsive environments.

Based on the premise of user-centric data extraction and decision making, smart applications support interactivity through interpretation of user gestures, region of interest, and user interactions with the surrounding environment's components. Thanks to the proliferation of inexpensive sensors, including image sensors, and embedded processors, unprecedented potential exists for novel real-time applications such as immersive human–computer interfaces for virtual reality, gaming, teleconferencing, smart presentations, and gesture-based control, as well as other human-centric applications such as abnormal event and accidental fall detection in assisted living and elderly care.

Many user-centric applications benefit from a user behavior model with which the system can tailor its services by learning a user's preferences, habits, and sensitivities, and by better interpreting or anticipating the user's state during interactions. Such models can be created online as the system engages with and observes the user's activities and interactions over time (see Chapter 15, New Frontiers in Machine Learning for Predictive User Modeling).

Through a variety of sensors, smart environments support their inhabitants, the users, by perceiving their actions and states and offering services in health, recreation, comfort, entertainment, and multimedia. Such services can invite, guide, stimulate, advise, and engage the user, with the aim of improving physical or mental health and well-being or serving educational and training purposes. The entertainment aspects of these services play an important role in their sustained usage by providing motivation and interest (see Chapter 16, Games and Entertainment in Ambient Intelligence Environments).

Applications based on camera systems in retail environments have been discussed in various contexts as a way to enhance a user's shopping experience. Smart-environment applications such as these, especially if based on imaging the user, need to pass the threshold of user acceptance to become marketable. To that end, they must take the issue of privacy of user information seriously and include solid privacy management in their design. This will give users the option to control the system when they are imaged and will offer them assurances about the safety of the sensed information. User acceptance studies can provide system designers with helpful hints at the early stages of technology development about how the system will eventually be perceived (see Chapter 17, Natural and Implicit Information-Seeking Cues in Responsive Technology).

Devices populating future smart environments need to provide nonexperts with easy-to-use and nonintrusive interfaces, and they must exploit natural communication. A spoken dialogue system is one of the key enabling technologies for a user-friendly human-centric interaction (see Chapter 18, Spoken Dialogue Systems for Intelligent Environments).

Besides upholding user privacy and offering unobtrusive interfaces, systems built to serve smart environments need to consider the user's ability to handle their installation and management. While much progress has been made in algorithm and solution development for home-based applications such as those relating to safety, health, well-being, and comfort, issues related to how these systems can be installed, operated, calibrated, trained, and fixed by the user have largely remained outside the scope of research and development. Interactions that are seamless and convenient for users are paramount in achieving acceptance and adoption of the technology (see Chapter 19, Deploying Context-Aware Health Technology at Home: Human-Centric Challenges).

CONCLUSIONS

Smart environment systems will enter people's daily life when their technological development is accompanied by and complemented with user-centric considerations of privacy, natural and unobtrusive interfaces, and user-friendly installation and setup. Visual, speech, and multimodal interfacing systems and methods are the technological foundations of numerous applications to serve the user. They will be accepted only when mechanisms that ensure truly human-centric operation are carefully incorporated in their design from the early stages of technology development.

This book offers examples of pioneering work in the area of human-centric interface design for AmI systems. The concepts, methods, and implementations described in its chapters provide a snapshot of the possibilities, each based on a different way of interfacing with the user or on a particular method of extracting information from user data. We hope that the concepts presented here will provide guidelines for researchers and developers working on smart environments to better envision the opportunities in the field based on a human-centric approach to user interface design.

ACKNOWLEDGMENTS

We would like to acknowledge the contribution of a number of people who helped make this book a reality. We are grateful to Tim Pitts of Elsevier for his encouragement and support of this project. Jeff Freeland offered us valuable editorial support. Many thanks to Melanie Benson and Greg Dezarn-O'Hare of Academic Press for helping with this book's organization. Finally, we are grateful to the leading researchers who agreed to contribute chapters. Their active and timely cooperation is highly appreciated.

Hamid Aghajan,
Ramón López-Cózar Delgado,
and Juan Carlos Augusto

Vision and Visual Interfaces

Face-to-Face Collaborative Interfaces

Aaron J. Quigley and Florin Bodea

*School of Computer Science and Informatics, Complex & Adaptive Systems
Laboratory, University College, Dublin, Ireland*

ABSTRACT

*The presentation of information as a large display and the use of such displays
to support collaboration in face-to-face activities have long been commonplace.
Computationally enhanced displays relying on the form factor of whiteboards,
surfaces, tables, benches, and desks now afford face-to-face* computer-supported
interaction *and collaboration not possible with classical desktop or mobile computing. This chapter provides an introduction to research and developments in
multitouch input technologies that can be used to realize large interactive tabletop or "surface user interfaces." Such hardware systems, along with supporting
software, allow for applications that can be controlled through direct touch or
multitouch. Further, a review of gestural interactions and design guidelines
for surface user interface design for collaboration is also provided.*

Key words: tabletop, HCI, surface user interface, gestural interface, design guidelines.

1.1 INTRODUCTION

People have been using large displays to present information for centuries. Ancient civilizations, including American Indian, Egyptian, Greek, Roman, and Mayan, used wall posters of papyrus, wall paintings, frescoes, and murals to announce and advertise social, economic, and political events [1]. As manufacturing and printing technologies became more advanced, ever larger displays proliferated. Now the many large static displays we see around us include billboards, conference posters, signs, and even the Goodyear blimp. Generally, such printed or fabricated displays are referred to as *static* as they offer limited interaction and cannot be easily repurposed. The use of lighting, animatronics, and mechanical movement has brought to some of these static displays an aspect of dynamism.

Large displays such as chalkboards were introduced over two centuries ago and remain in use today. Now bulletin boards and whiteboards are ubiquitous as well. Each type of display is employed in the sharing and communication of information in both face-to-face and asynchronous settings. These display technologies are simple and low cost because they are *reusable*. While many wouldn't consider a flat surface, such as a table, bench, or desk, to be a large display surface, it clearly is. Placing static objects or printed or written items on a blackboard or work surface allows one person or a group to easily organize large amounts of information and make them accessible to many others.

Display and projection technologies have transformed such static displays by adding *live* displayed or projected information. Novel forms of human computer interaction such as multitouch technology have further transformed these devices into interactive systems [3], as shown in Figure 1.1. Users can now interact directly with

FIGURE 1.1

Users sharing photos in Sharepic [2].

the displayed objects by simply touching the display, thus creating a sense of immediacy and naturalness. This sense of immediacy gives rise to a range of human–computer interactions and provides support for multiuser multisurface collaborative activities [4].

Other technologies are further helping to bridge the digital–physical divide by coupling real objects (eyeglasses, phones, pens, or blocks) with projected information. The aim is to weave such new forms of interaction and computation into the fabric of our lives until they are indistinguishable from it [5].

Systems exhibiting ambient intelligence (AmI) must consider the broader range of inputs now possible with current desktop, mobile, and gaming devices and applications. In practice everyday objects will become sites for sensing, output, and processing along with user input [6]. Examples of data or knowledge AmI systems can rely on as input involve spatial information, identity, environment, activity, schedules, and agendas, along with data that can be mined and inferred from other measurements or historical analysis.

Broadly speaking the range of implicit inputs to an AmI system can be called *context data* whether sensed or inferred. Context includes information from a human (physiological state), the sensed environment (environmental state), and the computational environment (computational state) that can be provided to alter an application's behavior [7, 8]. In contrast, explicit inputs from the user can include speech or movement of any kind. It is the explicit forms of human movement in face-to-face collaboration that are the focus of this chapter.

Large horizontal or vertical shared displays are an aspect of AmI or ubiquitous computing (UbiComp) in which computation is everywhere and computer functions are integrated in everything. As mentioned, computationally enhanced basic objects such as whiteboards, tables, benches, and desks allow enhanced forms of face-to-face computer-supported interaction and collaboration not possible with conventional desktop or mobile computing. For example, using digital photos the projected collaborative tabletop photo sharing in Figure 1.1 offers older people the social sharing and story telling common with physical photos. In Sharepic, users do not feel they are using a computer to collaborate; instead, the medium supports the actions directly. Ultimately, computer-supported face-to-face collaboration will become so common in bars, restaurants, schools, offices, and homes that no one will notice its presence, in spite of its power to enhance our lives.

The graphical user interface (GUI) of a personal computer relies on keyboard, screen, and mouse for input and output. GUIs typically offer the Window, icon, menu, pointer (WIMP) metaphor as an intuitive view of the computer, compared with the classical command line (textual) interface. Modern desktop operating systems are built around the GUI, WIMP, and keyboard/screen/mouse concepts, with interaction support for a single person. Technological advancements have moved computing beyond the desktop with the widespread adoption of mobile phones with keypads, PDAs with styli, tablets with styli, and touch screens. More recent developments have seen the adoption of game controller inputs or gesture-driven controls for game platforms.

In spite of these advancements, however, the tie between the single machine, the single application, and the single user remains. Typical desktop machines do not support two keyboards or two mice to allow people to enter information at the same time; game systems often split the screen, effectively carving out sections for each person; and combining personal devices (PDA with iPhone, say) into a collective ecosystem is often not possible.

Many AmI scenarios suggest radically new affordances and modes of interaction in the simplest and most basic operations of our daily lives. Two examples are turning a door handle while receiving haptic feedback on workflow status and clothing items that inform washing machines of their cleaning instructions. By contrast, the class of interface we consider here relies on common (e.g., face-to-face) interactions in well-understood social contexts such as meetings, or gatherings in a restaurant, as shown in the Microsoft Surface in Figure 1.2.[1] Technologies to realize such computationally enhanced experience include computer vision, speech recognition, image processing, RFID, and projected and embedded displays. However, making active many of the surfaces we interact with on a daily basis requires the computational support and power they offer to reside at the periphery of our attention and go unnoticed until needed. The challenge here is not providing the next-generation mouse and keyboard but instead ensuring that sites that already support natural face-to-face collaboration operate fluidly and seamlessly once computation is introduced.

Interactive displays that support multiple users and simultaneous interaction in typical face-to-face activities will become standard. A display's form factor typically defines its social benefits [10]. A mobile phone display can be comfortably viewed

FIGURE 1.2

Users sharing a map on the Microsoft Surface. Courtesy Microsoft.

[1]Copyright 2008 Microsoft. All rights reserved.

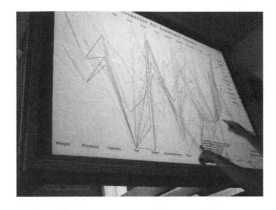

FIGURE 1.3

FTIR-based system displaying a parallel coordinate visualization [9].

by one user at a time; a large poster board is visible to multiple users simultaneously; an interactive surface such as the DiamondTouch [11] or the FTIR display shown in Figure 1.3 affords simultaneous interaction by many users. A display's physical constraints, such as real estate, orientation, and mass, strongly affect the social interaction it supports, and this is further constrained by the users' visual angle, territoriality, and capability to reach content and manipulate the display [3]. Interactive displays have been studied extensively in related work. Here the focus is on how touch or multitouch interactive displays can support face-to-face collaboration in AmI scenarios.

1.2 BACKGROUND

The classical GUI has been successfully used since its inception, but the limitations of basic mouse and keyboard input are obvious, leading to the demand for new input and interaction modalities that will enhance the interface. Available since the early 70s in various forms, touch-sensitive surfaces are one solution. The PLATO IV,[2] developed at the University of Illinois in 1972 and one of the first single-touch screens introduced, has a 16×16 array of touch-sensitive locations. One of the first multitouch systems was the *flexible machine interface* [12]. Here the touch-sensitive surface consisted of a frosted-glass sheet with special optical properties. When the sheet was touched, a black spot appeared that could be captured by the camera behind the sheet and recognized using simple computer vision.

---

[2]*http://en.wikipedia.org/wiki/Plato_computer.* Last accessed January 2009.

Importantly, this was only an input device; the user viewed the visual feedback on a different device.

Buxton[3] underscored the difference between touch tablets and touch screens as follows:

- *Touch tablets*. The touch-sensitive surface is not used for feedback display.
- *Touch screen*. The touch-sensitive surface is overlaid by the display.

The *soft machine* concept [13] builds on the classical hard machine concept (e.g., an oven or washing machine). It uses graphics software to generate images of controls (e.g., keys, pushbutton switches, and slides on the screen) to give the appearance of a hard machine. To ensure the illusion, the soft machine display is touch-sensitive, enabling a user to operate its controls by direct touch, as if they were physical controls. This connection between display and action increases the sense of immediacy in the interface.

The XEROX 5700 Electronic Printing System [14], the first commercial soft machine, has obvious parallels with the current generation of multitouch display prototypes and systems. In the original, all controls of the soft machine were on a black-and-white touch screen display. The Lemur,[4] an advanced example of a soft machine, released in 2003 is a multitouch music controller device with all controls (knobs and sliders) virtually created on the display. This interface is customizable to user preferences. Other advances such as haptic output can overcome the lack of tactile feedback on soft versions of hard machines. Sony's tactile touch screen feedback is based on an actuator, constructed as a multilayer sandwich of thin (0.28-μm) piezoceramic films, that "bends" the screen. The haptic effect can be coupled with visual or audio feedback to simulate the feel of buttons that click [15].

Rather than a dedicated sensing surface, alternative approaches often rely on computer vision for sensing. VideoPlace is a vision-based system capable of tracking hands and thus recognizing and interpreting a rich set of gestures [16]. Users are placed against a neutral background, making it possible to process their silhouette image. The system can detect when they "touch" the graphical objects projected on the wall in front of them and react to the contact. The concepts demonstrated in VideoPlace are used in current camera-based multitouch systems that are able to "see" in front of the display. Diffuse illumination or capacitance-based systems (described in detail in Section 1.4) can discriminate between touch and hover.

The Digital Desk [17] uses optical techniques to sense hands, fingers, and objects being moved on the desk's surface. It operates by projecting images on the desktop where documents can be placed. Using an overhead camera, it reacts to interaction with the objects on the desk and can scan the documents placed there. Although

---

[3]*http://www.billbuxton.com/multitouchOverview.html*. Last accessed January 2009.
[4]JazzMutant. *http://www.jazzmutant.com/*. Last accessed January 2009.

this is a front-projection system and occlusion can occur, the Digital Desk supports multitouch interaction through the use of both hands to rotate or scale documents or to manipulate objects on the desk.

Akin to the Digital Desk is Play Anywhere, a top-projection camera input system that allows multitouch user interaction [18]. It relies on a short-throw digital projector for top projection, an infrared illuminant, and an overhead camera to view the desk. These are all placed on the same stand, which makes this setup very portable because it can transform any flat surface into a multitouch sensitive display. The system can detect and track hands, fingers, and objects using a visual bar code scheme. The infrared illuminator illuminates the environment and causes a finger to cast an IR shadow on the display. If the shadow disappears, the system considers that the finger is touching the surface. By measuring the distance between the finger and its shadow, the system can also detect a hover.

More recent examples of touch-sensitive surface technologies include the Apple iTouch/iPhone product line and the SMART Table,[5] (shown in Figure 1.4). The SMART Table uses digital vision touch (DViT), which relies on small cameras embedded in a device around the rim of the display [19]. When an object enters the field of view (FOV), the angle within the FOV of the camera is calculated. The SMART Table is multitouch and, multiuser, designed for primary education applications. Other examples include ThinSight [20], developed for small LCD panels only, which supports multitouch input using hands and objects (or a stylus in N-trig's[6] case). ThinSight uses a 2D grid of retro-reflective optosensors (containing an IR light

FIGURE 1.4

SMART Table primary-education team-challenge application.

[6]*http://www.n-trig.com/*. Last accessed January 2009.

emitter and an optically isolated IR light detector, allowing it to emit light and to detect the intensity of incident light at the same time) placed behind an LCD panel. When a reflective object is placed in front of the panel, a part of the light is reflected back and detected by the optosensor. The data generated by the sensor grid is a low-resolution grayscale "image" that can be processed to extract information about the number of contact points and their position. N-trig uses a capacitive sensing system (i.e., signals are emitted that capacitively couple with users when they touch the surface) mounted in front of the LCD panel to detect touch, and a specialized sensor to detect and track the stylus.

1.3 SURFACE USER INTERFACE

A tangible user interface (TUI), initially termed a graspable user interface [22], as shown in Figure 1.5, is one that integrates both the representation and the control of computation in the same physical artifact. It helps provide physical form to computational artifacts and digital information, and, unlike a GUI, it "... *makes information directly graspable and manipulable with haptic feedback*" [21]. The informal definition of a touch screen given in Section 1.2 can be made more rigorous and broad when defined as a "surface user interface" (SUI), which relies on a self-illuminated (e.g., LCD) or projected horizontal or vertical interactive surface coupled with computation control on the same physical surface. As with a TUI, the outputs from and inputs to a SUI are tightly coupled. SUI-based touch screens range from small personal devices such as the iPhone to large public interactive surfaces such as the DiamondTouch.

SUIs are used in public places (kiosks, ATMs) or in small personal devices (PDAs, iPhones) where a separate keyboard and mouse cannot or should not be used. Basic SUIs have been common for over 20 years in the form of interactive kiosks, ATMs, and point-of-sale systems, which rely on touch-screen technology with simple button interfaces. The basic technologies in many products, such as the Nintendo DS with

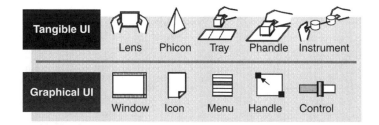

FIGURE 1.5

TUI instantiations of GUI elements [21]. Courtesy Brygg Ullmer.

its resistive touch screen, were established in hardware research decades ago. The recent heightened interest in SUIs such as the iPhone generally stems from the low cost of production and the interaction styles they afford beyond the desktop paradigm.

The current generation of SUIs suitable for face-to-face interaction are built on LCD displays or form-factored into walls or coffee tables. In their current form they cannot be considered a "basic object" in Weiser's vision. However, display technologies are now ubiquitous, and if SUI interaction styles can be woven into the environments and activities of everyday life and their industrial design improved, we can then achieve *invisibility in action*. As noted previously, the size of the display often determines the social benefits it supports. Thus, for face-to-face collaboration larger interactive horizontal or vertical surfaces are key. These have been researched and developed for over 20 years and from a technology perspective can be classified as front-projected, rear-projected, and self-illuminated.

For front-projected displays, the Digital Desk [17] is the seminal example. One application is a calculator based on a paper sheet with printed buttons. Pressing the paper buttons is recognized by a vision system and the current total is projected into the total square. DiamondTouch from MERL [11], Sony's SmartSkin [23], AudioPad [24], and TANGerINE [25] all rely on front projection onto a touch-sensitive surface or use computer vision for sensing. Front-projected systems may suffer from occlusion of the projected image or camera line of sight caused by body parts. Capacitive systems such as SmartSkin and DiamondTouch are described further in Section 1.4.2.

Rear-projected SUIs avoid the problem of occlusion of the projected image or a camera's line of sight. These large touch-sensitive SUIs can be seen in nightly newscasts, during political elections, and in other media. TouchLight, shown in Figure 1.6, relies on a rear-projected display and an infrared illuminant on a semi-transparent acrylic plastic plane fitted with HoloScreen material [26]. The reacTable has a horizontal orientation and can operate with physical objects and fiducial markers [27]. FTIR-based displays [28] rely on the total internal reflection (TIR) of light being frustrated by touch (see Section 1.4.1). The Microsoft Surface[7] is a commercial-level multitouch, multiuser interactive surface. Based on experience with TouchLight [26] the Microsoft Surface is realized using diffused illumination technology (described in detail in Section 1.4.1). For a comparison of diffused illumination with frustrated total internal reflection of light see Figure 1.10. The Microsoft Surface can detect input from multiple hands and fingers, and it uses multiple cameras so its video input has high resolution. In addition, it can detect and identify objects and their position on the table. Recent advances such as the UlteriorScape [29] use a combination of multiple rear projectors and lumisty film for viewpoint-dependent face-to-face collaborative displays.

Self-projected systems are typically developed around LCD or plasma screen technologies as shown in Figure 1.4. Advances such as ThinSight [20] may result in

---

[7]*http://www.microsoft.com/surface/index.html*. Last accessed December 2008.

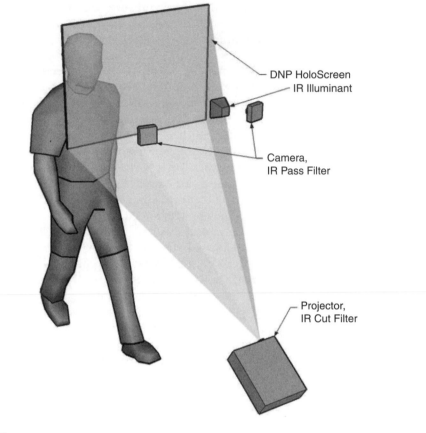

DNP HoloScreen
IR Illuminant

Camera,
IR Pass Filter

Projector,
IR Cut Filter

FIGURE 1.6

TouchLight physical configuration [26]. Courtesy Andy Wilson.

every future large screen being multitouch enabled. Alternatively, the OLED manufacturing process may be enhanced to form-factor IR LEDs and sensing elements directly into the same space as the pixels. Such developments would radically alter the nature of surface user interface research and development if all displays were *multitouch ready*.

1.4 MULTITOUCH

Multitouch SUIs can be mounted vertically on walls or horizontally on tables. They are capable of sensing the location of finger(s) when contact with the surface is made. The size of the surface can vary from a few inches to a few feet diagonally [30]. Buxton described the key features of SUIs in terms of touch tables which remain true today. Because multitouch SUIs have no mechanical intermediate device that can get lost or damaged, they are also appropriate for pointing tasks in moving or vibrating environments. Users can interact with all ten fingers at once compared to just one mouse per hand. Because of their simple one-piece construction they are suitable for intense use in clean or dirty environments.

As the most important advantage over mouse/keyboard interfaces is the possibility of multiple points of contact, experiments have been undertaken on two-handed input [31]. One experiment was composed of two tasks: selection and positioning and navigation and selection. The results show that for the first task all but one subject used both hands simultaneously and that parallel execution of subtasks led to a decrease in execution time from about 2.35 ms to 1.85 ms for novice users and from 1.8 ms to 1.6 ms for expert users. The second task was to select specific words from a document. The subjects were split again into novice and expert, but the general trend was the same: two-handed input completion times were lower than those for one-handed input by 15% for experts and 25% for novices. Also, the difference between expert and novice users when using two-handed input decreased significantly from 85% to 32% for one-handed input. These experiments demonstrate that splitting tasks between two hands leads to increased productivity, and that users tend to use both hands if possible, as such behavior is natural. When the opportunity presents itself and the task is suitable, users naturally revert to coordinated multi-hand interaction.

1.4.1 Camera-Based Systems

One of the first attempts at a large interactive display based on camera input was the Liveboard [32], which, although it used a stylus-based interaction method, was built on the principles used by the following prototypes. The pen used was cordless and had four buttons to control different states. These states gave Liveboard a slight advantage in this area over finger-touch displays. The pen sent a beam of optical light to the pen detection module behind the screen, from where the digitized pen position readings were transmitted to the PC through a serial port. The pen was accurate to less than 1 mm and could transmit 90 xy positions per second. Figure 1.7 is a diagram of the Liveboard prototype. A positive feature of Liveboard was that it could be operated from a distance; this allowed natural gestures such as sweeping motions to be used to execute operations, including scrolling.

HoloWall is a vertical touch-sensitive display [33], and as seen in Figure 1.8 its configuration is straightforward. The image together with IR light is projected from the back of the screen. When the hand approaches the screen, the IR light is reflected and the IR-sensitive camera captures the point of touch. The input image from the camera is processed and the touch points are separated from the background. HoloWall's advantage over Liveboard is that it can detect more than one point of contact and is easier to implement even for large displays. Because the IR

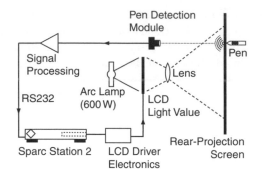

FIGURE 1.7

Functional diagram of Liveboard [32].

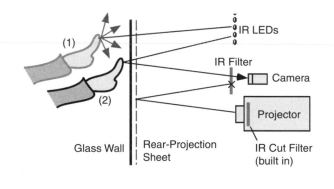

FIGURE 1.8

Configuration of the HoloWall [33]. Courtesy Jun Rekimoto.

light is projected from the back, it is not always possible to distinguish between a touch and a very close hover, as the light is reflected even when close to the surface.

TouchLight [26], as shown in Figure 1.6, relies on a setup similar to HoloWall's. However, here two cameras are used behind the screen and there is no diffusing projection surface. Instead, a different type of material is used on top of the acrylic sheet—namely, a DNP HoloScreen, which is a refractive holographic film that scatters light from a rear projector when the light hits it at a particular angle and is transparent to all other light. As there is no diffusing surface, the cameras can see beyond the surface and the system can achieve high-resolution imagery of objects on the surface. TouchLight supports user and face recognition capabilities and the scanning of documents. By using two cameras, TouchLight can determine how far objects are from the screen. After lens distortion correction, the images from both cameras are fused to obtain the final input image, which is used to recognize multiple touches and over-time gestures.

The metaDESK [34], developed as part of the Tangible Bits project [35], is a complex system with an almost horizontal top surface (Figure 1.9). This drafting table orientation is similar to that in many of the systems so far described (back-projected screen, IR lamps, and cameras) with the addition of active and passive lenses and a range of physical objects for interaction with the surface. The largest component of the metaDESK is a back-projected graphical surface for display of 2D geographical information within the Tangible Geospace prototype. The active lens is an arm-mounted flat-panel display and serves to display 3D geographical information projected in 2D on the desk's surface. This display panel is tracked by an Ascension Flock of Birds' 6-DOF magnetic-field position sensor. The passive lenses are created out of fiber-optic cluster material using a wooden frame, which makes it possible to visually simulate an independent display surface. The physical objects, or "phicons" (physical icons), are made of transparent acrylic backed with a "hot mirrors" material that makes them visible to the IR cameras but transparent to the eye. A computer vision system composed of two cameras located inside the desk performs the sensing in metaDESK together with magnetic-field position and electrical-contact sensors. The entire system is coordinated by three networked computers. metaDESK provides a user interface that supports physical interaction with digital information projected on a near-horizontal screen.

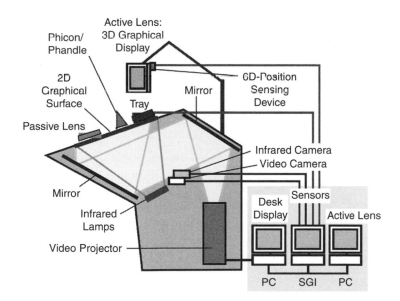

FIGURE 1.9

metaDESK system hardware architecture. Courtesy Jun Rekimoto.

The systems described thus far fall into the broad diffused illumination category, as shown in Figure 1.10(a). Both a camera and an IR illuminant are placed behind the screen/display surface. As objects (hand, finger, face, paper, etc.) approach the screen, they reflect the IR light back to the camera, which typically has a filter to limit the range of IR light it sees. The video from the camera is then passed to

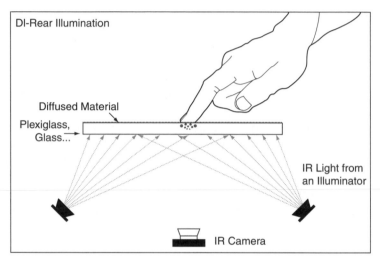

(a)

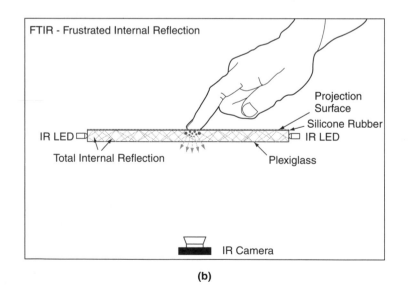

(b)

FIGURE 1.10

Diffused illumination (a) versus frustrated total internal reflection (b). Courtesy Seth Sandler.

software that determines blobs and tracks them, and determines gestures and other higher-order user actions. These hardware elements form only a limited portion of an overall SUI. Once gestures and actions are determined these must be passed to an end-user application.

FTIR multitouch displays rely on the TIR of light being frustrated (F) by a user's touch [36, 37, 28]. TIR occurs at the meeting point of light with mediums of a lower index of refraction. Depending on the angle of incidence, light is refracted and, when the angle is higher than a certain threshold, TIR occurs. When a different material (skin, say) makes contact with this medium it frustrates the TIR and scatters light out of its waveguide at the contact point, as shown in Figure 1.10(b).

Han's FTIR multitouch prototype [28] uses a sheet of acrylic with diamond-polished edges lit by high-power IR LEDs to effect the TIR. This is akin to the FTIR system shown in Figure 1.3. A camera behind the screen is equipped with a matching bandpass filter to cover just the frequency of the light emitted from the diodes. It captures the light frustrated by any object touching the acrylic, so multiple contact points can be detected. Here the camera captures at 30 fps with a 640×480 resolution, so image processing can be easily accomplished in real time on a commodity PC. The system works well in combination with rear projection when a projection screen is placed on top of the acrylic. This configuration ensures that there is no disparity between the display and interaction surfaces.

The success of Han's work owes more to the fluidity of prototype multitouch software applications than to any novelty of the FTIR approach itself [28]. Generally, a compliant surface is necessary between the acrylic and the projection screen as there is a slight delay after the moment the finger is lifted and until the contact effect completely dissipates. Without this, the finger leaves traces on the screen. The choice of compliant surface is particularly sensitive in an FTIR setup; to date there are no perfect solutions.

UlteriorScape [29] uses a combination of multiple rear projectors and lumisty film for viewpoint-dependent face-to-face collaborative displays. Multiple projectors are arranged so that light impacts a shared display along with secondary displays formed from the lumisty film. This allows both personal and public displays to be combined using a single rear-projected setting.

An alternate to the DI and FTIR approaches is DViT. The digital vision touch technology (DViT) from SMART Technologies [19] relies on camera input and image processing. Here two to four cameras are placed in the corners of the screen, facing diagonally across the surface rather than toward it. When the user touches the display using a finger or pointing device, the contact point coordinates are calculated by triangulation using the angle of the contact point relatively to all cameras. Once processed, the contact point is sent to the application as mouse clicks or as "electronic ink." This system enables the use of fingers instead of pointing devices such as a mouse or stylus, which makes it easy and intuitive for untrained users. The fact that the cameras are in the corners means that there is no technology in the display itself so the system is resistant to extended use. The drawback with this technology is that because it does not readily support multiple contact points, any additional contacts after the first one is detected may be ignored.

1.4.2 Capacitance-Based Systems

Camera-based systems as described in Section 1.4.1 typically cannot distinguish the input of different users—one touch looks very much like another. Software solutions to this problem are emerging in which intelligent decision making or user observation plays a key role in accurate user disambiguation. In contrast, DiamondTouch is a touch-sensitive input device that distinguishes the simultaneous input of multiple users (Figure 1.11(a)) [11]. Unlike other touch-sensitive surfaces, DiamondTouch is not sensitive to objects placed on the surface as it is not pressure sensitive. The top layer of the surface is made out of a durable material (e.g., PVC).

The basic layout of DiamondTouch can be seen in Figure 1.11(b). The table surface is built on a layer of eight embedded antennas, constructed from electrically conductive material, that are insulated from each other. A different electrical signal is sent to each one, and when touched, signals are capacitively coupled from beneath the touch point, through the user, into the receiver unit assigned to that user. Each antenna occupies a single area of the table and can be clearly identified. Initially the size of the antenna was 5×5 mm so a single touch activates at least three to four antennas in the same area.

As with all front-projection technologies, one of the problems with Diamond-Touch is that a user's hand interferes with the image (e.g., cast shadows), as shown in Figure 1.11(a). Another problem is the need for each user to maintain contact with her assigned antenna to ensure an effective capacitive coupling and hence identification. In spite of these issues, many applications, including planning, device coordination, mapping [38], and photo sharing [2], have been built using the DiamondTouch hardware.

An alternate form of capacitive sensing is employed by the SmartSkin [23]. The SmartSkin surface, as shown in Figure 1.12, is built on a mesh of transmitter/receiver electrodes. This enables identification of the contact point with the table as well as measurement of the distance between the hand and the table. When a hand approaches the table it capacitively couples the electrodes and causes a wave signal.

(a)   (b)

FIGURE 1.11

MERL DiamondTouch: (a) collaborative multiuser application; (b) schematic. Courtesy Circle Twelve.

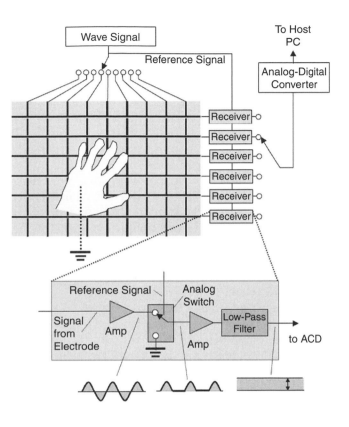

FIGURE 1.12

SmartSkin sensor configuration: A mesh-shaped sensor grid determines hand position and shape [23]. Courtesy Jun Rekimoto.

This makes it possible to measure the distance from the hand to the touch point. In practice, a dense sensor mesh enables such a system to determine the shape of the hand, which in turn increases the input capabilities.

Interaction techniques explored in SmartSkin include

- *Mouse emulation with distance measurement*. A hand's position is tracked in 2D to emulate the mouse, and the distance from the table is used as a mouse click. A threshold distance is used to distinguish between a mouse click and a release.
- *Shape-based manipulation*. The shape of the hand is used to move objects on the display without touching them.
- *Capacitance tags*. The use of objects coated with a conductive material was also explored. When placed on the table alone these tags have no effect, as they are not grounded. However, once a user touches them they are sensed. Such tags are used to realize knobs and sliders as TUI controls.

While capacitive systems are now prolific in small displays, including the Nintendo DS, the Apple iPhone, ATMs, and kiosks, they are currently a niche area of research and development for large-scale collaborative systems. Because of their inability to support rear projection and because of the actual or perceived cost of the hardware, camera-based systems now dominate for sensing multitouch input on large displays.

1.5 GESTURAL INTERACTION

A gesture is the movement of a body part to express meaning. Typical gestures such as pointing, waving, or nodding are made by the hand or the head as appropriate. Both simple gestures such as pointing and complex gestures, such as in sign language rely heavily on the cultural, geographical, or lingusitic frame of reference for their interpretation. Gesture recognition is the interpretation of human gestures using various inputs and computational processing. Almost any type of input device or system can be used to collect data on a user "gesture."

On an SUI, gestures are typically classified as single-point, multipoint, multi-hand, and whole-hand. SUIs that incorporate gesture recognition often suffer from problems of feedback and visibility—for example, "How do I perform the gesture," "How do I know what I just did was interpreted?" In this regard standards are important. This section reviews a standard gesture set that is well understood across SUI-based systems and that serves as a reference set in further SUI development.

FingerWorks[8] has developed a diverse range of input gestures for their iGesture Pad. These include simple mouse emulations—*point*, *click*, *double-click*, *right-click*, *drag/select*, and *scroll*,—and more advanced gestures for Web browsing—*touch and slide* for back and forward, *zoom in* or *zoom out*—relying on all five fingers expanding or contracting on the table as shown in Table 1.1. File operation commands—*open*, *save*, *new*, *print*—and simple editing commands—*cut*, *copy*, *paste*—are also supported, as described in Table 1.2. Basic application commands mapped to gestures include *exit, switch between applications*, and *minimize*, as shown in Table 1.3. FingerWorks was acquired by Apple and the influence of their gesture research and development can be seen across the Apple product line from multitouch gestures on the MacBook trackpad to the iPhone.

Although these examples are all multitouch but single-hand input, as the iGesture Pad was used for input purposes only, they indicate the diversity of gestures that can be mapped into input. Not all gestures are natural and intuitive, but, depending on the task at hand, users can adapt and learn.

---

[8]*Accessed July 2008 from: http://www.fingerworks.com.*

Table 1.1 Mouse and Web-Browsing Emulation Gestures

Gesture Type	Graphics	Action	Description
Mouse Emulation		Click	Tap any two adjacent fingers.
		Scroll	Touch and slide four fingers up/down. "Roll" fingers for fine scrolling.
		Double-click	Tap three adjacent fingers once.
		Right-click	Tap thumb, middle, and ring fingers.
		Drag/select	Touch and move three fingers.
		Point	Touch and move any two adjacent fingers.
Web Browsing		Back	Touch and slide thumb and three fingers left.
		Forward	Touch and slide thumb and three fingers right.

(Continued)

Table 1.1 Mouse and Web-Browsing Emulation Gestures—cont'd

Gesture Type	Graphics	Action	Description
		Zoom in	Touch and expand thumb and four fingers.
		Zoom out	Touch and contract thumb and four fingers.
		Find	Touch and pinch thumb and two fingers.

Source: http://www.fingerworks.com.

Table 1.2 Editing and File Operation Gestures

Gesture Type	Graphics	Action	Description
Editing		Cut	Touch and pinch thumb and middle finger.
		Copy	Tap thumb and middle finger.
		Paste	Touch and expand thumb and middle finger.

Table 1.2 Editing and File Operation Gestures—cont'd

Gesture Type	Graphics	Action	Description
		Undo/ redo	Touch and slide thumb and middle finger up/ down. Slide quickly and crisply to undo just one step, or gradually for multiple steps.
		Tab/ back tab	Touch and slide thumb and middle finger right/ left. Slide quickly and crisply for just one tab, or gradually for repetitive tabs.
File Operation		Open	Touch and rotate counterclockwise thumb and three fingers.
		Close	Touch and rotate clockwise thumb and three fingers.
		Save	Touch and contract thumb and three fingers.
		New	Touch and expand thumb and three inner fingers.
		Print	Prespread hand, then touch and further expand thumb and three outer fingers.

Source: http://www.fingerworks.com.

Table 1.3 Application Control Gestures

Gesture Type	Graphics	Action	Description
Application Control		Show desktop	Touch spread thumb and three fingers. Slide left.
		Exit application	Touch and rotate clockwise spread thumb and three fingers.
		Switch application	Spread hand, then touch three fingers and thumb and slide left or right. Slide crisply to advance just one window, or gradually to scroll through whole list.

Source: http://www.fingerworks.com.

1.6 GESTURAL INFRASTRUCTURES

The gesture and speech infrastructure (GSI) [39] was built using DiamondTouch and DViT technologies as described in Section 1.4. While it is a multimodal system (speech and gesture) the gestures GSI supports are very simple: one-finger pointing for selection, dragging, and panning; two-finger stretching for zooming in and out of a region; fist-stamping to create new objects; and palm-down wiping to delete objects. For example, a two-handed gesture might be multiple-object selection by surrounding an area with upright hands, used in many multitouch applications for grouping objects or as area selection. Sharepic includes a range of multihand and multitouch gestures such as two-handed copy and two-person reset (wherein two people can collaborate on a single two-handed (per person) gesture) [2].

RoomPlanner is furniture layout application developed with DiamondTouch technology [40]. It is designed for face-to-face work by two people sitting across a table who have a 2D overhead view of the room and the furniture. The interaction techniques here are more diverse than those in GSI or Sharepic. They are classified as follows:

- Single-finger input techniques for tapping and dragging (to select and move furniture in the room and to interact with the context-sensitive menu)
- Two-finger input techniques for rotation and scaling

- Single-hand techniques:
    - Flat hand on the table to rotate the display
    - Vertical hand to sweep the furniture pieces (as one would sweep objects across a real table top)
    - Horizontal hand on the table to display the properties of objects found in that area
    - Tilted horizontal hand with front projection to create a physical space where private information can be projected
- Two-handed techniques:
    - Both hands vertical, moving away from each other to spread furniture around the room
    - Both hands vertical, moving toward each other to bring objects in to the area delimited by them
    - Corner-shaped hands used to create a rectangular editing plane

1.6.1 Gestural Software Support

The NUI Snowflake system addresses the needs of third parties in the development of interfaces for collaborative multitouch interaction. While supporting both FTIR and DI, it uses computer vision and image processing to recognize motion, gestures, and multitouch interaction. Figure 1.13 shows a multiuser, multi-input collaborative photographic application running on an NUI Horizon device.

The DiamondSpin Toolkit [38] also supports third parties in the development of interfaces. Along with support for DiamondTouch, its main feature is a real-time polar-to-Cartesian transformation engine that enables around-the-table interactions. Among the applications built on top of the toolkit is Table for N, designed for a small number of people at a table creating, sketching, annotating, manipulating, and browsing various types of documents, including text, html, images, and video clips. Another application is UbiTable, which enables rapid display ecosystem formation

FIGURE 1.13

Collaborative photo-sharing application. Courtesy Natural User Interface Europe AB. Copyright 2008 Natural User Interface Europe AB. All rights reserved.

and content exchange between the UbiTable and other devices such as laptops, cameras, and PDAs.

CollabDraw uses the DiamondSpin Toolkit to enable collaborative art and photo manipulation [41]. Its hardware support is based on DiamondTouch. The notion of *cooperative gesturing* is introduced here, referring to gestures from multiple users interpreted by the system as one command. The system recognizes six basic hand inputs: single-finger, two-finger, three-finger, flat palm, single-hand edge, and two-hand edges. Collaborative gestures are also implemented by combining two or more basic gestures from different users. Eleven collaborative gestures were explored in this first prototype. For example, for drawing a stroke on the canvas, a touch on the surface with one finger by a user is necessary; in parallel another user can change the stroke's width or color. An interesting feature of the system is the ability to create collaborative gestures when more than two people are sitting at the table. One such gesture is stroke erasing, when all users around the table rub their palms back and forth to clean up the canvas. This is akin to the two-person reset introduced earlier [2].

1.7 TOUCH VERSUS MOUSE

The move from a standard mouse or even a multimouse setup to a fully touch-driven interface can introduce many human–computer interaction issues, such as keyboard input, accuracy of control, and fatigue. Preliminary user studies have been carried out to compare the differences between touch and mouse input and one-handed and two-handed input [42]. In line with earlier results [31], these experiments show the advantage of two hands, albeit, in this case, only over the use of two mouse devices. In the first part of the experiment user preference and performance for one-touch input, and mouse input were tested. As in prior studies [43] target selection time was very close between the two input modes. There was a slight advantage in touch mode, but this mode also had more selection errors, particularly when the distance to the target increased. The docking task showed an advantage of the mouse, suggesting that dragging the finger across long distances on the surface is inefficient. According to the first part of the experiment, for single-mode input the mouse was indicated and preferred by users. The results for the second experiment (a bimanual task) showed that users had trouble tracking the mouse pointers on the screen, leading to higher task completion times.

One user study [44] suggested that mouse pointers should be visually connected to give more clues about their position and to decrease the concentration required for operation. Direct-touch input using both hands had better completion times, but whereas there were no errors for close targets, touch was more error prone once the distance to the target increased. This was not the case with two-mouse input, where the error rates were constant, as in the first experiment.

Some of the errors with two-handed input were caused by the need for symmetrical movement of the hands; usually the nondominant hand is harder to control for precise tasks. As in real life, most tasks requiring both hands are asymmetrical [45], and an experiment focusing on different task types may show fewer errors with two-handed input.

Another problem with touch is the lack of precision in selection. Techniques for precise selection have been proposed [46, 47, 48, 43].

These studies provide evidence that multitouch is preferred to multimouse input, and that, even though in interactions where single-touch is sufficient, the mouse is more efficient. Touch input has other advantages such as reduced hand fatigue and enabled awareness of users action in a multiuser context.

1.8 DESIGN GUIDELINES FOR SUIs FOR COLLABORATION

Although the use of SUIs for supporting collaboration is a relatively new area of research, various design guidelines have been proposed [49, 50, 51]. This section discusses the key elements of these guidelines with respect to face-to-face interaction while keeping the original terminology from those sources.

Hardware Setup

- *Size*. Collaborative face-to-face systems must be considerably larger than traditional displays to support a number of users working together.
- *Configuration*. A tabletop or a wall display is task dependent. In the case of tabletop displays, which are more functional for face-to-face collaboration, the display space can be split into shared and private areas.
- *Input*. Each user should have at least one input mode (touch in the case of a touch-sensitive surface). To date, only the DiamondTouch can distinguish between different users' input. However, with the personal display spaces clearly separated, user identification can be realized at the application level with other multitouch systems as well.
- *Resolution*. Large displays suffer from low resolution for both output and input. The use of multiple projectors is possible but their cost is high. Touch input also has low resolution, and selecting small icons with the finger can be a challenge. Special techniques for precise selection should be considered depending on the face-to-face task at hand [46, 47, 52].
- *Interactive response*. In the case of face-to-face tasks, interaction can be computationally intensive. Preprocessing must be considered to reduce response delay.
- *Support for transitions between tabletop collaboration and external work*. There must be easy file transfer to personal devices for individual work.

- *Support for the use of physical objects*. The TUI prototypes described in Section 1.4 are examples of support for input through different objects. Also, special areas can be created on the sides of tables for objects that are not input devices.

Application-Level Guidelines

- *Support for mental models*. To interact freely with interface objects, users should be able to rearrange them according to their preferences for efficiency and comfort.
- *Representation changes*. Allow users access to various representations of the data, according to individual preference. As was shown in [53] seeing more than one representation of the same data can have a positive effect on the decision-making process.
- *Task history*. Keep track of interactions during the session for later discussion and reference.
- *Perception*. Some of the issues to be considered are user viewing angle, global and local legends, and strategic label placement [54]. Another issue is rotating representations so that all users at the table can have a clear view.

1.8.1 Designing the Collaborative Environment

According to [55] two types of basic operation are necessary within groupware systems for a fluid collaboration between users: *coordination* and *communication*.

Group coordination guidelines include:

- *Workspace organization*. Public and private display and work spaces are necessary.
- *Fluid transitions between activities*. There should not be much effort required to switch between different activities or stages within the same operation. This could entail provision of more than one input mode or addition of interface objects that can be easily manipulated.
- *Information access*. Rights and restrictions should be in place for different actions or access to data.
- *Collaboration styles*. Various collaboration styles should be supported. Multiple copies of documents must be made available for individual work, and concurrent access and interaction with shared data are necessary.

The communication guidelines are

- *Support for easy transitions between personal and group work*. Give users distinct work areas for individual work during group sessions.
- *Support for interpersonal interaction*. Take into account the fundamental mechanisms that people use in collaborative interactions. The ergonomics of the system must be considered to make it suitable for collaborative work.
- *Privacy*. Users should have control over how much of the data they want to expose to others.

1.9 CONCLUSIONS

The following usability issues, if ignored in practice, can hinder the development of any collaborative SUI-based application. They must be addressed each time an SUI-based system is to be considered.

- The user's stylus, fingers, and hands may partially occlude the interface.
- Interface elements may be difficult to select because of stylus, finger, or hand size.
- Users may suffer fatigue due to the range of human motion required.
- The screen surface can be damaged or dirty.
- There may be a lack of tactile feedback from passive screen surfaces.
- Calibration between the display (projector or LCD) and the sensing elements can become misaligned.

This chapter provided an overview of the core research and developments in multitouch display systems for surface user and face-to-face collaborative interfaces. We showed how these developments have impacted each other and the relative merits of each. We also discussed the notion of a surface user interface and how various forms of technology can be used to realize it for collaborative interaction. Tables 1.1 through 1.3 illustrated the types of gesture, action, and description SUIs should support. The chapter concluded with design guidelines for SUI's and how they can be applied to future interface design.

The ultimate goal of surface user interfaces in collaborative face-to-face activities is for people not to feel they are using a computer; instead, the visual elements should naturally support their actions. Ultimately, SUIs will become so commonplace in everyday life that no one will notice their presence. They will be aesthetic, powerful, and enhance our lives but so too will they be commonplace, obvious, and boring.

REFERENCES

[1] Christin A-M. A History of Writing from Hieroglyph to Multimedia. Flammarion; 2002.

[2] Apted T, Kay J, Quigley A. Tabletop sharing of digital photographs for the elderly. In: CHI '06: Proceedings of the SIGCHI Conference on Human Factors in Computing Systems. ACM Press; 2006. p. 781–90.

[3] Terrenghi L, Quigley A, Dix A. A taxonomy for and analysis of multi-person-display ecosystems. Journal of Personal and Ubiquitous Computing [Special Issue on interaction with coupled and public displays].

[4] Hao Jiang CF, Wigdor D, Shen C. System design for the wespace: Linking personal devices to a table-centered multi-user, multi-surface environment. In: Subramanian S, Izadi S, editors. Tabletop: 3rd Annual IEEE International Workshop on Horizontal Interactive Human-Computer Systems. IEEE Computer Society; 2008. p. 105–12.

[5] Weiser M. The computer for the 21st century. SIGMOBILE Mob Comput Commun Rev 1999; 3(3):3–11.

[6] Greenfield A. Everyware: The Dawning Age of Ubiquitous Computing. Peachpit Press; 2006.

[7] Kummerfeld B, Quigley A, Johnson C, Hexel R. Merino: Towards an intelligent environment architecture for multi-granularity context description. In: Cheverst K, de Carolis N, Kruger A, editors. Online Proceedings of the UM (User Modeling) 2003 Workshop on User Modeling for Ubiquitous Computing. 2003. p. 29–35. *http://www.di.uniba.it/ ubium03/quigley-6.pdf.*

[8] Dey AK, Hamid R, Beckmann C, Li I, Hsu D. Cappella: Programming by demonstration of context-aware applications. In: CHI '04: Proceedings of the SIGCHI Conference on Human Factors in Computing Systems. ACM Press; 2004. p. 33–40.

[9] Clear A, Shannon R, Holland T, Quigley A, Dobson S, Nixon P, 2009. Situvis: A visual tool for modeling a user's behaviour patterns in a pervasive environment, In: Brush A, Friday A, Tobø Y, (Eds.), Pervasive 2009: Proceedings of the 8th International Conference on Pervasive Computing, Springer-Verlag.

[10] Terrenghi L. Designing hybrid interactions through an understanding of the affordances of physical and digital technologies. Ph.D. thesis, Ludwig-Maximilians Universitä; 2007.

[11] Dietz P, Leigh D. DiamondTouch: A multi-user touch technology. In: UIST '01: Proceedings of the 14th Annual ACM Symposium on User Interface Software and Technology. ACM Press; 2001. p. 219–26.

[12] Mehta N. A flexible machine interface. Master's thesis, Department of Electrical Engineering, University of Toronto; 1982.

[13] Nakatani L, Rohrlich J. Soft machines: A philosophy of user-computer interface design. In: Proceedings of the SIGCHI Conference on Human Factors in Computing Systems. ACM Press; 1983. p. 19–23.

[14] Schuyten P. Xerox introduces intelligent copier. The New York Times September 25, 1980:D4.

[15] Poupyrev L, Maruyama S. Tactile interfaces for small touch screens. In: UIST '03: Proceedings of the 16th Annual ACM Symposium on User Interface Software and Technology. ACM Press; 2003. p. 217–20.

[16] Krueger M, Gionfriddo T, Hinrichsen K. Videoplace—an artificial reality. ACM SIGCHI Bull 1985;16(4):35–40.

[17] Wellner P. Interacting with paper on the DigitalDesk. Commun ACM 1993;36(7):87–96.

[18] Wilson A. Play Anywhere: A compact interactive tabletop projection-vision system. In: Proceedings of the 18th Annual ACM Symposium on User Interface Software and Technology. ACM Press; 2005. p. 83–92.

[19] I. Digital-Vision Touch. Digital-vision touch (dvit tm) technology white paper. Tech. Rep.

[20] Hodges S, Izadi S, Butler A, Rrustemi A, Buxton B. ThinSight: Versatile multitouch sensing for thin form-factor displays. In: Proceedings of the 20th Annual ACM Symposium on User Interface Software and Technology. ACM Press; 2007. p. 259–68.

[21] Ullmer B, Ishii H. Emerging frameworks for tangible user interface. IBM Syst J 2000;39(3–4):915–31.

[22] Fitzmaurice GW, Ishii H, Buxton WA. Bricks: laying the foundations for graspable user interfaces. In: Katz IR, Mack R, Marks L, Rosson MB, Nielsen J, editors. Proceedings of the SIGCHI Conference on Human Factors in Computing Systems (Denver, Colorado, United States, May 07–11, 1995). Conference on Human Factors in Computing Systems. New York, NY: ACM Press/Addison-Wesley Publishing Co; 1995. p. 442–9. DOI= http://doi.acm.org/10.1145/223904.223964.

[23] Rekimoto J. SmartSkin: An infrastructure for freehand manipulation on interactive surfaces. In: Proceedings of the SIGCHI Conference on Human Factors in Computing Systems: Changing Our World. Changing Ourselves; p. 113–20.

[24] Patten J, Recht B, Ishii H. Audiopad: A tag-based interface for musical performance. In: NIME '02: Proceedings of the 2002 Conference on New Interfaces for Musical Expression. National University of Singapore; 2002. p. 1–6.

[25] Baraldi S, Bimbo AD, Landucci L, Torpei N, Cafini O, Farella E, et al. Introducing tangerine: A tangible interactive natural environment. In: MULTIMEDIA '07: Proceedings of the 15th International Conference on Multimedia. ACM Press; 2007. p. 831–4.

[26] Wilson AD. TouchLight: an imaging touch screen and display for gesture-based interaction. In: Proceedings of the 6th international Conference on Multimodal interfaces (State College, PA, USA, October 13–15, 2004). ICMI '04. New York, NY: ACM; 2004. p. 69–76. DOI= http://doi.acm.org/10.1145/1027933.1027946.

[27] Jordà S, Kaltenbrunner M, Geiger G, Bencina R. The reactable*. In: Proceedings of the International Computer Music Conference (ICMC 2005). 2005. p. 379–82.

[28] Han JY. Low-cost multitouch sensing through frustrated total internal reflection. In: UIST '05: Proceedings of the 18th Annual ACM Symposium on User Interface Software and Technology. ACM Press; 2005. p. 115–8.

[29] Kakehi Y, Naemura T. Ulteriorscape: Interactive optical superimposition on a view-dependant tabletop display. In: Subramanian S, Izadi S, editors. Tabletop: 3rd Annual IEEE International Workshop on Horizontal Interactive Human-Computer Systems. IEEE Computer Society; 2008. p. 201–4.

[30] Buxton W, Hill R, Rowley P. Issues and techniques in touch-sensitive tablet input. In: Proceedings of the 12th Annual Conference on Computer Graphics and interactive Techniques SIGGRAPH '85. New York, NY: ACM; 1985. p. 215–24. DOI= http://doi.acm.org/10.1145/325334.325239.

[31] Buxton W, Myers B. A study in two-handed input. SIGCHI Bull. 17, 4 (Apr. 1986), 1986;321–6. DOI= http://doi.acm.org/10.1145/22339.22390.

[32] Elrod S, Bruce R, Gold R, Goldberg D, Halasz F, Janssen W, et al. Liveboard: a large interactive display supporting group meetings, presentations, and remote collaboration. In: Bauersfeld P, Bennett J, Lynch G, editors. Proceedings of the SIGCHI Conference on Human Factors in Computing Systems (Monterey, California, United States, May 03–07, 1992). CHI '92. New York, NY: ACM; 1992. p. 599–607. DOI= http://doi.acm.org/10.1145/142750.143052.

[33] Matsushita N, Rekimoto J. HoloWall: Designing a finger, hand, body, and object sensitive wall. In: Proceedings of the 10th Annual ACM Symposium on User Interface Software and Technology. ACM Press; 1997. p. 209–10.

[34] Ullmer B, Ishii H. The metadesk: Models and prototypes for tangible user interfaces. In: UIST '97: Proceedings of the 10th Annual ACM Symposium on User Interface Software and Technology. ACM Press; 1997. p. 223–32.

[35] Ishii H, Ullmer B. Tangible bits: Towards seamless interfaces between people, bits and atoms. In: CHI '97: Proceedings of the SIGCHI Conference on Human Factors in Computing Systems. ACM Press; 1997. p. 234–41.

[36] Mallos J. Touch position sensitive surface; U.S. patent 4,346,376 (Aug. 24). 1982.

[37] Kasday L. Touch position sensitive surface; U.S. patent 4,484,179 (Nov. 20). 1984.

[38] Shen C, Vernier FD, Forlines C, Ringel M. DiamondSpin: an extensible toolkit for around-the-table interaction. In: Proceedings of the SIGCHI Conference on Human Factors in Computing Systems (Vienna, Austria, April 24–29, 2004). CHI '04. New York, NY: ACM; 2004. p. 167–74. DOI= http://doi.acm.org/10.1145/985692.985714.

[39] Tse E, Greenberg S, Shen C. GSI demo: multiuser gesture/speech interaction over digital tables by wrapping single user applications. In: Proceedings of the 8th international Conference on Multimodal interfaces (Banff, Alberta, Canada, November 02–04, 2006). ICMI '06. New York, NY: ACM; 2006. p. 76–83. DOI= http://doi.acm.org/10.1145/1180995.1181012.

[40] Wu M, Balakrishnan R. Multi-finger and whole hand gestural interaction techniques for multi-user tabletop displays. In: Proceedings of the 16th Annual ACM Symposium on User Interface Software and Technology. ACM Press; 2003. p. 193–202.

[41] Morris MR, Huang A, Paepcke A, Winograd T. Cooperative gestures: multi-user gestural interactions for co-located groupware. In: Grinter R, Rodden T, Aoki P, Cutrell E, Jeffries R, Olson G, editors. Proceedings of the SIGCHI Conference on Human Factors in Computing Systems (Montréal, Québec, Canada, April 22–27, 2006). CHI '06. New York, NY: ACM; 2006. p. 1201-10. DOI= http://doi.acm.org/10.1145/1124772.1124952.

[42] Forlines C, Wigdor D, Shen C, Balakrishnan R. Direct-touch vs. mouse input for tabletop displays. In Proceedings of the SIGCHI Conference on Human Factors in Computing Systems (San Jose, California, USA, April 28 - May 03, 2007). CHI '07. New York, NY: ACM; 2007. p. 647-56. DOI= http://doi.acm.org/10.1145/1240624.1240726.

[43] Sears A, Shneiderman B. High precision touchscreens: design strategies and comparisons with a mouse. Int J Man-Mach Stud 1991;34(4):593–613. DOI= http://dx.doi.org/10.1016/0020-7373(91)90037-8.

[44] Balakrishnan R, Hinckley K. Symmetric bimanual interaction. In: Proceedings of the SIGCHI Conference on Human Factors in Computing Systems (The Hague, The Netherlands, April 01–06, 2000). CHI '00. New York, NY: ACM; 2000. p. 33–40. DOI= http://doi.acm.org/10.1145/332040.332404.

[45] Guiard Y. Asymmetric division of labor in human skilled bimanual action: The kinematic chain as a model. J Mot Behav 1987;19:486–517.

[46] Benko H, Wilson AD, Baudisch P. Precise selection techniques for multitouch screens. In: CHI '06: Proceedings of the SIGCHI Conference on Human Factors in Computing Systems. ACM Press; 2006. p. 1263–72.

[47] Albinsson P, Zhai S. High precision touch screen interaction. In: Proceedings of the SIGCHI Conference on Human Factors in Computing Systems. ACM Press; 2003. p. 105–12.

[48] Esenther A, Ryall K. Fluid DTMouse: better mouse support for touch-based interactions. In: Proceedings of the Working Conference on Advanced Visual interfaces (Venezia, Italy, May 23–26, 2006). AVI '06. New York, NY: ACM; 2006. p. 112-5. DOI= http://doi.acm.org/10.1145/1133265.1133289.

[49] Scott SD, Grant KD, Mandryk RL. System guidelines for co-located, collaborative work on a tabletop display. In: European Conference Computer-Supported Cooperative Work (ECSCW 2003), September 14, 2003, Finland: Helsinki; 2003.

[50] Isenberg P, Carpendale S. Interactive tree comparison for co-located collaborative information visualization. IEEE Trans Vis Comput Graph 2007;13(6):1232-9.

[51] Viegas F, Wattenberg M. Communication-minded visualization: A call to action. IBM Sys J 2006;45(4):801–12.

[52] Blanch R, Guiard Y, Beaudouin-Lafon M. Semantic pointing: Improving target acquisition with control-display ratio adaptation. In: CHI '04: Proceedings of the SIGCHI Conference on Human Factors in Computing Systems. ACM Press; 2004. p. 519-26.

[53] Zhang J, Norman D. Representations in distributed cognitive tasks. Cog Sci 1994;18(1):87-122.

[54] Yost B, North C. The perceptual scalability of visualization. IEEE Trans Vis Compu Graph 2006;12(5):837-44.

[55] Pinelle D, Gutwin C, Greenberg S. Task analysis for groupware usability evaluation: Modeling shared-workspace tasks with the mechanics of collaboration. ACM TOCHI 2003;10(4): 281–311.

Computer Vision Interfaces for Interactive Art

2

Andrew W. Senior[1]

Google Research, New York

Alejandro Jaimes[2]

Telefonica Research, Madrid, Spain

ABSTRACT

This chapter reviews the use of computer vision as an interface for the arts. We provide a taxonomy of vision-based art works and describe the major paradigms they follow. We also examine how the availability of inexpensive hardware and powerful free software tools is fueling an explosion in the use of computer vision for art interfaces, driving experimentation with new interface technologies, and enabling a new expressiveness in both performance and audience-interactive art.

[1]aws AT andrewsenior.com
[2]aj27 AT columbia.edu

Key words: computer vision, multimedia art, interactive art, tracking, performance, mirror interfaces, projector-camera systems.

2.1 INTRODUCTION

Vision is, for most people, the primary sense—our sense of presence in the world is most closely tied to the perceptions we receive through our eyes. Computer vision, by attempting to give computers the same sense of sight, opens up a new range of possibilities for sensing at a distance and for perceiving the world as humans do. For interactive art, vision is a unique modality by which a work can modulate its behavior according to conditions in its environment, whether by explicit user controls or by interpretation of visual occurrences without obvious causality.

This concept is directly related to the concept of ambient intelligence, with a twist: In art, reactions to the work need not be "intelligent" in the same sense that they might have to be, for example, in a digital home. "Ambient intelligence" reactions in interactive art are the artist's constructs and, as part of the work, can range from simple abstractions to complex physical movements of robots. Furthermore, such works are often implicitly human-centric from start to finish because they are conceived as part of an artistic concept. Computer vision in art is seldom discussed in ambient intelligence circles, but it is significant because some of the artworks and tools for art in many ways push the limits of technology in ambient spaces.

In this chapter we briefly introduce computer vision in the arts, with the goal of generating enough interest for the reader to explore further. There is a vast amount of information on the subject (from both art-critical and technical perspectives), as well as a large number of open-source software projects, artworks, tools, and performances that use computer vision. These "applications" of computer vision employ techniques ranging from simple background subtraction to state-of-the-art face detection, facial expression recognition, tracking, and many other technical subareas of computer vision. One key difference between the types of interactive arts we describe in this chapter and the technical work published in academic venues is that the systems/artworks are installed and "used" by many people (with no training) in public spaces, exhibitions, performances, and the like. This creates many real-world challenges for computer vision (and ambient intelligence) researchers, and great opportunities to "test" new technologies.

2.1.1 A Brief History of (Vision in) Art

Throughout history, art has been driven by technological change. New techniques and materials engender new styles of artistic expression. Computer vision is just one of the newest tools and is similarly powering changes in the arts as well as being a significant component in the burgeoning disciplines of new media and interactive art. As a sensing modality rather than a sensible medium, computer vision is not itself an art medium but rather a powerful tool that can be applied in many art forms, from photography and sculpture to dance and music.

One can find many precursors of computer vision art, such as the work of Muybridge [1], who used photography to understand human actions, and the original video games developed in the 1950s and 1960s. Electronic image sensors from the 1920s and 1930s through Bell Labs' CCD sensor introduced in 1969 laid the foundations for video art, such as the work of Nam June Paik. However, VideoPlace, introduced by Myron Krueger [2] in the 1970s, is often cited as the earliest true interactive video work of art (see Figure 2.1).

> *The VideoPlace System combines a participant's live video image with a computer graphic world. It also coordinates the behavior of graphic objects and creatures so that they appear to react to the movements of the participant's image in real-time. [3]*

Computer vision in art also has a strong historical link to performance—in particular, to the early happenings and multimedia performances of the 1960s (see Rush [4] for a general introduction to new media) or even to film (see Manovich [5] for a "film" perspective on new media). Vision in art can also be related to the concept of an active observer in "traditional" art, in which the main premise is that people "interact" with art (e.g., oil paintings) even if a work is not explicitly interactive.

Historical details are beyond the scope of this chapter. It may be sufficient to say that, although there are many resources on the history of new media, we are not aware of many that specifically focus on computer vision in the arts. (Levin's article [6], included in [7], is a notable exception.) Theoretical analysis of new media in art (including computer vision) is in the very early stages, and there are many active discussions on it in the arts community. As is natural, many of them occur online (see Section 2.6).

2.2 A TAXONOMY OF VISION-BASED ART

If we examine the work that uses computer vision techniques, we can see that a number of categories emerge. In this section we describe a taxonomy of computer-vision–based work and illustrate it with some notable examples. In doing so we identify several factors that we can use to categorize vision-based art. These are shown in Table 2.1.

The first division in our taxonomy is between works that use "live" vision and those that do not—that is, if images are captured in real-time and processed to generate an effect or whether existing images are somehow analyzed. (Examples of such noninteractive works are the *turbulence.org* commission "self portrait"[3] by Ham, which uses face recognition software to search for the artist's portrait on the flickr photo archive Website, and "Fingerbahn" (1998) by Levin,[4] which uses computer

---

[3]*transition.turbulence.org/Works/self-portrait/.*
[4]*acg.media.mit.edu/people/golan/photo/ps7/index.html.*

Table 2.1 Taxonomic Categories for Interactive Computer Vision Art
Live/stored images
Local/remote
Pixels/regions
People/object
Active/passive
Public/performers
Model-based/model-free
Location/shape/motion features

vision techniques to extract the ridges from a fingerprint still image and then adds virtual creatures that move along the ridges.

Among the works processing live video feeds, we can distinguish those that acquire the video locally—that is, in the same place as the viewer—from those that process a live feed from another location, whether outside the gallery or on the other side of the world. (For example "Suicide Box" by the Bureau for Inverse Technologies (Jeremijenko) placed a video camera below the Golden Gate Bridge to detect jumpers). In particular, among those with locally acquired live feeds are works that use computer vision to provide interactivity. We will examine these in more detail in this chapter.

We can distinguish levels of interpretation of the image. Some focus mainly on the pixel level, although these, such as "Light Tracer" by Willis (2005), could be said to use image-processing rather than computer vision algorithms. That work retains the maximum brightness of each pixel from a scene over time, producing an interface in which participants can draw—with their own bodies or with lights, cell phones, and so forth. "Couch Potato Farm" by Senior (2005)[5] uses motion from a live video feed together with pixel intensities in television signals to create artificial life forms in a hypothetical virtual ecosystem.

Like VideoPlace, some works extract edges or regions using simple thresholding or color keying. More complex algorithms such as background subtraction allow greater robustness to varying conditions. Finally, some works use high-level vision algorithms such as face detection or recognition. Vision-based motion capture technologies, commonplace in "offline" art production, also find their way into performance systems, allowing many degrees of freedom in human body poses to be captured, interpreted, and rerendered. Another way of looking at this

---

[5]*andrewsenior.com.*

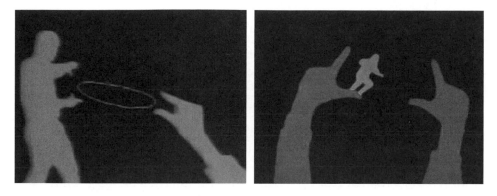

FIGURE 2.1

Krueger's VideoPlace.

increasing complexity is according to the level of modeling used by the vision algorithm. More complex effects such as object detection and tracking may use sophisticated modeling of an object (face, person, vehicle) rather than more generic model-free processing like background subtraction or motion detection.

We can also categorize vision-based interfaces according to subject matter. The subject of most works is people, but some are designed to detect particular (e.g., color-keyed) objects. In one version of "Audience Interaction" by Maynes-Aminzad [8] a beach ball is tracked by a camera as it is tossed around by an audience. Its position controls a video game. In another version, the audience leans to control a game. Other works are agnostic about their subject matter, looking for silhouettes or other visual features wherever they may occur. Of those that look at people or human activity we can distinguish the ones that face "the audience" or gallery-goers from those in which the cameras are directed at the performers, although much of the motivation of interactive art is precisely to blur this distinction.

2.3 PARADIGMS FOR VISION-BASED INTERACTIVE ART

Although we can classify individual works according to the preceding taxonomy, it is also possible to identify several major paradigms for computer-vision–based interactive art:

- Mirror interfaces
- Projector-camera systems
- Physical actuation
- Dance performance
- Musical performance

In this section we describe these paradigms, illustrating them with notable works.

2.3.1 Mirror Interfaces

A principal paradigm in interactive art is the presentation of a mirror-like surface to the viewer, representing the image seen by the camera. A striking series of mirror works devised by Danny Rozin[6] uses a variety of physical effects to produce light and dark pixels—from tilted wooden tiles in "Wooden Mirror" (1999) to retractable ball bearings in "Shiny Balls Mirror" (2003) (Figure 2.2). Rozin also produced a number of software mirrors that represent the image of the camera in a variety of ways. These simple mirror interfaces are, strictly, based on image processing rather than computer vision, since they use low-level, pixelwise operations. A work that uses a mirror paradigm while exploiting computer vision techniques is "Magic Morphin' Mirror" (1997) by Darrell et al. [9][7] (Figure 2.3). This presents the image captured by the camera as it would appear in a mirror except for faces, which, as one watches, begin to distort and warp. Here the faces are detected and tracked by a face detection algorithm, applying a complex pattern recognition system to control the mirror interface.

FIGURE 2.2

Rozin's "Shiny Balls Mirror."

[6]*www.smoothware.com/danny/.*
[7]*people.csail.mit.edu/trevor/Hallucinations.html.*

FIGURE 2.3

Darrell et al.'s "Magic Morphin' Mirror."

Another paradigm for visual art works is the camera-projector system. Such systems have been studied for a number of years as an interaction paradigm for computers [10]. They are often configured as augmented reality environments in which the projector projects an image into the space of the participants, which is the same area viewed by the camera. One early example of this is "Text Rain" (1999) by Utterback and Achituv,[8] in which falling letters gather like snow on the silhouette of the participants (Figure 2.4). A more recent work with a similar format is "Messa di

FIGURE 2.4

Utterback's "Text Rain."

[8]*www.camilleutterback.com/textrain.html.*

Voce" (2003) by Levin and Lieberman, with Blonk and La Barbara,[9] in which sounds from a microphone are visualized, for instance, as bubbles rising from the actors' heads which are tracked visually (Figure 2.5).

Camera-projector systems can be oriented horizontally as well as vertically. For example, "Boundary Functions" (1998) by Snibbe[10] (Figure 2.6) detects people with a camera and projects boundaries between their locations according to a Voronoi tessellation of the space. As pairs of participants move in the space, a line always

FIGURE 2.5

Jaap Blonk performing "Messa di Voce" by Levin et al.

FIGURE 2.6

Snibbe's "Boundary Functions."

[9]*tmema.org/messa/.*
[10]*www.snibbe.com/scott/bf/index.htm.*

separates them, evoking the metaphorical boundaries that separate people and providing a sharp visualization of the idea of "personal space."

"Diorama Table" (2005) is a whimsical work by Takahashi and Sasada [11] that also uses a camera pointed at a surface on which projections are based on what the camera sees (Figure 2.7). In this case users place objects (plates, cutlery, and so forth) on a table; virtual objects such as trains are then projected on the table, circling the objects. Users can rearrange the physical objects to redirect the behavior of the virtual objects. "Shadow Monsters" by Worthington,[11] a similar work, augments hand silhouettes with spines to turn them into monsters. Here, though, the coupling between sensing and projecting space is not necessary. "Subtitled Public" (2005) by Lozano-Hemmer[12] extends the camera-projector system by projecting words onto the people being tracked, while "Under Scan" by the same artist (2005) projects videos of faces into the shadows of pedestrians. "Ghost Pole Propagator" (2007) by Levin[13] uses a fundamental computer vision algorithm, known as "skeletonization," that reduces regions of a silhouette to a linear armature. In this case, the "skeletons" of different viewers are projected onto a nearby wall.

Other works employ computer vision less directly. Appropriating the technology of video surveillance systems, "You are here" by Snibbe[14] (2004) tracks gallery visitors across multiple cameras and presents their paths (as in Figure 2.8) in an interactive display, highlighting their own position. Video surveillance, with its privacy concerns and hints of Big Brother has been the theme of many art works [12] but few so far have used computer vision despite the extensive use of vision technologies in surveillance systems.

FIGURE 2.7

Takahashi et al.'s "Diorama Table."

---

[11]*www.worthersoriginal.com/.*
[12]*www.lozano-hemmer.com/.*
[13]*www.flong.com/projects/gpp/.*
[14]*www.snibbe.com/scott/public/youarehere/index.html.*

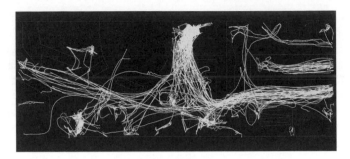

FIGURE 2.8

Snibbe's "You are here."

Yet another category is works that use computer vision to drive physical effects. Lozano-Hemmer's "Homographies" (2006) and "Standards and Double Standards" (2004) detect viewers and move physical objects (fluorescent lights and suspended belts, respectively) to reflect their presence, giving an uncanny sense of being watched, in the latter work, as the belts turn to "face" the viewer.

A particular variety of physical effects is the control of a robot. "Double-Taker (Snout)" (2008) by Levin, Hayhurst, Benders, and White[15] steers a huge eye on a robotic stalk (Figure 2.9) to stare at passersby, using visual detection and tracking to choose a subject. "Skeletal Reflections" by MacMurtrie (2000)[16] analyzes the posture of a viewer using two cameras, and matches the pose in a database of "art historical classical poses." A skeletal metal robot (Figure 2.10) then enacts the pose. "POMONA" by Senior[17] (2007) explores the domains of bioengineering, hybrids, and biofuels. In this work robotic–plant hybrids are steered by computer vision algorithms to maximize their exposure to the sun or to lights controlled by onlookers.

2.3.2 Performance

In recent years, as processing power increased at a reduced cost, it became more commonplace for vision to be used in live interactive performance. Groups that use computer vision in their performances include Dumb Type, Cie Incidents Mémorables, and Troika Ranch. For example, Winkler [13] uses vision-based motion tracking in live performance. Motion capture using markers has also been explored; one example is the work of Cunningham and Jones [14]. Audience participation, as described by Maynes-Aminzade et al. [8], constitutes one area of opportunity, although most works focus on the performers themselves, at different

---

[15]*www.flong.com/projects/snout/.*
[16]*amorphicrobotworks.org/works/skelli/fabrication.btm.*
[17]*andrewsenior.com/gallery/electronica/pomona.*

FIGURE 2.9

Levin's "Double-Taker (Snout)."

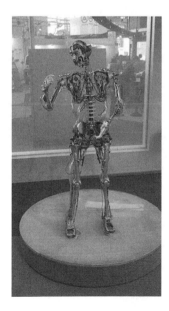

FIGURE 2.10

MacMurtrie's "Skeletal Reflections."

levels. In the work of Lyons et al. [15], a wearable camera pointing at the wearer's mouth interprets mouth gestures to generate MIDI sounds. The "mouthesizer" as a tool has been used in performances not only by itself (the performer moving her mouth to generate sounds) but also in combination with other instruments since the performer's hands remain free. The mouthesizer uses simple techniques to detect the shape of the performer's open mouth, while works such as that of Valenti et al. [16] use more sophisticated techniques (facial expression recognition) to sonify facial movements. In contrast, Hornof et al. [17] track eye movements to generate sounds, although it is not clear if their system has been used in a performance.

In the work of Paradiso and Sparacino [18], the camera tracks limbs so that the movements generate music, and in the work of Jean et al. [19] cameras track foot movement to generate sounds on a virtual keyboard.

Some of these systems are actually close to being additional tools for the performer, as well as an intricate part of the performance itself. In the "Live Cinema" work of Lew [20], computer vision is used to track fingers on a rear-projection screen: Multiple sensors are integrated so that finger motions on the screen, combined with other activities, determine what a VJ is projecting as a film. The system in this case is both a tool for the VJ and a performance element. "Audio d-touch" by Costanza et al. [21] uses computer vision to recognize basic patterns in small blocks placed on a table. As the performer moves the blocks, different sounds/variations are generated. This tool has also been used in combination with other instruments played by professional musicians. Some compositions explore intimate performance: In a body-drawing communicator for instant partners,[18] vision and a projection system are combined to allow two remote participants to draw on each other's bodies while lying in bed. Drawings are transmitted "live" between the two beds with the goal of creating a sense of communication that leverages the emotional quality of physical gesture.

2.4 SOFTWARE TOOLS

In this section we review some of the software tools that are available for artists who wish to use computer vision to provide interactivity in their work.

2.4.1 Max/MSP, Jitter, and Puredata

Max/MSP was originally created at IRCAM in the 1980s and has been in development since, in a commercial distribution (Max/MSP) and in a similar open-source "version" developed originally by the author (Puckette). Both environments use a visual programming interface for multimedia, music, and inputs from various sensors

---

[18]*www.distancelab.org/projects/mutsugoto/.*

including cameras (using plug-in modules such as Jitter for Max/MSP and framestein for puredata). The two software families have been used extensively over the years by musicians, designers, artists, and engineers in a wide range of applications, including performance art and installation.

2.4.2 EyesWeb

EyesWeb is an open-source software platform designed to support development of real-time multimodal distributed interactive applications. It was developed at the InfoMus Laboratory (at the Universidad de Genoa, where a project by the same name investigates real-time multimodal interaction) and has been used extensively in interactive performances and installations. The platform is similar to the Max/MSP family in that a visual programming language is used. However, while the original focus of Max/MSP was on music, EyesWeb was developed from the start with real-time multimodal interaction in mind.

2.4.3 processing

processing[19] by Reas and Fry [7] is a simplified programming environment modeled on the Java language (and compiled into Java to allow platform independence). It was designed for computer-generated video art around a frame-by-frame redrawing paradigm, but has built-in support for video and add-ons for sensors, including JMyron[20] by Nimoy for video capture.

2.4.4 OpenCV

OpenCV is an open-source library of computer vision algorithms, for users with significant programming cxpcricncc. It is writtcn in C++ and uscd for industrial computer vision applications. IIowever, it also provides complcx vision algorithms, including face detection, which run at high speed.

2.5 FRONTIERS OF COMPUTER VISION

The field of computer vision research has expanded tremendously in recent years as cameras, processing power, and storage have become abundant and affordable. Actual industrial systems have grown from those that perform highly constrained machine inspection to those that operate in the real world in domains as diverse and uncontrolled as video surveillance, biometric identification (particularly face recognition), fruit identification, and video indexing. The ubiquity of the Internet

---

[19]*processing.org.*
[20]*webcamxtra.sourceforge.net.*

and the open-source movement have led to wide sharing of research algorithms, putting them in the hands of adventurous and technically savvy artists. The breaking down of art/technology barriers in the field of new media has spawned artist-technologists as well as many collaborations between artists and technologists.

We expect this transfer and appropriation of technology to continue and accelerate as artists thirst for new and more complex effects. Recent developments of particular interest, which we predict will increasingly be seen in arts, are as follows:

- *Object detection*. Effective feature extraction and indexing have led to powerful algorithms to detect classes of objects (cars, bicycles, animals, etc.).
- *Mobile platforms*.
- *Face detection, identification, and analysis*. As algorithms for face processing improve, many new artistic effects based on recognizing people and understanding their facial expressions will be achievable.
- *Human tracking*. Works will harness improved tracking capabilities and will begin to extract more information more accurately about pose, whether of dancers or gallery-goers.
- *Video indexing and understanding*. Artists will use technologies to appropriate and mash up video sources from surveillance to home movies to television broadcasts.

The new technologies will spread from static installations to mobile devices as smartphones become widespread. One example is the Spellbinder system,[21] a gaming platform in which users take photographs of people, places, or objects with camera phones which are recognized on a server that controls game play.

2.6 SOURCES OF INFORMATION

Although many artists do not document their work in article form, many print and online publications provide not only technical details but also audio-visual documentation of performances and installations. In this section we list some of these resources, although they are not specific to computer vision.

- *Neural.it*.[22] An online and print magazine covering many types of work.
- *runme.org*.[23] An online user-contributed collection of software for art and software art.
- "Networked Performance."[24] A blog of *turbulence.org* that mainly deals with performance.

---

[21]*news.bbc.co.uk/2/hi/technology/6938244.stm*.
[22]*www.neural.it*.
[23]*www.runme.org*.
[24]*www.turbulence.org*.

- *Rhizome.org*.[25] An online community that includes a large database of artworks, documentation, interviews, and other texts.
- "we-make-money-not-art."[26] A blog about technology, art, and design.
- *Leonardo* and *Leonardo* Music.[27] Journals about art and technology.
- ACM Multimedia Interactive Art program.[28] A yearly technical multimedia conference that has an art track and exhibition.
- New Interfaces for Musical Expression (NIME) conference.[29] A conference on novel interfaces for musical expression.

2.7 SUMMARY

Ambient intelligence is an emerging field that promises to integrate many technologies that have been under development since the early days of computing (including algorithms in machine learning and other areas). A key component of an ambient intelligence platform is how it relates to humans and how humans relate to it. Computer vision can play a major role because it is unobtrusive (in relation to wearable sensors) and can sense a wide range of human actions and events. In the arts, computer vision has grown tremendously in recent years, precisely for these reasons.

In installation art, it is usually impractical for viewers (e.g., in a gallery or a museum) to wear specialized sensors. At the same time, the recent availability of feature-rich open-source (and affordable) computer vision toolkits for off-the-shelf hardware has allowed artists with few resources to create interesting compositions that run on basic laptops or PCs. For this reason, many artworks and interactive performances use computer vision techniques (often in combination with other sensors) for a wide range of purposes. These include detecting simple background changes and recognizing gestures, body parts, and objects. All of this is accomplished in the toughest conditions for a real-world application: before live audiences or in interactions with off-the-street "participants," and considering sociocultural issues that include the impact of technology (what may in part differentiate art from nonart). Thus, computer vision in the arts is perhaps the single most important ambient intelligence application to date, and in particular the most important example of human-centric interfaces for ambient intelligence.

ACKNOWLEDGMENTS

The authors would like to thank the artists who granted us permission to use images of their work in this chapter.

---

[25]*www.rhizome.org.*
[26]*www.we-make-money-not-art.com.*
[27]*www.mitpress.com.*
[28]*www.sigmm.com.*
[29]*www.nime.org.*

REFERENCES

[1] Muybridge E. The Human Figure in Motion. Dover; 1955.

[2] Krueger M. Artificial Reality. Addison-Wesley; 1983.

[3] Krueger M, Gionfriddo T, Hinrichsen K. VideoPlace—an artificial reality. ACM SIGCHI Bulletin 1985;16(4):35–40.

[4] Rush M. New Media in Art. Thames & Hudson; 2005.

[5] Manovich L. The Language of New Media. MIT Press; 2001.

[6] Levin G. Computer vision for artists and designers: Pedagogic tools and techniques for novice programmers. Journal of Artificial Intelligence and Society 20(4).

[7] Reas C, Fry B. Processing: A Programming Handbook for Visual Designers and Artists. MIT Press; 2007.

[8] Maynes-Aminzade D, Pausch R, Seitz S. Techniques for interactive audience participation. ICMI, IEEE; 2002.

[9] Darrell T, Gordon G, Woodfill J, Harville M. A virtual mirror interface using real-time robust face tracking. Workshop on Face and Gesture, No. 3. IEEE; 1998. p. 616–21.

[10] Workshop on Projector Camera Systems. *procams.org*.

[11] Takahashi K, Sasada S. Diorama table. ACM Multimedia 2005;1077–8.

[12] Levin T, Frohne U, Weibel P. CTRL [SPACE]: Rhetorics of Surveillance from Bentham to Big Brother. MIT Press; 2002.

[13] Winkler T. Fusing movement, sound, and video in falling up, an interactive dance/theatre production. In: Proceedings of the Conference on New Interfaces for Musical Expression. 2002.

[14] Dils A. The ghost in the machine: Merce Cunningham and Bill T. Jones. PAJ: A Journal of Performance and Art 2002;24(1):94–104.

[15] Lyons M, Haehnel M, Tetsutani N. Designing, playing, and performing, with a vision-based mouth interface. In: Proceedings of the Conference on New Interfaces for Musical Expression. 2003.

[16] Valenti R, Jaimes A, Sebe N. Facial expression recognition as a creative interface. In: Proceedings of the International Conference on Intelligent User Interfaces. 2008.

[17] Hornof A, Rogers T, Halverson T. Eyemusic: Performing live music and multimedia compositions with eye movements. In: Proceedings of the Conference on New Interfaces for Musical Expression. 2007. p. 299–300.

[18] Paradiso J, Sparacino F. Optical tracking for music and dance performance. In: Gruen A, Kahmen H editors. Optical 3-D Measurement Techniques IV. 1997. p. 11–8.

[19] Jean F, Albu A, Schloss W, Oriessen P. Computer vision-based interface for the control of meta-instruments. In: Proceedings of 12th International Conference on Human-Computer Interaction. ACM Press; 2007.

[20] Lew M. Live cinema: Designing an instrument for cinema editing as a live performance. In: Conference an New Interfaces for Musical Expression. 2004.

[21] Costanza E, Shelley S, Robinson J. Introducing audio d-touch: A novel tangible user interface for music composition and performance. In: Proceedings of the 6th International Conference on Digital Audio Effects. 2003.

CHAPTER

Ubiquitous Gaze: Using Gaze at the Interface

3

Dirk Heylen

*Human Media Interaction, University of Twente, Enschede,
The Netherlands*

ABSTRACT

In the quest for more natural forms of interaction between humans and machines, information on where someone is looking and how (for how long, with long or shorter gaze periods) plays a prominent part. The importance of gaze in social interaction, its manifold functions and expressive force, and the multiple factors that contribute to it, make it an interesting modality to explore in interaction. This can take many forms. Gaze can be used as a pointing device, similar to a mouse, but it can also be used in more subtle ways. The attention, interest, and other aspects of the mental state of the user may be inferred from gaze behaviors in context, and the system can react to it and adjust its behavior accordingly. This chapter reviews the use of gaze information at the interface in a number of scenarios ranging from the desktop to the ambient environment, including conversational interactions with robots and agents.

Key words: gaze, eye contact, gaze in computer-mediated communication, virtual agents and avatars, gaze in smart environments, user studies, measuring gaze, gaze as an input device, focus of attention, measuring and inferences, gaze in conversation, social variables.

3.1 INTRODUCTION

Gaze holds a special place as a communicative signal in our interactions. We look to see, and what we see can be other people looking, telling us what they are attending to. Unlike other senses, gaze can give us a fair idea of the visual information that others are perceiving. The accuracy of this type of judgment has been investigated in various experiments [1–7]. Gaze is essentially the basis of what makes the eyes the windows to the soul. Because we can see that others are looking at us and vice versa, the possibility of eye contact—mutual awareness of each other's presence and awareness—makes gaze important in social interactions. We use gaze to signal whether we are paying attention, to point, to show we are thinking, to beg, and to dominate.

Not surprisingly, gaze has received a fair amount of attention in human–computer interaction studies. These include research on gaze to reveal the interest of users when they are looking at a screen, on the use of gaze-aware interfaces, on the effects of gaze patterns of virtual humans interacting with people, and on the importance of mutual gaze in computer-mediated communication. In this chapter, we review the research on gaze in various types of interfaces, highlighting the interpretation of user gaze behaviors.

In the ambient intelligence vision for human–technology interaction, a central idea is that the computer disappears into the background, becoming invisible to users. The interface becomes transparent, and the computer performs actions not on the basis of command and control but on understanding the user's wishes through observing and interpreting his actions unobtrusively. Thus, the intelligence-enhanced attentive environment becomes a mind-reading machine. Besides this implicit mode of interaction, the ambient intelligence vision as laid down in the ISTAG Report ([8]) aims at "systems that engage in dialogue." This should be read as dialogue that resembles how people naturally interact, one form of which is the introduction of virtual humans or humanoid robots into the environment.

In this chapter we look at the role of gaze in both modes of interaction and at attempts to use gaze in traditional desktop interfaces. What can be inferred from gaze behaviors and what responses can be generated? What gaze behaviors should humanoids display in interaction? Before we survey the issues and proposals around these questions, we review some important findings on gaze in human interaction.

3.2 THE ROLE OF GAZE IN INTERACTION

Our eyes allow us to perceive our visual environment. This is the basic function of gaze, and all the others derive from it. Looking at the role of gaze direction in social interaction, where interactants are aware of each other's focus of attention, Kendon [9] distinguishes three main types of function: monitoring, expressive, and regulatory.

[W]e shall offer some suggestions as to the function of gaze-direction, both as an act of perception by which one interactant can monitor the behaviour of the other, and as an expressive sign and regulatory signal by which he may influence the behaviour of the other.

These functions are clearly interrelated, with the regulatory function seemingly building on the others. Consider for instance the following two regulatory functions taken from Kendon:

- By looking away, a speaker may signal her intention to continue to hold the floor, which might prevent the addressee from interrupting.
- Intermittent glances of a speaker at a listener are used to check how the message is received and to elicit a reaction.

In the second case, for instance, monitoring of the speaker works doubly: first to signal the listener; second—by the conventional rules of interaction—to regulate interactive behavior.

We started by saying that the primary function of gaze is visual perception, which translates as "monitoring" of the interlocutor in a conversational setting. The fact that it can serve a regulatory function derives from that, as the monitoring will be interpreted as volitional by the interlocutor and will therefore serve to indicate some intentional state. Such states can be quite diverse. Gaze plays a role in identification of an addressee, in the display attentiveness, in effecting turn transitions, and in requests for backchanneling [10–13]. Typical gaze patterns occur when doing a word search or when thinking. Gaze behavior may also reflect the social status of the participants. Looking away is often used to avoid distraction, to concentrate, or to indicate a desire not to be interrupted. It has been said that one looks at another person to obtain cues about mood and disposition and to establish or maintain social contact, so gazing away may reflect hesitation, embarrassment, or shyness. Gaze can also be used to locate referents in abstract space [14, 15].

Gaze may be used for a number of functions that build on the perceptive basis and the knowledge that it can be used as a signal, but clearly there are many factors besides utility that determine gaze behavior. Setting, type of conversation, relation between people (intimacy, role), physical condition (tiredness), cognitive load, emotional state [16–17], personality [19], social norms, gender [20]—all influence gaze behaviors. For overviews of these factors, see [21, 22].

Some of the factors just listed may be part of a deliberative effort by the gazer. For instance, one might deliberately look at an object, and point to it, when talking about it. Here gaze is used as a communicative signal much like a deictic pronoun or a pointing gesture with the hand or arm. Other patterns of gaze may have been learned and then become automatic—for instance, not gazing too long at a person because it violates a social rule. Still others are below awareness and come naturally. Some of these cannot be controlled—for instance, shutting the eyes in a reflex action.

From the point of view of the observer, gaze behaviors can be interpreted by others as indicative of the factors that cause or at least co-determine them. The behaviors thus become cues from which a range of interpretations of the gazer's mental state can be deduced [23, 24]. One of the challenges for automated systems is to develop similar mind-reading capabilities.

The presentation so far has focused more on functions of gaze and less on what makes up gaze behavior. While Kendon only discussed gaze *direction* in the examples above, this does not mean direction as such is the only parameter that needs to be considered. Another parameter that Kendon took into account in his analysis is the duration of gaze, which, for instance, differs typically between speakers and listeners.

> *Insofar as it is possible to speak of a typical pattern, it would appear to be this: during listening,* p *looks at* q *with fairly long* q*-gazes[1] . . . broken by very brief* a*-gazes, whereas during speaking he alternates between* q*- and* a*-gazes of more equal length, the* a*-gazes being longer than those that occur during listening. (p. 27)*

Gaze direction and duration are not the only parameters that are informative or that display typical patterns. In their study on the relation between gaze behaviors and impression management, Fukuyama et al. [25] took into account the amount of gaze, the mean duration of gaze, and the gaze points while averted. By systematically varying these parameters in their "eyes-only" agent, they showed how different impressions could be generated. In considering different parameters related to gaze, Poggi [26] went even further. For the analysis and interpretation of gaze she considered eyebrows and eyelids important. Eyelids, for instance, may blink or flap, vibrate, or partially shut. Furthermore, with respect to the eyes, she took into account aspects such as position, direction, humidity, focusing, and pupil dilation. The "language of the eyes" is not independent from other expressive parts of the face or the movements of the head, as the expressive faces in Figure 3.1 show.

The many factors that contribute to determining where and how people gaze make gaze a rich source for inferring mental states. However, they also make such inferences complex because there are always numerous confounding variables to be taken into account. Consider, for instance, duration, where a long, sustained gaze can be both intimidating and intimate.

Automatically detecting where a person is looking, measuring the amount of gaze and other features, is one challenge that gaze-aware interfaces encounter. A bigger challenge for them is to interpret gaze behaviors and provide appropriate reactions. In the following section we discuss several ways in which gaze has been used as an input device or where it has been used to infer information from human interactions.

---

[1]This should be read as a person (*p*) looks at the interlocutor (*q*) with fairly long gazes when listening. *a*-gazes are those away from the interlocutor.

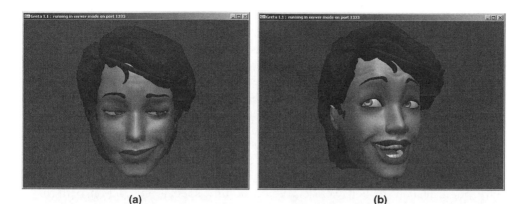

(a)

(b)

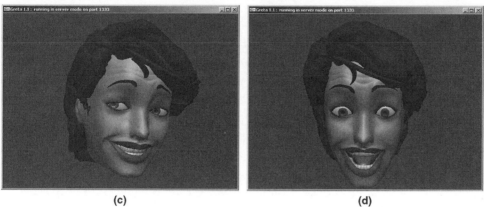

(c)

(d)

FIGURE 3.1

Expressive functions of gaze.

3.3 GAZE AS AN INPUT DEVICE

In the study of ambient intelligence, several paradigms of the interaction between the user and the computer-enhanced environment have been envisioned, as mentioned earlier. The intelligent environment is one that can perceive and interpret human actions without the user having to explicitly control the interaction. The computer and the interaction disappear into the background, invisible to the user but picking up and interpreting cues received from the user's gaze behavior, and adapting and reacting to if. If the intelligent environment can make sense of gaze behaviors, it may be able to infer the same information about the user's goals and desires, and other aspects of her mental and physical state, just as humans do.

We mentioned a second way in which a user can interact with technology in the ambient vision: the interface, personified as a virtual character or robot, serves as mediator, allowing modes of interaction that come naturally for humans. In this case, gaze plays a double role. Ideally, the agent not only can perceive and interpret the gaze of the user, but can display appropriate gaze behaviors itself.

Besides the settings in which gaze is used as an input channel, there are those in which gaze operates as an input device. In one, it can be used as a control and command interface where the user is conscious of the manipulations that can be performed. This resembles the way we regulate conversations, trusting that our interactants understand why we are looking at them or somewhere else, and how we intentionally look at places to communicate information. Opposed to this is the case where the system infers information about the user's mental state, which he may not himself be aware of. The type of interaction depends on the way gaze encodes information: conscious pointing toward action, unconscious and involuntary pupil dilation, or behaviors characteristic of a specific interaction pattern. In any of these visions, the goal of gaze as an input device is to make interaction "more natural." This ambition is clearly put forward by Jacob [27]:

> *Because eye movements are so different from conventional computer inputs, our overall approach in designing interaction techniques is, wherever possible, to obtain information from a user's natural eye movements while viewing the screen, rather than requiring the user to make specific trained eye movements to actuate the system. This requires careful attention to issues of human design.... (p. 260)*

Indeed, an important requirement for the interaction to be "natural" is knowing what comes naturally and thus how people use gaze. Methodologically this entails the following strategy (o.c.):

> *The goal is for human–computer interaction to start with studies of the characteristics of human communication channels and skills and then develop devices, interaction techniques, and interfaces that communicate effectively to and from those channels. We thus begin with a study of the characteristics of natural eye movements and then attempt to recognize appropriate patterns in the raw data obtainable from the eye tracker, turn them into tokens with higher-level meaning, and design interaction techniques for them around the known characteristics of eye movements. (p. 263)*

The notion of "natural" is rather general. Detailing this, Surakka et al. [28] summarize the main advantages of gaze used as an input device (relying in part on suggestions by [29–31]) with respect to bandwidth, effort, speed, comfort, learnability, and fun.

Bandwidth. Gaze-based techniques offer the means to extend the bandwidth of input.

Effort. Eye movements do not require conscious effort.

Speed. Gaze-based pointing techniques are faster than hand-based techniques: The eye selects the object of interest and the hand moves the cursor to the object.

Hands-free. Gaze-based input leaves the hands free.

Fun. The interaction can be more enjoyable.

Learnability. The interaction is easy to learn.

In line with these ideals, Edwards [32] lists the following requirements for useful gaze-based systems:

Recognition. They should be able to recognize eye movements.
No training. They should not require the user to learn or to use unnatural eye movements.
Calibration. They should calibrate automatically to the user and the situation.
Modes. They should recognize different user modes, such as searching for a target, thinking, reading, and so forth.

We will see in the following discussion that these advantages are not always easy to obtain, because the requirements may be difficult to meet. We start with gaze as input in traditional desktop settings and then look at conversational interfaces, concluding with ambient settings. We present several example applications and prototypes illustrating the main ideas. Given that a particular application may belong to more than one category, its discussion in a particular section does not limit it to that category alone.

3.3.1 **Eyes on the Desktop**

Jacob's work [27, 33] was primarily concerned with traditional desktop settings—window-icon-menu-pointer (WIMP) interfaces and the operations allowed by them, such as pointing and clicking—and their replacement by gaze movements and fixations captured by an eye-tracker. With his colleagues, Jacob developed interaction techniques for object selection, moving an object on the screen, scrolling, and menu selection. A similar group of operations was developed by other researchers. Salvucci and Anderson [30] created a gaze-added interface where the item on the screen to which the user is attending is highlighted and the user presses the control key to select a command.

This tradition of using eye gaze follows Bolt's [34] call for capturing and understanding natural modes of expression in the interface. In his World of Windows a screen containing many windows covers a complete wall; the display of the windows is organized by using eye gaze to indicate attention. Windows grow smaller when not looked at. Bolt was interested in large wall displays. Other researchers applied the use of gaze in combination with a traditional desktop.

Most of these applications rely on the assumption that eye gaze indicates attention or can be used for drawing attention by functioning as a pointing device. A main challenge in this work is that the information from gaze trackers is quite noisy and thus limited. To improve their quality, it is necessary to constrain the kinds of interactions allowed. But an even more important challenge is the fact that gaze and attention are not unequivocally related [35]. People may look somewhere without paying attention or without using the gaze direction as a pointing device.

Although the aim of this endeavor is to make use of natural commands that require no training, most of the early WIMP techniques were for command-and-control interaction tasks: selecting menu items, entering and editing text, clicking links.

These manipulations seem slightly against the spirit of natural interaction. Zhai [36] points out that such commands are indeed problematic:

> [T]he use of eye gaze in humans to perform control tasks does not tend to occur naturally. The eye, as a primary perceptual organ, does not function very well as a control organ. . . . [E]ye movements are not always under voluntary control. To load the visual perception channel with a motor-control task seems fundamentally at odds with natural behavior in which the eye searches for and takes in information from the world and in which the hand manipulates objects in that world. Other than for disabled users, the direct use of eye gaze for pointing does not appear very promising.

Some of the drawbacks of gaze-based interfaces mentioned in Surakka et al. [28] are that a person may look at an object without wanting to select it, which is known as the "Midas touch" problem. One solution lies in a better understanding of the precise mechanism of gaze behaviors—for instance, dwell time. Another solution considered in many studies and applications is the use of gaze as only one of several input modalities [37]. Zhai [36], for instance, combines manual and gaze input for pointing in his MAGIC system.

The combination of modalities and the use made of gaze information varies from system to system. Kuno and Ishiyama [38] presented a system where users can manipulate items on a screen by hand gestures. Because people may also use their hands when they are not engaged in manipulation, the system needs to infer whether or not they are issuing commands. Gazing at an object that can potentially be controlled by gestures will trigger command mode. In this case, gaze seems to be a natural intervention if people typically look at the interface when they want to use gestures, and do not want to use gestures when they look away. It appears from this and many other studies (as we will to see) that for gaze-based interfaces to work, the system should have a good understanding of the common practice of work, the ways in which humans use their eyes, and the physiology of the eyes themselves.

The following are examples of applications where gaze plays a part similar to that of input devices normally used in WIMP interfaces.

Typing and word processing. Several groups have tried to use gaze information to support or replace typing. Frey et al. [39] built the EASE system (Eye Assisted Selection and Entry) for selecting Chinese characters. Here gaze was used in combination with pressing a space bar to select the option [36].

Adaptive information presentation. "iTourist provides the user with tourist information about an imaginary city . . . , in the form of a map and photos of different places. . . . iTourist attempts to adapt its information output based on the user's interests and needs analyzed from the user's eye-gaze pattern" [40]. Hoekstra et al. [41] presented a system (shown in Figure 3.2) in which two virtual agents adapt their information on the basis of the user's gaze behaviors, which are taken to be indicative of attention. This attentive interface can also serve as an example of a gaze-aware conversational system (see the following).

FIGURE 3.2

Gaze-aware agents.

The Reading Assistant. Sibert et al. [42] built a reading assistant in which "the system uses eye tracking to trigger synthetic speech feedback as children read text from the monitor." Gaze is used to determine when to highlight and pronounce a word.

The use of gaze in these systems is not always the same. In some systems its pointing function is used; in others gazing at an object may indicate an interest in it. Most systems use gaze as a way to select an object in the scene. In the examples just described, a particular gaze behavior may be used as a trigger or other operations may function as a trigger to interpret the gaze behavior. In the systems to be discussed next, many similar interactions are present, but in combination with the modalities of speech and language, gaze has the potential to come closer to the way it functions in everyday human–human interaction.

3.3.2 Conversation-Style Interaction

A special type of multimodal interface that takes the idea of natural communication further than the gaze-based interfaces do is one where gaze is combined with speech and natural language interaction in an extended dialogue system. The motivation behind natural language interfaces is similar to that behind gaze-based interfaces. They are supposed to be easy to learn and "natural." Several authors claim that the use of gaze in combination with natural dialogue can alleviate problems with dialogue alone. In particular, gaze is used as a deictic device, helping to resolve underspecified referring phrases [43–45].

Below are a few examples of dialogue systems that rely on gaze input:

Determining processing. Morency et al. [46] used eye tracking to determine the cognitive load of the user and to differentiate periods when a user is thinking about a response from those when she is waiting for the agent or robot to take the turn.

Engagement. Koons and Flickner [47] described an attentive agent, PONG, "that watches the user, reacts to user actions, and conveys attention and emotion. PONG expresses happiness on seeing the user and sadness when the user leaves."

Humanoid robots. Many humanoid robots make use of gaze input to engage the user in action, understand the focus of user attention and engagement, and understand pointing gestures [48–50].

Empathy. Wang et al. ([51]) introduced ESA, the empathic software agent, where "eye movement tracking is used to monitor user's attention and interests, and to personalize the agent behaviors." ESA is used in a tutoring context, where the motivational state of the learner is partly determined by the focus of attention as detected by the gaze recognition system.

Toy robots. In the stuffed-toy robot, the gaze model consists of joint attention action for indirectly gaining the user's interest, and eye contact reaction for directly eliciting the user's favorable feeling [52].

Conversation disambiguation. Zhang [53] used gaze information to resolve speech ambiguities and correct speech recognition errors.

Conversational systems that use gaze as an input device try to determine whether the user is paying attention to the agent or robot or to other elements in the environment. This may guide the use of referring expressions used by the agent, help to disambiguate user utterances, be of use in regulating conversational flow (as when the system knows whether it is expected to take a turn), and increase engagement when the user notices the system is attentive. In the case of conversational interaction, in particular with embodied conversational systems, generating gaze behaviors becomes an important issue for interactive systems such as virtual agents and robots. Important issues in this case are the way humanoid gaze behaviors should be contingent on the the user's behaviors and his verbal expressions. Also, the expressive effects of different gaze behaviors are important to control, as several studies have pointed out. There is ample literature on modeling gaze behaviors in humanoids. See, for instance: [55–62].

Interaction with animated characters and robots is one side of the more natural form of communication hinted at in the ISTAG report [8]. Another side is moving the interface away from the desktop. Human–robot interaction is one form where this happens. In the next section, we look at interfaces that are increasingly becoming an integrated part of the smart environment.

3.3.3 Beyond the Desktop

Away from the desktop, recognition and interpretation of gaze behaviors can serve several functions. One can distinguish two main categories. The first is the recognition of gaze by objects and appliances in the environment that then activate or react to it. The second involves the interpretation of gaze behaviors to derive further information about user activities, particularly in a conversational setting. In this case the purpose is less to interface with a system than to understand human-to-human interactive behavior and have the system adapt or react to what is going on.

Ambient Displays

Bolt's [63] dynamic windows, mentioned earlier, are a good example of the first category, but they are still very close to the desktop kind of interaction. The same goes for the system of gaze-contingent displays proposed by Gepner et al. [64]. These are large displays in a smart or virtual environment where gaze is used for pointing to resolve underspecified reference phrases. Further away from desktop-like interactions is the example of driving a wheelchair [38, 65] using gaze or face direction. The goal is a wheelchair that can move as the user wishes, without the need for intentional commands. Because this is rather difficult, the studies used "behaviors which are done intentionally but so naturally that the user may not feel any burden." One can take this to be to a fairly "natural" way of making things happen, but it still needs conscious effort, much like we use gaze for pointing as an act of communication. Kuno and Ishiyama state this as follows:

> We use face direction. The wheelchair moves in the direction of the user's face. For example, it turns left if the user turns the face to the left. The user should know this fact and needs to move the head intentionally. However, it is a natural behavior to look in the direction where he/she intends to go. . . . Using face direction can remove a considerable part of . . . intentional operations, realizing a user-friendly interface. [38]

However, as with command-and-control desktop interfaces, there is a problem with natural, implicit commands. Kuno et al. [38] noted that people may turn their heads for other reasons than that they want to move in that direction. They attempted to solve this problem by having the unintentional command mode switch on or off as decided by the speed of the movements, as in their observational studies there was some evidence that the differences between moving the head for directing the wheelchair and for other intentions were related to differences in head movement velocity.

Two other examples of more ambient interfaces follow. The first is an interesting mixture of an attentive display and a simple conversational system in an ambient environment. The second is an attentive robot that is an instance of an ambient display and that exemplifies conversational style interaction.

  eyeCOOK. The system proposed by Bradbury et al. ([66]) is a multimodal attentive cookbook: The user can allow the system to choose the appropriate display mode using eye gaze. If a gaze is detected, the complete recipe is shown in a smaller font; also, when eye gaze is present the voice dialogues with the system allow it to be used for deictic references.

  vtoys. vtoys are robot-like toys that detect where people are and how many of them are in the scene and can make eye contact. Facial expressions and engagement behaviors are triggered by this information [67].

The use of gaze in a wheelchair and in eyeCOOK is not much different from its use on a desktop, in that in both cases gaze acts as a trigger for action with some degree of "nonintentionality." Studies on automatic detection of human behavior in smart meeting rooms or other smart environments where people meet and interact also treated gaze direction and what can be inferred from [68, 69]. Often head orientation acts as a proxy for gaze direction given that it is not possible to use fixed eye trackers in this setting, where people can move around freely, but only as camera images [70].

Human–Human Interaction in Ambient Environments

In various projects on ambient environments, researchers looked at how to detect and interpret the gaze behaviors of people interacting in the environment, for instance to infer who is talking and to indicate sides in a conversation.

With respect to participation status, there is a longer tradition in connecting gaze patterns and the question "Who is looking at whom?" to see how participants distribute their gaze depending on whether they are speaking or being addressed [9, 21, 71, 72]. Also, in ambient intelligence studies on automatic recognition, statistics about these patterns have been gathered from the various corpora. A general tendency is that speakers look less at listeners than vice versa. However, the figures vary according to the number of particants, the kind of conversation, and the presence and location of distractors (such as whiteboards or slide projections or objects that are being discussed or manipulated).

Besides the question of how well machines can detect participation status, some authors have raised the question of how well humans infer such information from looking at a conversational scene. Lunsford and Oviatt [73] and Terken et al. [74], for instance, looked at this question. The former found that with visual information only, people can judge with 57% accuracy who is talking to whom in multiparty conversations. Although one should take into consideration that they were looking at four-party conversations, this is not very high and shows the limits of what can be inferred from a scene.

In investigations of gaze in smart environments, the use made of this information is somewhat different, as it is not for control but for detecting particular activities in the scene and how people engage in the conversation, in what role. One application for which information about participant status (speakers, addressees) was considered is in video editing for presenting summaries of meetings [75]. Summarization and retrieval of fragments in multimedia archives of social encounters are the most important applications. Rienks et al. [76] provided examples of using the information gathered by the system within the interaction itself by means of proactive agents.

There is some diversity in the information derived from automatically observing gaze behaviors in social interaction. We list the most prominent ones here. Note that in most cases the detection of a behavior or mental state relies on gaze in combination with many other modalities.

Activity detection

What kind of activity are people engaged in? In a meeting typical activities are presentations, discussions, and brainstorming. The focus-of-attention patterns for these can be different. For instance, in presentations a presenter may be in front of a whiteboard or a screen, which draws the audiences's attention [68].

Interest level

Whether people show interest in the topic under discussion and are actively engaged in the conversation was in part determined from gaze information by Gatica-Perez et al. [77].

Hot spot detection

Yu et al. [69] used the degree of crossover of utterances and gaze changes, the number of nods, and feedback as indicators of hot spots. Hot spots in meetings are, intuitively speaking, periods where important things happen and where participants are highly involved in the discussion.

Participation status

Besides the question of who is speaking and who is listening, there is a more specific question: the listener actually being addressed. Automatically determining this was studied by various authors [78–82], taking the participants' focus of attention into account.

That the distribution of gaze direction (or head orientation at least) is sensitive to participation status (speaking/listening) is borne out by the histograms in Figure 3.3 [83], which show the azimuth angle of person 3 in a four-person meeting. They indicate the orientations taken over the whole meeting, over the period when person 1 was speaking and over the periods when person 3 was speaking.

Dialogue acts

Gaze information was used to classify certain dialogue acts in conversations, in particular feedback expressions [81, 84].

Interaction structure

Related to the previous two items is the work of Otsuka et al. [85] on the structure of interaction: "the action-reaction pairs of participants' behaviors such as question-and-answer and addressing followed by back-channel response."

Dominance and influence

Several authors looked at the detection of dominances (e.g., [86]). Otsuka et al. [87] also used gaze as an indication of addresseehood and based on these estimates found that "the amount of influence is based on the amount of attention paid to speakers in monologues and to persons with whom the participants interact during the dialogues."

Many of the studies made use of the insights about the role of gaze in social interaction referenced in Section 3.1. In contrast to control-and-command–like interfaces, they also made use of gaze behaviors that may not have been communicatively intended, focusing rather on patterns of behavior that are a by-product of other activities of participants who may not be aware of the patterns they exhibit and do not know that they may actually be contributing to controlling devices and services through their gaze behaviors.

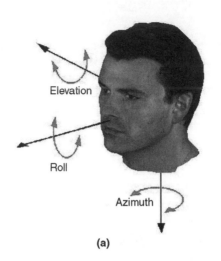

(a)

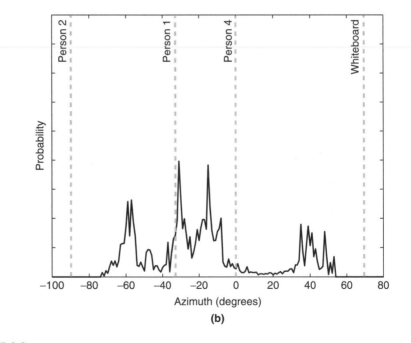

(b)

FIGURE 3.3

Distribution of azimuth angles for person 3 in meeting 3. (a) Azimuth, elevation, and roll angles; (b) entire meeting;

(Continued)

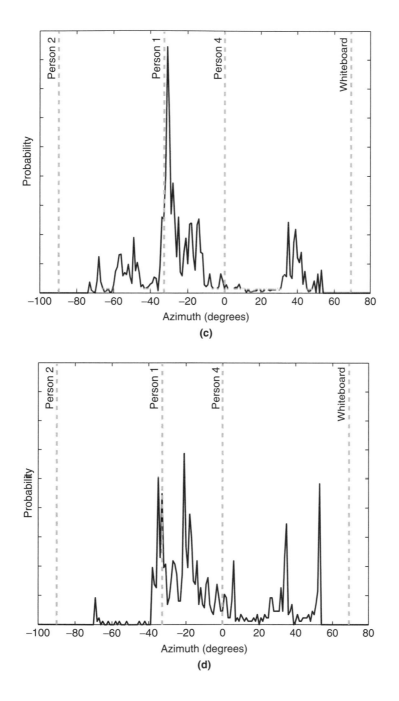

FIGURE 3.3—cont'd

(c) person 1 speaking; (d) person 3 speaking.

Besides the applications of summarization and retrieval mentioned earlier, another use that has been proposed for detecting information from human interactive behavior is in the context of remote participation. In this case, information about participation status and the focus of attention of co-located attendees is captured by the system and visualized in some way to remote participants. This use brings us to another kind of application for which capturing gaze is important: mediated communication. In the final section, we will briefly review the issues surrounding mediated communication and gaze.

3.4 MEDIATED COMMUNICATION

Videoconferencing over the Internet is becoming a relatively common means of interaction as bandwidth increases and the exchange of Webcam images becomes relatively stable. In mediated communication the affordances offered do not always allow the kind of natural interaction possible in face-to-face conversation. A particular channel of communication may be absent, or the capture and transmission of information and its subsequent presentation may not be completely faithful.

Research on videoconferencing and interaction has looked at the ways in which the limitations of technology and setting affect interaction quality. An important limitation in common videoconferencing, often pointed out, is that the setup does not provide for proper gaze contact, because looking at the person on the screen does not give the impression of being looked at, whereas looking at the camera does. This is misleading because, when looking at the camera, one does not see the other. Several, mostly partial, solutions to this problem have been proposed.

We list four approaches to eliminating angular deviation.

Smart setup. The "Multi-Attendant Joint Interface for Collaboration" (MAJIC) system was developed by Okada et al. [88]. It achieves gaze awareness by arranging video cameras and projectors. Life-size video images of participants are displayed on a large curved screen. Smart setup is also found in systems that use, for instance, half-mirrors [89].

Weak controlled gaze awareness. Ohno [90] presented a system that is meant not to render gaze accurately and faithfully but to have the user control a pointer in a mutual work space.

Avatars. Related to the solution by Ohno is one where information on the gaze of a participant is projected onto a robot or 3D avatar. This can be done by conscious control or by mapping the output of a gaze tracker to the avatar's eyes. Examples of this approach include [91–93].

Image manipulation. This technique consists of manipulating the rendering of information, as in the GAZE groupware system by Vertegaal [94]. A picture of the person was rotated on the screen of the other participants in accordance with where she was looking. Similarly, Jerald and Daily [95] and Lee and Jeon [96] used video editing to apply gaze correction in the image presented.

The mediated communication setting is in many ways different from the interfaces considered in the previous sections. The interaction is directed at communication between humans mediated by technology rather than with the technology as such. Mediation involves many techniques of capturing, interpreting, and rendering gaze that are similar or identical to those used in the previous applications. For instance, the use of robots or virtual humans as avatars relies on techniques used in conversational interfaces. Also, the goals of capturing and manipulating gaze information are much the same: to achieve more natural ways of communication.

3.5 CONCLUSION

Information on gaze behaviors has been important in the quest for more natural forms of interaction. The importance of gaze in social interaction, its manifold functions, and its expressive force, together with the multiple factors that contribute to it, make it an interesting interaction modality. We read a great deal about the intentions of others from their eyes. The eyes show attention and interest. They direct the attention of others and communicate a diversity of mental states.

The use of gaze information in the interface can take many forms. Gaze can be used as a pointing device, similar to a mouse. It can also be used in more subtle ways. Attention, interest, and other aspects of a user's mental state may be inferred by the machine from gaze behaviors in context. The system can react to them and adjust its behavior accordingly.

This chapter reviewed the use of gaze information at the interface in a number of scenarios, ranging from the desktop to the ambient environment, including conversational interactions with robots and agents. It showed how the various ways in which the eyes provide information can result in different interaction styles. One such style is command and control, where gaze is used, for instance, to point to an object of interest. In this case naturalness is only achieved if pointing with the eyes does indeed come naturally and there are not too many false positives (looking while not wanting to point). A more subtle use of gaze is found in attentive interfaces. These are assumed to guess the interest of a user, which triggers the system to adapt its style of presentation or which effects other changes in the environment without the user's conscious control.

Using gaze information at the interface is not without problems. Capturing gaze correctly is not always easy. Ascribing meaning to gaze behaviors is difficult, as many factors play a role and the behaviors are notoriously ambiguous and dependent on the context and the individual. Restricting the context can help.

Although not many everyday applications use gaze information, the numerous suggestions for its use show promise. As smart environments become smarter and our understanding of human action in them grows, the chances are that the potential for gaze in the interface will come to be fully realized.

REFERENCES

[1] Gibson JJ, Pick AD. Perception of another person's looking behavior. Am J Psychol 1963;76(3):386-94.

[2] Cline MG. The perception of where a person is looking. Am J Psychol 1967;80(1):41-50.

[3] Von Cranach ML, Ellgring JH. Problems in the recognition of gaze direction. In: Von Cranach I, Vine I, editors. Social Communications and Movement: Studies of Interaction and Expression in Man and Chimpanzee. Academic Press; 1973. p. 419-43.

[4] Vine I. Judgement of direction of gaze: an interpretation of discrepant results. British Journal of Social and Clinical Psychology 1971;10:320-31.

[5] Krüger K, Hückstedt B. Die Beurteilung von Blickrichtungen. Z Exp Angew Psychol 1969;16:452-72.

[6] Symons LA, Lee K, Cedrone CC, Nishimura M. What are you looking at? Acuity for triadic eye gaze. J Gen Psychol 2004;131(4):451-69.

[7] Poppe R, Rienks R, Heylen D. Accuracy of head orientation perception in triadic situations: experiment in a virtual environment. Perception 2007;36(7):971-9.

[8] ISTAG. Ambient intelligence: from vision to reality. European Commission; 2003.

[9] Kendon A. Some function of gaze direction in social interaction. Acta Psychologica 1967;32(6):22-63.

[10] Goodwin C. Notes on story structure and the organization of participation. Structures of social action. In: Atkinson JM, Heritage J, editors. Studies in Conversation Analysis. Cambridge University Press - Editions de la Maison des Sciences de l'Homme; 1984. p. 225-46.

[11] Duncan S. Some signals and rules for taking speaking turns in conversations. J Pers Soc Psychol 1972;23(2):283-92.

[12] Lerner G. Selecting next speaker: the context-sensitive operation of a context-free organization. Language in Society 2003;32:177-201.

[13] Novick DG, Hansen B, Ward K. Coordinating turn-taking with gaze. In: Proceedings of the International Conference on Spoken Language Processing (ICSLP'96). Philadelphia; 1996. p. 1888-91.

[14] Argyle M, Cook M. Gaze and Mutual Gaze. Cambridge University Press; 1976.

[15] Argyle M, Ingham R. The different functions of gaze. Semiotica 1972;7:32-49.

[16] Bonifacci P, Ricciardelli P. Emotional attention: effects of emotion and gaze direction on overt orienting of visual attention. Cognitive Processes 2008;9:127-35.

[17] Willis F, Hamm HK. The use of interpersonal touch in securing compliance. J Nonverbal Behav 1980;5(1):49-55.

[18] Calvo M, Lang PJ. Gaze patterns when looking at emotional pictures: motivationally biased attention. Motivation and Emotion 2004;28(3):221-43.

[19] Ellgring H. Nonverbal expression of psychological states in psychiatric patients. European Archives of Psychiatry and Neurological Sciences 1986;236:31-4.

[20] Bente G, Donaghy WC. Sex differences in body movement and visual attention: an integrated analysis of movement and gaze in mixed-sex dyads. J Nonverbal Behav 1988;22:31-58.

[21] Argyle M, Cook M. Gaze and Mutual Gaze. Cambridge University Press; 1976.

[22] Kleinke CL. Gaze and eye contact: a research review. Psychol Bull 1986;100(1):78-100.

[23] Perrett DI, Emery NJ. Understanding the intention of others from visual signals. Current Psychology of Cognition 1994;13:683-94.

[24] Baron-Cohen S. The reading the mind in the eyes test revised version: a study with normal adults, and adults with Asperger syndrome or high-functioning autism. J Child Psychiatry 2001;42:241-52.

[25] Fukayama A, Ohno T, Mukawa N, Sawaki M, Hagita N. Messages embedded in gaze of interface agents—impression management with agent's gaze. In: CHI '02: Proceedings of the SIGCHI Conference on Human Factors in Computing Systems. ACM Press; 2002. p. 41-8.

[26] Poggi I. Minds, Hands, Face and Body. Weidler Verlag; 2007.

[27] Jacob RJ. Eye tracking in advanced interface design. Virtual Invironments and Advanced Interface Design. In: Barfield W and Furness TA, Eds. Oxford University press, New York, NY, 1995. p. 258-88.

[28] Surakka V, Illi M, Isokoski P. Gazing and frowning as a new human-computer interaction technique. ACM Transactions on Applied Perception 2004;1(1):40-56.

[29] Sibert L, Jacob R. Evaluation of eye gaze interaction. In: Proceedings of the ACM SIGCHI Conference on Human Factors in Comuting Systems. ACM Press; 2000. p. 281-88.

[30] Salvucci DD, Anderson JR. Intelligent gaze-added interfaces. In: CHI 2000. ACM Press; 2000. p. 273-80.

[31] Jacob R, Karn K. Eye Tracking in Human-Computer Interaction and Usability Research: Ready to Deliver the Promises. Elsevier; 2003.

[32] Edwards G. A tool for creating eye-aware applications that adapt to changes in user behaviors. In: Assets '98: Proceedings of the Third International ACM Conference on Assistive Technologies. ACM Press; 1998. p. 67-74.

[33] Jacob R. Eye Movement-Based Human Computer Interaction Techniques: Toward Non-Command Interface. Ablex Publishing; 1993.

[34] Bolt RA. Eyes at the interface. In: Proceedings of the 1982 Conference on Human Factors in Computing Systems. ACM Press; 1982. p. 360-2.

[35] Groner R, Groner MT. Attention and eye movement control: an overview. European Archives of Psychiatry and Neurological Sciences 1989;239:9-16.

[36] Zhai S. What's in the eyes for attentive input. Commun ACM 2003;46(3):34-9.

[37] Oviatt S, Cohen P. Multimodal interfaces that process what comes naturally. Commun ACM 2000;43:45-53.

[38] Kuno Y, Ishiyama T. Combining observations of intentional and unintentional behaviors for human-computer interaction. In: CHI 1999. ACM Press; 1999. p. 238-45.

[39] Frey L, White K, Hutchinson T. Eye-gaze word processing. IEEE Trans Syst Man Cybern 1990;20:944-50.

[40] Qvarfordt P, Zhai S. Conversing with the user based on eye-gaze patterns. In: CHI 2005. ACM Press; 2005. p. 221-30.

[41] Hoekstra A, Prendinger H, Bee N, Heylen D, Ishizuka M. Highly realistic 3D presentation agents with visual attention capability. In: Smart Graphics, vol. 4569. Lecture Notes in Computer Science. Springer Verlag; 2007. p. 73-84.

[42] Sibert JL, Gokturk M, Lavine RA. The reading assistant: eye gaze triggered auditory prompting for reading remediation. In: UIST '00: Proceedings of the 13th Annual ACM Symposium on User Interface Software and Technology. ACM Press; 2000. p. 101-7.

[43] Byron D, Mampilly T, Sharma T, Xu V. Utilizing visual attention for cross-modal coreference interpretation. In: Proceedings of Context-05. Springer Verlag; 2005. p. 83-96.

[44] Campana E, Baldridge J, Dowding J, Hockey BA, Remington RW, Stone LS. Using eye movements to determine referents in a spoken dialogue system. In: PUI '01: Proceedings of the 2001 Workshop on Perceptive User Interfaces. ACM Press; 2001. p. 1-5.

[45] Prasov Z, Chai JY. What's in a gaze? The role of eye-gaze in reference resolution in multimodal conversational interfaces. In: Proceedings of the 13th International Conference on Intellient User Interface. ACM Press; 2008. p. 20-9.

[46] Morency L-P, Christoudias CM, Darrell T. Recognizing gaze aversion gestures in embodied conversational discourse. In: ICMI '06: Proceedings of the 8th International Conference on Multimodal Interfaces. ACM Press; 2006. p. 287-94.

[47] Maglio PP, Campbell CS. Attentive agents. Commun ACM 2003;46(3):47-51.

[48] Matsusaka Y, Tojo T, Kobayashi T. Conversation robot participating in group conversation. IEICE Transactions on Information and Systems 2003;1:26-36.

[49] Breazeal C. Designing Sociable Robots. MIT Press; 2002.

[50] Clodic A, Fleury S, Alami R, Chatila R, Bailly G, Brèthes L, et al. Rackham: an interactive robot-guide. In: IEEE International Workshop on Robots and Human Interactive Communication. Hatfield; 2006. p. 502-9.

[51] Wang H, Chignell M, Ishizuka M. Empathic tutoring software agents using real-time eye tracking. In: Eye Tracking Research and Application Symposium ETRA. ACM Press; 2006. p. 73-8.

[52] Yonezawa T, Yamazoe H, Utsumi A, Abe S. Gaze-communicative behavior of stuffed-toy robot with joint attention and eye contact based on ambient gaze-tracking. In: Proceedings of International Conference on Multimodal Interfaces. 2007. p. 140-5.

[53] Zhang Q, Go K, Imamiya A, Mao X. Overriding errors in a speech and gaze multimodal architecture. In: Intelligent User Interface (IUI). ACM Press; 2004. p. 346-8.

[54] Breitfuss W, Prendinger H, Ishizuka M. Automated generation of non-verbal behavior for virtual embodied characters. In: ICMI '07: Proceedings of the 9th International Conference on Multimodal interfaces. ACM Press; 2007. p. 319-22.

[55] Kim Y, Hill RW, Traum DR. Controlling the focus of perceptual attention in embodied conversational agents. In: AAMAS '05: Proceedings of the Fourth International Joint Conference on Autonomous Agents and Multiagent Systems. ACM Press; 2005. p. 1097-8.

[56] Breton G, Pelé D, Garcia C. Modeling gaze behavior for a 3D ECA in a dialogue situation. In: IUI '06: Proceedings of the 11th International Conference on Intelligent User Interfaces. ACM Press; 2006. p. 333-5.

[57] Cassell J, Thórisson KR. The power of a nod and a glance: envelope vs. emotional feedback in animated conversational agents. International Journal of Applied Artificial Intelligence 1999;13 (4-5):519-38.

[58] Cassell J, Pelachaud C, Badler N, Steedman M, Achorn B, Becket T, et al. Animated conversation: rule-based generation of facial expression, gesture and spoken intonation for multiple conversational agents. In: SIGGRAPH '94: Proceedings of the 21st Annual Conference on Computer Graphics and Interactive Techniques. ACM Press; 1994. p. 413-20.

[59] Cassell J, Nakano YI, Bickmore TW, Sidner CL, Rich C. Non-verbal cues for discourse structure. In: Meeting of the Association for Computational Linguistics. ACL Press; 2001. p. 106-15. Available from: *citeseer.ist.psu.edu/cassell01nonverbal.html*.

[60] Heylen DKJ, van Es J, Nijholt A, van Dijk EMAG. Controlling the gaze of conversational agents. In: van Kuppevelt J, Dybkjaer L, Bernsen NO, editors. Natural, Intelligent and Effective Interaction in Multimodal Dialogue Systems. Kluwer Academic Publishers; 2005. p. 245-62.

[61] Poggi I, Pelachaud C, de Rosis F. Eye communication in a conversational 3D synthetic agent. European Journal on Artificial Intelligence 2000;13(3):169–81.

[62] Lance B, Marsella S. The relation between gaze behavior and the attribution of emotion: an empirical study. In: Prendinger H, Lester JC, Ishizuka M, editors. Intelligent Virtual Agents (IVA). 2008. p. 1–14.

[63] Bolt R. Gaze-orchestrated dynamic windows. In: SIGGRAPH 81: Proceedings of the 8th Annual Conference on Computer Graphics and Interactive Techniques. ACM Press; 1981. p. 109–19.

[64] Gepner D, Simonin J, Carbonell N. Gaze as a supplementary modality for interacting with ambient intelligence environments. In: Constantine Stepahnids, Universal Access in HCI (part II). Springer-Verlag; 2007. p. 848–57.

[65] Yanco H. Wheelesley: a robotic wheelchair system. In: Indoor Navigation and User Interface. Springer-Verlag; 1998. p. 256–68.

[66] Bradbury JS, Shell JS, Knowles CB. Hands on cooking: towards an attentive kitchen. In: CHI '03: Extended Abstracts on Human Factors in Computing Systems. ACM Press; 2003. p. 996–7.

[67] Haritaoglu I, Cozzi A, Koons D, Flickner M, Zotkin DN, Duraiswami R, et al. Attentive toys. In: Proceedings of International Conference on Multimodal Interfaces. ACM Press; 2001. 1124–7.

[68] McCowan I, Gatica-Perez D, Bengio S, Lathoud G, Barnard M, Zhang D. Automatic analysis of multimodal group actions in meetings. IEEE Trans Pattern Anal Mach Intell 2004;27(3):305–17.

[69] Yu Z, Ozeki M, Fujii Y, Nakamura Y. Towards smart meeting: enabling technologies and a real world application. In: Proceedings of International Conference on Multimodal Interfaces. ACM Press; 2007. p. 86–93.

[70] Stiefelhagen R, Zhu J. Head orientation and gaze direction in meetings. In: CHI 2002. ACM Press; 2002. p. 858–9.

[71] Vertegaal R. Look who's talking to whom. Ph.D. thesis. University of Twente; 1998.

[72] Weisbrod RM. Looking behavior in a discussion group. Term paper. Cornell University; 1965.

[73] Lunsford R, Oviatt S. Human perception of intended addressee during computer-assisted meetings. In: Proceedings of International Conference on Multimodal Interfaces. ACM Press; 2006. p. 20–7.

[74] Terken J, Joris I, de Valk L. Multimodal cues for addressee-hood in triadic communication with a human information retrieval agents. In: Proceedings of International Conference on Multimodal Interfaces. ACM Press; 2007. p. 94–101.

[75] Takemae Y, Otsuka K, Mukawa N. Video cut editing rule based on participants' gaze in multiparty conversation. In: Proceedings of the 11th ACM International Conference on Multimedia. ACM Press; p. 303–306.

[76] Rienks R, Nijholt A, Barthelmess P. Pro-active meeting assistants: attention please! AI & Society. The Journal of Human-Centred Systems 2009;23(2):213–31.

[77] Gatica-Perez D, McCowan I, Zhang D, Bengio S. Detecting group interest-level in meetings. In: Proceedings of International Conference on Acoustics, Speech and Signal Processing (ICASSP). 2005. p. 489–92.

[78] Jovanovic N, op den Akker R, Nijholt A. Addressee identification in face-to-face meetings. In: Proceedings of the European Chapter of the ACL. ACL Press; 2006. p. 169–76.

[79] van Turnhout K, Terken J, Bakx I, Eggen B. Identifying the intended addressee in mixed human-human and human-computer interaction from non-verbal features. In: Proceedings of the 7th International Conference on Multimodal Interfaces. ACM Press; 2005. p. 175–82.

[80] Katzenmaier M, Stiefelhagen R, Schultz T. Identifying the addressee in human-human-robot interactions based on head pose and speech. In: Proceedings of the 6th International Conference on Multimodal Interfaces. ACM Press; 2004. p. 144–51.

[81] Matsusaka Y, Enomoto M, Den Y. Simultaneous prediction of dialog acts and address types in three-party conversations. In: Proceedings of International Conference on Multimodal Interfaces. ACM Press; 2007. p. 66–73.

[82] Otsuka K, Yamato J, Takemae Y, Murase H. A probabilistic inference of multi-party conversation structure based on Markov-switching models of gaze patterns, head directions, and utterances. In: Proceedings of International Conference on Multimodal Interfaces. ACM Press; 2005. p. 191–8.

[83] Rienks RJ, Poppe R, Heylen D. Differences in head orientation behavior for speakers and listeners: an experiment in a virtual environment. Transactions on Applied Perception, to appear. 2010;7(1).

[84] Heylen D, op den Akker H. Computing backchannel distributions in multiparty conversations. In: Cassell J, Heylen D, editors. Proceedings of the ACL Workshop on Embodied Language Processing. ACL Press; 2007. p. 17–24.

[85] Otsuka K, Sawada H, Yamato J. Automatic inference of cross-modal nonverbal interactions in multiparty conversations. In: Proceedings of International Conference on Multimodal Interfaces. ACM Press; 2007. p. 255–62.

[86] Rienks R, Heylen D. Automatic dominance detection in meetings using easily obtainable features. In: Bourlard H, Renals S, editors. Revised Selected Papers of the 2nd Joint Workshop on Multimodal Interaction and Related Machine Learning Algorithms, vol. 3869. Lecture Notes in Computer Science. Springer Verlag; 2006. p. 76–86.

[87] Otsuka K, Yamato J, Takemae Y, Murase H. Quantifying interpersonal influence in face-to-face conversations based on visual attention patterns. In: CHI 2005. ACM Press; 2005. p. 1175–80.

[88] Okada K, Maeda F, Ichikawa Y, Matsushita Y. Multiparty video conferencing at virtual social distance. In: Conference on Computer Supported Cooperatiue Work CSCW 94. 1994. p. 385–93.

[89] Ishii H, Kobayashi M. Clearboard: a seamless medium for shared drawing and conversation with eye contact. In: CHI 1992. ACM Press; 1992. p. 525–32.

[90] Ohno T. Weak gaze awareness in video-mediated communication. In: CHI 2005. ACM Press; 2005. p. 1709–12.

[91] Morita T, Mase K, Hirano Y, Kajita S. Reciprocal attentive communication in remote meeting with a humanoid robot. In: Proceedings of International Conference on Multimodal Interfaces. ACM Press; 2007. p. 228–35.

[92] Heylen D, Poel M, Nijholt A. Using the ICAT as avatar in remote meetings. In: Proceedings Multimodal Signals: Cognitive and Algorithmic Issues. Springer; 2009. p. 60–6.

[93] Garau M, Slater M, Bee S, Sasse MA. The impact of eye gaze on communication using humanoid avatans. In: Proceedings of the Conference on Human Factors in Computing Systems (CHI'01). ACM Press; 2001. p. 309–16.

[94] Vertegaal R. The GAZE groupware system: mediating joint attention in multiparty communication and collaboration. In: Proceedings of the Conference on Human Factors in Computing Systems (CHI'99). ACM Press; 1999. p. 294–301.

[95] Jerald J, Daily M. Eye gaze correction for videoconferencing. In: Eye Tracking Research and Application Symposium ETRA'02; 2002. p. 77–81.

[96] Lee I, Jeon B. Enhanced video communication using gaze correction with simplified 3D warping and single camera. In: Multimedia Databases and Image Communication MDIC. Springer; 2001. p. 213–24.

Exploiting Natural Language Generation in Scene Interpretation

Carles Fernández, Pau Baiget, Xavier Roca, and Jordi Gonzàlez

Computer Vision Centre, Universitat Autònoma de Barcelona, Bellaterra, Spain

ABSTRACT

The analysis of human behaviors in image sequences is currently restricted to the generation of quantitative parameters describing where and when motion is being observed. However, recent trends in cognitive vision demonstrate that it is becoming necessary to exploit linguistic knowledge to incorporate abstraction and uncertainty in the analysis and thus enhance the semantic richness of reported descriptions. Toward this end, natural language generation will in the near future constitute a mandatory step toward intelligent user interfacing. Moreover, the characteristics of ambient intelligence demand this process to adapt to users and their context—for example, through multilingual capabilities. This chapter addresses the incorporation of a module for natural language generation into an artificial cognitive vision system, to describe the most relevant events and behaviors observed in video sequences of a given domain. We introduce the required stages to convert conceptual predicates into natural language texts. Experimental results are provided for multilingual generation in various application domains.

Key words: natural language generation, computational linguistics, cognitive vision system, situation analysis.

4.1 INTRODUCTION

The introduction of natural language (NL) interfaces into vision systems has become popular for a broad range of applications. In particular, they have become an important part of surveillance systems, in which human behavior is represented by predefined sequences of events in given contexts [4]. Scenes are evaluated and automatically translated into text by analyzing the contents of the images over time and deciding on the most suitable predefined pattern that applies in each case.

Such a process is referred to as human sequence evaluation (HSE) in [5]. HSE takes advantage of cognitive capabilities for the semantic understanding of observed situations involving humans. It aims to automatically evaluate generally complex human behavior from image sequences in restricted discourse domains. In our case, the domain of interest has been restricted to urban outdoor surveillance environments.

4.2 RELATED WORK

This automatic analysis and description of temporal events was earlier tackled by Marburger et al. [12], who proposed an NL dialogue system in German to retrieve information about traffic scenes. Recent methods for describing human activities from video images were reported by Kojima et al. [9, 10], and automatic visual surveillance systems for traffic applications were studied by Buxton and Gong [1] and Nagel [13] among others. These approaches present one or more specific limitations such as textual generation in a single language, surveillance for vehicular traffic applications only, restrictions for uncertain data, or very rigid environments.

There exist interesting approaches in some of the specific tasks presented here. Hovy [6] described work in discourse generation using discourse structure relations, especially regarding automated planning and generation of text containing multiple sentences. Emele et al. [2] proposed an architecture for the organization of linguistic knowledge for multilingual generation based on typed feature structures. More recently, Lou et al. [11] discussed a general framework for semantic interpretation of vehicle and pedestrian behaviors in visual traffic surveillance scenes.

We aim to build a system that addresses the aforementioned limitations—
monolingual generation, exclusivity of the application domain, uncertainty management, and rigidness—by following the proposals of HSE in order to generate NL
descriptions of human behavior appearing in controlled scenarios. Several considerations have been taken into account for the design of such a system toward
this goal:

- The resulting system should be flexible enough to: (1) enable a multilingual
  generation of discourse in natural language with average external users, and
  (2) enable such a discourse to address the communication of complex events
  happening in the observed scenario—for example, interactions among entities
  from more than one application domain (surveillance over both pedestrians
  and vehicles), contextualization of actions in a metric-temporal framework,
  or statements about reasoned interpretations for certain situations.
- This system has also been restricted to cover a defined domain of interest, given by
  the outdoor inner city scenario used and the model of possible situations to expect.
  As a result, we work with particularized linguistic models, which, however, must
  still be able to automatically produce natural descriptions of the occurring facts.

Experimental results have specialized in a single type of scenario in order to study
the problems in depth, rather than achieve a supposedly generally applicable solution. This agrees with the situatedness property of cognitive systems [18]. Two
particular scenes have been considered, which contain complex situations resulting from the interaction of pedestrians and vehicles in an outdoor environment
(see Figure 4.1). Both consist of crosswalk scenes, in which pedestrians, cars, and
objects appear and interact. In the first scene, four pedestrians cross a road in
different ways. Several behaviors appear in the second scene; displacements, meetings, crossings, object disposals, and more complex situations such as abandoned
objects, danger of being run over, and thefts. Hence, we consider the first scene

(a) (b)

FIGURE 4.1

(a) Crosswalk scene showing simple behavior. (b) Crosswalk scene including more complex
behaviors and interactions.

as simpler than the second one in terms of complexity of the behaviors, interactions, and the semantic analysis required to extract interpretations from them. The recording was obtained using a distributed system of static cameras, and the scenarios were modeled a priori.

Section 4.3 discusses the importance of ontologies in natural interfacing systems, and introduces a conceptual framework for the proposed cognitive vision system. Section 4.4 provides a brief overview of the results obtained at the vision and conceptual levels. In Section 4.5, we detail the main stages and tasks accomplished specifically by the NL generation (NLG) module. In Sections 4.6 and 4.7, some results are shown and evaluated. Section 4.8 highlights some general ideas and concludes the work.

4.3 ONTOLOGY-BASED USER INTERFACES

Interacting with end users is one of the main underlying ideas of the HSE framework, and hence it articulates the mechanisms proposed at the highest level of the evaluation. Figure 4.2 shows the general layout of the surveillance-oriented cognitive vision system in which the NLG module is found. As seen in the figure, the interaction level is based on a bidirectional communication between machine-user and user-machine, undertaken by the NLG and NLU modules, respectively. Even though the two modules are thought to be independent, the range and representations of knowledge must adapt to this overall scheme: That is the goal of the ontology.

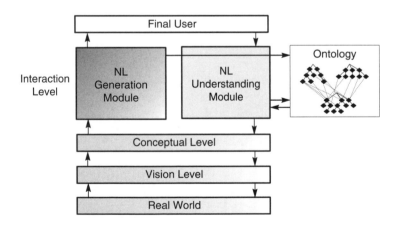

FIGURE 4.2

The NLG module transforms the conceptualized results provided by the vision algorithms into NL text to be presented to external users. Although NLG and NLU use independent mechanisms and grammars, they are both governed by a central ontology, which provides/restricts domain knowledge to the whole stage.

Ontologies are particularly adequate for unifying knowledge. An ontology acts as a central repository of all concepts that are relevant to a certain application, and it informs us about the way these concepts interrelate. In our case, this is firstly useful to provide two independent processes—NLG and NLU—with common underlying semantics. In addition, ontologies help restrict the open universe of possible requests for the system to a closed set of plans provided by the application domain. This is especially useful for NLU, since it helps solve the inherent vagueness of the language of user queries by linking them to a limited set of concepts that can be identified by the system. Hence, we may wonder: Are ontologies only valuable for understanding tasks and not useful for generation? The answer is, not necessarily.

Ontologies provide a consistent and well-organized repository of knowledge, which is mandatory to connect with stored meaningful data but which can also state several semantic properties of the conceptual framework in the domain of interest. This means that we can inform the generation process about the type of knowledge we are describing, thus enabling content-based operations such as filters for the *amount* or *type* of information we produce. Such a capability is mandatory for a natural and user-friendly interface.

In the proposed HSE-based system, we organize the information according to the kind of expressiveness given to the situations that we detect and describe. Talmy organized conceptual material in a cognitive manner by analyzing what he considered crucial parameters in conception: space and time, motion and location, causation and force interaction, and attention and viewpoint [17]. For him, semantic understanding involves the combination of these domains in an integrated whole. Our classification of situations mostly agrees with these structuring domains: We organize semantics in a linear fashion, ranging from structural knowledge in vision processes (quantitative pose vectors) to uncertain, intentional knowledge based on attentional factors (high-level interpretations). This classification is structured as shown Tables 4.1 and 4.2.

The next section gives a better idea of how these concepts are instantiated from visual information captured by a camera system.

4.4 VISION AND CONCEPTUAL LEVELS

The vision level acquires relevant visual content from the scenes by using a distribution of cameras. The detection and capture of interesting objects within the images is accomplished at this stage by means of segmentation and tracking procedures that capture the motion information [7, 16]. As a result, a series of quantitative measurements over time is provided for each detected target, such as positions, velocities, and agent orientations.

In our case, we distinguish among different concepts within a scene: agents (e.g., pedestrians and vehicles); objects (e.g., movable objects like bags or relevant static elements of the scenario such as benches); locations for interesting areas of the

Table 4.1 Knowledge-Based Classification of Human Motion Representations. The three last categories guide the process of interpretation.

	Description	Examples for		
		Agent	Body	Face
Pose Vectors	Array of static configurations over time	Trajectory of locations	Sequence of postures, gestures	Sequence of expressions
Status	Dynamic interpretation of static elements	*Stopped: sitting? standing?*	*Standing: moving head up and down*	*Serious expression: worry? concentration?*
Contextualized Event	Disambiguation using information from other levels	*Standing in front of scene object*	*Nod? search for something?*	*Staring at scene object*
Interpreted Behavior	Hypothesis of interpretation using complete scene knowledge	*"A person is searching for information on the timetables of the subway station"*		

Table 4.2 Taxonomy of some of the Main Concepts from the Event/Situation Taxonomy of the Ontology. This taxonomy classifies the generated descriptions according to their content.

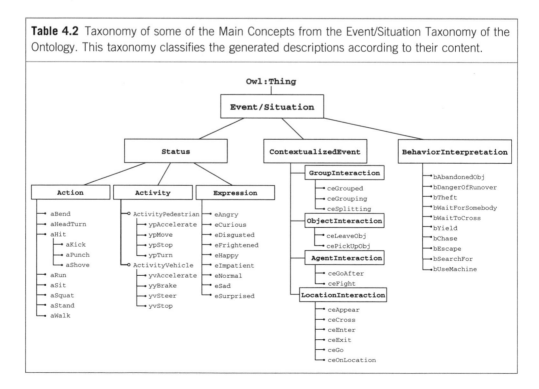

scenario (e.g., sidewalks, crosswalks, or waiting regions); and events for the actions, situations, or behaviors expected in a domain of interest.

Although we could express the observed facts in a quantitative way, such as "The vehicle moved to the right at a speed of 23 km/h," natural language is more inclined to be vague and inexact and to use fuzzy prototypical concepts in order to evaluate facts in linguistic terms. Thus, it would be better to say that the vehicle is moving at low, medium, or high speed depending on the context of this observation, to deal with the inherent uncertainty of the assertions and to better relate and categorize the situations we observe.

The conceptual level accomplishes the conversion from quantitative to qualitative information. First, spatiotemporal data is represented by means of logical predicates created for each frame of the video sequence, in which numerical information is represented by its membership to predefined fuzzy functions. For example, a zero, small, average, or high tag can be assigned, depending on the instantaneous velocity value (V) for an agent (Figure 4.3). Apart from categorizing instantaneous facts, a scenario model also enables us to situate agents and objects in meaningful regions of the recorded location (e.g., crosswalks, sidewalks, or waiting zones).

Nevertheless, we obtained a large collection of basic geometric facts—information about geometric properties such as positions and velocities—that needs to be filtered so that relevant information and patterns are extracted from it. Specifically, our aim is to detect admissible sequences of occurrences, which will contextualize geometric and temporal information about the scene and allow us to interpret the situation an agent is in. For instance, a sequence in which an agent walks

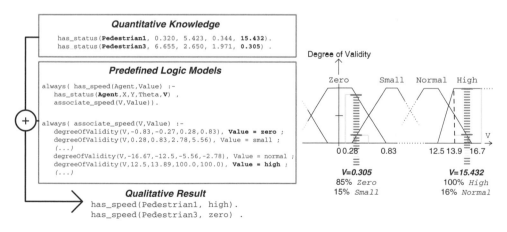

FIGURE 4.3

Conversion from quantitative to qualitative values. The numerical value of velocity for an agent (last field of has_status) at a time step is linked to the most probable membership of the has_speed fuzzy function.

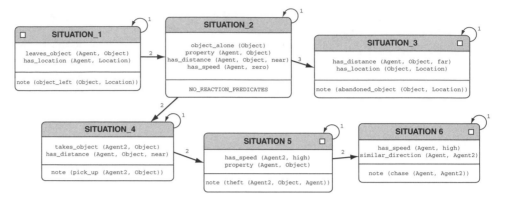

FIGURE 4.4

Situation graph trees are used to model situations and behaviors as predefined sequences of basic events. The situation graph shown, part of a SGT, allows for complex inferences such as abandoned objects, chasings, or thefts by means of high-level note predicates.

by a sidewalk and stops in front of a crosswalk probably means that this agent is waiting to cross.

Situation graph trees are the specific tool used to build these models [2, 5], as shown in Figure 4.4. They connect a set of defined situations by means of prediction and specialization edges. When a set of conditions is asserted, a high-level predicate is produced as an interpretation of a situation. An interesting property at this point is that the produced notes are much closer to a linguistic reading, since they interrelate and put into context different semantic elements such as locations, agents, and objects. Nevertheless, these expressions still maintain language independence and hence are a good starting point for multilingual text generation. More information about this situational analysis can be found in [3].

4.5 THE NLG MODULE

NLG can be seen as a subfield of both computer science and cognitive science. Because it focuses on computer systems that can automatically produce understandable texts in a natural human language, it is concerned with computational models of language and its use. NLG has often been considered as a process of choice, in which the most suitable means must be selected to achieve some desired end [15].

The set of situations that need to be expressed are modeled and made available to the purposed NLG module, so that the module's main goal consists of selecting one unique form of expressing that information in a clear and natural way for each of the languages considered. This module is then built from a deterministic point of

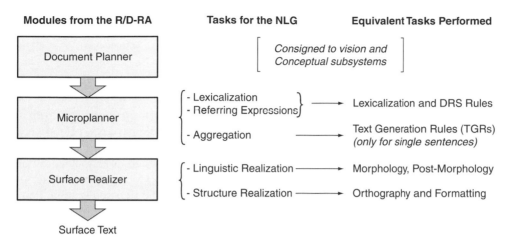

Modules from the R/D-RA   **Tasks for the NLG**   **Equivalent Tasks Performed**

Document Planner — [Consigned to vision and Conceptual subsystems]

Microplanner
- Lexicalization
- Referring Expressions } ⟶ Lexicalization and DRS Rules
- Aggregation ⟶ Text Generation Rules (TGRs) (only for single sentences)

Surface Realizer
- Linguistic Realization ⟶ Morphology, Post-Morphology
- Structure Realization ⟶ Orthography and Formatting

Surface Text

FIGURE 4.5

Schema of the Reiter/Dale Reference Architecture [16], including the tasks related to each module that are necessary for a natural language generator.

view, since it deals with already known situational models. Reiter and Dale [15] presented a roadmap of the main tasks to be solved regarding NL text generation. Their proposed architecture model (Figure 4.5) includes three modules:

- *A document planner*, which produces a specification of the text's content and structure (i.e., what has to be communicated by the NLG), using both domain knowledge and practical information to be embedded into text.
- *A microplanner*, in charge of filling in the missing details regarding the concrete implementation document structure (i.e., how the information has to be communicated: distribution, referring expressions, level of detail, voice, etc.).
- *A surface realizer*, which converts the abstract specification given by the previous stages into real text, possibly embedded within some medium. It involves traversing the nodal text specification until the final presentation form.

Our system is based on this generic approach and enhances it by including multilingual capabilities and situation-guided content planning. Visual trackers acquire basic quantitative information about the scene, and the reasoning system decides how this information needs to be structured, provides coherency to the results, and carries out inferences based on predefined conceptual and situational models. All of these tasks are related to the document planner since they provide the structured knowledge to be communicated to the user. Other tasks, such as microplanning and surface realization, are specifically included in the NLG module.

The NLG module receives high-level semantic predicates from the reasoning stage, which are eventually converted into surface text. This is a sequence of words, punctuation symbols, and markup annotations to be presented to the end user.

There are several tasks to cover in carrying out this process; they have been structured into the following stages:

Stage 1: discourse representation
Stage 2: lexicalization
Stage 3: surface realization

Also, the set of lemmata for the domain of interest has to be extracted from a restricted corpus of the specific language. The different corpora have been elaborated based on the results of several psychophysical experiments on motion description collected from a significant number of native speakers of the target language. In our case, ten people independently contributed to the corpus with their own descriptions of the sample videos, according to the capabilities of the tracking system. Four languages were implemented for this scenario: Catalan, English, Italian, and Spanish.

4.5.1 Representation of the Discourse

The chosen approach to implement semantics for NL generation is based on discourse representation theory [8], which allows the semantic structures representing linguistic information contained in NL sentences to be constructed in predicate logic formalism. Semantic relationships are stated by means of discourse representation structures (DRSs). Here, the inverse process is implemented, consisting of the retrieval of NL text from logic predicates by defining a set of DRS construction and transformation rules for each language.

DRSs are semantic containers that relate referenced conceptual information to linguistic constructions [8]. A DRS always consists of a so-called universe of referents and a set of conditions that express characteristics of these referents, relations between them, or even more complex conditions including other DRSs in their definition. These structures contain linguistic data from units that may be larger than single sentences, since one of the ubiquitous characteristics of DRSs is their semantic cohesiveness for an entire discourse.

One of the main semantic characteristics to take into account is cohesiveness. When a contextual basis is explicitly provided, the maintenance of the meaning of a discourse, including its cross-references, relations, and cohesion, can be granted. A particularly interesting and comprehensible example of discourse cohesion is anaphoric pronominalization, which allows the generation of some referring expressions; for instance, we typically discard "The pedestrian waits to cross. The pedestrian crosses," in favor of "The pedestrian waits to cross. S/he crosses."

Using such structures, we can point out the cross-references existing among the semantic constituents of a predicate. The classification of linguistically perceived reality into thematic roles (e.g., agent, object, location) is commonly used in contemporary linguistics-related applications as a possibility for the representation of semantics, and it justifies the use of computational linguistics for describing content extracted by vision processes. In the current implementation, these constituents can be classified as agents, objects, locations, and events/situations.

Given that a situational analysis is accomplished for each detected agent, we take previously mentioned information about the focused agent as a basis to decide on referenced expressions or full descriptions. An example that shows how semantic representation and contextualization are undertaken by a DRS is illustrated in Figure 4.6. DRSs also facilitate subsequent tasks for sentence generation. The syntactical features of a sentence are provided by so-called text generation rules (TGRs), which establish positions of the discourse elements within a sentence for a particular language. Because of the specific goals for this system, simple sentences are used for effective communication.

The question of how to address temporal references also arises at the semantic level. A natural possibility consists of tensing a statement of recent observations in the present perfect (e.g., "He has turned left") and handling inferences in the present (e.g., "He waits to cross"), although there is a certain flexibility in tense selection. A discourse referent for the utterance time of discourse (n) is required, so that the rest of the temporal references t_i can be positioned with respect to it (Figure 4.6).

Conceptual Facts: *(linguistic-oriented predicates)*

$$\cdots$$

```
  5 : 150   !   kick (agent_1, vending_machine)
171 : 213   !   stare (agent_2, agent_1)
```

Discourse Representation and Contextualization:

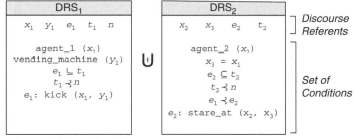

Context *(1st predicate)*   Preliminary DRS *(2nd predicate)*

Linguistic Results:

"**agent_1** kicked the vending machine. Next, **agent_2** stared at him."

FIGURE 4.6

A pattern DRS allows the conversion of a stream of conceptual predicates into a string of textual symbols. Here two predicates are validated. The first one instantiates a DRS, which serves as context for the following asserted facts. Once a new predicate is validated, it instantiates another DRS, which merges with that context, thus providing a new context for subsequent facts. The temporal order of the events is stated by including them within time variables ($e_1 \subseteq t_1$), placing these variables in the past ($t_1 \prec n$), and marking precedence ($e_1 \prec e_2$).

4.5.2 Lexicalization

As stated in [15], lexicalization is the process of choosing words and syntactic structures to communicate the information in a document plan, that is, the interpreted knowledge of logical predicates within a defined domain. Concretely, we will have to map the messages from the predicates, now linked by DRSs, into words and other linguistic resources that explain the semantic contents we want to communicate. It is difficult to bound the lexicalization process to a single module, since the mappings from semantic to linguistic terms are accomplished at several stages of the architecture. In this section we focus on lexicalization of prior knowledge (i.e., agents, objects, and locations), which have to be known beforehand.

The lexicalization step can be seen as a mapping process, in which the semantic concepts identifying different entities and events from the selected domain are attached to linguistic terms referring to those formal realities. This step works as an actual dictionary, providing the required lemmata that will be a basis for describing the results using natural language. Parsing processes will be in charge of traversing the syntactical structures obtained by the text generation rules and replacing the semantic identifiers with their suitable linguistic patterns. Figure 4.7 is an example of lexicalization for two previously known identifiers of semantic regions from the scenario.

4.5.3 Surface Realization

The surface realization stage is completed in two steps. First a morphological process is applied to each word and partially disambiguates the individual abstraction of that word by means of morphological attributions such as gender or number. These attributions can be propagated on the semantic relations previously established by the DRSs among the lemmata of a single piece of discourse. After that, a

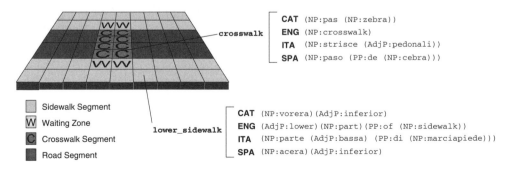

FIGURE 4.7

Example depicting lexicalization for locations, in which a linguistic structure is associated with a semantic region of the scenario for each considered language. Only basic structural information is represented here, although morphological characteristics are also provided to the linguistic terms at this step.

Table 4.3 Examples of Simple Morphological Rules in Catalan, English, and Italian. Rules 1 and 2, in English, allow reducing the participle tag of a verb for two exceptions and producing the word form. Rule 3 produces the participle in general. The other rules, for Catalan and Italian, deal with prosodic manipulation: Rule 4 covers the contractions of a preposition with a determiner, and Rules 5 and 6 are for apostrophication, when certain words appear in front of a word with an initial vowel.

$$(1)\ \langle"go"\rangle \begin{bmatrix} verb \\ particip. \end{bmatrix} \xrightarrow{\text{ENG}} \langle"gone"\rangle[verb]$$

$$(2)\ \langle"meet"\rangle \begin{bmatrix} verb \\ particip. \end{bmatrix} \xrightarrow{\text{ENG}} \langle"met"\rangle[verb]$$

$$(3)\ \langle\alpha\rangle \begin{bmatrix} verb \\ particip. \end{bmatrix} \xrightarrow{\text{ENG}} \langle\alpha + "ed"\rangle[verb]$$

$$(4)\ \langle"a"\rangle[prep.] + \langle"el"\rangle \begin{bmatrix} determ. \\ masc. \\ sing. \end{bmatrix} \xrightarrow[\text{ITA}]{\text{CAT}} \langle"al"\rangle \begin{bmatrix} prep. \\ determ. \\ masc. \\ sing. \end{bmatrix}$$

$$(5)\ \langle"de"\rangle[prep.] + \langle vowel + \alpha\rangle \xrightarrow[\text{ITA}]{\text{CAT}} \langle"d'"\rangle[prep.] + \langle vowel + \alpha\rangle$$

$$(6)\ \langle\alpha\rangle \begin{bmatrix} determ. \\ sing. \end{bmatrix} + \langle vowel + \beta\rangle \xrightarrow[\text{ITA}]{\text{CAT}} \langle"l'"\rangle[determ.] + \langle vowel + \beta\rangle$$

---

set of post-morphological rules is conceived to enable interactions among predefined configurations of words, thus affecting the final surface form of the text. This additional step is indispensable for many languages, in which certain phenomena force the surface form to change: contractions ($a + el \rightarrow al$, in Spanish) or order variation ($es + va + en \rightarrow se$ '$n\ va$, in Catalan). Table 4.3 lists examples of morphological rules included in the grammar used for parsing.

Finally, a general scheme for the entire process of generation is shown in Figure 4.8. The sentence "He is waiting with another pedestrian" is generated step by step from logical predicates for the English language. The center column contains the tasks being performed, the right column indicates the output obtained after each task.

4.6 EXPERIMENTAL RESULTS

Here we provide some results for the two scenes considered (Table 4.4). For the first crosswalk scene, textual descriptions in Catalan, English, and Spanish have been selected for Agents 3 and 4, respectively. They include agents appearing or leaving, interactions with locations, and basic interpretations such as waiting with others to

```
pedestrian(ag2), has_speed(ag2,zero),
pedestrian(ag3), has_speed(ag3,zero),
    ag2 <> ag3, on_waiting_line(ag2)
```
Logical Relations in FMTHL   (Logical Predicates)

```
            waiting_with(ag2,ag3)
                 pedestrian(ag2)
                 pedestrian(ag3)
```
Lexicalization Rules   (DRSs, Lemmata)

Event:	waiting(ag2)
Attribute:	with (ag3)
Agent:	pedestrian(ag2)
Object:	pedestrian(ag3)

Syntax

Text Generation Rules (TGRs) + DRSs   (Syntactical Form / Sentence with Referring Expressions)

"pedestrian wait with pedestrian"

REG

"he wait with another pedestrian"

Morphology   (Word Forms)

"he is waiting with another pedestrian"

Orthography and Formatting   (Surface Text)

"He is waiting with another pedestrian."

FIGURE 4.8

Generation of the sentence "He is waiting with another pedestrian" from logical predicates and for the English language.

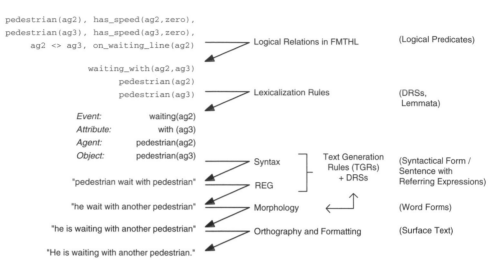

Table 4.4 Experimental Results for the First Scene

Pedestrian 3 (Catalan)	Pedestrian 3 (English)
203 : Lo vianant surt per la part inferior dreta.	203 : The pedestrian shows up from the lower right side.
252 : Va per la vorera inferior.	252 : S/he walks on the lower sidewalk.
401 : S'espera per creuar.	401 : S/he waits to cross.
436 : S'està esperant amb un altre vianant.	436 : S/he is waiting with another pedestrian.
506 : Creua pel pas zebra.	506 : S/he enters the crosswalk.
616 : Va per la vorera superior.	616 : S/he walks on the upper sidewalk.
749 : Se'n va per la part superior dreta.	749 : S/he leaves by the upper right side.

Table 4.4 Experimental Results for the First Scene—cont'd

Pedestrian 4 (Spanish)	Pedestrian 4 (English)
523 : El peatón aparece por la parte inferior izquierda.	523 : The pedestrian shows up from the lower left side.
572 : Camina por la acera inferior.	572 : S/he walks on the lower sidewalk.
596 : Cruza sin cuidado por la calzada.	596 : S/he crosses the road carelessly.
681 : Camina por la acera superior.	681 : S/he walks on the upper sidewalk
711 : Se va por la parte superior izquierda.	711 : S/he leaves by the upper left side.

cross or crossing in a dangerous way (i.e., crossing the road directly without looking for vehicular traffic). The average measured time for generating a single sentence was 3 milliseconds, with a Pentium D 3.20 GHz and 2.00 GB RAM.

Table 4.5 shows results for the second scene in Catalan, Italian, and English. In this case there exist more complex interactions and interpretations of events, such as abandoned objects, dangers of runover, thefts, and chasings.

4.7 EVALUATION

Thirty native English speakers were recruited from among different sources in five countries. Less than one-third of the subjects were members of a computer science department, and none of them had an NLP background. Subjects were told to describe both sequences in a natural and linguistically correct manner, using the expressions they considered most suitable. Only the results concerning the second sequence (the one showing vehicular traffic) are presented, since they contain a greater number of facts, enable more subjective interpretation, and thus better state the main problems of our approach.

The ground truth of the second sequence contained 30 basic facts, and so a limitation was imposed to make subjects describe a number of facts, between 20 and 40, in order to deal with comparable levels of detail. However, they were free to include

Table 4.5 Some Experimental Results for the Second Scene

(…)
470 ! Un vianant surt per la part superior asquerra.
470 ! A pedestrian appears from the upper left side.
470 ! Un pedone compare nella parte superiore sinistra.
492 ! Lo vianant camina per la vorera superior.
492 ! Il pedone cammina sulla parte alta del marciapiede.
492 ! The pedestrian walks on the upper part of the sidewalk.
583 ! Gira pac a la dreta per la part superior de lo pas zebra.
583 ! S/he turns right in the upper part of the crosswalk.
583 ! Gira a destra sulla parte alta delle strisce pedonali.
591 ! S'ha parat allà mateix.
591 ! S/he has stopped in the same place.
591 ! Si fermato in questa posizione.
615 ! Ha dixat l'objecte a terra.
615 ! S/he has left an object.
615 ! Ha lasciato un oggetto in terra.
630 ! Un nou vianant surt per la part superior dreta.
630 ! A new pedestrian appears from the upper right side.
630 ! Un altro pedone compare nella parte superiore destra.
642 ! Lo vianant camina per la vorera superior.
642 ! The pedestrian walks on the upper part of the sidewalk.
642 ! Il pedone cammina sulla parte alta del marciapiede.

(…)
687 ! L'objecte pareix haver astat dixat a la part superior de lo pas zebra.
687 ! The object seems to have been abandoned in the upper part of the crosswalk.
687 ! L'oggetto sembra che sia stato abbandonato nella parte alta delle strisce pedonali.
692 ! Lo primer vianant s'ha trobat en lo segon vianant allà mateix.
692 ! The first pedestrian has met the second pedestrian in the same place.
692 ! Il primo pedone si è incontrato con il secondo pedone in questa posizione.

(…)
822 ! Un vehicle pareix que astà a punt d'atropellar lo primer vianant.
822 ! A danger of runover between the first pedestrian and a vehicle seems to have been detected.
822 ! Un veicolo ha rischiato d'investire il primo pedone.
(…)

them in either single or compound sentences; for example, "A kid runs, then falls down, and finally gets up again" was considered as three events in one sentence. Table 4.9 presents statistical graphs concerning the population and the basic results of the experiment.

4.7.1 Qualitative Results

A qualitative comparison between the generated data and the collected set was carried out regarding several concerns: The main objective at a semantic level has been to detect the differences between the set of facts detected by the subjects and that generated by the system. We also wanted to learn the mechanisms of reference used and which types of words, expressions, and connectors were being employed most often. These were compared to our choices. When considering the facts to compare to the inputs, those having closely related meanings were gathered together, e.g., *notice-realize*, and *run after-chase-chase after*.

- A practical rule for simplicity is deduced from the results. The majority of cases avoid obvious explanations that can be logically derived from a more expressive linguistic choice. When one states "A man walks down the sidewalk," there is no need to include "A man appears." Also, there is no need to state that a person is "bending" when picking up an object; that is obvious when the object is known to be on the ground.
- The greater difference regarding expressiveness occurs when the subjects deduce the agent intentions via context using common sense—for instance, "He waves his hands in amazement that the car didn't stop" or "He seemed somewhat hesitant." Sometimes, situations in the scene are anticipated, such as "A person is walking to the zebra crossing to meet someone." These constructions are very useful in discourse.
- One of the main tasks lacking in the described generation system is the aggregation of simple sentences into more complex and expressive ones, using mechanisms such as coordination or subordination. This has the main advantage of emphasizing certain elements of the discourse. For instance, "After crossing the street they stop, one of them puts his bag on the ground, and while they are talking, another guy comes and snatches the bag" prioritizes the object left over the crossing and the theft over the talk.
- The use of certain adverbs, adjectives, and other complementary words has been seen as leading toward a richer discourse. These include "nearly hit by an oncoming vehicle," "jumps back in surprise," "moves back slightly," and "they only crossed the street halfway."

4.7.2 Quantitative Results

To retrieve some quantitative measures of the adequacy of the proposed generation, we provide some statistical results that compare the frequencies of use of the two sets of facts: those generated and those collected. The main purpose is to decide up to which point the current capabilities of the vision-tracking and conceptual-reasoning levels enable us to provide natural results.

Figure 4.9 shows statistics about the NL generation experiment. Based on these sorted results, we easily identify facts that should be included, replaced, or removed from the current set. The list of descriptions generated by the system contains many of the most frequent facts: The system generates 100% of those used by more than half of the participants and 77.8% of those employed above the average share of facts (25.9%). The average share was computed as the average of the proportions of the facts in the whole list.

- First, we notice some of facts referring to the same situations in different ways, such as "danger of runover" and "almost hit/knock down/run over pedestrians" and "pass without stopping/not let pedestrians cross." Selecting suitable terms depends on the purposed application, and hence it is not identified as a main concern.

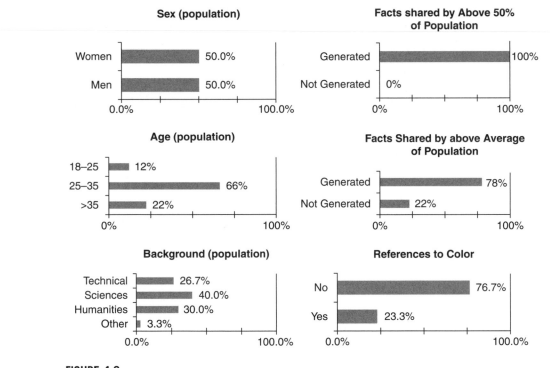

FIGURE 4.9

Statistics about the NL generation experiment for English and the outdoor sequence. The population consisted of 30 subjects from different backgrounds. The left column contains information about the population; the right column shows quantitative results about the evaluation and comparison with the facts used.

- Concerning facts to add, the most significative are those referring to the conversation and interactions between the first two pedestrians ("talk," "shake hands," "greet each other," "wave," "chat"). This points out an actual limitation of the tracking system, which as yet cannot provide such detailed information about body postures.
- Some of the facts used should be discarded. Some features were detected that seem to indicate that facts are not interesting enough to be included in the final text. These include being obvious (reach the other side after crossing, bend to take an object), being an uncommon expression (having an exchange, motioning someone somewhere), being too subjective (two people being friends), or guessing emotions (seem confused, angry, or surprised). When a situation can be interpreted in more than one way, each interpretation receives less support than a unique one, so that uncertainty is another factor to consider.

It is also interesting that just about one-quarter of the population included color references to support their descriptions. Most of these (above 70%) used a single reference, for the "white car," which is the only agent with a very distinctive color.

4.8 CONCLUSIONS

From the qualitative considerations, we notice a great difficulty: how to balance objectively certain hard facts with more expressive but also more uncertain facts to obtain a consistent description of what is happening, at the same time making the generated text relevant and communicative. The system should be enhanced with a richer use of complementary words; on the other hand, simple sentences should be aggregated as needed to lead the discourse to defined goals. Some behavioral models should be included as well in order to introduce interpretations regarding agent intentionality.

The quantitative results obtained provide objective information about the facts that should be considered. However, some of the less frequently used facts are appropriate for description, such as people "having brief exchanges" or a pedestrian "motioning" to someone somewhere. This suggests running new experiments, where subjects can choose among different expressions to refer to the situations observed. In this way, the subjects would not be hampered by not finding a suitable expression.

Regarding multilinguality, the system performed in the same way and presented the same problems in English as in the other languages considered.

Most of the limitations for the described NLG module are clearly determined by the restrictive domain of work. The linguistic models need to be extended as new situations are detected by the HSE system, since the content to be communicated is provided entirely by the ontology by means of situational analysis. The deterministic approach chosen limits the variety of produced sentences, but ensures that the output results will be linguistically correct, since they obey the constructions proposed by native speakers and encoded in the models.

The modular architecture proposed for the NLG subsystem apparently allows the common stages to remain unchanged, disregarding the incorporation of new languages or the enlargement of the detection scope. So far, the addition of a new language has required only the extension of DRS rules and parsing grammars, which allows for a fast and effective implementation of similar languages.

Future work includes an enhancement of the microplanner to support sentence aggregation. This will allow ordering the information structured in single sentences and mapping it to more complex sentences and paragraphs. Discourse representation theory has been proved consistent to accomplish this task [8].

ACKNOWLEDGMENTS

This work is supported by EC grants IST-027110 for the HERMES project and IST-045547 for the VIDI-Video project, and by the Spanish MEC under projects TIN2006-14606 and CONSOLIDER-INGENIO 2010 (CSD2007-00018). Jordi Gonzàlez also acknowledges the support of a Juan de la Cierva Post-doctoral fellowship from the Spanish MEC.

APPENDIX LISTING OF DETECTED FACTS SORTED BY FREQUENCY OF USE

Here we present the percentages of use for the facts detected by subjects. Facts are described schematically (Ped = Pedestrian, Veh = Vehicle, Obj = Object). Shadowed facts are currently those used for automatic generation. We use line separators to state those percentages that appear above average and below 10%.

Used	Fact
100%	Ped1 leaves object1
100%	Peds1,2 cross / try to cross / walk to other side / want to cross
90.0%	Ped1 walks
86.7%	Ped2 leaves Obj2
83.3%	Ped3 runs / runs off / runs away
83.3%	Peds1,2 enter crosswalk / cross / go across / go on crossing
83.3%	Veh2 gives way / stops / wait for them to cross
80.0%	Ped2 chases / chases after / runs after Ped3
70.0%	Ped3 picks up / grabs / snatches Obj2
63.3%	Peds1,2 meet / stand close
60.0%	Ped3 appears / enters
50.0%	Ped3 crosses

Used	Fact
50.0%	Ped3 steals / thief
50.0%	Peds2 walks / comes
46.7%	Ped3 walks / approaches / comes
46.7%	Veh1 passes without stopping / not allowing them to cross
46.7%	Veh2 appears / comes
43.3%	Peds1,2 back up and stop / pull back
43.3%	Peds1,2 talk / chat / have a conversation (upper crosswalk)
40.0%	Ped1 stops / reaches crosswalk (ped1)
40.0%	Ped2 appears
40.0%	Peds1,2 stop / stand (lower crosswalk)
40.0%	Veh1 appears / comes
36.7%	Peds1,2 notice/realize/see Ped3
36.7%	Veh1 almost hits / knocks down / runs over Peds1,2
33.3%	Peds2,3 run
33.3%	Peds1,2 shake hands (upper)
26.7%	Ped1 holds briefcase / ... with a bag
26.7%	Peds1,2 greet each other
26.7%	Peds1,2 talk / converse / chat (lower crosswalk)
23.3%	Ped1 appears
20.0%	Ped1,2 keep on talking / while they talk (while crossing)
20.0%	Peds1,2 stop at Veh1
20.0%	Veh2 arrives / approaches at the crossing pass
16.7%	Object1 abandoned / forgotten
13.3%	Ped2 waves / attracts attention of Ped1
13.3%	Peds1,2 shake hands (lower crosswalk)
13.3%	Peds1,2 still talking / keep on chatting (lower crosswalk)
13.3%	Peds2,3 leave
13.3%	Veh1 accelerates / goes on
13.3%	Veh1 reaches / runs toward / approaches
13.3%	Veh2 exits / passes by
10.0%	danger of run over / about to run over
10.0%	Ped1 eventually follows the chase
10.0%	Ped1 stays watching
10.0%	Peds1,2 start talking (lower crosswalk)
10.0%	Ped3 does not notice / ignores Obj1
10.0%	Ped3 walks away from them
10.0%	shout at the driver
10.0%	Veh2 accelerate /drives on
6.7%	Ped1 says hello to Ped2
6.7%	Ped1 spins around confused / looks on bewildered / seems hesitant

Used	Fact
6.7%	Ped1 walks away
6.7%	Ped2 reaches / arrives to Ped1
6.7%	Ped2 tries to recover / reclaims his bag
6.7%	Peds1,2 complain against / protest to car driver / raise / wave hands
6.7%	Peds1,2 do not notice Ped3
6.7%	Peds1,2 do not pay attention when crossing
6.7%	Peds1,2 reach to the other side
6.7%	Peds1,2 say goodbye to each other
6.7%	Peds1,2 wait to let Veh2 pass
6.7%	Veh1 leaves
3.3%	brief exchange between Peds1,2
3.3%	Ped1 checks road
3.3%	Ped1 motions Ped2 to cross
3.3%	Ped1 motions Ped2 to cross
3.3%	Peds1,2 have a brief exchange
3.3%	Peds1,2 out of range of vehicles
3.3%	Ped2 tells Ped1 about Ped3
3.3%	Ped3 bends down
3.3%	Ped3 ducks
3.3%	Ped3 notices Obj2
3.3%	Ped3 stops near Obj2
3.3%	Peds 1,2 seem to be friends
3.3%	Peds1,2 are angry at Veh1
3.3%	Peds1,2 are surprised
3.3%	Peds1,2 communicate
3.3%	Peds1,2 let the car continue its way
3.3%	Peds1,2 wait for car to pass
3.3%	Veh1 brakes up

REFERENCES

[1] Buxton H, Gong S. Visual surveillance in a dynamic and uncertain world. AI Magazine 1995;78(1–2):431–59.

[2] Emele M, Heid U, Momma S, Zajac R. Organizing linguistic knowledge for multilingual generation. In: Proceedings of the 13th Annual Conference on Computational Linguistics, vol. 3. Association for Computational Linguistics; 1990. p. 102–7.

[3] Fernandez C, Baiget P, Roca X, Gonzàlez J. Semantic annotation of complex human scenes for multimedia surveillance. In: Tenth Congress of the Italian Association for Artificial Intelligence (AI*IA). Springer LNAI; 2007. p. 698–709.

[4] Gerber R, Nagel H-H. Representation of occurrences for road vehicle traffic. Artificial Intelligence 2008;172(4–5):351–91.

[5] Jordi Gonzàlez, Daniel Rowe, Javier Varona, F. Xavier Roca, "Understanding Dynamic Scenes based on Human Sequence Evaluation", Image and Vision Computing, Volume 27, Issue 10, Pages 1433-1444, September, 2009.

[6] Hovy EH. Automated discourse generation using discourse structure relations. Artificial Intelligence 1993;63(1-2):341-85.

[7] Huerta I, Rowe D, Mozerov M, Gonzàlez J. Improving Background Subtraction Based on a Casuistry of Colour-Motion Segmentation Problems. 3rd ed. IbPRIA: Springer LNCS; 2007. p. 475-82.

[8] Kamp H, Reyle U. From Discourse to Logic. Kluwer Academic Publishers; 1993.

[9] Kojima A, Izumi M, Tamura T, Fukunaga K. Generating natural language description of human behavior from video images. In: ICPR. IAPR; 2000. p. 728-31.

[10] Kojima A, Tamura T, Fukunaga K. Natural language description of human activities from video images based on concept hierarchy of actions. International Journal of Computer Vision 2002;50(2):171-84.

[11] Lou J, Liu Q, Tan T, Hu W. Semantic interpretation of object activities in a surveillance system. In: ICPR, IAPR; 2002. p. 777-80.

[12] Marburger H, Neumann B, Novak H. Natural language dialogue about moving objects in an automatically analyzed traffic scene. In: IJCAI-81; 1982.

[13] Nagel H-H. Steps toward a cognitive vision system. AI Magazine 2004;25(2):31-50.

[14] Nevatia R, Zhao T, Hongeng S. Hierarchical language-based representation of events in video streams. In: Proc. IEEE Workshop on Event Mining. IEEE; 2003.

[15] Reiter E, Dale R. Building Natural Language Generation Systems. Cambridge University Press; 2000.

[16] Rowe D, Rius I, Gonzàlez J, Villanueva J. Improving tracking by handling occlusions. In: 3rd ICAPR. Springer LNCS; 2005. p. 384-93.

[17] Talmy L. Toward a Cognitive Semantics, vol. 1: Concept Structuring Systems. Bradford Books; 2000.

[18] Wilson R, Keil F, editors. The MIT Encyclopedia of the Cognitive Sciences. Bradford Books; 2001.

The Language of Action: A New Tool for Human-Centric Interfaces

5

Yiannis Aloimonos

CVL (Computer Vision Laboratory), UMIACS (Institute for Advanced Computer Studies) Cognitive Science Program, Computer Science Department, University of Maryland, College Park, Maryland

Gutemberg Guerra-Filho

Sensory-Motor Intelligence Laboratory, Department of Computer Science and Engineering, University of Texas at Arlington, Arlington, Texas

Abhijit Ogale

Google Corporation, Mountain View, California

ABSTRACT

One of the major goals of human-centric interfaces is for humans to interact with robots or other machines as they do with other humans. To achieve this we need to analyze and interpret human activity sensed by a variety of sensors. In order to develop useful technology and a subsequent industry around human-centric interfaces, we need to proceed in a principled fashion. This chapter suggests that human activity can be expressed in a language, a special language with its own phonemes, its own morphemes (words), and its own syntax. This language can be inferred using machine learning techniques applied to gargantuan amounts of data collected by cameras or other sensor networks. Developing sensory-motor language will create bridges among several disciplines. It will also provide a hierarchical structure that can lead to a successful industry. We point to a research program and the application of its early realizations to a few domains.

5.1 INTRODUCTION

User interface designers today focus on nontraditional interfaces that make use of each of the five human senses. In principle, then, we could design interfaces where a human would interact with a machine as he would with another human. In this chapter we focus on vision. If machines equipped with vision sensors are able to understand our movements and actions, this understanding can become the basis of a new breed of human-centric interfaces. The measurements in such an interface are accomplished with sensor networks [24, 35].

One can easily see that building a specific human-centric interface requires a set of rules and patterns. In an elder care situation, for instance, doctors or primary caregivers would use an in-home human-centric interface to monitor activity levels, detect "fall" or "stuck" situations, and prevent elders from engaging in risky behaviors. In another situation, when a human centric interface is serving people with various challenges, we need to understand gestures.

How are we going to achieve this? For every new application, must we come up with the rules and patterns? This is what is happening today in the state of the art. In recent literature, we note a number of very interesting approaches for interpreting the sensory data stream.

Many of these approaches are based on very simple features that can be extracted from the data, yet such features could be sufficient for solving a specific problem. One interesting example is determining the amount of time a person spends at a particular location. Because of the vast amount of training data, the appropriate distributions of timing could be built and used for inference [31, 33, 51].

Looking into the future, however, it is clear that we must adopt a more basic approach. After all, human-centric interfaces "sense" interacting and behaving humans. In other words, the human-centric interfaces of the future will need to interpret human activity. In the sequel, a research program along this line of thought is outlined, assuming that the sensors are ordinary video cameras. Section 5.2 introduces the multimodal aspect of human activity, and Section 5.3 points to the possibilities for learning. Sections 5.4 and 5.5 get into some of the details, and Sections 5.6 and 5.7, respectively, show applications to health and artificial cognitive systems.

5.2 HUMAN ACTION

One of the important lessons from the field of neuroscience [7, 15, 26, 43] is the model of action shown in Figure 5.1. Before the command is sent to the muscle, a copy (the efference copy) is kept. The efference copy can be used with forward models and predicted feedback in order to "think" about an action without actually doing it. In other words, we have inside our minds abstract representations of actions, our own and others'. It is these representations that sensor networks of the future should be extracting.

Knowledge of actions is crucial to our survival. Hence, human infants begin to learn actions by watching and imitating those performed by others. With time, they learn to combine and chain simple actions to form more complex actions. This process can be likened to speech, where we combine simple constituents called phonemes into words, and words into clauses and sentences.

The analogy does not end here: Humans can recognize as well as generate both actions and speech. In fact, the binding between the recognitive and generative aspects of actions is revealed at the neural level in the monkey brain by the presence of mirror neuron networks. These are neuron assemblies that fire when a monkey observes an action (e.g., grasping) and when the monkey performs the same action [15]. All these observations lead us to a simple hypothesis: *Actions are effectively characterized by a language*. This language has its own building blocks (phonemes), its own words (lexicon), and its own syntax.

The realm of human actions (e.g., running, walking, lifting, pushing) may be represented in at least three domains: visual, motor, and linguistic. The visual domain covers human actions when visually observed. The motor domain covers the underlying control sequences that lead to observed movements. The linguistic domain covers symbolic descriptions of actions (natural languages such as English, French, and others). Thus, it makes sense to take the hierarchical structure of

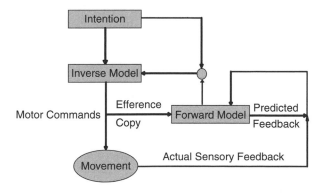

FIGURE 5.1

Contemporary model of human action representation.

natural language (e.g., phonology, morphology, and syntax) as a template for structuring not only the linguistic system that describes actions but also the visual and motor systems. One can define and computationally model visual and motor control structures that are analogous to basic linguistic counterparts: phonemes (the alphabet), morphemes (the dictionary), and syntax (the rules of combination of entries in the dictionary) using data-driven techniques grounded in actual human movement data. Cross-domain relations can also be modeled, yielding a computational model that grounds natural language descriptions of human action in visual and motor control models. Since actions have a visual, motor, and natural language, converting from one space to another becomes a language translation problem (see Figure 5.2).

Thus we should be after a methodology for grounding the meaning of actions, ranging from simple movement to intentional action (e.g., from *A* to *B*), by combining the (up to now hypothesized) grammatical structure of action (motor and visual) with the grammatical structure of planning or intentional action. In this way, having an understanding of the grammar of this language, we should be able to parse the measurements from the sensors. For example, a video would be "parsed" in a manner analogous to the parsing of natural language.

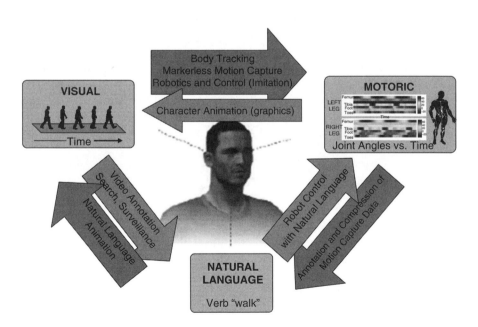

FIGURE 5.2

Three action spaces (visual, motoric, and natural language) and their mappings. Many problems in today's HCC, HCI, and HRI involve translation from one space to another (e.g., video annotation, natural language character animation, imitation).

5.3 LEARNING THE LANGUAGES OF HUMAN ACTION

By language we refer to what is conventional in modern computer science and computational linguistics—namely, a system consisting of three intertwined subsystems: phonology, morphology, and syntax [25]. *Phonology* is concerned with identifying the primitives (phonemes/letters) that make up all actions. Phonemic differences are often defined as the smallest change in the surface form (of speech) that signals a difference in meaning. A distinction that is phonemic in one language may not be phonemic in another. *Morphology* is concerned with the rules and mechanisms that combine the primitives into morphemes (words/basic actions). Morphemes are the basic units of language that have standalone meanings. For example, "unwanted" has three morphemes: *un-*, *want*, and *-ed*; "cat" and "dog" have one morpheme each; "cats" has two morphemes (*-s* meaning plural). *Syntax* is concerned with the mechanisms that combine words (actions) into sentences (complex, composite actions/behavior). There may be a theoretically deeper reason for cross-modal similarities, with the analogy being real in humans, in the sense that there is a "grammar of thought" reflected in natural language but that also structures other cognitive domains.

With regard to motoric actions, we do not need to reach down to the level of neurons and muscles (motors and actuators) to create measurements. After all, we are interested not in a neural theory of action but in a framework that advances sensor network interpretation. Instead, we can consider a higher-level description like the one provided by motion capture systems (see Figure 5.3). Currently, such systems are moving into the real world in the form of suits one can wear beneath ones clothing that allow collecting motoric data for thousands of actions in natural settings. This data can be imported into commercial animation/graphics packages such as Poser and Motion Builder to produce videos from any viewpoint of the motoric actions. We can also acquire video data of the person wearing the motion capture suit and performing actions. As a result, we have for the first time access to a very large amount of data containing actions in motoric space (joint angles versus time) and visual space (images). In today's *zeitgeist*, we can apply techniques from statistics and learning to compress the information in our data set. If we are able to represent all these actions efficiently, we will indeed have a language [37, 49, 56].

There are two main ways to go about this. One way (a *learning approach*) is to let the data decide, that is, to obtain through grammatical induction techniques [37] a probabilistic grammer generating all the actions in an observation set. The other way (a *synthetic modeling approach*) is to impose an a priori model for the primitives (phonemes) and then, through appropriate learning or compression, discover the morphological grammars as well as the syntax.

It is by now clear that we should be studying not only the visual space of action—even though that is the input from our sensor networks—but the motoric space as well. The lesson from the neurosciences suggests that when humans see and understand an action they do so through an internal act that captures the essence of the action. In other words, they map the observed action to their own "potential" movements. From the viewpoint of the sensor network engineer, the additional motor space is an unexpected benefit.

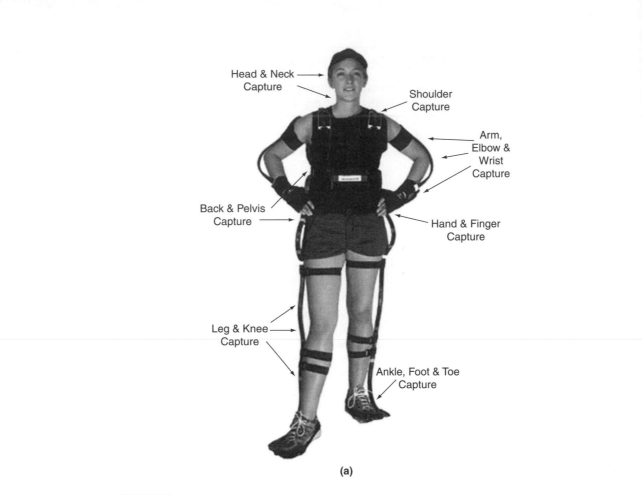

(a)

FIGURE 5.3

Motion capture suit. (a) Suit providing data from human movement in a wireless manner. Motion capture data amounts to 3D trajectories of the joints.

(Continued)

5.3.1 **Related Work**

There is not much previous work on a language for action. A system that comes closest in spirit to our work was developed more than ten years ago for handling eye movements. By turning the eye movement data into a string of symbols, Juhola [28] developed a finite automaton (the equivalent of a regular grammar) to represent it. Aside from this, researchers have only come close to the idea of primitives, and primitives are the first step to a language.

Recent work points to evidence that voluntary actions are made of simpler elements, called here primitives, that are connected to each other either serially or in

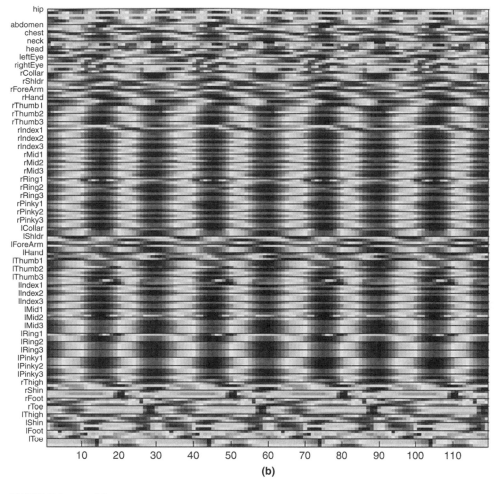

FIGURE 5.3—cont'd

(b) Equivalent representation actually captured by the suit showing a time evolution of joint angles. For each joint (vertical axis) there are at most three varying rotation angles over time (horizontal axis). Each "row" is a ID function (grayscale).

parallel (i.e., simultaneously). This modularity provides the system with much versatility and learning flexibility. To some scientists, motor primitives basically amount to motor schemas or control modules [10, 27, 47] and may be specific to a task. Their basic feature is that many different movements can be derived from a limited number of primitives through appropriate transformations, and that these movements can be combined through a well-defined set of rules to form more complex actions (see for example the movemes of [10] or the modules of [47]). Primitives can be kinematic, dynamic, or kinematodynamic. They are extracted using statistical techniques like PCA (principal component analysis), HMM (hidden Markov models), and others.

At the behavioral level many studies have concentrated on reaching and grasping, gait and balance, and posture and locomotion. Reaching movements appear to be coded in terms of direction and extent [18] and to be composed of discrete submovements, all with a similar stereotypical, serially concatenated shape and overlapping in time [8, 12, 40]. Motor primitives have also been examined for human and monkey grasping and object manipulation. Prehension (e.g., lifting a full cup) consists of reaching, orienting the hand, and grasping. These three actions are executed as a unified, coordinated, complex act even though they can be combined in a variety of ways. In tasks such as grasping, not only must the positions of the fingers and motions be appropriately selected and preplanned, but the forces exerted on the object must be controlled to achieve the goal while securing a stable grasp.

Finger movements and forces have been decomposed into basic synergies based either on uncontrolled manifold or on inverse dynamics computations. Hand gestures also consist of primitives or more complicated sequences that can be decomposed into a series of more elementary units of activity. Of particular interest are the motor (or muscle) synergies. These are simultaneous activations of several muscles that produce a torque about a joint or a force in a particular direction. EMG recordings from frog hind limb muscles have been analyzed to test whether natural behavior shows synergies among groups of muscle activities for an entire set of natural behaviors. Similar attempts have been made to find muscle synergies during human posture and locomotion [6, 11, 13, 30, 38, 42, 44, 50, 55].

More recently, through the technique of non-negative matrix factorization, muscle synergies during a postural task in the cat [52] have been successfully identified. Since several synergies are assumed to act on a given muscle, the total activation of that muscle is the sum of activations due to all the synergies. Of particular importance here is the work of d'Avella and Bizzi [9]. They employed a similar approach to extract amplitudes and timing relationships among muscle activations during natural behaviors in intact animals. A combination of synergies shared across behaviors and those for specific behaviors captured the invariance across the entire observed data set. These results support a modular organization of the motor controller; the motor output of these modules is combined to control a large set of behaviors.

Fod et al. [14] extracted primitives by k-means clustering of the projection of high-dimensional segment vectors onto a reduced subspace. Kahol et al. [29] used the local minimum in total body force to detect segment boundaries. Nakazawa et al. [36] measured similarities of motion segments according to a dynamic programming distance and clustered them with a nearest-neighbor algorithm. Wang et al. [54] segmented gestures with the local minima of velocity and local maxima of change in direction. These segments were hierarchically clustered into classes using hidden Markov models to compute a metric.

Of special importance to this work is the finding that electrical micro-stimulation in the primary motor and premotor cortex of the monkey causes complex movements involving many joints and even several body parts [19, 20]. These actions are very similar to gestures in the monkey's natural repertoire. Micro-stimulation at each site causes the arm to move to a specific final posture. Thus there appears to be evidence for a cortical map of joint angles (or a cortical representation of limb or body postures). There is also growing evidence of cortical coding not only of kinematic and dynamic variables but also of more global features (segment geometrical shape or the order of the segments within the sequence [3, 17].

5.4 GRAMMARS OF VISUAL HUMAN MOVEMENT

We believe that the place to begin a discussion about actions and their recognition is to first ask the question: What do we really mean by actions? When humans speak of recognizing an action, they may be referring to a set of visually observable transitions in the human body, such as "raise right arm," or an abstract event, such as "a person entered the room." We recognize that the former requires only visual knowledge about allowed transitions or movements of the human body, whereas the latter requires much more than that. It requires that we know about rooms and the fact that they can be "entered" and "exited," and about the relationships of these abstract linguistic verbs to lower-level verbs having direct visual counterparts. Current work [39] deals with the automatic view-invariant recognition of low-level visual verbs that involves only the human body. The visual verbs enforce the visual syntactic structure of human actions (allowed transitions of the body and viewpoint) without worrying about semantic descriptions.

In [39], each training verb or action a is described by a short sequence of key pose pairs $a = \langle (p_1, p_2), (p_2, p_3), \ldots, (p_{k-1}, p_k) \rangle$, where each pose p_i belongs to P, and P is the complete set of k observed (allowed) poses. Note that for every consecutive pair, the second pose in the earlier pair is the same as the first pose in the later pair, since they correspond to the same time instant. This is so because what we really observe in a video is a sequence of poses, not pose pairs. Hence, if we observe poses (p_1, p_2, p_3, p_4), we build the corresponding pose pairs as $\langle (p_1, p_2), (p_2, p_3), (p_3, p_4) \rangle$. Each pose p_i is represented implicitly by a family of silhouettes (images) observed in m different viewpoints: $p_i = (p_i^1, p_i^2, \ldots, p_i^m)$. The set of key poses and actions is directly obtained from multi-camera multi-person training data without manual intervention. A probabilistic context-free grammar (PCFG) is automatically constructed to encapsulate knowledge about actions, their constituent poses, and view transitions.

During recognition, the PCFG is used to find the most likely sequence of actions seen in a single-viewpoint video. Thus, in this language the phonemes are multiview poses of the human body, and actions amount to transitions among them. Given a sequence (after detecting the human silhouette), the issue at hand is how to find a representative sequence of key poses to describe the action seen. For a given sequence of frames, we define a *keyframe* as one where the average of the optical flow magnitude of foreground pixels (pixels lying inside the human silhouette) reaches an extremum. Note that the optical flow is measured in the reference frame of the foreground. That is, the mean optical flow of the foreground is first subtracted from the flow value at each foreground pixel. Hence, given frames $f_1, \ldots, f_n$ and the 2D optical flow $u_1(x, y), \ldots, u_n(x, y)$ for each frame, we find the extrema of a discrete function denoting deviation of the flow from the average mean flow (see Figure 5.4). In other words, these are points of high average acceleration. The intuition behind this criterion is that frames where this value reaches a minimum indicate flow reversals that occur when the body reaches an extreme pose. Frames at the maxima are points where the body is exactly between two extreme configurations and is in the middle of a transition undergoing large overall movement.

Since our training videos consist of synchronized multiview data for each action, we perform keyframe extraction in each view separately, and each view v yields a set of key time instants $\{t_{v_1}, t_{v_2}, t_{v_3}, \ldots\}$. For each action a, the union of these sets of key time instants from all views gives the complete set of key time instants $\{t_1, t_2, t_3, \ldots\}$ for that action. Corresponding to each key time instant t_i, we obtain a pose p_i as a multiview set of silhouette images $p_i = (p_i^1, p_i^2, \ldots, p_i^m)$. Thus, each action is represented by a short sequence of key multiview pose pairs, as described earlier. The entire process requires no human intervention. The keyframe extraction process is fairly robust and insensitive to the accuracy of optical flow estimation, since it only uses averages of the flow.

One can easily develop a method to automatically construct a PCFG using our multiview training data set, which is separate from our singleview test data set. Note that we are specifying a PCFG, and not learning it, so the term *training data* is not used in the strictest sense. In the previous step, we used multiview training videos to find a sequence of key poses for all of the training actions.

From this data, we wish to find the complete set of unique key poses of the body. It is clear that a particular key pose (such as "standing upright") may be common to many actions. However, since we used independent training videos for each action, we must first identify such common poses automatically so that we avoid redundant representations.

Therefore, given a set of training actions $\{a, b, c, \ldots\}$ and the recovered multiview pose sequence pairs for each action, $a = \langle (p_{a_1}, p_{a_2}), (p_{a_2}, p_{a_3}), \ldots \rangle$, $b = \langle (p_{b_1}, p_{b_2}), (p_{b_2}, p_{b_3}), \ldots \rangle$ and so on, the task is to identify the complete set $P = \{p_1, p_2, p_3 \ldots, p_n\}$ of unique poses, where a pose p_i belonging to P represents, say, equivalent poses $p_{a_1}, p_{b_4}, p_{c_2}$.

To do this, we can first create the set $P_o = \{p_{a_1}, p_{a_2}, \ldots, p_{b_1}, p_{b_2}, \ldots, p_{c_1}, p_{c_2}, \ldots\}$ of all observed key poses (with possible repetitions) from all actions. If the silhouettes for two poses p_i and p_j match in each of the m views, the poses are considered to be the same. We register two silhouette images using phase correlation in the Cartesian and log-polar space, which is invariant to 2D translation, rotation, and scaling. In the registered images, the ratio of the sizes of the intersection set (overlap) of the silhouettes to the union set must be close to 1 for the silhouettes to match, which is

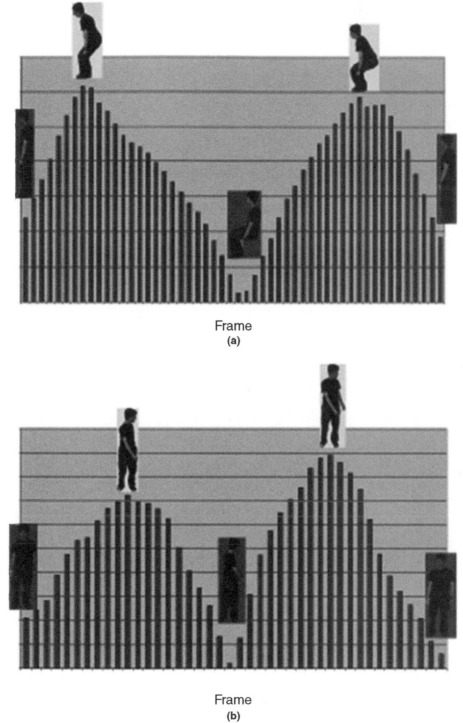

FIGURE 5.4

Keyframe extraction for two videos showing the sit/stand (a) and turn (b) actions. The plots show the value found using deviation from mean flow and the resulting keyframes (acceleration extrema).

decided with a threshold. If the silhouettes for two poses match in all views, the poses are considered to be the same. This procedure allows us to map the observed set of key poses P_o to a smaller set of unique key poses P. After this is done, each action is relabeled using the mapping $P_o \rightarrow P$ from P_o to P, so that we finally get representations such as $a = \langle (p_5, p_2), (p_2, p_7), \ldots \rangle$, $b = \langle (p_3, p_5), (p_5, p_1), \ldots \rangle$, and so on.

Constructing a PCFG is straightforward. Figure 5.5 shows examples of a training set. Figure 5.6 shows all unique 3D poses in the data set. Figures 5.7 and 5.8 show recognition results (parsing). Since it is based on the whole silhouette, the grammar,

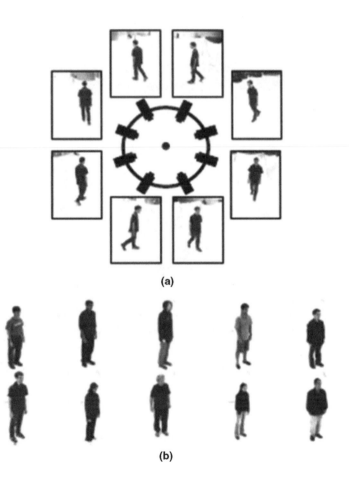

(a)

(b)

FIGURE 5.5

Examples of a training set: (a) eight viewpoints; (b) ten people performing various actions;

(Continued)

(c)

FIGURE 5.5—cont'd

(c) key poses for a person in one of the views.

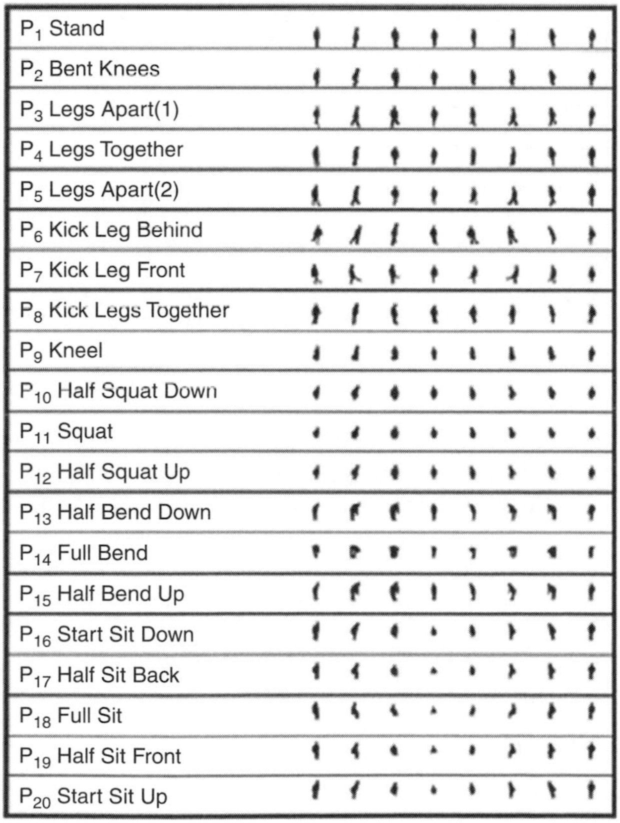

P_1 Stand	
P_2 Bent Knees	
P_3 Legs Apart(1)	
P_4 Legs Together	
P_5 Legs Apart(2)	
P_6 Kick Leg Behind	
P_7 Kick Leg Front	
P_8 Kick Legs Together	
P_9 Kneel	
P_{10} Half Squat Down	
P_{11} Squat	
P_{12} Half Squat Up	
P_{13} Half Bend Down	
P_{14} Full Bend	
P_{15} Half Bend Up	
P_{16} Start Sit Down	
P_{17} Half Sit Back	
P_{18} Full Sit	
P_{19} Half Sit Front	
P_{20} Start Sit Up	

FIGURE 5.6

Set of 39 unique 3D key poses extracted from all videos in the training data set. Each pose is shown as a collection of silhouettes in eight viewpoints.

(Continued)

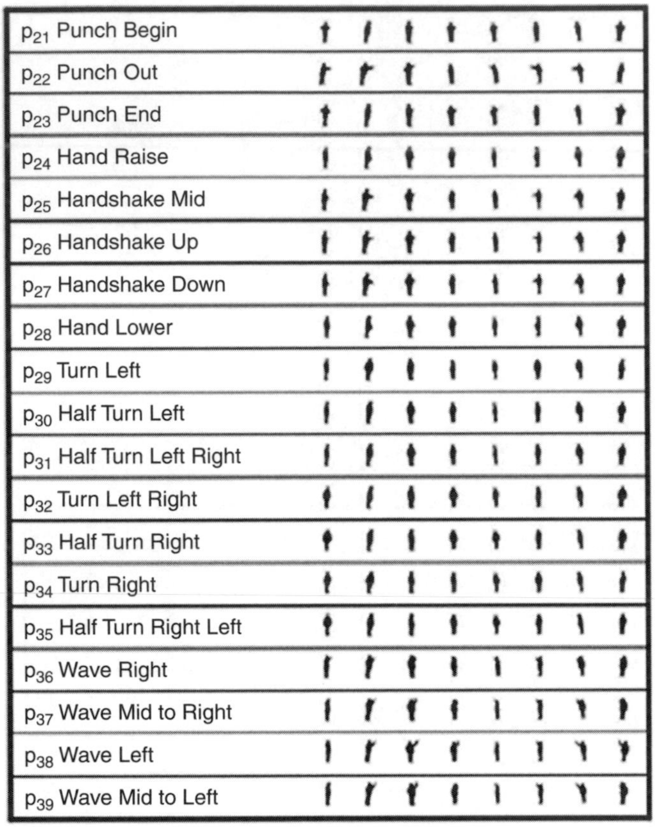

p_{21} Punch Begin	↑	✓	↑	↑	↑	↓	↘	↑	
p_{22} Punch Out	↑	↑	↑	↓	↘	↗	↑	↙	
p_{23} Punch End	↑	✓	↑	↑	↑	↓	↘	↑	
p_{24} Hand Raise	↓	✓	↑	↑	↓	↓	↓	↑	
p_{25} Handshake Mid	↑	↑	↑	↓	↓	↑	↑	↑	
p_{26} Handshake Up	↑	↑	↑	↓	↘	↑	↑	↑	
p_{27} Handshake Down	↑	↑	↑	↓	↓	↑	↑	↑	
p_{28} Hand Lower	↓	✓	↑	↑	↓	↓	↓	↑	
p_{29} Turn Left	↓	↑	↑	↓	↓	↓	↓	✓	
p_{30} Half Turn Left	↓	↑	↑	↑	↓	↓	↓	↑	
p_{31} Half Turn Left Right	↓	↑	↑	↑	↘	↓	↓	↑	
p_{32} Turn Left Right	↑	✓	↑	↑	↓	↓	↘	↑	
p_{33} Half Turn Right	↑	✓	↓	↑	↑	↓	↘	↑	
p_{34} Turn Right	↑	↑	↓	↓	↑	↑	↘	↘	
p_{35} Half Turn Right Left	↑	↑	↓	↑	↑	↑	↘	↑	
p_{36} Wave Right	✓	↑	↑	↓	↘	↘	↓	↑	
p_{37} Wave Mid to Right	↓	✓	✓	↓	↘	↘	↘	↑	
p_{38} Wave Left	↓	✓	✓	✓	↓	↘	↘	↓	
p_{39} Wave Mid to Left	↓	✓	✓	✓	↓	↘	↘	↓	

FIGURE 5.6—cont'd

is somewhat restricted. A powerful generalization involves body parts, including facial expressions. The phonemes in such a grammar are images of body parts. It is feasible to construct filters that detect body parts, and we have applied this idea to the detection of the whole human silhouette by developing human visual filters (see Fig. 5.9). Generalizations of such approaches to body parts are a fruitful research topic.

5.5 GRAMMARS OF MOTORIC HUMAN MOVEMENT

Motoric languages still remain hidden, although considerable progress has been made with the human activity language, HAL [21–23] and the Behaviourscope Project [32]. The fundamental question is related to the phonemes or primitives of the language, called here *kinetemes*.

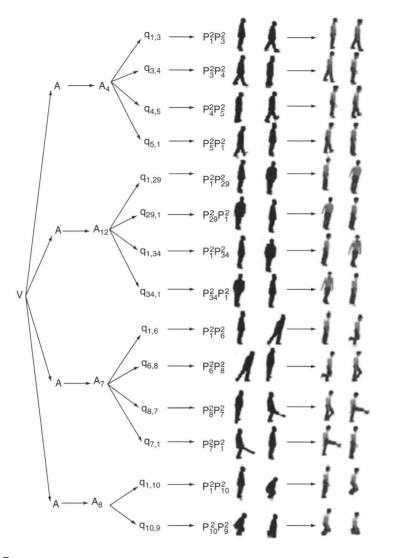

FIGURE 5.7

Parse tree obtained for the input video whose keyframes are arranged in pairs shown on the right. The parsed sequence consists of four actions: A_4, A_{12}, A_7, and A_8 (walk, turn, kick, and kneel, respectively).

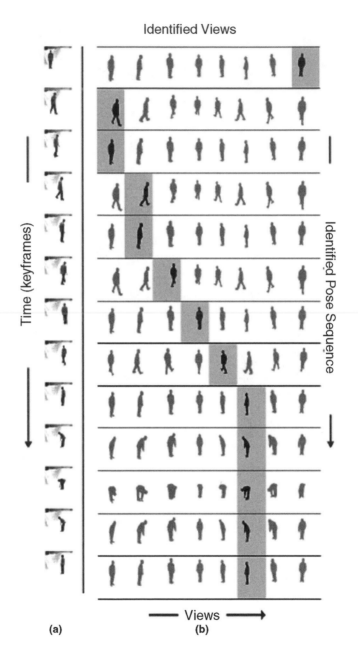

FIGURE 5.8

Changing viewpoint. (a) Detected keyframes in the input (time increases from top to bottom). The subject turns while walking and then picks something up. (b) Each row, containing eight images, collectively describes a 3D pose. Each element of the row shows a viewpoint. Detected viewpoints are marked in dark gray. Note that the figure does not display the parse tree, but only the changes in viewpoint.

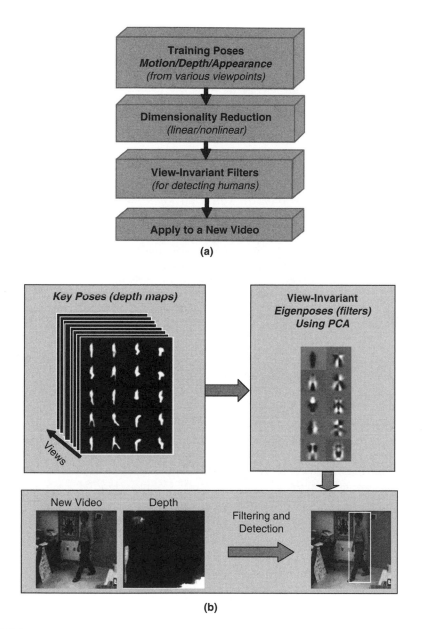

FIGURE 5.9

Developing visual human filters for detecting humans and their parts. (a) Basic pipeline;
(b) example using depth.

5.5.1 Human Activity Language: A Symbolic Approach

HAL is a language learned from motion capture data. Our database does not consist of actions in any specific domain; instead, it contains general activities covering locomotion, nonlocomotion, and manipulative and interactive actions. Phonology takes the name **kinetology** in our approach, and the phonemes become **kinetemes**.

Each degree of freedom (DOF) i in a model for the articulated human body, denoted as *actuator*, corresponds to a time-varying function J_i. The value $J_i(t)$ represents the joint angle of a specific actuator i at a particular instant t. In kinetology, our goal is to identify the motor primitives (segmentation) and to associate them with symbols (symbolization). This way, kinetology provides a nonarbitrary grounded symbolic representation for human movement. While *motion synthesis* is performed by translating the symbols into motion signals, *motion analysis* uses this symbolic representation to transform the original signal into a string of symbols used in the next steps of our linguistic framework.

To find motion primitives, the joint angle function is divided into segments. The *segmentation* process starts by assigning a state to each instant (see Fig. 5.10(a)). Adjacent instants assigned to the same state belong to the same segment. The state is chosen from a set that includes all possible sign combinations of angular derivatives (e.g., velocity, acceleration, and jerk). For example, considering angular velocity (J') and angular acceleration (J''), there are four possible states: $\{ J'_i(t) \geq 0$ and $J''_i(t) \geq 0;$ $J'_i(t) \geq 0$ and $J''_i(t) < 0; J'_i(t) < 0$ and $J''_i(t) \geq 0;$ and $J'_i(t) < 0$ and $J''_i(t) < 0\}$.

Once the segments are identified, we keep three attribute values for each one: the state, the angular displacement (i.e., the absolute difference between initial angle and final angle), and the time length. Each segment is graphically displayed as a filled rectangle, where the grayscale intensity represents its state, the vertical width corresponds to angular displacement, and the horizontal length denotes time length. Given a compact representation, these attributes are used in the reconstruction of an approximation for the original motion signal and in the symbolization process. The *symbolization* process consists of associating each segment with a symbol such that the segments corresponding to different performances of the same motion are associated with the same symbol (see Figure 10(c)). In the context of finding patterns in time-series data, there is a vast literature on this problem that goes beyond the limits of this chapter. A simple solution is hierarchical clustering. This approach is based on a distance metric that measures the similarity between different segments.

Given the segmentation for motion data, the symbolization output is a set of strings that defines a data structure denoted as an *actiongram* (see Figure 10(d)). An actiongram A has n strings $A_1, \ldots, A_n$. Each string A_i corresponds to an actuator of the human body model and contains a (possibly different) number of m_i symbols. Each symbol $A_i(j)$ is associated with a segment.

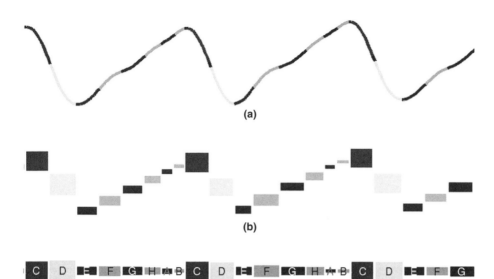

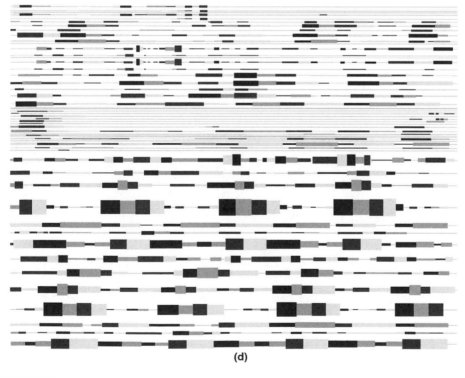

FIGURE 5.10

Kinetological system. The horizontal axis is time. (a) Geometric representation; (b) segmentation; (c) symbolization; (d) actiongram.

It is worth nothing that a kinetological system can be defined in both simple and complex ways. The system just described uses the signs of both the first and second derivative of the human movement function. However, it could have used only the first. In that case, we would have only light gray and dark gray rectangles as before, with the length and width of each having the same meaning (see Figure 5.11).

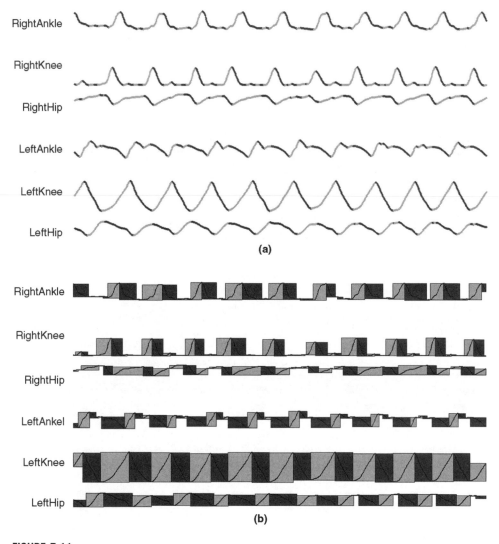

FIGURE 5.11

A simpler kinetological system. (a) Human motion data. Joint angle functions (right ankle, right hip, right knee, left ankle, left hip, and left knee) assigned to states corresponding to positive velocity (light gray) and negative velocity (dark gray). (b) Kineteme sequences for the functions at the top.

The approach used to learn HAL is by now clear. Our algorithms work with thousands of representations like the one in Figure 5.10(d), with the goal of finding structure in these rectangles of various sizes. This structure is of two kinds: along each row (joint) and among different rows (synergies—as one part of the body performs some motion, another part simultaneously performs a correlated motion). For example, analysis of the patterns derived from the proposed grammar shows common motion invariances across widely varying movement types, suggesting common mechanisms for movement production independent of the end effector. We list three interesting results:

(a) *Common substructures in different actions*. Figure 5.12 shows language strings for one joint for different verbs (actions) in our database, using a kinetological system like the one in Figure 5.11. Note the differences and similarities, as many different actions share kinetemes.

(b) *Adverbial modeling*. HAL also has adverbs that in general characterize the manner of the action. Adverbial modeling requires the introduction of parameters such as speed, location in space (which could be provided as a direction in retinal coordinates), and force. Here we give an example using the walk forward action. In this case, our motion samples are walk actions at 40 different speeds regularly spaced from 0.1 to 4.0 miles per hour. Figure 5.13 shows these sample motions for the "right knee flexion-extension" actuator.

Actually, we show a single cycle of the walk action normalized in time. The motion curves are colored according to speed: lighter gray for slower walks and darker gray for faster walks. Note that, for the speed-varying motions, the most variability in the curves is at the maxima and minima points. Coincidently, these points are the borders of motion segments. With this in mind, we aim at modeling how these extreme points behave in time and space (i.e., position, varying velocity, acceleration, and jerk) according to the speed parameter. We consider a single extreme point e and denote its time and space in the motion as $t_e(s)$ and $q_e(s)$, respectively. We discover from the motion data that a straight line approximates these functions fairly well (see Fig. 5.14). This way, only two values are required to model each extreme point behavior according to the speed parameter, which means that we can easily relate the symbolic descriptions at different speeds.

(c) *The semantics of the action language*. Imagine two people A and B. A moves toward B holding an object (a book). He extends his hand toward B, B grabs the book, and A turns around and walks away. Just witnessed is the intentional act of *giving*. We have collected in our lab human motion measurements from this event using video. Our grammars parsed this volume of data and came up with a number of descriptions, such as A walks toward B and A extends his hand while holding an object. Figure 5.15 shows this story at the top using a few representative video frames. The parsing is shown below each frame (time stamp) in the form of a classic semantic network. It basically encodes the information of the parsing.

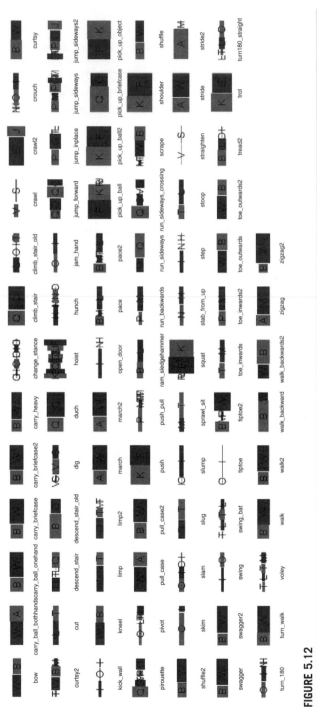

FIGURE 5.12

"Right hip flexion-extension" motion patterns for 87 actions in our praxicon. The first action in the first row is "bow." The tenth action in the second row is "jump forward," and so on. Every pattern is a sequence of kinetemes, which are the light and dark gray rectangles of different dimensions (length corresponding to time, width corresponding to the difference in angles at the beginning and end of the kineteme). Rectangles of similar dimensions and grayscale intensity become the same symbol. The symbolization system places a label on each rectangle, such as W, A, B, Q. These are the symbols of our language, the distinct kinetemes. The action "limp" (the third action in the third row) consists of the kineteme L followed by the kineteme T. The action "jump-forward" consists of the sequence QDQG, and the action "kick wall" (the first action in the third row) consists of the kinetemes IOI. Note how different actions share kinetemes. Also note how the symbolization system, which is data driven, assigns "symbols" to different kinetemes (a few dark gray rectangles of similar sizes are categorized as A, and so on).

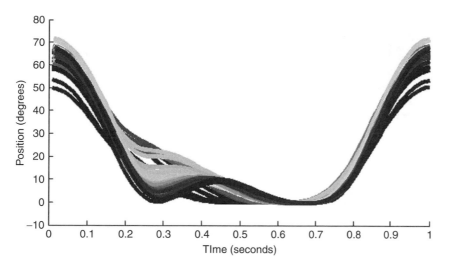

FIGURE 5.13

Human motion measurements from walking action at different speeds.

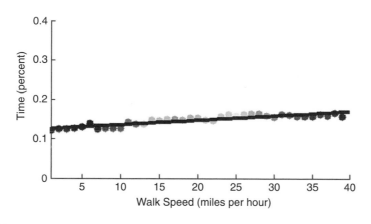

FIGURE 5.14

Extreme points (maxima and minima) of the functions in Figure 5.13 lie along a straight line. This means that all functions in Figure 5.13 can be represented together with two parameters.

Now we examine a definition of the abstract action *give*. To keep it simple, *give* (A, B, x) amounts to A holds x, sometime later B also holds x, and sometime later only B holds x. The gestures are important (such as A extends his hand), but we do not need to incorporate them here to make our point.

If we translate this to the language of Figure 5.15, *give* becomes a graph, which is isomorphic to a subgraph of the global cognitive model. In this case then grounding

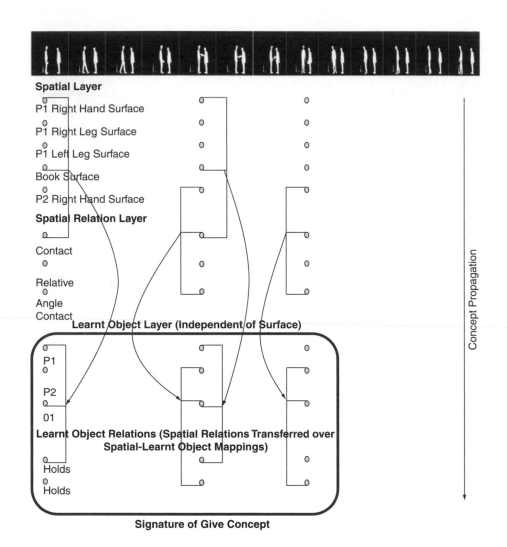

FIGURE 5.15

Grounded cognitive model representing the interaction of two subjects shown at the top with a few keyframes of the video. Parsing is shown below in the form of a semantic network (nodes and relations). P1 and P2 refer to the two subjects, O refers to the object. The definition of an abstract predicate, such as *give*, can be found inside the cognitive model—it is actually a subgraph of the total cognitive model graph. Below each frame at the top is a network showing the relationship between P1, P2, and O. The subgraph inside the dark frame is the signature of the abstract predicate *give* saying that P1 had the object at some time, at a future time both P1 and P2 were holding the object, and at another time later only P2 held the object.

the meaning of *give* amounts to subgraph isomorphism (matching the graph denoting *give* to a subgraph of the cognitive model graph).

The nouns in HAL are the body parts and the objects participating in the action, the verbs are the actions themselves, and the adjectives are the poses (modifying the body parts). The adverbs, as discussed, define the style of the action. Finally, let us briefly discuss what the HAL words look like.

We define *sequential learning* as a technique to infer the structure of a single sequence of symbols A_i. This structure corresponds to a forest of binary trees (see Figure 5.16), where each node in a tree is associated with a context-free grammar rule in a normal form. Initially, the sequential learning algorithm computes the number of occurrences for each *digram*, A *diagram* is a pair of adjacent symbols, in string A_i. A new grammar rule $N_c \rightarrow \alpha\beta$ is created for the diagram $\alpha\beta$ with the current maximum frequency. The algorithm replaces each occurrence of $\alpha\beta$ in string A_i with the created nonterminal N_c. The entire procedure is repeated until diagrams occur more than once. For example, the set of rules inferred for the CFG displayed in Figure 5.16 is $\{N_1 \rightarrow AB, N_2 \rightarrow CD, N_3 \rightarrow EF, N_4 \rightarrow BN_1, N_5 \rightarrow N_2 N_3, N_6 \rightarrow N_5G, N_7 \rightarrow N_6N_4\}$.

A sequential learning algorithm keeps merging adjacent root nodes into single rules and, consequently, overgeneralization happens when "unrelated" rules are generalized. Of course, this would not be enough for capturing the structure of the action. We need to know which joints move together. We call this *parallel learning* and use it to concurrently infer a grammar system as the structure of all strings $A_1, \ldots, A_n$ in the actiongram A. In parallel learning, nodes are merged only if the new rule is synchronized with other rules in different CFG components of a grammar system. This way, overgeneralization is avoided since synchronization guarantees a relationship between the merged rules.

This is achieved through the use of a parallel communicating grammar system (PCGS) with rule synchronization [41]. See for example Figure 5.17, which shows the model for just two joints. Not only do we discover structure (the trees) along each row, but we also find which two nodes in the two trees correspond to simultaneous movements. This is denoted by the introduction of an additional node in the graph.

Figure 5.18 shows a HAL word (carry something heavy). We have arranged the essential actuators in a circle and have omitted the graph denoting synchronous motion.

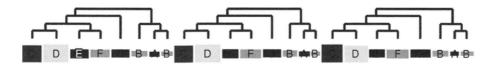

FIGURE 5.16

Sequential learning on a single string of an actiongram.

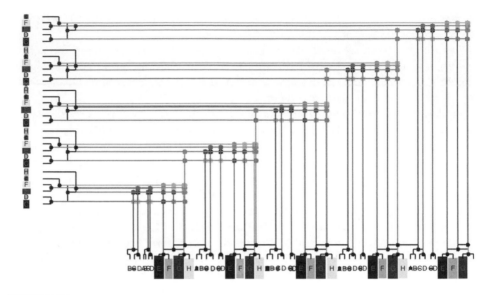

FIGURE 5.17

Two CFGs (binary trees corresponding to hip and knee flexion/extension) of a grammar system for the walk action related by synchronized rules representing synergies.

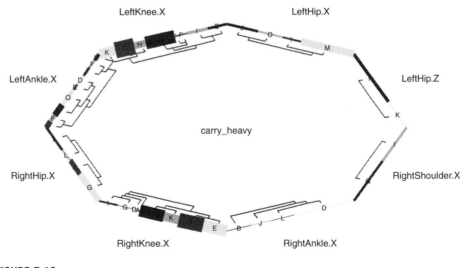

FIGURE 5.18

5.5.2 A Spectral Approach: Synergies

As we saw in Figure 5.3, motoric action data amounts to a set of 1D functions and, for most actions, there is a high degree of coordination among the different joints. This is evident in that figure, where we immediately see two sets of rows (of 1D functions) that "go together." These are the synergies [34, 53]. The brain cannot generate a large number of independent control movements (which is why juggling is hard). It generates a few, and those are sufficient to generate any movement. The trick is to send the same signal to a group (or a subset) of muscles. Of course, not all of these muscles will move in the same way. Instead, there appears to be a *coordination* step, where the signal is transformed using a number of simple operations and then is sent to the appropriate muscles. The basic signal, the group of muscles, and the coordination parameters constitute the motor synergy. Thus, it makes sense to use the motor synergies as primitives and to look for a grammar of motor synergies.

In this a case, if such a grammar exists, the system will operate as in Figure 5.19. The grammar generates strings of control symbols, the control generates a control signal, and coordination generates coordinated signals. A critical property of this system is that it does not need to be applied only to muscles. It could be applied to images, thus providing a fundamentally new way of recognizing human action from video. We can learn the visual spatiotemporal pattern for each synergy (see Figure 5.20). Thus, our learning problem amounts to reversing the directions in the earlier figures. We start from joint angle data or video and learn coordination/synergies, control functions, and subsequently a grammar.

It turns out that this is feasible. We will walk through a specific example. The assumption is that we have at our disposal very large amounts of motion capture

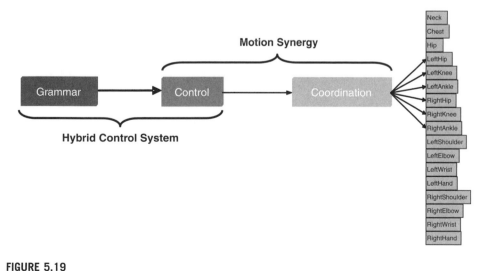

FIGURE 5.19

Motion generation.

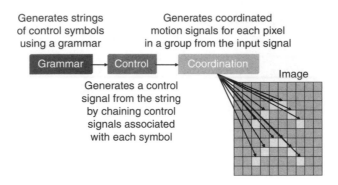

FIGURE 5.20

Grammar of motion synergies. Using animation/graphics packages, we generate the visual patterns created by synergies.

data, which can be annotated (for each action there is a label or verb) or can be continuous data from someone's behavior that is segmented using the technique of incremental PCA. Here, we concentrate on the actual processing. Consider the data shown in Figure 5.21(a). To discover the synergies, one approach is to find which ones of these 1D functions (joint angles over time) are "spectrally" similar. We focus

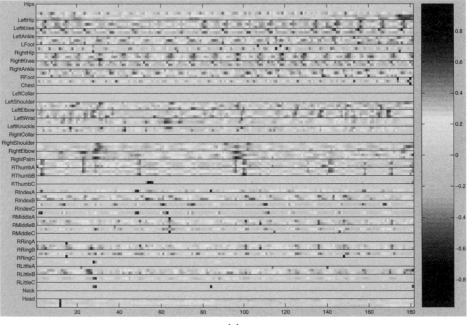

(a)

FIGURE 5.21

Spectral similarity: (a) motion capture data. Stationary jogging while moving the right hand (rubbing) on the chest.

(Continued)

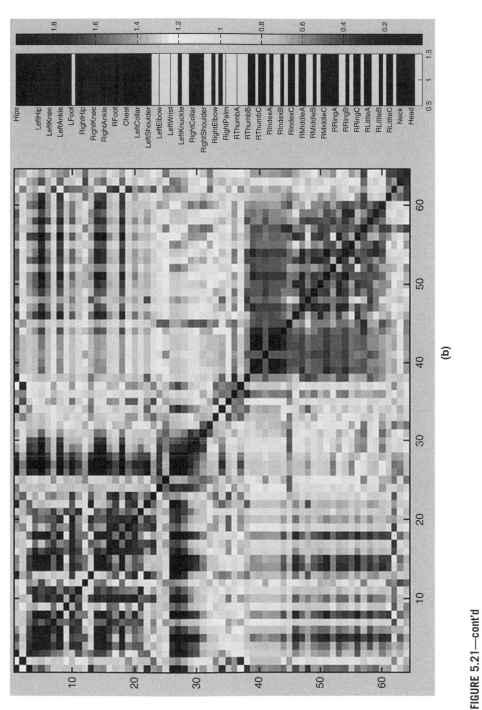

FIGURE 5.21—cont'd

(b) similarity matrix and groups of joints.

on spectral similarity since our goal is to find one signal, a 1D function that generates all of the 1D functions in the synergy.

First we group joint angles together based on their *spectral similarity*. If $s_i(t)$ and $s_j(t)$ are two joint angle time series and $f_i(\omega)$ and $f_j(\omega)$ are their respective Fourier transforms, we find a similarity matrix by multiplying the Fourier transforms (see Figure 5.21(b)). This is used for clustering the joints into coordinated groups and finding control symbols. As Figure 5.21(b) shows, this clustering provides three groups of joints: (one of stationary joints and two synergies: group 1 (dark gray) and group 2 (light gray)). Let us concentrate on the first group—that is, on a subset of the data from Figure 5.21(a) (see Figure 5.22).

Now we need to discover one 1D function that can easily generate all the functions (rows) of Figure 5.22. We achieve this by allowing changes in four parameters (scale, translation, amplitude, and DC shift).

Figure 5.23 shows the basic function that can generate all rows of Figure 5.22 and an even more basic function (a wavelet) that generates the basic one. Figure 5.24 describes our approach in more detail. The grammar generates basic functions, in this case wavelets. These are the phonemes of the new language. The control

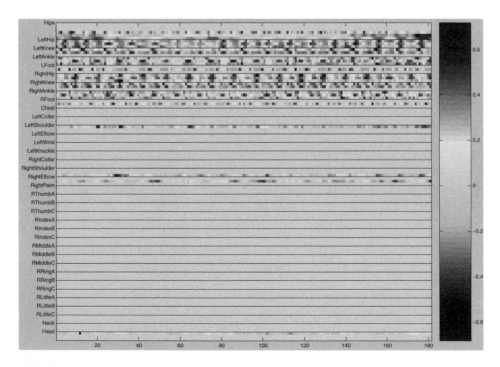

FIGURE 5.22

A potential synergy subset of data in group 1 of Figure 5.21(b).

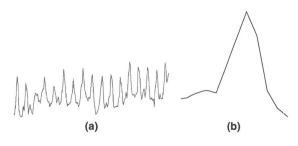

FIGURE 5.23

Basic functions: (a) control signal; (b) basic control function (wavelet).

mechanism turns this wavelet into a control signal, which is given to the coordination mechanism, which by assigning different values for the four parameters of translation, scale, amplitude, and DC shift, generates the signals for each joint. By identifying phonemes in our new language as wavelets in the appropriate space, we can now, as before, build our language with grammatical induction techniques. A long sequence of actions can be processed into a sequence of wavelets that each refer to a group of joints, each of which possesses four parameters. These represent the (often simultaneous) synergies.

The basic problem for future research is the discovery (or design) of the primitives in human movement [10, 27, 47]. Let us assume that these control symbols will

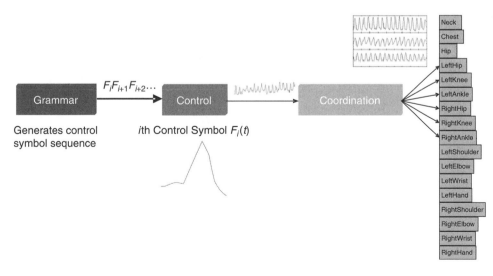

FIGURE 5.24

Grammars of wavelets for motion synergies.

be some form of basic function, say a wavelet. Then Figure 5.24 explains how a grammar of wavelets can produce human action, by generating control symbols (wavelets) that a control mechanism turns into a function, which in turn can generate all the functions in the synergy by changing a few parameters for each joint.

Ultimately, one is interested in visuo-motor representations. In terms of Figure 5.2, we are interested in developing a map from the visual to the motoric space. Given that we can acquire the visual data of someone wearing a motion capture suit, it becomes feasible to learn this map from a very large number of examples.

5.6 APPLICATIONS TO HEALTH

Human-centric interfaces, equipped with a grammar of human actions, are a very important tool in a variety of areas, including health. Movement, because it is universal, easily detectable, and measurable, is a window into the nervous system. Using, for the most part, measurements of human movement, behavioral neuroscience has seen major accomplishments, such as documenting milestones in human development and establishing a relationship between brain and behavior in typical and atypical populations. The measurements are obtained with a cornucopia of sophisticated techniques, ranging from infrared and video to magnetic approaches, RFID, and wireless sensor networks (with their advantages and disadvantages regarding accuracy, portability, intrusion, and cost). In the future, these measurements will be taken in "smart environments." However, despite the tremendous progress in measuring human movement, we still do not know, for example, how to track motor decline in the elderly during daily life activities at home and in the workplace. With regard to Parkinson's disease, we still do not know how to assess, in quantitative terms, the effectiveness (over time) of a new medicine. With regard to autism, we still do not know how social interaction deficits are manifested in body gestures so that an early diagnosis is possible. Why can we not yet deal with such problems?

It is clear that these problems have characteristics that are beyond the state of the art. To track the evolution of Parkinson's disease it is not enough to just perform measurements of human movement; we have to look at these measurements in a new, holistic sense. We must group them into subsets that have "meaning" and then find global patterns and relationships in them. With regard to tracking motor decline, we need to interpret long sequences of measurements as interactions between two or more people. In the case of autism, we need to be able to pinpoint idiosyncratic characteristics of whole-body gestures or of a series of actions and interactions. In other words, we need to move to the next step, which is to study the structure of human action in a way that encompasses group dynamics. For this, we need a new tool that can sift through the gargantuan amount of data collected about human movement and structure it so that we can refer not only to individual movements but also to actions, subactions, sequences of actions, and interactions and plans. This tool will create representation of action at different levels of abstraction. It will be a human activity language of the kind envisioned in this chapter.

5.7 APPLICATIONS TO ARTIFICIAL INTELLIGENCE AND COGNITIVE SYSTEMS

Human–machine communication requires partial conceptual alignment for effective sharing of meaning. Concepts are the elementary units of reason and linguistic meaning, and they represent the cognitive structures underlying phonemes/words. A commonly held philosophical position is that all concepts are symbolic & abstract and therefore should be implemented outside the sensorimotor system. In this way, the meaning of a concept amounts to the content of a symbolic expression, a definition of the concept in a logical calculus. This is the viewpoint that elevated artificial intelligence to the mature scientific and engineering discipline it is today. Despite the progress, text-based (natural language processing (NLP)) technologies are still unable to offer viable models of semantics for human–computer interaction. Imagine, for example, a situation where a human user is interacting with a robot around a table of different colored/shaped objects. If the human were to issue the command "Give me the red one" or "Give me the long one," both the manually coded and statistical models of meaning employed in text-based NLP would be inadequate. In both models, the meaning of a word is based only on its relations to other words.

However, there is another viewpoint regarding the structure of concepts, which states that concepts are grounded in *sensorimotor representations*. This sensorimotor intelligence considers sensors and motors in the shaping of cognitive hidden mechanisms and knowledge incorporation. There are a number of studies in many disciplines (neurophysiology, psychophysics, cognitive linguistics) suggesting that the human sensorimotor system is indeed deeply involved in concept representation. The functionality of Broca's region in the brain and the mirror neurons theory suggests that perception and action share a symbolic structure that provides common ground for sensorimotor tasks (e.g., recognition and motor planning) and higher-level activities.

Perhaps the strongest support for the sensorimotor theory comes from the work of Rosch et al. [16, 45]. The classic view assumed that categories formed a hierarchy and that there was nothing special about the categories in the middle. In hierarchies such as vehicle/car/sports car or furniture/chair/rocking chair [45], the categories in the middle, according to Rosch, *are* special—they are at the basic level. One can get a mental image of a car or a chair but not of a piece of furniture or a vehicle in general. We have motor programs for interacting with chairs, but not with pieces of furniture. In addition, words for basic-level categories tend to be learned earlier, to be shorter, to be more frequent, to be remembered more easily, and so on. Thus, the basic-level category is the one at which we interact optimally in the world with our bodies. The consequence is that categorization is embodied, given by our interactions.

In the example given before, in order for the robot to successfully "give me the red one," it must be able to link the meaning of the words in the utterance to its perception of the environment. Thus, recent work on grounding meaning has focused on how words and utterances map onto physical descriptions of the environment:

in the form of either perceptual representations or control schemas [2, 4, 5, 46, 48]. Here is the critical point. If we can make a language out of the sensorimotor representations that arise from our actions (in general, interactions with our environment), then we can obtain *abstract descriptions* of human activity from nontext (language) data (sensory and motor). These representations are immediately useful since they can ground basic verbs (e.g., walk, turn, sit, kick). It is intuitively clear that we humans understand a sentence like "Joe ran to the store" not because we check "ran" in the dictionary but because we have a sensorimotor experience of running. We know what it means to "run," we can "run" if we wish, we can think of "running." We have functional representations of running that our language of action provides.

While such physical descriptions are useful for some classes of words (e.g., colors, shapes, physical movements), they may not be sufficient for more abstract language, such as that for intentional action. This insufficiency stems from the fact that intentional actions (i.e., actions performed with the purpose of achieving a goal) are highly ambiguous when described only in terms of their physically observable characteristics. Imagine a situation in which one person moves a cup toward another person and says the unknown word "trackot." Based only on the physical description of this action, one might come to think of "trackot" as meaning anything from "give cup" to "offer drink" to "ask for change." This ambiguity stems from the lack of contextual information that strictly perceptual descriptions of action provide.

A language of action provides a methodology for grounding the meaning of actions, ranging from simple movement to intentional acts (e.g., "walk to the store" versus "go to the store," "slide the cup to him" versus "give him the cup"), by combining the grammatical structure of action (motoric and visual) with the well-known grammatical structure of planning or intent. Specifically, one can combine the bottom-up structure discovered from movement data with the top-down structure of annotated intentions. The bottom-up process can give us the actual hierarchical composition of behavior; the top-down process gives us intentionally laden interpretations of those structures. It is likely that top-down annotations will not reach down to visual-motor phonology, but they will perhaps be aligned at the level of visuo-motor morphology or even visuo-motor clauses.

5.8 CONCLUSIONS

Human-centric interfaces not only promise to dominate our future in many applications, but might also begin a new phase in artificial intelligence by studying meaning through the utilization of both sensorimotor and symbolic representations, using machine learning techniques on the gargantuan amounts of data collected. This will lead eventually to the creation of the praxicon, an extension of the lexicon that contains sensorimotor abstractions of the items in the lexicon [1]. The entire enterprise may be seen in light of the emerging *network science*, the study of human behavior not in isolation but in relation to other humans and the environment. In this endeavor, languages of human action will play a very important role.

ACKNOWLEDGMENTS

The support of NSF, NIH, and the European Union (under the POETICON project) is gratefully acknowledged.

REFERENCES

[1] The POETICON. The Poetics of Everyday Life: Grounding Resources and Mechanisms for Artificial Agents. Project funded under the 7th Framework, European Union, *www.poeticon.eu*.

[2] Arbib M, Iberall T, Lyons D. Schemas that integrate vision and touch for hand control. In: Vision, Brain, and Cooperative Computation. MIT Press; 1987. p. 489-510.

[3] Averbeck B, Chafee M, Crowe D, Georgopoulos A. Neural activity in prefrontal cortex during copying geometrical shapes. I. Single cells encode shape, sequence, and metric parameters. Exp Brain Res 2003;150(2):127-41.

[4] Bailey D, Chang N, Feldman J, Narayanan S. Extending embodied lexical development. In: Proceedings of the Annual Meeting of the Cognitive Science Society. 1998. p. 84-9.

[5] Bailey D, Feldman J, Narayanan S, Lakoff G. Modeling embodied lexical development. In: Proceedings of the Annual Meeting of the Cognitive Science Society. 1997. p. 19-24.

[6] Berthier N, Rosenstein M, Barto A. Approximate optimal control as a model for motor learning the kinematics of reaching by a dynamical arm. Psychol Rev 2005;112:329-46.

[7] Buccino G, Lui F, Canessa N, Patteri I, Lagravinese G, Benuzzi F, et al. Neural circuits involved in the recognition of actions performed by nonconspecifics: An FMRI study. J Cogn Neurosci 2004;16(1):114-26.

[8] Citman A, Massaquoi S, Takahashi K, Ebner T. Kinematic analysis of manual tracking in monkeys: Characterization of movement intermittencies during a circular tracking task. J Neurophysiol 2004;91:901-11.

[9] d'Avella A, Bizzi E. Shared and specific muscle synergies in natural motor behaviors. Proc Natl Acad Sci U S A 2005;102(8):3076-81.

[10] del Vecchio D, Murray R, Perona P. Decomposition of human motion into dynamics-based primitives with application to drawing tasks. Automatica 2003;39:2085-98.

[11] Doeringer J, Hogan N. Intermittency in preplanned elbow movements persists in the absence of visual feedback. J Neurophysiol 1998;80(4):1787-99.

[12] Fishbach A, Roy S, Bastianen C, Miller L, Houk J. Kinematic properties of on-line error corrections in the monkey. Exp Brain Res 2005;164(4):442-57.

[13] Flash T, Henis E. Arm trajectory modifications during reaching towards visual targets. J Cogn Neurosci 1991;3(3):220-30.

[14] Fod A, Matarić M, Jenkins O. Automated derivation of primitives for movement classification. Autonomous Robots 2002;12(1):39-54.

[15] Gallese V, Fadiga L, Fogassi L, Rizzolatti G. Action recognition in the premotor cortex. Brain 1996;119(2):593-609.

[16] Gallese V, Lakoff G. The brain's concepts: The role of the sensory-motor system in conceptual knowledge. Cognitive Neuropsychology 2005;22(3-4):455-79.

[17] Georgopoulos A, Schwartz A, Kettner R. Neuronal population coding of movement direction. Science 1986;233(4771):1416-9.

[18] Ghez C, Favilla M, Ghilardi M, Gordon J, Bermejo J, Pullman S. Discrete and continuous planning of hand movements and isometric force trajectories. Exp Brain Res 2004;115 (2):217-33.

[19] Graziano M, Patel K, Taylor C. Mapping from motor cortex to biceps and triceps altered by elbow angle. J Neurophysiol 2004;92:395-407.

[20] Graziano M, Taylor C, Moore T, Cooke D. The cortical control of movement revisited. Neuron 2002;36(3):349-62.

[21] Guerra-Filho G, Aloimonos Y. Understanding visuo-motor primitives for motion synthesis and analysis. Computer Animation and Virtual Worlds 2006;17(3-4):207-17.

[22] Guerra-Filho G, Aloimonos Y. A language for human action. IEEE Computer Magazine 2006;40(5):60-9.

[23] Guerra-Filho G, Fermüller C, Aloimonos Y. Discovering a language for human activity. In: Proceedings of AAAI 2005 Fall Symposium: "From Reactive to Anticipatory Cognitive Embodied System." 2005. p. 70-7.

[24] Han C-C, Kumar R, Shea R, Kohler E, Srivastava M. A dynamic operating system for sensor nodes. In: Proceedings of the International Conference on Mobile Systems, Applications, and Services (Mobisys). 2005. p. 163-76.

[25] Jackendorf R. The Architecture of the Language Faculty. MIT Press; 2000.

[26] Jeannerod M. Object oriented action. In: Bennett K, Castiello U, editors. Insights into the Reach to Grasp Movement. Elsevier and North-Holland; 1994. p. 3-15.

[27] Jenkins O, Mataric M. Automated derivation of behavior vocabularies for autonomous humanoid motion. In: Proceedings of the International Conference on Autonomous Agents. 2003. p. 225-32.

[28] Juhola M. A syntactic method for analysis of saccadic eye movements. Pattern Recogn 1986;19 (5):353-9.

[29] Kahol K, Tripathi P, Panchanathan S. Automated gesture segmentation from dance sequences. In: Proceedings of IEEE International Conference on Automatic Face and Gesture Recognition. 1983. p. 883-8.

[30] Lacquaniti F, Terzuolo C, Viviani P. The law relating the kinematic and figural aspects of drawing movements. Acta Psychologica 54(1-3):115-30.

[31] Liao L, Fox D, Kautz H. Location-based activity recognition using relational Markov networks. In: Proceedings of the International Joint Conference on Artificial Intelligence. 2005.

[32] Lymberopoulos D, Ogale A, Savvides A, Aloimonos Y. A sensory grammar for inferring behaviors in sensor networks. In: Proceedings of Information Processing in Sensor Networks (IPSN). 2005. p. 251-9.

[33] Lymberopoulos D, Teixeira T, Savvides A. Detecting patterns for assisted living using sensor networks. In: Proceedings of the IEEE International Conference on Sensor Technologies and Applications (SensorComm). 2007. p. 590-6.

[34] Mussa-Ivaldi F, Bizzi E. Motor learning through the combination of primitives. Philos Trans R Soc Lond B Biol Sci 2000;355:1755-69.

[35] Nachman L. New tinyos platforms panel: imote2. In: Proceedings of the International TinyOS Technology Exchange. 2005.

[36] Nakazawa A, Nakaoka S, Ikeuchi K, Yokoi K. Imitating human dance motions through motion structure analysis. In: Proceedings of IEEE/RSJ International Conference on Intelligent Robots and Systems. 2002. p. 2539-44.

[37] Nevill-Manning C, Witten I. Identifying hierarchical structure in sequences: A linear-time algorithm. Journal of Artificial Intelligence Research 1997;7:67-82.

[38] Novak K, Miller L, Houk J. Features of motor performance that drive adaptation in rapid hand movements. Exp Brain Res 2003;148(3):388-400.

[39] Ogale A, Karapurkar A, Aloimonos Y. View invariant modeling and recognition of human actions using grammars. In: Proceedings of the Workshop on Dynamical Vision at ICCV'05. 2005. p. 115-26.

[40] Pasalar S, Roitman A, Ebner T. Effects of speeds and force fields on submovements during circular manual tracking in humans. Exp Brain Res 2005;163(2):214-25.

[41] Păun G. On the synchronization in parallel communicating grammar systems. Acta Informatica 1993;30(4):351-67.

[42] Polyakov P, Flash T, Abeles M, Ben-Shaul Y, Drori R, Zoltan N. Analysis of motion planning and learning in monkey scribbling movements. In: Proceedings of the Biennial Conference of the International Graphonomics Society. 2001. p. 78-83.

[43] Rao R, Shon A, Meltzoff A. A Bayesian model of imitation in infants and robots. In: Imitation and Social Learning in Robots, Humans, and Animals. Cambridge University Press; 2005.

[44] Rohrer B, Fasoli S, Krebs H, Volpe B, Frontera W, Stein J, et al. Submovements grow larger, fewer, and more blended during stroke recovery. Motor Control 2004;8(4):472-83.

[45] Rosch E. Categorization. In: Ramachandran V, editor. The Encyclopedia of Human Behavior. Academic Press; 1994.

[46] Roy D. Semiotic schemas: A framework for grounding language in action and perception. Artificial Intelligence 2005;167(1-2):170-205.

[47] Schaal S, Ijspeert A, Billard A. Computational approaches to motor learning by imitation. Philos Trans R Soc Lond B Biol Sci 2003;358:537-47.

[48] Siskind J. Grounding the lexical semantics of verbs in visual perception using force dynamics and event logic. Journal of Artificial Intelligence Research 2001;15:31-90.

[49] Solan Z, Horn D, Ruppin E, Edelman S. Unsupervised learning of natural languages. Proc Natl Acad Sci U S A 2005;102(33):11629-34.

[50] Sternad D, Schaal S. Segmentation of endpoint trajectories does not imply segmented control. Exp Brain Res 1999;124(1):118-36.

[51] Teixeira T, Savvides A. Lightweight people counting and localizing in indoor spaces using camera sensor nodes. In: Proceedings of the ACM/IEEE International Conference on Distributed Smart Cameras (ICDSC). 2007. p. 36-43.

[52] Ting L, Macpherson J. A limited set of muscle synergies for force control during a postural task. J Neurophysiol 2005;93:609-13.

[53] Viviani P. Do units of motor action really exist? In: Heuer H, editor. Generation and Modulation of Action Patterns. Springer; 1986. p. 201-16.

[54] Wang T-S, Shum H-Y, Xu Y-Q, Zheng N-N. Unsupervised analysis of human gestures. In: Proceedings of IEEE Pacific Rim Conference on Multimedia. 2001. p. 174-81.

[55] Woch A, Plamondon R. Using the framework of the kinematic theory for the definition of a movement primitive. Motor Control 2004;8(4):547-57.

[56] Wolff J. Learning syntax and meanings through optimization and distributional analysis. In: Levy Y, Schlesinger I, Braine M, editors. Categories and Processes in Language Acquisition. Lawrence Erlbaum Associates; 1988. p. 179-215.

Speech Processing and Dialogue Management

CHAPTER

Robust Speech Recognition Under Noisy Ambient Conditions

6

Kuldip K. Paliwal

School of Microelectronic Engineering, Griffith University, Brisbane, Australia

Kaisheng Yao

Speech Component Group, Microsoft Corporation, Redmond, Washington

ABSTRACT

Automatic speech recognition is critical in natural human-centric interfaces for ambient intelligence. The performance of an automatic speech recognition system, however, degrades drastically when there is a mismatch between training and testing conditions. The aim of robust speech recognition is to overcome the mismatch problem so the result is a moderate and graceful degradation in recognition performance. In this chapter, we provide a brief overview of an automatic speech recognition system, describe sources of speech variability that cause mismatch between training and testing, and discuss some of the current techniques to achieve robust speech recognition.

Key words: automatic speech, recognition, robust speech recognition, speech enhancement, robust speech feature, stochastic matching, model combination, speaker adaptation, microphone array.

6.1 INTRODUCTION

Ambient intelligence is the vision of a technology that will become invisibly embedded in our surroundings, enabled by simple and effortless interactions, context sensitive, and adaptive to users [1]. Automatic speech recognition is a core component that allows high-quality information access for ambient intelligence. However, it is a difficult problem and one with a long history that began with initial papers appearing in the 1950s [2, 3]. Thanks to the significant progress made in recent years in this area [4, 5], speech recognition technology, once confined to research laboratories, is now applied to some real-world applications, and a number of commercial speech recognition products (from Nuance, IBM, Microsoft, Nokia, etc.) are on the market. For example, with automatic voice mail transcription by speech recognition, a user can have a quick view of her voice mail without having to listen to it. Other applications include voice dialing on embedded speech recognition systems.

The main factors that have made speech recognition possible are advances in digital signal processing (DSP) and stochastic modeling algorithms. Signal processing techniques are important for extracting reliable acoustic features from the speech signal, and stochastic modeling algorithms are useful for representing speech utterances in the form of efficient models, such as hidden Markov models (HMMs), which simplify the speech recognition task. Other factors responsible for the commercial success of speech recognition technology include the availability of fast processors (in the form of DSP chips) and high-density memories at relatively low cost.

With the current state of the art in speech recognition technology, it is relatively easy to accomplish complex speech recognition tasks reasonably well in controlled laboratory environments. For example, it is now possible to achieve less than a 0.4% string error rate in a speaker-independent digit recognition task [6]. Even continuous speech from many speakers and from a vocabulary of 5000 words can be recognized with a word error rate below 4% [7]. This high level of performance is achievable only when the training and the test data match. When there is a mismatch between training and test data, performance degrades drastically.

Mismatch between training and test sets may occur because of changes in acoustic environments (background, channel mismatch, etc.), speakers, task domains, speaking styles, and the like [8]. Each of these sources of mismatch can cause severe distortion in recognition performance for ambient intelligence. For example, a continuous speech recognition system with a 5000-word vocabulary raised its word error rate from 15% in clean conditions to 69% in 10-dB to 20-dB signal-to-noise ratio (SNR) conditions [9, 10]. Similar degradations in recognition performance due to channel mismatch are observed. The recognition accuracy of the SPHINX speech recognition system on a speaker-independent alphanumeric task dropped from 85% to 20% correct when the close-talking Sennheiser microphone used in training was replaced by the omnidirectional Crown desktop microphone [11]. Similarly, when a digital recognition system is trained for a particular speaker, its accuracy can be easily 100%, but its performance degrades to as low as 50% when it is tested on a new speaker.

To understand the effect of mismatch between training and test conditions, we show in Figure 6.1 the performance of a speaker-dependent, isolated-word recognition system on speech corrupted by additive white noise. The recognition system uses a nine-word English e-set alphabet vocabulary where each word is represented by a single-mixture continuous Gaussian density HMM with five states. The figure shows recognition accuracy as a function of the SNR of the test speech under (1) mismatched conditions where the recognition system is trained on clean speech and tested on noisy speech, and (2) matched conditions where the training and the test speech data have the same SNR.

It can be seen from Figure 6.1 that the additive noise causes a drastic degradation in recognition performance under the mismatched conditions; with the matched conditions, however, the degradation is moderate and graceful. It may be noted here that if the SNR becomes too low (such as −10 dB), the result is very poor recognition performance even when the system operates under matched noise conditions. This is because the signal is completely swamped by noise and no useful information can be extracted from it during training or in testing.

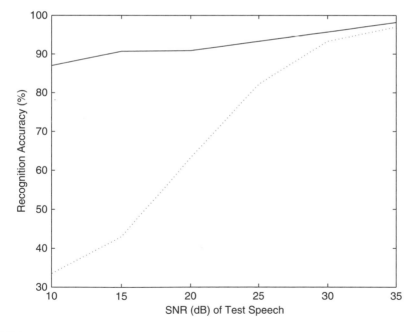

FIGURE 6.1

Effect of additive white noise on speech recognition performance under matched and mismatched conditions: training with clean speech (dotted line); training and testing with same-SNR speech (solid line).

When a speech recognition system is deployed in a real-life situation for ambient intelligence, there is bound to be a mismatch between training and testing that causes severe deterioration in recognition performance. The aim of a robust speech recognition system is to remove the effect of mismatch and achieve performance that is as graceful as obtained under matched conditions.

Note that devices used for ambient intelligence are usually small, low power, low weight, and (very important) low cost. A successful speech recognition system therefore needs to consider factors of practical implementation and system usage. These challenges include but are not limited to dealing with large volumes of incoming recognition requests, prompt response, and hardware constraints such as low memory and fixed-point arithmetic on DSP chips.

In this chapter, we provide only a glimpse of robust speech recognition and describe briefly some of the popular techniques used for this purpose. (For more details, see [12–21].) We will focus here mainly on techniques to handle mismatches resulting from changes in acoustic environments (e.g., channel and noise distortions). Some of these are equally applicable to mismatches resulting from speaker variability. The chapter is organized as follows: Section 6.2 provides a brief overview of the automatic speech recognition process. Different sources of variability in speech signals are discussed in Section 6.3. Robust speech recognition techniques are briefly described in Section 6.4. Section 6.5 concludes the chapter.

6.2 SPEECH RECOGNITION OVERVIEW

The objective of an automatic speech recognition system is to take the speech waveform of an unknown (input) utterance, and classify it as one of a set of spoken words, phrases, or sentences. Typically, this is done in two steps (as shown in Figure 6.2). In the first step, an acoustic front-end is used to perform feature analysis

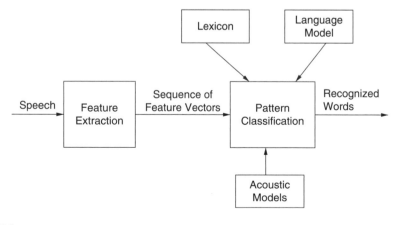

FIGURE 6.2

Block diagram of an automatic speech recognition system.

of the speech signal at the rate of about 100 frames per second to extract a set of features. This produces a sequence of feature vectors that characterizes the speech utterance sequentially in time.

The second step deals with pattern classification, where the sequence of feature vectors is compared against the machine's knowledge of speech (in the form of acoustics, lexicon, syntax, semantics, etc.) to arrive at a transcription of the input utterance.

Currently, most speech recognition systems use a statistical framework to carry out the pattern classification task, and they generally recognize the input speech utterance as a sequence of words. Consider a sequence of feature vectors,

$$\mathbf{Y} = \{\mathbf{y}_1, \mathbf{y}_2, \ldots, \mathbf{y}_T\}$$

representing the T frames of the input speech utterance. The task of the system is to find a word sequence,

$$W = \{w_1, w_2, \ldots, w_K\}$$

that maximizes the a posteriori probability of the observation sequence $\mathbf{Y}$; that is, the recognized word sequence,

$$\hat{W} = \{\hat{w}_1, \hat{w}_2, \ldots, \hat{w}_{\hat{K}}\}$$

is given by the following equation:

$$\hat{W} = \underset{W}{\operatorname{argmax}} \ \Pr(W|\mathbf{Y}) \tag{6.1}$$

In this Equation (6.1), maximization of the a posteriori probability $\Pr(W|\mathbf{Y})$ is over all possible word sequences $\{w_1, w_2, \ldots, w_K\}$ for all possible values of K. For a large-vocabulary continuous-speech system, this is a computationally exorbitant task. Fast search algorithms are available in the literature to carry it out [22–24].

Applying Bayes's rule and noting that $\Pr(\mathbf{Y})$ is independent of W, Equation (6.1) can be written as

$$\hat{W} = \underset{W}{\operatorname{argmax}} \ \Pr(\mathbf{Y}|W) \cdot \Pr(W) \tag{6.2}$$

This is known as the maximum a posteriori probability (MAP) decision rule in the statistical pattern recognition literature [25].

Equation (6.2) indicates that we need two probabilities $\Pr(\mathbf{Y}|W)$ and $\Pr(W)$ to carry out the recognition task. These are computed through the acoustic and language models, respectively, which are briefly described as follows:

Acoustic models. The acoustic models are used to compute the probability $\Pr(\mathbf{Y}|W)$. To do this, we need the probability of an observed sequence of feature vectors for each of the words in the vocabulary. This is done by representing each word by a hidden Markov model (HMM) [27] and estimating the HMM parameters from an independent (and preferably large) speech data set during the training phase. To capture the sequential nature of speech, the left-to-right HMMs are used to model individual words. For a large-vocabulary continuous-speech recognition system, it is not possible to have one HMM for each word, so we seek smaller units (subword units) to characterize these probabilities. Examples of subword units are phonemes, demisyllables, and syllables. If there are M phonemes in the (English) language, we can have M HMMs, each estimated from the training data belonging to a particular phoneme. These are called context-independent models. For a large-vocabulary speech recognition system, such models are not adequate, and one requires context-dependent modeling to get good recognition performance.

Current recognition systems use HMMs for all possible left and right contexts for each phoneme (triphone models). Once the acoustic models (in the form of HMMs) are available for individual subword units (e.g., triphones) from the training phase, the word models are constructed from the subword models according to the transcription of the words (in terms of subword units) contained in the lexicon.

Language model. The language model is used to compute the probability $\Pr(W)$. Note that $\Pr(W)$ is independent of the observed feature vector sequence $\mathbf{Y}$. Like acoustic models, the language model is estimated from a large, independent corpus of training data. Among different language models proposed in the literature, the N-gram model (where N is typically 2, 3, or 4) is perhaps the most popular and simplest for representing the syntactic, semantic, and pragmatic sources of knowledge. In it, the probability of the current word depends on $N-1$ preceding words. Thus, it is very effective for capturing local dependencies between words. In an N-gram model, the probability $\Pr(w_k|w_1,w_2,\ldots,w_{k-1})$ is approximated by $\Pr(w_k|w_{k-1},w_{k-2},\ldots,w_{k-N+1})$. As an example, we show the procedure for calculating the probability $\Pr(W)$ using the trigram model ($N=3$).

$$
\begin{aligned}
\Pr(W) &= \Pr(w_1, w_2, \ldots, w_K) \\
&= \prod_{k=1}^{K} \Pr(w_k|w_1, w_2, \ldots, w_{k-1}) \\
&= \prod_{k=1}^{K} \Pr(w_k|w_{k-1}, w_{k-2})
\end{aligned}
\tag{6.3}
$$

Thus, we compute the acoustic and language models in the training phase from the data available for training the speech recognizer. Let us denote the set of acoustic models (i.e., subword HMMs) by $\Lambda_{\mathbf{X}}$ and the set of N-gram models by Υ_W. Then the MAP decision rule (Equation (6.2)) can be written in terms of these models as follows:

$$
\hat{W} = \underset{W}{\operatorname{argmax}} \ \Pr(\mathbf{Y}|W, \Lambda_{\mathbf{X}}) \cdot \Pr(W|\Upsilon_W)
\tag{6.4}
$$

During the test phase, the recognizer uses the acoustic and language models to compute the probabilities $\Pr(\mathbf{Y}|W, \Lambda_{\mathbf{X}})$ and $\Pr(W|\Upsilon_W)$ and to carry out the recognition of the input utterance according to the MAP decision rule given by Equation (6.4).

6.3 VARIABILITY IN THE SPEECH SIGNAL

Robust speech recognition deals with the mismatch between the training and testing conditions. Most of this mismatch is due to variability in the speech signal resulting from various sources, some of which are listed here:

Background noise. When speech is recorded in a given acoustic environment, the resulting signal is the sum of the speech produced by a speaker and the background (or ambient) noise. This additive noise generally has a colored spectrum, whose shape depends on the source that generates it. In an office environment, background noise results from sources such as computers, printers, typewriters, air conditioners, telephones, fans, background, conversations, and so forth. In a moving-car environment, it can be due to engine, wind, tires, road, and the like. Sources of background noise for other environments (such as a telephone booth, industrial plant, plane cockpit) can also be easily identified. Depending on the source, the background noise can be stationary (e.g., a fan or an air-conditioner) or nonstationary (e.g., a moving car).

   Though spectral shape as well as level of background noise causes a degradation in recognition performance, the latter has a greater effect. When the background noise is at a relatively high level, it produces the Lombard effect [29], which changes even the characteristics of the speech signal produced by a given speaker.

Room reverberation. Room reverberation causes a convolutional distortion; that is, the reverberated speech signal can be modeled as a convolution of the intended speech signal, with the impulse response characterizing the distortion. The amount of reverberation distortion is determined by the room acoustics and the position of speaker and microphone within the room. When a speaker is at a relatively large distance from the microphone, the reverberation distortion becomes serious and can significantly affect speech recognition performance [30].

Microphone characteristics. A microphone acts on the speech signal as a linear filter (approximately) and causes convolution distortion. Since different types of microphones have different frequency responses, their mismatch during training and test conditions causes severe recognition performance degradation [11].

Transmission channel. When a speech recognizer is accessed through a telephone or mobile phone, the transmission channel used is totally unknown and unpredictable. This causes mismatch between training and testing, and speech recognition performance suffers because of it. A transmission channel acts like a linear filter on the speech signal and causes convolution distortion. Mobile telephony introduces another distortion, resulting from speech coders, which also affects recognition performance adversely [31].

Intra-speaker variability. When a person speaks the same word twice at different times of day, the resulting utterances show different acoustic characteristics. This intra-speaker variability is mainly caused by changes in the health and emotional state of the speaker.

Inter-speaker variability. Inter-speaker variability is one of the main sources of mismatch between training and testing conditions and is a major cause of the degraded performance of a speech recognizer. Differences in the length and shape of the vocal tract, dialect, pronunciation, and articulatory habits are some examples of this variability.

Most of the sources of speech variability discussed produce additive distortion (e.g., background noise) and/or convolution distortion (e.g., microphone mismatch) in the speech signal. A common model that describes these distortions and helps in understanding robust speech recognition techniques (discussed in the next section) is as follows:

$$\mathbf{y}_t = \mathbf{x}_t * \mathbf{h}_t + \mathbf{w}_t \tag{6.5}$$

where the symbol $*$ denotes the convolution operation and the subscript t is the time index. $\mathbf{x}_t$ and $\mathbf{y}_t$ are the clean speech signal and the distorted signal, respectively. $\mathbf{h}_t$ and $\mathbf{w}_t$ each denote convolution distortion and the additive noise signal. In this equation, both distortions are nonstationary, but they can be assumed stationary for simplicity of analysis. Further assuming that $\mathbf{y}_t$, $\mathbf{x}_t$, and $\mathbf{w}_t$ are uncorrelated, we have a power spectrum after the short-time Fourier analysis of the distorted signal as

$$P_{yy}(m, f) = P_{xx}(m, f)|H(f)|^2 + P_{ww}(f) \tag{6.6}$$

where f is the frequency variable and m is the frame index; $H(f)$ denotes the Fourier transform of $\mathbf{h}_t$; and $P_{yy}(m, f)$, $P_{xx}(m, f)$, and $P_{ww}(f)$ are the power spectra of $\mathbf{y}_t$, $\mathbf{x}_t$, and $\mathbf{w}_t$, respectively. If there is only convolution distortion present in the signal, Equation (6.6) can be written as

$$\log P_{yy}(m, f) = \log P_{xx}(m, f) + 2\log |H(f)| \tag{6.7}$$

When the signal is corrupted by additive noise distortion (i.e., there is no convolution distortion), then Equation (6.6) can be written as

$$P_{yy}(m, f) = P_{xx}(m, f) + P_{ww}(f) \tag{6.8}$$

Equations (6.6), (6.7), and (6.8) form the basis of a number of the robust speech recognition techniques discussed in the next section.

6.4 ROBUST SPEECH RECOGNITION TECHNIQUES

As mentioned earlier, robust speech recognition deals with the problem resulting from the mismatch between training and testing. A speech recognizer is considered robust if it (approximately) maintains good recognition performance even if this mismatch exists.

Some researchers believe that one can solve the mismatch problem by increasing the size of the training data set and including all possible speech variations in it. However, this approach, called matched training or multi-condition training, solves the problem only to some extent. The models computed from this large training data set may be diffused and diluted (i.e., they may have large variance). As a result, their performance may be relatively poor for all test conditions. By increasing the size of the training data set and including all possible speech variations in it, one is only improving generalization capability at the cost of recognition performance.

To really solve the robust speech recognition problem, one has to understand the basic characteristics of the speech signal and the effect of different sources of distortion and variability, and then capture this knowledge during the feature extraction and acoustic-modeling stages. If the mismatch still remains, one must use small amounts of adaptation data prior to testing the recognition system for fine tuning.

In this chapter, we concentrate on the mismatch between training and testing conditions resulting from variability in the speech signal. This means that we have to handle the mismatch between the acoustic models $\Lambda_{\mathbf{X}}$ and the observation sequence $\mathbf{Y}$, without worrying about the language model Υ_W.

6.4.1 Speech Enhancement Techniques

The aim of a speech enhancement system is to suppress the noise in a noisy speech signal. For robust speech recognition, such a system is used as a preprocessor to a speech recognizer. Since it produces a clean speech signal, no changes in the recognition system are necessary to make it robust. A number of speech enhancement techniques have been reported in the literature [32]. They include spectral subtraction [33, 34, 41], Wiener and Kalman filtering [35], MMSE estimation [36], comb filtering [32], subspace methods [37, 38], and phase spectrum compensation [39, 40].

These techniques were originally developed with the aim of improving the intelligibility of noisy speech, but they can be used for robust speech recognition as well. The technique that has been used most for this purpose is spectral subtraction, in which the power spectrum of clean speech $P_{xx}(m, f)$ is estimated by explicitly subtracting the noise power spectrum $P_{ww}(f)$ from the noisy speech power spectrum $P_{yy}(m, f)$ using Equation (6.8). This requires information about the noise power spectrum, which can be estimated from the nonspeech frames detected by voice activity detection (VAD). However, it is not always possible to detect the nonspeech frames correctly, which affects the estimation of the noise power spectrum and may result in poor speech enhancement. Hence, a practical spectral subtraction scheme has the form

$$\hat{P}_{xx}(m, f) = \begin{cases} P_{yy}(m, f) - \alpha P_{ww}(f) & \text{if } \hat{P}_{xx}(m, f) \geq \beta P_{ww}(f) \\ \\ \beta P_{ww}(f) & \text{otherwise} \end{cases} \tag{6.9}$$

where α is an oversubtraction factor and β sets a spectral floor to avoid the enhanced spectra from becoming negative. Wiener filtering, which is closely related to spectral subtraction [44], was recently used in an industrial standard [45, 46] for speech recognition.

Since VAD itself is hard to tune for correct determination of speech and nonspeech events, especially in low SNR and highly nonstationary noise conditions, there are methods that estimate the noise power spectrum without VAD. In [42, 43], based on the observations that speech and background noise are usually statistically independent and that the power spectrum $P_{yy}(m, f)$ frequently decays to the noise power spectrum $P_{ww}(f)$, minimum statistics methods estimated the noise power spectrum by tracking and smoothing spectral minima in each frequency band.

Phase spectrum compensation (PSC) [39, 40] is a recently proposed approach to speech enhancement in which the noisy magnitude spectrum is recombined with a changed phase spectrum to produce a modified complex spectrum. During synthesis, the low-energy components of the modified complex spectrum cancel out more than the high-energy components, thus reducing background noise.

The PSC procedure is as follows. First, the noisy speech signal y_t is transformed via N-point short-time Fourier transform into the complex spectrum $Y(m, k)$ at frame m. Second, the noisy complex spectrum is offset by an additive real-valued frequency-dependent $\Xi(k)$ function:

$$Y_\Xi(m, k) = Y(m, k) + \Xi(k) \tag{6.10}$$

where $\Xi(k)$ should be anti-symmetric about $F_s/2$ (half the sampling rate). A simple anti-symmetric $\Xi(k)$ function may be as follows:

$$\Xi(k) = \begin{cases} +\xi & 0 \le k < \dfrac{N}{2} \\ -\xi & \dfrac{N}{2} \le k \le N - 1 \end{cases} \tag{6.11}$$

where ξ is a real-valued constant and N is the length of frequency analysis assumed to be even. $Y_\Xi(m, k)$ is used to compute the changed phase spectrum through the arctangent function

$$\angle Y_\Xi(m, k) = \arctan\left(\frac{Im\{Y_\Xi(m, k)\}}{Re\{Y_\Xi(m, k)\}}\right) \tag{6.12}$$

where $Im\{\cdot\}$ and $Re\{\cdot\}$ denote imaginary and real operators, respectively. The phase spectrum is combined with the noisy magnitude spectrum to produce a modified complex spectrum:

$$\hat{X}_\Xi(m, k) = |Y(m, k)| e^{j\angle Y_\Xi(m, k)} \tag{6.13}$$

In the synthesis stage, the complex spectrum of Equation (6.13) is converted to a time-domain representation. Because of the additive offset introduced in Equation (6.10), the modified complex spectrum $\hat{X}_\Xi(m, k)$ may not be conjugate symmetric and the resulting time-domain signal may be complex. In the proposed PSC method, the imaginary component is discarded. The enhanced signal $\hat{x}_t$ is produced by employing the overlap-and-add procedure.

All of the above methods can be tuned to achieve a certain degree of noise reduction at the cost of some speech distortion. Note that, for an ASR system, speech distortion is usually difficult to compensate for, but residual noise remaining after speech enhancement can be post-processed using techniques discussed later in this chapter. Hence, an optimal set of speech enhancement parameters for ASR systems usually allows more residual noise than that for a human listener. For this reason, the optimal speech enhancement parameters for ASR and for a human listener can be very different.

6.4.2 Robust Feature Selection and Extraction Methods

Selection of proper acoustic features is perhaps the most important task in the design of a robust speech recognition system, as it directly affects system performance. These features should be selected with the following criteria in mind:

- They should contain the maximum information necessary for speech recognition.
- They should be insensitive to speaker characteristics, manner of speaking, background noise, channel distortion, and so forth.
- We should be able to estimate them accurately and reliably.
- We should be able to estimate them through a computationally efficient procedure.
- They should have a physical meaning (preferably consistent with the human auditory perception process).

Obviously, it is very difficult to select a set of acoustic features that satisfies all of these requirements, and a great deal of research has gone into identifying them (see [54, 58–60, 62] and references therein for different front-ends).

Once the features are selected, the task of the acoustic front-end is to extract them from the speech signal. It does this by dividing the signal into overlapping time frames and computing the values of the features for each frame. The complexity of the acoustic front-end depends on the type of features selected. They may be as simple as the energy and zero-crossing rate of the waveform during each frame. A better, but more complex, method for feature analysis is based on the source/system model of the speech production system. It is generally considered that the system part of this model represents the vocal tract response and contains most of the linguistic information necessary for speech recognition. The power spectrum of each speech frame contains information about the source part (in the form of a fine structure) and vocal tract system part (in the form of a smooth spectral envelope). The acoustic front-end computes the smooth spectral envelope from the power spectrum by removing the fine structure. Once the envelope is estimated, it can be represented in terms of a few parameters (such as cepstral coefficients). These parameters are used as acoustic features in a speech recognition system. Human listeners, in contrast, can recognize speech even in the presence of large amounts of noise and channel distortions. Therefore, it is argued that the acoustic front-end can be made more robust to these distortions by utilizing the properties of the human auditory system.

The Mel filter-bank analysis procedure [55] is based on the fact that the frequency sensitivity of the human ear is greater at low frequencies than at high frequencies. Therefore, the analysis computes the power spectrum of a given speech frame by using a nonuniform filter bank, where filter bandwidth increases logarithmically with filter frequency (according to the Mel scale). The Mel frequency cepstral coefficients (MFCCs) representing the smooth spectral envelope are computed from the power spectrum using homomorphic analysis. The MFCC feature and its time derivatives [56] are now the most widely used speech features. Inclusion of time derivatives in the feature set improves recognition performance in matched as well as mismatched acoustic conditions [69].

PLP analysis [57] uses more detailed properties of the human auditory system than does Mel filter-bank analysis to compute the power spectrum. In addition to a nonuniform filter bank (where filters are spaced according to the Bark scale), it uses an equal loudness curve and the intensity-loudness power law to better model the auditory system. The cepstral features are estimated from the resulting power spectrum using LP analysis.

Recent discriminative feature extraction methods [64, 65, 67] use a posteriori probabilities of a set of models that are related to classification accuracy. For example, the tandem features [64] are computed with a multilayer perceptron (MLP) to first discriminatively transform multiple feature vectors (typically several frames of MFCC or PLP features). The outputs of the MLPs approximate the a posteriori probabilities of selected phones given the snapshot of these input frames. For the a posteriori probabilities to be used as input to HMM, they are transformed by principal component analysis (PCA). Training MLPs increases the a posteriori probabilities of the selected phones in comparison to the probabilities of competing phones. It is found that augmenting the feature with other features such MFCCs and PLPs is preferable when training and testing environments have mismatches [66].

The feature-space minimum phone error (fMPE) method [67] is another example of discriminative feature extraction. Using a discriminative training method [68], it estimates a matrix to transform a high-dimension vector consisting of a posteriori probabilities of Gaussian components in HMM into a time-dependent vector that adds to the original input vector. These Gaussian components are further updated on the extracted feature. The procedures for estimating the transform and for updating the Gaussian components are repeated several times. It is interesting that the fMPE feature is not appended to the original feature vector, as is common with other feature extraction methods such as the previously mentioned tandem feature or the delta/acceleration parameters. A discussion in [114] suggests that fMPE may be analyzed in light of feature compensation methods such as SPLICE [113] (see Section 6.4.4).

Heteroscedastic linear discriminant analysis (HLDA) [71] defines an objective function of discrimination using the actual covariance of Gaussian components in HMM as follows,

$$Q_{HLDA}(\mathbf{A}) = \sum_{n} \gamma_n \log \frac{|\mathbf{A}|\Sigma_b \mathbf{A}^T}{\mathbf{A}\Sigma^{(n)}\mathbf{A}^T} \tag{6.14}$$

where γ_n is the total occupation posterior probability of component n, and $\Sigma^{(n)}$ is its covariance; Σ_b is the between-class covariance. The matrix $\mathbf{A}$ is not constrained to be full rank, so it can have fewer rows than columns, which results in dimension reduction.

By maximizing the objective function, HLDA allows decorrelation of the elements in feature vectors while rotating them to achieve dimension reduction with little loss of discrimination. In practice, five to nine adjacent frames of feature vectors are concatenated, forming a slice with about 200 feature dimensions. The slice is then analyzed using HLDA, and the feature dimensions can be reduced to, say, 39. Since much of the discrimination of the original high-dimensional slice is kept, HLDA-processed features can yield improved performance over those with similar dimension but without such processing.

6.4.3 Feature Normalization Techniques

Variability not related to discriminating speech content may be reduced by feature normalization techniques. For instance, cepstral mean normalization (CMN) [72] assumes that the interfering distortion is stationary and convolutional (see Equation (6.7)), and suppresses it by subtracting the long-term cepstral mean vector (over the input utterance) from the current cepstral vector. This technique is currently very popular for overcoming channel mismatch distortion. When the channel is slowly varying with time, its effect can be eliminated by highpass filtering (e.g., RASTA) of the sequence of cepstral feature vectors [73, 76].

Cepstral variance normalization (CVN) [77] reduces mismatches by normalizing the second moment of the distribution of speech to a fixed value. It is usually combined with CMN and other techniques, such as speaker adaptation, and yields good results. Some embedded speech recognition systems [78] use CMN and CVN because of their low implementation costs. CMN and CVN are further extended in [79] to equalize histograms of training and testing data.

Vocal tract length normalization (VTLN) warps the frequency axis of the magnitude spectrum to reduce the shifting of formant frequencies due to speaker variations. This is achieved by linearly scaling the filter bank center frequencies within the front-end feature extraction to approximate a canonical formant frequency scaling [80]. Given a previously trained acoustic model, a grid search on likelihoods against different frequency-warping parameters is performed to find the optimal likelihood of an utterance. Once all utterances are normalized, the acoustic models are re-estimated. This is repeated until the VTLN parameters of all utterances are stabilized. It was observed in [81] that VTLN may be considered a special type of maximum-likelihood linear regression method (see Section 6.4.5, subsection Adaptation-Based Compensation).

6.4.4 Stereo Data-Based Feature Enhancement

In some applications, stereo data may be available. For instance, hands-free microphones can be placed in a car to collect noisy speech along with speech collected via close-talking microphones. It is also possible to generate noisy speech by artificially adding noise to clean speech. Stereo data can be used to estimate mapping from noisy to clean speech, and this mapping can be used to enhance noisy speech features in the testing phase.

Usually, a minimum mean-square error (MMSE) scheme [82, 83, 86, 113] is used to enhance the feature vector:

$$\hat{X}_t = \boldsymbol{\varepsilon}\,(\mathbf{X}_t|\mathbf{Y}_t) \tag{6.15}$$

The noisy observation $\mathbf{y}_t$ is assumed to be distributed in multiple Gaussian components $\sum_n c_n N(\mathbf{y}_t; \mu_y^{(n)}, \Sigma_y^{(n)})$ with a mixture weight c_n for Gaussian component n. This is similar for clean speech distribution. Assuming that the clean speech $\mathbf{x}_t$ and the noisy speech are distributed jointly within each component n, an estimate of the clean speech in the component is

$$\begin{aligned}
\boldsymbol{\varepsilon}\left(\mathbf{x}_t|\mathbf{y}_t, n\right) &= \mu_x^{(n)} + \Sigma_{xy}^{(n)}(\Sigma_y^{(n)})^{-1}(\mathbf{y}_t - \mu_y^{(n)}) \\
&= \mathbf{A}^{(n)}\mathbf{y}_t + \mathbf{b}^{(n)}
\end{aligned} \tag{6.16}$$

Because there are correlations among clean and noisy speech, as shown in $\Sigma_{xy}^{(n)}$, matrix $\mathbf{A}^{(n)}$ is usually full, representing a rotation from $\mathbf{y}_t$ to the cleaned speech $\mathbf{x}_t$. $\mathbf{b}^{(n)}$ serves as a bias within the component. The MMSE estimate (Eq. 6.15) is then a weighted average of the above estimates, with weights being a posteriori probabilities of Gaussian components given a noisy observation sequence.

The SPLICE method [113] assumes only bias $\mathbf{b}^{(n)}$ to be estimated within each Gaussian component n. Using stereo data, a training procedure estimates the bias as

$$\mathbf{b}^{(n)} = \frac{\sum_t \gamma_n(t)(\mathbf{x}_t - \mathbf{y}_t)}{\sum_t \gamma_n(t)} \tag{6.17}$$

where

$$\gamma_n(t) = \frac{c_n N(\mathbf{y}_t; \mu_y^{(n)}, \Sigma_y^{(n)})}{\sum_n c_n N(\mathbf{y}_t; \mu_y^{(n)}, \Sigma_y^{(n)})} \tag{6.18}$$

is the a posteriori probability of Gaussian component n given noisy observation $\mathbf{y}_t$. During testing, at each time t, a Gaussian component n^* is selected as $n^* = \operatorname{argmax}_n \gamma_n(t)$ and the enhanced feature is obtained by subtracting the bias of the selected Gaussian component from noisy observation as $\hat{x}_t = \mathbf{y}_t - \mathbf{b}^{n^*}$.

When stereo data is not available, statistics in a noisy environment may be predicted using a model of the environment. This type of method is described in Section 6.4.5.

6.4.5 The Stochastic Matching Framework

This section describes methods in a stochastic matching framework [94] that can further improve the performance of features extracted as discussed in Sections 6.4.1 through 6.4.4. To achieve this, knowledge of acoustic models is usually employed. In a typical stochastic matching scenario, HMMs are computed during the training phase from a large collection of data coming from a number of speakers and environments. Stochastic matching is carried out for a new speaker or environment either in feature-space or in model space using a small amount of speaker-specific or environment-specific adaptation data.

Let us denote this adaptation data by $\mathbf{Y}$, and let us assume that the transcription of $\mathbf{Y}$ is available. Let us denote this transcription by W. This data is utilized to design a transformation $\mathbf{G}_\theta$ in the model space:

$$\Lambda_\mathbf{Y} = \mathbf{G}_\theta(\Lambda_\mathbf{X}) \tag{6.19}$$

or a transformation F_θ in the feature-space:

$$\hat{\mathbf{Y}} = \mathbf{F}_\theta(\mathbf{Y}) \tag{6.20}$$

The functional forms of the transformations are assumed to be known from our prior knowledge of the source of mismatch, and θ are the associated parameters. These parameters are estimated so as to provide the best match between the transformed models $\Lambda_\mathbf{Y}$ and the adaptation data $\mathbf{Y}$, or the enhanced feature $\hat{\mathbf{Y}}$ and the original model $\Lambda_\mathbf{X}$. Usually, the maximum likelihood formulation is used to estimate $\hat{\theta}$ for model space adaptation as follows:

$$\hat{\theta} = \underset{\theta}{\mathrm{argmax}}\, \mathrm{Pr}(\mathbf{Y}|\theta, W, \Lambda_\mathbf{X}) \cdot \mathrm{Pr}(W|\Upsilon_W) \tag{6.21}$$

The maximization in this equation can be carried out using the expectation-maximization (EM) algorithm [94]. Parameters for feature-space enhancement can be similarly derived.

We may categorize methods in stochastic matching according to the following criteria

- Whether a parametric function representing environment distortions is used
- Whether a method works in model space or in feature-space

Model-Based Model Adaptation

One way to achieve robust speech recognition is by training a new set of models from scratch every time the test condition changes. These models may be saved on a large disk and be invoked whenever a working condition is detected [88, 89]. This approach requires a large disk space for saving the models, which is very expensive for applications such as embedded speech recognition.

Another approach [11, 84, 87, 90, 106, 107, 111] is to capture some information about the mismatch during the training phase and use it for model adaptation. The mismatch may be modeled as a parametric transformation of HMM parameters, and the parameters may be meaningful. Using Equations (6.7) and (6.8), the joint additive and convolutive distortion compensation method (JAC) [90] relates a noisy observation in the log-spectral domain to clean speech log-spectra $\log P_{xx}(m, f)$, additive noise $\log P_{ww}(f)$, and channel distortion $H(f)$ as

$$
\begin{aligned}
\log P_{yy}(m, f) &= \log(P_{xx}(m, f)|H(f)|^2 + P_{ww}(f)) \\
&= \log P_{xx}(m, f) + \log|H(f)|^2 + \log\left(1 + \frac{P_{ww}(f)}{P_{xx}(m, f)|H(f)|^2}\right) \\
&= \log P_{xx}(m, f) + \log|H(f)|^2 + g(P_{xx}(m, f), |H(f)|^2, P_{ww}(f))
\end{aligned} \tag{6.22}
$$

where

$$g(x,y,z) = \log\left(1 + \exp(\log z - \log x - \log y)\right) \tag{6.23}$$

To use the functions just described to represent effects in the model space, at every Gaussian component n, we expand them using a first-order Taylor series around clean speech mean $\mu_x^{(n)}$, noise mean μ_n, and channel distortion mean μ_b as

$$
\begin{aligned}
\log P_{yy}(m,f) \approx\ & C^{-1}(\mu_x^{(n)} + \mu_b) + g(C^{-1}\mu_x^{(n)}, C^{-1}\mu_b, C^{-1}\mu_n) \\
& + \mathbf{G}_x(C\log P_{xx}(m,f) - \mu_x^{(n)}) + \mathbf{G}_b(C\log|H(f)|^2 - \mu_b) \\
& + \mathbf{G}_n(C\log P_{ww}(f) - \mu_n)
\end{aligned}
\tag{6.24}
$$

where C and C^{-1} each denote the discrete cosine transformation and its inverse. $\mathbf{G}_x$, $\mathbf{G}_b$, and $\mathbf{G}_n$ each denote the first-order differential of noisy observation $\log P_{yy}$ (m,f) with respect to clean speech, channel distortion, and noise.

The channel distortion and noise mean may be estimated using the EM algorithm. Given these estimations, JAC reduces the mismatch caused by channel distortion and noise by transforming clean speech mean $\mu_x^{(n)}$ to noisy speech mean $\hat{\mu}_y^{(n)}$ as

$$\hat{\mu}_y^{(n)} = \mu_x^{(n)} + \mu_b + C g(C^{-1}\mu_x^{(n)}, C^{-1}\mu_b, C^{-1}\mu_n) \tag{6.25}$$

Whereas JAC compensates mean $\mu_x^{(n)}$ only, the parallel model combination (PMC) [87] method and VTS methods [84] further compensate distortion effects on speech covariance. In addition to the distortions parameters μ_b and μ_n, the original clean speech model mean $\mu_x^{(n)}$ can be updated [115].

These methods provide a framework for incorporating independent concurrent signals (speech and noise) using a parametric function with a small number of meaningful parameters. The nonlinear function (Eq. 6.25) allows the acoustic model mean to be quickly adapted to noisy conditions, thus allowing robust performance in slowly time-varying noise [106–108]. This is also very useful for embedded speech recognition [85] in mobile environments, where distortion parameters μ_b and μ_n must be estimated from the utterance in use and noise conditions for one utterance can be very different from those for others.

The computational cost of model-space methods is usually high because they apply the nonlinear function (Eq. 6.25) on every speech mean. In [112], a scheme was devised to reduce the number of times that (Eq. 6.25) is computed, so that the JAC method can still be applied on embedded devices with very limited computational resources. In this method, clean speech mean vectors are first vector-quantized to have a centroid mean vector $\mu_x^{c(n)}$ for every cluster $c(n)$. Then, for each cluster, the following bias is computed:

$$\mathbf{b}^{c(n)} = \mu_b + C g(C^{-1}\mu_x^{c(n)}, C^{-1}\mu_b, C^{-1}\mu_n) \tag{6.26}$$

which represents the last two terms in function (Eq. 6.25). Finally, this bias is applied to every mean vector within the cluster to compensate environment distortion effects.

Model-Based Feature Enhancement

Similar to the model-based model adaptation method, model-based feature enhancement methods [82, 91–93, 109, 110] use a parametric function of distortion and an optimal estimation of the function's parameters. In VTS-based feature enhancement method [109, 110], a clean-speech GMM, together with the estimate of distortion parameters, is used to produce a GMM for noisy speech. Statistics of noisy speech can be predicted by VTS decomposition of (Eq. 6.22) around the clean speech mean vector, noise, and channel distortion. For example, for a Gaussian component n, the noisy speech mean vector $\mu_y^{(n)}$ can be predicted using equation (Eq. 6.25). The variance of noisy speech, $\Sigma_y^{(n)}$, can be similarly derived. With the noisy-speech GMM, the a posteriori probability of component n given a noisy observation can be estimated in Equation (6.18). We can then obtain an estimate of clean speech $\mathbf{x}_t$ using (Eq. 6.15) and

$$\varepsilon(\mathbf{x}_t|\mathbf{y}_t, n) = \mathbf{y}_t - \mu_b - Cg(C^{-1}\mu_x^{(n)}, C^{-1}\mu_b, C^{-1}\mu_n) \qquad (6.27)$$

In the feature-space methods, clean-speech GMMs for enhancement have far fewer Gaussian components than do those in acoustic models for recognition. Therefore, the cost for computing the nonlinear function $g(\cdot)$ on every Gaussian component in the feature-space methods is much lower than that in model-space model adaptation methods (Section 6.4.5). However, since the latter can adapt every parameter in HMMs for speech recognition, they compensate environment effects in much more detail than does enhancement of feature vectors alone, and so, usually perform better than model-based feature enhancement methods.

Adaptation-Based Compensation

The methods in this section, although originally developed for speaker adaptation, are equally useful for handling other sources of mismatch (background noise, microphone, and channel mismatch distortion). They follow the same concept in (Eq. 6.19) for model-space and (Eq. 6.20) feature-space stochastic matching, but do not necessarily use a parametric function with parameters representing environment distortions. The several functional forms include a simple cepstral bias [94–96], linear affine transformation [97–99], and nonlinear transformation realized through an MLP [100]. The linear affine transformation is currently the most popular choice, and the resulting formulation (given by Eq. (6.21)) is called maximum likelihood linear regression (MLLR) [98, 99]. Particularly, feature-space MLLR, or fMLLR, is a variant of MLLR that has the same linear transforms applied on means and covariance. In fMLLR, the adapted mean $\hat{\mu}^{(n)}$ and covariance $\hat{\Sigma}^{(n)}$ at Gaussian component n are

$$\hat{\mu}^{(n)} = \mathbf{A}\mu^{(n)} + \mathbf{b}$$
$$\hat{\Sigma}^{(n)} = \mathbf{A}\Sigma^{(n)}\mathbf{A}^T$$

where $\mathbf{A}$ and $\mathbf{b}$ are, respectively, the transformation matrix and the bias. The likelihood of observation $\mathbf{y}_t$ at Gaussian component (n) can be expressed as

$$\Pr(\mathbf{y}_t|\theta, \Lambda_X) = |\mathbf{A}|^{-1}N(\mathbf{A}^{-1}(\mathbf{y}_t - \mathbf{b}); \mu^{(n)}, \Sigma^{(n)}) \qquad (6.28)$$

Because this likelihood computation does not change the model parameters, fMLLR is appealing in applications where modifying HMM parameters is expensive.

To improve performance of linear affine transformations, it is a common and powerful practice to use a regression tree. When the amount of adaptation data is limited, a global transform can be tied to all Gaussian components. With sufficient data, a transform can be specific to a leaf node of the regression tree that represents a group of Gaussian components sharing some common characteristics. With sufficient data, then, these components are adapted in the sense of piecewise linear transformations, which can to some extent compensate any nonlinear distortions.

Instead of using transformation-based adaptation, one can adapt the HMMs directly using the MAP algorithm [101, 102]. MAP incorporates prior knowledge of HMM parameters to get the MAP estimate for the new speaker using speaker-specific or environment-specific adaptation data. For a particular Gaussian mean, with prior mean $\mu_0^{(n)}$, the estimate is

$$\mu^{(n)} = \frac{\tau \mu_0^{(n)} + \sum_{t=1}^{T} \gamma_n(t) \mathbf{y}_t}{\tau + \sum_{t=1}^{T} \gamma_n(t)} \tag{6.29}$$

where τ controls the balance between the maximum likelihood estimate of the mean from the data and the prior mean, and $\gamma_n(t)$ is the posterior probability of Gaussian component n at time t given the observation sequence.

Though the MAP algorithm provides an optimal solution, it converges slowly and requires a relatively large amount of adaptation data. For better and faster adaptation, MAP can be combined with transformation-based methods [105, 120–123]. Another way to improve MAP's convergence speed is through structural MAP (SMAP) [124]. In SMAP, Gaussian components are organized into a tree structure and a mean offset at each layer is estimated for the Gaussians in it. At the root of the tree, the offset is an average of the maximum likelihood estimate of its mean shift and its a priori mean shift. This offset is then propagated to its children. The mean offset at a child is an average of the maximum likelihood estimate of its mean shift and this propagated prior mean shift from its parent. The computation is carried on recursively from the root of the tree to the leaves.

There has been some recent interest in fast adaptation techniques (such as cluster adaptive training (CAT) [103, 125], speaker-adaptive training (SAT) [26], eigenvoice techniques [126], and eigen-MLLR [104, 127]). Unlike MLLR and MAP, these methods use information about the characteristics of an HMM set for particular speakers or environments. They may be seen as an extension of speaker clustering. Rather than taking a hard decision about speaker style, which may lead to adaptation fragmentation and a poor choice of speaker group, these methods form a weighted sum of "speaker cluster" HMMs, and use this interpolated model to represent the current speaker. The few parameters of these interpolation weights can be viewed as representing a new speaker in a "speaker space" spanned by these "speaker clusters."

The number of parameters in these methods can be controlled to be far smaller than the number of parameters to be estimated in other methods. For example, for a full-matrix MLLR transform, the number of parameters is $D \times (D + 1)$, and D is the feature vector size. The simplest MLLR with diagonal transformation and a bias vector has $2 \times D$ parameters to be estimated. For a feature vector with 39 dimensions, the full-matrix MLLR transform has 1560 parameters and the simplest MLLR has 78. However, it is reported in [103] that, with only 8 speaker clusters, a CAT method can outperform MLLR.

It is important in these fast adaptation methods to have proper "speaker space." Otherwise, they can easily saturate their performance. Differences among these methods mainly lie in how the "speaker space" is formed. CAT uses individual speaker cluster models, which have a common variance and mixture weights and only their Gaussian mean values vary. Thus the mean for a particular Gaussian for a particular speaker is

$$\hat{\mu} = \sum_k \lambda_k \mu_k \tag{6.30}$$

where λ_k is a specific weight of mean vector μ_k in cluster k.

In fact, not only can CAT be fast because of the small number of λ_k to be estimated during recognition, but its performance can be as good as that of an MLLR-adapted system. This is achieved using a scheme that updates these cluster means during training. That is, in CAT both weight λ_k and speaker cluster μ_k are iteratively and jointly updated during training. During testing, only weights need to be estimated.

A variant of CAT represents cluster mean μ_k using a set of MLLR transforms of a "canonical model" as follows:

$$\mu_k = \sum_l c_l \mathbf{A}_{kl} \mu_0 \tag{6.31}$$

where μ_0 is the canonical mean. $\mathbf{A}_{kl}$ are the MLLR transformations, and c_l is the weight of transformation $\mathbf{A}_{kl}$. The number of parameters to be estimated during training is the number of parameters in the MLLR transforms plus that in the "canonical model," which could be lower than that in the CAT scheme in (Eq. 6.30). This variant of CAT, when combined with speaker adaptive training (SAT) [26], has been widely applied.

The eigenvoice technique [126] differs from CAT in that it finds cluster speakers using principle component analysis (PCA) of sets of "supervectors" constructed from all of the mean values in speaker-dependent HMMs [126]. Weights λ_k are estimated as they are in CAT, however, there is no update of speaker clusters. A variant of the eigenvoice technique represents cluster speakers using PCA of sets of MLLR transforms that are applied on a speaker-independent and environment-independent HMM [104, 127].

Uncertainty in Feature Enhancement

The previously mentioned feature-space methods, albeit low in cost, make point estimates of cleaned speech as if the estimates were exactly the original clean speech $\mathbf{X}$. Since the clean speech may be difficult to recover, especially in conditions such as negative instantaneous SNR, models for recognition need to be adapted to be "aware" of the conditions' inaccuracy. One widely used and simple approach is retraining of models from enhanced features. For example, in [113], the SPLICE feature enhancement method is combined with matched condition training to obtain a lower word-error rate than achieved with feature enhancement alone.

Uncertainty decoding is a recent approach that uses an estimated degree of uncertainty, which may mask some undesirable distortion effects. In [118, 119], the MAP decision rule (Eq. 6.4) is modified to incorporate uncertainty due to noise **N** as follows:

$$
\begin{aligned}
\hat{W} &= \operatorname*{argmax}_{\mathbf{W}} \Pr(W|\Upsilon_W)\Pr(\mathbf{Y}|W,\Lambda_{\mathbf{X}}) \\
&= \operatorname*{argmax}_{\mathbf{W}} \Pr(W|\Upsilon_W)\int_{\mathbf{X}}\Pr(\mathbf{Y}|\mathbf{X},\theta)\Pr(\mathbf{X}|W,\Lambda_{\mathbf{X}})d\mathbf{X}
\end{aligned}
\tag{6.32}
$$

where the likelihood of noisy speech, given clean speech, is evaluated as follows:

$$
\Pr(\mathbf{Y}|\mathbf{X},\theta) = \int_{\mathbf{N}}\Pr(\mathbf{Y}|\mathbf{X},\mathbf{N})\Pr(\mathbf{N}|\theta)d\mathbf{N}
\tag{6.33}
$$

A natural choice for approximating (6.33) is to use M Gaussian components. At time t, we then have

$$
\Pr(\mathbf{y}_t|\mathbf{x}_t,\theta) = \sum_{m=1}^{M}\Pr(m|\theta)\Pr(\mathbf{y}_t|\mathbf{x}_t,m,\theta)
\tag{6.34}
$$

We may train the Gaussian components based on noisy speech, and then

$$
\Pr(m|\theta) \approx \Pr(m|\mathbf{y}_t,\theta)
\tag{6.35}
$$

Further approximation can be done by choosing the most likely component m^*. Then we have

$$
\Pr(\mathbf{y}_t|\mathbf{x}_t,\theta) \approx \Pr(\mathbf{y}_t|\mathbf{x}_t,m^*,\theta)
\tag{6.36}
$$

This conditional likelihood is plugged into (Eq. 6.32). At time t, (Eq. 6.32) is a convolution of Gaussian components. Assuming $\mathbf{y}_t$ is linearly transformed from $\mathbf{x}_t$, we have

$$
\Pr(\mathbf{y}_t|\theta,\Lambda_{\mathbf{x}}) = \sum_{n}c_n\mathrm{N}(\mathbf{A}^{m^*}\mathbf{y}_t+\mathbf{b}^{m^*};\mu_x^{(n)},\Sigma_x^{(n)}+\Sigma_b^{m^*})
\tag{6.37}
$$

Compared to the feature enhancement in the fMLLR described in Section 6.4.5, the additional cost is a result of adding global variance $\Sigma_b^{m^*}$ to the original variance $\Sigma_x^{(n)}$ of each component. If this global variance is diagonal, the additional cost is insignificant.

In addition to incorporating uncertainty, another advantage of this decision rule is that one may choose a simplified model to evaluate $\Pr(\mathbf{Y}|\mathbf{X},\theta)$. In the simplest scheme [116], a single Gaussian is used to model noisy speech, so that a global variance is used in (Eq. 6.37) to enlarge the original Gaussian variance of the clean acoustic model. With more Gaussian components used, (Eq. 6.37) becomes a cluster-dependent computation that has Gaussian component variances enlarged with a cluster-dependent variance, and uses cluster-dependent speech enhancement. A simpler scheme in [117] uses cluster-dependent enhancement of speech but applies a global variance to enlarge the original Gaussian variances.

6.4.6 Special Transducer Arrangement to Solve the Cocktail Party Problem

It has been observed that a speech recognizer can be made robust to adverse acoustic environments if the transducers can be favorably arranged. In the simplest case, if we use a unidirectional microphone and place it near the mouth, we can reduce distortion due to background noise and reverberation. This will improve the SNR of the recorded speech. If we use two microphones, one to capture the noise signal and the other to pick up the noisy speech signal, we can apply adaptive filtering algorithms, such as least mean squares (LMS), to achieve speech enhancement. This cancels both stationary and nonstationary noise and improves recognition performance in the presence of noise [47, 48].

What is more challenging to state-of-the-art speech recognition systems is recognizing speech in the presence of competing speech-like distortions. This is known as the cocktail party problem [20], and it is very apparent in hands-free speech recognition applications (e.g., teleconferencing, a moving car), where it is not possible to use a close-talking microphone. The common wisdom is to apply a set of well-spaced microphone arrays and to properly fuse the signals they recorded. With an adaptive beamforming procedure used jointly with a source localization procedure [49–52], the SNR of speech is increased in both stationary and nonstationary acoustic environments (background noise and reverberation). In addition to beamforming, there is independent component analysis (ICA) [53], a recent approach for enhancement of desired speech experiencing types of other interference. ICA assumes mutual statistical independence between the desired speech and interference. Both beamforming and ICA may introduce some distortions to the enhanced speech signal. To deal with the problem, we can use methods introduced in previous sections (e.g., CMN) to remove some residual distortion in the enhanced signal.

6.5 SUMMARY

In this chapter, we addressed robust speech recognition for ambient intelligence. Mismatch between training and testing conditions causes severe degradation in speech recognition performance. The aim of robust speech recognition is to overcome this mismatch so that degradation in performance becomes moderate and graceful. We concentrated here on mismatch resulting from variability in the speech signal. The sources for this variability include additive background noise, channel and microphone mismatches, speaker mismatch, and different accents, stress types, and speaking styles.

A number of widely used robust speech recognition techniques were briefly described. These range from simple to complex. To build a robust system for ambient intelligence, it is a good idea to start with simple approaches, including feature normalization methods such as CMN, which have advantages of easy implementation and low computational cost. To further boost robustness, we may use a proper adaptation method such as MLLR.

However, in some situations involving ambient intelligence, these approaches may not be sufficient. For instance, MLLR requires larger amounts of adaptation data than do methods that use a parametric function of environment effects on clean speech. The parametric function allows model space adaptation or feature-space enhancement with small amounts of data. Thus, if high performance is required with small amounts of adaptation data, some model-based methods can be used, but they may not be applied to any feature types or to compensate any distortion types. For instance, CVN cannot work with the parametric function (6.24) in JAC.

In the design of a practical robust speech recognition system for ambient intelligence, computational complexity is a very important factor. Thus, it is worthwhile to revise robust speech recognition methods in order to achieve simplified procedures, albeit with some performance losses. Balancing performance and computational cost for robust speech recognition for ambient intelligence will be a design art.

REFERENCES

[1] Aghajan H, Augusto J, Delgado R. Human-Centric Interfaces for Ambient Intelligence. Elsevier; 2009.

[2] Davis KH, Biddulph R, Balashek S. Automatic recognition of spoken digits. J Acoust Soc Am 1952;24:637.

[3] Dudley H, Balashek S. Automatic recognition of phonetic patterns in speech. J Acoust Soc Am 1958;30:721–32.

[4] Lee CH, Soong FK, Paliwal KK, editors. Automatic Speech Recognition: Advanced Topics. Kluwer Academic Publishers; 1996.

[5] Young S. A review of large-vocabulary continuous-speech recognition. IEEE Signal Processing Magazine 1996;13:45–57.

[6] Li J, Lee CH. Soft margin feature extraction for automatic speech recognition. Proc INTERSPEECH 2007;30–3.

[7] Macherey W, Haferkamp L, Schluter R, Ney H. Investigations on error minimizing training criteria for discriminative training in automatic speech recognition. Proc INTERSPEECH 2005;2133–6.

[8] Junqua JC. Impact of the unknown communication channel on automatic speech recognition: A review. Proc EUROSPEECH 1997;KN29–32.

[9] Parihar N, Picone J, Pearce D, Hirsch H. Performance analysis of the AURORA large vocabulary baseline system. EUSIPCO 2004;553–6.

[10] Yeung S-K, Siu M-H. Improved performance of AURORA 4 using HTK and unsupervised MLLR adaptation. Proc INTERSPEECH 2004;161–4.

[11] Acero A, Stern RM. Environmental robustness in automatic speech recognition. Proc ICASSP 1990;849–952.

[12] Junqua JC, Haton JP, editors. Robustness in Automatic Speech Recognition. Kluwer Academic Publishers; 1996.

[13] Juang BH. Speech recognition in adverse environments. Computer Speech and Language 1991;5:275-94.

[14] Gong Y. Speech recognition in noisy environments: A survey. Computer Speech and Language 1995;16:261-91.

[15] Furui S. Recent advances in robust speech recognition. In: Proc. ESCANATO Workshop on Robust Speech Recognition for Unknown Communication Channels. 1997. p. 11-20.

[16] Bellegarda JR. Statistical techniques for robust ASR: Review and perspectives. Proc EURO-SPEECH 1997;KN33-6.

[17] Lee CH. Adaptive compensation for robust speech recognition. In: Proc. IEEE Workshop on Automatic Speech Recognition and Understanding. 1997. p. 357-64.

[18] Lee CH. On stochastic feature and model compensation approaches to robust speech recognition. Speech Communication 1998;25:29-47.

[19] Woodland PC. Speaker adaptation for continuous density HMMs: A Review. In: ITRW on Adaptation Methods for Speech Recognition. 2001. p. 11-9.

[20] Huang XD, Acero A, Hon H-W. Spoken Language Processing: A Guide to Theory, Algorithm and System Development. Prentice Hall PTR; 2001.

[21] Hirsch H-G, Pearce D. The AURORA experimental framework for the performance evaluation of speech recognition systems under noisy environments. Proc ASR 2000;181-8.

[22] Ney H, Aubert X. Dynamic programming search strategies: From digit strings to large vocabulary word graphs. In: Lee CH, Soong FK, Paliwal KK, editors. Automatic Speech Recognition: Advanced Topics. Kluwer Academic Publishers; 1996. p. 384-411.

[23] Gopalakrishnan PS, Bahl LR. Fast search techniques. In: Lee CH, Soong FK, Paliwal KK, editors. Automatic Speech Recognition: Advanced Topics. Kluwer Academic Publishers; 1996. p. 413-28.

[24] Schwartz R, Nguyen L, Makhoul J. Multiple-pass search strategies. In: Lee CH, Soong FK, Paliwal KK, editors. Automatic Speech Recognition: Advanced Topics. Kluwer Academic Publishers; 1996. p. 429-56.

[25] Duda RO, Hart PE. Pattern Classification and Scene Analysis. Wiley; 1973.

[26] Anastasakos T, McDonough J, Schwartz R, Makhoul J. A compact model for speaker-adaptive training. Proc ICSLP 1996;2:1137-40.

[27] Rabiner LR. A tutorial on hidden Markov models and selected applications in speech recognition. Proc IEEE 1989;77:257-86.

[28] Rabiner L, Juang BH. Fundamentals of Speech Recognition. Prentice Hall; 1993.

[29] Junqua JC, Anglade Y. Acoustic and perceptual studies of Lombard speech: Application to isolated-words automatic speech recognition. Proc ICASSP 1990;841-4.

[30] Nakamura S, Takiguchi T, Shikano K. Noise and room acoustics distorted speech recognition by HMM composition. Proc ICASSP 1996;69-72.

[31] Lilly BT, Paliwal KK. Effect of speech coders on speech recognition performance. Proc ICSLP 1996;2344-7.

[32] Lim JS, Oppenheim AV. Enhancement and bandwidth compression of noisy speech. Proc IEEE 1979;67:1586-604.

[33] Boll SF. Suppression of acoustic noise in speech using spectral subtraction. IEEE Trans Acoust, Speech Signal Proc ASSP-27 1979;113–20.

[34] Berouti M, Schwartz R, Makhoul J. Enhancement of speech corrupted by additive noise. Proc ICASSP 1979;208–11.

[35] Paliwal KK, Basu A. A speech enhancement based on Kalman filtering. Proc ICASSP 1987;177–80.

[36] Ephraim Y, Malah D. Speech enhancement using a minimum mean-square error log-spectral amplitude estimator. IEEE Trans Acoust Speech Signal Proc 1985;33(2):443–5.

[37] Dendrinos M, Bakamidis S, Carayannis G. Speech enhancement from noise: A regenerative approach. Speech Commun 1991;10(2):45–57.

[38] Ephraim Y, Trees HV. A signal subspace approach for speech enhancement. IEEE Trans. Speech Audio Proc 1995;3(4):251–66.

[39] Wójcicki K, Milacic M, Stark A, Lyons J, Paliwal KK. Exploiting conjugate symmetry of the short-time Fourier spectrum for speech enhancement. IEEE Sign Proc Lett 2008;15:461–4.

[40] Stark A, Wójcicki K, Lyons J, Paliwal KK. Noise driven short-time phase spectrum compensation procedure for speech enhancement. Proc INTERSPEECH 2008;549–53.

[41] Van Compernolle D. Noise adaptation in a hidden Markov model speech recognition system. Comput Speech Lang 1989;3:151–67.

[42] Martin R. Spectral subtraction based on minimum statistics. In: Proc. European Signal Processing Conference. 1994. p. 1182–5.

[43] Martin R. Noise power spectral density estimation based on optimal smoothing and minimum statistics. IEEE Trans Speech Audio Proc 2001;9(5):504–12.

[44] Virag N. Signal channel speech enhancement based on masking properties of the human auditory system. IEEE Trans Speech Audio Proc 1999;7(2):126–37.

[45] Agarwal A, Cheng YM. Two-stage Mel-warped Wiener filter for robust speech recognition. Proc ASRU 1999;67–70.

[46] ETSI. Standard speech processing, transmission and quality tests (STQ); distributed speech recognition; front-end feature extraction algorithm; compression algorithms. ETSI ES 201 108, v1.1.2. 2004.

[47] Powell G, Darlington P, Wheeler P. Practical adaptive noise reduction in the aircraft cockpit environment. Proc ICASSP 1987;ETSI ES 201 108, v1.1.2. 2004.

[48] Nakadai Y, Sugamura N. A speech recognition method for noise environments using dual inputs. Proc ICSLP 1990;1141–4.

[49] Flanagan JL, Johnston JD, Zahn R, Elko GW. Computer-steered microphone arrays for sound transduction in large rooms. J Acoust Soc Amer 1985;78:1508–18.

[50] Silverman HF, Kirtman SE. A two-stage algorithm for determining talker location from linear microphone data. Comput Speech Lang 1992;6:129–52.

[51] Omologo M, Svaizer P. Acoustic source location in noisy and reverberant environment using CSP analysis. Proc ICASSP 1996;921–4.

[52] Lleida E, Fernandez J, Masgrau E. Robust continuous speech recognition system based on a microphone array. Proc ICASSP 1998;241–4.

[53] Bell A, Sejnowski T. An information-maximization approach to blind separation and blind deconvolution. Neural Comput 1995;7:1129–59.

[54] Picone JW. Signal modeling techniques in speech recognition. Proc IEEE 1993;81(9):1215–47.

[55] Davis SB, Mermelstein P. Comparison of parametric representations for monosyllabic word recognition in continuously spoken sentences. IEEE Trans Acoust, Speech Signal Proc 1980;28(4):357-60.

[56] Furui S. Speaker-independent isolated word recognition using dynamic features of speech spectrum. IEEE Trans Acoust Speech Signal Proc 1986;34:52-9.

[57] Hermansky H. Perceptual linear predictive (PLP) analysis of speech. J Acoust Soc Am 1990;87(4):1738-52.

[58] Paliwal KK, Sagisaka Y. Cyclic autocorrelation-based linear prediction analysis of speech. Proc EUROSPEECH 1997;279-82.

[59] Johnston JD, Brandenburg K. Wideband coding—Perceptual considerations for speech and music. In: Furui S, Sondhi MM, editors. Advances in Speech Signal Processing. Marcel Dekker; 1992. p. 109-49.

[60] Lilly BT, Paliwal KK. Auditory masking based acoustic front-end for robust speech recognition. In: Proc. IEEE Region 10 Conf. on Speech and Image Technologies for Computing and Communications. 1997. p. 165-8.

[61] Varga A, Moore R. Hidden Markov model decomposition of speech and noise. Proc ICASSP 1990;845-8.

[62] Paliwal KK. Spectral subband centroids as features for speech recognition. In: Proc. IEEE Workshop on Automatic Speech Recognition and Understanding. 1997. p. 124-31.

[63] Paliwal KK. Decorrelated and filtered filter-bank energies for robust speech recognition. Proc EUROSPEECH 1999;85-8.

[64] Hermansky H, Ellis D, Sharma S. Tandem connectionist feature stream extraction for conventional HMM systems. Proc ICASSP 2000;1635-8.

[65] Zhu Q, Stolcke A, Chen B, Morgan N. Using MLP features in SRI's conversational speech recognition system. In: Proc. 9th European Conference on Speech Communication and Technology. 2005. p. 2141-4.

[66] Benitez C, Burget L, Chen B, Dupont S, Garudadri H, Hermansky H, et al. Robust ASR front-end using spectral-based and discriminant features: Experiments on the Aurora tasks. Proc EUROSPEECH 2001;429-32.

[67] Povey D, Kingsbury B, Mangu L, Saon G, Soltau H, Zweig G. fMPE: Discriminatively trained features for speech recognition. Proc ICASSP 2005;961-4.

[68] Povey D, Woodland PC. Minimum phone error and I-smoothing for improved discriminative training. Proc ICASSP 2002;105-8.

[69] Hanson BA, Appelbaum TH, Junqua JC. Spectral dynamics for speech recognition under adverse conditions. In: Lee CH, Soong FK, Paliwal KK, editors. Automatic Speech Recognition: Advanced Topics. Kluwer Academic Publishers; 1996. p. 331-56.

[70] Theodoridis S, Koutroumbas K. Pattern recognition. Academic Press Elsevier.

[71] Kumar N, Andreou AG. Heteroscedastic discriminant analysis and reduced rank HMMs for improved speech recognition. Speech Communication 1994;26:283-97.

[72] Atal BS. Effectiveness of linear prediction characteristics of the speech wave for automatic speaker identification and verification. J Acoust Soc Amer 1974;55:1304-12.

[73] Geller D, Umbach RH, Ney H. Improvements in speech recognition for voice dialing in car environment. In: Proc. ECSA Workshop on Speech Processing in Adverse Conditions. 1992. p. 203-6.

[74] Murveit H, Butzberger J, Weintraub M. Reduced channel dependence for speech recognition. In: Proc. Speech and Natural Language Workshop (DARPA). 1992. p. 280-4.

[75] Hermansky H, Morgan N. RASTA processing of speech. IEEE Trans Speech Audio Proc 1994;2(4):578-89.

[76] Aikawa K, Singer H, Kawahara H, Tohkura Y. A dynamic cepstrum incorporating time-frequency masking and its application to continuous speech recognition. Proc ICASSP 1993;2:668-71.

[77] Haeb-Umbach R, Aubert X, Beyerlein P, Klakow D, Ullrich M, Wendemuth A, et al. Acoustic modeling in the Philips Hub-4 continuous speech recognition system. In: Proc. DARPA Broadcast News Transcription and Understanding Workshop.

[78] Iso-Sipila J, Moberg M, Viikki O. Multi-lingual speaker-independent voice user interface for mobile devices. Proc ICASSP 2006;1081-4.

[79] Hilger F, Ney H. Quantile based histogram equalization for noise robust large vocabulary speech recognition. IEEE Trans Speech Audio Proc 2006;14(3):845-54.

[80] Lee L, Rose R. Speaker normalization using efficient frequency warping procedures. Proc ICASSP 1996.

[81] Pitz M, Ney H. Vocal tract normalization as linear transformation of MFCC. Proc EUROSPEECH 2003;1445-8.

[82] Stern RM, Acero A, Liu FH, Ohshima Y. Signal processing for robust speech recognition. In: Lee CH, Soong FK, Paliwal KK, editors. Automatic Speech Recognition: Advanced Topics. Kluwer Academic Publishers; 1996. p. 357-84.

[83] Cui X, Afify M, Gao Y. MMSE-based stereo feature stochastic mapping for noise robust speech recognition. Proc ICASSP 2008;4077-80.

[84] Moreno P, Raj B, Stern RM. A vector Taylor series approach for environment independent speech recognition. Proc ICASSP 1996;733-6.

[85] Yao K, Netsch L, Viswanathan V. Speaker-independent name recognition using improved compensation and acoustic modeling methods for mobile applications. Proc ICASSP 2006;173-6.

[86] Neumeyer L, Weintraub M. Probabilistic optimum filtering for robust speech recognition. Proc ICASSP 1994;1:417-29.

[87] Gales MJF, Young SJ. An improved approach to the hidden Markov model decomposition of speech and noise. Proc ICASSP 1992;233-6.

[88] Akbacak M, Hansen J. Environmental sniffing: Robust digit recognition for an in-vehicle environment. Proc EUROSPEECH 2003;2177-80.

[89] Zhang Z, Furui S. Piecewise-linear transformation-based HMM adaptation for noisy speech. Proc ASRU 2001;159-62.

[90] Gong Y. A method of joint compensation of additive and convolutive distortions for speaker-independent speech recognition. IEEE Trans Speech Audio Proc 2005;13:975-83.

[91] Varga AP, Moore RK. Simultaneous recognition of concurrent speech signals using hidden Markov model decomposition. Proc EUROSPEECH 1991;1175-8.

[92] Rose R, Hofstetter E, Reynolds D. Integrated models of speech and background with application to speaker identification in noise. IEEE Trans Speech Audio Proc 1994;2:245-57.

[93] Ephraim Y. Gain adapted hidden Markov models for recognition of clean and noisy speech. IEEE Trans Signal Proc 1992;40:1303-16.

[94] Sankar A, Lee CH. A maximum likelihood approach to stochastic matching for robust speech recognition. IEEE Trans. Speech Audio Proc 1996;4:190-202.

[95] Rahim MG, Juang BH. Signal bias removal by maximum likelihood estimation for robust telephone speech recognition. IEEE Trans. Speech Audio Proc 1996;4:19-30.

[96] Zhao Y. An acoustic-phonetic based speaker adaptation technique improving speaker independent continuous speech recognition. IEEE Trans Speech Audio Proc 1994;2:380-94.

[97] Digalakis VV, Rtischev D, Neumeyer LG. Speaker adaptation using constrained estimation of Gaussian mixtures. IEEE Trans Speech Audio Proc 1995;3:357-66.

[98] Leggetter CJ, Woodland PC. Flexible speaker adaptation for large vocabulary speech recognition. Comput Speech Lang 1995;9:171-86.

[99] Gales MJF, Woodland PC. Mean and variance adaptation within the MLLR framework. Comput Speech Lang 1996;10:249-64.

[100] Abrash V, Sankar A, Franco H, Cohen M. Acoustic adaptation using nonlinear transformations of HMM parameters. Proc ICASSP 1996;729-32.

[101] Lee CH, Lin CH, Juang BH. A study on speaker adaptation of the parameters of continuous density hidden Markov models. IEEE Trans Signal Proc 1991;39:806-14.

[102] Gauvain JL, Lee CH. Maximum a posteriori estimation for multivariate Gaussian mixture observations of Markov chains. IEEE Trans Speech Audio Proc 1994;2:291-8.

[103] Gales MJ. Cluster adaptive training of hidden Markov models. IEEE Trans Speech Audio Proc 2000;8(4):417-28.

[104] Mak B, Hsiao R. Kernel eigenspace-based MLLR adaptation. IEEE Trans Audio, Speech Lang Proc 2007;15(3):784-95.

[105] Digalakis VV, Neumeyer LG. Speaker adaptation using combined transformation and Bayesian methods. IEEE Trans Speech Audio Proc 1996;4:294-300.

[106] Kim NS. Non-stationary environment compensation based on sequential estimation. IEEE Signal Proc Lett 1998;3:57-9.

[107] Yao K, Paliwal KK, Nakamura S. Noise adaptive speech recognition based on sequential parameter estimation. Speech Commun 2004;42:5-23.

[108] Yao K, Nakamura S. Sequential noise compensation by sequential Monte Carlo method. In: Dietterich TG, Becker S, Ghahramani Z, editors. Advances in Neural Information Processing Systems 14. MIT Press; 2001. p. 1205-12.

[109] Kim DY, Un C, Kim NS. Speech recognition in noisy environments using first-order vector Taylor series. Speech Commun 1998;24:39-49.

[110] Acero A, Deng L, Kristjansson T, Zhang J. HMM adaptation using vector Taylor series for noisy speech recognition. Proc ICSLP 2000;869-72.

[111] Sagayama S, Yamaguchi Y, Takahashi S, Takahashi J. Jacobian approach to fast acoustic model adaptation. Proc ICASSP 1997;835-8.

[112] Yao K. Systems and methods employing stochastic bias compensation and Bayesian joint additive/convolutive compensation in automatic speech recognition. U.S. Patent 20070033027, 2007.

[113] Deng L, Acero A, Plumpe M, Huang XD. Large vocabulary speech recognition under adverse acoustic environments. Proc ICSLP 2000;806-9.

[114] Deng L, Wu J, Droppo J, Acero A. Analysis and comparison of two speech feature extraction/compensation algorithms. IEEE Signal Proc Lett 2005;2(6):477-80.

[115] Hu Y, Huo Q. Irrelevant variability normalization based HMM training using VTS approximation of an explicit model of environmental distortions. Proc INTERSPEECH 2007;1042–2045.

[116] Arrowwood J, Clements M. Using observation uncertainty in HMM decoding. Proc ICSLP 2002;3:1561–4.

[117] Deng L, Droppo J, Acero A. Dynamic compensation of HMM variances using the feature enhancement uncertainty computed from a parametric model of speech distortion. IEEE Trans. Speech Audio Proc 2005;13:412–21.

[118] Gales MJ, van Dalen RC. Predictive linear transforms for noise robust speech recognition. Proc ASRU 2007;59–64.

[119] Liao H, Gales MJ. Issues with uncertainty decoding for noise robust automatic speech recognition. Speech Commun 2008;50:265–77.

[120] Zavaliagkos G, Schwartz R, McDonough J. Maximum a posteriori adaptation for large scale HMM recognizers. Proc ICASSP 1996;725–8.

[121] Nagesh V, Gillick L. Studies in transformation-based adaptation. Proc ICASSP 1997;1031–4.

[122] Ishii J, Tonomura M. Speaker normalization and adaptation based on linear transformation. Proc ICASSP 1997;1055–8.

[123] Siohan O, Chesta C, Lee CH. Joint maximum a posteriori adaptation of transformation and HMM parameters. IEEE Trans Speech Audio Proc 2001;9(4):417–28.

[124] Shinoda K, Lee CH. A structural Bayes approach to speaker adaptation. IEEE Trans Speech Audio Proc 2001;9:276–87.

[125] Gales MJF. Cluster adaptive training for speech recognition. Proc ICSLP 1998;1783–6.

[126] Kuhn R, Nguyen P, Junqua JC, Goldwasser L, Niedzielski N, Fincke S, et al. Eigenvoices for speaker adaptation. Proc ICSLP 1998;1771–4.

[127] Chen KT, Liau WW, Wang HM, Lee LS. Fast speaker adaptation using eigenspace-based maximum likelihood linear regression. Proc ICSLP 2000;742–5.

Speaker Recognition in Smart Environments

7

Sadaoki Furui

Department of Computer Science, Tokyo Institute of Technology, Tokyo, Japan

ABSTRACT

This chapter describes the principles of speaker recognition and their application in smart environments. Speaker recognition is the process of recognizing the speaker using speech signals, which can be classified as speaker identification and verification. Speaker identification is the process of determining from which of the registered speakers a given utterance comes; speaker verification is the process of accepting or rejecting the identity claimed by a speaker. Speaker recognition can also be classified as text dependent, text independent, and text-prompted. Spectral envelope and prosody features of speech are normally used as speaker features. To accommodate intra-speaker variations in signal characteristics, it is important to apply parameter domain and/or likelihood domain normalization/adaptation techniques. High-level features, such as word idiolect, pronunciation, phone usage, and prosody, have recently been investigated in text-independent speaker verification. Speaker diarization, an application of speaker identification technology, is defined as the task of deciding "who spoke when," in which speech versus nonspeech decisions are made and speaker changes are marked in the detected speech. Speaker diarization allows searching audio by speaker and makes speech recognition results easier to read.

Key words: speaker identification, speaker verification, speaker diarization, cepstrum

7.1 PRINCIPLES AND APPLICATIONS OF SPEAKER RECOGNITION

Speaker recognition is the process of automatically recognizing who is speaking using speaker-specific information in speech waves [1–3]. Many applications have been considered for speaker recognition. These include secure access control by voice, customizing services or information to individuals by voice, indexing or labeling speakers in recorded conversations or dialogues, surveillance, and criminal and forensic investigations involving recorded voice samples. Currently, the most frequently mentioned application is access control, which includes voice dialing, banking transactions over a telephone network, telephone shopping, database access services, information and reservation services, voice mail, and remote access to computers. Speaker recognition technology, as such, is expected to create new services in smart environments and make daily life more convenient.

Speaker diarization, in which an input audio channel is automatically annotated with speakers, has been actively investigated. It is useful in speech recognition, facilitating the searching and indexing of audio archives, and increasing the richness of automatic transcriptions, making them more readable. Another important application of speaker recognition technology is as a forensics tool [4].

7.1.1 Features Used for Speaker Recognition

Speaker identity is correlated with physiological and behavioral characteristics of an individual's speech production system. These characteristics derive from both the spectral envelope (vocal tract characteristics) and the supra-segmental features (voice source characteristics). The most commonly used short-term spectral measurements are cepstral coefficients and their regression coefficients [5]. The cepstral coefficient (cepstrum) is the (inverse) Fourier transform of the log of the signal spectrum. In the spectrum domain, a nonuniform spacing of bandpass filters is often used for reflecting perceptual criteria that allot approximately equal perceptual contributions for each filter. Mel scale or Bark scale filters provide a spacing approximately linear in frequency below 1000 Hz and logarithmic above.

The cepstrum has many interesting properties. Since it represents the log of the signal spectrum, signals that can be represented as the cascade of two effects that are products in the spectral domain are additive in the cepstral domain. Also, pitch harmonics, which produce prominent ripples in the spectral envelope, are associated with high-order cepstral coefficients. Thus, the set of cepstral coefficients truncated, for example, at order 12 to 24 can be used to reconstruct a relatively smooth version of the speech spectrum. The spectral envelope obtained is associated with vocal tract resonances and does not have the variable, oscillatory effects of the pitch excitation. One of the reasons that cepstral representation is more effective than other representations for speech and speaker recognition is this property of separability of source and tract.

As for the regression coefficients, typically the first- and second-order coefficients—that is, derivatives of the time functions of cepstral coefficients—are extracted at every frame period to represent spectral dynamics. These regression coefficients are respectively referred to as delta-cepstral and delta-delta-cepstral coefficients. It has been shown in experiments that such dynamic feature measurements are fairly uncorrelated with the original static feature measurements and provide improved speaker recognition performance.

As supra-segmental features, fundamental frequency and energy, particularly when measured as a function of time over a sufficiently long utterance, have been shown to be useful for speaker recognition. Such time sequences, or "contours," are thought to represent characteristic speaking inflections and rhythms associated with individual speaking behavior. Pitch and energy measurements have an advantage over short-time spectral measurements in that they are more robust to many kinds of transmission and recording variations and distortions, since they are not sensitive to spectral amplitude variability. However, because speaking behavior can be highly variable because of both voluntary and involuntary activity, pitch and energy can acquire more variability than short-time spectral features and are more susceptible to imitation.

To increase robustness under noisy conditions, research has been conducted on multimodal speaker recognition systems in which visual features—typically lip movement—are combined with spectral features. "High-level" behavioral character-istics, which refer to individual choice of words and phrases and other aspects of speaking styles, have also been investigated.

7.1.2 Speaker Identification and Verification

Speaker recognition can be classified as speaker identification and speaker verifica-tion, as shown in Figure 7.1. Identification is the process of determining from which of the registered speakers a given utterance comes. Verification is the process of

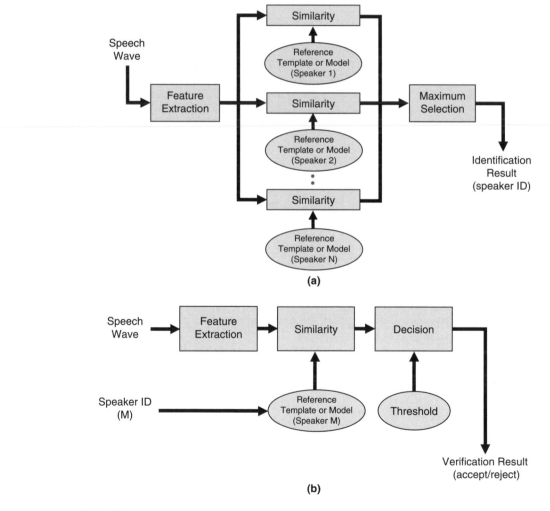

FIGURE 7.1

Basic structures of speaker (a) identification and (b) verification systems.

accepting or rejecting the identity claimed by a speaker. Most of the applications in which voice is used to confirm identity are classified as speaker verification.

In speaker identification, an utterance from an unknown speaker is analyzed and compared with speech models of known speakers. The unknown speaker is identified as the one whose model best matches the input utterance. In speaker verification, an identity is claimed by an unknown speaker, whose utterance is compared with a model for the registered speaker (customer) whose identity is being claimed. If the match is good enough—that is, above a threshold—the claim is accepted. A high threshold makes it difficult for different speakers (impostors) to be accepted by the system, but it carries the risk of falsely rejecting customers. Conversely, a low threshold enables valid users to be accepted consistently, but risks accepting impostors. To set the threshold at the acceptable level of customer rejection (false rejection) and impostor acceptance (false acceptance), data showing distributions of customer and impostor scores is necessary. For this, one or more enrollment sessions are required in which training utterances are obtained from customers. Many speaker recognition systems include an updating facility in which test utterances are used to adapt speaker models and decision thresholds.

The fundamental difference between identification and verification is the number of decision alternatives. In identification, that number is equal to the size of the population, whereas in verification there are only two choices, acceptance or rejection, regardless of population size. Therefore, identification performance decreases as population size increases, whereas verification performance approaches a constant independent of the size of the population, unless the distribution of physical characteristics of speakers is extremely biased.

In "open-set" identification, a reference model for an unknown speaker may not exist. In this case, an additional decision alternative, "the unknown does not match any of the models," is required. Verification can be considered a special case of open-set identification in which the known population size is one. In either verification or identification, an additional threshold test can determine whether the match is sufficiently close to accept the decision or, if not, to ask for a new trial. Speaker diarization can be classified as open-set speaker identification.

7.1.3 Text-Dependent, Text-Independent, and Text-Prompted Methods

Speaker recognition methods can be text dependent (fixed passwords) or text independent (no specified passwords). The former requires the speaker to provide utterances of key words or sentences, the same text being used for both training and recognition. The latter does not rely on a specific text being spoken. Text-dependent methods are usually based on template/model-sequence-matching techniques in which the time axes of an input speech sample and reference templates or reference models of the registered speaker are aligned; the similarities between them are then accumulated from the beginning to the end of the utterance. Because this method can directly exploit voice individuality associated with each phoneme or syllable, it generally achieves higher recognition performance than the text-independent method.

In applications such as forensics and surveillance, predetermined key words, as in text-dependent methods, cannot be used. Moreover, human beings can recognize speakers irrespective of the content of the utterance. For these reasons, text-independent methods have attracted more attention. Another advantage to text-independent recognition is that it can be done sequentially, until a desired significance level is reached, without the speaker having to repeat key words again and again.

Both text-dependent and text-independent methods have a serious weakness. They can easily be circumvented because someone can play back the recorded voice of a registered speaker uttering key words or sentences into the microphone and be accepted as the registered speaker. Another problem is that people often do not like text-dependent systems because they do not want to utter their identification number (e.g., their social security number) within the hearing of other people. To cope with these problems, some methods use a small set of words, such as digits, as key words, and each user is prompted to utter them in a given sequence that is randomly chosen every time the system is used [6, 7]. Even this method, however, is not reliable, since it can be circumvented with advanced electronic recording equipment that can reproduce key words in a requested order. Therefore, a text-prompted speaker recognition method has been proposed in which password sentences are completely changed every time [8].

7.2 TEXT-DEPENDENT SPEAKER RECOGNITION METHODS

Text-dependent speaker recognition can be classified as DTW (dynamic time warping) or HMM (hidden Markov model) based.

7.2.1 DTW-Based Methods

In DTW each utterance is represented by a sequence of feature vectors, generally short-term spectral feature vectors, and the trial-to-trial timing variation of utterances of the same text is normalized by aligning the analyzed feature vector sequence of a test utterance to the template feature vector sequence using a DTW algorithm. The overall distance between the test utterance and the template is used for the recognition decision. When multiple templates are used to represent spectral variation, distances between the test utterance and the templates are averaged and then used to make the decision. The DTW approach has trouble modeling statistical variation in spectral features.

7.2.2 HMM-Based Methods

An HMM can efficiently model the statistical variation in spectral features. Therefore, HMM-based methods have achieved significantly better recognition accuracies than have DTW-based methods [9].

7.3 TEXT-INDEPENDENT SPEAKER RECOGNITION METHODS

In text-independent speaker recognition, generally the words or sentences used in recognition trials cannot be predicted. Since it is impossible to model or match speech events at the word or sentence level, the following four method types have been investigated.

7.3.1 Methods Based on Long-Term Statistics

Long-term sample statistics of various spectral features, such as mean and variance over a series of utterances, have been used. Long-term spectral averages are extreme condensations of the spectral characteristics of a speaker's utterances and, as such, lack the discriminating power of the sequences of short-term spectral features used as models in text-dependent methods.

7.3.2 VQ-Based Methods

A set of short-term training feature vectors of a speaker can be used directly to represent her essential characteristics. However, such a direct representation is impractical when the number of training vectors is large, since the amount of memory and computation required become prohibitive. Therefore, attempts have been made to find efficient ways of compressing the training data using vector quantization (VQ) techniques.

VQ codebooks, consisting of a small number of representative feature vectors, are used to efficiently characterize speaker-specific features [6, 10–12]. In the recognition stage, an input utterance is vector-quantized using the codebook of each reference speaker; the VQ distortion accumulated over the entire input utterance is used to make the recognition determination.

Along with memoryless (frame-by-frame) VQ-based method, non-memoryless source-coding algorithms have been studied using a segment (matrix) quantization technique [13]. The advantage of a segment quantization codebook over a VQ codebook representation is its characterization of the sequential nature of speech events. A segment-modeling procedure for constructing a set of representative time-normalized segments called "filler templates" has been proposed [14]. The procedure, a combination of k-means clustering and dynamic programming time alignment, handles temporal variation.

7.3.3 Methods Based on Ergodic HMM

The basic structure here is the same as that of the VQ-based method, but a multiple-state ergodic HMM (i.e., all possible transitions between states are allowed) is used instead of a VQ codebook (see Figure 7.2). The ergodic HMM classifies speech segments into one of the broad phonetic categories corresponding to the HMM states.

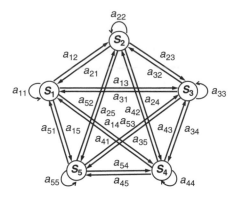

FIGURE 7.2

Five-state ergodic HMM for text-independent speaker recognition.

Over a long time scale, the temporal variation in speech signal parameters is represented by stochastic Markovian transitions between states. The automatically obtained categories are often characterized as strong voicing, silence, nasal/liquid, stop burst/post silence, frication, and so forth [15].

The VQ-based method has been compared with the discrete/continuous ergodic HMM-based method, particularly from the viewpoint of robustness against utterance variations [16]. It was found that the continuous ergodic HMM method is far superior to the discrete ergodic HMM method and that it is as robust as the VQ-based method when enough training data is available. However, the VQ-based method is more robust when few data are available. Speaker identification rates using continuous HMM were investigated as a function of the number of states and mixtures. It was shown that speaker recognition rates strongly correlate with the total number of mixtures, irrespective of the number of states. This means that information on transitions between different states is ineffective for text-independent speaker recognition.

A technique based on maximum-likelihood estimation of a Gaussian mixture model (GMM) representation of speaker identity [17] is one of the most popular methods. It corresponds to the single-state continuous ergodic HMM. Gaussian mixtures are noted for their robustness as a parametric model and for their ability to form smooth estimates of rather arbitrary underlying densities.

The VQ-based method can be regarded as a special (degenerate) case of a single-state HMM, with a distortion measure being used as the observation probability.

7.3.4 Methods Based on Speech Recognition

The VQ- and HMM-based methods use phoneme-class-dependent speaker characteristics contained in short-term spectral features through implicit phoneme-class recognition. In other words, phoneme classes and speakers are simultaneously recognized. On the other hand, in speech-recognition-based methods, phonemes or phoneme classes are explicitly recognized, and then each phoneme/phoneme-class segment in the input speech is compared with speaker models or templates corresponding to it.

A five-state ergodic linear predictive HMM for broad phonetic categorization has been investigated [18]. In this method, feature selection is performed after frames that belong to particular phonetic categories have been identified. In the training phase, reference templates are generated and verification thresholds are computed for each phonetic category. In the verification phase, after phonetic categorization, a comparison with the reference template for each particular category provides a verification score for it. The final verification score is a weighted linear combination of the scores for each category. The weights are chosen to reflect the effectiveness of particular categories of phonemes in discriminating between speakers, and they are adjusted to maximize verification performance. Experimental results show that verification accuracy can be considerably improved by this category-dependent weighted linear combination method.

A speaker verification system using 4-digit phrases was tested, under actual field conditions, for a banking application. Input speech was segmented into individual digits using a speaker-independent HMM [19]. The frames within the word boundaries for a digit were compared with the corresponding speaker-specific HMM digit model and the Viterbi likelihood score was computed. This was done for each of the digits making up the input utterance. The verification score was defined to be the average normalized log-likelihood score over all digits in the utterance.

A large-vocabulary speech recognition system was also used for speaker verification [20]. In this approach a set of speaker-independent phoneme models were adapted to each speaker. Verification consisted of two stages. First, speaker-independent speech recognition was run on each of the test utterances to obtain phoneme segmentation. Second, the segments were scored against the adapted models for a particular target speaker. The scores were normalized by those with speaker-independent models. The system was evaluated using the 1995 NIST-administered speaker verification database, which consists of data taken from the Switchboard corpus. The results showed that this method did not outperform Gaussian mixture models.

7.4 TEXT-PROMPTED SPEAKER RECOGNITION

In this method, key sentences are completely changed every time [8, 21]. The system accepts the input utterance only when it determines that the registered speaker uttered it. Because the vocabulary is unlimited, prospective impostors cannot know in advance the sentence they will be prompted to say. This method not only accurately recognizes speakers but also rejects an utterance whose text differs from the prompted text, even if it is by a registered speaker. Thus, a recorded and played-back voice can be correctly rejected.

Speaker-specific phoneme models are the basic acoustic units in this method. One of the major issues is how to properly create them when using training utterances of a limited size. The phoneme models are represented by Gaussian mixture continuous or tied-mixture HMMs, and they are created by adapting speaker-independent phoneme models to each speaker's voice.

In the recognition stage, the system concatenates the phoneme models of each registered speaker to create a sentence HMM, according to the prompted text. Then the likelihood of the input speech against the sentence model is calculated and used for speaker verification. The robustness of this method has been confirmed through various experiments.

7.5 HIGH-LEVEL SPEAKER RECOGNITION

High-level features such as word idiolect, pronunciation, phone usage, and prosody have been successfully used in text-independent speaker verification [22]. Typically, high-level feature recognition systems produce a sequence of symbols from the acoustic signal and then perform recognition using the symbol frequency and co-occurrence. In an idiolect approach, word unigrams and bigrams from manually transcribed conversations are used to characterize a particular speaker in a traditional target/background likelihood ratio framework. The use of support vector machines in speaker verification based on phone and word sequences obtained using phone recognizers was proposed in [23]. The benefit of these features was demonstrated in the "NIST extended data" task for speaker verification; with enough conversational data, a recognition system can become "familiar" with a speaker and achieve excellent accuracy. The corpus was a combination of phases 2 and 3 of the Switchboard-2 corpus. Each training utterance in the corpus consisted of a conversation side that was nominally 5 minutes in length (approximately 2.5 minutes of speech) recorded over a landline telephone. Speaker models were trained using 1 to 16 conversation sides. These methods need utterances of at least several minutes—much longer than those used in conventional speaker recognition methods.

7.6 NORMALIZATION AND ADAPTATION TECHNIQUES

How can we normalize intra-speaker variation in likelihood (similarity) values in speaker verification? The most significant factor in automatic speaker recognition is variation in signal characteristics from trial to trial (inter-session variability, or variability over time). Variations arise from the speaker herself, from differences in recording and transmission conditions, and from noise. Speakers cannot repeat an utterance precisely the same way from trial to trial. It is well known that samples of the same utterance recorded in one session are much more highly correlated than tokens recorded in separate sessions. There are also long-term trends in voices [24, 25].

It is important for speaker recognition systems to accommodate these variations. Adaptation of the reference model as well as the verification threshold for each speaker is indispensable to maintaining high recognition accuracy over a long period. To compensate for the variations, two types of normalization techniques have been tried—one in the parameter domain and the other in the distance/similarity domain. The latter technique uses the likelihood ratio or a posteriori probability. In adapting HMMs to noisy conditions, various techniques, including HMM composition (parallel model combination [PMC]) [26], have proved successful.

7.6.1 Parameter Domain Normalization

A typical normalization technique in the parameter domain is spectral equalization (the so-called "blind equalization" method), which has been confirmed effective in reducing linear channel effects and long-term spectral variation. It is especially effective for text-dependent speaker recognition using sufficiently long utterances. In this method, cepstral coefficients are averaged over the duration of an entire utterance, and the averaged values are subtracted from the cepstral coefficients of each frame (cepstral mean subtraction [CMS]) [5, 27]. This compensates fairly well for additive variation in the log spectral domain; however, it unavoidably removes some text-dependent and speaker-specific features and so is inappropriate for short utterances. It has also been shown that time derivatives of cepstral coefficients (delta-cepstral coefficients) are resistant to linear channel mismatches between training and testing [5, 28].

7.6.2 Likelihood Normalization

A normalization method for likelihood (similarity or distance) values that uses a likelihood ratio has been proposed [7]. The likelihood ratio is the ratio of the conditional probability of the observed measurements of the utterance, assuming the claimed identity is correct, to the conditional probability of the observed measurements, assuming the speaker is an impostor (normalization term). Generally, a positive log-likelihood ratio indicates a valid claim, whereas a negative value indicates an imposter. The likelihood ratio normalization approximates optimal scoring in a Bayesian sense.

However, likelihood normalization is unrealistic because conditional probabilities must be calculated for all reference speakers, which is computationally expensive. Therefore, a set of "cohort speakers," who are representative of the population distribution near the claimed speaker, is chosen for calculating the normalization term. Cohort speakers can also be those who are typical of the general population. In fact, it was reported that a randomly selected, gender-balanced background speaker population outperformed a population near the claimed speaker [29].

Another normalization method is based on a posteriori probability [8, 30]. The difference between normalization based on likelihood ratio and that based on a posteriori probability is whether or not the claimed speaker is included in the impostor speaker set for normalization: The cohort speaker set in the likelihood ratio method does not include the claimed speaker, whereas the normalization term for the a posteriori probability method is calculated using a set of speakers that includes the claimed speaker. Experimental results indicate that both normalization methods almost equally improve speaker separability and reduce the need for speaker-dependent or text-dependent thresholding, compared with scoring using only the model of the claimed speaker [30, 31].

A method in which the normalization term is approximated by the likelihood of a world model representing the population in general was proposed in [32]. This method has an advantage in that the computational cost for calculating the normalization term is much smaller than that for the original method since it does not need to sum the likelihood values for cohort speakers. Also proposed was a method based on tied-mixture HMMs in which the world model is fashioned as a pooled mixture representing the parameter distribution for all registered speakers [30]. A single background model for calculating the normalization term has become the predominate approach in speaker verification systems.

Because these normalization methods neglect absolute deviation between the claimed speaker's model and the input speech, they cannot differentiate highly dissimilar speakers. It was reported that a multilayer network decision algorithm makes effective use of the relative and absolute scores obtained from the matching algorithm [7].

Yet another approach is a family of normalization techniques in which the scores are normalized by subtracting the mean and then dividing by standard deviation, both terms having been estimated from the (pseudo) imposter score distribution. Different possibilities are available for computing the imposter score distribution: Znorm, Hnorm, Tnorm, Htnorm, Cnorm, and Dnorm [33]. State-of-the-art text-independent speaker verification techniques associate one or more parameterization-level normalization approaches (CMS, feature variance normalization, feature warping, etc.) with world model normalization and one or more score normalizations.

7.6.3 HMM Adaptation for Noisy Conditions

Increasing the robustness of speaker recognition techniques against noisy speech or speech distorted by a telephone is a crucial issue in real applications. Rose et al. [34] applied the HMM composition (PMC) method [26, 35] to speaker identification under noisy conditions. HMM composition combines a clean-speech HMM and a background-noise HMM to create a noise-added speech HMM. To cope with the variation in signal-to-noise ratio (SNR), Matsui and Furui [36] proposed a method in which several noise-added HMMs with various SNRs were created and the HMM that had the highest likelihood value for the input speech was selected. A speaker decision was made using the likelihood value corresponding to the selected model. Experimental application of this method to text-independent speaker identification and verification in various kinds of noisy environments demonstrated considerable improvement in speaker recognition.

7.6.4 **Updating Models and A Priori Thresholds for Speaker Verification**

How to update speaker models to cope with gradual changes in voices is an important issue. Since we cannot ask every user to provide many utterances across different sessions in real situations, it is necessary to build each speaker model based on a small amount of data collected in a few sessions, and then update the model using speech data collected when the system is used.

Setting the a priori decision threshold for speaker verification is another important issue. In most laboratory speaker recognition experiments, the threshold is set a posteriori to the system's equal error rate (EER). Since it cannot be set a posteriori in real situations, we need practical ways to set it before verification. It must be set according to the relative importance of the two errors, which depends on the application.

These two problems are intrinsically related. Methods for updating reference templates and the threshold in DTW-based speaker verification have been developed [5]. An optimum threshold was estimated based on the distribution of overall distances between each speaker's reference template and a set of utterances by other speakers (inter-speaker distances). The inter-speaker distance distribution was approximated by a normal distribution, and the threshold was calculated by the linear combination of its mean value and standard deviation. The intra-speaker distance distribution was not taken into account in the calculation, mainly because it is difficult to obtain stable estimates of it from small numbers of training utterances. The reference template for each speaker was updated by averaging new utterances and the present template after time registration. These methods have been extended and applied to text-independent and text-prompted speaker verification using HMMs [37].

Various model adaptation and compensation techniques have been investigated for GMM based speaker recognition methods. McLaren et al. [38] proposed two techniques for GMM mean super-vector SVM classifiers: inter-session variability modeling and nuisance attribute projection. Preti et al. [39] proposed an unsupervised model adaptation technique that includes a weighting scheme for the test data based on the a posteriori probability that a test belongs to the target customer model.

7.7 **ROC AND DET CURVES**

7.7.1 **ROC Curves**

Measuring false rejection and acceptance rates for a given threshold condition provides an incomplete description of system performance. A general description can be obtained by varying the threshold over a sufficiently large range and tabulating the resulting false rejection and acceptance rates. A tabulation of this kind can be summarized in a receiver operating characteristic (ROC) curve, first used in psychophysics. The ROC curve is obtained by assigning the probability of correct

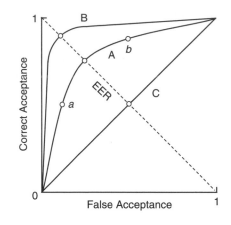

FIGURE 7.3

Receiver operating characteristic (ROC) curves; performance examples of three speaker recognition systems: A, B, and C.

acceptance (1 − false rejection rate [FRR]) and the probability of incorrect acceptance (false acceptance rate [FAR]) to the vertical and horizontal axes, respectively, and varying the decision threshold, as shown in Figure 7.3 [3].

The figure exemplifies the curves, A, B, and C, for three systems. Clearly, the performance of curve B is consistently superior to that of curve A, and curve C corresponds to the limiting case of purely chance performance. Position *a* in the figure corresponds to the case in which a strict decision criterion is employed, and position *b* corresponds to a case involving a lax criterion.

The point-by-point knowledge of the ROC curve provides a threshold-independent description of all possible functioning conditions of the system. For example, if a false rejection rate is specified, the corresponding false acceptance rate is obtained as the intersection of the ROC curve with the horizontal straight line indicating the false rejection.

The EER is a commonly accepted overall measure of system performance. It corresponds to the threshold at which the false acceptance rate is equal to the false rejection rate. The EER point corresponds to the intersection of the ROC curve with the straight line of 45 degrees, indicated in Figure 7.3.

7.7.2 DET Curves

It is now standard to plot the error curve on a normal deviate scale [40], in which case the curve is known as the "detection error trade-offs" (DETs) curve. False rejection and false acceptance rates are assigned to the vertical and horizontal axes, respectively. With the normal deviate scale, a speaker verification system whose customer and impostor scores are normally distributed, regardless of variance, will result in a linear scale with a slope equal to −1. The better the system is, the closer

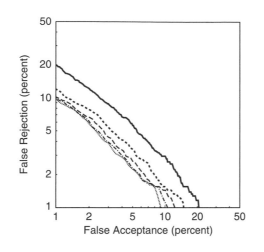

FIGURE 7.4

Examples of the DET curve.

to the origin the curve is. In practice, score distributions are not exactly Gaussian but are quite close to it. Thus, the DET curve representation is more easily readable than the ROC curve and allows for a comparison of system performance over a large range of operating conditions. Figure 7.4 shows a typical example of DET curves. The EER point corresponds to the intersection of the DET curve with the first bisector curve.

In NIST speaker recognition evaluations, a cost function defined as a weighted sum of the two types of errors is chosen for use as the basic performance measure [41]. This cost, referred to as C_{DET} is defined as

$$C_{DET} = (C_{FR} \times P_{FR} \times P_C) + (C_{FA} \times P_{FA} \times (1 - P_C)) \tag{7.1}$$

where P_{FR} and P_{FA} are false rejection (FR) and false acceptance (FA) rates, respectively. The required parameters in this function are the cost of FR (C_{FR}), the cost of FA (C_{FA}), and the a priori probability of a customer (P_C).

7.8 SPEAKER DIARIZATION

Continually decreasing cost and increasing storage capacity and network bandwidth facilitate the use of large volumes of audio, including broadcasts, voice mails, meetings, and other "spoken documents." There is a growing need to apply automatic human language technologies to achieve efficient and effective indexing, searching, and accessing of these information sources. Extracting the words spoken in audio using speech recognition technology provides a sound base for these tasks, but the transcripts do not capture all the information the audio contains. Other technologies are needed to extract metadata that can make the transcripts more readable and provide context and information beyond a simple word sequence. Speaker turns and sentence boundaries are examples of such metadata, both of which help provide a richer transcription of the audio, making transcripts more readable and potentially helping with other tasks such as summarization, parsing, and machine translation.

Speaker diarization, also called speech segmentation and clustering, is defined as deciding "who spoke when." Here speech versus nonspeech decisions are made and speaker changes are marked in the detected speech. Nonspeech is a general class consisting of music, silence, noise, and so forth, that need not to be broken out by type. Speaker diarization allows searching audio by speaker, makes transcripts easier to read, and provides information that can be used in speaker adaptation in speech recognition systems.

A prototypical combination of key components in a speaker diarization system is shown in Figure 7.5 [42]. The general approach in speech detection is maximum-likelihood classification with Gaussian mixture models (GMMs) trained on labeled training data. The simplest system uses just speech/nonspeech models, while a more complex system uses four speech models for the possible combinations of gender (male or female) and bandwidth (low/narrow bandwidth: telephone; high bandwidth: studio). Noise and music are explicitly modeled in several systems, having classes for speech, music, noise, speech+music, and speech+noise. When operating on unsegmented audio, Viterbi segmentation using the models is employed to identify speech regions.

The aim of change detection is to find points in the audio stream likely to be change points between audio sources. If input to this stage is the unsegmented

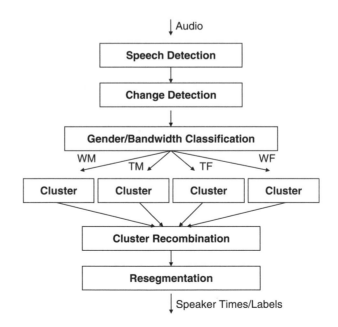

FIGURE 7.5

Prototypical diarization system (W: wide bandwidth, T: narrow/telephone bandwidth, M: male, F: female).

audio stream, the change detection looks for both speaker and speech/nonspeech change points. If a speech detector classifier has been run first, the change detector looks for speaker change points within each speech segment. The most general approach to change detection is a variation on the Bayesian information criterion (BIC) technique, which searches for change points within a window using a penalized likelihood ratio test of whether the data in the window is better modeled by a single distribution (no change point) or two different distributions (change point).

The aim of gender/bandwidth classification is to partition the segments into common groupings of these classes to reduce the load on subsequent clustering. Clustering for both gender and bandwidth is typically done using maximum-likelihood classification with GMMs trained on labeled training data.

The purpose of clustering is to associate or cluster segments from the same speaker. Clustering ideally produces one cluster for each speaker in the audio, with all segments from that speaker in it. The predominant approach used in diarization systems is hierarchical, agglomerative clustering with a BIC-based stopping criterion.

Cluster recombination is a relatively recent approach in which state-of-the-art speaker recognition modeling and matching are used as a secondary stage for combining clusters.

The last stage of the resegmentation found in many diarization systems is resegmentation of the audio via Viterbi decoding (with or without iterations) using the final cluster and nonspeech models. The purpose of this stage is to refine the original segment boundaries and/or to fill in short segments that may have been removed for more robust processing in the clustering stage.

7.9 MULTIMODAL SPEAKER RECOGNITION

Although the most commonly used features for speaker recognition are cepstral coefficients and their regression coefficients, several other features are often combined to increase the robustness of the system under a variety of environmental conditions, especially for additive noise. The most typical additional features are fundamental frequency and visual information related to lip movement.

7.9.1 Combining Spectral Envelope and Fundamental Frequency Features

Matsui and Furui [11, 12] tried a method using a VQ codebook for long feature vectors consisting of instantaneous and transitional features calculated for both cepstral coefficients and fundamental frequency. Because the fundamental frequency cannot be extracted from unvoiced speech, there were two separate codebooks for voiced and unvoiced speech for each speaker. A new distance measure was introduced to take into account intra- and inter-speaker variability and to deal with the problem of outliers in the distribution of feature vectors. The outlier vectors correspond to intersession spectral variation and to the difference between the phonetic content of the training texts and that of the test utterances. It was confirmed that, although fundamental frequency achieved only a low recognition rate by itself, recognition accuracy was greatly improved by combining the fundamental frequency with cepstral features.

Asami et al. [43] proposed a speaker verification method using fundamental frequency extracted via the Hough transform, which is a robust image-processing technology effective in reliably extracting fundamental frequency values under noise. Multistream HMMs were used to integrate fundamental frequency and cepstral features. Stream weights and a threshold for verification decisions were simultaneously optimized by combining linear discriminant analysis (LDA) and Adaboost. Experiments were conducted using utterances contaminated by white, in-car, or elevator-hall noise at various SNRs. The results show that fundamental frequency improves verification performance in various noisy environments, and that the stream weight and threshold optimization method effectively estimates control parameters so that FA and FR rates are adjusted to achieve equal error-rates.

7.9.2 Combining Audio and Visual Features

Much recent interest has focused on audiovisual speaker verification systems that combine speech and image information. As visual information, lip movement is widely used. The audiovisual combination helps improve system reliability. For instance, while background noise has a detrimental effect on the performance of voice, it has no influence on lip information. Conversely, although the performance of lip recognition systems depends on lighting conditions, lighting has no effect on voice quality.

The combination of information (audiovisual fusion) can be treated as a problem of either classifier combination or pattern classification. For example, for systems that can only provide decisions, a majority voting method can be used. If the outputs of classifiers are compatible (e.g., in the form of posterior probabilities), they can be linearly combined (sum rule) or multiplied together (product or log-linear rule). Besides these combination methods, researchers have also suggested considering the outputs of individual classifiers as feature vectors and using classifiers such as support vector machines, binary decision trees, and radial basis function networks to classify the vectors [44, 45].

7.10 OUTSTANDING ISSUES

There are many outstanding issues in the area of speaker recognition. The most pressing for implementing practical and uniformly reliable systems for speaker verification are rooted in problems associated with variability and insufficient data.

As described earlier, variability is associated with trial-to-trial variations in recording and transmission conditions and speaking behavior. The most serious variations occur between enrollment sessions and subsequent test sessions and result in models that are mismatched to test conditions. Most applications require reliable system operation under a variety of environmental and channel conditions and require that variations in speaking behavior be tolerated. Insufficient data refers to the unavailability of enough data to provide representative models and accurate decision thresholds. This is a serious and common problem because most applications require systems that operate with the smallest practicable amounts of training data recorded in the fewest number of enrollment sessions (preferably one).

The challenge is to find techniques that compensate for these deficiencies. A number of techniques have been mentioned that provide partial solutions, such as cepstral subtraction for channel normalization and spectral subtraction for noise removal. An especially effective technique for combating both variability and insufficient data is updating models with data extracted from test utterances. Studies have shown that model adaptation, properly implemented, can improve verification significantly with a small number of updates. It is difficult, however, for model adaptation to respond to large, precipitous changes. Moreover, this risks the possibility that customer models might be updated and captured by impostors.

A desirable feature for a practical speaker recognition system is reasonably uniform performance across a population of speakers. Unfortunately, in a typical speaker recognition experiment there is a substantial discrepancy between the best-performing individuals—the "sheep"—and the worst—the "goats." Although this has been widely observed, there are virtually no studies focusing on its origin. Speakers with no observable speech pathologies, and for whom apparently good reference models have been obtained, are often observed to be "goats." It is possible that such speakers exhibit large amounts of trial-to-trial variability, beyond the ability of the system to provide adequate compensation.

Speaker recognition techniques are related to research on improving speech recognition accuracy by speaker adaptation, improving synthesized speech quality by adding the natural characteristics of voice individuality, and converting synthesized voice individuality from one speaker to another. Studies on speaker diarization, automatically extracting individual utterances of each speaker from conversations/dialogues/meetings involving more than two participants have appeared as an extension of speaker recognition technology. Increasingly, speaker segmentation and clustering are being used to aid the adaptation of speech recognizers and to supply metadata for audio indexing and searching. These techniques are becoming important in various applications using speaker-related information in smart environments.

REFERENCES

[1] Furui S. Speaker-independent and speaker-adaptive recognition techniques. In: Furui S, Sondhi MM, editors. Advances in Speech Signal Processing. Marcel Dekker: 1991. p. 597–622.

[2] Furui S. Recent advances in speaker recognition. In: Proc. First International Conference on Audio- and Video-based Biometric Person Authentication. Switzerland: Crans Montana: 1997. p. 237–52.

[3] Furui S. Digital Speech Processing, Synthesis, and Recognition. 2nd ed. Marcel Dekker: 2000.

[4] Kunzel HJ. Current approaches to forensic speaker recognition. In: Proc. ESCA Workshop on Automatic Speaker Recognition, Identification and Verification. Martigny, Switzerland: 1994. p. 135–41.

[5] Furui S. Cepstral analysis technique for automatic speaker verification. IEEE Trans Acoust Speech, Signal Proc 1981;29(2):254–72.

[6] Rosenberg AE, Soong FK. Evaluation of a vector quantization talker recognition system in text independent and text dependent modes. Comput Speech Lang 1987;2(3–4):143–57.

[7] Higgins A, Bahler L, Porter J. Speaker verification using randomized phrase prompting. Digital Signal Proc 1991;1:89–106.

[8] Matsui T, Furui S. Concatenated phoneme models for text-variable speaker recognition. In: Proc. IEEE International Conference on Acoustics, Speech, and Signal Processing, vol. 2. Minneapolis, MN: 1993. p. 391–4.

[9] Naik J, Netsch M, Doddington G. Speaker verification over long distance telephone lines. In: Proc. IEEE International Conference on Acoustics, Speech, and Signal Processing, vol. 1. Glasgow, Scotland: 1989. p. 524–7.

[10] Li K-P, Wrench Jr EH. An approach to text-independent speaker recognition with short utterances. In: Proc. IEEE International Conference on Acoustics, Speech, and Signal Processing. Boston, MA: 1983. p. 555–8.

[11] Matsui T, Furui S. Text-independent speaker recognition using vocal tract and pitch information. In: Proc. International Conference on Spoken Language Processing, vol. 1. Kobo, Japan: 1990. p. 137–40.

[12] Matsui T, Furui S. A text-independent speaker recognition method robust against utterance variations. In: Proc. IEEE International Conference on Acoustics, Speech, and Signal Processing, vol. 1. Toronto, Ontario: 1991. p. 377–80.

[13] Juang B-H, Soong FK. Speaker recognition based on source coding approaches. In: Proc. IEEE International Conference on Acoustics, Speech, and Signal Processing, vol. 1. Albuquerque, NM: 1990. p. 613–6.

[14] Higgins AL, Wohlford RE. A new method of text-independent speaker recognition. In: Proc. IEEE International Conference on Acoustics, Speech, and Signal Processing, vol. 2. Tokyo, Japan: 1986. p. 869–72.

[15] Poritz AB. Linear predictive hidden Markov models and the speech signal. In: Proc. IEEE International Conference on Acoustics, Speech, and Signal Processing, vol. 2. Paris, France: 1982. p. 1291–4.

[16] Matsui T, Furui S. Comparison of text-independent speaker recognition methods using VQ-distortion and discrete/continuous HMMs. In: Proc. IEEE International Conference on Acoustics, Speech, and Signal Processing, vol. 2. San Francisco, CA: 1992. p. 157–60.

[17] Rose RC, Reynolds RA. Text independent speaker identification using automatic acoustic segmentation. In: Proc. IEEE International Conference on Acoustics, Speech, and Signal Processing, vol. 1. Albuquerque, NM: 1990. p. 293–6.

[18] Savic M, Gupta SK. Variable parameter speaker verification system based on hidden Markov modeling. In: Proc. IEEE International Conference on Acoustics, Speech, and Signal Processing, vol. 1. Albuquerque, NM: 1990. p. 281–4.

[19] Rosenberg AE, Lee C-H, Gokcen S. Connected word talker verification using whole word hidden Markov models. In: Proc. IEEE International Conference on Acoustics, Speech, and Signal Processing, vol. 1. Toronto, Ontario: 1991. p. 381–4.

[20] Newman M, Gillick L, Ito Y, McAllaster D, Peskin B. Speaker verification through large vocabulary continuous speech recognition. In: Proc. International Conference on Spoken Language Processing, vol. 4. Philadelphia, PA: 1996. p. 2419-22.

[21] Matsui T, Furui S. Speaker adaptation of tied-mixture-based phoneme models for text-prompted speaker recognition. In: Proc. IEEE International Conference on Acoustics, Speech, and Signal Processing, vol. 1. Adelaide, Australia: 1994. p. 125-8.

[22] Doddington G. Speaker recognition based on idiolectal differences between speakers. In: Proc. EUROSPEECH. Aalborg, Denmark: 2001. p. 2521-4.

[23] Campbell WM, Campbell JP, Reynolds DA, Jones DA, Leek TR. High-level speaker verification with support vector machines. In: Proc. IEEE International Conference on Acoustics, Speech, and Signal Processing, vol. 1. Montreal, Quebec: 2004. p. 73-6.

[24] Furui S, Itakura F, Saito S. Talker recognition by longtime averaged speech spectrum. Trans IECE 55-A 1972;1(10):549-56.

[25] Furui S. An analysis of long-term variation of feature parameters of speech and its application to talker recognition. Trans IECE 57-A 1974;12:880-7.

[26] Gales MJF, Young SJ. HMM recognition in noise using parallel model combination. In: Proc. EUROSPEECH, vol. 2. Berlin, Germany: 1993. p. 837-40.

[27] Atal BS. Effectiveness of linear prediction characteristics of the speech wave for automatic speaker identification and verification. J Acoust Soc Am 1974;55(6):1304-12.

[28] Soong FK, Rosenberg AE. On the use of instantaneous and transitional spectral information in speaker recognition. IEEE Trans Acoust Speech, Signal Pro ASSP-36 1988;(6):871-9.

[29] Reynolds D. Speaker identification and verification using Gaussian mixture speaker models. In: Proc. ESCA Workshop on Automatic Speaker Recognition, Identification and Verification. 1994. p. 27-30.

[30] Matsui T, Furui S. Similarity normalization method for speaker verification based on a posteriori probability. In: Proc. ESCA Workshop on Automatic Speaker Recognition, Identification and Verification. 1994. p. 59-62.

[31] Rosenberg AE, DeLong J, Lee C-II, Juang B H, Soong FK. The use of cohort normalized scores for speaker verification. In: Proc. International Conference on Spoken Language Processing, vol. 1. Banff, Alberta: 1992. p. 599-602.

[32] Carey MJ, Parris ES. Speaker verification using connected words. Proc Institute of Acoustics 1992;14(part 6):95-100.

[33] Bimbot F, Bonastre J-F, Fredouille C, Gravier G, Magrin-Chagnolleau I, Meignier S, et al. A tutorial on text-independent speaker verification. EURASIP App Signal Proc 2004;(4): 430-51.

[34] Rose RC, Hofstetter EM, Reynolds DA. Integrated models of signal and background with application to speaker identification in noise. IEEE Trans Speech Audio Proc 1994;2(2):245-57.

[35] Martin F, Shikano K, Minami Y. Recognition of noisy speech by composition of hidden Markov models. In: Proc. EUROSPEECH, vol. 2. Berlin, Germany: 1993. p. 1031-4.

[36] Matsui T, Furui S. Speaker recognition using HMM composition in noisy environments. Comput Speech Lang 1996;10(2):107-16.

[37] Matsui T, Furui S. Robust methods of updating model and a priori threshold in speaker verification. In: Proc. IEEE International Conference on Acoustics, Speech, and Signal Processing, vol. 1. Atlanta, GA: 1996. p. 97-100.

[38] McLaren M, Vogt R, Baker B, Sridharan S. A comparison of session variability compensation techniques for SVM-based speaker recognition. In: Proc. INTERSPEECH. Antwerp, Belgium: 2007. p. 790–3.

[39] Preti A, Bonastre J-F, Matrouf D, Capman F, Ravera B. Confidence measure based unsupervised target model adaptation for speaker verification. In: Proc. INTERSPEECH. Antwerp, Belgium: 2007. p. 754–7.

[40] Martin A, Doddington G, Kamm T, Ordowski M, Przybocki M. The DET curve in assessment of detection task performance. In: Proc. EUROSPEECH, vol. 4. Rhodes, Greece: 1997. p. 1895–8.

[41] Martin A, Przybocki M. The NIST speaker recognition evaluations: 1996–2001. In: Proc. 2001: A Speaker Odyssey – The Speaker Recognition Workshop. Crete, Greece: 2001. p. 39–43.

[42] Tranter SE, Reynolds DA. An overview of automatic speaker diarization systems. IEEE Trans Audio, Speech, Lang Proc 2006;14(5):1557–95.

[43] Asami T, Iwano K, Furui S. Evaluation of a noise-robust multi-stream speaker verification method using F_0 information. Trans IEICE E91-D 2008;(3):549–57.

[44] Cheung M-C, Mak M-W, Kung S-Y. A two-level fusion approach to multimodal biometric verification. In: Proc. IEEE International Conference on Acoustics, Speech, and Signal Processing, vol. 5. Philadelphia, PA: 2005. p. 485–8.

[45] Campbell WM, Campbell JP, Reynolds DA, Singer E, Torres-Carrasquillo PA. Support vector machines for speaker and language recognition. Comput Speech Lang 2006;20(2–3): 210–29.

Machine Learning Approaches to Spoken Language Understanding for Ambient Intelligence

8

Minwoo Jeong and Gary Geunbae Lee

*Department of Computer Science and Engineering,
Pohang University of Science and Technology, Pohang, Korea*

185

ABSTRACT

Spoken language understanding (SLU) has received recent interest as a component of spoken dialogue systems to infer intentions of the speaker and to provide natural human-centric interfaces for ambient intelligence. The goal of SLU is to map natural language speech to a frame structure that encodes its meaning. While most approaches based on rule-based parsing often succeeded before the 1990s, for academic and industrial fields the paradigm has shifted from knowledge-based to statistical. Statistical SLU automatically learns patterns from data in a supervised or semi-supervised fashion. The statistical framework is growing into a more powerful tool for SLU using modern machine learning methods. This chapter discusses the concept of learning to understand human language using modern machine learning techniques, and presents a machine learning–based formalism for modeling the SLU problem, focusing on goal-oriented slot-filling dialogue systems. It also addresses some advanced issues that should be examined for ambient intelligence environments. To reduce computational costs, we present efficient algorithms for learning and applying SLU, because some applications for ambient intelligence have limited computation resources. Then we describe a transfer learning framework for SLU modeling, in which multiple tasks and domain knowledge can be incorporated. Finally, to assess the feasibility of our methods, two novel problems for statistical SLU are demonstrated.

Key words: spoken language understanding, slot-filling dialogue system, machine learning approach, conditional random fields, transfer learning.

8.1 INTRODUCTION

Recent advances in computing devices and ambient intelligence technology have created a new paradigm for human-centric interfaces. In the current vision of ambient intelligence, computing will become invisibly embedded in our natural surroundings, be present whenever needed, and be enabled by simple and effortless interactions that are adaptive to users and context sensitive [36]. Speech and dialogue-based interfaces are expected to provide such interactions in a natural and human-centric way. The technological challenges in establishing these interfaces are nontrivial, however. In particular, these interfaces would operate normally while the computing devices could *understand* human speech or language. Spoken language understanding (SLU) is the study of methods of analyzing human spoken language and extracting a semantic structure from speech.

SLU has been extensively studied in the last decade by the language-processing and speech communities. It covers many spoken language problems such as utterance classification, speech summarization, spoken-document retrieval, speech-to-speech translation, and information extraction from speech. In particular, SLU has received much recent interest as a part of spoken dialogue systems to infer speaker intentions and to provide natural human–computer interfaces [8, 23, 25, 34]. Its goal in spoken dialogue applications is to extract semantic meanings from speech signals, using semantics that are differently defined in a variety of applications. For slot-filling dialogue systems, the semantics are usually structured by a frame that might include a dialogue act, a named entity, and a semantic role.

In the past two decades, many statistical and knowledge-based approaches were developed (see [8] and references therein). The paradigm proposed for SLU is shifting from knowledge-based to statistical. Statistical SLU can automatically learn from training examples annotated with corresponding semantics. Although a rule-based approach often achieves good performance in commercial systems, a data-driven statistical approach is more robust and feasible because it is more portable and because semantic labeled data is less expensive to build for a new domain. Moreover, the statistical framework is growing into a more powerful tool for SLU through modern machine learning methods; for example, the system can reduce the labeling effort by active or semi-supervised learning [33] and can incorporate prior knowledge into statistical models [29].

This chapter presents the concept of learning to understand spoken language and presents a machine learning–based formalism for modeling SLU problems that focuses on goal-oriented dialogue systems. In a supervised learning framework, statistical SLU is formulated as a sequential modeling task, which is fundamental in scientific fields, especially in speech and natural language processing, where many problems of sequential data can be formulated as sequential labeling or sequence classification. In slot-filling spoken dialogue systems, the problem in SLU is to extract object names and user intention from user utterances. Recognizing an object is a matter of sequential labeling, and identifying user intent is a matter of sequence classification. To deal with these problems, this chapter introduces state-of-the-art probabilistic models, termed *conditional random fields* (CRFs), which are conditional distributions over complex structured data (including sequential data) in which the output variables are mutually dependent or constrained. CRFs have been applied in many scientific fields, including the processing of large scale natural language data.

Despite the clear potential of CRFs, applying them to SLU for ambient intelligence (AmI) remains a significant challenge. In this chapter, we explore more advanced issues in learning SLU problems for ambient intelligence.

First, AmI computing devices usually have restricted computational resources; thus a developer should consider the time and space complexities of SLU learning algorithms. To do this, we present fast and efficient algorithms to make training and decoding of large-scale CRFs more appropriate for ambient intelligence applications with low computation power.

Second, typical learning methods for statistical classification can be extended to transfer learning, where a model trained to learn one task is used to improve another model devoted to a related task. We apply transfer learning to statistical SLU and present a novel probabilistic model: triangular-chain CRFs. Our proposed method jointly represents the sequence and meta-sequence labels in a single graphical structure that both explicitly encodes their dependencies and preserves uncertainty between them. Finally, we assess two applications of statistical SLU; these are components of spoken-dialogue interfaces for two AmI projects: (1) automatic call centers and (2) intelligent robotics and smart-home services.

The remainder of this chapter is structured as follows. Section 8.2 gives the background and general formalism of SLU for spoken dialogue systems. Section 8.3 reviews the CRFs closely related to the statistical SLU problem. Section 8.4 presents efficient algorithms for inference and learning of large-scale CRFs. Section 8.5 addresses transfer learning for SLU and introduces triangular-chain CRFs. Section 8.6 applies triangular-chain CRFs to SLU, where dialogue act (DA) and named entity (NE) tasks can be correlated. The empirical results in spoken dialogue for the automatic call center demonstrate an improvement in the domains of both dialogue act classification and named entity recognition.

In Section 8.7 triangular-chain CRFs are applied to a multi-domain SLU problem, in which data and knowledge from multiple domains can be incorporated. The empirical results in intelligent robot and smart-home applications show that our model effectively learns multiple domains in parallel and allows use of domain-independent patterns among domains to create a better model for the target domain. Finally, Section 8.8 presents our conclusion and an overview of remaining challenges.

8.2 STATISTICAL SPOKEN LANGUAGE UNDERSTANDING

In this section, we will explain SLU for slot-filling dialogue systems and its learning paradigm.

8.2.1 Spoken Language Understanding for Slot-Filling Dialogue System

SLU has received much interest as a means to provide a natural human–computer dialogue interface for spoken dialogue systems. For practical dialogue systems, it aims to fill the domain-specific frame slots by interpreting a speech-recognized utterance. The dialogue system manages the frame history to process dialogue flow. This type of dialogue system is referred to as *slot-filling* (Figure 8.1); such systems have been widely adopted as dialogue management frameworks.

The goal of SLU for slot-filling dialogue applications is to extract meanings from natural language speech and to infer the speaker's intention. To understand the user utterance, most SLU systems define a semantic frame—that is, a formal structure of predicted meanings consisting of slot/value pairs. This frame is usually divided into two main components: dialogue act (DA) and named entity (NE). The DA represents the meaning of an utterance at the discourse level, which is approximately the equivalent of the *intent* or *subject slot* in practical dialogue systems. The NE is an identifier of an entity such as a person, location, organization, or time. In this chapter we define NE as the domain-specific semantic meaning of a word. Figure 8.2(a),

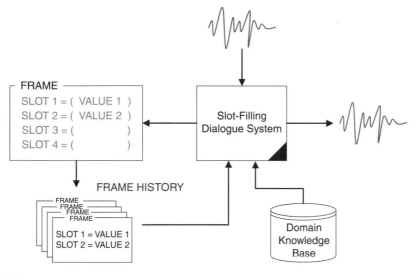

FIGURE 8.1

Logical diagram of the slot-filling dialogue system.

```
<frame domain='ATIS'>
  <utt>Show me flights from Denver to New York on Nov. 18th</utt>
  <slot type='DA' name='show_flight'/>
  <slot type='NE' name='from.city'>Denver</slot>
  <slot type='NE' name='to.city'>New York</slot>
  <slot type='NE' name='none.month'>Nov.</slot>
  <slot type='NE' name='none.day_number'>18th</slot>
</frame>
```

(a)

utt	Show	me	flights	from	Denver	to	New	York	on	Nov.	18th
					from.		to.	to.		none.	none.
NE	O	O	O	O	O				O		
					city-B		city-B	city-1		month-B	day-number-B
DA	show_flight										

(b)

FIGURE 8.2

Examples of a semantic frame representation of air travel service domains: (a) XML format;
(b) sequential data format.

for example, shows the semantic frame structure, based on an XML representation, for an air travel information service. To develop a goal-oriented slot-filling dialogue system, we therefore attempt to understand the user utterance based on two subproblems: DA and NE extractions.

To formalize these two SLU problems, we use statistical classification, which can be categorized as sequential labeling and sequence classification. Given a sequence of observations, the former predicts "a sequence of labels"; the latter, "a single label." Thus, the problem of recognizing NEs is one of sequential labeling, and the problem of identifying DAs is one of sequence classification. In particular, NE recognition requires assigning a label to a phrase rather than to a word. The standard method for dealing with this segmentation is to use "BIO" encoding [28], in which the slot labels are drawn from a set of classes constructed by extending each label by X-B, X-I, or O. Here, X-B means "Begin a phrase of slot X," X-I means "Continue a phrase of slot X," and O means "Not in a phrase." Figure 8.2(b), for example, shows an utterance, the NE tags, and the DA for an air travel information service.

8.2.2 Sequential Supervised Learning

In machine learning formalism, statistical SLU can be thought of as a sequential supervised learning problem, which is fundamental to many statistical approaches in speech and language processing. Let $\mathbf{x} \in X$ be a random vector that we observe, and $\mathbf{y} \in \mathcal{Y}$ be a random vector that we wish to predict. For example, in the NE tagging task, $\mathbf{x}$ may be a sequence of words and $\mathbf{y}$ may be a sequence of NE tags. (For the DA task, we of course assume that the size of random vector $\mathbf{y}$ is one, $|\mathbf{y}| = 1$.) To simplify the model, we typically assume that the lengths of two vectors are equal; consequently, a paired sequence $(\mathbf{x}, \mathbf{y})$ denotes $(x_1, y_1, x_2, y_2, \ldots, x_T, y_T)$. For any scalar variable x or y, we write that $x \in X_a$ and $y \in \mathcal{Y}_a$, where X_a is an atomic set of the input space (i.e., the size of vocabulary) and $\mathcal{Y}_a$ is an atomic set of the output space (i.e., the finite set of labels). Note that the output space $\mathcal{Y}$ is a natural extension of the atomic sets $\mathcal{Y}_a$—that is, $\mathcal{Y} = \mathcal{Y}_a \times \mathcal{Y}_a \times \ldots \times \mathcal{Y}_a$. Intuitively, $\mathcal{Y}$ can be thought of as the set of all possible paths in a $|y_a| \times T$ mesh, where T is the column size of vector $\mathbf{y}$. Let $\mathcal{D} = \{\mathbf{x}^{(i)}, \mathbf{y}^{(i)}\}_{i=1,\ldots,N}$ be a set of N training examples.

Now we are interested in the general problem of learning functions $f : X \to \mathcal{Y}$ between input spaces X and discrete output spaces $\mathcal{Y}$ based on a training example $\mathcal{D}$. We define a discriminant function $F : X \times \mathcal{Y} \to \mathbb{R}$ over input-output pairs, from which we can derive a prediction by maximizing F over the response variable for a specific given input $\mathbf{x}$. Hence, the general form of our hypotheses f is

$$f(\mathbf{x}; \boldsymbol{\lambda}) = \arg\max_{\mathbf{y} \in \mathcal{Y}} F(\mathbf{x}, \mathbf{y}; \boldsymbol{\lambda}) \tag{8.1}$$

where $\boldsymbol{\lambda} = \{\lambda_k\}$ denotes a parameter vector. Each function F can be seen as a score function that measures the compatibility of pairs $(\mathbf{x}, \mathbf{y})$. In this chapter, we restrict the space of F to linear or log-linear equations over some feature representation $\phi = \{\phi_k\}$, which is defined on the joint input-output space as

$$F(\mathbf{x}, \mathbf{y}; \boldsymbol{\lambda}) \triangleq \begin{cases} \boldsymbol{\lambda}^T \phi(\mathbf{x}, \mathbf{y}) & \text{(linear)} \\ Z(\mathbf{x})^{-1} \exp(\boldsymbol{\lambda}^T \phi(\mathbf{x}, \mathbf{y})) & \text{(log-linear)} \end{cases} \qquad (8.2)$$

where $\boldsymbol{\lambda}^T \phi(\mathbf{x}, \mathbf{y}) = \sum_k \lambda_k \phi_k(\mathbf{x}, \mathbf{y})$ and $Z(\mathbf{x})$ is a partition function that ensures that the probability sums to one for the log-linear case. That is, $Z(\mathbf{x})$ is defined as $Z(\mathbf{x}) \triangleq \sum_{\mathbf{y} \in \mathcal{Y}} \exp(\boldsymbol{\lambda}^T \phi(\mathbf{x}, \mathbf{y}))$, and $F(\mathbf{x}, \mathbf{y}; \boldsymbol{\lambda})$ is defined as $F(\mathbf{x}, \mathbf{y}; \boldsymbol{\lambda}) = p_{\boldsymbol{\lambda}}(\mathbf{y}|\mathbf{x})$.

Note that input sequence $\mathbf{x}$ and output sequence $\mathbf{y}$ are significantly correlated by a complex structure. In the sequential supervised learning task, the structure is simplified to a left-to-right sequence. Following this assumption, we can factorize the parameter vector as

$$\phi(\mathbf{x}, \mathbf{y}) = \sum_{t=1}^{T} \phi(\mathbf{x}, y_t, \mathbf{y}_{t-1:b}, t) \qquad (8.3)$$

$$\boldsymbol{\lambda}^T \phi(\mathbf{x}, \mathbf{y}) = \sum_{t=1}^{T} \boldsymbol{\lambda}^T \phi(\mathbf{x}, y_t, \mathbf{y}_{t-1:b}, t) \qquad (8.4)$$

where $\mathbf{y}_{t-1:b} = (y_{t-1}, y_{t-2}, \ldots, y_b)$ and $b \geq 1$.

Learning function f is obtained by optimizing loss function $\mathcal{R}$ given training data $\mathcal{D}$. We find $\boldsymbol{\lambda}^*$ by loss minimization criteria as

$$\boldsymbol{\lambda}^* = \arg\min_{\boldsymbol{\lambda}} \mathcal{R}(\mathcal{D}; \boldsymbol{\lambda}) = \arg\min_{\boldsymbol{\lambda}} \sum_{\mathcal{D}} \Delta(\mathbf{y}^{(n)}, f(\mathbf{x}^{(n)}; \boldsymbol{\lambda})) \qquad (8.5)$$

where $\Delta(\cdot, \cdot)$ is an arbitrary loss function in which $\Delta : \mathcal{Y} \times \mathcal{Y} \to \mathbb{R}$. For a linear model, one typically assumes 0–1 loss defined as

$$\Delta(\mathbf{y}, \mathbf{y}^*) = \begin{cases} 1 & \text{if } \mathbf{y} \neq \mathbf{y}^* \\ 0 & \text{otherwise} \end{cases}$$

For the log-linear model, on the other hand, we define log-loss as data likelihood by

$$\Delta(\mathbf{y}, \cdot) = -\log F(\mathbf{x}, \mathbf{y}; \boldsymbol{\lambda}) \qquad (8.6)$$

where $F(\mathbf{x}, \mathbf{y}; \boldsymbol{\lambda}) \triangleq p_{\boldsymbol{\lambda}}(\mathbf{y}|\mathbf{x})$.

In the machine learning community, the family of techniques for solving such learning problems is generally known as structured prediction or structured learning. Several state-of-the-art structured learning algorithms exist, including structured perceptron [5], conditional random fields (CRFs) [18], maximum-margin Markov networks, support vector machines for structured outputs [32], and search-based structured prediction [6]. Developers have many choices for learning the function $F(\mathbf{x}, \mathbf{y}, \boldsymbol{\lambda})$ using any structured prediction method.

In this chapter, we focus on CRFs, which are log-linear models as defined in Equation (8.2). While both linear and log-linear models are popular in natural language and machine learning fields, there is a clear reason to apply CRFs to SLU problems. CRFs are probabilistic models learned by maximum likelihood estimation, and thus they naturally estimate posterior probability $p_\lambda(\mathbf{y}|\mathbf{x})$. This characteristic is important in spoken dialogue applications because spoken language causes many errors in automatically recognized speech. Many recent studies have achieved state-of-the-art results on SLU tasks using CRFs [12, 20, 27, 35].

8.3 CONDITIONAL RANDOM FIELDS

CRFs are undirected graphical models that are used to specify the conditional probability of an assignment of output labels given a set of input observations [18]. This section reviews a basic CRF type—linear-chain CRFs, which are closely related to the sequential supervised learning of SLU.

8.3.1 Linear-Chain CRFs

Linear-chain CRFs are conditional probability distributions over label sequences which are conditioned on the input sequences [18, 31]. In linear-chain CRFs, one assumes that input and output sequences are significantly correlated by a left-to-right chain structure. Formally, they are defined as follows. Let $\mathbf{x}$ be a random vector that we observe, and $\mathbf{y}$ be a random vector that we wish to predict. A first-order linear-chain CRF defines conditional probability for a label sequence $\mathbf{y}$ to be

$$p_\lambda(\mathbf{y}|\mathbf{x}) = \frac{1}{Z(\mathbf{x})}\prod_{t=1}^{T}\Psi_t(y_t, y_{t-1}, \mathbf{x}) \tag{8.7}$$

where Ψ_t is the local potential, which denotes the factor at time t. $Z(\mathbf{x})$ is a partition function that ensures the probabilities of all state sequences summed to one. That is, $Z(\mathbf{x})$ is defined as $Z(\mathbf{x}) \triangleq \sum_y \prod_{t=1}^{T}\Psi_t(y_t, y_{t-1}, \mathbf{x})$. Note that $\Psi_t(y_t, y_{t-1}, \mathbf{x}) = \Psi_t(y_t, \mathbf{x})$ if $t = 1$.

We assume that the potentials factorize according to a set of features $\{\phi_k\}$ as

$$\Psi_t(y_t, y_{t-1}, \mathbf{x}) = \underbrace{\Psi_t^1(y_t, \mathbf{x})}_{observation} \cdot \underbrace{\Psi_t^2(y_t, y_{t-1})}_{transition} \tag{8.8}$$

$$\Psi_t^1(y_t, \mathbf{x}) = \exp\left(\sum_k \lambda_k^1 \phi_k^1(y_t, x_t)\right) \tag{8.9}$$

$$\Psi_t^2(y_t, y_{t-1}) = \exp\left(\sum_k \lambda_k^2 \phi_k^2(y_t, y_{t-1})\right) \tag{8.10}$$

where the feature functions can encode any aspect of the observation, $\phi_k^1(y_t, x_t)$, and can also encode a state transition, $\phi_k^2(y_t, y_{t-1})$, centered at the current

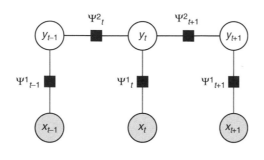

FIGURE 8.3

Linear-chain CRFs: An open node denotes a random variable; a shaded node has been set to its observed value.

time, t.[1] Large positive values for parameters λ_k^1 and λ_k^2 indicate a preference for such an event, while large negative values make the event unlikely. Figure 8.3 shows a graphical model for linear-chain CRFs.

When the dependencies between y_t and y_{t-1} are excluded, this special case is identical to a logistic regression model (known as a maximum entropy classifier in the natural language community [2]). A logistic regression model can therefore be viewed as an unstructured version of a CRF in which state transitions are ignored and the probability of sequence $p_\lambda(\mathbf{y}|\mathbf{x})$ is a product of per-state probability $p_\lambda(y_t|x_t)$ as follows:

$$p_\lambda(\mathbf{y}|\mathbf{x}) = \prod_{t=1}^{T} \underbrace{\frac{1}{Z(x_t)} \exp\left(\sum_k \lambda_k^1 \phi_k^1(y_t, x_t) \right)}_{p_\lambda(y_t|x_t)} \tag{8.11}$$

where $Z(x_t)$ is a per-state partition function, $Z(x_t) \triangleq \sum_{y_t} \exp\left(\sum_k \lambda_k^1 \phi_k^1(y_t, x_t)\right)$. To provide a unified view, we call the probability distribution $p_\lambda(y_t|x_t)$ the zero-order CRF. Note that this is a special case of linear-chain CRFs in which the length of input vector $\mathbf{x}$ is just one. Therefore, parameter estimation and inference algorithms for linear-chain CRFs can also be applied in a zero-order CRF.

8.3.2 Parameter Estimation

Estimation of linear-chain CRF parameters can be performed using conditional maximum log likelihood. Let $\mathcal{D} = \{(\mathbf{x}^{(n)}, \mathbf{y}^{(n)}) : 1 \leq n \leq N\}$ denote a training set and

---

[1]Although CRFs allow the score of a transition $y_{t-1} \rightarrow y_t$ to depend on the current observation vector as $\phi_k^2(y_t, y_{t-1}, \mathbf{x})$, for clarity we show that the transition receives the same score as $\phi_k^2(y_t, y_{t-1})$ regardless of the input. This model is defined as an HMM-like linear-chain CRF in [32]. We keep the same factorization throughout the chapter, but our formulae can be extended to allow the transition to depend on the observations with minor changes.

$\lambda = \{\lambda_k\} \in \mathbb{R}^K$ denote a parameter vector. Overfitting can be reduced by applying a regularization term to penalize a parameter vector whose norm is too large. A common choice of penalty is a spherical Gaussian prior with mean $\mu = 0$ and covariance matrix $\Sigma = \sigma^2 I$. The objective function is then defined as

$$\mathcal{L}(\lambda) = \sum_{n=1}^{N}\sum_{t=1}^{T}\sum_{k=1}^{K}\lambda_k\phi_k\left(y_t^{(n)}, y_{t-1}^{(n)}, \mathbf{x}^{(n)}\right) - \sum_{n=1}^{N}\log Z\left(\mathbf{x}^{(n)}\right) - \sum_{k=1}^{K}\frac{\lambda_k^2}{2\sigma^2} \qquad (8.12)$$

where for clarity ϕ_k represents a feature function for all local functions ϕ_k^1 and ϕ_k^2. This function is known to be convex, which guarantees convergence to the global optimum.

Differentiating Equation (8.12) can give the optimal parameter vector λ^* as

$$\frac{\partial\mathcal{L}}{\partial\lambda_k} = \underbrace{\sum_{n=1}^{N}\sum_{t=1}^{T}\phi_k(y_t^{(n)}, y_{t-1}^{(n)}, \mathbf{x}^{(n)})}_{E_{\tilde{p}}\langle\phi_k\rangle} - \underbrace{\sum_{n=1}^{N}\sum_{t=1}^{T}\sum_{y,y'}\phi_k(y, y', \mathbf{x}^{(n)})p_\lambda(y, y'|\mathbf{x}^{(n)})}_{E_p\langle\phi_k\rangle} - \frac{\lambda_k}{\sigma^2} \qquad (8.13)$$

where $E_{\tilde{p}}$ is the empirical distribution of training data and E_p denotes the expectation with respect to distribution p_λ. E_p can be efficiently calculated by dynamic programming (described in Section 8.4). After calculating $E_{\tilde{p}}$ and E_p, numerical optimization techniques can be used to estimate the parameters of linear-chain CRFs. We optimize the parameters using a limited-memory version of the quasi-Newton method (L-BFGS), which uses approximation to the Hessian [21]. The L-BFGS method converges super-linearly to the solution, so it can be an efficient optimization technique for large-scale problems.

8.3.3 Inference

There are two common inference problems for linear-chain CRFs. First, the marginal distributions and $Z(\mathbf{x})$ must be calculated during training. Second, the most likely labeling $\mathbf{y}^* = \arg\max_{\mathbf{y}} p_\lambda(\mathbf{y}|\mathbf{x})$ must be computed during prediction. Both inference problems are efficiently performed by forms of dynamic programming known as forward-backward and Viterbi algorithms [18].

The marginal probability distributions and the partition function $Z(\mathbf{x})$ are calculated via the forward-backward algorithm. We introduce notation for forward-backward recursions. The forward values $\alpha_t(i)$ are the sum of the unnormalized scores for all partial paths starting at $t = 0$ and converging at $y_t = i$ at time t. The backward values $\beta_t(i)$ similarly define the sum of unnormalized scores for all partial paths starting at time $t + 1$ with state $y_{t+1} = j$, continuing until the end of the sequences, $t = T + 1$.

We define the forward vector $\alpha_t(\cdot)$ and the backward vector $\beta_t(\cdot)$ as follows:

$$\alpha_t(i) \triangleq \sum_{i\in\mathcal{Y}_a}\Psi_t(i, j, \mathbf{x})\cdot\alpha_{t-1}(i) \qquad (8.14)$$

$$\beta_t(i) \triangleq \sum_{j\in\mathcal{Y}_a}\Psi_t(j, i, \mathbf{x})\cdot\beta_{t+1}(j) \qquad (8.15)$$

where the base values of α are defined by $\alpha_0(i) = 1$ if $i = \mathbf{start}$ and $\alpha_0(i) = 0$ otherwise. Similarly, the base values of β are defined by $\beta_{T+1}(i) = 1$ if $i = \text{end}$ and $\beta_{T+1}(y_{T+1}) = 0$ otherwise. The probabilities often involved in forward-backward recursions become too small to be represented with numerical precision, however. One solution to this problem is to normalize each of the vectors α_t and β_t to sum to 1, thereby magnifying small values [31].

In the forward backward algorithm for linear-chain CRFs, recursion can be used to show that the sum of final α yields the mass of all state sequences; thus $\alpha_{T+1}(\text{end}) = \sum_{i=1}^{I}\alpha_T(i)$. Then we define $Z(\mathbf{x})$ as

$$Z(\mathbf{x}) \triangleq \sum_{y \in \mathcal{Y}} \prod_{t=1}^{T} \Psi_t(y_t, y_{t-1}, \mathbf{x}) = \alpha_{T+1}(\text{end}) \tag{8.16}$$

Finally, using forward-backward recursions, we can define the marginal distributions as follows:

$$p_\lambda(y_t = i|\mathbf{x}) = \frac{\alpha_t(i)\beta_t(i)}{Z(\mathbf{x})} \tag{8.17}$$

$$p_\lambda(y_{t-1} = j, y_t = i|\mathbf{x}) = \frac{\alpha_{t-1}(j)\Psi_t(y_t, y_{t-1}, \mathbf{x})\beta_t(i)}{Z(\mathbf{x})} \tag{8.18}$$

The graphical interpretation of marginals is given in Figure 8.4.

To compute the globally most probable assignment $\mathbf{y}^* = \text{argmax}_{\mathbf{y} \in \mathcal{Y}}\, p_\lambda(\mathbf{y}|\mathbf{x})$, we can use a similar dynamic programming technique, in which all summations in Equation (8.14) are replaced by maximization. This yields the δ recursion:

$$\delta_t(i) = \max_{j \in y_a} \Psi_t(y_t = i, y_{t-1} = j, \mathbf{x})\delta_{t-1}(j)$$

$$= \Psi_t^1(y_t = i, \mathbf{x})\left(\max_{j \in y_a} \Psi_t^2(y_t = i, y_{t\ 1} = j)\delta_{t-1}(j) \right) \tag{8.19}$$

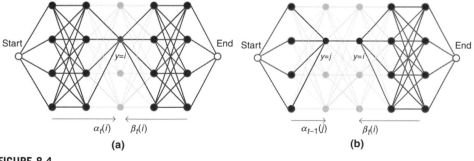

(a)   **(b)**

FIGURE 8.4

Marginal distributions for linear-chain CRFs: (a) All paths might pass a node $y_t = i$, $p_\lambda(y_t = i\,|\mathbf{x})$; (b) all paths might pass an edge $y_{t-1} = j$, $y_t\,t = i$, $p_\lambda\,(y_{t-1} = j,\ y_t = i|\mathbf{x})$.

8.4 EFFICIENT ALGORITHMS FOR INFERENCE AND LEARNING

SLU systems encounter a conflict between their limited computing power and the computational complexity of their algorithms. Most applications for ambient intelligence typically assume that the system has limited computation resources. However, many SLU problems involve large sets of slot/value attributes, even for domain-specific dialogue systems. A huge set of attributes—that is, a large state space $\mathcal{Y}$ and huge set of feature vectors ϕ—causes high time and space complexities; hence, systems may require considerable computation time and memory. Reducing these complexities is an important research area in machine learning. To tackle this problem, efficient algorithms should be developed to make CRFs more feasible for ambient intelligence environments. In this section, we explore two advanced methods for CRFs to reduce computation requirements: fast inference algorithms and feature selection algorithms.

8.4.1 Fast Inference for Saving Computation Time

The time complexity of inference for linear-chain CRFs is $O(T|\mathcal{Y}_a|^2|)$, where T is the size of the sequence. An exact inference can be conducted efficiently if $|\mathcal{Y}_a|$ is not large. When it is, however, the inference is often prohibitively expensive. This problem can be alleviated by introducing approximate inference methods based on the reduction of the search spaces to be explored.

The basic idea is that the output state space $\mathcal{Y}$ can be reduced to a smaller partial space $\mathcal{A}$. Intuitively, there are a large number of *unseen* or *unsupported* transitions $y_{t-1} \rightarrow y_t$—that is, only a small part of the possible labeling set is informative. Formally, the sequence label set can be decomposed as $\mathcal{Y} = \mathcal{A} \cup \mathcal{A}^c$, where $\mathcal{A}$ is the active set of labels and $\mathcal{A}^c$ is the remaining set. In this case, the inference algorithm need not calculate marginals or maximums (more generally messages) to label $\mathcal{A}^c$ precisely, and this fact can be exploited by ignoring paths that consist of unsupported transitions. This is achieved by fixing the paths' potentials to some constant value ω. We call this scheme *a partial-space inference* because the full-space $\mathcal{Y}$ is reduced to a small partial space $\mathcal{A}$. For tasks in which the partial state space is sufficiently small (i.e., $|\mathcal{A}| < |\mathcal{Y}|$), both decoding times and training times are remarkably reduced in linear-chain CRFs.

Now we formally describe the partial-space inference algorithm by introducing ω. For clarity, we first define the local factors as

$$\Psi_{t,i}^1 \triangleq \Psi_t^1(y_t = i, \mathbf{x}) \tag{8.20}$$

$$\Psi_{j,i}^2 \triangleq \Psi_t^2(y_{t-1} = j, y_t = i) \tag{8.21}$$

Then we reformulate the α recursion as follows:

$$
\alpha_t(i) = \sum_{j \in \mathcal{Y}_a} \Psi^1_{t,i} \Psi^2_{j,i} \alpha_{t-1}(j)
$$

$$
= \Psi^1_{t,i} \left(\sum_{j \in \mathcal{A}_i} \Psi^2_{j,i} \alpha_{t-1}(j) + \sum_{j \in \mathcal{A}^c_i} \omega \alpha_{t-1}(j) \right)
$$

$$
= \Psi^1_{t,i} \left(\sum_{j \in \mathcal{A}_i} \Psi^2_{j,i} \alpha_{t-1}(j) + \sum_{j \in \mathcal{A}^c_i} \omega \alpha_{t-1}(j) + \sum_{j \in \mathcal{A}_i} \omega \alpha_{t-1}(j) - \sum_{j \in \mathcal{A}_i} \omega \alpha_{t-1}(j) \right)
$$

$$
= \Psi^1_{t,i} \left(\sum_{j \in \mathcal{A}_i} \left(\Psi^2_{j,i} - \omega \right) \alpha_{t-1}(j) + \omega \right)
$$

(8.22)

where $\mathcal{A}_i$ is an active set of atomic labels of $\mathcal{Y}_a$ given the label $y_t = i$, and ω is a shared transition parameter value for the set $\mathcal{A}^c_i$, in which the transition score is shared across all unsupported transitions. That is, $\Psi^2_{j,i} = \omega$. Note that $\mathcal{Y}_a = \mathcal{A}_i \cup \mathcal{A}^c_i$, and the sum of all α at time t is scaled to equal $1 - \Sigma_i \alpha_t(i) = 1$. Because unsupported transitions are calculated simultaneously using ω, the complexity of Equation (8.22) is reduced to $O(T|\mathcal{A}_i||\mathcal{Y}_a|)$. Modified α recursion is illustrated in Figure 8.5.

Similarly, β recursion can be reformulated as

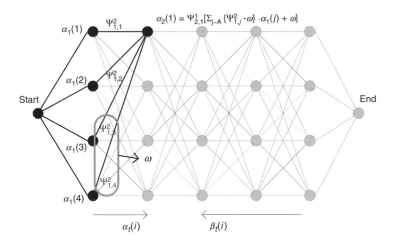

FIGURE 8.5

Illustration of partial space α recursion: Unsupported transitions $\Psi^2_{j,i}$ (depicted in edges) are fixed by a value ω.

$$\beta_{t-1}(j) = \sum_{i \in \mathcal{Y}_a} \Psi^1_{t,i} \Psi^2_{j,i} \beta_t(i)$$

$$= \sum_{i \in \mathcal{A}_j} \Psi^1_{t,i} \Psi^2_{j,i} \omega \beta_t(i) + \sum_{i \in \mathcal{A}^c_j} \Psi^1_{t,i} \omega \beta_t(i)$$

$$= \sum_{i \in \mathcal{A}_j} \Psi^1_{t,i} \Psi^2_{j,i} \beta_t(i) + \sum_{i \in \mathcal{A}^c_j} \Psi^1_{t,i} \omega \beta_t(i) + \sum_{i \in \mathcal{A}_j} \Psi^1_{t,i} \omega \beta_t(i) - \sum_{i \in \mathcal{A}_j} \Psi^1_{t,i} \omega \beta_t(i) \qquad (8.23)$$

$$= \sum_{i \in \mathcal{A}_j} \Psi^1_{t,i} \left(\Psi^2_{j,i} - \omega \right) \beta_t(i) + \omega \sum_{i \in \mathcal{Y}} \Psi^1_{t,i} \beta_t(i)$$

Lastly, we can derive modified Viterbi recursion to predict a best sequence of output given a new test point $\mathbf{x}$ as

$$\delta_t(i) = \max_{j \in \mathcal{Y}_a} \Psi^1_{t,i} \Psi^2_{j,i} \delta_{t-1}(j)$$

$$= \Psi^1_{t,i} \left(\max_{j \in \mathcal{Y}_a} \Psi^2_{j,i} \delta_{t-1}(j) \right) \qquad (8.24)$$

$$= \Psi^1_{t,i} \left(\max\{ \max_{j \in \mathcal{A}_i} \Psi^2_{j,i} \delta_{t-1}(j), \max_{j \in \mathcal{A}^c_i} \omega \delta_{t-1}(j) \} \right)$$

Key issues for implementing the partial space inference are selecting $\mathcal{A}$ and ω. A feasible set of $\mathcal{A}$ is first defined heuristically or statistically. The simplest method is to prune transitions that never or rarely occur in training examples. This is a simple feature selection heuristic that can be generalized using general feature selection methods, in which we can select the active transition set $\mathcal{A}$ using some computational measures. Next the value of ω should be determined. The theory for partial space inference is independent of the specific value of ω, but the detailed algorithms are usually implemented in different ways. There are three algorithms:

- $\omega = 1$. In this case, we set $\Psi^2_{j,i} = 1$ for unsupported transitions, that is, $\lambda^2_k = 0$. Intuitively, we move zero-parameters ($\lambda^2_k = 0$) from the inside to the outside of the summation in Equations (8.22), (8.23), and (8.24); hence, we call this the *zero-out* method. Note that this exactly calculates α, β, and δ values if the unsupported transition features are not parameterized in the model.

- $\omega = 0$. In this case we also ignore the transition scores $\Psi^2_{j,i}$ and the previous values for recursion, such as $\alpha_{t-1}(j)$ and $\beta_t(i)$. That is, we remove unsupported transitions and observations. This scheme is closely related to the beam search method. In particular, if $\mathcal{A}_i$ is defined by the quantity α_{t-1}, it is dynamically selected by removing the state i with $\alpha_{t-1}(i) < \varepsilon$. This special case of pruning was published as the "sparse forward-backward using minimum divergence beam" algorithm [22].

- $\omega = c$. This assigns a constant value c for $\mathcal{A}^c$, labeling rather than ignoring them. The value of c is estimated in the training phase, so c is a shared parameter for $\mathcal{A}^c$. This method leads to more robust parameter estimation if the unsupported transition features potentially affect the model's performance. Known as the tied potential method, this algorithm exploits the regularities of the transition features (y_{t-1}, y_t) [4].

Although it was derived for the linear-chain case, the algorithm can be easily extended to the general structured case. Using it, we expect to achieve fast training and prediction for more complex structures. The empirical results will be presented in Section 8.6.3.

8.4.2 Feature Selection for Saving Computation Memory

In many natural language tasks, input vectors may include rich and largely unconstrained features (e.g., words, prefixes and suffixes, capitalization, n-grams, part-of-speech tags, phrase chunk labels, syntactic parse trees, membership in domain-specific lexicons). Moreover, the feature functions ϕ_k are ordinarily chosen to have a binary form; hence, the function space of ϕ is likely to be high-dimensional. For example, [30] used 3.8 million features to match state-of-the-art results in a standard natural language task. Such a huge set is problematic because it imposes significant memory and time requirements.

A standard approach to alleviate this problem is the use of feature selection techniques that reduce irrelevant features. Many machine learning publications present methods based on significance tests (e.g., information gain) or dimensionality reduction (e.g., principal components analysis). In this section, we introduce an alternative for selecting features based on the automatic feature induction algorithm [14, 19, 24]. This is a novel and efficient method for feature selection in an exponential model, especially for CRFs.

To select a relevant subset from a large collection of features, we begin by specifying the feature gain, which measures the effect of adding a feature. Feature gain is defined as the improvement in log likelihood in training data.

Definition 1. $\mathcal{L}^{old}(\boldsymbol{\lambda})$ *is the log likelihood of the previous model, and $\mathcal{L}^{new}(\boldsymbol{\lambda}, \mu)$ is the log likelihood for a new model where μ is a parameter of an adding feature to be found and $\varphi(y, \mathbf{x})$ is a corresponding feature function. Feature gain is thus the difference between the new and the old log likelihood as $\Delta \mathcal{L}(\boldsymbol{\lambda}, \mu) = \mathcal{L}^{new}(\boldsymbol{\lambda}, \mu) - \mathcal{L}^{old}(\boldsymbol{\lambda})$.*

The feature induction algorithm greedily finds the subset of features that improves the log likelihood. That is, our goal is to iteratively select a set of candidates that maximizes the gain $\Delta \mathcal{L}(\boldsymbol{\lambda}, \mu)$ and then adds it to the training data. This algorithm can be summarized by two computations: calculating $\mathcal{L}^{old}(\boldsymbol{\lambda})$ and calculating $\mathcal{L}^{new}(\boldsymbol{\lambda}, \mu)$. Calculating $\mathcal{L}^{old}(\boldsymbol{\lambda})$ is equivalent to learning the CRF model mentioned in Section 8.3.2. The remaining step is estimation of the new log likelihood $\mathcal{L}^{new}(\boldsymbol{\lambda}, \mu)$. Unfortunately, when a new feature $\varphi(y, \mathbf{x})$ is included, the optimal values of all parameters $\boldsymbol{\lambda}$ change. We therefore assume that the addition of a feature $\varphi(y, \mathbf{x})$ affects only μ, leaving the other parameters unchanged. Then we can find the optimal parameter μ^* to achieve maximum feature gain as in the following equation:

$$\Delta \mathcal{L}(\boldsymbol{\lambda}, \mu^*) = \max_{\mu} \Delta \mathcal{L}(\boldsymbol{\lambda}, \mu) = \max_{\mu} (\mathcal{L}^{new}(\boldsymbol{\lambda}, \mu) - \mathcal{L}^{old}(\boldsymbol{\lambda})) \qquad (8.25)$$

The algorithm iteratively calculates the feature gain and selects the features with the highest values. Each iteration requires optimization of parameter μ.

Following [19, 24], the mean field approximation allows us to treat the calculation of $p_\lambda(\mathbf{y}|\mathbf{x})$ as an independent inference problem rather than as a sequential inference problem. That is, we approximate $p_\lambda(\mathbf{y}|\mathbf{x})$ by the mean field $p_\lambda(\mathbf{y}|\mathbf{x}) = \prod_t p_\lambda(\mathbf{y}_t|\mathbf{x}_t)$. This is the independent product of marginal distributions at each position t. Moreover, we can take advantage of ignoring the transition feature $\Psi_t^2(y_{t-1}, y_t)$ to calculate a gain of the feature. Thus, we can calculate the marginal probability of state y with an adding feature given observation $\mathbf{x}$ separately.

Formally, we approximate the log-likelihood $L(\boldsymbol{\lambda}, \mu)$ as

$$L(\boldsymbol{\lambda}, \mu) = \sum_{i=1}^{N} \log p_{\lambda+\mu}(\mathbf{y}|\mathbf{x}) \approx \sum_{i=1}^{N} \log \prod_{t=1}^{T_i} p_{\lambda+\mu}(y_t|x_t) = \sum_{i=1}^{N} \sum_{t=1}^{T_i} \log p_{\lambda+\mu}(y_t|x_t) \qquad (8.26)$$

Note that $p_{\lambda+\mu}(y_t|x_t)$ is a zero-order CRF model and can be easily calculated. Because all training positions are independent, we can remove the time index t and replace Equation 8.26 with $\sum_{i=1}^{M} \log p_{\lambda+\mu}(y|x)$, where M is the total number of independent training samples $\left(= \sum_{i=1}^{N} \sum_{t=1}^{T_i} 1\right)$ that is equal to the number of words in the training data. By adding a new candidate feature, we obtain an additional feature model:

$$p_{\lambda+\mu}(y|x) = \frac{\exp(\sum_k \lambda_k \phi_k(y, x) + \mu\varphi(y, x))}{Z(x)}$$

$$= \frac{\exp(\sum_k \lambda_k \phi_k(y, x) + \mu\varphi(y, x))}{\sum_y \exp(\sum_k \lambda_k \phi_k(y, x) + \mu\varphi(y, x))} = \frac{p_\lambda(y|x) \exp(\mu\varphi(y, x))}{\sum_y p_\lambda(y|x) \exp(\mu\varphi(y, x))} \qquad (8.27)$$

The feature gain can be calculated on the old model that was trained in previous iterations. With the candidate feature set, the gain is derived as

$$\Delta L(\boldsymbol{\lambda}, \mu) = \underbrace{\sum_{i=1}^{M} \log\left(p_{\lambda+\mu}\left(y^{(i)}|\mathbf{x}^{(i)}\right)\right) - \frac{\mu^2}{2\sigma^2} - \sum_{k=1}^{K} \frac{\lambda_k^2}{2\sigma^2}}_{L^{new}(\boldsymbol{\lambda}, \mu)} - \underbrace{\left(\sum_{i=1}^{M} \log\left(p_\lambda\left(y^{(i)}|\mathbf{x}^{(i)}\right)\right) - \sum_{k=1}^{K} \frac{\lambda_k^2}{2\sigma^2}\right)}_{L^{old}(\boldsymbol{\lambda})}$$

$$= \sum_{i=1}^{M} \log\left(\frac{\exp(\mu\varphi(y^{(i)}, \mathbf{x}^{(i)}))}{\sum_y p_\lambda(y^{(i)}|\mathbf{x}^{(i)}) \exp(\mu\varphi(y^{(i)}, \mathbf{x}^{(i)}))}\right) - \frac{\mu^2}{2\sigma^2} \qquad (8.28)$$

$$= \sum_{i=1}^{M} \mu\varphi(y^{(i)}, \mathbf{x}^{(i)}) - \sum_{i=1}^{M} \log\left(\sum_y p_\lambda(y^{(i)}|\mathbf{x}^{(i)}) \exp(\mu\varphi(y^{(i)}, \mathbf{x}^{(i)}))\right) - \frac{\mu^2}{2\sigma^2}$$

While estimating the gain, we can efficiently assess many candidate features in parallel by assuming that the old features remain fixed. The optimal value of μ^* can be calculated by Newton's method. The first-order derivatives are

$$\Delta L'(\boldsymbol{\lambda}, \mu) = \sum_{i=1}^{M} \varphi\left(y^{(i)}, \mathbf{x}^{(i)}\right) - \sum_{i=1}^{M} \sum_y p_{\lambda+\mu}\left(y^{(i)}|\mathbf{x}^{(i)}\right) \varphi\left(y^{(i)}, \mathbf{x}^{(i)}\right) - \frac{\mu}{\sigma^2} \qquad (8.29)$$

And the second-order derivatives are

$$\Delta \mathcal{L}''(\boldsymbol{\lambda}, \mu) = -\sum_{i=1}^{M}\sum_{y} p_{\lambda+\mu}\left(y^{(i)}|\mathbf{x}^{(i)}\right)\left\{\varphi\left(y^{(i)}, \mathbf{x}^{(i)}\right)^2 \right.$$

$$\left. -\varphi\left(y^{(i)}, \mathbf{x}^{(i)}\right)\sum_{y'} p_{\lambda+\mu}\left(y'^{(i)}|\mathbf{x}^{(i)}\right)\varphi\left(y'^{(i)}, \mathbf{x}^{(i)}\right)\right\} - \frac{1}{\sigma^2} \tag{8.30}$$

Finally, we can obtain the optimum parameter via a Newton update:

$$\mu^{new} = \mu^{old} - \frac{\Delta \mathcal{L}'(\boldsymbol{\lambda}, \mu^{old})}{\Delta \mathcal{L}''(\boldsymbol{\lambda}, \mu^{old})} \tag{8.31}$$

Using this scheme, we can select a small number of candidates and retrain the model using them. We iteratively perform the selection algorithm with some stop conditions (maximum number of iterations or no added features up to the gain threshold). We use only the zero-order CRF model for the feature induction procedure, so the resulting algorithm is quite efficient. Empirical results of modeling nonlocal dependency in SLU tasks demonstrate that the proposed algorithm is efficient and effective [14].

8.5 TRANSFER LEARNING FOR SPOKEN LANGUAGE UNDERSTANDING

In this section, we present a *transfer-learning* approach to the SLU problem in which tasks and knowledge from multiple domains can be incorporated. To implement SLU with transfer learning, we introduce a novel probabilistic model: *triangular-chain CRFs* [15], which effectively learns multiple tasks in parallel and allows use of domain-independent patterns among domains to create a better model for the target domain.

8.5.1 Transfer Learning

The current standard SLU system often uses a cascade or pipeline architecture where all subproblems are sequentially solved. In the cascade architecture, SLU examines user utterances to first predict particular NEs and then infer user intent, or DAs. In another example in multi-domain SLU, the current standard system often uses a domain detection method that classifies the user utterance into a predefined domain type. The classified utterance is forwarded to a domain-dependent SLU module where the semantic frame is defined for that domain.

In the pipeline architecture, each SLU module is learned using task-dependent data, and typical learning methods can be used. However, the pipeline architecture has a significant drawback: Current modules cannot use the information from modules used later in the process. Our insight is that the related processes of SLU can be learned simultaneously to improve the performance of each. To achieve this capability, we introduce transfer learning for multi-domain SLU.

In transfer learning, a model trained to learn one task is used to improve another model that is devoted to a related task. In the machine learning literature, transfer learning is typically divided into two types. When the input distribution changes but the output labels remain the same, the problem is called *domain adaptation* [6]. When the output labels are also allowed to change, the problem is called *multi-task learning* [2]. Most approaches to both problems aim to find a way of altering the classifier that was learned on the source task (or source domain) to fit the specifics of the target task (or target domain).

The key idea in our approach is to concurrently solve the two related problems of sequence labeling and sequence classification using transfer learning, especially multitask learning. In this framework, we jointly predict the best labels $(\mathbf{y}^*, z^*)$ using a probabilistic model $p(\mathbf{y}, z|\mathbf{x})$ that is trained from the joint data $(\mathbf{x}^{(n)}, \mathbf{y}^{(n)}, z^{(n)})_{n=1}^{N}$. Our framework regards $\mathbf{y}$ as a *sequence* and z as a *topic* (meta-sequence information), so the problem can be viewed as one of multi-topic sequence labeling. The goal is to learn dependencies between sequences and their corresponding topics; these dependencies provide information relevant to improving the performance of this approach. Intuitively, co-occurrence patterns between $\mathbf{y}$ and z are important because they can be exploited to improve prediction accuracy in both methods. This intuition is applied to probabilistic sequence modeling to develop a novel method, triangular-chain CRFs.

8.5.2 Triangular-Chain Conditional Random Fields

A probability distribution $p(\mathbf{y}, z|\mathbf{x})$ can be learned using triangular-chain CRFs, which are defined as follows. Let a random vector $\mathbf{x}$ be a sequence of input observations, a random vector $\mathbf{y}$ be a sequence of output labels that we wish to predict, and a random variable z be an output variable that indicates a topic or meta-sequence information. For example, in joint prediction of DAs and NEs [13], $\mathbf{x}$ may be a word sequence, $\mathbf{y}$ may be an NE sequence, and z may be a DA (or the speaker's intent). We can write the data as $(\mathbf{x}, \mathbf{y}, z) = (x_0, z, x_1, y_1, x_2, y_2, \ldots, x_T, y_T)$, where x_0 indicates an observation feature variable for topic z. Using this additional notation, we can integrate other knowledge into the model, say a history of DAs and of system actions and user profiles available in the dialogue manager. Then we formally define the triangular-chain CRFs as follows.

Definition 2. *Let $\mathbf{y}$ and $\mathbf{x}$ be random vectors, z be a random variable, λ be a parameter vector, and $\{\Phi_k\}$ be a set of real-valued feature functions. Then a triangular-chain conditional random field is a conditional probability distribution $p_\lambda(\mathbf{y}, z|\mathbf{x})$ that takes the form*

$$p_\lambda(\mathbf{y}, z|\mathbf{x}) = \frac{1}{Z(\mathbf{x})} \prod_{t=1}^{T} \left(\Psi_t(z, y_t, y_{t-1}, \mathbf{x}) \right) \cdot \Phi(z, \mathbf{x}) \tag{8.32}$$

where Ψ_t and Φ are the potentials over triangular-chain graphs and $Z(\mathbf{x})$ is a partition function defined to ensure that the distribution is normalized as

$Z(\mathbf{x}) \triangleq \sum_{\mathbf{y},z} \prod_{t=1}^{T} (\Psi_t(z,y_t,y_{t-1},\mathbf{x})) \cdot \Phi(z,\mathbf{x})$, *and where ϕ_k and λ parameterize the potentials Ψ_t and Φ.*

Triangular-chain CRFs have local factors that are divided by time-dependent potential Ψ_t and time-independent potential Φ. Thus, Ψ_t applies to the state of a sequence at time t and Φ applies to the entire sequence. Accordingly, a triangular-chain structure is constructed with these two factors. Obviously, Φ plays a prior role in classifying z. If we assume that Φ is uniform, then z depends only on $\mathbf{x}_{1:T} = \{x_1,\ldots,x_T\}$ and $\mathbf{y}_{1:T} = \{y_1,\ldots,y_T\}$.

Figure 8.6 shows a graphical model for the triangular-chain CRF, which can be seen as an integration of a linear-chain CRF and a zero-order CRF. Thus, variables and potentials can naturally derive from the two: From zero-order CRFs, $\mathbf{x}_0$ is an observation and Φ is a potential function for predicting z; from linear-chain CRFs, $\{x_t\}$ for $t = 1,\ldots,T$ are observations and Ψ_t are potential functions for predicting $\mathbf{y}$. We combine a linear-chain and a zero-order CRF by adding probabilistic connections between $\mathbf{y}$ and z—that is, adding edges between them in an undirected graphical model. In addition, the links between z and $\{x_t\}$ are appended to represent the relations of topic and sequence. In other words, the observation of sequence data is assumed to depend on topic.

Now we describe two configurations for triangular-chain CRFs.

Model1

We assume that a random variable z directly influences random vectors $\mathbf{x}$ and $\mathbf{y}$. Then we factorize Ψ_t and Φ as follows:

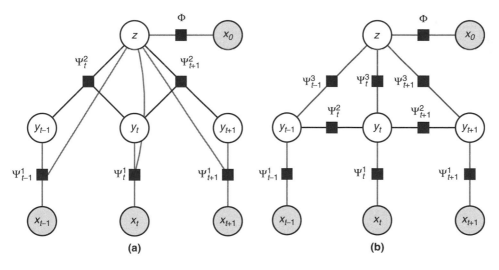

(a)   (b)

FIGURE 8.6

Graphical representations of triangular-chain CRFs. In factor graphs Model1 (a) and Model2 (b), a solid square denotes a local factor to be used for inference.

$$\Psi_t(z, y_t, y_{t-1}, \mathbf{x}) = \underbrace{\Psi_t^1(z, y_t, \mathbf{x})}_{observation} \cdot \underbrace{\Psi_t^2(z, y_t, y_{t-1})}_{transition} \tag{8.33}$$

$$\underbrace{\Phi(z, \mathbf{x})}_{prior} = \exp\left(\sum_k \lambda_k^0 \phi_k^0(z, x_0)\right) \tag{8.34}$$

$$\Psi_t^1(z, y_t, \mathbf{x}) = \exp\left(\sum_k \lambda_k^1 \phi_k^1(z, y_t, x_t)\right) \tag{8.35}$$

$$\Psi_t^2(z, y_t, y_{t-1}) = \exp\left(\sum_k \lambda_k^2 \phi_k^2(z, y_t, y_{t-1})\right) \tag{8.36}$$

We call this a *hard-constraint* model (MODEL1). The feature functions encode any aspect of the observation $\phi_k^1(z, y_t, x_t)$ and the transition $\phi_k^2(z, y_t, y_{t-1})$ for the sequence, centered at the current time, t; and the observation for topic, $\phi_k^0(z, x_0)$. Note that both $\phi_k^1(z, y_t, x_t)$ and $\phi_k^2(z, y_t, y_{t-1})$ represent the z-dependent transitions and observations, so the assignment of sequence labels is highly dependent on topic z. Figure 8.6(a) shows the factor graph representation [19] of MODEL1 for visualizing the model's factor and structures.

Model2

We can derive a special case of MODEL1 by setting $\Psi_t^1(z, y_t, \mathbf{x}) = \Psi_t^1(y_t, \mathbf{x})$. This factorization is reasonable for some applications, such as topic-dependent speech recognition. The topic z (e.g., speaker, genre, or dialogue act) influences the language model as $\Psi_t^2(z, y_t, y_{t-1})$, but the emission of the speech $\mathbf{x}$ depends only on the words $\mathbf{y}$, not on the topic, as in $\Psi_t^1(y_t, \mathbf{x})$. Furthermore, we can derive a more factorized model by assuming that the state transition $y_{t-1} \to y_t$ is independent of the topic z.

We assume that a random variable z does not directly influence random vectors $\mathbf{x}$. For clarity, we assume that z is independent of $\mathbf{x}_{1:T}$ given $\mathbf{y}_{1:T}$. Then we factorize Ψ_t and Φ as follows:

$$\Psi_t(z, y_t, y_{t-1}, \mathbf{x}) = \underbrace{\Psi_t^1(y_t, \mathbf{x})}_{observation} \cdot \underbrace{\Psi_t^2(y_t, y_{t-1})}_{transition} \cdot \underbrace{\Psi_t^3(z, y_t)}_{z-\mathbf{y}\ edge} \tag{8.37}$$

$$\Psi_t^3(z, y_t) = \exp\left(\sum_k \lambda_k^3 \phi_k^3(z, y_t)\right) \tag{8.38}$$

We call this a *soft-constraint* model (MODEL2). It has the same factors Ψ_t^1 and Ψ_t^2 as in linear-chain CRFs (Equations (8.9) and (8.10)) and has the same factor Φ as in MODEL1 (Equation (8.34)). Ψ_t^3 denotes a soft constraint of interdependency between z and $\mathbf{y}$. We assume that the state transition is the same for all values of z; that is, z operates as an observation feature to predict a sequence of labels. Figure 8.6(b) shows the factor graph representation of MODEL2.

MODEL2 requires only $|\mathcal{Y}_a| \times |\mathcal{Z}|$ additional memory to store dependencies between $\mathbf{y}$ and z, and so if should have a smaller parameter size than MODEL1.

This characteristic reduces the time complexity in large-scale applications. Theoretically, the time complexities of inference in MODEL1 and MODEL2 are the same. In practice, especially with large-scale data, MODEL2 can calculate the potentials more efficiently than MODEL1 can because local factors for the observations and transitions, Ψ_t^1 and Ψ_t^2, are calculated z times more often in MODEL1.

8.5.3 Parameter Estimation and Inference

Similar to linear-chain CRFs, parameter estimation of triangular-chain CRFs can be performed using conditional maximum log likelihood. Let $\{(\mathbf{x}^{(n)}, \mathbf{y}^{(n)}, z^{(n)}): 1 \leq n \leq N\}$ denote a training set and $\boldsymbol{\lambda} = \{\lambda_k\} \in \mathbb{R}^K$ denote a parameter function for $p(\mathbf{y}|z, \mathbf{x})$ and $p(z|\mathbf{y}, \mathbf{x})$ as follows:

$$\mathcal{L}^1(\boldsymbol{\lambda}') = \sum_{n=1}^{N}\sum_{t=1}^{T} \log p_{\boldsymbol{\lambda}'}\left(y_t^{(n)}|y_{t-1}^{(n)}, y_{t+1}^{(n)}, z^{(n)}, \mathbf{x}^{(n)}\right) \tag{8.39}$$

$$\mathcal{L}^2(\boldsymbol{\lambda}') = \sum_{n=1}^{N} \log p_{\boldsymbol{\lambda}'}\left(z^{(n)}|\mathbf{y}^{(n)}, \mathbf{x}^{(n)}\right) \tag{8.40}$$

Then merge them to seed the training procedure for triangular-chain CRFs.

There are two common inference problems for triangular-chain CRFs: (1) computing the marginal distributions for $p_{\boldsymbol{\lambda}}(z, y_t|\mathbf{x})$, $p_{\boldsymbol{\lambda}}(z, y_t, y_{t-1}|\mathbf{x})$, and $p_{\boldsymbol{\lambda}}(z|\mathbf{x})$ for the gradient calculation and computing a partition function $Z(\mathbf{x})$; and (2) computing the Viterbi decoding to predict a new instance. Intuitively, the former is used to estimate the parameter vector in training, and the latter is executed for evaluating testing data.

Triangular-chain CRFs form parallel linear-chain structures so that there are $|Z|$ planes of linear-chain search space and one plane corresponding to a realization of one z. Figure 8.7 describes the search space in triangular-chain CRFs, where

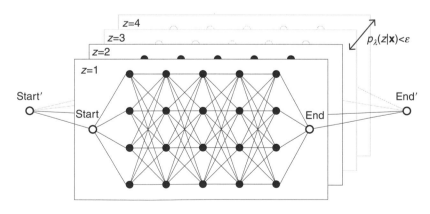

FIGURE 8.7

Search space in a triangular-chain CRF. Each plane corresponds to one linear-chain CRF which has a **start** and an **end** node. All planes are parallel but are connected by the **start'** and **end'** nodes.

a 3-dimensional space is explored rather than a 2-dimensional space. Note that no path connects to nodes on other planes. Thus, the inference of triangular-chain CRFs straightforwardly uses $|\mathcal{Z}|$-way parallel inferences for linear-chain CRFs. Therefore, for a value of $z = k$, we perform the inference on the k space and repeat this procedure for all values of z using a modified Viterbi decoding algorithm to find the best path in the parallel search spaces.

To decrease the time complexity, the pruning method is employed to reduce the space of $\mathcal{Z}$ by removing planes with $p_\lambda(z|\mathbf{x}) < \varepsilon$ [15]. We easily calculate $p_\lambda(z|\mathbf{x})$. Because $Z(z, \mathbf{x})$ should be calculated before pruning is performed, α recursions are finished first. Thus, we apply the pruning method only during training. If we wish to predict the best labels without marginal probabilities in predicting a new instance, we can omit calculation of $Z(\mathbf{x})$; hence we cannot prune less confident planes. However, we can take advantage of the pruning method in some applications that require marginal probabilities (e.g., active learning). The pruning technique reduces training time, allowing triangular-chain CRFs to be scaled for large-scale problems.

8.6 JOINT PREDICTION OF DIALOGUE ACTS AND NAMED ENTITIES

Current state-of-the-art SLU systems use cascade or pipeline schemes [10], which are often derived by training the NE model; the schemes then use the model's prediction as a feature for the DA classifier. The NE plays an important role in identifying the DA; it can thus also improve the performance of the DA classifier in cascading scheme. However, the cascade approach has a significant drawback: The NE recognition module cannot take advantage of information from the DA identification module. Our assumption here is that the problems of modeling DA and modeling NE are significantly *correlated*; that is, DA information influences the NE recognition task and vice versa. Thus, we need to concurrently optimize the DA and NE models. This problem can be solved using a complex model to reflect inter-dependency between the two. The triangular-chain CRFs are thus applied to the joint SLU task.

This section evaluates triangular-chain CRFs in a real-world dialogue application for ambient intelligence: an automated call center. Our method is found to perform better for SLU tasks since it effectively captures the dependencies between NEs and DAs. Empirical results show an improvement in both DA classification and NE recognition.

8.6.1 Data Sets and Experiment Setup

We evaluated our method on two goal-oriented dialogue data Sets: **Air-Travel** (English; travel agency service—DARPA-Communicator) and **Telebank** (Korean; automated response system for a banking service). All data Sets were collected and annotated to develop spoken dialogue systems that consist of annotated DAs and NEs. In practice, a realistic dialogue system for human–computer interfaces functions best if the dialogue is short and restrictive. In these data Sets, the average

Table 8.1 Statistics of Dialogue Data Sets

Data Set	Sent	Words	DA	NE	$|x|$	$|Y|$	$|z|$
Air-Travel	5138	25,024	5138	10,237	3632	110	21
Telebank	2238	16,480	2238	2278	1813	33	25

utterance consisted of less than 5 to 8 words and the average number of classes per utterance was 1 to 3. Both data Sets are summarized in Table 8.1. Figure 8.8 depicts the statistics for annotation. Each plot shows relative DA and NE class frequencies and depicts ranked class IDs. The class IDs are ordered from most to least frequent.

All data Sets were evaluated, with the results averaged over 10-fold cross-validation (CV) with a 90/10 split of the data. As a standard, precision and recall were computed; these were evaluated on a per-entity basis and combined into a micro-averaged F_1 score ($F_1 = 2PR/(P + R)$). The significance of our results was verified using the McNemar paired test [10], which is based on individual labeling decisions to compare the correctness of two models.

For NE recognition, we selected feature templates such as current word, ± 2-context words, bigrams, distance-n bigrams, and prefix and suffix features. The bag-of-words and bag-of-bigrams techniques were used for DA classification. Both linear-chain and triangular-chain CRFs were trained for 100 iterations with a Gaussian prior variance of 10. In addition, the methods were evaluated for both text and spoken input. For spoken input, the HTK-based recognition system was used [40]. The word error rates for **Air-Travel** and **Telebank** were 27.18% and 20.79%, respectively.

8.6.2 Comparison Results for Text and Spoken Inputs

To evaluate our method, we compared two versions of our model against five baseline models. Our models were

JOINT1 and JOINT2. These are versions of our proposed methods. They were obtained by training DAs and NEs jointly, which jointly optimized the DA and NE tasks in the training step and also jointly extracted the $(\hat{y}, \hat{z})$ pair in the prediction step. The triangular-chain CRF MODEL1 and MODEL2 were used for the joint SLU system. During training, a pseudo-likelihood parameter was used as an initial weight (estimated in 20 iterations) and the planes were pruned to ϵ of 0.001.

The baseline models were

INDEP. This model was obtained by training DA and NE classifiers independently, a process that completely ignores the other classifier's outputs. We used the zero-order CRF as a DA classifier and the first-order linear-chain CRF as an NE classifier.

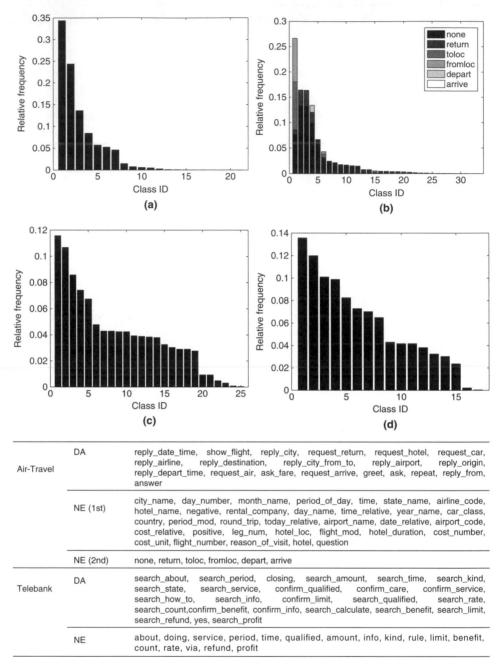

FIGURE 8.8

Annotation for dialogue data Sets: (a) DA, Air-Travel; (b) NE, Air-Travel; (c) DA, Telebank; (d) NE, Telebank; (E) DA and NE lists. All classes are ordered by their class ID. In Air-Travel data Set, the NE category has a two-level hierarchy: 33 first-level classes and 6 second-level classes, for a total of 110 class combinations.

CASCADE1. This model was obtained using NE prediction. We first extracted the NE and then augmented a DA feature vector with it for DA classification. The result of NE prediction was the same as that of INDEP, so it was not reported.

CASCADE2. This model was obtained using DA prediction. It is an inverse pipeline system of CASCADE1 since we first identified the DA and then used it to augment a feature vector for NE classification. In this model, the result of DA prediction was the same as that of INDEP.

RERANK1. This model was obtained by rescoring the n-best results of the NE classifier. We first produced n-best NE sequences, and the DA classifier then exploited this information. Finally, the best score was selected by interpolation: $p = \gamma p(z|\mathbf{x}) + (1 - \gamma)p(\mathbf{y}|\mathbf{x})$, which can be viewed as a joint extraction method where learning is not jointly optimized. We empirically set the best parameters as $n = 5$ and $\gamma = 0.2$.

RERANK2. This model was obtained by rescoring the n-best results of the DA classifier. It is an inverse system of RERANK1 ($n = 10$ and $\gamma = 0.8$).

Our method performed better than the baseline systems. Tables 8.2 and 8.3 show the experimental results for text and speech input, respectively. The results of CASCADE1 and CASCADE2 show that DAs are useful for predicting NEs and vice versa. However, the cascade approach cannot improve both tasks. While the approach of RERANK1 and RERANK2 improves both DA and NE performance, the reranking method reduces the overall performance of SLU. Because of the limit of n-best lists, the reranking method based on the cascade model cannot take advantage of interdependencies and finds a local solution. Moreover, RERANK1 and RERANK2 often do not pass

Table 8.2 Results for Dialogue Data (Text)

Method	Air-Travel		Telebank	
	F_1(DA)	F_1(NE)	F_1(DA)	F_1(NE)
INDEP	92.09±1.03	90.67±0.80	95.09±1.68	92.88±1.49
CASCADE1	92.70±1.20†	N/A	96.36±1.23*	N/A
CASCADE2	N/A	94.34±0.49*	N/A	92.97±1.34
RERANK1	92.75±1.13*	89.75±0.82	96.32±1.27*	92.18±1.81
RERANK2	92.56±1.10*	94.39±0.56*†	95.42±1.64*	93.16±1.18
JOINT1	92.96±0.89*	93.78±0.83*	96.51±1.49*	93.47±1.79
JOINT2	**93.07±1.21*†**	**94.42±1.38*†**	**96.93±1.33*†**	**93.53±1.26***

Note: F_1 scores are averaged over 10-fold CVs with standard errors.
*Statistically, these results are significantly better than the INDEP model, p < 0.05.
†Statistically, these results are significantly better than the CASCADE model, p < 0.05.

Table 8.3 Results for Dialogue Data (ASR)

Method	Air-Travel		Telebank	
	F_1(DA)	F_1(NE)	F_1(DA)	F_1(NE)
INDEP	78.44±1.26	75.67±1.32	90.04±1.33	84.67±2.59
CASCADE1	79.00±1.62	N/A	90.85±2.04	N/A
CASCADE2	N/A	78.88±1.24*	N/A	84.77±1.83
RERANK1	79.04±1.59	74.74±1.28	91.10±2.01	83.64±2.66
RERANK2	78.82±1.43	78.90±1.19*	90.02±1.32	85.01±1.94
JOINT1	**79.41±1.25***	78.21±1.37*	**91.36±1.27***	**85.93±2.43*†**
JOINT2	78.76±1.08	**78.92±1.17***	91.19±2.11*	85.42±2.50*†

Note: F_1 scores are averaged over 10-fold CVs with standard errors.
*Statistically, these results are significantly better than the INDEP model, $p < 0.05$.
†Statistically, these results are significantly better than the CASCADE model, $p < 0.05$.

the McNemar test, compared with INDEP and CASCADE. Thus, the reranking approach is not the best one for joint extraction.

Our JOINT system significantly improves performance by exploiting the dependence between DAs and NEs. On most F_1 scores, the JOINT model improves over INDEP, CASCADE, and RERANK. Also, the differences in accuracy between JOINT and other systems are statistically significant (p values are calculated using the McNemar test). Note that the result of the McNemar test comparing JOINT and RERANK is similar to that comparing JOINT and CASCADE. This shows that DAs and NEs are valuable to each other and that joint learning and inference can improve the performance of both tasks.

8.6.3 Comparison of Space and Time Complexity

For practicality, we evaluated the space and time complexity for **Air-Travel** data. Table 8.4 summarizes the results, which are averaged on 10-fold CV. The decoding time is measured per utterance. For INDEP, the zero-order CRF and linear-chain CRF were run individually, and parameter values and times were aggregated. Whereas INDEP has no parameter values for the dependencies between y and z, CASCADE, RERANK, and JOINT need more spaces to store the joint features. There are no significant differences among the training times of INDEP, CASCADE, and RERANK. However, decoding in RERANK is more expensive because it has the additional tasks of performing n-best searches and rescoring.

Our algorithm originally required 51,936 seconds to train JOINT1 and 37,364 seconds to train JOINT2. To reduce the time complexity, we used the INIT and PRUNE methods so that the parameter weights were learned within 36,464 seconds by JOINT1 and 21,472 seconds by JOINT2. Trained log likelihoods were -1865.18 for JOINT1 (full) and -1944.30 for JOINT2 (full). The decoding times were 106.2 milliseconds for JOINT1 and 46.1 milliseconds for JOINT2. This was a consequence of the

Table 8.4 Comparison of Space and Time Complexity for Air Travel

Method	Parameters	Training Time (seconds)	Decoding Time (milliseconds)
INDEP	8124	2250	5.2
CASCADE1	8356	2278	5.3
CASCADE2	8377	2252	5.4
RERANK1	8356	2278	78.5
RERANK2	8377	2252	50.1
JOINT1 (full)	17,826	36,464	106.2
JOINT2 (full)	8377	21,472	46.1
JOINT1 (zero-out)	11,942	5504	11.1
JOINT2 (zero-out)	8377	3647	8.2

time complexity of triangular-chain CRFs, which is linear in state space size $|\mathcal{Z}|$. (Note that $|\mathcal{Z}| = 21$, and training and decoding times were approximately 20 times those of INDEP.) We reduced the time complexity using the zero-out method described in Section 8.4.1. The averaged number of $|\mathcal{A}_i|$ was 12.38, while a full state set $|\mathcal{Y}|$ was 110. This method had the limitation that a novel instance that does not appear in training data is impossible to decode, but in practice the partial space constraint model remarkably reduced the inference times without significant loss of performance. F_1 scores for DA and NE classification (ASR) are 78.28 and 77.43 for JOINT1 (zero-out) and 78.97 and 78.56 for JOINT2 (zero-out). These results indicate that triangular-chain CRFs can be scaled up for large-scale applications.

8.7 MULTI-DOMAIN SPOKEN LANGUAGE UNDERSTANDING

Multi-domain spoken dialogue systems have attracted attention because of the increased need for a simple and convenient interface for multitasking. To this end, the system should have multiple semantics and agents to process tasks in multiple domains. Two problems in multi-domain SLU are *domain detection* and *semantic tagging*. Our main claim is that the domain detector in a pipeline architecture cannot exploit the results of subsequent components in the SLU process. That is, the domain type is classified only by the lexical features (or some acoustic features) from the speech recognizer rather than by the semantics produced by domain-dependent SLU. Moreover, any detection error is propagated to subsequent stages, which causes errors in dialogue flow. To reduce the effect of propagated errors, we introduce a multi-domain SLU system in which the tasks of domain detection and SLU can be learned together to simultaneously improve the performance of each process [16].

The main contribution of this section is a method for solving the multi-domain SLU problem through transfer learning techniques. First, we approach SLU modeling in multiple domains as a multitask learning problem, where we learn domain detection and semantic tagging simultaneously. For this, we use a novel structured probabilistic model—triangular-chain CRFs—with which we combine a node for domain type and a linear-chain structure for semantic tags by adding probabilistic connections in an undirected graphical model framework. A second contribution is that we address the problem of adapting the multi-domain SLU model by introducing a new factor function to transfer domain portability into the proposed triangular-chain CRF model.

8.7.1 Domain Adaptation

To enhance the feasibility of our model, we introduce another type of transfer learning, domain adaptation. In multitask learning, the task being learned varies; that is, the finite sets of output labels in source and target tasks differ [3]. For example, in our problem the finite output spaces of $\mathcal{Y}$ and $\mathcal{Z}$ are different; $\mathcal{Y}$ also varies among domains. In fact, one assumption in domain adaptation is that the finite sets of source and target tasks are equivalent, which is not true for our system. Still, we have empirical evidence that domain adaptation techniques may apply to our problem, although differences between the finite sets make the problem more difficult.

Our evidence is that we observe some labels for DAs and NEs overlapping in realistic dialogue data. For example, person name and time-related information commonly appear in both the "television program guide" and the "schedule management task" domain. Thus, in our multi-domain SLU problem, the tasks being learned vary but remain closely related. We believe that we can exploit these common labeling sets to learn the target task from the source task, especially when the amount of data in the target domain is small.

To exploit source domain data in learning about the target domain, we extend our multi-domain SLU models by adding a new factor that is shared across all domains. Specifically, the potential functions Ψ_t are partitioned into domain-dependent and domain-independent factors. The latter are used to predict the best semantic tag assignment in all domains and to guide the improvement of weight factors for common labels.

Formally, we define the Ψ_t factors as follows:

$$\Psi_t(d, y_t, y_{t-1}, \mathbf{x}) = \underbrace{\Psi_t^d(z, y_t, y_{t-1}, \mathbf{x})}_{domain-dependent} \cdot \underbrace{\Psi_t^i(y_t, y_{t-1}, \mathbf{x})}_{domain-independent} \tag{8.41}$$

$$\Psi_t^d(z, y_t, y_{t-1}, \mathbf{x}_t) = \underbrace{\Psi_t^1(z, y_t, \mathbf{x})}_{observation} \cdot \underbrace{\Psi_t^2(z, y_t, y_{t-1})}_{transition} \tag{8.42}$$

$$\Psi_t^i(y_t, y_{t-1}, \mathbf{x}_t) = \underbrace{\Psi_t^1(y_t, \mathbf{x})}_{observation} \cdot \underbrace{\Psi_t^2(y_t, y_{t-1})}_{transition} \tag{8.43}$$

where Ψ_t^d is domain dependent and Ψ_t^i is domain independent. Ψ_t^d and Ψ_t^i each have observation and transition components (Equations (8.43) and (8.44)).

The domain-independent factors do not include a variable for z. This simple modification gives a better interpretation of our model: It can learn both domain-dependent and domain-independent patterns. Empirically, domain adaptation is effective for our multi-domain SLU problems because domain-independent factors and their parameters are useful for predicting data points that do not occur in the target domain but do appear in other domains.

Domain adaptation is important for both performance improvement and domain portability. If we extend a new domain from an existing model, especially with a small set of training data, the domain adaptation techniques are potentially useful because we expect that some features shared by the target domain are sufficiently trained in the source domain. In this way, modeling multi-domain SLU with transfer learning improves the model's extensibility and portability.

8.7.2 Data and Setup

We evaluated our method on six goal-oriented Korean dialogue data Sets (Table 8.5) for intelligent robotics and smart-home applications: **EPG** (an electronic television program guide), **Schedule** (a schedule management task), **Object** (an object search and delivery service in a mobile robot), **Guide** (a building guide), **Navigation** (a navigation guide for restaurants), and **Weather** (a weather information service). Figure 8.9 depicts the statistics for annotation. Each plot shows relative DA and NE class frequencies and the class IDs ranked from most to least frequent. All data Sets were collected and annotated by human users in a wizard-of-Oz situation [1]. For the NE task, we selected feature templates such as current word, ±2-context words, bigrams, trigrams, distance-2 bigrams, and prefix and suffix features. We did not use syntactic features such as part-of-speech tags and parse trees. Traditional morphological analyzers and parsers often fail to produce accurate results because our data Sets are mostly conversational and often ungrammatical. For the DA and domain type classification tasks, we used the bag-of-words and bag-of-bigrams techniques.

Table 8.5 Statistics of Dialogue Data Sets

Data Set	Dialogue Examples	Sentences	DA Classes	DA Features	NE Classes	NE Task Features
EPG	338	2509	21	129k	22	846k
Schedule	336	430	13	15k	17	111k
Object	194	362	6	5k	13	68k
Guide	742	1997	17	69k	22	528k
Navigation	581	972	10	28k	16	272k
Weather	135	574	7	5k	10	45k

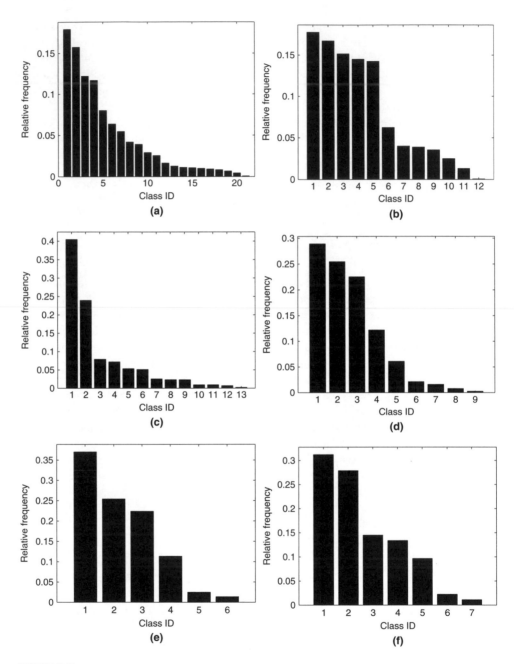

FIGURE 8.9

Annotation for dialogue data Sets: (a) DA, EPG; (b) NE, EPG; (c) DA, Schedule; (d) NE, Schedule; (e) DA, Object; (f) NE, object.

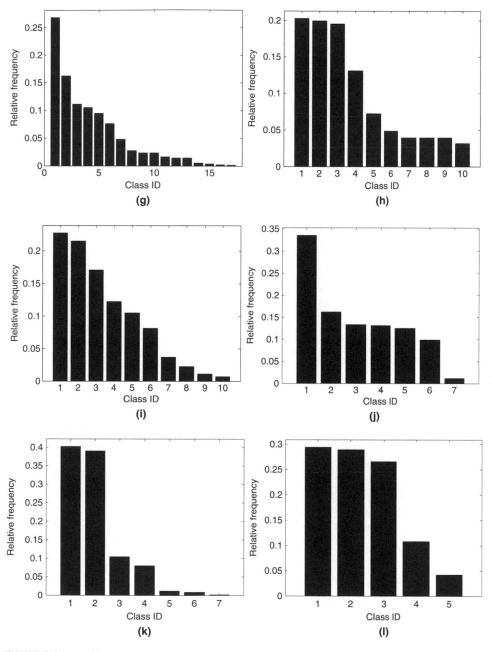

FIGURE 8.9—cont'd

(g) DA, Guide; (h) NE, Guide; (i) DA, Navigation; (j) NE, Navigation; (k) DA, Weather; (l) NE, Weather.

(Continued)

EPG	DA	search_program, change_channel, record_prg, unknown, tv_on, search_start_time, vol_up, alarm_epg, search_person, search_channel, tv_off, search_topic, search_current_time, search_prg_date, bright_up, vol_down, none, search_end_time, recommend_prg, search_current_date, bright_down
	NE	epg_genre, epg_channel, epg_program, timex_time, timex_date, timex_order, per_name, per_role, num_count, epg_topic, epg_type, timex_period
Schedule	DA	search_phone, search_schd, call_phone, none, search_schd_loc, search_schd_time, search_schd_per, unknown, add_schd, alarm_schd, add_phone, del_schd, search_current_time
	NE	per_name, timex_date, tel_type, timex_time, per_title, event, tel_name, tel_num, loc_keyword
Object	DA	bring_object, none, search_object, inform_object, unknown, move_object
	NE	ref, object, obj_drink, obj_cup, loc_place, timex_time, timex_date
Guide	DA	none, search_loc, unknown, guide_loc, search_person, search_contact, deliver_object, search_event, search_schd, alarm_piro, bring_object, search_current_time, inform_loc, call_person, search_current_date, search_object, search_floor
	NE	loc_room_name, per_name, per_title, ref, loc_building, obj_print, timex_time, timex_date, object, event
Navigation	DA	search_route, guide_loc, confirm_route, search_loc, select_route_type, none, confirm_loc, search_contact, ask_route_type, start_navi
	NE	loc_address, loc_name, route_type, loc_keyword, loc_from, loc_road, ref
Weather	D	none, search_weather, search_temperature, search_rainy_prob, ask_city_list, ask_state_list, unknown
	NE	timex_date, loc_city, weather_type, loc_state, timex_time

(m)

FIGURE 8.9—cont'd

(m) DA and NE lists. All classes are ordered by their class ID.

All data Sets were evaluated, with the results averaged over 5-fold CV with an 80-training/20-testing split of the data. Specifically, we split the training and test sets at the dialogue rather than the sentence level. As a standard, precision (P) and recall (R) were computed and evaluated on a per-entity basis and then combined into a micro-averaged F_1 score ($F_1 = 2PR/(P + R)$). The significance of our results was determined by the McNemar paired test for proportions [9], which uses individual labeling decisions to compare the correctness of two models. All experiments were conducted over the transcriptions (Text) and 1-best speech recognition output (ASR) of utterances. For spoken inputs, the HTK-based recognition system was used. The overall word error rate was 19.09% averaged over 10 speakers.

8.7.3 Comparison Results

For evaluation, we compared two versions of our model against three baseline models. Our models were

JOINT. This model was obtained by multitask learning for multi-domain SLU models and is the same as JOINT1 in Section 8.6.

JOINT+A. Like JOINT, this model was obtained by multitask learning for multi-domain SLU models, but included domain adaptation. We added domain-independent parameters Ψ_t^i, which can capture cross-domain features to leverage domain portability. All settings were the same as in the JOINT model.

The baseline models were

ORACLE. This model was obtained using true domain types. It assumes complete domain detection, so we used it to demonstrate the effectiveness of our method. We used the zero-order CRF as a DA classifier and the first-order linear-chain CRF as an NE classifier. Both CRFs were trained for 200 iterations with a Gaussian prior variance of 10.

CASCADE. This model is the same as the CASCADE2 model in Section 8.6.

RERANK. This model is the same as the RERANK2 model in Section 8.6.

Before implementing the multi-domain SLU systems, we inspected the data Sets. We observed that some utterances are totally domain independent—for example, short ones such as "Thanks," "Yes," and "No." To deal with these, we added an extra domain description, "GEN." However, we did not report this result because the general domain has no NE tag or only one DA tag, "none."

First, we show that multitask learning for multi-domain SLU is a feasible solution (see Tables 8.6, 8.7, 8.8, and 8.9). For both NE and DA tasks in both Text and ASR experiments, the errors of CASCADE are generally higher than those of ORACLE. The only exception is the result for domain A in the DA task. This irregular situation occurred because the data contained "unknown" labels. As our data was collected by real users in a wizard-of-Oz situation, some dialogues occurred that could not be processed by SDS. CASCADE could process "unknown" in other domains, but had difficulty processing it in domain A. The results of the RERANK model are closely similar to those of CASCADE. Our proposed method, JOINT, outperforms both.

Interestingly, some results using JOINT are significantly better than those obtained using ORACLE, the main reason for which is that JOINT was trained using multi-domain

Table 8.6 Results of Multi-Domain SLU for the NE Task (Text)

Model	Detection Errors	Understanding Errors					
		EPG	Schedule	Object	Guide	Navigation	Weather
ORACLE	N/A	91.1±1.5	90.1±4.6	92.8±2.1	96.8±0.9	96.5±0.9	96.8±1.4
CASCADE	94.0±0.8	90.3±1.5	90.0±5.1	89.8±4.0	94.8±1.1	95.0±1.1	95.9±1.5
RERANK	94.1±0.8	90.4±1.6	90.0±4.6	89.8±4.0	95.2±1.1[†]	95.2±1.1	95.7±1.3
JOINT	95.5±0.4[*]	91.0±1.4[†]	90.5±3.4	**90.5±5.0**	96.0±0.7[†]	**95.7±0.7[‡]**	94.4±1.8
JOINT+A	**95.7±0.5[*]**	**91.6±1.4[*]**	**92.5±2.8[†]**	90.4±3.3	**96.1±1.1[‡]**	95.7±1.0[‡]	**97.2±1.5[‡]**

Note: *Mean and Standard error of percent detection error over 5-fold CVs.*
[*]*Statistically, this result is significantly better than the CASCADE model, p ≤ 0.001.*
[†]*Statistically, this result is significantly better than the CASCADE model, p = 0.05.*
[‡]*Statistically, this result is significantly better than the CASCADE model, p = 0.01.*

Table 8.7 Results of Multi-Domain SLU for the DA Task (Text)

Model	Detection Errors	Understanding Errors					
		EPG	Schedule	Object	Guide	Navigation	Weather
ORACLE	N/A	80.1±1.3	89.6±1.2	92.5±2.0	88.8±0.7	97.5±0.9	80.5±6.6
CASCADE	94.0±0.8	80.6±1.1	83.1±1.2	87.5±6.1	86.5±1.2	95.8±1.0	78.3±6.5
RERANK	94.2±0.7	80.7±1.1	83.9±1.3	88.0±5.8	87.0±1.0†	95.9±1.2	78.8±5.7
JOINT	**96.3±0.4***	80.8±1.6	**86.2±2.1***	92.8±2.4*	**87.9±1.1***	**97.3±0.6***	**80.0±7.4†**
JOINT+A	96.2±0.5*	**81.0±1.7**	86.1±2.5*	**93.0±3.1***	87.6±0.9‡	97.2±0.7*	79.7±7.3

Table 8.8 Results of Multi-Domain SLU for the NE Task (ASR)

Model	Detection Errors	Understanding Errors					
		EPG	Schedule	Object	Guide	Navigation	Weather
ORACLE	N/A	78.1±2.4	86.3±2.1	77.3±12.2	85.7±4.3	91.8±1.6	90.2±4.5
CASCADE	87.9±3.2	76.0±2.9	84.4±4.1	69.4±12.4	82.1±4.7	89.3±2.6	89.5±4.4
RERANK	88.0±3.2	76.3±2.9	84.7±3.4	68.4±11.6	82.2±4.8	89.8±2.1	89.0±4.4
JOINT	**92.3±1.6***	78.0±2.8*	86.8±2.3	77.0±3.8‡	**84.9±4.1‡**	90.9±1.2‡	91.1±4.1†
JOINT+A	92.3±2.0*	**78.9±2.8***	**88.1±4.4†**	**79.5±4.6***	84.8±4.4‡	**91.1±1.1‡**	**91.9±1.8†**

Table 8.9 Results of Multi-Domain SLU for the DA Task (ASR)

Model	Detection Errors	Understanding Errors					
		EPG	Schedule	Object	Guide	Navigation	Weather
ORACLE	N/A	70.1±2.5	82.9±5.9	85.6±4.5	73.6±6.0	93.8±2.7	75.8±4.1
CASCADE	87.9±3.2	69.1±2.6	78.5±5.6	79.4±5.0	73.6±6.0	91.3±3.3	71.1±4.9
RERANK	88.1±3.2	69.6±2.6	**78.8±4.8**	80.7±5.3	73.6±6.0	92.0±3.1	**72.0±4.5**
JOINT	89.1±2.4*	70.1±2.4	74.2±4.4	82.4±2.4†	**73.8±7.3**	92.8±1.0†	71.9±5.2
JOINT+A	**89.3±2.6***	**70.5±1.7†**	77.0±3.4	**84.4±3.5†**	**73.8±7.3**	**93.1±0.5†**	71.7±5.1

data whereas ORACLE was trained using only domain-dependent data. This means that learning with multi-domain data gains some benefit from large data Sets. In our analysis, we observed that some features that commonly appear in two or more domains strengthen each other. Most results using JOINT are significantly better than those using CASCADE.

Second, we show that domain adaptation is useful for our multi-domain SLU problem. Although the output sets vary in domains, which makes adaptation more difficult, the results for Joint+A are often better than those for Joint and Oracle (Tables 8.6, 8.7, 8.8, and 8.9, bottom rows). This implies that learning with auxiliary source data is often better than learning with only target domain data. Also, this result leads us to conclude that exploiting transfer learning is appropriate for multi-domain SLU. While Joint+A achieved better performance for the NE task, it often failed to improve the performance of the DA task. The major reason for this is that DA tag sets often disagree; that is, there were few common labels in domain-dependent semantic tagging data Sets (on average, 4 to 5 for NE and 1 to 2 for DA). For practical SDS, the semantics for DA are totally domain dependent.

Third, for practicality we evaluated space and time complexity. Table 8.10 summarizes the results, which are averaged on 5-fold CV. For Oracle, the zero-order and linear-chain CRFs were run individually. While this model has no parameters to describe the dependencies between y and z, Cascade, Rerank, and Joint need more space to store the joint features. There are no significant differences among the training times of Oracle, Cascade, and Rerank. However, decoding in Rerank is more expensive because it has the additional tasks of n-best searching and rescoring. Training times for Joint and Joint+A were much longer than for the other models. Joint's training times were 6625 seconds for the NE model and 681 seconds for the DA model. Using Joint+A, they were 9859 for the NE model and 1993 for the DA model. Decoding times were in milliseconds for all models and were thus negligible.

Finally, we show that the domain adaptation method potentially improves the performance of multi-domain SLU. To validate this hypothesis, we plotted the learning curves of Joint and Joint+A with different sizes of target-domain data (Figure 8.10). For all domains except **Navigation**, Joint+A has a lower error rate than Joint, which demonstrates that domain adaptation is especially helpful when the target domain data Set is small. This observation indicates that transfer learning can improve the portability of multi-domain SLU. Because our problem is more

Table 8.10 Comparison of Space and Time Complexity (NE/DA)

Method	Parameters (1000)		Training Time (seconds)		Decoding Time (milliseconds)	
	NE	DA	NE	DA	NE	DA
Oracle	1870	258	261	10	1.0	0.2
Cascade	1885	273	264	13	3.6	0.6
Rerank	1885	273	264	13	7.0	1.1
Joint	1890	268	6625	681	3.5	0.6
Joint+A	1983	296	9859	1993	5.4	1.2

Note: *Decoding time measured per utterance.*

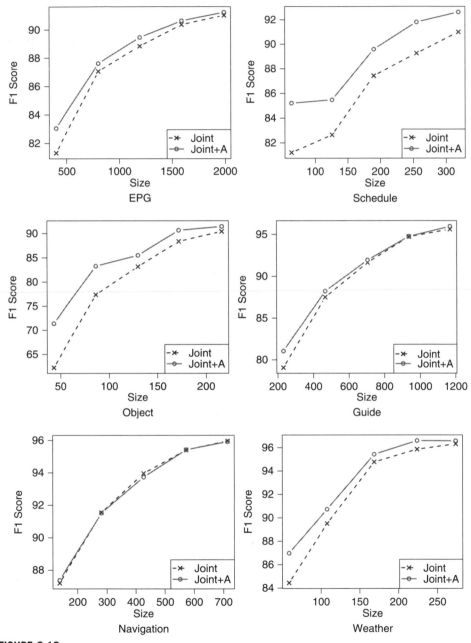

FIGURE 8.10

Learning curves for multi-domain NE recognition using the JOINT and JOINT+A models in six target domains. Percent error rate averaged over 5-fold CVs with transcripts.

complex than those in traditional domain adaptation, we believe that the adaptation method described here improves performance and portability in large-scale SDS. An extensive experiment on large-scale multi-domain SLU, where the domains are close to each other, remains our future work.

8.8 CONCLUSION AND FUTURE DIRECTION

This chapter introduced the use of statistical machine learning methods to understand spoken language. Statistical SLU was formalized by sequential supervised learning, in which the DA and NE recognition tasks were formulated as sequential labeling and sequence classification. State-of-the-art learning techniques for sequential supervised learning were introduced, most of which can be described by a loss minimization framework in linear and log-linear models. In particular, CRFs have been widely adopted for solving statistical SLU because of well-founded probabilistic theory and empirical evidence.

Despite the clear potential of machine learning approaches in SLU, developing practical methods for ambient intelligence and smart environments remains a significant challenge. To address this problem, this chapter presented two advanced applications of statistical SLU for ambient intelligence. First, we addressed efficient learning and inference of large-scale CRFs by applying two methods: (1) partial-space inference for saving time, and (2) feature selection for reducing memory requirements. Second, we addressed transfer learning for statistical SLU, where multiple tasks and domain knowledge can be incorporated. To this end, a novel probabilistic model, triangular-chain CRFs, was proposed to concurrently solve the two related problems of sequence labeling and sequence classification. An attractive feature of our method is that it represents multiple tasks in a single graphical model, thus naturally embedding their mutual dependence. We applied triangular-chain CRFs to two novel applications: joint prediction of NEs and DAs and multi-domain SLU.

Researchers have begun to study machine learning methods to improve performance and adaptability for practical SLU. The main drawback of the supervised learning method is that assembling training data is expensive. To alleviate this problem, methods of active and semi-supervised learning to reduce annotation requirements were presented [35]. Some studies attempt to incorporate human-crafted knowledge to compensate for the lack of data when building statistical SLU (e.g., [31]).

Another problem with the supervised learning method is how to use the acoustic information from a speech recognizer to develop robust SLU. The output of a speech recognizer contains rich information, such as n-best lists, word lattices, and confidence scores, which many researchers have tried to utilize to improve SLU performance as well as to provide useful information for dialogue management [12, 30].

Exploiting structural information to overcome long-distance dependency is another significant challenge. He and Young [13] described an approach using a hidden vector state model that extends the basic hidden Markov model for encoding hierarchical structures. More recently, some primary works proposed ways to deal with dependency beyond *n*-grams using statistical approaches such as nonlocal feature selection [16] and syntactic/semantic tree kernels [22] in discriminative learning. As a consequence of extensible studies of statistical approaches for SLU, we believe that the recent advances in machine learning and the development of practical SLU systems expand the ambient intelligence paradigm.

ACKNOWLEDGMENTS

This work was supported by the Intelligent Robotics Development Program, one of the 21st Century Frontier R&D Programs funded by the Ministry of Knowledge Economy of Korea.

REFERENCES

[1] Ammicht E, Gorin A, Alonso T. Knowledge collection for natural language spoken dialogue systems, In: Proceedings of the European Conference on Speech Communication and Technology (EUROSPEECH). Budapest: Hungary, 1999. p. 1375-8.

[2] Berger AL, Pietra SD, Pietra VD. A maximum entropy approach to natural language processing. Computational Linguistics 1996;22(1):39-71.

[3] Caruana R. Multitask learning. Machine Learning 1997;28(1):41-75.

[4] Cohn T. Efficient inference in large conditional random fields. In: Proceedings of the European Conference on Machine Learning (ECML). 2006. p. 606-13.

[5] Collins M. Discriminative training methods for hidden Markov models: Theory and experiments with perceptron algorithms. In: Proceedings of the Conference on Empirical Methods in Natural Language Processing (EMNLP). 2002. p. 1-8.

[6] Daumé H III. Practical Structured Learning Techniques for Natural Language Processing. PhD thesis, University of Southern California: 2006.

[7] Daumé H III, Marcu D. Domain adaptation for statistical classifiers. Journal of Artificial Intelligence Research 2006;26:101-26.

[8] De Mori R, Béchet F, Hakkani-Tür D, McTear M, Riccardi G, Tur G. Spoken language understanding for conversational systems. Signal Processing Magazine, Special Issue on Spoken Language Technologies 2008;25(3):50-8.

[9] Gillick L, Cox S. Some statistical issues in the comparison of speech recognition algorithms. In: Proceedings of the IEEE International Conference on Acoustics, Speech and Signal Processing (ICASSP). 1989. p. 532-5.

[10] Gupta N, Tur G, Hakkani-Tür D, Bangalore S, Riccardi G, Gilbert M. The AT&T spoken language understanding system. IEEE Transactions on Audio, Speech, and Language Processing 2006;14(1):213-22.

[11] Hakkani-Tür D, Béchet F, Riccardi G, Tur G. Beyond ASR 1-best: Using word confusion networks in spoken language understanding. Computer Speech and Language 2006;20(4): 495-514.

[12] Jeong M, Lee GG. Exploiting non-local features for spoken language understanding. In: Proceedings of the Joint International Conference on Computational Linguistics and Association of Computational Linguistics (COLING/ACL). Australia: Sydney, 2006. p. 412–9.

[13] Jeong M, Lee GG. Jointly predicting dialogue act and named entity for spoken language understanding. In: Proceedings of the IEEE/ACL 2006 Workshop on Spoken Language Technology. 2006. p. 66–9.

[14] Jeong M, Lee GG. Practical use of non local features for statistical spoken language understanding. Computer Speech and Language 2008;22(2):148–70.

[15] Jeong M, Lee GG. Triangular-chain conditional random fields. IEEE Transactions on Audio, Speech and Language Processing 2008;16(7):1287–302.

[16] Jeong M, Lee GG. 2009. Multi-domain spoken language understanding with transfer learning. Speech Comm.; to appear.

[17] Kschischang FR, Frey BJ, Loeliger HA. Factor graphs and the sum-product algorithm. IEEE Transactions on Information Theory 2001;47(2).

[18] Lafferty J, McCallum A, Pereira F. Conditional random fields: Probabilistic models for segmenting and labeling sequence data. In: Proceedings of the International Conference on Machine Learning (ICML). 2001. p. 282–9.

[19] McCallum A. Efficiently inducing features of conditional random fields. In: Proceedings of the Conference on Uncertainty in Artificial Intelligence (UAI). 2003. p. 403.

[20] Moschitti A, Riccardi G, Raymond C. Spoken language understanding with kernels for syntactic/semantic structures. In: Proceedings of the IEEE Workshop on Automatic Speech Recognition and Understanding (ASRU). Kyoto: Japan, 2007.

[21] Nocedal J, Wright SJ. Numerical Optimization. Springer: 1999.

[22] Pal C, Sutton C, McCallum A. Sparse forward-backward using minimum divergence beams for fast training of conditional random fields. In: Proceedings of the IEEE International Conference on Acoustics, Speech and Signal Processing (ICASSP). 2006.

[23] Peckham J. Speech understanding and dialogue over the telephone: An overview of the ESPRIT SUNDIAL project. In: Proceedings of the Workshop on Speech and Natural Language. Pacific Grove: CA, 1991. p. 14–27.

[24] Pietra SD, Pietra VD, Lafferty J. Inducing features of random fields. IEEE Trans Pattern Anal Mach Intell 1997;19(4):380–93.

[25] Price PJ. Evaluation of spoken language systems: The ATIS domain. In: Proceedings of the Workshop on Speech and Natural Language. Hidden Valley: PA, 1990. p. 91–5.

[26] Ramshaw LA, Marcus MP. Text chunking using transformation-based learning, In: Proceedings of the 3rd Workshop on Very Large Corpora; 1995. p. 82–94.

[27] Raymond C, Riccardi G. Generative and discriminative algorithms for spoken language understanding. In: Proceedings of INTERSPEECH. Antwerp: Begium, 2007.

[28] Raymond R, Béchet F, Mori RD, Damnati G. On the use of finite state transducers for semantic interpretation. Speech Comm 2006;48(3–4):288–304.

[29] Schapire R, Rochery M, Rahim M, Gupta N. Incorporating prior knowledge into boosting. In: Proceedings of the International Conference on Machine Learning (ICML). 2002.

[30] Sha F, Pereira F. Shallow parsing with conditional random fields. In: Proceedings of the Conference of the North American Chapter of the Association for Computational Linguistics and Human Language Technology (NAACL/HLT). 2003. p. 134–41.

[31] Sutton C, McCallum A. An introduction to conditional random fields for relational learning. In: Getoor L, Taskar B, editors. Introduction to Statistical Relational Learning. MIT Press: 2006.

[32] Tsochantaridis I, Hofmann T, Joachims T, Altun Y. Support vector learning for interdependent and structured output spaces. In: Proceedings of the International Conference on Machine Learning (ICML). 2004.

[33] Tur G, Hakkani-Tür D, Schapire RE. Combining active and semi-supervised learning for spoken language understanding. Speech Comm 2005;45(2):171–86.

[34] Walker M, Rudnicky A, Prasad R, Aberdeen J, Bratt E, Garofolo J, et al. DARPA communicator: Cross-system results for the 2001 evaluation. In: Proceedings of the International Conference on Spoken Language Processing (ICSLP). 2002. p. 269–72.

[35] Wang Y, Lee J, Mahajan M, Acero A. Statistical spoken language understanding: From generative model to conditional model. In: Wo on Advances in Structured Learning for Text and Speech Processing NIPS. 2005.

[36] Weber W, Rabaey JM, Aarts EHL, editors. Ambient Intelligence. Springer-Verlag: 2005.

The Role of Spoken Dialogue in User–Environment Interaction

9

Michael McTear

University of Ulster, Newtownabbey, Northern Ireland

ABSTRACT

Spoken dialogue systems have traditionally been deployed for automated self-service interactions in which users employ spoken language on the telephone to perform well-defined tasks such as making travel inquiries and reservations. Recently more open-ended applications have been developed, for example, to support senior citizens and people with disabilities in the management of daily activities within smart homes, or to provide drivers and pedestrians with route planning and point-of-interest information. This chapter reviews the role of spoken dialogue in such environments. It begins by describing and comparing the functions and technical characteristics of different spoken dialogue applications, including voice control, call routing, voice search, and question answering. This is followed by a review of recent research that illustrates the current state of the art in spoken dialogue systems for ambient intelligence environments, and, finally, an overview of challenges and future prospects for this emerging technology.

Key words: spoken dialogue systems, voice search, question answering, dialogue initiative, dialogue state representation.

9.1 INTRODUCTION

Ambient intelligence has been defined as "a digital environment that proactively, but sensibly, supports people in their daily lives" [1]. Two essential requirements for computer systems operating in such environments are context awareness and natural interaction. Context awareness includes relevant information about the physical environment, such as location, lighting, temperature, noise level, network connectivity, and communication bandwidth, as well as information about the people in the environment, such as physical and mental states [2, 3]. Natural interaction involves the ability to communicate in an intelligent and cooperative manner, for example, much like a human assistant who is aware of various characteristics of the user, including her physical and emotional state, location, tastes, desires, and habits [4]. Spoken dialogue, which is the most natural mode of communication between humans, is now being applied successfully to many aspects of human–computer interaction [5]. The aim of this chapter is to examine the potential contribution of spoken dialogue technology to ambient intelligence environments.

It is important to distinguish systems in which speech can be used as input or output, from systems in which it is used interactively, as in a dialogue. Those that accept spoken input from users are often described as voice control systems. Voice control of a computer or electronic device has been available for the past two decades and is particularly useful for people with physical disabilities. There are a number of systems within the domain of home automation, such as programming a VCR, navigating an electronic TV program guide, or setting an oven's cooking time and temperature. Phone-based applications include voice dialing, composing and sending emails and text messages, and managing applications such as address books and calendars, automotive applications include inputting navigation instructions and controlling devices within the car. In all of these applications speech is used to issue commands, and the system's response involves carrying out the required action. There are also systems that accept spoken input to record information for data entry, such as medical reports or accident reports for insurance companies. For these systems the information interpreted by the system is transcribed either into predefined forms or rendered as a dictated document. Finally there are systems that respond to spoken queries by outputting displays of information, such as a list of TV programs. What all of these systems have in common in their most basic forms is that they accept speech as input but do not output speech to the user or engage in a dialogue. Thus, they cannot be viewed as interactive speech systems.

Spoken language can also be used to send messages. Examples of such applications in everyday use include talking clocks, elevators that announce the opening and closing of doors and arrival at each floor, microwave ovens that advise when the door is opened or closed and what functions and cooking time have been selected, self-service systems at supermarket checkouts that instruct customers on their use, and GPS-based satellite navigation systems that provide step-by-step instructions on how to reach a desired destination. There are also systems such as screen readers that provide support for people with visual impairment when using computers.

Spoken output can be generated from data gathered by a system or device. For example, data could be gathered from sensors and interpreted in some way, and an appropriate spoken message could be delivered to the user. Systems known as outbound IVR (interactive voice response) can phone a customer and output information—for example, that a flight has been delayed. Such systems vary in complexity, from those that simply output prerecorded messages according to predetermined conditions—say, arriving at the third floor in an elevator—to those that dynamically construct a message, such as a navigation system incorporating the next street name in a route, or a sensor-based system generating a spoken message, using text-to-speech synthesis to render text as audio output. Again, these systems in their most basic forms do not accept spoken input from the user, so they cannot be viewed as interactive speech systems.

Spoken dialogue systems are interactive, as they engage users in a dialogue. The dialogue may be minimal, consisting of a single exchange between the user and the system, but more typically there are several turns of extended interaction in which the system and the user interact in order to achieve some goal. Voice control systems may be implemented as spoken dialogue systems, since even simple tasks such as programming an oven or a washing machine cannot always be accomplished with a single command or query.

This chapter will examine the technological requirements for spoken dialogue systems in ambient intelligence environments. Currently many commercially operational systems are able to automate a variety of customer services, such as providing flight information, weather forecasts, sports results, and share prices. They can also support transactions such as booking hotels, renting cars, making payments, or downloading ringtones for mobile phones. These systems free human operators from mundane tasks that can be easily automated and for which spoken dialogue is a natural mode of communication.

Research laboratories across the world are continually pushing the frontiers by developing systems with advanced capabilities that provide a more conversational interface and deal with more difficult tasks, such as troubleshooting a faulty piece of equipment for a customer or planning the evacuation of a disaster area. Some research is concerned with making systems more human-like, for example, by enabling them to recognize the emotional states of their users and by similarly displaying appropriate emotions in the course of a dialogue. However, only recently have spoken dialogue systems begun to be developed for more ambitious applications in environments involving ambient intelligence.

The remainder of this chapter is organized as follows. Section 9.2 introduces several types of interactive speech systems and compares them in terms of their functions and technical characteristics. Section 9.3 presents an architecture for the main components of an interactive speech system and describes how they differ according to the type of application in which they are used. Section 9.4 reviews some projects in which spoken dialogue systems have been developed for use in ambient environments. Section 9.5 examines specific issues and challenges for spoken dialogue technology in such environments. Section 9.6 summarizes the main issues raised in the chapter.

9.2 TYPES OF INTERACTIVE SPEECH SYSTEMS

Several types of interactive speech systems enable users to interact with their environment, including voice control of appliances and devices, call routing to a desired destination, voice search to retrieve information (e.g., a telephone number or address), question answering, and task performance. A wide range of techniques have been applied in these different systems, especially for interpreting user input and handling interactions. Although they can all be considered spoken dialogue systems, in practice each system type has evolved separately. This section outlines briefly the main characteristics of each type of system and then provides a more detailed account of the technologies involved.

Voice control systems enable users to control their environment using speech. These systems are particularly useful for people with physical disabilities for whom it is difficult to manipulate objects, but they are also used more generally in situations where the user's hands or eyes are otherwise occupied—for example, when driving a car. Voice control of personal computers to replace mouse events has been available for some time, while more recently systems have become available to control household appliances, such as ovens, refrigerators, washing machines, and dishwashers [6], and to control devices in cars [7].

The main characteristic of voice control systems is that there is a finite set of commands that they can recognize and map directly to a set of applicable actions. In their most basic forms they cannot be described as dialogue systems since the interaction comprises just a spoken command and the system's response (or lack of response if the command is not recognized). However, more advanced systems are being developed that incorporate dialogue technology to help clarify the command or to request additional parameters that may need to be specified to complete the action. The following example illustrates this (based on [6]):

User: Wash my clothes by the time I come back from work.
System: When are you going to come back?

User: At eight o'clock in the evening.
System: Which washing program?
User: Soft, 30°C.
System: Washing machine programmed.

Call routing involves classifying customer calls made to a business such as a customer-care center and routing them to the correct destination. One of the earliest examples to be deployed commercially was the AT&T How May I Help You? (HMIHY) system, which handles around 15 million calls per month [8, 9]. HMIHY greets users with an open-ended prompt that encourages fairly free-form spoken language input. The system determines the class of call from a set of 14 possible classes and extracts data relevant to the query either from the initial utterance or through a subdialogue. For example, given the user query *I have a question about my bill for October*, the system would classify it as the type ASK(BILL) and extract the item DATE with the value *October*. In many cases the dialogues are short: In a corpus of 4692 dialogues in several experimental trials of the system with real customers, 23% consisted of only two exchanges [10]. However, more extended dialogues are possible to collect values for a set number of attributes relevant to a particular call type and also to handle misunderstandings, as in the following example (from [10]):

S1: AT&T: How may I help you?
U1: I need to [uh] put a call on my calling card, please.
S2: May I have your card number please?
U2: 7 6 5 4 3 2 1 0 9 8 7 6 5 4.
S3: What number would you like to call?
U3: 8 1 4 7 7 7 6 6 6 6 [misunderstood].
S4: May I have that number again?
U4: 8 1 4 7 7 7 6 6 6 6.
S5: Thank you.

In **voice search** the system responds to a spoken query, usually by looking up the information in a database [11]. To date the most common application of voice search is directory assistance, where the user specifies a query such as *Thai restaurants near the train station* and the system responds with a list of matches, usually with additional information such as telephone number and address. A number of commercial systems have become available recently [12]. What differentiates them from voice control and call routing is that they have a very large semantic space (or set of destination classes), often consisting of millions of entries. For this reason, techniques such as statistical classification of the user's input are not possible since sufficient data is generally not available to train the classifier. Dialogue management may also be required to disambiguate the query if the user's intent is unclear, or to elicit additional constraints to narrow down the scope of the query if the list of matches is too large.

The following example illustrates how the system presents various items of information in a way that allows the user to narrow down the query scope (from [13]):

User: Tell me about restaurants in London.

System: I know of 596 restaurants in London. All price ranges are represented. Some of the cuisine options are Italian, British, European, and French.

User: I'm interested in Chinese food.

System: I know of 27 restaurants in London that serve Chinese cuisine. All price ranges are represented. Some are near the Leicester Square tube station.

User: How about a cheap one?

System: I know of 14 inexpensive restaurants that serve Chinese cuisine. Some are near the Leicester Square tube station. Some are in Soho.

Question answering is concerned with providing answers to natural language questions, such as *How many species of spider are there?* [14]. Unlike traditional text-based Web search, where the search engine retrieves a ranked set of documents, in question answering the system retrieves answers. Ask.com is a well-known question-answering system for general queries, while various companies, such as AT&T and Ikea, provide question-answering services that supply customers with information about products and services.

Interactive question answering has two dimensions. In the first, follow-up questions are asked that often require discourse processing, as in reference and ellipsis resolution. For example, a follow-up to the question about species of spider could be *How many are poisonous to humans?* The second dimension involves dialogue processing, which could involve questions by the system to refine the user's question or suggest an alternative, more appropriate one, or further questions by the user that extend the topic. As with voice search, question-answering systems must be able to process a wide range of unpredicted input. In contrast to voice search, which usually accesses a database as its knowledge source, question answering typically accesses collections of unstructured documents, for example, on the World Wide Web [15].

The term **spoken dialogue** has traditionally been applied to systems that help the user perform a well-defined task, such as obtaining flight information or making hotel reservations. The parameters of the task are known in advance and the dialogue system is specifically designed for the task with a set of system prompts to elicit the required information.

According to [16] there have been three generations of spoken dialogue systems:

- *Informational*, in which the system retrieves information for the user.
- *Transactional*, in which the system assists the user in a transaction.
- *Problem solving*, in which the system supports the user in solving a problem, for example, troubleshooting a malfunctioning piece of equipment such as a cable modem.

The input requirements for dialogue systems can range from highly restricted input, where the system elicits single-word or minimal responses to carefully designed prompts, to less constrained input that can be specified in a set of grammatical rules and to free-form input that requires more complex interpretation mechanisms. Whereas voice search and question answering may provide answers to one-shot queries, spoken dialogue is required when it is necessary to elicit a number of items of information from the user that could not be easily acquired within a single input. Given that the tasks for which spoken dialogue systems have traditionally been designed are well defined, evaluation of system performance has generally involved measuring the extent to which the task can be accomplished successfully within an acceptable time and to the satisfaction of the user [17, 18].

A new type of dialogue system is evolving that provides conversational companionship to users, such as the elderly (see Section 9.4.4). Support (or companionship) is provided over a longer period of time compared with the short-term interaction typical in a task-based dialogue system, and often a long-term relationship may develop. This type of system is likely to require different criteria for its evaluation.

Table 9.1 summarizes this overview of interactive speech systems, specifying their main functions, the types of input they handle, and the types of output they generate, as well as the knowledge sources they draw on.

Table 9.1 Classification of Interactive Speech Systems

Application Type	Function	Input	Output	Knowledge Source
Voice Control	Control environment	Finite set of spoken commands	Action	Mapping of commands and related actions
Call Routing	Route telephone calls	Free-form speech	Transfer to desired destination	Mapping of spoken language inputs to set of destinations
Voice Search	Retrieve information (e.g., address)	Free-form speech	Retrieve item of information (e.g., address)	Structured information (e.g., database)
Question Answering	Retrieve answer to question	Free-form spoken question	Answer in form of sentence or short paragraph	Unstructured information (e.g., Web)
Spoken Dialogue	Information Transactions Problem solving	From constrained (e.g., single-word) to free-form speech	Response to query Clarification requests Further questions	Typically databases

9.3 THE COMPONENTS OF AN INTERACTIVE SPEECH SYSTEM

Although there are major differences in the technologies used by the different inter-active speech systems, common to all of them are the main processing components indicated in the high-level architecture depicted in Figure 9.1.

The flow of interaction is as follows. When the user asks a question, her words are captured by an audio device such as a microphone and passed to the *automatic speech recognition (ASR)* component, which outputs a string of words. This string is then analyzed by the *spoken language understanding (SLU)* component, which outputs a formal representation of its semantics (or meaning) in a form relevant to the back-end application. This representation is taken by the *dialogue manager (DM)*, which processes the input in relation to the task at hand (indicated here at a high level of abstraction as the *external knowledge* component) and decides what message to output to the user. The *response generation* component composes the message, which may involve taking the results of a database query and integrating them into one or more sentences of text. This text is then passed to the *text-to-speech synthesis (TTS)* component, which outputs the words as speech. The process can con-tinue in loops, resulting in a speech-based dialogue between the user and the system.

Each of the components described here is the subject of research in its own right, but for a spoken dialogue system to function properly all of the com-ponents must be linked in an end-to-end process. How the components work and the types of data passed between them vary. In the remainder of this section the input and output elements of the dialogue process will be described in a little more detail; the dialogue management process will be discussed in Section 9.3.3.

9.3.1 Input Interpretation

As indicated in Figure 9.1, the first stage of analysis is recognition of the user's input. This involves returning a sequence of words by matching a set of models, acquired

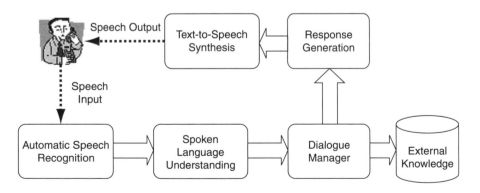

FIGURE 9.1

Architecture of a spoken dialogue system.

in a prior training phase, with the incoming speech signal that constitutes the user's utterance. ASR is a probabilistic pattern-matching process whose output is a set of word hypotheses, often referred to as an *n*-best list, or word graph. In some dialogue systems the first-best hypothesis is chosen and passed to SLU for further analysis. However, given that this hypothesis may not be correct, there is merit in maintaining multiple recognition hypotheses so that alternatives can be considered at a later processing stage. For a detailed account of speech recognition, particularly in noisy ambient environments, see [19].

Given a string of words from the ASR component, the SLU component analyzes it to determine its meaning. SLU is a complex process that can be carried out in a variety of ways. The traditional approach involves two stages: syntactic analysis, to determine the constituent structure of the recognized string, and semantic analysis, to determine the meaning of the constituents. This approach is motivated by research in theoretical and computational linguistics and it provides a deeper level of understanding by capturing fine-grained distinctions that might be missed in alternative approaches that aim to extract the meaning directly without recourse to syntactic analysis. Meaning is often represented using logical formulae or alternatively in terms of dialogue acts that represent the user's intent, that is, whether the utterance was meant as a question, a command, a promise, or a threat [20, 21].

In many spoken dialogue systems the meaning of the utterance is derived directly from the recognized string using a *semantic grammar*. A semantic grammar uses phrase structure rules as a syntactic grammar does, but its constituents are classified in terms of function or meaning rather than syntactic categories. Generally semantic grammars for spoken dialogue and other natural language systems are domain specific. So, for example, a system involving flights will have categories relevant to the flight domain, such as AIRLINE, DEPARTURE AIRPORT, and FLIGHT NUMBER, whereas a system involving banking will have categories such as ACCOUNT, BALANCE, and TRANSFER. The output of the parsing of an input string using a semantic grammar is usually a set of key words representing the main concepts expressed. A domain-specific dialogue act may also be the output of this analysis, accompanied by values extracted from the input string that fill slots in a frame. For example, *a flight from Belfast to Malaga* might be represented as

Intent: Flight_reservation
DepartCity: BFS
ArrivalCity: AGP

Both approaches described involve grammars constructed by a developer who creates the grammar rules, often on the basis of a corpus of texts from a relevant domain. An alternative approach is to derive statistical models of a language automatically from such texts by learning mappings between input strings and output structures [22, 23]. These models are easier to create as they involve annotating data rather than manually authoring grammars. Moreover, they can be easily adapted to new data and are more robust to the unpredictable and irregular output of the ASR process. They can also utilize efficient decoding methods to extract meaning from the input, thus avoiding many of the problems that arise with traditional parsing algorithms. Using statistical methods also provides a principled way to maintain multiple speech recognition and language understanding hypotheses based on probability distributions, and these can be used subsequently to drive the dialogue management process [24].

Different methods for language understanding have been used in some of the speech-based interactive systems described earlier. For example, *named entity extraction* can be used to locate named entities within the input string. There are predefined categories, such as person name, location, date, phone number, company name, that are relevant to the application. Extraction involves associating stretches of text with the named entities. Rule-based methods can be used to create patterns for named entities, as in the AT&T SLU system, in which grammar rules in the form of regular expressions were compiled into finite state acceptors [9]. Statistical methods can also be used—for example, in the HMIHY (How May I Help You) system, mappings were learned between strings and named entities. The output can be a list of named entities and their values, or, as in the case of the AT&T SLU system, a dialogue act representing the user's intent along with the named entities and their values. Thus, the user utterance *I want credit for ten dollars* would be output as

Request (Credit) monetary.amount=$10

Another approach, involving the classification of utterances using a set of predefined classes, has been used in call-routing applications. It could also be used in any application where the purpose is to determine the user's intent. The previous example illustrates this type of classification, where the user's intent was identified as REQUEST(CREDIT).

Classification can be rule or statistics based. In rule-based classification, rules map patterns of text into a finite set of categories; in statistical classification, salient phrases are extracted from data, clustered into grammar fragments, and associated with call types using statistical decision rules. In the AT&T SLU system, rules were used initially to bootstrap the system and then adapted using a learning algorithm when more data became available.

Classification is applicable where there is a relatively small and finite set of categories into which strings can be placed, and, in the case of machine learning, where there is sufficient data to support the training of a statistical classifier. Voice search, which supports a large semantic space in terms of potential input, is not suitable for this approach [11].

This description of the ASR and SLU components of a spoken dialogue system suggests a serial model in which the results of the ASR stage are passed to SLU for the next stage of analysis. However, there are a number of alternative approaches, one of which is to apply post-processing to the results of the ASR stage before proceeding to SLU. [25] uses a noisy channel model of ASR errors for this task, while [26] uses statistical models of words and contextual information to determine corrections. It is also possible to use evidence from later stages in the interpretation process. For example, [27, 28] use combinations of features at various levels, including ASR and SLU probabilities, as well as semantic and contextual features to reorder the *n*-best hypotheses from the ASR stage.

9.3.2 Output Generation

Generation of system output has received less attention in the research literature in comparison with interpretation of user input. Output generation consists of response generation, in which the message to be spoken to the user is constructed, and text-to-speech synthesis (TTS), in which the text is synthesized as a waveform and output as speech. In most commercial systems response generation is a fairly trivial task involving the insertion of items retrieved from the database into a predefined response template. However, considerable effort is devoted to issues such as prompt design since the quality of the output can have a major impact on the user's acceptance of the system; moreover, carefully designed prompts play an important role in constraining the user's response and thus in supporting the ASR and SLU processes [29].

Response generation can be viewed as two tasks: content planning and content realization. Content planning involves determining what to say by selecting and ranking options from the content to be expressed; planning the use of discourse relations, such as comparison and contrast, in order to present the information in a meaningful way; and adapting the information to the user's perceived needs and preferences. Content realization is concerned with how to express the content in terms of grouping different propositions into clauses and sentences, generating appropriate referring expressions, and using appropriate discourse cues.

As with other components of a spoken dialogue system, strategies for response generation can be handcrafted using rules to determine the desired output, or they can be learned using statistical methods. For an overview of natural language text generation see [30]. The use of TTS systems in ambient intelligence environments is discussed in [31].

9.3.3 Dialogue Management

The dialogue manager, the central component of a spoken dialogue system, accepts interpreted input from the ASR and SLU components, interacts with external knowledge sources, produces messages to be output to the user, and generally controls the dialogue flow. The dialogue management process can be viewed in terms of two main tasks:

- *Dialogue modeling*. Keeping track of the state of the dialogue.
- *Dialogue control*. Making decisions about the next system action.

Dialogue modeling provides the information used for dialogue control. Dialogue state information may include a record of what has been said so far in the dialogue, such as the propositions and entities that have been discussed (dialogue history). The extent to which this information is shared (or grounded) between the system and the user may also be recorded. Another type of information is the task record, which describes the information to be gathered in the dialogue. This record, often referred to as a form, frame, template, or status graph, is used to determine what information has been acquired by the system and what information is still needed. In simple methods of dialogue control this information may be encoded implicitly in a dialogue graph or in a form consisting of one or more slots to be filled with values elicited in the course of the dialogue.

One of the most advanced approaches to the representation of dialogue state information is information state theory [32], in which a wide range of information might be represented, including the user's mental state, such as beliefs, desires, and intentions; discourse obligations, such as the obligation to acknowledge a previous turn or respond to a question; overall goals and immediate goals and plans (or agenda). To date most approaches to dialogue modeling have maintained a single hypothesis about the current dialogue state. An alternative is to maintain multiple dialogue state hypotheses to which probabilities are assigned (see, for example, [24, 33–36]. Although such models are more complex, they have the advantage that they can incorporate more information, such as all of the n-best lists from the ASR and SLU components, including confidence scores, and can combine this information with context-specific expectations about user behavior in a principled way. Keeping track of multiple hypotheses also enables the system to reinterpret previous utterances and behaviors at a later point in the dialogue if an error is discovered.

Dialogue control involves deciding what to do next in the context of the current dialogue state. Decisions may include prompting for more input, clarifying or grounding the previous input, or outputting some information. These decisions may be pre-scripted, with choices based on factors such as the confidence levels associated with the user's input. For example, if the confidence levels are above a certain threshold, the system can assume that it has correctly interpreted the input and can proceed to its next action; if the levels are low, it may first try to verify that it has interpreted the input correctly or even ask the user to repeat her utterance.

These decisions can be anticipated at design time and hardcoded into the dialogue control. However some methods of dialogue control may involve decisions made dynamically based on reasoning about the current dialogue state and using evidence from a combination of domain and dialogue knowledge sources. Thus in addition to confidence scores from the ASR and SLU components, the DM may take other factors into account such as the relative importance of the information elicited, what needs to be achieved in the task at hand, the user's needs and preferences, and the dialogue history. There may also be mechanisms to enable the system to adapt its output and style of interaction to different users as well as sophisticated ways of detecting and handling errors.

Dialogue control can be viewed in terms of two dimensions:

- *Dialogue initiative*. Who has control over the dialogue.
- *Dialogue flow*. How dialogue control is implemented.

There are three types of dialogue initiatives. In a *system-directed dialogue*, the system is in control and prompts the user for input. This is the most common dialogue control type in current commercial systems, where typically a user requests a service; the system then asks a series of questions in order to collect the values for a database query that will provide the requested information. The following is a simple example (from [5]):

System: Where are you traveling to?
User: London.
System: What day do you wish to travel?
User: Friday.
System: At what time?
User: 9 a.m.

A major advantage of system-directed dialogues is that, since the dialogue flow is determined in advance, the user can be restricted to a small set of possible responses, to achieve more constrained and more accurate ASR and SLU.

In a *user-directed dialogue* (or user-initiative) the user controls the dialogue, as in question-answering (QA) systems. The following is an example (from [5]):

User: How many employees living in the London area earn more than 50,000?
System: Fifty four.
User: How many are female?
System: Eleven.
User: And managers?
System: Nine.

Because the user is allowed to ask unconstrained questions, often involving discourse phenomena such as ellipses, the system requires more advanced speech- and language-processing capabilities.

Finally, in *mixed-initiative dialogue* both system and user can take the initiative, as in naturally occurring conversations, to ask questions, change topics, and so on. The following example illustrates ([5]):

System: Where are you flying to?
User: I want to fly to London on Friday.
System: At what time?
User: Are there any cheap flights?

This dialogue begins with a system initiative. However, the user does not answer the system's second question but instead asks a question about cheap flights, taking the initiative and changing the topic. Mixed-initiative dialogue systems also require more advanced speech- and language-processing capabilities and, possibly, mechanisms for assessing the relevance of a topic change to the overall purpose of the dialogue and for deciding whether to follow the user's initiative or to maintain the system's agenda.

The term *mixed-initiative* has also been used, in a more restricted sense, in VoiceXML systems, where the user can volunteer more information than requested, as in the user's first response in the previous example [37]. Here the system has to keep track of the information provided by the user so as not to ask redundant questions – in this case, about the day of travel. A typical data structure used for this purpose is the *form*, as described earlier.

Dialogue flow can be implemented in several ways using

- Dialogue scripts
- Frames and slot filling
- Agent-based methods

Dialogue scripts define the actions that can be taken at each point (or state) of the dialogue. This method is also known as *finite-state dialogue control*. All of the predicted states of the dialogue, as well as the transitions between them, can be depicted in a graph, which can be represented diagrammatically provided there are not too many states and action choices. This approach is used for system-directed dialogues, but not for user-directed or mixed-initiative dialogues since the dialogue states cannot be predicted in advance.

Frame-based dialogue control is more flexible. Frames consist of slots that are filled with values elicited from the user. In a dialogue dealing with flights, for example, a frame is likely to have slots for departure and destination locations, times, dates, airlines, and so on. The aim is to fill these slots by gathering values from the user and then to retrieve records from a database that satisfy the user's constraints. This type of dialogue has also been referred to as *form-filling*. While it is possible to fill such a form using a dialogue script, in which the order of the system's questions is predetermined, the added value of frame-based control is that it supports more flexible dialogues by allowing the user to fill in the slots in different orders and combinations. For example, if the user responds to the system's initial prompt with more than one value, as in the previous example, these slots can be filled and the system can then ask for values for any slots that remain open. Thus the flow of the dialogue is not predetermined but depends on information the user provides in response to the system's prompts.

True mixed-initiative dialogues are similar to naturally occurring conversation, where either participant can introduce new topics, ask questions, request clarification, and so on. Methods for implementing them are the subject of research and have often been referred to as *agent-based dialogue control*, since they may involve some attempt to model dialogue as a process of collaboration between intelligent conversational agents. TRIPS is an example of an intelligent dialogue agent [38, 39]. In such a system, compared with script-based and frame-based approaches, the dialogue evolves dynamically based on the current context, which may take the form of a plan being developed by the system or the user, as in TRIPS, or some representation of the dialogue context that is updated as a result of each dialogue event, as in information state theory.

Generally the choice of dialogue management strategy is determined by the application. Task-based spoken dialogue systems are usually implemented using a form-filling approach in which the dialogue model is a form with slots to be filled and the dialogue control is either system directed or VoiceXML mixed-initiative. Systems for voice control, voice search, and question answering are typically user driven but may involve some degree of initiative switch in which the system takes control to constrain or otherwise redirect the dialogue. One interesting line of research is multi-strategy dialogue managers that can adopt different dialogue control styles depending on factors such as user experience and recognition conditions [40]. Generally in applications for ambient environments, more flexible approaches to dialogue management are needed (see Section 9.5).

The approaches to dialogue management discussed so far require careful design and handcrafting of rules, strategies, and dialogue models [29, 41]. However, a major problem is that it is difficult to design all the rules required to cover all aspects of dialogue management, particularly when taking into account the uncertainties that pervade every level of dialogue, from recognizing the words spoken to understanding the intentions behind them. An alternative is to use a data-driven method involving statistical machine learning. Three such approaches can be distinguished: supervised learning, utility maximization, and reinforcement learning (RL).

Supervised learning can be used when there is a corpus of examples of the optimal decisions to make in a dialogue [42, 43]. From such a labeled corpus, a stochastic dialogue model can be learned (or estimated) that can be applied to new dialogues that are similar to those recorded in the corpus.

With *utility maximization* the idea is to specify priorities for the system in terms of a real-valued objective function; optimization then determines what action to take in a given state in order to maximize that function. The action with the maximum immediate utility is selected (see, for example, [33, 34]).

In *reinforcement learning*, the priorities of the dialogue system are specified in a (real-valued) reward function and an optimization algorithm is applied to choose actions that maximize that function. In other words, the designer specifies the desired outcomes and the algorithm works out the details. The optimal policy consists of choosing the best action at each state in the dialogue to achieve a given success metric, such as successful and efficient dialogue completion, or some measure of user satisfaction. In the first applications of RL in spoken dialogue systems, dialogue was formalized as a Markov decision process (MDP) (see, for example, [44]); more recently partially observable Markov decision processes (POMDPs) have been used to handle the various uncertainties inherent in dialogue interactions (see, for example, [24]).

The advantages and disadvantages of data-driven approaches are the subject of much active research. Their role in applications for ambient environments will be discussed further in Section 9.5.

9.4 EXAMPLES OF SPOKEN DIALOGUE SYSTEMS FOR AMBIENT INTELLIGENCE ENVIRONMENTS

A number of recent research projects investigated the application of spoken dialogue technology in ambient intelligence environments. A selection of these will be reviewed in this section. CHAT is concerned with spoken dialogue systems in cars across a number of domains. SmartKom involves spoken and multimodal communication in three environments: a public kiosk information system, a home-based system for device control and information services, and a mobile environment for drivers and pedestrians. SmartWeb addresses open-domain information retrieval using spoken language question answering. The TALK project deals with multimodal dialogue interaction involving various devices and services in the home and car. Finally, the COMPANIONS project addresses issues in assisting senior citizens with everyday tasks and accessing information through an embodied conversational agent.

9.4.1 CHAT

CHAT is a joint NIST ATP project involving Bosch RTC, CSLI (Stanford University), Volkswagen (U.S.), and SRI International [7]. The CHAT system currently operates in the entertainment (MP3 player), navigation, and Web services (restaurant finder) domains and employs state-of-the art technologies in robust speech recognition and spoken language understanding, flexible dialogue management, and optimization of output content. This contrasts with current in-car speech systems that are based on the command-and-control paradigm in which drivers use a carefully designed set of voice commands to control audio and navigation devices and operate the phone in hands-free mode [45]. Such systems are limited in several ways. First, there is no flexibility in what can be spoken by the user, who has to learn and remember the particular commands that are available for each device. This potentially contributes to the cognitive load on the driver, who must pay full attention to the primary task of driving. Another issue is that, in current systems it is not easy to add new devices and functionalities as this requires the addition of new vocabularies and commands that also must be learned and memorized. Finally, the technology for voice-based command-and-control applications is insufficient for more advanced applications such as online information search and Web-based services that require more sophisticated natural language processing and dialogue modeling capabilities.

Currently most spoken dialogue systems operate within a single domain or, as in the Galaxy Communicator systems [46], across a predefined and limited domain. CHAT allows users to switch easily between the domains that are currently supported. The following is an example:

User: Switch to restaurant.
System: OK, switched to the restaurant finder.
User: Can you find me a Chinese restaurant in Palo Alto with good service?
System: There are 11 Chinese restaurants in Palo Alto with good service.

User: Switch to navigation.
System: OK, switched to navigation.
User: Take me to Little Garden Restaurant, but stop by the Bosch Page Mill Office.

User: Switch to music player.
System: OK, switched to MP3 music player.
User: What songs do you have by Alicia Keys?

In these examples the user makes explicit statements to switch domains. Implicit domain switching is also possible. For example, the user has selected a restaurant in the restaurant domain and then says, *Find me a fast route to restaurant XYZ*, without explicitly saying *Switch to navigation*. Keeping track of multiple threads related to different devices and domains is achieved through a dynamically evolving dialogue move tree, which classifies and interprets user utterances in terms of the current dialogue context and selects from a set of possible system responses [28].

Robustness is important in speech recognition in noisy environments as well as in other aspects of the conversational process, such as extracting the meaning of the input in relation to the current context and recovering from errors. Imperfect speech, which includes disfluencies, incomplete references to names, and phrase fragments, along with inexactly memorized names, contributes to problems in speech recognition and language understanding. Solutions include the use of separate n-gram name models, a disfluency language model, and a multi-component language understanding module that uses deep linguistic processing but with a back-off strategy using shallow semantic parsing. Special dialogue strategies are used for error handling, including combining information from the n-best output from the spoken language understanding module, the possible dialogue moves, and the dialogue [27].

An important consideration for in-car spoken dialogue systems is that the interaction should not divert drivers from their primary task of driving. The content optimizer controls the amount of information to be output to the driver, especially in the case of lengthy lists of results, by proposing extra criteria to narrow the results down. Additionally, when no result is returned from the database, the user constraints are relaxed. These measures were shown to lead to increased user satisfaction [47], while for other measures an overall task completion rate of 98% was achieved for navigation tasks and an average of 2.3 turns were required to complete the tasks, indicating a high level of dialogue efficiency.

9.4.2 SmartKom and SmartWeb

SmartKom is a multimodal dialogue system developed through a large-scale project funded by the German Federal Ministry of Education and Research and involving 12 partners across academia and industry [48]. It supports collaborative, multimodal dialogues that include face-to-face interaction with an embodied conversational agent (Smartakus) in three environments:

- *Public*. A kiosk-based help system for tasks such as telephoning, faxing, and e-mailing, retrieving information about movies, making ticket and seat reservations, and biometrical authentication [49].
- *Home*. An infotainment companion to operate various TV appliances—for example, VCR programming—and an intelligent interface to the electronic program guide (EPG) to browse and create personalized program listings [50].
- *Mobile*. A mobile travel companion to be used in the car as well as while walking to assist with navigation and point-of-interest information retrieval [51, 52].

SmartKom required a collaborative dialogue between the user and the system to define and elaborate tasks as well as monitor their execution. Given the range of modalities available for input and output—speech, gesture, facial expression—the technical challenges included seamless fusion and mutual disambiguation of the input as well as plan-based methods for multimodal fission and adaptive output presentation. The system was based on a distributed, blackboard component architecture that used a publish/subscribe approach for distributed event notification. Knowledge was represented in a series of ontologies that include a domain-independent top-level ontology combined with multiple domain-specific ontologies [53].

An important consideration in SmartKom's development was to integrate the various devices and environments to support ubiquitous access to information using any device while providing a seamless user interface within a single dialogue system. This required the ability to manage physical connections when users changed devices and to represent how different modalities were supported on a particular device. For example, the user could transition from a pedestrian to a driving scenario in a car, requiring a change from PDA to in-car device and a change of permissible modalities from multimodal input and presentation to speech-based input and output.

The following interaction with the kiosk-based system SmartKom Public illustrates a combination of modalities available to the user and the system in a scenario involving movie information, ticket ordering, and seat reservation (from [49]):

User: I'd like to go to the movies tonight.
Smartakus: (presents a list of movies and a map)
Here is a selection of tonight's movies.
I've marked the cinemas on the map.
User: (points to the cinema "Kamera" on the map)
What's on here?
Smartakus: (presents the programme of the cinema "Kamera")
These are tonight's movies at the "Kamera"
User: (points to *Matrix:Reloaded*)
Tell me more about this movie?
Smartakus: (presents additional information)
Here is more information on *Matrix:Reloaded*
User: I'd like two tickets for this film at 8 pm.
Smartakus: (presents seat plan of the "Kamera")

Where do you want to sit?
User: (encircles specific seats)
Here.
Smartakus: (highlights the selected seats on the plan)
Is this correct?
User: Exactly.
Smartakus: I reserved the seats.
Your reservation code is 42.

While the SmartKom Public system offered high communication bandwidth and high quality in input and output results, its mobile systems were technically challenging in terms of device capabilities, noisy environments, and a dynamically changing context while walking or driving.

The main applications for SmartKom Mobile were navigation, route planning, and parking (including location, hours of operation, available parking spaces, and fees). The system also supported dialogues about points of interest using interactive maps whose semantic representation supported the dialogue. Thus the user could ask for particular objects represented on the map; the system could also behave proactively, for example, by generating a message about an interesting landmark the user was approaching and offering a more detailed description of it.

SmartKom is based on a distributed and modular architecture consisting of a large number of components whose successful integration is crucial for robust, real-time performance. Its dialogue management component is of particular relevance here. In SmartKom the Dialogue Manager plans and performs dialogic interaction between the user and the system, as represented by the embodied conversational agent Smartakus, and plans and executes interaction with system components and applications. Users communicate their wishes to Smartakus, who provides a unified and personalized interface to the system's functionalities [54].

Dialogue management is accomplished through a planning module combined with a dialogue move engine. The module devises the system's actions by adopting a goal and then chaining backward from it, executing plan operators and invoking subplans to resolve preconditions of the operators. For example, sending a fax requires the user to state the fax number; a subplan can be initiated to elicit this information. The subplan is carried out as a communication game, which consists of a sequence of moves by each participant—in this case, request–response. Composite games can be constructed from basic games through concatenation or nesting.

The dialogue manager maintains a stack of goals and integrates the user's utterances and inputs into an overall dialogue plan. The user can cooperate with the system and allow that plan to be followed. However, there is also scope for the user to make contributions not expected within the plan or to provide information in a different sequence from that anticipated. In such cases the plan has to be revised and modified. In the fax application, for example, if the user says something like *I want to send it to Alex*, the system can replan the dialogue and, instead of asking the user to type in Alex's fax number, initiate an address book search to find it. In another situation, the user might suspend the dialogue temporarily, for example, in a driving emergency. Then the system should be able to suspend the interaction and resume the dialogue after a short time, still taking into account changes that might have occurred in the intervening period.

SmartKom works in multiple domains and on various devices, but the dialogues it supports are domain specific – for example, cinema information, TV programs, or driving routes. A follow-up project known as SmartWeb, uses the Web as a knowledge base and exploits the machine-understandable content of semantic Web pages for intelligent question answering [55]. SmartWeb also supports task-oriented dialogues for Web services that involve online form filling, but in this case the system forwards the query to the external service rather than simulating the service within the dialogue.

In the SmartWeb scenario a user asks questions about a visit to a Football World Cup stadium in 2006. Input modalities include speech over a Bluetooth headset, gestures based on pen input to a smart phone, a face camera, biosignals, and haptic feedback on the handlebars of a BMW motorbike. Output is in the form of multimodal displays. Questions can be about players, events, weather information, and services available through the Web such as a navigation to the stadium.

The following are examples of questions, translated from the original German, that can be handled by SmartWeb (from [56]):

Who won the 1954 final?
Show me the goal from the match between France and Senegal.
What is playing at the cinemas in Saarbrucken tonight?
Where is this movie playing?
Are there any traffic jams between Karlsruhe and Berlin?

Answers are obtained from the Web using named entity extraction to obtain information about persons, objects, and locations named in the query. The question analysis process is ontology driven, resulting in a paraphrase of the question and a semantic representation in XML format. The user interface is context aware in that it supports the user in different roles: driver, motorcyclist, pedestrian, and spectator. As with SmartKom, a major emphasis in the SmartWeb project is an infrastructure that can handle multimodal, open-domain question answering and requests for services within a Semantic Web framework using standard interfaces and protocols.

Unlike SmartKom, SmartWeb supports a limited dialogue consisting mainly of single question–answer pairs. However, follow-up questions are possible based on the results displayed on the browser. For example, looking at the display of previous World Cup champions, the user can point to a team and ask *How often did this team win?* The system uses multimodal reference resolution to resolve the referent of the query and compose an answer.

9.4.3 **TALK**

TALK (Talk and Look: Tools for Ambient Linguistic Knowledge) was a three-year, EU-funded project involving nine partners from academia and industry [57]. Similar to SmartKom, TALK was concerned with multimodal dialogue interaction involving various devices and services in the home and car, and its main aim was to make dialogue systems more conversational, robust, and adaptive. The theoretical basis for dialogue management in TALK is information state update (ISU) [32] developed in previous projects such as SIRIDUS [58] and TRINDI [59]. ISU provides a rich formalism for the representation of dialogue context, which is essential for the multitasking and event-driven dialogues typical of in-car interaction.

One goal of the project was to develop ISU to make it reusable for different languages, modalities, and application domains. Another was to develop techniques for the automated learning of optimal dialogue strategies from corpora of human interactions modeled using ISU [60]. Demonstrator systems developed included the SAMMIE in-car dialogue system installed in a BMW test car [61] and the MIMUS home automation system that allowed users to control devices in the home using voice and mouse clicks [62, 63].

SAMMIE supports multimodal interaction with an MP3 database and player; the user controls the player with commands to play, pause, and select tracks. The interpretation module supports reference resolution—for example, *the second one*—as well as list processing with and without constraints—for example, *Show me all albums by the Beatles*. Dialogue management is mixed-initiative, as shown in the following example in which the user begins with a command to play a song and the system responds with queries to narrow down the command scope:

> User: Please play *Irgendwie, Irgendwo, Irgendwann.*
> System: Would you like the album or the song?
> User: The song.
> System: By which of these two artists: Nena or Eisfeld?
> User: By Nena.

SAMMIE's dialogue management involves modeling the interaction as collaborative problem solving within ISU. Collaborative problem solving uses objects such as objective, recipe, constraint, evaluation, situation, and resource to model the solution at a domain-independent level [64]. The model is then applied to a domain using inheritance and instantiation of domain-specific types and objects from the abstract objects. ISU, in common with similar approaches, provides methods for the integration of utterance information, including grounding status, decisions for what the system should do and output next, and preparation and realization of communicative intentions.

To demonstrate SAMMIE's ability to process unrestricted spoken input and mixed-initiative strategies, a command-and-control version was constructed that simulated state-of-the-art state-based dialogue control. It was found that SAMMIE provided a number of advantages: Users did not have to learn sets of command words and they could switch tasks easily in comparison with the more restricted interaction provided by a menu-based system. A second application domain for tourist information was also developed to demonstrate the reusability of the domain-independent system architecture, showing that it was possible to develop a fully working prototype for a different domain within a relatively short time.

The MIMUS system supports users in the home environment. It was implemented as a set of collaborative agents interacting with a common knowledge source in the form of an OWL ontology. As in SAMMIE, ISU drives dialogue management. The dialogue manager uses the ontology to answer queries from the user and as a resource for the resolution of reference phenomena—for example, which lamp is being referred to in an ambiguous command such as *Turn off the lamp in the kitchen* when there is more than one switched on. Following a dialogue move, update rules are triggered that result in runtime changes to the ontology.

Ontologies play a major role in the TALK project. In addition to providing a representation for objects in the home that changes dynamically during the course of an interaction, they automatically generate grammar rules for the interpretation of multimodal and multilingual input [65]. The advantage of this approach is that coherence and completeness can be ensured between domain knowledge and linguistic knowledge and that new grammars can be developed quickly for the ASR and SLU modules using the same mechanism.

In addition to the demonstration projects just described, TALK addressed several research issues, including the role of ontologies and the use of ISU in dialogue. A major research focus was the development of methods to support the automatic learning of dialogue strategies from examples of human interactions [24, 66]. Other contributions of the project include the collection of corpora for the automatic training of dialogue systems [67, 68] as well as the development of user simulators to support large-scale empirical studies of user–system interactions without the need for large groups of users [69, 70].

9.4.4 COMPANIONS

COMPANIONS was a four-year, EU-funded project involving a consortium of 16 partners across 8 countries [71]. Its aim was to assist senior citizens in carrying out everyday tasks and to provide them easy access to information, using a variety of devices ranging from PCs to handhelds and supporting interaction with small robots and embodied conversational agents [72]. The main technologies involved were speech and natural language processing, emotion processing and the social use of language, and dialogue management.

COMPANIONS had two demonstrators: a health and fitness companion and a senior companion. The purpose of the health and fitness companion was to monitor information about a user's eating habits and fitness activities in support of a healthy lifestyle. The senior companion was designed as a conversational partner, providing access to information and services, helping with everyday tasks, entertaining, and chatting with them about experiences and memories evoked by photographs.

Dialogue management in COMPANIONS required a different approach from the form-filling method used widely in traditional task-based dialogue systems. Because the goal of the interaction was to provide personal assistance and companionship, the interactions were less clearly defined. Moreover, whereas in traditional systems each interaction is normally modeled as a single event, COMPANIONS aimed to model the development of a longer-term relationship between user and conversational agent. There was also a range of interfaces available, such as avatars, talking heads, and small robots, compared to just the telephone in traditional systems. Finally, information gathered by the system included not only speech but images, in the form of photos, as well as information about the user's location and physical state while taking exercise, in the form of GPS and sensor data.

COMPANIONS handled these dialogue management issues through a distributed, agent-based architecture using an object-oriented approach in which inheritance separated generic dialogue behavior from domain-specific dialogue actions. Information and functionalities were shared across components in the distributed system. The agents were specialized software components that carried out specific dialogue actions. In the health and fitness companion, which was based on the Jaspis architecture [73], agents were specialized for particular tasks, such as handling speech recognition errors or presenting information in a particular way. There could also be different agents for the same task, for example, to provide speech output in different languages. This feature enabled the system to adapt dynamically to both situation and user. The selection of a specific agent was made dynamically based on scores calculated by the evaluators, which scored each agent according to its applicability within a given dialogue situation. Each evaluator scored each agent and the agent that received the highest score was selected to deal with the current dialogue situation, which included information on current input, dialogue context, and user preferences.

A similar approach was used for the senior companion demonstrator, in which there were two types of agents: behavior agents that handled a particular conversational task such as DISCOVER USER NAME or READ NEWS, and control agents that determined which behavior agent should run at a particular time [74]. Inter-agent communication was based on the publish/subscribe mechanism that was used in SmartKom.

While in SmartKom domain knowledge was represented in a series of ontologies, in the health and fitness companion there was a cognitive model that actively processed domain information [75]. This involved reasoning and learning about the domain as well as updating the cognitive model with new information that was acquired during the dialogue. In the senior companion this functionality was performed in the working memory, which, in addition to keeping track of relevant predicates and objects, tried to keep its knowledge consistent, actively forgetting old knowledge and automatically inferring new knowledge [74].

The dialogue manager in each system made use of domain information to control the dialogue. In the health and fitness companion it maintained and updated a dialogue state consisting of a dialogue history tree, a stack of active dialogue topics, and the current user input (including ASR confidence scores and n-best lists) [75]. In the senior companion a stack was used to deal with user interruptions when an agent was in the process of executing a dialogue sequence [74]. Each dialogue behavior was placed on the stack so that the currently running behavior was the one at the top. If a new behavior was initiated, as in a user interruption, it was pushed to the top of the stack, above the interrupted behavior. When completed it was popped and the original behavior resumed. In a special case, items could be removed from any position in the stack, for example, if the user made reference to an item further down. Behaviors could also be removed from the stack if they had been inactive for some time—in other words, when the topic was no longer relevant.

9.5 CHALLENGES FOR SPOKEN DIALOGUE TECHNOLOGY IN AMBIENT INTELLIGENCE ENVIRONMENTS

The preceding sections described the components of spoken dialogue systems and reviewed recent research involving spoken dialogue for ambient intelligence environments. This section outlines some of the challenges that this research must address.

9.5.1 Infrastructural Challenges

A spoken dialogue system cannot operate in a vacuum. This is particularly the case for systems that will operate in ambient intelligence environments, where the infrastructure can be viewed in terms of an operational layer, an intelligent layer, and the ambient intelligence layer [76].

The operational layer includes elements required to make the system work, such as hardware, operating systems, and communications. Traditionally, spoken dialogue systems have been linked to the telephone to provide a range of customer services, but the use of other handheld devices such as mobile phones and PDAs is increasing, particularly for multimodal input and output. Spoken dialogue can also be implemented on public service kiosks and, indeed, on any type of equipment that can embed devices for capturing and outputting speech. These devices may take the form of avatars that provide a lifelike character for the interaction.

Network communications are another aspect of the operational layer. Often speech-based applications use distributed systems to overcome issues such as processing power and footprint. For example, handheld devices run on limited resources and so resource-intensive applications such as speech recognition often run on a server rather than on the client device itself. For efficient and seamless functioning, a level of network integration is required that is both cost effective and reliable.

At the intelligent layer are the various applications and knowledge sources accessed by the system. Spoken dialogue systems traditionally were used to access information residing in databases, such as flight times, stock quotes, or hotel prices.

Now other sources of information are being used, such as Web pages that are parsed for content and RSS news feeds. Applications involving transactions are often conducted through Web-based APIs, for example, to buy goods from an online service provider. Various resources are accessed as part of the processing required by a spoken dialogue application: large databases of pronunciations, street names, and directory listings, large grammars in multiple languages, and ontologies that represent the domain knowledge.

Finally, within the ambient intelligence layer are the locations for these systems. In addition to the home there are a number of mobile environments in which spoken dialogue can be used, such as a car, pedestrian sidewalks, and public transport. In addition to the technical challenges of such diverse environments—as noise, requirements for seamless and uninterrupted communications, and the ability to function on a range of devices, for example—there are many issues concerning usability, acceptability, and adaptability to users of all types.

9.5.2 Challenges for Spoken Dialogue Technology

A number of challenges concern specific aspects of spoken dialogue technology, including methods for dialogue control, representation of dialogue and user states, and the use of learning to enable systems improvement over time.

In traditional dialogue systems dialogue control is often achieved using methods that are appropriate to the application—for example, system-directed for applications involving predetermined services and transactions, and user initiative for more open-ended applications such as voice search and question answering. Mixed-initiative dialogue has been explored mainly in research systems involving collaborative problem solving or human-like conversation.

In ambient intelligence environments dialogue control will need to be more open and more diverse. On occasion users will want to query the system for information using unrestricted natural language, but it might be necessary for the system to switch to a more constrained dialogue to elicit particular details. Within a system-directed dialogue users may also wish to query or clarify things with the system, or take over the initiative to introduce a different topic. Or it might be necessary for the system to interrupt the ongoing dialogue because there is some important information to be conveyed. More generally, dialogues may be less well structured than the form-filling variety in which the interaction is determined by a sequence of slots to be filled. They may be more opportunistic and distributed, as the user obtains some information from one application and then switches seamlessly to a different application, perhaps to engage in a casual conversation.

The implications of open-ended dialogue control are that it will be necessary to maintain more comprehensive models of dialogue and user states in order to support users as they move between applications and environments. Various models have been developed to support the various aspects of dialogue management, such as ISU. It will be necessary to extend these models to deal with the more transient and opportunistic dialogues that occur in ambient intelligence environments.

Finally, there is a need for systems that can learn over time as a result of their interactions with users and adapt their behavior to both the user and the situation. While much progress has been made in machine learning–based dialogue management, the applications using it have generally involved fairly simple form filling where the parameters to be learned are simple. Major challenges are to be expected when learning is extended to the more open-ended environments of ambient intelligence.

9.6 CONCLUSIONS

This chapter described the main characteristics of spoken dialogue applications and explored how spoken dialogue technology can be applied to the more open-ended environments of ambient intelligence. Spoken dialogue technology is a multidisciplinary field that has attracted considerable attention over recent years. It is likely that many of the challenges and issues raised in this chapter will be the subject of future research, resulting in advances in the underlying technologies and providing support for a wide range of users, including senior citizens and people with disabilities as well as, more generally, users who require assistance in managing their everyday activities.

REFERENCES

[1] Augusto JC, McCullagh P. Ambient intelligence: Concepts and applications. International Journal of Computer Science and Information Systems 2007;4(1):1–28.

[2] Schilit B, Adams N, Want R. Context-aware computing applications, In: IEEE Workshop on Mobile Computing Systems and Applications (WMCSA'94). Santa Cruz, CA; 1994. p. 89–101.

[3] Bolchini B, Curino C, Quintarelli E, Schreiber FA, Tanca L. A data-oriented survey of context models. SIGMOD Record 2007;36(4):19–26.

[4] Lafuente-Rojo A, Abascal-González J, Cai Y. Ambient intelligence: Chronicle of an announced technological revolution. UPGRADE 2007;8(4):8–12.

[5] McTear M. Spoken Dialogue Technology: Toward the Conversational User Interface. Springer; 2004.

[6] Gárate A, Herrasti N, López A. GENIO: An ambient intelligence application in home automation and entertainment environments. In: Joint sOcEUSAI Conference. Grenoble, France. 2005. p. 241–5.

[7] Weng F, Yan B, Feng Z, Ratiu F, Raya M, Lathrop B, et al. CHAT to your destination. In: Keizer S, Bunt T, Paek T, editors. Proceedings of the 8th SIGdial Workshop on Dialogue and Discourse. Antwerp, Belgium. 2007. p. 79–86.

[8] Gorin A, Riccardi G, Wright J. How may I help you? Speech Comm 1997;23(1-2):113–27.

[9] Gupta N, Tür G, Hakkani-Tür D, Bangalore S, Riccardi G, Gilbert M. The AT&T Spoken Language Understanding System. IEEE Transactions on Speech Audio Processing 2006; 14(1):213–22.

[10] Walker M, Langkilde-Geary I, Wright-Hastie H, Wright J, Gorin A. Automatically training a problematic dialogue predictor for the HMIHY spoken dialogue system. Journal of Artificial Intelligence Research 2002;16:293–319.

[11] Wang YY, Yu D, Ju YC, Acero A. An introduction to voice search. IEEE Signal Processing Magazine 2008;25(3):29–37.

[12] Acero A, Bernstein N, Chambers R, Ju YC, Li X, Odell J, et al. Live search for mobile: Web services by voice on the cellphone. In: IEEE Conference on Acoustics, Speech and Signal processing (ICASSP'08). Las Vegas, NV; 2008. p. 5256–9.

[13] Polifroni J, Walker MA. An analysis of automatic content selection algorithms for spoken dialogue system summaries, In: Proceedings of the IEEE/ACL 2006 Workshop on Spoken Language Technology (SLT); Aruba; 2006.

[14] Voorhees E. QA Track overview (TREC) 2001. In: Ninth Text REtrieval Conference (TREC-9). Gaithersburg, MD; 2001. p. 1–15.

[15] Gilbert M, Feng J. Speech and language processing over the Web. IEEE Signal Processing Magazine 2008;25(3):18–28.

[16] Pieraccini R, Huerta J. Where do we go from here? Research and commercial spoken dialog systems, In: Proceedings of the 6th SIGdial Workshop on Dialogue and Discourse. Lisbon, Portugal; 2005. p. 1–10.

[17] Möller S, Smeele P, Boland H, Krebber J. Evaluating spoken dialogue systems according to de-facto standards: A case study. Computer Speech and Language 2007;21(1):26–53.

[18] Möller S, Engelbrecht K-P, Kuhnel C, Naumann A, Wechsung I, Weiss B. Evaluation of multimodal interfaces for ambient intelligence. In: Aghajan H, López-Cózar Delgado R, Augusto JC, editors. Human-Centric Interfaces for Ambient Intelligence. Elsevier 2009.

[19] Paliwal K, Yao K. Robust speech recognition under noisy ambient conditions. In: Aghajan H, López-Cózar Delgado R, Augusto JC, editors. Human-Centric Interfaces for Ambient Intelligence. Elsevier 2009.

[20] Traum DR, Hinkelman EA. Conversation acts in task-oriented spoken dialogue. Computational Intelligence 1992;8(3):575–99.

[21] Jurafsky D. Pragmatics and computational linguistics. In: Horn LR, Ward GL, editors. The Handbook of Pragmatics. Blackwell; 2004.

[22] De Mori R, Bechet F, Hakkani-Tür D, McTear M, Riccardi G, Tur G. Spoken language understanding. IEEE Signal Processing Magazine 2008;25(3):50–8.

[23] Jeong M, Lee GG. Machine learning approaches to spoken language understanding. In: Aghajan R, López-Cózar Delgado R, Augusto JC, editors. Human-Centric Interfaces for Ambient Intelligence. Elsevier; 2009.

[24] Williams JD, Young SJ. Partially observable Markov decision processes for spoken dialog systems. Computer Speech and Language 2007;21(2):393–422.

[25] Ringger E, Allen JF. Error correction via a postprocessor for continuous speech recognition. In: Proceedings of the IEEE International Conference on Acoustics, Speech, and Signal Processing. Atlanta, GA; 1996. p. 427–30.

[26] López-Cózar R, Callejas Z. ASR post-correction for spoken dialogue systems based on semantic, syntactic, lexical and contextual information. Speech Comm 2008;50(8-9):745–66.

[27] Purver M, Ratiu F, Cavedon L. Robust interpretation in dialogue by combining confidence scores with contextual features. In: Proceedings of INTERSPEECH 2006. Pittsburgh, PA; 2006. p. 1–4.

[28] Lemon O, Gruenstein A. Multithreaded context for robust conversational interfaces: Context-sensitive speech recognition and interpretation of corrective fragments. ACM Transactions on Computer–Human Interaction (ACM TOCHI) 2004;11(3):241–67.

[29] Cohen M, Giangola J, Balogh J. Voice User Interface Design. Addison-Wesley; 2004.

[30] Fernández C, Baiget P, Roca X, González J. Exploiting natural language generation in scene interpretation. In: Aghajan H, López-Cózar Delgado R, Augusto JC, editors. Human-Centric Interfaces for Ambient Intelligence. Elsevier; 2009.

[31] Bulut M, Narayanan S. Speech synthesis in ambient intelligence environments. In: Aghajan H, López-Cózar Delgado R, Augusto JC, editors. Human-Centric Interfaces for Ambient Intelligence. Elsevier; 2009.

[32] Larsson S, Traum D. Information state and dialogue management in the TRINDI dialogue move engine toolkit. Natural Language Engineering 2000;5(34):323–40.

[33] Paek T, Horvitz E. Uncertainty, utility, and misunderstanding: A decision-theoretic perspective on grounding in conversational systems. In: AAAI Fall Symposium on Psychological Models of Communication. North Falmouth, MA; 1999. p. 85–92.

[34] Paek T, Horvitz E. Conversation as action under uncertainty. In: Proceedings of 6th Annual Conference on Uncertainty in Artificial Intelligence. San Francisco, CA; 2000. p. 455–64.

[35] Higashinaka R, Sudoh K, Nakano M. Incorporating discourse features into confidence scoring of intention recognition results in spoken dialogue systems. Speech Comm 2006;48(3–4): 417–36.

[36] Williams JD, Young SJ. Scaling POMDPs for spoken dialog management. IEEE Transactions on Audio, Speech, and Language Processing 2007;15(7):2116–29.

[37] Voice Extensible Markup Language (VoiceXML) Version 2.0. W3C Recommendation; 2004. http://www.w3.org/TR/voicexml20/.

[38] Allen JF, Byron DK, Dzikovska M, Ferguson G, Galescu L, Stent A. Towards conversational human-computer interaction. AI Magazine 2001;22(4):27–38.

[39] Allen JF, Ferguson G, Stent A. An architecture for more realistic conversational systems. In: Proceedings of the Intelligent User Interfaces (IUI-01). Santa Fe, NM; 2001. p. 1–8.

[40] Chu SW, O'Neill I, Hanna P. Using multiple strategies to manage spoken dialogue. In: Proceedings of INTERSPEECH 2007. Antwerp, Belgium; 2007. p. 158–61.

[41] Balentine B, Morgan DP. How to Build a Speech Recognition Application. 2nd ed. EIG Press; 2002.

[42] Griol D, Hurtado LF, Segarra E, Sanchis E. A statistical approach to spoken dialog systems design and evaluation. Speech Comm 2008;50(8–9):666–82.

[43] Lee C, Jung S, Jeong M, Lee GG. CHAT and goal-oriented dialog together: A unified example-based architecture for multi-domain dialog management. In: Proceedings of the IEEE/ACL 2006 Workshop on spoken language technology (SLT). Aruba: 2006.

[44] Levin E, Pieraccini R, Eckert W. A stochastic model of human–machine interaction for learning dialog strategies. IEEE Transactions on Speech and Audio Processing 2000;8(1):11–23.

[45] Berton A, Regel-Brietzmann P, Block H, Schachtl S, Gehrke M. How to integrate speech-operated Internet information dialogs into a car. In: Proceedings of INTERSPEECH 2007. Antwerp: Belgium; 2007.

[46] Seneff S, Hurley E, Lau R, Pao C, Schmid P, Zue V. Galaxy-II: A reference architecture for conversational system development. In: Proceedings of INTERSPEECH 1998. Sydney, Australia; 1998. p. 931–4.

[47] Pon-Barry H, Weng F, Varges S. Evaluation of content presentation strategies for an in-car spoken dialogue system. In: Proceedings of INTERSPEECH 2006. Pittsburgh, PA: 2006. p. 1930–3.

[48] Wahlster W, editor SmartKom: Foundations of Multimodal Dialogue Systems. Springer; 2006.

[49] Horndasch A, Rapp H, Röttger H. SmartKom-Public. In: Wahlster W, editor. SmartKom: Foundations of Multimodal Dialogue Systems. Springer; 2006. p. 471–92.

[50] Portele T, Goronzy S, Emele M, Kellner A, Torge S, te Vrugt J. SmartKom-Home: The interface to home entertainment. In: Wahlster W, editor. SmartKom: Foundations of multimodal dialogue systems. Springer; 2006. p. 493–503.

[51] Berton A, Bühler D, Minker W. SmartKom-Mobile car: User interaction with mobile services in a car environment. In: Wahlster W, editor. SmartKom: Foundations of Multimodal Dialogue Systems. Springer; 2006. p. 523–37.

[52] Malaka R, Häuler J, Aras H, Merdes M, Pfisterer D, Jöst M. SmartKom-Mobile: Intelligent interaction with a mobile interface. In: Wahlster W, editor. SmartKom: Foundations of Multimodal Dialogue Systems. Springer; 2006. p. 505–22.

[53] Wahlster W. Dialogue systems go multimodal: The SmartKom experience. In: Wahlster W, editor. SmartKom: Foundations of Multimodal Dialogue Systems. Springer; 2006. p. 3–27.

[54] Löckelt M. Plan-based dialogue management for multiple cooperating applications. In: Wahlster W, editor. SmartKom: Foundations of Multimodal Dialogue Systems. Springer; 2006. p. 301–16.

[55] Reithinger N, Bergweiler S, Engel R, Herzog G, Pfleger N, Romanelli M. A look under the hood—design and development of the first SmartWeb system demonstrator, In: Proceedings of the Seventh International Conference on Multimodal Interfaces: Trento. Italy; 2005.

[56] Reithinger N, Herzog G, Blocher A. SmartWeb—mobile broadband access to the Semantic Web. In: KI—Künstliche Intelligenz, vol. 2/07. Faculty for Artificial Intelligence of the "Gesellschaft fr Informatik e.V." (GI); 2007. p. 30–3.

[57] TALK project. http://www.talk-project.org/.

[58] SIRIDUS project. http://www.ling.gu.sc/projekt/siridus/.

[59] TRINDI project. http://www.ling.gu.se/projekt/trindi/.

[60] Lemon O, Georgila K, Stuttle M. An ISU dialogue system exhibiting reinforcement learning of dialogue policies: Generic slot-filling in the TALK in-car system, EACL (demo session). Trento: 2006.

[61] Becker T, Blaylock N, Gerstenberger C, Korthauer A, Perera N, Pitz M, et al. D5.3: In-Car Showcase Based on TALK Libraries. IST-507802 Deliverable 5.3. 2007.

[62] Pérez G, Amores G, Manchón P. A Multimodal Architecture for Home Control for Disabled Users. In: Proceedings of the IEEE/ACL 2006 workshop on spoken language technology (SLT). Aruba; 2006.

[63] Amores G, Pérez G, Manchón P. MIMUS: A multimodal and multilingual dialogue system for the home domain. In: Proceedings of the ACL 2007 Demo and Poster Sessions. Prague, Czechoslovakia: 2007. p. 1–4.

[64] Blaylock N, Allen JF. A collaborative problem-solving model of dialogue. In: Proceedings of the SIGdial Workshop on Discourse and Dialog. Portugal: Lisbon; 2005. p. 200–11.

[65] Pérez G, Amores G, Manchón P, González D. Generating multilingual grammars from OWL ontologies. In: Research in Computing Science, vol. 18. Advances in Natural Language Processing 2006; p. 3–14.

[66] Rieser V, Lemon O. Using machine learning to explore human multimodal clarification strategies. In: Proceedings of the IEEE/ACL 2006 Workshop on Spoken Language Technology (SLT). Aruba: 2006.

[67] Kruijff-Korbayova I, Becker T, Blaylock N, Gerstenberger C, Kaisser M, Poller P, et al. The SAMMIE corpus of multimodal dialogues with an MP3 Player. In: Proceedings of "International Conference on Language Resources and Evaluation" (REC 06); 2006. p. 2018–23.

[68] Manchón P, del Solar C, Amores G, Pérez G. The MIMUS Corpus, In: Proceedings of "International Conference on Language Resources and Evaluation" (LREC 06), International Workshop on Multimodal Corpora From Multimodal Behavior Theories to Usable Models. Genoa, Italy; 2006. p. 56–9.

[69] Georgila K, Henderson J, Lemon O. User simulation for spoken dialogue systems: Learning and evaluation. In: Proceedings of INTERSPEECH 2006. Pittsburgh, PA; 2006. p. 1–4.

[70] Schatzmann J, Weilhammer K, Stuttle MN, Young S. A survey of statistical user simulation techniques for reinforcement-learning of dialogue management strategies. Knowledge Engineering Review 2006;21(2):97–126.

[71] Mival O, Benyon D. Introducing the Companions Project: Intelligent, persistent, personalised interfaces to the Internet. In: Sas C, Ormerod T, editors. Proceedings of the 21st British HCI Group Annual Conference (HCI 07); 2007.

[72] Catizone R, Dingli A, Pinto H, Wilks Y. Information extraction tools and methods for understanding dialogue in a companion, In: Proceedings of the Sixth International Conference on Language Resources and Evaluation (LREC 08) Marrakech, Morocco; 2008.

[73] Turunen M, Hakulinen J, Rih K-J, Salonen E-P, Kainulainen A, Prusi P. An architecture and applications for accessibility systems. IBM Systems Journal 2005;44(3):485–504.

[74] Pinto H, Wilks Y, Catizone R, Dingli A. The Senior Companion Multiagent Dialogue System, In: Proceedings of the Seventh International Joint Conference on Autonomous Agents and Multi-Agent Systems (AAMAS 08); 2008. p. 1245–8.

[75] Hakulinen J, Turunen M. Interoperability and knowledge representation in distributed health and fitness companion dialogue system. In: Proceedings of the Workshop on Speech Processing for Safety Critical Translation and Pervasive Applications. Manchester. England; 2008. p. 2431.

[76] Ramos C, Augusto JC, Shapiro D. Ambient intelligence—the next step for artifical intelligence. IEEE Intelligent Systems 2008;23(2):15–8.

Speech Synthesis Systems in Ambient Intelligence Environments

10

Murtaza Bulut

Philips Research, Eindhoven, The Netherlands

Shrikanth S. Narayanan

Viterbi School of Engineering, University of Southern California, Los Angeles, California

ABSTRACT

In this chapter, the state of the art in speech synthesis systems and the components necessary to incorporate ambient intelligence characteristics in them are discussed. Possible implementation issues and their challenges are stated, and directions for future advances are outlined.

Key words: intelligent, adaptive, affective, flexible speech synthesis systems, situation- and environment-dependent functionality.

10.1 INTRODUCTION

Ambient intelligence (AmI) is a vision of the future for human-centric environments and applications [1–5]. As highlighted in the different chapters of this book, the AmI concept comprises broad areas of interest including visual, physiological, audio, and speech processing. In this chapter the emphasis will be on speech processing and specifically on speech synthesis.

Spoken interaction is probably the most effective means of human communication. Speech is an essential characteristic of humans that sets them apart from other species. It has evolved to become extremely flexible, variable, and consequently very complex. Speech is a medium for transmitting not only meaning but emotions, personal characteristics, culture, and environment. For machines to better communicate and interact with humans, it is essential that they have some human abilities, including the critical ability to speak.

In the past, and to date, human–machine interactions have been predominantly unidirectional or limited in interaction. With advances in artificial intelligence, machines are becoming more intelligent, evolving toward smart companions for humans. It is reasonable to assume that, instead of being mere processors of commands, future machines will be able to assist humans in making better decisions by taking appropriate initiative and providing specific comments and suggestions.

As a common and comfortable communication channel, speech will be one of the important mediums for the future human–machine communication. This requires that machines be able to generate speech that is adaptive to the environment and user actions, needs, and emotions, that can change with time and context, and that has the appropriate affective qualities. Naturally, synthetic speech must be as close as possible to natural human speech. For some applications artificial voice characteristics, such as voices of robots and cartoon characters, may be acceptable.

While current speech synthesis systems have made significant strides, they are far from producing speech synthesizers that have the flexibility and richness of their natural human counterparts. They can produce intelligible speech that is arguably pleasant to human ears, but they are limited in terms of affective processing of both input text and speech parameters. Additionally, synthesizing user-specific voices quickly and in a scalable fashion is still largely unsolved. The generated output is not easily adaptable to different environments and listener needs. The adaptive functionality requires capabilities for environment and user monitoring, change detection, and for making appropriate decisions and reactions; all performed in a reasonable time. Such capabilities require intelligent and adaptive natural language and signal processing. Incorporating these functionalities in speech synthesis systems is a challenging but necessary task for ambient intelligence environments.

To better visualize the areas of interest, challenges, and opportunities in speech synthesis, a short hypothetical scenario can be beneficial.

Every morning Thomas Green reviews his daily agenda with the help of a speech synthesizer that reads the agenda items to him in an energizing tone. Speech is presented synchronously with the visual information. Timing, content, length, and affective characteristics of the speech are adjusted to what Thomas is doing and feeling. Thomas can communicate with the speech synthesis system either manually or through the automatic speech recognizer. He can interrupt the system to give instructions and to make additions and corrections. The system is capable of understanding the instructions and responding in a timely manner.

Thomas knows that he has an important presentation scheduled for today. He instructs the system to prepare a 15-minute summary of his slides before leaving home. The summary is prepared within seconds, and Thomas starts listening to it using his cell phone while walking toward his car. The loudness, duration, and pitch of the synthesized speech is adjusted naturally to emphasize the important points. While inside his car, Thomas continues listening to the summary using the speech synthesizer in his car. The summary contains technical slides including complex mathematical equations, which Thomas wants to be explained in detail. The synthesis system changes the format of the presentation and explains the equations slowly and carefully, while making sure Thomas is satisfied. His satisfaction is assessed automatically from his voice, eye movements, facial gestures, and changes in body temperature and pressure sensors.

While listening to the slides, Thomas receives a call from his friend. The synthesizer automatically stops. His friend is speaking in Spanish; however, Thomas hears the English translation as if his friend were speaking English. At the other end, his friend hears Thomas speaking Spanish. After the call, the summary of presentation continues. Once it is completed, the speech synthesis system, although not instructed, also reads one of Thomas' favorite poems. This is a pleasant surprise to Thomas. "My assistant is always in a good mood, and it always knows what I want and like," he thinks. Thomas enjoys this very much.

In this scenario, the presentation by the speech synthesizer is masterfully blended with the surrounding environment and the user's activities. The system has high computational power and so can operate fast, and it has natural language-processing capabilities such as summarization, translation, language generation, and text interpretation. Also important, it can operate on different devices, both stationary and mobile, and in different locations.

This chapter describes state-of-the-art speech synthesis technology and shows how it can be incorporated into AmI environments. In addition, it outlines possible implementation challenges and future opportunities.

Section 10.2 presents a general outline of an AmI communication system that is able to generate and combine outputs from different modalities. Section 10.3 describes the state of the art in speech synthesis and summarizes different signal generation algorithms. Emotional speech generation is outlined in Section 10.4, and the characteristics of speech synthesizers for ambient intelligence interfaces are discussed in Section 10.5. Section 10.6 concludes the chapter.

10.2 SPEECH SYNTHESIS INTERFACES FOR AMBIENT INTELLIGENCE

The ambient intelligence vision is built on the concept of utilizing all possible information from potentially different sources. As part of an AmI environment, speech synthesis systems will have access to all of this information as well. In this section, the role of speech synthesis in ambient intelligence interfaces is described. The presented system is useful for identifying major components, stimulating ideas about size and complexity, and formulating future applications.

As illustrated in Figure 10.1, in an ambient intelligence environment, information collected and processed by the microprocessors can be stored in a potentially distributed database unit. Both past and present information is available. The processing of the sensor data typically entails some form of a pattern classification involving comparison of the collected data to the defined (i.e., trained) models in order to learn the situation. Present and past data is used together, but is weighted differently. The processed and organized informative data consists of facts and scientific assumptions (branch 004 in Figure 10.1) about user state and actions. As an example, consider an in-home application where, by analyzing the conversation between a husband and a wife, the processor can learn its topic and details (e.g., *They will go shopping at the closest supermarket, Albert Heijn, to buy groceries and then will go to the electronics store, Media Markt*). It can also sense the emotions of the husband (e.g., *Somewhat unhappy*).

The learned information is supplied to the idea generator, which can be viewed as an artificial intelligence (AI) module, *a brain*, that can understand the situation.

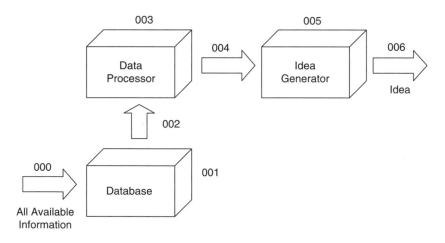

FIGURE 10.1

Data-processing and idea-generating components of an ambient intelligent speech synthesis system.

The idea generator processes the collected data and produces intelligent outputs describing the environment and user state. The outputs, which in this case are called ideas or concepts, are various descriptors such as transmission medium, user characteristics, user emotions, environment conditions, user actions, and action purpose. They are *ideas* about what is going on and what actions to take.

Returning to the example, the output in this case can be a thought: *The husband is not happy because his preference is first to go to Media Markt and then to Albert Heijn. He thinks that there may not be enough time to go to both places. However, he also knows that there is a need to buy groceries.* Evaluating the available information, the idea generator (block 005) "thinks" *The couple should go to Albert Heijn* because it knows that *there is nothing to cook for a dinner.* Also, it knows that *next weekend a big sale will start at Media Markt* (note that this information may or may not be known to the couple). In the processing of all this information, an idea is generated. This idea is to suggest that the couple *go to Albert Heijn now and to Media Markt next week.*

Once the idea is conceived, it is processed by the idea processor (Figure 10.2). The purpose is to find material to realize (i.e., to express) the idea. This step can be viewed as a decision about specifics: what to say, what to show, what to do, and so forth. For our example, the following message can be prepared for the husband: *"I understand that you want to go to the Media Markt, but today may not be the best time to do so. Look at this (showing the video of the LCD TV that he plans to buy). The TV that you want to buy will be on sale next week and you'll get it for 500 Euros less. Besides, there is nothing to cook for today"* (showing his favorite food on the screen and some videos of him eating it).

Note that at this stage nothing is said or shown (it will be later; see Figure 10.4); only the specifics of the material to be used are precisely defined. As noted, the output will be, in general, multimodal, it will be context sensitive, and it will contain speech, video, audio, and maybe some ambiance components such as light and smell effects. The content from these different modalities will be presented simultaneously, so it

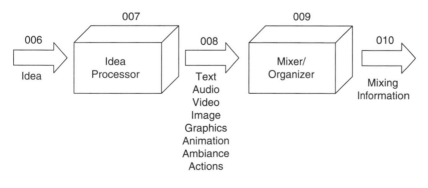

FIGURE 10.2

Content and mixing information generation.

needs to be annotated, aligned, and modified as necessary to ensure that it is appropriately mixed. The required mixing information is generated by the mixer (block 009) and transmitted to the different processors that are processing the data to prepare the final output signals.

One such processor is the text-to-speech (TTS) synthesizer (Figure 10.3). In it the input text is first processed by the text processor to find the correct pronunciation. This takes several steps, which include semantic disambiguation and conversion of special symbols, numbers, and abbreviations to words (see Section 10.3.1). Then the pronunciation is found by lexicon lookup and by using letter-to-sound (i.e., letter-to-phone) rules. Once the phones are determined they are mapped to the existing speech units. This mapping can be by selecting the best matching speech units from the speech database or by generating the sound using appropriate filtering techniques (see Section 10.3.2). During speech sound generation, the desired prosody is also taken into account. The prosody information is supplied by the prosody generator (see Section 10.3.3) based not only on the text but on *the ideas* (branch 006) and *the mixing information* (branch 010).

The generated speech is examined for spectral discontinuities, and necessary post-filtering operations are performed (Figure 10.4). Moreover, additional modifications in the prosody content can be performed to smooth and fine-tune the speech output (block 017). The final output is then mixed with the outputs from the different modalities and presented to users, who now watch and listen to a skillfully prepared message. Like the content, the right time and context of the presentation are critical. The right time can be determined automatically based on the learned user profiles. Alternatively, an indicator (blinking light, color change, vibrations from wearable sensors, etc.) may first notify the users of a new message, which can then be played if desired.

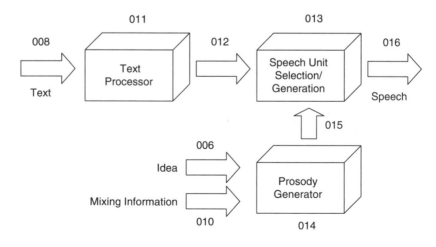

FIGURE 10.3

Text-to-speech synthesis.

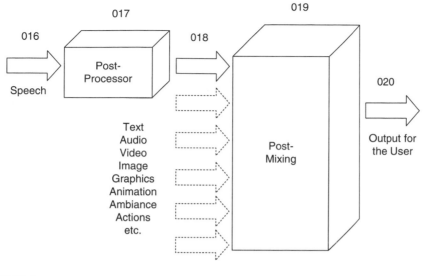

FIGURE 10.4

Post-mixing and presentation to the user.

It is important to note that, although not shown explicitly in the figures, all of the processors can communicate with each other. Also note that there is a continuously ongoing interaction between the described system and its users. Similar to human-to-human interaction, where verbal and nonverbal information is exchanged at every moment, the AmI system continuously observes the user, adapting the output to the user's need and actions to ensure that the right information is presented at the right time and to the right person.

The described system is a high-level representation of AmI interfaces with speech synthesis capabilities. In the next section, we take a closer look at the different components of speech synthesizers.

10.3 SPEECH SYNTHESIS

As shown in (Figure 10.3), a traditional speech synthesis system consists of four major components: text generator, text processor, speech unit generator, and prosody generator.

10.3.1 Text Processing

The text generator module evaluates the environment and user characteristics to generate a text, annotated with tags and labels indicating punctuation, emotions, pauses, important words, voice changes, stress points, and so forth. These annotations are required by other modules in the system for the generation of the appropriate prosody contours and for the selection or generation of the most appropriate speech units. The number of tags used is dependent on the application and on the amount of control desired. While in some cases a single tag per sentence may be sufficient (e.g., for short sentences), in other cases individually tagged words and syllables may be required (e.g., in systems built for entertaining and/or educating children). Tags can also specify how the mixing of sources from different modalities will be performed to ensure that the speech output is adequately prepared and mixed.

In the input text for traditional speech synthesis systems, there are usually no annotations other than punctuation. The input is plain (or raw) text—hence the term *text-to-speech*.

The text data is processed to find the word equivalent of every character cluster that will be vocalized. This is normally described with terms such as front-end processing, natural language processing, or linguistic processing. It entails going through the input text multiple times to transcribe it [6–8], which can be rather complicated since the transcriptions are context, language, and application sensitive. As examples, we can consider the processing of numbers, abbreviations, acronyms, symbols, foreign words, and homographs.

Numbers can be digits, dates, roman numerals, measures, fractions, mathematical expression, and so on. All of these representations can have different pronunciations depending on intended usage and language. For example, in U.S. English, the number 1997 should be pronounced as *one thousand nine hundred and ninety seven* when it represents a count (e.g., 1997 people), and as *nineteen ninety seven*, when used as a year (e.g., Sept. 25, 1997). As another example, the fraction 2/3 can be pronounced as *two-thirds* or as *February the third*. It is interesting that many of the available TTS systems have difficulty finding the correct pronunciation of the sentence *2/3 of the students will be absent on 2/3*, unless they have special rules that address such cases. Mathematical expressions are also challenging. Current TTS systems are trained for general expressions and therefore can hardly manage mathematical expressions at all. Special cases such as pronunciation of 1–0 as *one–love* for tennis and as *one–zero* for soccer requires special context-dependent rules.

Abbreviations, acronyms, special characters, and symbols need to be properly dealt with as well. For example, the natural language processor should be able to differentiate if *dr.* is used as *doctor* or *drive* and if *ft.* indicates *fort* or *feet*. In informal writing and e-mail, where formal rules are rarely followed, performance of the text normalization algorithms can degrade significantly.

Homographs are words that have the same spelling but different valid pronunciations (e.g., *read, present, live, lead*). For intelligibility of generated speech output, it is important that they are properly handled.

Once the words corresponding to the character clusters in the text are determined, grapheme-to-phoneme mapping is performed. This is done with lookup tables (i.e., lexicons) and letter-to-sound rules [6, 9, 10]. A lexicon is a dictionary showing the phonetic transcription of words. In addition to phonemes, it usually includes part-of-speech (POS) tags and annotations indicating syllable structure and stress points. Letter-to-sound rules are mathematical formulations that map letters to sounds using rules such as *When X follows Y pronounce it as Z*. Here X and Y can represent individual letters or broader sound classes such as fricatives or vowels.

For phonetic languages like Spanish, high-accuracy phonetic transcriptions can be generated with a relatively small number of letter-to-sound rules that are combined with a lexicon to handle exceptional cases such as foreign words and names. For nonphonetic languages like English, a complete lexicon containing pronunciations of all words is critical to ensure good-quality output. In English synthesizers the letter-to-sound rules are used as a backup to cope with words missing from the lexicon. Foreign words and names are examples.

Considering the large number of variations that are possible, phoneme combinations selected through letter-to-sound rules can be far from the actual pronunciations. When used as part of an intelligent, sophisticated system, such as an ambient intelligence interface, mispronunciations can have undesired effects. Users can become distracted, annoyed, and even angry. A user-centric synthesis system should be thus able to automatically learn the correct pronunciations from the user through implicit or explicit examples. Such adaptation capabilities, require the integration of automatic speech recognition (ASR), and, in fact, both ASR and TTS are essential for human-centric ambient intelligence communication systems. Such learning capabilities increase the mutual connection and trust between AmI interfaces and users.

When the phonetic transcription of the input text is ready, it is passed to the speech synthesis unit, which is described next.

10.3.2 Speech Signal Synthesis

In the speech synthesis unit there are two major components, which can be connected in a parallel, serial, or hybrid architecture. These are the speech unit generator and/or selector and the prosody generator, and their function is to transform the phonetic transcriptions into speech signals—that is, to perform phoneme-to-sound mapping. As one might expect, numerous approaches are used for this transformation, each with its advantages and limitations.

There is a trade-off between speech signal modification flexibility and speech quality (i.e., how good the synthesized speech sounds to human ears). Modifying natural speech decreases speech quality, so the modifications should be adjusted to keep modification artifacts imperceptible to humans. Two main techniques can be specified; speech signal *generation* and speech signal *selection*. These can be further divided into categories such as articulatory, formant, LPC, HMM, statistical, and waveform concatenation synthesis [9].

In the prosody generator, characteristics such as fundamental frequency, duration, and amplitude, are specified. The prosody parameters are modified according to the content and context of the message being conveyed. This requires taking into account several factors, such as the desired output emotions, emphasis, strength, meaning, and target users. The techniques employed for prosody generation are summarized in Section 10.3.3.

Articulatory Synthesis

Articulatory synthesis is one possible signal generation technique. It has great potential that has not yet been fully explored. Most likely, it will become one of the major means of producing human-quality speech in the future.

In articulatory speech synthesis, the movements of articulators are parameterized. These articulators are lips, teeth, tongue, glottis, and velum. The movement of air in the cavities is also modeled. Since the method is based on the mathematical modeling of physiological and physical parameters, in principle, it is possible to generate different speaking styles and effects with ease.

Mermelstein's model [11, 12] is popular. It controls the movement of jaw, tongue body, lips, velum, and hyoid. Timing, position, and shape of the articulator parameters are also mathematically modeled.

Although research on generating speech by directly modeling the movement of the articulators has a long history, it has not been popular. A major reason for this has been the lack of data that can inform the construction of an accurate model. Because of this, currently the approach in articulatory synthesis largely depends on mathematical and heuristics-driven models that control the shape, position, and movement of the articulators. As one would expect, these are not always adequate. With the collection of more data, statistical models will be possible. With these, one can expect the naturalness of the produced speech to increase considerably.

Articulatory data collection has increased in recent years. For example, in [13, 14] articulatory data was collected to analyze the movement of articulators in relation to affective content variation (see Figures 10.5 and 10.6). Such data collection and analysis efforts are promising for future developments in articulatory speech synthesis research.

Formant Synthesis

Formant synthesis is the most popular speech synthesis method. The commonly used Klatt synthesizer [15], shown in Figures 10.7 and 10.8, consists of filters connected in parallel and in series. The parallel model, whose transfer function has both zeros and poles, is suitable for the modeling of fricatives and stops. The cascade (series) model is an all pole model and is suitable for voiced sounds. The filters model the spectral envelope of sounds and have resonance frequencies tuned according to the formant frequencies of the phonemes. The parameters required for synthesis are formant frequency, bandwidth, and amplitude (including amplitude of voicing, frication, aspiration, sinusoidal voicing, and several others). The excitation signal is a periodic train of impulses for voiced sounds, shaped noise for voiced fricatives, and random noise–like signals for fricatives.

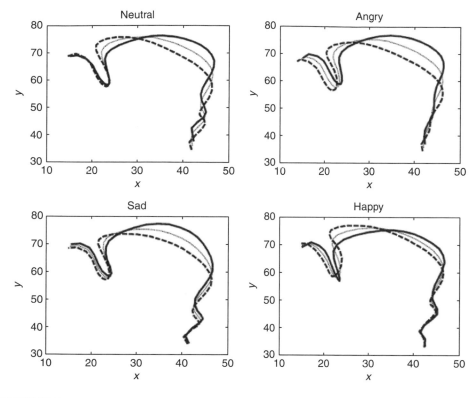

FIGURE 10.5

Tongue shape variation associated with the first principal component analysis (PCA) component plotted as a function of emotion. The dotted line represents each mean tongue shape. Variations can be interpreted as dominant linguistic articulations modulated by emotional components. Reproduced from [13].

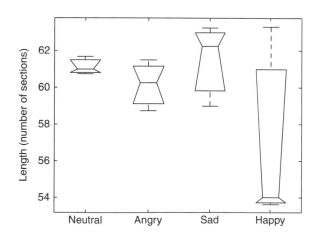

FIGURE 10.6

Distribution of vocal tract length covered by tongue contour for different emotions. Reproduced from [14].

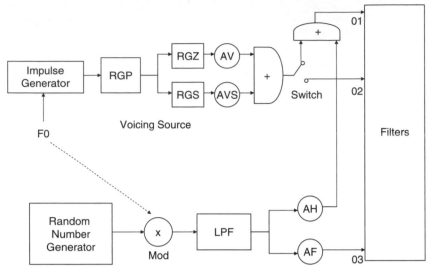

FIGURE 10.7

Klatt formant synthesizer excitation-signal generation. The excitation signal is a periodic train of impulses for voiced sounds, shaped noise for voiced fricatives, and a random-noise–like signal for fricatives. Adapted from [15].

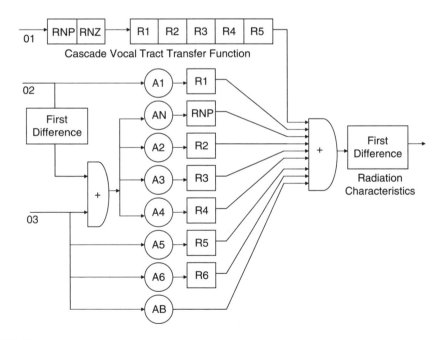

FIGURE 10.8

Klatt formant synthesizer filters: parallel model suitable for modeling fricatives and stops; series model suitable for voiced sounds. R1–R6: second-order IIR filters; RNP: nasal resonance; RNZ: nasal zero; A1-AB: gains; SW: switch; RGP: low-pass filter; RGZ and RGS: bandpass filter. Adapted from [15].

For the synthesis of different phonemes, formant frequencies and formant bandwidths are updated every 5 to 10 ms. These values are derived from the locus theory of speech production using the target formant values for each phoneme stored in lookup tables together with transition times and slope parameters. Examples of target formants for a male speaker are shown in Table 10.1.

Formant synthesizers have low memory requirements and can run on small, power-efficient devices. Their generated speech output is intelligible and can be modified easily to obtain different voice and emotion characteristics [16, 17]. This makes them attractive for education and research and for portable devices. For the generated synthetic speech output, reasonably good speech quality can be achieved with well-tuned parameters. However, parameter tuning is a challenging task. If done automatically naturalness may suffer; if done manually, it is highly time consuming and laborious.

Formant synthesizers are a good option for devices where power consumption is the main concern, so one would expect their popularity to continue in the future. It is essential to note the trade-off between computational power and power efficiency (i.e., devices with high computation power consume much power), since it will be one of the main concerns and challenges in the development of ambient intelligence interfaces [18].

Concatenative Synthesis

The generation of natural-sounding speech using parametric (rule-based) format and articulatory synthesizers depends significantly on how well the system parameters are tuned. Considering the number of existing parameters, this task requires considerable effort, especially when manual intervention is necessary.

Table 10.1 Target Formant Frequency and Bandwidth (in Hertz) for a Male Speaker

Phoneme	F1	F2	F3	B1	B2	B3
/b/	200	900	2100	65	90	125
/ch/	300	1700	2400	200	110	270
/r/	330	1060	1380	70	100	120
/s/	400	1400	2700	200	95	220
/aa/	700	1220	2600	130	70	160
/ih/	400	1800	2670	50	100	140
/ow/	540	1100	2300	80	70	70
/uh/	450	110	2350	80	100	80

Note: *Adapted from [15].*

Because of these limitations, synthesizers utilizing natural speech data and minimizing the amount of modifications have gained popularity. Referred to as concatenative (or corpus-driven), these systems [19] represent the state of the art in text-to-speech synthesis today. They are based on the concept of gathering very large amounts of speech data from human subjects and using it as it is (or with minimal modifications in their prosody) to generate the desired novel output by means of concatenation (which requires some smoothing between the concatenated units). With these techniques it is possible to synthesize very realistic and natural sounding speech [19, 20].

As is clear from the stated description, the most critical component of a corpus-driven synthesizer is the quality of the collected data [21]. Collecting "good" data is not a simple task, especially when a very large database is desired. If the data is to be collected quickly, it will require a tremendous effort from the voice talent, and, therefore, is practically impossible. If done over a period of time, it may be difficult to achieve consistency (e.g., recording settings, speech characteristics). Additionally, the specific techniques used for the data collection (e.g., if isolated words, nonsense words, sentences, and so forth are recorded) have a significant impact on speech quality [20].

In concatenative synthesizers, the process for a given input phoneme string consists of first finding the best matching speech units. The match is described in terms of two cost functions: target cost and concatenation cost. The target cost is a measure of how well the prosody and spectral characteristics of the desired output unit matches the existing units. Concatenation cost is a measure of how well the selected unit blends with its neighbor units to achieve the desired co-articulation effects and smooth inter-unit transitions.

The size of the concatenated speech units can vary depending on the application. These units can be phones, diphones, demisyllables, words, phrases, and sentences. Diphones and demisyllables have been the most popular. By concatenating the speech units in the middle of a phone (diphones) or in the middle of a vowel (demisyllables), which are more stable regions in comparison to phone boundaries, the transition effects between different units are minimized. Note that, in addition to only a single type of speech unit, units of different lengths can be used depending on the application.

When speech synthesizers are built for specific and limited domains, the content and prosodic characteristics of all possible expressions are well known or predictable. Hence, one can easily collect many different examples of speech units, including not only phonemes but also words or even longer expressions. In such cases, the generated speech is in many cases comparable to natural human speech [20].

The strong dependence on the database is the main limitation of concatenative speech synthesizers. In general, the allowed modifications in prosody and spectral characteristics are limited, so it is not easy to generate new speaking styles or voices. Moreover, these synthesizers are not robust since the expansion of the database is only possible if the same recording conditions and speakers are used, which can be very challenging after a period of time.

10.3.3 Prosody Generation

Once the linguistic processing of text is completed, the next step is generating the prosody parameters, which will be used in the generation or selection of the speech units. In traditional speech synthesizers text is the only available input. As described in Section 10.2, future synthesizers will process not only text but also the state of the user and the surrounding environment. Mixing information will also be considered.

The primary prosody parameters are F0 contour, duration, and energy of the speech signal. At this stage, spectral envelope shape and fine spectral characteristics can also be modified. The purpose of the modifications is to increase the richness and naturalness of the synthesized speech to make it as close to human speech as possible.

Research on prosodic processing for speech synthesis has a long and rich history (a summary of different approaches can be found in [22]). Because F0 has received the most attention, there are many theories for modeling F0 contour variations. Duration (also referred to as timing) modification and prediction have also been studied in detail. The literature on energy modification for speech synthesis is relatively small compared to that on F0 and duration. However, based on recent results showing its importance [23], energy can also be considered a major prosody component. It is especially important in affective content generation [24] when combined with other parameters.

Three main approaches can be followed for prosody generation: rule based, statistics based, and no modification [22]. Rule-based approaches rely on a specific set of rules to determine the required prosody values. These rules may be specified at phoneme, syllable, word, phrase, and even larger scales. The function, location, and neighbors of the processed unit are taken into account to find the required timing and F0 parameters for synthesis. Usually preset initial values are modified within some ranges (specific percentage increase or decrease) based on the rules. Examples of the rule-based approach are Klatt's duration model [25] and Jilka et al.'s [26] tones and break indices (ToBI) [27] F0 model.

Statistical approaches rely on large amounts of data [7] that is carefully labeled to ensure good training. Labeling and proper annotation of data are laborious tasks that require significant manual effort. The speech units for which prosodic labels will be generated are described as in the rule-based approach, but with many more parameters. The statistical method is a powerful one because complex relations can be easily learned by the machine and natural-sounding prosody can be generated. The Tilt model [28] is a good example of statistical intonation modeling.

Once the desired parameter values are determined, the speech sounds are synthesized (e.g., in the formant synthesizer) or modified (e.g., in the concatenative synthesizer) according to the generated prosody. Different techniques can be used to perform these modifications [9, 29]. Some of the most popular are PSOLA [30], LPC [9], sinusoidal model [31], and HNM [3, 32]. Each has its advantages and limitations; generally, however, one can argue that modifying recorded speech degrades its natural quality.

With large data sets containing many examples of the same speech units (e.g., phonemes) recorded with different pitch and duration [20], synthesis can potentially be performed without prosody modifications.

10.3.4 Evaluation of Synthetic Speech

Speech synthesis systems can be evaluated in terms of different requirements, such as speech intelligibility, speech naturalness, system complexity, and so forth [9]. For ambient intelligence applications it is reasonable to assume that new evaluation criteria will be required—for example, emotional influence on the user, ability to get the user to act, mastery over language generation, and whether the system takes the environmental variables into account and adjusts its behaviors accordingly.

Some of the just mentioned evaluation criteria are for the complete system presented in Figures 10.1, 10.2, 10.3, and 10.4. Having evaluation criteria for the whole system is reasonable because a single misperforming component would negatively impact how the system is perceived by humans.

10.4 EMOTIONAL SPEECH SYNTHESIS

Emotional characteristics of speech can be modified by changing the speech prosody parameters such as fundamental frequency, duration, and amplitude of different sounds [34–39]. In addition to prosody, spectral characteristics also carry emotional information. A system that can control these parameters can generate varieties of emotional speech. By limiting the number of modifications, high-quality results can be achieved. For instance, using a database of happy emotional speech, such modifications can be used to synthesize different nuances of happiness expression.

Both formant and concatenative synthesizers have been successfully used for emotional speech synthesis. In [16] each emotion was parameterized using the variables in the DECtalk formant synthesizer (version 3.0) (this system was called the Affect Editor). A similar approach was followed in [40] to build a fully automated system called HAMLET. In both systems, which operated at the phoneme level, speech prosody, voice quality, and articulation were modified. Another formant synthesizer Emosyn [35], modifies pitch mean, range and variation, pitch contour in phrase and syllable level, F0 flutter, syllable intensity, speech rate, phonation type, vowel precision, and lip spreading.

In a concatenative speech synthesis system [41], where pitch and duration of the concatenated segments were modified, it was shown that affective samples can be successfully generated. The copy synthesis experiments for English [36] and Spanish

[42] showed that if the correct prosody parameters and emotional speech units are used, high-quality emotional speech can be achieved.

A novel technique for modifying speech characteristics to produce emotional speech is described in [43]. The described emotion-to-emotion transformation (ETET) system is illustrated in Figure 10.9, which shows three main blocks, denoted 1, 2, and 3, performing spectral envelope modifications at the phoneme level, prosody modifications at POS tag level, and prosody modification at the voiced/unvoiced region level, respectively. Inputs required are a speech signal (utterance), the input speech emotion, phoneme labels and boundaries, POS tags and boundaries, and the desired output emotion. The output is a resynthesized version of the input signal that possesses the desired emotion characteristics. In its current state, the system operates on isolated input utterances and the input emotion is assumed to be neutral. The target emotions for which the system was evaluated were anger, happiness, and sadness. ETET is robust and can be trained and modified to handle longer speech segments, such as paragraphs, and to include new input and/or target emotion categories.

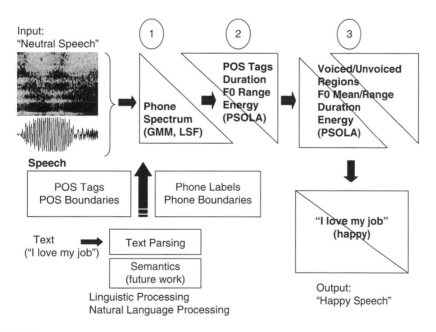

FIGURE 10.9

Multi-level emotion-to-emotion transformation (ETET) system based on the modification of speech acoustic features at different time scales. Taken from [43].

10.5 DISCUSSION

Ambient intelligence environments are designed to improve quality of life. They consist of "calm" [44] (i.e., "invisible" [45]) microprocessors operating in accord and processing incoming data. The resulting output is transmitted to the user either in a direct (e.g., speech) or indirect (e.g., ambiant) manner.

A speech synthesis system that talks to the user is an example of direct communication, which can take place in many instances and for various purposes, such as alerting, informing, answering, entertaining, and educating. The conditions under which such services are provided can vary. Also, naturally, users can vary significantly based on time, sex, age, education, experience, culture, scientific and emotional intelligence, needs, wealth, and so forth.

It is practically impossible to formulate specific rules for each of these conditions. Nevertheless, ambient intelligence systems should be able to cope with them all. This is a challenging but not insurmountable task. As a result of the "training" they receive starting right from birth, humans are fairly adept at doing this. With advances in sensing, computing, and machine learning, similar capabilities by machines for enhancing AmI-driven communication is becoming increasingly possible. One of the biggest challenges is finding and using adequate amounts of the right data.

AmI speech synthesis databases should be continuously updated to reflect new variations in the data. When new data is collected, it should be automatically uploaded to the existing system. Additionally, users should be able to collect their own data so they can "teach" the system to talk with their own voices. Having control over the system and over the level and amount of information provided to it can be a pleasant, personalized experience and it can help build trust, resulting in strong ties between humans and machines.

A human-like speech synthesis system should be able to account for environment and human factors and should generate its output accordingly, which requires it to generate speech as natural and flexible as human speech. This is achievable through hybrid systems incorporating model-based approaches supported by large databases covering many different speech sounds, and by having speech production and modification algorithms that do not produce perceptible speech quality distortions.

Statistical parametric synthesizers [46] are an emerging research area, pioneered by HMM-based synthesis techniques [47]. They provide an effective way to learn patterns from data. The ease of voice quality modification and adaptation provided by parametric methods makes them an attractive tool for synthesis. The main limitation of HMM-based techniques, however, is their vocoder (buzzy) speech quality.

In daily life we are not always in clean, noise-free conditions. By adapting the quality of the generated output to the transmission medium and material—for instance, embellishing the output signal with audio soundtrack—or targeting the attention of users to different modalities such as video and avatars, or by presenting the output as the voice of a virtual character (e.g., a talking duck or a talking refrigerator), it may be easier to generate outputs that will be perceived by users as natural.

10.5.1 Ambient Intelligence and Users

The interaction between user and speech synthesizer can be explicit or implicit. As in traditional human–machine interactions, an example of explicit interaction is when the user selects the input information to be synthesized. In implicit human–machine interaction, the output is generated in a more natural way, similar to human–human interaction, without any explicit extra user input. Moreover, the generated output is integrated seamlessly with the user's actions and needs so that it is "trivial" (i.e., normal, somewhat expected, part of the process) and thus "invisible" [44, 45] to the user. Implicit human–machine interaction is the integral vision of ambient intelligence interfaces [48].

A speech synthesis system can be perceived as "invisible" by having human-like characteristics, such as the ability to generate meaningful, understandable, logical, pleasant, and affective speech at the right place, at the right time, and to the right person.

10.5.2 Future Directions and Challenges

In summary, the characteristics of an AmI speech synthesizer are as follows:

- Synthesized speech output should be understandable, pleasant, and free of any distracting pronunciation errors and spectral discontinuity artifacts. It should have the appropriate affective and semantic characteristics.
- The synthesizer should be able to synthesize informal writing, nongrammatical expressions, complex technical papers, and mathematical expressions.
- Synthetic speech can resemble natural human speech; however, this may not always be necessary. Some users may prefer the machines to sound different from humans.
- It should be easy for users to modify the machine's voice characteristics. Moreover, users should be able to create their own synthetic voices.
- Synthetic speech output should be generated quickly so that efficient and realistic human–machine interactions are possible.
- Synthesized speech should be presented at the right time in a manner that is nonintrusive and nondistracting to users.
- The content and presentation of the material should be automatically tailored to user needs.

With the current technology, synthesis of human-like natural speech is possible if concatenative synthesizers with large speech databases are used. However, such synthesizers are not flexible in the sense that the allowed modifications in prosody and voice characteristics are limited. In contrast, rule-based synthesizers are flexible but are not always pleasant sounding. Clearly, this trade-off is the main challenge in building synthesizers that are flexible, adaptive, and human-like. It is possible to lessen the trade-off by synthesizing nonhuman voices. For both human and nonhuman voices, however, the appropriate affective and semantic characteristics are critical.

Enabling synthetic speech to possess the right affective characteristics requires the correct prosody and frequency domain characteristics to be generated, which requires assessing and understanding content, context, user, and environment. Intelligent systems capable of processing past and present information, and capable of generating realistic models for predicting the future, are needed.

The text-processing capabilities of current systems need to be improved so that both informal and technical writing, special symbols, foreign words, and so forth are handled properly. Speech synthesizers should be capable of text summarization, spelling error correction, and translation. Given adequate data, these are all achievable to some extent using existing natural language processing algorithms. However, processing time needs to be improved to ensure that human–machine interactions are not interrupted unexpectedly. Quick response time requires high computational power, which can be challenging to achieve considering the cost and power consumption requirements of AmI devices for home environments [18].

Adaptation of synthesized speech to users requires additional capabilities, such as real-time dialogue interruption and content adaptation, which are not present in traditional speech synthesizers. One can expect many of the above mentioned functionalities to be available in laboratory environments within the next few years [49]. For them to become common in home environments, however, cost- and power-efficient solutions are needed. These solutions require significant advances not only in data- and language-processing algorithms but also in hardware chip design and production [18].

10.6 CONCLUSIONS

In this chapter, we summarized the state of current speech synthesis technology, outlined its essential highlights and limitations, and projected future opportunities in the context of human-centric AmI interfaces. The goal is speech synthesis systems in AmI environments that will be able to produce the right speech at the right place and time and to the right person. This is a highly challenging task that requires multidisciplinary research in several fields.

ACKNOWLEDGMENTS

The authors would like to thank to Carlos Busso and Aki Harma for their valuable comments and suggestions.

REFERENCES

[1] Aarts E. Ambient intelligence: A multimedia perspective. IEEE Multimedia 2004;11(1):12–9.

[2] Riva G, Vatalaro F, Davide F, Alcaniz M, editors. Ambient Intelligence: The Evolution of Technology, Communication and Cognition towards the Future of Human-Computer Interaction. IOS Press; 2005.

[3] Philips-Research. Ambient intelligence. Password, Philips Research Technology Magazine 2005;23(May).

[4] Cook DJ, Das SK, editors. Smart Environments, Technologies, Protocols, and Applications. Wiley-Interscience; 2005.

[5] Wright D, Gutwirth S, Friedewald M, Vildjiounaite E, Punie Y, editors. Safeguards in a World of Ambient Intelligence. Springer; 2008.

[6] Dutoit T. An Introduction to Text-to-Speech Synthesis. Kluwer Academic Publishers; 1996.

[7] Jurafsky D, Martin JH. Speech and Language Processing: An Introduction to Natural Language Processing, Computational Linguistics, and Speech Recognition. Prentice-Hall, Inc; 2000.

[8] Sproat R. Springer Handbook of Speech Processing. Springer; 2008.

[9] O'Shaughnessy D. Speech Communications Human and Machine. 2nd ed. IEEE Press; 2000.

[10] Black A, Taylor P. The Festival speech synthesis system: System documentation. Technical report HCRC/TR-83. Human Communications Research Centre, University of Edinburgh; 1997.

[11] Mermelstein P. Articulatory model for the study of speech production. J Acoust Soc Am 1973;53:1070–82.

[12] Rubin P, Baer T, Mermelstein P. An articulatory synthesizer for perceptual research. J Acoust Soc Am 1981;70:321–8.

[13] Lee S, Bresch E, Narayanan S. An exploratory study of emotional speech production using functional data analysis techniques. In: Proceedings of the 7th International Seminar on Speech Production. Ubutuba, Brazil: 2006.

[14] Lee S, Bresch E, Adams J, Kazemzadeh A, Narayanan S. A study of emotional speech articulation using a fast magnetic resonance imaging technique. In: Proceedings of INTER SPEECH ICSLP. Pittsburg, PA: 2006.

[15] Klatt D. Software for a cascade/parallel formant synthesizer. J Acoust Soc Am 1980; 67(3):971–95.

[16] Cahn JE. The generation of affect in synthesized speech. Journal of the American Voice I/O Society 1990;8(July):1–19.

[17] Murray I, Arnott J. Synthesizing emotions in speech: Is it time to get excited?. In: Proceedings of INTERSPEECH. Philadelphia, PA. 1996. p. 1816–9.

[18] Man HD. Ambient intelligence: Gigascale dreams and nanoscale realities. In: Solid-State Circuits Conference 2005, Digest of Technical Papers (ISSCC 2005) IEEE International Volume, vol. 1. 2005. p. 29–35.

[19] Dutoit T. Springer Handbook of Speech Processing. Springer; 2008. p. 437–55.

[20] Schroeter J. Circuits, Signals, and Speech and Image Processing. CRC Press; 2006.

[21] Syrdal AK, Conkie A, Stylianou Y. Exploration of acoustic correlates in speaker selection for concatenative synthesis. In: Proceedings of ICSLP. vol. 6. Sydney, Australia: 1998. p. 2743–6.

[22] van Santen J, Mishra T, Klabbers E. Springer Handbook of Speech Processing. Springer; 2008.

[23] Kochanski G, Grabe E, Coleman J, Rosner B. Loudness predicts prominence: Fundamental frequency lends little. J Acoust Soc Am 2005;118(2):1038-54.

[24] Bulut M, Lee S, Narayanan S. Analysis of emotional speech prosody in terms of part of speech tags. In: Proceedings of INTERSPEECH EUROSPEECH. Antwerp, Belgium: 2007. p. 626-9.

[25] Klatt D. Frontiers of Speech Communication Research. Academic Press; 1979. p. 287-300.

[26] Jilka M, Mohler G, Dogil G. Rules for the generation of ToBI based American English intonation. Speech Comm 1999;28:83-108.

[27] Silverman K, Beckman M, Pitrelli J, Ostendorf M, Wightman C, Price P, et al. ToBI: A standard for labeling English prosody. In: International Conference on Spoken Language Processing. Canada: Banff, Alberta; 1992. p. 867-70.

[28] Taylor P. Analysis and synthesis of intonation using the Tilt model. J Acoust Soc Am 2000; 107(3):1697-714.

[29] Schroeter J. Springer Handbook of Speech Processing. Springer; 2008.

[30] Moulines E, Charpentier F. Pitch-synchronous waveform processing techniques for text-to-speech synthesis using diphones. Speech Comm 1990;9(December):453-67.

[31] Quatieri TF. Discrete-Time Speech Signal Processing: Principles and practice. Prentice Hall; 2001.

[32] Stylianou Y. Harmonic plus noise models for speech, combined with statistical methods, for speech and speaker modification. Ph.D. dissertation. Ecole Nationale Superieure des Telecommunications; 1996.

[33] Syrdal A, Stylianou Y, Garrison L, Conkie A, Schroeter J. TD-PSOLA versus harmonic plus noise model in diphone based speech synthesis. In: Proceedings of ICASSP, vol. 1. Seattle, Washington. 1998. p. 273-6.

[34] Ladd DR, Silverman KEA, Tolkmitt F, Bergmann G, Scherer KR. Evidence for the independent function of intonation contour type, voice quality, and F0 range in signaling speaker affect. J Acoust Soc Am 1985;78(2):435-44.

[35] Burkhardt F, Sendlmeier WF. Verification of acoustical correlates of emotional speech using formant-synthesis. In: Proceedings of the ISCA workshop on speech and emotion. 2000. p. 151-6.

[36] Bulut M, Narayanan S, Syrdal AK. Expressive speech synthesis using a concatenative synthesizer. In: International Conference on Spoken Language Processing. Denver, CO. 2002. p. 1265-8.

[37] Iida A, Campbell N, Higuchi F, Yasumura M. A corpus-based speech synthesis system with emotion. Speech Comm 2003;40:161-87.

[38] Pitrelli JF, Bakis R, Eide EM, Fernandez R, Hamza W, Picheny MA. The IBM expressive text-to-speech synthesis system for American English. IEEE Transactions on Audio, Speech, and Language Processing 2006;14(4):1099-108.

[39] Schroder M. Emotional speech synthesis—a review. In: Proceedings of EUROSPEECH. Aalborg. 2001. p. 87-90.

[40] Murray IR, Arnott JL. Implementation and testing of a system for producing emotion-by-rule in synthetic speech. Speech Comm 1995;16(4):175-205.

[41] Murray IR, Edgington MD, Campion D, Lynn J. Rule-based emotion synthesis using concatenated speech. In: Proceeding of the ISCA Workshop on Emotion and Speech. Newcastle, Northern Ireland: 2000. p. 173-7.

[42] Montero JM, Gutierrez-Arriola J, Colas J, Enriquez E, Pardo JM. Analysis and modelling of emotional speech in Spanish. In: International congress of phonetic sciences. San Francisco, CA. 1999. p. 957–60.

[43] Bulut M. Emotional speech resynthesis. Ph.D. dissertation. University of Southern California; 2008.

[44] Weiser M, Brown JS. Designing calm technology. http://www.ubiq.com/hypertext/weiser/calmtech/calmtech.htm; 1995.

[45] Heer J, Khooshabeh P. Seeing the invisible. In: Workshop on Invisible & Transparent Interfaces, Advanced Visual Interfaces. Lecce, Italy: 2004.

[46] Black A. CLUSTERGEN: A statistical parametric synthesizer using trajectory modeling. In: Proceedings of INTERSPEECH. Pittsburgh, PA. 2006.

[47] Tokuda K, Yoshimura T, Masuko T, Kobayashi T, Kitamura T. Speech parameter generation algorithms for HMM-based speech synthesis. In: Proceedings of ICASSP. Istanbul, Turkey. 2000. p. 1315–8.

[48] Schmidt A. Ambient Intelligence: The Evolution of Technology, Communication and Cognition towards the Future of Human-Computer Interaction. IOS Press; 2005.

[49] Intille SS, Larson K, Tapia EM, Beaudin J, Kaushik P, Nawyn J, et al. Using a live-in laboratory for ubiquitous computing research. In: Fishkin PNKP, Schiele B, Quigley A, editors. Proceedings of PERVASIVE 2006 LNCS 3968. Springer-Verlag; 2006. p. 349–65.

Multimodal Interfaces

Tangible Interfaces for Ambient Augmented Reality Applications

11

Mark Billinghurst, Raphaël Grasset, and Hartmut Seichter

Human Interface Technology Laboratory New Zealand (HIT Lab NZ), University of Canterbury, Christchurch, New Zealand

ABSTRACT

Ambient intelligence has the goal of embedding context-sensitive technology into the user's surroundings. In many ways augmented reality (AR) is complementary to this in that AR interfaces seamlessly enhance the user's real environment with a virtual information overlay. The two merge in context-aware ambient AR applications, allowing users to easily perceive and interact with the interface using the AR overlay of the real world. In this chapter we describe how tangible interaction techniques can be used to design human-centric interfaces for ambient AR applications. Examples will be drawn from current and previous research in augmented reality and ambient interfaces, and design guidelines will be given to show how human-centric tangible AR interfaces can be developed.

Key words: augmented reality, tangible user interfaces, interaction design.

11.1 INTRODUCTION

One of the overarching goals of human–computer interaction is to make the computer vanish and allow technology to invisibly assist people in their everyday real-world tasks. Over the last several decades there have been a number of compelling visions presented showing how this may be achieved, such as Weiser's concept of ubiquitous computing [1], Norman's invisible computing [2], and Fishkin's embodied interaction [3].

Currently, ambient intelligence (AmI) has the goal of embedding context-sensitive technology in the user's surroundings. AmI is defined as "digital environments that are sensitive and responsive to the presence of people" [4]. Thus, AmI research involves the convergence of several earlier research ideas, including ubiquitous or pervasive computing, intelligent systems, context awareness, and an appreciation of the social interactions of objects in environments [5].

We are particularly interested in how to create AmI interfaces that are easy to interact with. In this chapter we describe one approach for developing ambient AR interaction techniques. We begin with a detailed rationale for using AmI interfaces and then review both AR and ambient AR interfaces. In Section 11.2 we present related work in these areas, and in Section 11.3 we outline our design approach. We present some design guidelines in Section 11.4, and case studies showing how these guidelines can be applied in Section 11.5. Finally, in Section 11.6 we describe authoring tools for building ambient AR interfaces.

11.1.1 Rationale for Ambient AR Interfaces

The notions of ambient environments and ambient interfaces are closely related to design ideas that eliminate the need for explicit functionality cues. One such approach is Le Corbusier's counter-functional design methods that aimed to remove the need for an inherent functional design.

Human–computer interface designers have investigated how to eliminate the need for functional cues and explicit expression of interfaces. Negroponte et al. [6] called for the interface to dissolve completely as an unneeded interference between human and technology. This means that the interface as an entity is removed from user perception, which in turn removes important glue between the mind and the machine. In order for this interaction method to succeed it is necessary to merge output and input into one entity. Fishkin et al. [3] called this approach *embodied interaction*, declaring the diminishment of the seam between device and input and output.

Beyond merging input and output, interactive environments still require *explicit user interaction* in order to enhance the environment [7]. One approach to this is through *tangible user interfaces* (TUIs) [8], which allow the user to interact with digital content by manipulating real objects, or so-called tangible bits. The design of tangible bits is of utmost importance to gain the user's immediate understanding.

Another approach is through use of *augmented reality* (AR), which involves the visual enhancement of the real world. In AR applications virtual images are seamlessly combined with the user's view of reality, and so the relationship between the real and the virtual environment is important to explore.

Ambient AR interfaces combine these ideas into a computational extension of the real world by implementing a spatial, sensual, and logical appendix to a physical entity. *Ambient AR applications* are those that use AR technology to represent context information from an ambient interface. For example, Rauhala et al. [9] developed an ambient AR interface that shows the temperature distribution of building walls (Figure 11.1). They embedded temperature sensors in room walls and then wirelessly sent temperature information to a mobile phone AR interface. When the user pointed her phone at the wall, on the screen she could see a virtual image of

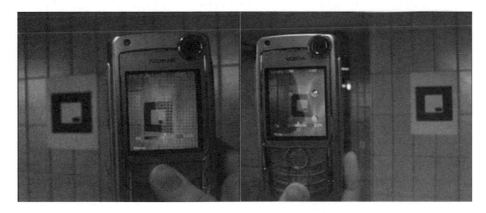

FIGURE 11.1

Ambient AR interface showing real-time temperature information superimposed over the real world (courtesy Malinda Rauhala).

the current temperature distribution superimposed over a live video view of the real world. As can been seen, AR technology provides a natural way to make visible the invisible context information captured by the ambient interface application.

11.1.2 Augmented Reality

Providing information display to the user is a key element in invisible interfaces. Many ambient intelligence applications use traditional screen-based or projected displays. However, AR is one of the more interesting approaches for doing this.

In augmented reality applications, three-dimensional computer graphics are superimposed over real objects, typically viewed through head-mounted or hand-held displays. The three key attributes of an AR application are that it combines real and virtual images, it is interactive in real time; and the virtual imagery is registered with the real world [10]. In many ways augmented reality is complementary to ambient intelligence in that the latter captures context while AR seamlessly enhances the user's real environment with virtual information display in context. The two merge in context-aware ambient AR applications, so that users can easily perceive and interact with the interface using an AR overlay of the real world.

Although AR technology is very promising, much research needs to be conducted on how to interact with ambient AR information. Substantial research on augmented reality exists, but much of it has focused on the underlying technology (such as tracking and display devices) rather than on user experience and interaction techniques. As Ishii says, the AR field has been primarily concerned with "considering purely visual augmentations" [8] and interaction with AR environments has usually been limited to either passive viewing or simple browsing of virtual information registered to the real world (as in Rauhala's example). Few systems provide tools that let the user interact with, request, or modify this information effectively and in real time. Furthermore, even basic interaction tasks, such as manipulation, copying, annotation, and dynamically adding and deleting virtual objects from the AR scene have been poorly addressed.

One possible approach for designing ambient AR interaction techniques is through a *tangible augmented reality (tangible AR) metaphor*. Tangible AR interfaces are those in which

- Each virtual object is registered to a physical object.
- The user interacts with virtual objects by manipulating the corresponding tangible objects.

The physical objects and interactions are as important as the virtual imagery and provide a very intuitive way to interact with the AR interface.

In this chapter we describe how tangible interaction techniques can be used to design ambient AR applications. Users already know how to manipulate real-world objects and so by building interaction techniques around object manipulation very intuitive interfaces can be developed.

11.2 **RELATED WORK**

Our research work is based on earlier work in augmented reality, ambient interfaces, and tangible user interfaces. In this section we review related work in interaction techniques in each of these areas.

11.2.1 **From Tangibility**...

Tangible user interfaces (TUIs) describe physical objects that are able to translate user actions into input events in the computer interface. They are an implementation of the approach described as "direct manipulation" by Shneiderman et al. [11], who described immediacy and haptic quality as important in fostering physical engagement with an object for the purpose of lowering the mental load. They identified three core properties of direct manipulation ([11], p. 251):

- Continuous representation of the object of interest
- Physical actions or labeled buttons instead of complex systems
- Rapid incremental, reversible operations whose impact on the object of interest is immediately visible

Hutchins et al. [12] found two main benefits of information retrieval through direct manipulation. First, the user is relieved of interpreting the representation and consequently can focus on the goal rather than the process. Second, the mnemonics are tied to an external instance and as such do not change modes. Therefore, a direct link between object and action is maintained—a crucial aspect of tangible AR interfaces.

Ullmer and Ishii [13] introduced an important distinction between tangible bits and painted bits on the basis of the nature of menus as they have commonly been used. The interface inherently changes if it is painted and yields a variety of modes. In contrast, tangible interfaces link their representations to physical appearance. Based on their experience with the metaDESK interface, Ullmer and Ishii envisioned a set of systems that would interact on the basis of physical and digital pervasiveness. The metaDESK itself was an interactive table for urban planning with several modes of access using tangible objects. A later version with multiple modes of interaction and visualization was the Luminous Table [14]. Another example of explicit tangible interaction in an AR interface can be found in the AR interior design tool of Kato et al. [15].

Tangibility and the need for direct manipulation are important concepts for interaction with ambient interfaces. Physical representation is only a small part of these concepts. More important is logic representation, which provides an important clue to the understanding of information. For example, the universal constructor installation of Frazer et al. [16] used the metaphor of urban structures for a networked system. In it actual cubes represented the spatial relationship of autonomous working units interconnected as nodes. It was thus essential for the users to understand the flow of information between the nodes, and ambient meaning was conveyed through the link between real and virtual objects.

11.2.2 . . . To the AR Tangible User Interface

When a new interface medium is developed, it typically progresses through the following stages:

1. Prototype demonstration
2. Adoption of interaction techniques from other interface metaphors
3. Development of new interface metaphors appropriate to the medium
4. Development of formal theoretical models for predicting and modeling user interactions

The earliest virtual reality (VR) systems were used just to view virtual scenes. Then interfaces such as 3DM [17] explored how elements of the desktop WIMP metaphor could be used to enable users to model immersively and to support more complex interactions. Interaction techniques such as Go-go [18] were later developed that were unique to virtual reality. Most recently, researchers are attempting to arrive at a formal taxonomy for characterizing interaction in virtual worlds and building virtual interfaces in a systematic manner [19].

In many ways AR interfaces have barely moved beyond the first stage. The earliest AR systems were used to view virtual models in a variety of application domains, such as medicine [20] and machine maintenance [21]. These were ideal for viewing 3D information, but provided little support for creating or modifying AR content. More recently, researchers have begun to address this deficiency. The AR modeler of Kiyokawa and Takemura [22] uses a magnetic tracker to allow users to create AR content, while the Studierstube [23] and EMMIE [24] projects use tracked pens and tablets for selecting and modifying AR objects. Still, these attempts have largely been based on existing 2D and 3D interface metaphors from desktop or immersive virtual environments.

In a similar way, ambient intelligence interaction methods have been limited. Previous work often relied on the sensing of context cues as a way of interacting with applications [25]. One example would be turning off the ring tone on a phone when the user joins a meeting already in progress. Physical proximity [26], location [27], user activity, and interaction with physical objects [28] have all been used as context cues for interaction. However, there has been little development of theories of interaction for AmI research, except, perhaps, for the concept of implicit human–computer interaction (iHCI) advanced by Schmidt [29], which takes the user's context into account. Schmidt identified a number of research areas to be addressed in developing a theory of interaction for ambient intelligence, including the problem of the user's perception of invisible context information. This is one area where AR technology could be useful.

In our work we are trying to develop interface metaphors that will move ambient AR applications beyond mere 3D information browsers. In augmented reality there is an intimate relationship between 3D virtual models and the physical objects they enhance. This suggests that one promising research direction may arise from taking advantage of the familiarity of everyday physical objects for effective manipulation of virtual objects.

Although intuitive to use, with TUI interfaces information display can be a challenge. It is difficult to dynamically change an object's physical properties, so most displays use image projection on objects or augmented surfaces. In tangible interfaces that use 3D graphics there is often also a disconnect between the task space and the display space. For example, in the Triangles work [30], physical triangles were assembled to tell stories, but the visual representations of the stories were shown on a separate monitor distinct from the physical interface.

Presentation and manipulation of 3D virtual objects on projection surfaces is also difficult [31], particularly when trying to support multiple users, each with an independent viewpoint. Most important, because the information display is limited to a projection surface, users are not able to pick virtual images off the surface and manipulate them in 3D space as they would a real object.

So we see that current tangible interfaces provide very intuitive manipulation of digital data but limited support for viewing 3D virtual objects. In contrast, current AR interfaces provide an excellent interface for viewing virtual models but limited support for interaction and space-multiplexed input devices. A promising new AR interface metaphor arises from combining the enhanced display possibilities of augmented reality with the intuitive manipulation of tangible user interfaces. We call this *tangible augmented reality* and in the next section show how it can be used to provide design guidelines for ambient intelligence interfaces.

11.3 DESIGN APPROACH FOR TANGIBLE AR INTERFACES

11.3.1 The Tangible AR Interface Concept

The combination of TUI and AR provides an interaction metaphor called *tangible AR*. The key elements are that each virtual object is registered to a physical object and that the user interacts with virtual objects by manipulating the corresponding tangible objects. Thus in the tangible AR approach physical objects and interactions are as important as the virtual imagery and provide a very intuitive way to interact with the AR interface.

The key benefit of the tangible AR metaphor is that it can support seamless interaction between real and virtual worlds. The goal of computer interfaces is to facilitate seamless interaction between the user and his computer-supported task. In this context, Ishii defined a seam as a discontinuity or constraint in interaction that forces the user to shift among a variety of spaces or modes of operation [8].

Seams that force a user to move between interaction spaces are referred to as functional, while those that force the user to learn new modes of operation are referred to as cognitive. In the previous section we described how tangible user interfaces provide seamless interaction with objects, but may introduce a discontinuity or functional seam between the interaction space and the display space. In contrast, most AR interfaces overlay graphics on the real-world interaction space and so provide a spatially seamless display. However, they often force the user to learn techniques for manipulating virtual content that differ from normal physical object manipulation, or to use a different set of tools for interacting with real and virtual objects. Thus, AR interfaces may introduce a cognitive seam. By combining these two approaches, however, we can develop a seamless interface.

In the AmI context, tangible AR could be used to provide a seamless way of interacting with content. For example, Schmidt [29] discussed the design goal of invisible integration with everyday objects in AmI applications, enabling the same objects to be used for tangible AR interaction. Objects such as the Active Badge [32] and MediaCup [33] are digitally enhanced artifacts that have the familiar affordances of their nonenhanced equivalents (a name badge and a cup). Users thus have some idea of how to use the AmI objects based on familiarity with their nondigital counterparts.

11.4 DESIGN GUIDELINES

One of the most important outcomes of the tangible AR metaphor is that it will provide a set of design guidelines for developing effective interfaces. In designing these interfaces three key elements must be considered (Figure 11.2):

- The *physical elements* in the system
- The *visual and audio display elements*
- The *interaction metaphor* that maps interaction with the real world to virtual object manipulation

A tangible AR interface provides true spatial registration and presentation of 3D virtual objects anywhere in the physical environment, while at the same time allowing users to interact with this virtual content using the same techniques they would use with a physical object. An ideal tangible AR interface thus facilitates seamless display and interaction, removing the functional and cognitive seams found in traditional AR and tangible user interfaces. This is achieved by using design principles learned from TUIs, including

- The use of physical controllers for manipulating virtual content
- Support for spatial 3D interaction techniques (such as object proximity)

FIGURE 11.2

Key elements of a tangible AR interface.

- Support for both time-multiplexed and space-multiplexed interaction
- Support for multi-handed interaction
- Matching the physical constraints of the object to the needs of the interaction task
- Support for parallel activity where multiple objects are being manipulated
- Collaboration between multiple participants

Our central hypothesis is that ambient AR interfaces that follow these design principles will provide completely seamless interaction with virtual content and so will be extremely intuitive to use. In the next section we provide case studies to show how these design guidelines can be applied.

11.5 CASE STUDIES

In this section we show how tangible AR design guidelines have been applied in three AR interfaces: the AR Lens, MagicBook, and AR Tennis. These case studies provide examples of how the same approach can be applied in AmI interfaces.

11.5.1 AR Lens

In 1993 Bier et al. [34] introduced the MagicLens™, a visual filter over pictorial or textual information offering the possibility of interacting with a local area of the data. For example, Figure 11.3(a) illustrates a Gaussian curvature lens displayed

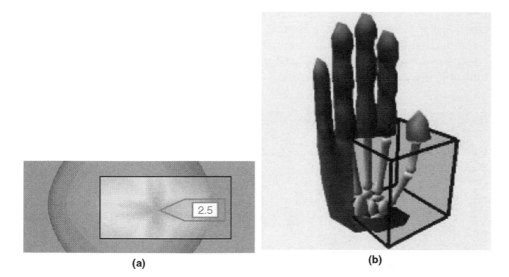

(a)   (b)

FIGURE 11.3

(a) Original MagicLens from Bier (courtesy Eric Bier). (b) 3D MagicLens defined by Viega (courtesy John Viega).

above the rendering of a 3D model. This technique can be used for scientific visualization (multivariate data), photography (image-processing filter), information visualization, and so forth.

Bier's 2D lens was movable over the content with a mouse (or any other device), but he also introduced a second device to edit the content (toolglass widgets). The MagicLens idea was extended to the third dimension by Viega et al. [35] when he proposed the use of a volumetric lens (illustrated in Figure 11.3(b)).

In 2004, Looser et al. [36] built on Bier's work to develop the AR MagicLens. In this case the MagicLens technique enabled the user to see relevant information in multilayered AR data sets superimposed over the real world. Looser used tangible AR design guidelines when designing the physical elements, the visual display elements, and the dedicated interaction metaphor in the AR lens interface.

Figure 11.4 illustrates the Tangible AR MagicLens and its use in an earth visualization (Figure 11.4(a)) and an architectural application (Figure 11.4(b)).

The three parts of the AR MagicLens are:

Physical elements. There are two physical elements to the interface; (1) a handheld trackball mouse with an attached visual tracking element, and (2) a sheet of tracking patterns that serve as a ground plane to the virtual model. In addition, the user wears a video see-through head-mounted display (HMD) to view the AR content.

Visual display elements. In the architectural application the ARToolKit tracking library [37] and osgART graphics library [38] are used to show a virtual building model overlaid on a user's view of the real world. This model is made up of several layers such as internal framing, the walls, and electrical wiring.

Interaction metaphor. AR technology is used to create the illusion that the user is using a real magnifying glass to look inside the virtual model. The interaction technique is based on the metaphor of a real lens: The user moves the physical handle of the AR lens to navigate the content as she would using a real magnifying glass.

(a)   (b)

FIGURE 11.4

Tangible MagicLens.

In the architectural application the user can hold the AR lens over the house model and then use buttons on the trackball controller to turn the different layers of the house model on and off (see Figure 11.4(b)). In this way he can see inside the model, such as to the framing behind the walls, and have an X-ray view of the content. The interaction is extremely natural because the user just has to move the handheld mouse to see into a different part of the model. In addition to supporting intuitive interaction, a key benefit of the AR lens is that it is a focus+context technique, filtering a focus area of interest while keeping the surrounding context visible.

11.5.2 AR Tennis

Mobile devices are one of the more popular potential platforms for ambient interfaces. The rapid growth of mobile phone use, combined with new location-based services and sensing technologies on the phones themselves, could be applicable to a number of AmI applications. Moreover, mobile processing and graphics power has increased to the point that mobile phones can be used for AR application as well. In 2004 Molhring created the first mobile phone AR application [62], while in 2005 Henrysson ported the ARToolKit tracking library to the Symbian platform [40]. It is clear that combining mobile AR visualization with AmI sensing and middleware can produce a number of interesting mobile AmI applications.

However, research still needs to be conducted on the best interface metaphors for these applications. As with the AR lens, TAR interaction techniques can be applied to mobile phone AR experiences. One example of this is the AR Tennis game [41] developed at the HIT Lab NZ. This is a collaborative AR application that allows two users to play an augmented-reality version of tennis on their mobile phones.

In AR Tennis the three parts of the interface are

Physical elements. The two physical elements to the interface are (1) a handheld mobile phone and (2) a sheet of tracking patterns that serve as a ground plane to the virtual model.

Visual display elements. Vision-based AR tracking is used to superimpose a virtual tennis court over the real tracking patterns and to show a virtual ball in motion.

Interaction metaphor. This is a real tennis game where the mobile phones become the racquets that hit a virtual ball across the court.

The AR tennis application uses a set of three ARToolKit tracking markers arranged in a line (see Figure 11.5(a)). When a player points the camera phone at the markers she sees a virtual tennis court model superimposed over the real world. As long as one or more markers are in the field of view, the virtual tennis court will appear. This marker set is used to establish a global coordinate frame in which both of the phones are tracked.

A single ball initially appears on one of the phones. To serve the ball the player points her phone at the court and hits the 2 key. Once the ball is in play there is

(a)   (b)

FIGURE 11.5

(a) Playing AR tennis; (b) hitting the ball over the net.

no further need to use the keypad. The player only has to move her phone in front of the ball. A simple physics engine is used to bounce the ball off the court and to respond when the player hits it (Figure 11.5(b)). Each time the ball is hit a small sound is played and the phone of the player who hits it vibrates, providing multi-sensory cues.

The direction and position vectors of the ball are sent to the other phone using Bluetooth, and the physics simulations are synchronized in each round. When receiving data the device switches state from outgoing to incoming and checks for contact with the racket. Both devices check for collision with the net and if the ball is bounced outside the court. If an incoming ball is missed one of the player serves.

The game was tested on Nokia 6600 and 6630 phones, which have a screen resolution of 176×208 pixels. The video resolution is 160×120 pixels. The Nokia 6600 has a 104-Mhz ARM processor and can run the application at around 3 to 4 frames per second. In contrast the 6630 has a 210-Mhz ARM processor and achieves frame rates of up to 7 frames per second.

As can be seen, the AR Tennis application implements a simple tangible AR interaction metaphor, in which the phone is transformed into a tennis racquet that can hit the ball. This metaphor is very easy to understand and enables players to immediately grasp the game. In user studies [41] players reported that they preferred an AR view of the opponent to a non-AR view and found the tennis application very simple and intuitive to use.

11.5.3 MagicBook

The MagicBook [42] is another example of a tangible AR interface based on TUI design guidelines. The underlying concept is an augmented-reality book that combines the benefits of the real and virtual worlds by overlaying 3D virtual content on real book pages.

In the MagicBook application the three parts of the interface are

Physical elements. A real book with tracking markers on each page.
Visual display elements. Three-dimensional virtual models that can pop out of the pages of the real book.
Interaction metaphor. A book, where the user can change the virtual scene simply by turning the page.

Figure 11.6(a) shows the prototype MagicBook. Each page can be tracked using ARToolKit tracking and visually augmented with 3D virtual and audio content that can be seen through a handheld display (Figure 11.6(b)). The interaction metaphor reproduces the way a person uses a real book: opening it, turning pages, looking at a page. The simplicity of this metaphor ensures an intuitive and highly usable system.

Since the development of the original MagicBook, there have been many demonstrations of the concept. Earlier work explored how to improve the technical limitations of the book (markerless tracking, nonrigid tracking, etc.) and how to use this concept in different domains (education, training, entertainment, cultural heritage, etc.). Figure 11.7 shows some examples [43, 44].

Recent work has focused on AR interaction in the MagicBook interface. In [45], Grasset et al. identified three generic categories of interaction with a MagicBook:

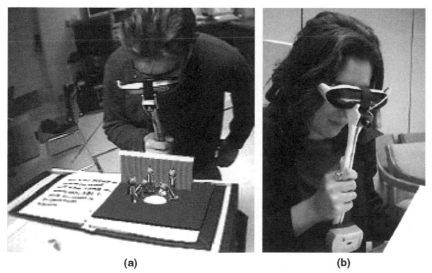

(a)   (b)

FIGURE 11.6

(a) Original MagicBook concept; (b) details of the interaction device.

(a)　　　　　　　　(b)

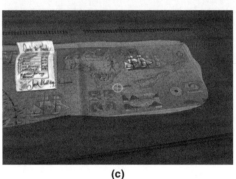

(c)

FIGURE 11.7

Examples of MagicBook: (a) AR Volcano (b) the Black Magic Book, (c) the House That Jack Built AR.

tangible, gestural, and gaze-based. Other researchers explored the use of physical sensors or actuators embedded in the book [46, 47], providing another way for the reader to interact with it. The ideal interaction techniques depend on context and use in a classroom (a controlled environment), in a library (a large number of users), or in the home (adaptable to room conditions). Important questions need to be answered, such as how to adapt the interaction techniques to the book format and how to provide guidance to the user without interfering with the content.

To address these questions, Grasset et al. [45] developed a conceptual framework for mixed-reality books that provides a more formal description of earlier work and deals with future development. They applied the general reality–virtuality continuum presented by Milgram et al. [48] to a new continuum dedicated to the mixed-reality book (see Figure 11.8).

What we can learn from the MagicBook is how the generic tangible AR design guidelines underlie a need to develop adapted design guidelines for specific user contexts. The potential complexity of a MagicBook interface fosters research

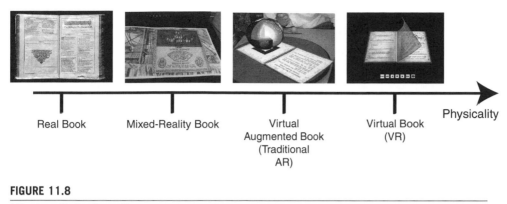

FIGURE 11.8

Mixed-reality book continuum.

on a dedicated conceptual framework for mixed-reality books. There is a similar need for conceptual frameworks in ambient AR interfaces in general.

To explore the design space of ambient AR interfaces software libraries and tools for developing new tangible AR interfaces are needed. The next section will introduce research on authoring tools to simplify the task of the researcher, developer, and end user.

11.6 TOOLS FOR AMBIENT AR INTERFACES

High-level AR authoring tools address the need for interactivity and thus user input in AR environments. They are essential in providing a pathway for interface designers to prototype or create ambient interfaces. Development of these tools can be on different levels: high-level GUI-driven, feature-rich tools, frameworks for programming environments, and low-level development libraries for computer vision or input fusion. Mostly, one level sits on top of another, and the various authoring tools are geared toward a certain application domain.

11.6.1 Software Authoring Tools

A number of software tools have been developed for high-level AR authoring. For example, DART [49], a plug-in for Adobe Director, has inherent access to the wealth of pre-existing infrastructure. Imagetclar [50] introduces a more rigid framework that is capable only of compile-time definition of interactions. In comparison, APRIL [51] addresses the connection between real and virtual environments with a much higher-level framework. It provides an extensible AR authoring platform based on XML descriptions, but interactions are implemented in noninterpretive languages through the XML parser.

In our work we are developing ComposAR [52], which is unique compared to other AR authoring tools in its ability to support different levels of interaction. We follow a similar approach to [53] by extending the notion of a fiducial marker into a sensor. The intermediate level of the system implements an *action-reaction* mechanism that imitates Newtons' physics paradigm. To distinguish the different levels where input and output are connected, we describe the chain of events through *sensors, triggers*, and *actions*.

Sensors provide a raw live data stream into the authoring environment. They include keyboards, mice, and other conventional input devices. The data provided by these sensors is elevated to the state of "information" only once it is interpreted by a *trigger*, which evaluates the input and decides whether or not to invoke an *action*. An example of this process is the monitoring of a marker's visibility. Currently ComposAR provides basic interaction based on a standard repertoire common in AR applications, including that based on fiducial proximity, occlusion, tilting, and shaking.

Through this very rough abstraction, ComposAR can provide a convenient way to create a broad variety of interfaces, including ambient displays and simulations (Figure 11.9). As ambient interfaces react to low-level data, this methodology allows us to quickly create demonstrations that act on data from an RSS feed or the tilt sensor in a desktop computer. Because this approach is even net transparent, displays and sensors can be meshed.

11.6.2 Hardware Authoring Tools

In addition to software authoring tools for ambient AR interfaces, there is a need for hardware tools for rapid prototyping. The design and development of AR tangible interfaces have demonstrated the need for tools that can easily integrate physical

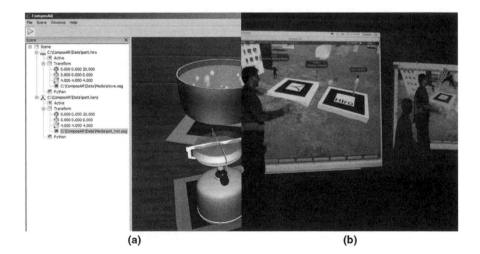

(a)   (b)

FIGURE 11.9

(a) ComposAR simulating boiling water with a TUI to allow real-world proximity sensing.
(b) Projection screen installation with ComposAR in combination with a SecondLife art piece.

actuators and sensors into ambient AR applications. By combining a tangible inter-face with intelligible sensors, users can benefit from a new range of design possibilities such as kinetic movement, skin sensitivity, and sustainable power. In the past it was difficult to explore such designs because of the high level of hardware skills required and the difficulty of integrating the technology in software. However, more affordable and intuitive solutions have emerged.

Simple programming microcontroller boards (like the Arduino [54]) can be remotely read or controlled from a standard PC. USB or wireless components have also become simple and easily integrated into an electronic interface. The research community has pursued the goal of creating physical computing elements that are easily integrated into the user interface. In this section we present a few examples in this category.

The Phidgets toolkit [55] combines a set of independent sensors that are pluggable through a USB port. A low-level software interface allows users to plug them in at run-time and access them through a .NET interface. The CALDER toolkit [56] introduces a similar approach, but adds wireless components. The iStuff framework [57] facilitates support of distributed sensors and actuators through a transparent network interface and an API based on system events. Papier-Mâché [58] supports RFID in an event-based toolkit integrated with other technologies such as computer vision tracking. It also has high-level tools for the developer, through a visual debugging interface, and monitoring tools.

These toolkits are in large part oriented toward developers with good programming skills and a good understanding of hardware processing; thus they are inaccessible to a large range of users. Furthermore, few of them are integrated with general libraries for developing augmented reality or virtual reality applications.

One way to make these tools more accessible is through a visual programming interface. For example, in the Equator project, ECT has a visual interface for building applications that support a large range of physical sensors [59]. Support for AR has recently been added to this library ([60]). Recently we proved the feasibility of using ComposAR [52] with physical input devices [61].

We have been developing a generic hardware toolkit supporting a number of physical actuators and sensors (Figure 11.10). Called Pandora's Box, our toolkit is a multi-language library that uses a client server approach for access to various hardware toolkits (e.g. Arduino, In-house, T3G). It is being integrated into the ComposAR software toolkit to create an all-in-one solution for easy development of physical, ambient, and visually augmented interfaces.

A number of research areas remain. A transparent interface for multiple hardware devices is still challenging and needs more development and testing. Standardization and a more generic interface for electronic boards and sensors will help with this. Research is also needed on methods for user access to sensors. How, for example, can sensors be visually represented? How easily can they be configured? How can sensors be combined and high-level information provided to the end user in a relevant way? Initial work has been conducted in this area, for example, with flow control diagrams, but their generic nature makes them difficult for novice end users.

FIGURE 11.10

Rescaling a 3D model with physical sensors using Pandora's Box.

11.7 CONCLUSIONS

Ambient intelligence interfaces present interesting challenges in terms of how to represent the AmI information to the user and how the user should interact with AmI applications. While many AmI applications use implicit human–computer interaction and so do not require explicit user input, the majority do require some active user intervention.

In this chapter we described the concept of ambient AR interfaces in which augmented reality can be used to make visible the invisible data in AmI applications. Ambient AR interfaces provide a way to achieve this.

One benefit of this approach is that it also supports the use of a tangible AR interaction metaphor for interacting with AmI applications. In tangible AR tangible user interface input methods combine with AR display methods to create very intuitive AR applications. Using this metaphor we can produce design guidelines that will make it easier to develop good AR interfaces. Several case studies were described to show how these design guidelines can be applied.

The work presented in this chapter is an interesting beginning, but there are still some significant directions for future research. One of the most important is hardware and software authoring tools. For ambient AR applications to become widespread better tools are necessary. As discussed in this chapter, some work has begun in this area, but it is still far too difficult for nonprogrammers to develop AmI prototype applications. If the design community is going to engage in this research they will need tools that can match the way they work.

A second important area of research is in user evaluation of the ambient AR interaction techniques we are exploring. The tangible AR interaction metaphor is interesting, but its value will only be shown through more rigorous user studies that compare its ease of use with that of other methods.

REFERENCES

[1] Weiser M. The computer for the 21st century. Sci Am 1991;265(3):94-104.

[2] Norman D. The Invisible Computer: Why Good Products Can Fail, the Personal Computer Is So Complex, and Information Appliances Are the Solution. MIT Press; 1999.

[3] Fishkin KP, Moran TP, Harrison BL. Embodied user interfaces: Towards invisible user interfaces. In: Proceedings of the IFIP TC2/TC13 WG2.7/WG13.4 Seventh Working Conference on Engineering for Human-Computer Interaction. Kluwer; 1999. p. 1-18.

[4] Gaggioli A. Ambient Intelligence. IOS Press; 2005 (Chapter, Optimal Experience in Ambient Intelligence).

[5] Shadbolt N. Ambient Intelligence. IEEE Intelligent Systems.

[6] Negroponte N. Being Digital & Stoughton. IEEE Intelligent Systems archive 2003;18(4):2-3.

[7] Rekimoto J, Nagao K. The world through the computer: Computer augmented interaction with real world environments. In: UIST '95: Proceedings of the 8th Annual ACM Symposium on User Interface and Software Technology. ACM Press; 1995. p. 29-36.

[8] Ishii H, Ullmer B. Tangible bits: Towards seamless interfaces between people, bits and atoms. In: CHI '97: Proceedings of the SIGCHI Conference on Human Factors in Computing Systems. ACM Press; 1997. p. 234-41.

[9] Malinda Rauhala AH, Gunnarsson AS. A novel interface to sensor networks using handheld augmented reality. In: Proceedings of Mobile HCI; 2006. p. 145-8.

[10] Azuma RT. A Survey of Augmented Reality. Presence: Teleoperators and Virtual Environments 1997;6(4):355-85.

[11] Shneiderman B. The Future of Interactive Systems and the Emergence of Direct Manipulation. University of Maryland Press; 1982.

[12] Hutchins EL, Hollan JD, Norman DA. Direct manipulation interface. Human-Computer Interaction 1985;1(4):311-38.

[13] Ullmer B, Ishii H. The metadesk: Models and prototypes for tangible user interfaces. In: UIST '95: Proceedings of the Conference on User Interface Software Technology. ACM Press; 1997. p. 223-32.

[14] Underkoffler J, Ishii H. URP: A luminous-tangible workbench for urban planning and design. In: CHI '99: Proceedings of the Conference on Human Factors in Computing System. ACM Press; 1999. p. 386-93.

[15] Kato H, Billinghurst M, Imamoto K, Tachibana K. Virtual object manipulation on a table-top AR environment. In: ISAR '00: International Symposium on Augmented Reality; 2000. p. 111-9.

[16] Frazer JH, Frazer JM, Frazer PA. Intelligent physical three-dimensional modelling systems. In: SIGGRAPH '80: Proceedings of the Annual Conference on Computer Graphics and Interactive Techniques; 1980. p. 359-70.

[17] Butterworth J, Davidson A, Hench S, Olano MT. 3DM: A three-dimensional modeler using a head-mounted display. In: SI3D '92: Proceedings of the 1992 Symposium on Interactive 3D Graphics. ACM Press; 1992. p. 135-8.

[18] Poupyrev I, Billinghurst M, Weghorst S, Ichikawa T. The go-go interaction technique: Non-linear mapping for direct manipulation in V. In: UIST '96: Proceedings of the 9th Annual ACM Symposium on User Interface Software and Technology. ACM Press; 1996. p. 79-80.

[19] Gabbard JL. A taxonomy of usability characteristics in virtual environment. Master's thesis. Virginia Polytechnic Institute and State University; 1997.

[20] Bajura M, Fuchs H, Ohbuchi R. Merging virtual objects with the real world: Seeing ultrasound imagery within the patient. In: SIGGRAPH '92: Proceedings of the 19th Annual Conference on Computer Graphics and Interactive Techniques. ACM Press; 1992. p. 203–10.

[21] Feiner S, Macintyre B, Seligmann D. Knowledge-based augmented reality. Commun ACM 1993;36(7):53–62.

[22] Kiyoshi Kiyokawa NY, Takemura H. A collaboration support technique by integrating a shared virtual reality and a shared augmented reality. In: Proceedings of ISMC 1999;6:48–53.

[23] Schmalstieg D, Fuhrmann A, Hesina G. Bridging multiple user interface dimensions with augmented reality. In: Proceedings of ISAR. 2000. p. 20–9.

[24] Butz A, Höllerer T, Feiner S, Macintyre B, Beshers C. Enveloping users and computers in a collaborative 3D augmented reality. In: IWAR '99: Proceedings of the International Workshop on Augmented Reality. 1999. p. 35–44.

[25] Bill N. Schili, Norman Adam, Roy Wan. Context-aware computing applications. In: First International Workshop on Mobile Computing Systems and Applications. 1994. p. 85–90.

[26] Kirsh D. The intelligent use of space. Journal of Artificial Intelligence 1995;73(1-2):31–68.

[27] Schilit WN. A system for context-aware mobile computing. Ph.D. thesis. Columbia University; 1995.

[28] Schmidt MBA, Gellersen HW. There is more to context than location. Interactive Applications of Mobile Computing, Neuer Hochechulscheiftenverlag, Rostok.

[29] Schmidt A. Ambient Intelligence. IOS Press; 2005 (Chapter A. Interactive Context-Aware Systems Interacting with Ambient Intelligence, 159–78).

[30] Gorbet MG, Orth M, Ishii H. Triangles: Tangible interface for manipulation and exploration of digital information topography. In: CHI '98: Proceedings of the SIGCHI Conference on Human Factors in Computing Systems. ACM Press/Addison-Wesley; 1998. p. 49–56.

[31] Fjeld M, Voorhorst F, Bichsel M, Lauche K, Rauterberg M, Krueger H. Exploring brick-based navigation and composition in an augmented reality. In: HUC '99: Proceedings of the 1st International Symposium on Handheld and Ubiquitous Computing. Springer-Verlag; 1999. p. 102–16.

[32] Want FR, Hopper A, Gibbons J. The active badge location system. ACM Transactions on Information Systems 1992;10(1):42–7.

[33] Beigi ASM, Gellersen H-W. Mediacups: Experience with design and use of computer-augmented everyday objects. Computer Networks, Special Issue on Pervasive Computing 2001;35(4):401–9.

[34] Bier EA, Stone MC, Pier K, Buxton W, Derose TD. Toolglass and Magic Lenses: The See-Through Interface; 1993. p. 73–80.

[35] Viega GWJ, Conway MJ, Pausch R. 3D magic lenses. In: Proceedings of the 9th Annual ACM Symposium on User Interface Software and Technology. ACM Press; 1996.

[36] Looser J. Through the looking glass: The use of lenses as an interface tool for augmented reality interfaces, In: Proceedings of GRAPHITE '04. ACM Press; 2004. p. 204–11.

[37] Kato H, Billinghurst M. Marker tracking and HMD calibration for a video-based augmented reality conferencing system. In: IWAR '99: Proceedings of the 2nd IEEE/ACM International Workshop on Augmented Reality. IEEE Computer Society; 1999. p. 85.

[38] Looser J, Grasset R, Seichter H, Billinghurst M. (2006) OSGART—A pragmatic approach to MR. In: 5th IEEE and ACM International Symposium on Mixed and Augmented Reality (ISMAR 06): Industrial Workshop; 2006. p. 22-5.

[39] Anabuki M, Kakuta H, Yamamoto H, Tamura H. Welbo: An embodied conversational agent living in mixed reality space. In: CHI '00: Extended Abstracts on Human Factors in Computing Systems. ACM Press; 2000. p. 10-1.

[40] Henrysson A, Ollila M. UMAR: Ubiquitous mobile augmented reality. In: MUM '04: Proceedings of the 3rd International Conference on Mobile and Ubiquitous Multimedia. ACM Press; 2004. p. 41-5.

[41] Henrysson A, Billinghurst M, Ollila M. AR tennis. In: SIGGRAPH '06: ACM SIGGRAPH 2006 Sketches. ACM Press; 2006. p. 13.

[42] Billinghurst M, Kato H, Poupyrev I. The Magicbook: A transitional AR interface. Computers and Graphics 2001;25:745-53.

[43] Woods E, Billinghurst M, Looser J, Aldridge G, Brown D, Garrie B, et al. Augmenting the science centre and museum experience. In: GRAPHITE '04: 2nd International Conference on Computer Graphics and Interactive Techniques in Australasia and South east Asia. 2004. p. 230-6.

[44] Grasset R, Duenser A, Seichter H, Billinghurst M. The mixed reality book: A new multimedia reading experience. In: CHI '07: Extended Abstracts on Human Factors in Computing Systems. ACM Press; 2007. p. 1953-8.

[45] D. A. B. M. R. Grasset A, Duenser , Billinghurst M. Design of a mixed-reality book: Is it still a real book? In: Proceedings of ISMAR. 2008.

[46] Back M, Cohen J, Gold R, Harrison S, Minneman S. Listen reader: An electronically augmented paper-based book. In: CHI '01: Proceedings of the SIGCHI Conference on Human Factors in Computing Systems. ACM Press; 2001. p. 23-9.

[47] de G?tzen ARD. Continuous sonic interaction in books for children. In: International forum: Less is more—Simple Computing in an Age of Complexity. 2005.

[48] Milgram P, Takemura H, Utsumi A, Kishino F. Augmented reality: A class of displays on the reality virtuality continuum. In: SPIE, Telemanipulator and Telepresence Technologies, vol 2351. p. 282-92.

[49] MacIntyre B, Gandy M, Dow S, Bolter JD. DART: A toolkit for rapid design exploration of augmented reality experiences. In: Proceedings of the 17th Annual ACM Symposium on User Interface Software and Technology. 2004. p. 197-206.

[50] Owen C, Tang A, Xiao F. Imagetclar: A blended script and compiled code development system for augmented reality, citeseer.ist.psu.edu/owen03imagetclar.html; 2003.

[51] Ledermann F, Schmalstieg D. APRIL: A high-level framework for creating augmented reality presentations. In: VR '05: Proceedings of the IEEE Conference on Virtual Reality 2005; 2005. p. 187-94.

[52] Seichter H, Looser J, Billinghurst M. Composar: An intuitive tool for authoring AR applications. IEEE 2008;177-8.

[53] Hampshire A, Seichter H, Grasset R, Billinghurst M. Augmented reality authoring: Generic context from programmer to designer. In: OZCHI '06: Proceedings of the Australasian Computer-Human Interaction Conference. 2006.

[54] Arduino. www.arduino.cc.

[55] Greenberg S, Fitchett C. Phidgets: Easy development of physical interfaces through physical widgets. In: UIST '01: Proceedings of the 14th Annual ACM Symposium on User Interface Software and Technology. ACM Press; 2001. p. 209–18.

[56] Lee JC, Avrahami D, Hudson SE, Forlizzi J, Dietz PH, Leigh D. The calder toolkit: Wired and wireless components for rapidly prototyping interactive devices. In: DIS '04: Proceedings of the 5th Conference on Designing Interactive Systems. ACM Press; 2004. p. 167–75.

[57] Ballagas R, Ringel M, Stone M, Borchers J. iStuff: A physical user interface toolkit for ubiquitous computing environments. In: CHI '03: Proceedings of the SIGCHI Conference on Human Factors in Computing Systems. ACM Press; 2003. p. 537–44.

[58] Klemmer SR, Li J, Lin J, Landay JA. Papier-Mâché: Toolkit support for tangible input. In: CHI '04: Proceedings of the SIGCHI Conference on Human Factors in Computing Systems. ACM Press; 2004. p. 399–406.

[59] Greenhalgh C, Izadi S, Mathrick J, Humble J, Taylor I. ECT: A toolkit to support rapid construction of UBICOMP environments. In: UBICOMP 2004; 2004.

[60] Hampshire A, Seichter H, Grasset R, Billinghurt M. Augmented reality authoring: Generic context from programmer to designer. In: OZCHI 06: Proceedings of the Australasian Human–Computer Interaction Conference; 2006.

[61] Hong D, Looser J, Seichter H, Billinghurst M, Woo W. A sensor based interaction for ubiquitous virtual reality systems. IE 2008;75–8.

[62] Moehring M, Lessig C, Bimber O. Video see-through AR on consumer cell phones. In: Proceedings of International Symposium on Augumented and Mixed Reality (ISMAR'04); 2004. p. 252–3.

Physical Browsing and Selection—Easy Interaction with Ambient Services

12

Pasi Välkkynen, Johan Plomp, and Timo Tuomisto

VTT Technical Research Centre of Finland, Tampere, Finland

303

ABSTRACT

Physical browsing is an interaction paradigm that associates digital information with physical objects. It can be regarded as analogous to browsing the Web: The physical environment contains links to digital information; by selecting them, various services can be activated. Physical browsing is based on selecting a physical world target with a mobile terminal—for example, an RFID tag with a mobile phone equipped with a suitable reader device. Selection causes information related to the target to be displayed on the mobile terminal, some service related to the target object to be "activated," or the mobile terminal to be connected to another device in the ambient intelligence environment.

Key words: physical browsing, physical selection, affordance, RFID tag, interaction.

12.1 INTRODUCTION TO PHYSICAL BROWSING

In ambient intelligence, computing devices are embedded into the physical environment so that users can interact with them at the same time as they interact with the physical environment. The various devices are connected to each other and have various sizes and input and output capabilities depending on their purpose. Together they provide services to the user that may go beyond their separate capabilities. Interaction in such an environment, where the physical and digital worlds are intertwined, calls for new paradigms. Browsing and selection tasks now go beyond the screen into the physical world, and a mouse is no longer sufficient to point at the target objects.

Interaction with services embedded in the physical environment first requires their discovery. Users must perceive the availability, purpose, capabilities, and way of use of these affordances, whose subsequent use involves a number of selection tasks to indicate, for example, objects of interest, choices, targets for interaction, and sources of information. While in the familiar desktop environment a series of pointing, clicking, and dragging actions manipulate objects on the screen; similar interaction techniques can now be developed for physical browsing and manipulating data associated with the physical objects. Because of the diverse nature of the physical world, there is a large variety of solutions for implementing these browsing and selection tasks and associated interaction paradigms.

In physical browsing, the interaction happens via a mobile terminal—such as a mobile phone or a personal digital assistant (PDA). The links are implemented as tags that can be read by the terminal—for example, radio frequency identifier (RFID) tags that are read with a mobile phone augmented with an RFID reader. The basis of physical browsing is physical selection—the interaction task through which the user tells the mobile terminal which link to activate. A selection is followed by an action. Say the tag contains a universal resource identifier (URI, or Web address);

the mobile phone may then display the associated Web page in the browser. The displayed information will be related to the physical object itself, creating an association between the object and its digital counterpart.

Physical selection, an interaction task for ubiquitous computing, tells the user's mobile terminal which physical object the user wants to interact with. It is based on tags that identify physical objects or store a physical hyperlink to digital information related to the object to which attached. The user selects the hyperlink by touching, pointing, or scanning the tag with a mobile terminal equipped with an appropriate reader. Physical selection can be implemented with various technologies, such as RFID tags and readers, infrared transceivers, and optically readable tags and mobile phone cameras.

In this chapter, we will first describe the physical browsing concept and highlight physical selection as a user interaction task. Selection methods such as touching, pointing, and scanning will be presented and illustrated with examples from various domains: the desktop computing, laser pointers, virtual environments, and mobile terminal–based ubiquitous computing settings. Subsequently we will elaborate the architecture and technologies for implementing physical selection functionality and managing the associated user interaction events and data. Finally, we will attempt to provide some insight into the further development of these paradigms.

12.2 WHY AMBIENT SERVICES NEED PHYSICAL BROWSING SOLUTIONS

With the vision that an abundance of ambient services will in time become available, we need ways to choose the ambient service of our interest. First, the services must advertise themselves—it must be obvious to users which services are available. Some might be available anywhere, others at a particular location. More specifically, some might be associated with objects in the environment. We can view these services as affordances of the environment. When the user looks at a Web page or a user interface on a computer screen, there are certain cues that help her understand where to click—for example, buttons with a 3D effect to suggest an object that can be pressed, and links to a Website are in blue and underlined.

While such cues are easy to understand, much of this knowledge is based on non-explicit conventions. Likewise we need conventions to give hints to visitors to a smart space on how to detect available services. One possibility is to have all services broadcast their presence on a handheld device. As we cannot expect people to be watching their mobile devices all the time, the services might also need to be indicated by visual cues. On the other hand, cues should be subtle enough not to disturb the environment too much. This is a challenge for designers. Visualization of physical hyperlinks is discussed briefly in the next section.

When the users detect ambient services, they select one and start using it. This is where other physical browsing technologies come in. The AmI services may convey their presence by means of a tag (visual or RFID). Selecting one may be by touching or pointing at it so that interaction may start. These two service selection procedures—together with the broadcasting method previously mentioned—are instances of physical browsing technologies. They are indispensable in searching for ways to connect the physical world to the virtual world. In the future using services embedded in the environment may become as matter of fact as switching on the light by means of a switch next to the door.

12.3 PHYSICAL SELECTION

Physical selection is the method by which the user accesses the ambient service; it is therefore an important aspect of putting these services into use. For physical selection, we introduce three selection methods: touching, pointing, and scanning.

12.3.1 Concepts and Vocabulary

A *tag* is the technical device that a *reader* embedded in a mobile terminal can read. There are several implementation technologies for tags and their corresponding readers—for example RFID tags and readers—which are introduced in Subsection 12.5.2.

The tag implements a *link*, or physical hyperlink, which is something the user sees and interacts with by physical selection. Thus, the user selects links and the reader reads tags in the terms of this chapter. Optimally, the user should not have to know the implementation details of the tag; the mobile terminal hardware takes care of those. In the real world, with its diverse technologies, incompatible readers, and varying reading ranges, this goal is often not met.

Physical selection is an interaction task. Through physical selection, users tell the terminal what physical object they want to interact with.

After selection, typically some *action* occurs. This can be displaying information related to the physical object to which the tag is attached, or it may be any digital service the terminal offers. Selection and action are independent of each other [1], and the selection method should not affect the action. Also, as Bowman and Hodges [6] state, it is important to consider grabbing (selection) and manipulation (action) as separate issues.

Physical browsing [16] in this chapter means the entire process of selecting a link in an ambient intelligence environment and obtaining the information or service related to it. We choose to include in the term "browsing" all services activated by physical selection, be it traditional information retrieval or connecting to ambient services or other devices.

12.3.2 Touching

Touching is a centimeters-range selection method in which the user brings the terminal very close to the tag to select it. Touching requires that either the mobile terminal or the tag sense the proximity of the other. If the communication range of the implementation technology is very short, as for example in near-field RFID, touching is implemented "for free." If the range is longer, there has to be a technique for determining which tag is closest to the reader. That can be accomplished in various ways, such as power analysis or periodically limiting the communication range to a few centimeters.

Touching (Figure 12.1) is the most direct and unambiguous selection method. It is suitable for selecting links near the user and in environments in which link density is high. When touching a link, the user has to know the exact location of the tag and even the placement of the reader inside the terminal. Positioning the mobile terminal over the target requires hardly any adaptation of the normal sensorimotor task of touching, and equals the positioning of any tool on target. This makes touching with a mobile terminal a "natural" selection method.

12.3.3 Pointing

Pointing (Figure 12.2) is a long-range selection method suitable for selecting one tag from a distance. The distance depends on the communication range of the implementation technology, but ideally should be several meters [31] or as much as needed for the user to select a visible tag. To point at a link, the user has to know its exact location.

FIGURE 12.1

User touching a tag attached to a poster.

FIGURE 12.2

User pointing at a tag attached to a poster.

Implementation of pointing is heavily dependent on the technology. Some technologies, such as infrared, are easy to make directional whereas others, such as RFID, typically have more or less uniform spherical reading fields and special methods are required to determine the relative alignment of the reader and the tag.

12.3.4 Scanning

Scanning (Figure 12.3) is a long-range selection method that combines the physical location of the user and the graphical user interface of the mobile terminal. When the user scans for links, all links within the reading range are displayed in a list from which the user will be able to select. Scanning for nearby Bluetooth devices with a mobile phone is a familiar example of scanning. The implementation of scanning requires a long reading range, preferably several meters, and a uniform spherical reading field so that all tags within range will be read.

FIGURE 12.3

User scanning for links.

Scanning is suitable for situations in which the user does not know the exact locations of the links or what is available in the environment. Touching and pointing are more direct selection methods when link location and content are known. One of the main challenges with scanning is naming the links for display so that the user can predict what action will follow from his selection. In this chapter, our focus will be on touching and pointing because, as extra-terminal selection methods, they are more interesting in the physical world setting than intra-terminal scanning selection.

12.3.5 Visualizing Physical Hyperlinks

Web browsing has established ways to indicate the existence of a hyperlink: An embedded link within text may have a different color, font, or style from the other text. When the cursor is hovered or rolled over the link, the link's visual look changes—a tooltip appears to display, for example, its address or title.

In physical selection, visual cues in, for example, posters for touch-sensitive areas may resemble the hyperlinks in Web browsers. However—unlike display devices— the target cannot present focusing or hovering information. This can only be presented on a mobile terminal, and selection and subsequent action must be confirmed by some additional user action, which produces a trade-off between ease of use and security. If security is preferred, the user is required to perform another step to confirm the selection and action in addition to bringing the terminal close to the target. The confirmation can be done within the normal graphical user interface of the terminal, or the user can touch the target again to confirm her action. If ease of use is preferred, the hovering phase is left out and touching always means selection: The target application is responsible for confirming the action with the user.

Outside printed physical objects—such as posters—cues provided by normal hyperlinks are not available: Users have to rely only on symbols printed on the tags. Various symbols exist to indicate the physical browsing paradigm or access technology. A good example of the variation in touching symbols can be found in [2]. We suggested symbols that inform the user about the physical selection method and the type of action within the tag [33].

12.4 SELECTION AS AN INTERACTION TASK

To better understand physical selection, it is necessary to look at selection in other, more established computing environments. Selection of an object for interaction is one of the basic tasks found in many environments. In this chapter, desktop computer systems, immersive virtual environments, and laser pointers are discussed in relation to physical selection. This section is a modified version of a chapter by the same name in [34].

In addition to selection technologies based on wireless electro-magnetic transmission (such as RFID or Bluetooth), there exist other selection technologies for connecting digital and physical entities. Visual codes can be read with mobile devices and interaction with them resembles a mix between touching and pointing. Another technology, RedTacton, transmits data through the body of the user, allowing for example exchanging business cards by shaking hands.

12.4.1 Selection in Desktop Computer Systems

Foley et al. [9] proposed an organization of interaction techniques based on the tasks for which they are used. Their emphasis was on graphics applications, but their organization is somewhat applicable even to ubiquitous computing applications. Its basis was an analysis of the contemporary input devices and the input techniques they were able to perform. Card et al. [7] criticized Foley et al. organization, saying, "the limitation of the scheme is that the categories are somewhat ad hoc and there is no attempt at defining a notion of completeness for the design space." Still, organization of interaction techniques into interaction tasks is useful.

In their analysis, Foley et al. [9] found six fundamental interaction tasks:

- *Select* (the user makes a selection from a set of alternatives)
- *Position* (the user specifies a position—for example, screen coordinates)
- *Orient* (the user specifies an angle)
- *Path* (the user specifies a set of positions and orientations)
- *Quantify* (the user inputs a numeric value)
- *Text entry* (the user inputs a string value)

Of these, selection is the most interesting one for physical browsing. Foley et al. [9] divided the selection task into different selection techniques. *Indirect pick* is a selection technique in which the selectable object is displayed and the user can pick it directly from the screen. Direct pick technologies in graphical user interfaces can be a light pen and a touch-sensitive screen. In *simulated pick with cursor match,* a cursor is positioned over the desired visible object using a locator device like a mouse.

Direct pick can be seen to roughly correspond to physical selection by touching. Simulated pick roughly corresponds to physical selection by pointing. From this analysis it can also be seen that selecting an object by touching is more direct than selecting it by pointing, which in turn is more direct than selection by scanning.

12.4.2 About the Choice of Selection Technique

English et al. [8] stated that the important factors in the choice of selection techniques are (1) the mix of other operations required of the select-operation hand, (2) the ease of the hand getting to and gaining control of a given selection device, and (3) the fatigue effects of the associated operating posture of the technique. Although their experiments were based on an early desktop computer and different selection devices for it, the basic principles can be considered valid in physical selection techniques as well. In particular, the fatigue effects may prove important with touching and pointing. Additionally, the first item in Foley's list—the mix of operations—can be presumed to affect the selection techniques. For example, the basic pointing sequence includes several operations: aligning the terminal toward the target, pressing a button to trigger the selection, and bringing the terminal back close enough to see the result of the selection.

Foley et al. [9] saw time, accuracy, and pleasantness as the primary criteria for the quality of interaction design. These criteria are met in different degrees by the same interaction technique, depending on (1) the context of the task, (2) the experience and knowledge of the user, and (3) the physical characteristics of the interaction device. Therefore, interaction techniques "should not be selected in isolation from knowledge of the other techniques at use at approximately the same time. The performance of a complete action generally involves a series of tasks to be carried out almost as a single unit" [9]. The context of interaction techniques is especially relevant in ubiquitous computing environments in which the interaction is intended to be as natural as possible and it is more unpredictable than in constrained desktop environments.

We built a physical browser prototype that supports all three selection methods, touching, pointing, and scanning [30]. We found that users are willing to use touching only if the target is within reach (about 1.1 meters); otherwise, they prefer pointing at the target [32]. The most important result from an evaluation was that there is a need for several alternative selection methods, and the users should have the freedom to choose depending on their situation.

12.4.3 **Selection in Immersive Virtual Environments**

Selecting an object for further interaction is one of the most fundamental actions in a virtual environment [6, 18, 27]. Interaction with virtual objects requires some way to indicate to the system the interaction target.

Virtual environments typically support direct user interaction, which allows interaction techniques such as hand tracking, gesture recognition, pointing, and gaze direction to specify task parameters, including object selection [27, 18]. This interaction paradigm supports natural mapping between user actions and the action results. In such an environment, object selection can be performed directly: If an object is within reach, the user can select it by extending a hand and touching it, in a similar manner to touching objects in physical selection. Selection typically involves using a button or a gesture to signal the system that the chosen object is the one the user wants.

The two primary selection technique categories in virtual environments are local and at a distance [18, 6]. If the object is out of reach, an at-a-distance technique is needed. Selecting a remote object for manipulation in a virtual environment bears some resemblance to the same task in a physical environment. Remote selection can be done by arm extension or ray casting. Arm extension requires a graphical system to show how far the virtual hand of the user is extended and thus is not suitable for physical environments without augmented reality displays. Ray casting, on the other hand, is similar to physical selection by pointing. In ray casting, a light ray (such as a virtual laser beam or spotlight) projects from the hand of the user, typically when a specific button is pressed. By intersecting the ray with the desired object and releasing the button, the object is attached to the ray and is ready for manipulation. Other techniques for selecting objects in virtual environments include gaze direction, head orientation, voice input, and list selection, which is similar to physical selection by scanning.

According to Mine [18], feedback is essential for selection in virtual environments. The user must know when the object is ready for selection—that is, when, for example, the pointing beam is intersecting with it. The user must also obtain feedback about a successful selection. Bowman and Hodges [6] stated that it is important to consider selection and manipulation as separate issues, which supports our view of selection and action as orthogonal phases of interaction.

12.4.4 Selection with Laser Pointers

In addition to physical selection by pointing, laser pointing has been used as an input technique for large projected screens. As ubiquitous computing becomes more common, rooms will contain computer-controlled devices, appliances, and displays [37]. In these nondesk situations, users will need to interact with display surfaces at a distance [21]. For users who are distant from the screen, the most natural way to select objects is to point at them [19]. A popular interaction scheme is to track a laser pointer beam on the display surface with a camera. The drawback here, with regard to tag-based physical selection, is that the target area must be tracked with a camera, and so laser pointing can be used only in suitably instrumented environments.

Kirstein and Müller [17] developed a system in which a common laser pointer can be tracked by a video camera. The pointer works as an input device, freeing the user from the physical connection that traditional input devices require. The user moves the laser pointer on the display area, and the camera detects the point on the projection screen. The image is analyzed, and mouse control signals (up, down, move) are derived from the detected beam and sent to the computer. Applications in the computer do not notice whether a regular mouse or a laser pointer is used.

Olsen and Nielsen's [21] approach was similar to Kirstein and Müller's, but they argued that such a simple mapping (mouse up, down, move) is insufficient for general information manipulation. They described a full suite of interactions and an implementation to accomplish them.

As in the system of Kirstein and Müller, laser pointers are used to interact with information on a large projected display. The difference is that Olsen and Nielsen did not directly translate laser pointer events to mouse events. In addition to laser on, laser off, and laser move they had events for the laser being off for an extended period of time and for it being held in one place for an extended period. They developed laser-specific user interface widgets that respond to these new events, dividing them into button, enumeration, scrollable (numbers, dates, and times), text, and list categories. Their view was thus that interaction with a laser pointer requires a specific user interface, separate from the application on the projected display. The results of the user study Olsen and Nielsen performed indicate that laser-based interactions on a projected screen are clearly slower than using a mouse.

Myers et al. [20] stated that interaction techniques using laser pointers tend to be imprecise, error prone, and slow. In addition to the technological problems (for example, there is no mouse button in a common laser pointer), inherent human limitations cause difficulties for laser pointer interaction:

- Users do not know exactly where the laser beam will hit when they turn it on, and it takes about one second to move it to the desired position.
- The hands are unsteady, causing the beam to wiggle approximately 0.10 to 0.17 degrees (mostly vertically) depending on the design of the pointing device (a PDA was found to be the most stable).
- When the button is released, the beam often shifts away from the target before going off.

For these reasons, a new interaction style is needed. Myers et al. [19] suggested a new approach to previous work—that is, to use pointing for referencing a broad area of interest. The laser pointer indicates the region of interest and the item in that region is copied to the user's handheld device. Myers et al. called this interaction style *semantic snarfing*. "Snarfing" [25] refers to grabbing the contents of a large screen to a handheld device, "semantic" refers to the fact that the meaning, or semantics, of the grabbed object is often needed, instead of a picture or an exact copy of the interface, because the interaction capabilities of handheld devices are limited. In addition to interacting with displays, users can "snarf" the user interface of a remote appliance to their mobile device, which is similar to physical selection by pointing.

The human limitations Myers et al. described also apply to physical selection by pointing. It does not matter whether the user is trying to point at a widget on a projected display or at a physical object; he does not know where the laser beam will be when he first turns it on (at least until he has had considerable practice with his personal device). If the laser beam alone is used to trigger a pointable tag, the problem of shaky hands makes the selection more difficult, as does the potential shift when the pointing button is released. Myers et al. stated that, because of wiggling, graphical user interface widgets designed for laser pointer interaction should be fairly big. This holds true also for pointable tags if only laser triggering is used, meaning that the tag should, for example, have an array of photosensitive sensors.

To counteract some of the problems Myers et al. described, we decided to trigger a tag in our own pointing implementation [30] as soon as the laser beam hit it. The initial location of the beam is still somewhat problematic because, if there happens to be a tag under the beam when it is still in the wrong location, the wrong tag will be triggered.

The semantic snarfing of Myers et al. can also be used to extend our view of pointing and scanning. Since "snarfing" refers to grabbing the contents of a large area to the screen of the mobile terminal for further examination, we can imagine it as "directional scanning." The final selection still requires intra-device interaction as in scanning, but the user can better indicate her intention to the terminal. This also shows that our three selection methods can easily be extended or combined to form new ones.

12.4.5 The Mobile Terminal as an Input Device

Ballagas et al. [3] used the taxonomy of Foley et al. [9] as a framework for their analysis of mobile phones as ubiquitous computing input devices. They noted that, although Foley et al. performed their analysis in a desktop graphical user interface context, the interaction tasks they found could be applied to ubiquitous computing. The most interesting interaction task in the analysis for this chapter is that of selection. In ubiquitous computing, selection is used to choose a physical object to operate upon. Ballagas et al. divided it into the following interaction techniques:

- *Direct pick of tagged objects* (the user selects a tag with a tag reader–equipped mobile terminal)
- *Direct pick with camera* (the user selects the target using a camera embedded in the mobile terminal)
- *Direct pick by laser pointer* (the user selects the target by pointing at it with a laser pointer)
- *Voice recognition* (the target is selected based on the user's utterance)
- *Gesture recognition* (the target is selected based on a user's physical gesture)

The direct pick techniques correspond most closely to physical selection as defined in this chapter. Ballagas et al. [3] defined the mobile RFID reader system by Want et al. [36], laser pointer–activated photosensitive tags [22], and the RFIG lamps [24] as *direct pick of tagged objects*. Common to all of these systems is that physical objects contain identification tags, which can be read with a mobile device to effectively select the physical object via the tag.

The *direct pick with camera* technique is similar to *direct pick of tagged objects*, but Ballagas et al. [3] chose to differentiate between visual and electronically readable tags. Although they did not mention it in the article, tag reading with a camera differs somewhat from that with an RFID reader. A camera-based interaction typically shows the visual tag on the mobile terminal screen to help the user align it to the camera field of vision. RFID tag readers are somewhat less sensitive to alignment of the reader relative to the camera, although the reader generally works better if its antenna and the tag antenna are aligned parallel to each other.

The third direct pick technique, *direct pick by laser pointer*, considers such systems as semantic snarfing by Myers et al. [20] (see previous subsection). Typical for this technique is that the laser pointer beam is monitored with a camera in the ubiquitous computing environment.

12.5 IMPLEMENTING PHYSICAL SELECTION

While for human beings selection unambiguously establishes a mental link between the user and the target, the realization of such an association in the virtual world is not trivial. Both user and target have a presence in the physical world—that is, the user is a human being and the target is a physical object—but not necessarily in the virtual world. Instead, there are digital counterparts in the virtual world that act as the proxies of these objects. The virtual representation (presence) of the selection means that these digital counterparts will exchange information. The amount of information may vary—in some cases a single notification of selection may be sufficient; in other cases complete addresses and even content may be passed. The communication may have a single direction, either from pointer to target or vice versa, or be bidirectional. The act of selection ends when the pointer and target counterparts have exchanged sufficient information to establish an association. Note that actual knowledge of selection may be on the side of the user or the target, or on both.

12.5.1 Implementing Pointing

Capturing the act of pointing requires the assistance of pointing devices and/or pointing receptors that are able to detect the physical link established. A range of technologies may be applied here, both active and passive. The actual action following the selection may need different technologies and use different channels for communication. Figure 12.4 is an overview of the components involved. Note that some components may be combined in one device.

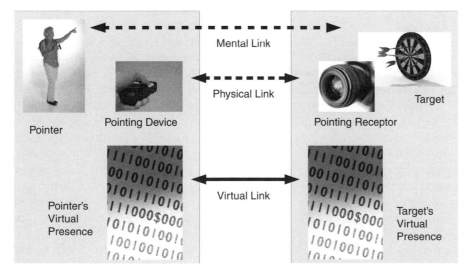

FIGURE 12.4

Mental, physical, and virtual links in pointing.

One view of pointing can be found by examining how the selection device and target can be active or passive and how that affects selection. We use pointing in the following examples, but touching is analogous: Either the selection device or the target (tag) must be active in the selection.

Pointing without device. When no device is used for pointing, the pointing receptor in practice consists of several cameras. The camera system observes the position and pose of the user and derives whether a pointing action appears. The pointing action typically needs to be mapped to a 3D model of the environment to find its target. This is a demanding task, requiring advanced computer vision methods. The advantage is that the user does not need to carry any devices and the target can be any appropriately modeled physical object (in a fixed location). The virtual presence of both user and target can be in the same software environment. An early example of such a system is the "finger-pointer" by Fukumoto et al. [10]. Later systems are more robust and able to cope with multiple users [35].

Pointing with an active device at a passive target. The best example of this is pointing at a visual tag with a camera, which reads the tag identifier. Here the camera, together with its vision software, is the only active pointing device. The virtual presence of the pointer, the active part, is aware of the pointing action. Based on the ID of the tag, it can establish an association with the virtual presence of the target via a lookup mechanism. The visual tags may be targets on their own, but they are usually attached to the physical target. This method has been applied in augmented reality setups not only to provide the object IDs but also to use the tags as anchors to render additional information near the relevant objects using head-mounted displays. Rekimoto and Agatsuka demonstrated this in their CyberCode environment [26].

Selecting an active target with a simple pointing device. A simple pointing device can be a laser or a light beam. It is active in the sense that it needs energy, but it does not provide any information to the target (unless modulated). Sensing the pointing action is now left to the target, which can detect the light beam by means of a suitable sensor. Knowledge of the selection is only at the target and, while this may be sufficient for some applications, the lack of information about the pointer may be cumbersome. A combination of presence information (for example, which users are in the room) and timing might provide a work-around for this problem.

Pointing device and target are both active. In a similar setup, the pointing device might add its ID as a modulation of the light beam. In this way the target knows which pointer is selecting it. The association with the pointer can be established by looking up the ID of the pointer in a table or registry. A more elaborate version might add a light source to the target and a sensor to the pointer to allow a bidirectional communication link to be established. Some solutions have made use of amplified and directional IrDA (infrared data association) links to achieve this. See for example [4], where a laser was added to aid in the positioning of the pointer because the IR beam was invisible. IrDA tags

Table 12.1 Pointing Devices and Targets According to Activity

Pointing Device	Passive Target	Active Target
None	—	Camera-based pointing gesture recognition system
Simple	Selection of reflective target (no identification of pointer or target)	Selection by laser or light beam
Active	Pointing by means of camera; target is visual tag or recognizable object	Pointing with modulated light source or directed RF

tend to be power-consuming, giving rise to more power-economic solutions as proposed by Strömmer et al. [29]. Patel opted to modulate the laser beam itself [22]. For a summary of the combinations of pointing device/target activity, see Table 12.1.

12.5.2 Implementing Touching

There are several short-range selection technologies, such as optically readable tags and mobile phone cameras, but in this chapter we focus on radio frequency identification (RFID). RFID uses electromagnetic inductance for communication and for powering up a passive tag. An RFID tag has an antenna and a transponder, which contains a unique identifier. Depending on the processing power of the transponder, RFID tags range from those solely identifying themselves to contactless smart cards, or cards having their own microprocessor and operating system.

RFID as an Implementation Technology

Touching must somehow be sensed, and the touched object identified—either by the target or by the mobile terminal. In RFID systems, the reader of a mobile terminal serves as a sensor for RFID tags in its range. If the range is small, the touch selection method is built into the system. The longer the range, the more tag reading resembles scanning. As RFID tags require no direct contact, touching is sometimes replaced by waving. Tapping is also used, although physical contact is an artifact not required for proximity detection. We exclude contact smart cards from physical selection, as they have to be inserted in a specific slot. Table 12.2 presents some common reading ranges of contactless smart cards and other RFID tags.

Touching is brought to mobile phones by near-field communication (NFC) operating at 13.56-MHz frequency. NFC uses a well-established communication technology based on electromagnetic induction between wired loops in the near field. NFC devices are capable of reading or writing common RFID tags and communicating with other NFC devices, including NFC-enabled mobile phones. Moreover, they can function as ISO 14443 or as FeliCa contactless smart cards and can be used for ticketing and other payment applications.

Table 12.2 Reading Ranges and Data Transfer Rates of Common RFID Tags		
Tag Type	**Range**	**Transfer Rate (kbps)**
Close Coupling Smart Cards	1 cm	9.6
Proximity Coupling Cards	10 cm	106–424
LF Tags	50 cm	Low
Vicinity Coupling Cards	1.5 m	6.7–45
UHF Tags (2.4 GHz)	1.5 m	1.6–424
UHF Tags (860–960 MHz)	4 m	10–640

If a target (RFID tag) distance to an electromagnetic source (reader) is much less than the wavelength of the electromagnetic field, the target is in the source's near field. If the source is a coil antenna, it produces a magnetic field, which induces in the near field a current in the receiving coil antenna of the target. If the target is a passive RFID tag, this magnetic induction is capable of powering the tag and the microprocessor within it. Information is passed between the source and the target by modulating the amplitude of the signal. The induction term of the electromagnetic field declines proportionally to $1/r^2$ to the distance r between the source and target, making the communication very short range, typically on the same order as the diameter of the coil. With mobile terminals, the range for NFC communication is only a few centimeters. In the far field—that is, at distances much higher than the wavelength—the propagating electromagnetic field dominates and field strength declines in proportion to $1/r$. UHF (ultra high frequency) tags operate in the far field, use electromagnetic backscatter for communication, and can have a reading range of several meters.

The higher the frequency of the electromagnetic field, the more penetration in water and metal is affected. This limits the use of RFID tags on such surfaces: On metallic surfaces or packages containing liquids, special antennas on dielectric substrate are required.

Semi-passive tags contain an internal battery to power the tag's chip, but the communication still uses power from the reader. Active tags use the energy of the battery also for transmission, leading to a reading range that is too long for touching. A touching selection method for these tags may be implemented by extra proximity sensors or by temporarily decreasing the reader electromagnetic field strength.

User Interaction Considerations

The duration of touch should not matter for successful touch operation; artificially prolonged touch is not necessary. Otherwise, the user should get feedback on the ongoing touch operation. Information exchange between interacting devices can only occur within the short period the tag is in the reading range of the touching device; which the time required for data exchange should never exceed. When touching with fingers, cutaneous receptors—mechanoreceptors and temperature receptors in the skin—provide information. However, if the duration of data transfer exceeds the time available for communication, visual or haptic feedback—for example, the vibration of a mobile terminal—is required to avoid interrupting the touch operation.

Ideally when touching, only the near proximity of the tag and the reader should matter—not the relative alignment. Magnetic induction is strongest when the coils are aligned parallel to each other. If they are perpendicular, forming a T shape, neither energy nor information is exchanged. Aligning the mobile terminal's antenna parallel to its display plane means that a tag has to be accessed by at least partially aligning the mobile terminal with the tag. When the tag is on the wall, slightly below eye level, visual feedback is also facilitated via the mobile terminal display unit.

12.5.3 Other Technologies for Connecting Physical and Digital Entities

In addition to selection technologies based on wireless electro-magnetic transmission (such as RFID or Bluetooth), there exist other selection technologies for connecting digital and physical entities. Visual codes can be read with mobile devices and interaction with them resembles a mix between touching and pointing. Another technology, RedTacton, transmits data through the body of the user, allowing for example exchanging business cards by shaking hands.

Visual Technologies for Mobile Terminals

The need to speed up grocery checkout by automatically reading an identifier associated with a product was apparent in the middle of the 20th century. In 1949 Woodland and Silver [38] filed a patent for an apparatus to translate optically readable patterns on products: The patent included drawings of a line pattern similar to modern ID barcodes, and a bulls-eye pattern consisting of concentric spheres. The bulls-eye pattern may be regarded as a simple 2D code and is part of many modern 2D barcode systems. Using visual code as a database rather than just as an index to information led to the development 2D visual codes, still called 2D barcodes for historical reasons. Many of them are in the form of a matrix and are also called matrix codes. They are read by image scanners or cameras equipped with CCD (charge coupled device) or CMOS (complementary metal oxide semiconductor) imaging technology.

The Sharp J-SH09, with its 0.3-megapixel camera, appeared in 2002. It was the first mobile phone to read 2D barcode and JAN (Japanese EAN) code [13]. For reading by the camera phone, the visual tag is aligned by viewing it through the LCD screen. It is recognized by pattern recognition software and its contents are read. Further activity often requires user acceptance.

There are many types of 2D barcode, the most common being the Japanese QR-Code and Data Matrix created in the United States. The visual tags come in increasing module (unit information) sizes, allowing more information to be packed into the tags. The QR-Code is widely used in Japan in advertisements, posters, newspapers, vending machines, e-tickets, and the like, for physical browsing. Typically visual tags contain a URL as information. However, several index-based 2D barcodes have been developed to improve readability with standard mobile terminals [13].

A comparison of the suitability of different 2D barcodes and decoding software for mobile phones has been made [13]. However, the rapid development of camera technology, built-in autofocus, increased pixel density, and enhanced processing speed and algorithms make any state-of-the-art comparison quickly obsolete. As an example of evolving technology, in 2008 Sony introduced a 12-megapixel CMOS unit (compare this to the first 0.3-megapixel camera phone) with built-in auto-focus to appear in 2009 high-end mobile phones. Technology development enables ever increasing information density in visual tags at higher reading distances. It should be noted, however, that the physical size of the visual tag can also be increased to gain access at high distances. Building walls can be covered with posters and visual tags of corresponding size: These tags can be pointed to and read from across the street with standard camera phones.

Visual codes have two clear advantages over RFID tags: With printable RFID technology in its infancy, barcodes are still cheaper to manufacture and easier to attach to targets. Nearly every modern mobile terminal is capable of reading 2D barcodes, whereas NFC phones are still, in 2009, a rarity among consumers.

Using camera phones to access visual tags originally resembled touching, as the targets were normally kept in close proximity. With improvements in imaging technology and pattern recognition algorithms, camera phone–based physical browsing more and more resembles physical selection by pointing. There may be one usability caveat involved in pointing: With no steering beam the user still has to point through the phone's LCD display and thus view the target through the screen, which is inferior to viewing the target with the naked eye.

Body Communication

Personal area networking using intra-body communication was first explored in the 1990s [39]. In addition to communication between wearable devices by touching, information is passed from one person to another or to any other object. NTT developed this networking technology under the name RedTacton.[1] A RedTacton-enabled mobile terminal need not be at hand but may be kept in a pocket. Users can exchange business cards just by shaking hands, or go through a door just by touching the door knob. The technology for intra-body communication is complex because of its small signals and many disturbing factors. Novel technologies allow rather high (10-MB/s) communication speeds [28], permitting credible data transfer scenarios.

However, many touch-related scenarios challenge this paradigm, as possible visual or other feedback provided by the mobile terminal is not aligned with the user's visual field, which is focused on controlling the touch operation. Park et al. addressed some of the technical and usability issues in their touch and play (TAP) system [23]. Also, the advantage of this technology over other, abundantly available short-range wireless networks is doubtful [11]. Still, if the environment provides enough feedback for the touch operation, the paradigm works: In opening a door, the handle, lock, or the door itself—not the mobile device—may provide enough (visual and other) feedback to support touch selection.

---

[1]*www.redtacton.com*

12.6 INDICATING AND NEGOTIATING ACTIONS AFTER THE SELECTION EVENT

Selecting a target is only the first step in physical browsing. Next the action needs to be indicated and performed. It goes beyond the scope of this chapter to elaborate on all possible actions that may follow a selection event as they are domain specific, but wc will identify some general trends and issues to take into account.

12.6.1 Activation by Selection

The selection of a target may be sufficient to start an action. The equivalent is clicking on a link in a browser or a button on a user interface. Note, however, that these basic WIMP interface actions also consist of pointing at the target, or positioning a finger over a button and pushing it (on the mouse). Whether or not mere pointing at a target should be sufficient to start an action depends on usability. For example, how likely is accidentally pointing at a target? What is the penalty if a target is accidentally triggered? Similar considerations apply to speech interfaces and gaze-based interaction. In the latter case one's gaze is wandering from target to target continuously. Selection can then be done by using a second cue, such as pressing a button or blinking the eyes, or by fixing one's gaze at a target for a specified time. Likewise for target selection by means of pointing, a minimum fixation time or additional button (on the pointer) may solve the accidental selection problem. Note that turning a beam used for the selection on and off is similar to the button option, except that pointing might need to take place with no guiding beam (this is also the case for IR pointing). If a selection can be casily repeated, double-click equivalents may be implemented—that is, selecting a target multiple times in a certain time frame. In fact, a whole vocabulary of codes could be developed using Morse-code selection styles. As we are not aware of any implementations using this method, we assume that activation by selection is limited to initiating one predefined action per pointer/target pair.

From Subsection 12.5.1 we know that the selection information is either at the target side or at the pointer side, or both, depending on the implementation technology. The actual recipient of the action may even be a third object, possibly residing elsewhere (we use the term "recipient" here to avoid confusion with the target). When the recipient resides at the pointer and the pointer receives the selection information, there is no problem. Nor is there a problem if the target receives the information and the recipient is associated with it. In all other cases communication between the active pointer or target and the recipient needs to be established. This might be done via existing communication channels.

The action that can be invoked using this method is usually limited to one specific action per pointer/target pair, but note that different pairs give rise to various actions. For example, by having a set of targets in range, with each representing a choice of menu, the actual choice can be made by selecting one of them. Also, the internal state of the pointer and the target may affect the action. For example, pointing at a business card target tag with a phone in calling mode may start a phone call to the indicated person, while doing the same with the address book open may load the card information into the book. If the pointer and the target have different internal states, the result of the selection may be complex, even unpredictable. This is an important issue to take into account when designing such systems. Keränen et al. addressed it in the Tag Manager they proposed as a software solution [15].

12.6.2 Action Selection by a Different Modality

The use of a button together with pointing technology is an example of a second modality for invoking the action. When using several buttons, different actions may be invoked while pointing at a single target. A simple example of this is a TV remote control, which is (deliberately) not very directional, so the pointing is quite rudimentary (e.g., all similar TVs in a shop will react).

Another option is the use of speech. In combination with the selection of a target, the intended action can be invoked by a spoken command. Depending on the speech system, this can vary from simple commands from a predefined vocabulary to complex questions or the start of a dialogue. The microphone may be located in the environment or integrated with either the pointer or the target. An early implementation of a system using a combination of pointing and speech was Put-That-There by Bolt et al. [5]. Pointing was not done in a real environment but at a screen. A more recent example features a robot taking instructions by means of speech and pointing gestures [12].

Because we use our hands and arms for pointing, it is quite natural to consider gestures for the invocation of an action. The problem that often arises is that gestures subsequent to a pointing action are likely to cause the focus of the action to be lost. This can be remedied by allowing some time for the action gesture after a selection has occurred. Technically, gestures can be recognized by a camera-based system in the environment, a camera in the pointing device, or sensors integrated in the pointing device. In the case of a camera-based system in the environment, the pointing and action-invoking gestures form a sequence the system recognizes. When a camera implemented in the pointing device is used for the pointing action, it may recognize subsequent gestures. For example, a turn in either direction around the axis or moving the pointing device in a certain direction can easily be recognized by analyzing the camera image (possibly by following the position and orientation of the visual tag in it). Motion sensors allow for very free movements, resulting in a vocabulary of semantic gestures that can be associated with certain actions [14].

12.6.3 Actions by Combining Selection Events

Instead of invoking an action based on a selection event and a subsequent action indication, actions can result from a series of selection events. The WIMP equivalent of this is, for example, a drag-and-drop operation. By first selecting an object and subsequently a destination for it, the object is moved to that destination. Also, a path can be defined if the pointing direction is followed for a longer time. This is only possible for a limited number of pointing techniques.

A particularly interesting application of subsequent selection events is establishing associations between (passive) objects in the environment. An example is two objects that cannot be directly associated with each other, either because they cannot be moved or because they only feature passive targets. The association can be used to establish a communication link. Consider a laptop and a beamer. By first pointing to the laptop and then to the beamer, the presentation on the laptop can be shown on the beamer. Naturally this requires that both can be connected via the Internet or wirelessly. This kind of interaction paradigm was developed by Kindberg et al. in their CoolTown [16].

12.6.4 Physical Selection in Establishing Communication

Touching and pointing allow the user to select a single, known link in the physical environment, while scanning allows him to display all available links on the mobile terminal screen and select one from there. In scanning, associating the scanned information (the name of the device or service) to the real-world physical object is a challenge. Touching and pointing avoid this ambiguity. With touching, secure exchange of cryptographic information is possible because the extremely short communication range makes eavesdropping difficult; thus it is a safe and easy-to-use method for establishing communication between active objects.

In Bluetooth, any two Bluetooth devices form a trusted pair: Whenever they detect each other, the paired devices automatically accept communication, bypassing authentication. The near-field communication (NFC) protocol whitepaper [13] proposes using NFC devices to establish a Bluetooth connection by touch and connect. This is implemented within "Bluetooth simple pairing," which protects against eavesdropping and man-in-the-middle attacks. When communicating devices touch each other, both discovery information and cryptographic information is passed. The former is used when establishing the connection; the latter, during authentication.

Similarly, the Wi-Fi Alliance has introduced Wi-Fi protected setup to ease the setup of security-enabled Wi-Fi networks in the home and small office environments. Strong security is a requirement of Wi-Fi–certified devices, but enabling it has been difficult. NFC can be used as an alternative channel for exchanging authentication information, limiting the possibility of security attacks. Ideally, touching should be used for the selection of communicating objects and other local communication protocols for further communication.

12.7 CONCLUSIONS

In this chapter, we presented physical browsing, a mobile device–based user interaction paradigm for ambient intelligence. We discussed the need for physical browsing and how a target can first be physically selected from the real world and then how an action follows the selection. There are different selection methods for different situations. Touching is a short-range method for unambiguously selecting objects very close to the user. Pointing is a long-range method for selecting a target from afar when the user knows the location of the link. Scanning is different from these two methods in that it can be used to search the entire nearby environment for links; these links are then presented on the mobile terminal graphical user interface, from which the user can continue the selection process.

Physical selection was compared to selection in other environments for user interaction: desktop computing, virtual environments, and projection screen interaction with laser pointers. We discussed different technologies for implementing touching and pointing, and the user interaction considerations related to them. Finally, we discussed the action phase of physical browsing and how ambient services can be activated based on physical selection and how devices can easily establish communication with each other when selected.

Physical selection should be seen as a basic building block of ambient intelligence user interfaces. It can be combined with actions to create more complicated user interactions. Much work is still needed to fully understand multi-device interaction, especially that involving two active partners. For example, what do users expect to happen if they bring their NFC-equipped mobile phones into touch range and the phones are in a certain state? Should they open a communication link, transfer to the other phone what is displayed in the first one, exchange contact information, ask each other what to do? These will be interesting challenges.

Physical selection will be needed for mobile device–based ambient intelligence, and it will become more common in the near future. At the time of writing, several companies offer RFID readers for PDAs, mainly intended for use in logistics. Nokia has so far released four readers for their mobile phones, the latest of which is intended for consumer use. Many camera phones are capable of reading visual tags, and the first commercial experiments have already been conducted. To truly enable mobile device–based ambient services, some method for easily and simply selecting a physical hyperlink will be needed.

REFERENCES

[1] Ailisto H, Korhonen I, Plomp J, Pohjanheimo L. Realising physical selection for mobile devices. 2003. p. 38–41.

[2] Arnall T. A graphic language for touch-based interactions. In: Proc. Mobile Interaction with the Real World. 2006. p. 18–22.

[3] Ballagas R, Borchers J, Rohs M, Sheridan JG. The smart phone: a ubiquitous input device. Pervasive Computing 5(1):70-7.

[4] Beigl M. Point & Click — Interaction in smart environments, handheld and ubiquitous computing. In: Gellersen, editor. LNCS 1707. Springer; 1999. p. 311-3.

[5] Bolt RA. "Put-that-there": Voice and gesture at the graphics interface. In: Proceedings of the 7th Annual Conference on Computer Graphics and interactive Techniques. SIGGRAPH '80. ACM Press; p. 262-70.

[6] Bowman DA, Hodges LF. An evaluation of techniques for grabbing and manipulating remote objects in immersive virtual environments. In: Proc. Symposium on Interactive 3D Graphics. ACM Press; 1997. p. 35-8.

[7] Card SK, Mackinlay JD, Robertson GG. The design space of input devices. In: Proc. SIGCHI Conference on Human Factors in Computing Systems. ACM Press; 1990. p. 117-24.

[8] English WK, Engelbart DC, Berman ML. Display-selection techniques for text manipulation. IEEE Transactions on Human Factors in Electronics 1967;8(1):5-15.

[9] Foley JD, Vallace L, Chan P. The human factors of computer graphics interaction techniques. IEEE Comput Graph Appl 1984;4(11):13-48.

[10] Fukumoto M, Suenaga Y, Mase K. "Finger-Pointer": Pointing interface by image processing. Computer and Graphics 18(5):633-42.

[11] Goldstein H. Loser: a touch too much. IEEE Spectrum 2006;43(1):24-5.

[12] Holzapfel H, Nickel K, Stiefelhagen R. Implementation and evaluation of a constraint-based multimodal fusion system for speech and 3D pointing gestures. In: Proc. 6th International Conference on Multimodal Interfaces, ICMI '04. ACM; 2004. p. 175-82.

[13] Kato H, Tan KT. Pervasive 2D barcodes for camera phone applications. IEEE Pervasive Computing 6(4):76-85.

[14] Kela J, Korpipää P, Mäntyjärvi J, Kallio S, Savino G, Jozzo L, et al. Accelerometer-based gesture control for a design environment. In: Personal and Ubiquitous Computing. Springer; 2005. p. 285-99.

[15] Keränen H, Pohjanheimo L. Tag Manager, a mobile phone platform for physical selection services. In: Proc. International Conference on Pervasive Services (ICPS'05). IEEE; 2005. p. 405-12.

[16] Kindberg T, Barton J, Morgan J, Becker G, Caswell D, Debaty P. People, places, things. Mobile Networks and Applications 2002;7(5):365-76.

[17] Kirstein C, Müller H. Interaction with a projection screen using a camera-tracked laser pointer. Proceedings Multimedia Modeling 1998;191-2.

[18] Mine MR. Virtual environment interaction techniques. In: Technical report TR95-018. University of North Carolina; 1995.

[19] Myers BA, Peck CH, Kong D, Miller R, Long AC. Interacting at a distance using semantic snarfing. In: Proc. 3rd International Conference on Ubiquitous Computing, LNCS 2201. Springer-Verlag; 2001. p. 305-14.

[20] Myers BA, Bhatnagar R, Nichols J, Peck CH, Kong D, Miller R, et al. Interacting at a distance: measuring the performance of laser pointers and other devices. In: Proc. CHI 2002. ACM Press; 2002. p. 33-40.

[21] Olsen DR, Nielsen T. Laser pointer interaction. In: Proc. CHI 2001. ACM Press; p. 17-22.

[22] Patel SN, Abowd GD. A 2-way laser-assisted selection scheme for handhelds in a physical environment. In: Proc. UBICOMP LNCS 2864. Springer-Verlag; 2003. p. 200-7.

[23] Park DG, Kim JK, Bong SJ, Hwang JH, Hyung CH, Kang SW. Proc. 4th Annual IEEE International Conference on Pervasive Computing and Communications (PERCOM'06), IEEE 2006.

[24] Raskar R, Beardsley P, van Baar J, Wang Y, Dietz P, Lee J. RFIG lamps: interacting with a self-describing world via photosensing wireless tags and projectors. In: ACM SIGGRAPH 2004 Papers. ACM Press; 2004. p. 406-15.

[25] Raymond ES. The New Hacker's Dictionary. 3rd ed. MIT Press; 1996.

[26] Rekimoto J, Ayatsuka Y. Cybercode: designing augmented reality environments with visual tags. In: Proc. DARE 2000 on Designing Augmented Reality Environments. ACM Press; 2000. p. 1-10.

[27] Robinett W, Holloway R. Implementation of flying, scaling and grabbing in virtual worlds. In: Proc. Symposium on Interactive 3D Graphics. ACM Press; 1992.

[28] Shinagawa M, Fukumoto M, Ochiai K, Kyuragi H. A near-field-sensing tranceiver for intrabody communication based on the electrooptic effect. IEEE Transactions on Instrumentation and Measurement 2004;53(6):1533-8.

[29] Strömmer E, Suojanen M. Micropower IR Tag—a new technology for ad-hoc interconnections between hand-held terminals and smart objects. In: Smart Objects Conference sOc'; 2003.

[30] Tuomisto T, Välkkynen P, Ylisaukko-oja A. RFID tag reader system emulator to support touching, pointing and scanning. In: Advances in Pervasive Computing. Austrian Computer Society; 2005. p. 85-8.

[31] Välkkynen P, Pohjanheimo L, Ailisto H. Physical browsing. In: Ambient Intelligence, Wireless Networking, and Ubiquitous Computing. Artech House; 2006. p. 61-81.

[32] Välkkynen P, Niemelä M, Tuomisto T. Evaluating touching and pointing with a mobile terminal for physical browsing. In: Proc. NordiCHI 2006. ACM Press; 2006. p. 28-37.

[33] Välkkynen P, Tuomisto T, Korhonen I. Suggestions for visualising physical hyperlinks. In: Proc. Pervasive Mobile Interaction Devices; 2006. p. 245-54.

[34] Välkkynen P. Physical Selection in Ubiquitous Computing. Edita; 2007.

[35] Yamamoto Y, Yoda I, Sakaue K. Arm-pointing gesture interface using surrounded stereo cameras system. In: Proc. 17th International Conference on Pattern Recognition (ICPR'04). 2004. p. 965-70.

[36] Want R, Fishkin KP, Gujar A, Harrison BL. Bridging physical and virtual worlds with electronic tags. In: Proc. SIGCHI Conference on Human Factors in Computing Systems. ACM Press; 1999. p. 370-7.

[37] Weiser M. Some computer science issues in ubiquitous computing. Commun ACM 1993;36(7):75-84.

[38] Woodland NJ, Silver B. Classifying Apparatus and Method. U.S. Patent 2.612.994.

[39] Zimmerman TG. Personal Area Networks (PAN): Near-Field Intra-Body Communication. Master's Thesis, Massachusetts Institute of Technology; 1995.

Nonsymbolic Gestural Interaction for Ambient Intelligence

13

Matthias Rehm

Multimedia Concepts and Applications, Department of Applied Informatics, University of Augsburg, Augsburg, Germany

ABSTRACT

Our gestural habits convey a multitude of information of different levels of granularity that can be exploited for human–computer interaction. Gestures can provide additional or redundant information accompanying a verbal utterance, they can have a meaning in themselves, or they can provide the addressee with subtle clues about personality or cultural background. Gestures are an extremly rich source of communication-specific and contextual information for interactions in ambient intelligence environments. This chapter reviews the semantic layers of gestural interaction, focusing on the layer beyond communicative intent, and presents interface techniques to capture and analyze gestural input, taking into account nonstandard approaches such as acceleration analysis and the use of physiological sensors.

Key words: gesture recognition, emotion, personality, culture.

13.1 INTRODUCTION

Imagine a student who must give an important presentation in front of a university board to apply for funding of his Ph.D. work. During this presentation, the student exhibits an unusually high number of hand gestures. An obvious explanation for this excessive show of hand movements is that the speaker is nervous because it is an important event. This interpretation follows more or less Burgoon's [4] definition of nonverbal communication as "behaviors other than words that form a socially shared coding system ... [and] have consensually recognizable interpretations" (p. 231). Thus, even if in a specific situation the behavior is not intentional (e.g., excessive gesturing) it conveys meaning relevant to the interaction. Watzlawick et al. [44] put this fact concisely by saying that one cannot not communicate. In this chapter, we concentrate on such aspects of gestural interaction that are not directly related to intentional communicative content but convey additional meanings below it.

13.2 CLASSIFYING GESTURAL BEHAVIOR FOR HUMAN-CENTRIC AMBIENT INTELLIGENCE

Gestural behavior has mainly been investigated as a co-verbal phenomenon, focusing on the meaning (intentionally) conveyed by the speaker. Gestures in this sense accompany utterances and give sometimes redundant, sometimes additional information about the speaker's message. For instance, a speaker might recount a story about his child losing a balloon. He might illustrate the utterance "and then the balloon flew up and away" by raising his right hand in a straight line, emphasizing what is said, that the balloon flew up. He could also accompany this utterance with a hand movement that mirrors the actual ascent of the balloon: raising the hand, and moving it to the right and then to the left. This gesture gives information that goes beyond what was explicitly said.

McNeill [31] established a solid foundation for this perspective, presenting a taxonomy and coding scheme for conversational gestures. He distinguished between adaptor, beat, emblem, deictic, iconic, and metaphoric gestures. Adaptors include every hand movement to other parts of the body (e.g., scratching one's nose). Beats are rhythmic gestures that may emphasize certain propositions made verbally or that may even link different parts of an utterance. Emblems are gestures that are meaningful in themselves, without an accompanying utterance, but highly culture-specific. An example is the American "OK" gesture, which in Italy is interpreted as an insult. Deictic gestures identify referents in the gesture space. They can be real, such as the addressee, or they can be abstract, such as pointing to the left and the right while uttering the words "the good and the bad." Iconic gestures depict spatial or shape-oriented aspects of a referent, such as using two fingers to indicate someone walking while uttering "he went down the street." Lastly, metaphoric gestures are difficult in that they visualize abstract concepts by the use of metaphors, such as using a box gesture to visualize "a story." This is the conduit metaphor that makes use of the idea of a container, in this case a container holding information.

Similar taxonomies were introduced by Kendon [24] and Ekman and Friesen [13], who distinguished emblems, illustrators, regulators, affect displays, and adaptors. Emblems and adaptors are comparable to McNeill's categories; illustrators summarize McNeill's iconic, deictic, and metaphoric gestures. Affect displays are movements triggered by emotional states, like Ekman's [12] basic emotions of fear, anger, joy, suprise, sadness, and disgust. Their relationship with body movements remains a bit unclear; the face is identified as the main display for emotions. Finally, regulators are all movements that do not fall into one of the other categories and that are identified by Ekman and Friesen as necessary to structure the flow of conversation.

In this chapter, we look at a different level of gesture semantics. For an ambient intelligence system, more subtle features of gestural activity can provide relevant contextual information for successful interactions. Therefore, the focus here is not primarily on the symbolic or communicative content of a gesture—whether intentional or not—but rather on the way a gesture is performed—that is, qualitative features of movements and their interpretation.

To provide pervasive assistance in complex computing environments it does not suffice to restrict the analysis and interpretation of body movements to finding an appropriate gesture class. It is necessary to focus on the diverse aspects of body movements, which not only provide emblematic information but have a whole range of communicative functions [3, 4] and even allow identification of inherent user characteristics like identity [29], personality [15], and cultural background [36]. Such a shift in perspective allows infering additional information about the user's patterns of activities and relating that to cognitive or emotional user states. These can be the user's identity, her personality, her current or expected emotional state or mood, her current or expected state of arousal/concentration, and so forth.

Coming back to the example at the beginning of the chapter, we can speculate a bit more on what his behavior reveals about the speaker. Our first guess was that he might be nervous because it is an important presentation. On the other hand, the excessive use of hand gestures might also be attributable to the speaker's extrovert personality, perhaps strengthened by his nervousness. Or the interpretation that his gesturing is excessive might be our misconception because we are used to more controlled hand movements in our culture, but in the speaker's culture this might just be standard behavior to underline personal engagement in a topic. These possibilities make it clear that such nonsymbolic, qualitative information can be the source for recognizing a wide range of contextual effects by analyzing a user's gestures. At the same time, they underline the complexity of the task, as the interpretation of the recognized features is not restricted to a single contextual variable and might be quite ambiguous. Thus, in the long run it will be necessary to come up with an integrated approach to analyzing the qualitative features of gesture usage.

As we have seen, a number of contextual factors relie on gestural activity as an input channel. In the rest of this chapter, contextual influences such as emotional state, personality, and cultural background are examined. Beforehand, however,

Table 13.1 General Qualitative Features of Gestural Activity for Nonsymbolic Interpretation

Feature	Efron	Gallaher	de Meijer
Location	Plane of gesture		Vertical/sagittal direction
Distance	Closeness		
Spatial Extent	Radius	Constricted versus expansive	
Speed	Tempo	Tempo	Velocity
Activation		Gesture frequency/quantity	
Fluidity		Jerky versus smooth	
Power			Force
Body	Body parts—touch	Body parts—posture	Trunk/arm movement

three attempts are introduced that categorize gestural activity apart from its co-verbal content and that serve as a guideline for analyzing the qualitative features of gestural activity. Table 13.1 summarizes and groups the important features from these attempts.

In a study on cultural differences in gesturing (see also Section 13.5), Efron [11] defined three dimensions for categorizing gestural activity:

Spatiotemporal. This category is based on formal features that allow us to describe how a gesture is realized, taking into account the radii of the gesture, the plane in which it is performed (*xy*, *xz*, or *yz*), which body parts are employed, and the speed ("tempo").

Interlocutional. What Efron calls interlocutional aspects can best be summarized by Hall's [17] notion of "proxemics," that is, the way interlocutors use the space available in their face-to-face encounters. This category describes if interlocutors stand close to each other or farther away in such an encounter, if they exhibit frequent body contacts like touching the other's lower arm, or if they gesture while grasping an object, which can be used to emphasize the speaker's intention.

Co-verbal. The last category describes the relationship of gestures and the content of utterances and is thus in accordance with the gestural taxonomies of McNeill and Ekman and Friesen, which concentrate on gestures as a co-verbal phenomenon.

A similar set of features can be found in Gallaher's work on personal style (see also Section 13.4). Gallaher [15] reviewed work on expressive movements and showed that intra-individual consistencies exist across a wide range of behavior. For instance, someone who is walking fast is likely to also gesture at a high speed, talk faster, and speak louder. Thus, analyzing "tempo" (the speed of movement) allows us to draw conclusions about more general aspects of a speaker. Gallaher defined a set of expressivity features, which she related to aspects of personality but which, like Efron's spatiotemporal and interlocutional aspects, are general enough to serve as features for other contextual variables as well. In her analysis, Gallaher focused not only on body movements but also on other aspects of nonverbal behavior like facial expressions or speech volume. A factor analysis revealed four dimensions that summarize the qualitative features. The following lists (mainly) movement-related features from these dimensions:

Expressiveness. This dimension describes which parts of the body are used. Moreover, the frequency (i.e., how often and how many gestures are used), speed, and spatial extent of gestures are features that describe the expressiveness of movements.

Expansiveness. To describe how much space a speaker is taking up for gestures, the expansiveness dimension is introduced. The features here are the spatial extent of gestures and the distance from a speaker to his addressee in face-to-face encounters. An example of a non-movement-related feature of expansiveness is speech volume.

Coordination. The only movement-related feature of the coordination dimension is fluidity, which describes if the movements of a gesture are smooth or jerky.

Animation. The animation dimension is described for instance by postures such as slumped versus erect shoulders or by the speed of gesture or other behaviors such as speech.

These dimensions are stable across time and raters. The overlap in features like spatial extent (expressiveness, expansiveness) and speed (expressiveness, animation) shows again that such qualitative features contribute to different interpretations of behavior. What is evident is that some of the features analyzed by Gallaher are consistent with the features defined by Efron for studying cultural differences in gesture usage.

De Meijer [10] explored how specific body movements are perceived and what impression they give about the subject's emotional state. He first defined seven dimensions of body movement that describe in a qualitative way how a specific movement is performed:

- *Trunk movement*. Stretching, bowing
- *Arm movement*. Opening, closing
- *Vertical direction*. Upward, downward
- *Sagittal direction*. Forward, backward
- *Force*. Strong, light
- *Velocity*. Fast, slow
- *Directness*. Direct, indirect

These movement qualities were then related to the user's different emotional states (see Section 13.3). Again, it is apparent that there is an overlap in features used to describe body movements in the approaches of Gallaher and Efron. The first two dimensions correspond to some of Efron's spatiotemporal aspects and Gallaher's expressive features; the third and fourth, to Efron's location features; the sixth, to the tempo or speed feature in Efron's spatiotemporal aspects and to Gallaher's expressiveness and animation dimensions. Additonally, de Meijer introduced the force that is used to perform a movement and the feature directness, which unfortunately remains a bit vague and unclear.

As noted, Table 13.1 summarizes the different movement characteristics used by Efron, Gallaher, and de Meijer. Although their analyses focused on very different determinants of behavior—cultural background versus personality versus emotional state—there is some overlap in the relevant features, making them a promising starting point for analyzing gestural activity for ambient intelligence systems on a nonsymbolic level.

13.3 EMOTIONS

Since Picard's seminal book [34], affective interactions have increasingly become the center of interest for human–computer interaction given that emotions—our own or those attributed to others—play a fundamental role on different levels of our communicative and decision-making behavior, as was convincingly shown by Damasio [9]. Especially in situations where the user experiences negative emotions like frustration and/or anger, the interaction might greatly benefit from the system's ability to take the user's state into account in its next move, either to prevent the user from breaking up the interaction altogether or, in the ideal case, to change the user's emotional state and his attitude toward the system to provide a more positive interaction experience.

Whereas it is undeniable that our faces often reveal our emotional state in face-to-face encounters (e.g., [14]), the mapping between body movements and emotional states is still a matter for discussion. For instance, de Meijer's [10] controlled study of how specific body movements are perceived and what impression they give about the subject's emotional state which is defined by twelve emotion categories: Ekman's basic emotions [12] (joy, grief, anger, fear, surprise, disgust), additional categories by Izard [20] (interest, shame, contempt), and some so-called emotional attitudes taken from Machotka [30] (sympathy, antipathy, admiration). Relating given movements to one of the twelve emotion categories allowed de Meijer to identify the qualitative movement features and their combinations that play a central role in the perception of that emotion. The dimensions are related to the parameters identified in the previous section and take into account body parts, location, speed, and power of movements. A number of correlations were found. In particular, the difference between positive and negative emotions was reliably distinguishable. As a general result of this study, de Meijer was able to define movement profiles for emotions. Thus, single qualitative features were not realiable enough to distinguish emotions, but more complex combinations of movement features had high predictive value.

A similar study was conducted by Walbott [43], who tried to correlate specific movements with specific emotional states. Walbott was more cautious in his account, stating that the quality of a body movement cannot be directly mapped to an emotional state, but it is indicative of an emotion's quantity, that is, its intensity. Vice versa, differences in body movement are sometimes explained by the intensity of a given emotion rather than a difference between emotional states. Nevertheless, his results showed distinctive patterns of movement and postural behavior for some of the studied emotions.

In his study Walbott used 14 emotional categories: elated joy, happiness, sadness, despair, fear, terror, cold anger, hot anger, disgust, contempt, shame, guilt, pride, and boredom. Twelve actors (six male, six female) acted out these 14 emotions in two scenarios, uttering nonsense sentences to prevent emotional priming by the content of the utterace. In all, 1344 samples were recorded under these conditions, and 224 takes were selected from this database, for the analysis. The coding system introduced by Walbott is a combination of a categorical approach similar to Ekman and Friesen's for emotions: expressive parameters (activity, spatial extension, power/dynamics) for qualitative movement features, and posture coding following Bull's ideas [3].

Table 13.2 outlines expressive movement profiles for some of the studied cmotions. What becomes evident for hot anger and elated joy is the influence of the emotions' intensity on the expressive profile. On the other hand, this data shows that it is feasible to distinguish between low-intensity emotions like disgust and contempt based on the expressive features.

Crane and Gross [8] showed not only that emotions can be recognized in the body movements of others but also that body movements are affected by felt emotions. Four emotions plus a neutral state were elicited (angry, sad, content, joy, and no emotion); the subjects were then asked to walk across the room, and their movement was recorded by video and motion capture. Afterwards, they gave a self-report on the felt emotion. Additionally, recordings were rated by observers, who could choose from ten emotions. Although emotions were recognized beyond

Table 13.2 Walbott's Correlations Between Emotion Categories and Movement Profiles

Emotion	Activity	Spatial Extent	Power
Hot Anger	High	High	High
Elated Joy	High	High	High
Happiness	-	-	Low
Disgust	-	Low	-
Contempt	Low	-	-
Sadness	-	-	Low
Despair	-	High	-
Boredom	Low	Low	Low

chance (62% of anger trials, 76% of sad trials, 74% of content trials, 67% of joy trials, 83% of neutral trials), the observers' ratings did not necessarily correspond to the self-reports of the subjects, making evident a fundamental problem with studies of this kind. Actors or laypersons are instructed to display emotions, or emotions are elicited by specific means, and subjects then rate these expressions. Because this happens in a laboratory setting, the displayed emotions might be not felt but simply acted. Thus, although humans are able to interpret body movements as having affective content, it cannot be guaranteed that a person exhibiting such movements really feels the emotion attributed to him.

It remains to be seen if these results scale up to natural situations. Crane and Gross analyzed movement taking qualitative features into account. Their results show that apart from the speed and velocity of the walking movement, posture and limb motions are affected that also play a crucial role in hand gestures. Sadness especially seems to influence movement qualities of the arms and hands. The spatial extent—measured in this case by shoulder and elbow ranges—is significantly less compared to all the other emotions (i.e., anger, content, and joy). Categorizing the elicited emotions according to valence and activation dimensions gives another insight. Emotions in the high activation group (anger, joy) show a higher spatial extent in elbow flexions.

Some words are in order on the emotional models used in the studies and applications presented here. Most of them rely either on categorical approaches, like Ekman's [12] basic emotions, or on dimensional approaches, which date back as far as Wundt [46]. Categorical approaches define distinct emotion categories that are often claimed to be universal and that can be mapped to specific behavior routines such as facial displays or—as we saw—to expressive movement features. Dimensional approaches, on the other hand, define emotions as a continuous phenomenon, taking up to three dimensions into account:

- *Arousal* denotes the intensity of a felt emotion.
- *Valence* denotes if this emotion is positive or negative.
- *Dominance* denotes if the emotion is more outgoing (e.g., anger) or more self-directed (e.g., fear).

Crane and Gross combined both types of model in their analysis to capture the effects of the intensity of an emotion. As was also shown by Walbott, intensity is a crucial influence on gestural activity.

Kapur and colleagues [21] presented a system trained to detect four basic emotions based on movement patterns and performed with a recognition rate similar to that of a human observer. The emotions were sadness, joy, anger, and fear. To create the necessary database, motion capture data was collected for five subjects, who were told to represent the emotional states by movement. Five hundred samples were collected (i.e., every subject performed every emotion 25 times). To capture the dynamics of the movements, their velocity and acceleration, as well as the position of body parts, were used as features. No further movement analysis was conducted. That is, movements were taken into account as whole samples.

As Kapur et al.'s system was able to perform similarly to a human observer, the employed features seem to represent a promising starting point for the recognition task.

Bernhardt and Robinson [2] went a step further and presented a machine learning approach that takes the inner structure of movements into account to allow for a more context-dependent classification of emotions based on movement patterns. To this end, they built on work by Bull [3], which showed that affective states can be recognized from body movements, and developed a recognition framework by defining motion primitives that were used to recognize affective states. Such primitives were created by clustering motion samples found in specific contexts.

To exemplify their approach the researchers considered a very small context, "knocking at a door." They made use of a database containing around 1200 knocking motions recorded by motion capture and performed in affective ways to express neutral, happy, angry, and sad. The clustering approach was based on some a priori knowledge that allowed for segmenting the knocking movement into four phases: (1) lift arm, repeatedly (2) knock, (3) retract, and (4) lower arm. To determine the affective states, features were calculated on the motion primitives similar to those described in Section 13.2 (general names given in parentheses): maximum distance of hand from body (body parts), average hand speed (speed), average hand acceleration (power), and average hand jerk (fluidity). The same features were calculated for the elbow. Bernhardt and Robinson's recognition algorithm first segmented a motion into motion primitives for each of the four phases, then calculated the expressive features to classify its affective content. Their results showed that this approach is very promising, with recognition rates far above chance—up to 92% for the four-class problem.

Castellano et al. [6] compared the applicability of a time-series classification approach (dynamic time warping) with feature-based approaches (nearest neighbor, Bayesian network, decision trees) for recognizing emotions based on nonpropositional gestural qualities. Movements were described by power (amplitude), speed, fluidity, activation, and velocity. To train and test the approach, ten subjects were asked to provide gestures for eight emotional states (anger, despair, interest, pleasure, sadness, irritation, joy, and pride). These were chosen because they are equally distributed in the two-dimensional valence–arousal space. Each subject repeated each gesture three times, resulting in 240 gestures. The approach then focused only on four emotions (joy, anger, pleasure, sadness), which represent the four quadrants of the valence–arousal space. Consequently, it was based on a very small sample size of 30 samples for each emotion, and it remains to be shown if the results scale up.

Apart from the movement features mentioned, Castellano and colleagues calculated some second-order statistical features, like initial and final slope, initial and final slope of the main peak, maximum, mean, and so on, on the motion cues. It is unclear why this was necessary and how the recognition rates benefited from the inclusion of these features. Results showed that expressive motion cues allow discrimination between high- and low-arousal emotions and between positive and negative emotions. This is in line with Walbott's results (see above), who showed that such motion cues are a good predictor of the intensity of emotions.

Shan et al.'s [39] work on emotion recognition is in line with Efron's analysis. They focused on spatiotemporal aspects for modeling body gestures that allow for recognizing emotional states. Instead of defining specific spatiotemporal features as Efron did, they analyzed video sequences without investing further knowledge in the definition of specific features. They used spatial and temporal filters to identify regions and time-series that showed strong spatial or temporal activity.

Shan et al.'s work was based on the general assumption that, although a strong variance can be seen in how a gesture is made, spatiotemporal features related to emotions are stable over subjects. Features were directly calculated on the video image as points of interest in space-time, derived by employing spatial (Gaussian) and temporal (Gabor) filters on the video image. To classify emotions, a clustering approach was used to identify movement prototypes based on these interest points. Recognition rates using support vector machines ranged between 59% and 83% for a seven-class problem (anger, anxiety, boredom, disgust, joy, puzzlement, surprise). To train their recognition system they used a database containing around 1900 videos. Additionally they showed that fusing information from gestural activity and facial expressions can result in higher recognition rates.

To sum up, a number of studies demonstrated the correlation between the qualitative features of gestural activity, as described in Section 13.2, and emotional states. However, they also showed that this correlation is not unambiguous and sometimes allows us to derive only the intensity of an emotion or its valence, not the distinct emotion itself. Some first approaches to automatically recognizing emotions based on such correlations were presented that are very promising but that, at the moment, lack comparability because of the different sets of emotions and quite different databases that were employed for training and testing the recognition techniques.

13.4 PERSONALITY

Whereas the analysis of emotional states has become very popular in recent years, other contextual factors influencing interactions, such as personality or cultural heuristics for behavior, have not been its central focus although, for instance, Gallaher's expressive parameters have been defined to capture the relation between body movements and personality.

Ball and Breese [1] presented a first model for integrating personality as a factor influencing gestural behavior. To this end, they defined a Bayesian network to model the causal relations between gestural activity and posture and personality traits. Their model was based on studies that show that people are able to reliably interpret personality traits based on movement features. The approach used was primarily concerned with conveying the personality of an embodied agent by characteristic movements. However, because they modeled this relation with a Bayesian network, the same approach can be employed to recognize the user's personality based on his movement characteristics, which were already modeled in the network. Apart from defining specific postures and gestures that are most likely to occur in correlation with a given personality, qualitative characteristics like frequency, speed, and timing of a gesture were integrated to convincingly convey information about personality.

To integrate personality as a contextual factor influencing the movements of an embodied agent, Pelachaud [33] drew from Gallaher's analysis of personal style to define expressive features that serve as control parameters for the animation (gestures and face) of a virtual character. The aim of this work was to create individual rather than generic behaviors for an agent, in this case to achieve some kind of personal style. To this end, she defined a set of six parameters, which were based on Gallaher's dimensions: spatial extent, speed, fluidity, power, repetivity, and quantity. Perception studies were conducted, showing that combinations of these parameters establish consistent behavior patterns like sluggishness or vigorous movements. Moreover, the participants were able to recognize the differences in some of these parameters, with good results for spatial extent and speed, and not so good results for fluidity and power.

Karpouzis and colleagues [22] presented a gesture recognition system that takes the same parameters into account to extract quantitative information related to gestural expressivity from the user's hand movements: spatial extent, speed, fluidity, power, and repetition. As in Pelachaud's work, expressivity was not restricted to hand movements but took head movements and facial expressions into account as well. Spatial extent, for instance, applies to hand and head movement if this movement is wider or narrower; for facial expressions it applies to increased versus decreased muscular contraction.

Caridakis and colleagues [5] combined both approaches to realize a system that mimics the behavior of a human by a virtual agent based on the recognized expressive features and the agents' corresponding profiles. The general idea was that the agent is not directly mirroring the user's behavior but instead, by extracting the expressive parameters, its individual behavior is modified to fit the user's expressive behavior profile. Thus, the same gesture is realized by the agent qualitatively differently depending on the set of parameters. For instance, the user might show an expression of sadness accompanied by slow and narrow movements. To mirror this behavior in the agent, the agent's behavior profile for this emotion is combined with the user's expressive parameters to result in a display of the same emotion with a similar profile that nevertheless is idiosyncratic for this agent. This example application represents a first step in analyzing the user's gestural activity as a basis for deriving information about his personality profile.

13.5 CULTURE

Labarre [28] reviewed a large body of evidence on the cultural differences in using and interpreting body movements, including gesture repertoires that have specific meanings in a given culture (emblems). A most embarrasing situation might occur if someone uses such emblematic gestures unconsciously in interactions with people from other cultures. As earlier noted, the best known example might be the

American "OK" sign formed by thumb and index finger, which in Italy is a severe insult. Another example taken from Labarre is a gesture, in which the open right hand is raised to the face, with the thumb on the bridge of the nose. This is used by the Toda in South India to express respect, but an almost identical gesture is used in Germany to mock (i.e., it is a sign of disrespect). Thus, the recognition of specific gestures may give interesting insights into the cultural background of the user or it may cause severe problems in interpreting the semantic content of the gesture if the cultural background is not known. Again, the quality of the movement can serve as necessary evidence for a successful disambiguation.

The kinesthetic features defined by Efron [11] (see Section 13.2) were derived from his study of cultural differences in gesturing, but so far very few approaches take this information into account in an interactive ambient intelligence system. In his study, Efron examined differences in gesturing between Italian and Jewish immigrants as well as assimilated subjects from the same cultural groups. Based on his large amount of data (around 2500 subjects), he could show significant differences in all categories he analyzed: spatiotemporal, interlocutionary, and co-verbal aspects (see Section 13.2). With his sample of assimilated subjects (those already living for a long time in the United States), he was also able to show that differences vanish, giving clear evidence that differences in gestural activity are a learned cultural heuristic. An example of the differences he found is that, whereas Italian subjects used their whole arm for gesturing, Jewish subjects kept their upper arms close to the body, resulting in movements from the elbow downward (i.e., in narrower movements).

This empirical evidence of cultural differences in gestures on the spatiotemporal level is accompanied by a number of anecdotal references in the literature. Hall [16], for instance, gave a number of such references to culture-specific differences in gesture usage. Similar information can be found in Ting-Toomey [41], who found, for instance, that Germans use more gestures than Japanese and that Southern Europeans gesture more frequently then Northern Europeans. As we saw in Section 13.2, Efron's spatiotemporal and interlocutionary aspects are very similar or identical to Gallaher's expressive dimensions [15], which she used to distinguish personal gesturing styles. This implies again that these dimensions might also be useful for describing cultural differences in gesture use.

Rehm and colleagues [37] presented a corpus study designed to shed light on specific differences in gesture usage in individualistic and collectivistic cultures, with the aim of deriving expressive profiles for these cultures as a way to adapt the behavior of virtual agents to a user's cultural background. They recorded around 20 hours of interactions in Germany (21 pairs) and Japan (26 pairs). Their analysis focused on nonverbal behavior such as gesture and postures. Gestural expressivity was analyzed, focusing on parameters that had been proven successful in animating a virtual agent [33]: spatial extent, speed, overall activation, fluidity, and power.

Results from this corpus analysis show significant differences in the expressive profiles of participants from the two cultures. The frequency of gesture use is consistent with information from the literature [41] in that a significant difference can be seen in the number of gestures used in the German and the Japanese samples.

German participants use over three times more gestures than Japanese participants on average. Other significant differences were found for the expressive parameters spatial extent and speed.

Rehm et al. [36] gave an example of how this information can be used to infer the cultural background of the user based on his gestural expressivity. They presented a Bayesian network model of cultural influences on expressivity for analyzing the user's expressive behavior and deriving his cultural background. Culture in their approach was defined as a dimensional model following Hofstede's suggestions [18]. A given culture was thus a point in a five-dimensional space where dimensions described dichotomies such as individualistic versus collectivistic or high-power versus low-power distance. Table 13.3 gives cultural profiles for four example countries.

Hierarchy. This dimension describes the extent to which different distributions of power are accepted by less powerful members. According to Hofstede, more coercive and referent power (based on personal charisma and identification with the powerful) is used in societies scoring high on the hierarchy dimension; more reward, legitimate, and expert power, in those scoring low.

Identity. Here the degree to which individuals are integrated into a group is defined. On the individualist side, ties between individuals are loose, and each member is expected to take care of himself. On the collectivist side, members are integrated into strong, cohesive in-groups.

Gender. The gender dimension describes the distribution of roles between genders. In feminine cultures roles differ less than in masculine cultures, where competition is accepted and status symbols are important.

Uncertainty. Tolerance for uncertainty and ambiguity is defined in this dimension. It indicates to what extent the members of a culture feel uncomfortable in unstructured situations that are novel, unknown, surprising, or different from usual. Whereas uncertainty-avoiding cultures have rules to avoid unknown situations, uncertainty-accepting cultures are tolerant of situations different from what they are used to and have as few rules as possible.

Orientation. This dimension distinguishes long- and short-term orientation. The values associated with long-term orientation are thrift and perseverance, whereas those associated with short-term orientation are respect for tradition, fulfilling social obligations, and saving face.

Table 13.3 Hofstede's Ratings on a Scale from 1 to 100 for Selected Countries

	Hierarchy	Identity	Gender	Uncertainty	Orientation
Germany	35	67	66	65	31
Japan	54	46	95	92	80
Sweden	31	71	5	29	33
US	40	91	62	46	29

According to Hofstede [18], nonverbal behavior is strongly affected by cultural affordances. The identity dimension, for example, is tightly related to the expression of emotions and acceptable emotional displays in a culture, in that, for instance, individualistic cultures tolerate individual expressions of anger more easily than do collectivistic cultures. Hofstede et al. [19] explicitly examined the differences that arise in the use of sound and space for the five dimensions. By relating the results from their corpus study to Hofstede's dimensional model, Rehm and colleagues showed how a user's expressive gestural behavior can be recognized with high accuracy and then used to infer the user's position on Hofstede's cultural dimensions. With this contextual information it becomes possible to modify the behavior of an interactive system.

13.6 RECOGNIZING GESTURAL BEHAVIOR FOR HUMAN-CENTRIC AMBIENT INTELLIGENCE

In Part I of this book, vision-based techniques for gesture recognition were presented in depth. Here the focus is on input techniques that make use of sensoric equipment to allow more private interactions. Although vision-based techniques present the most unobstrusive method for movement analysis and have proven very successful for recognizing gestural activity (perhaps apart from some minor occlusion problems), they may present a severe threat to privacy in ambient intelligence environments if the user is unaware of the vision device and does not know which information is being processed, such as affective state, personality traits, or cultural background. Thus, obstrusive input methods might be more appropriate for sensitive personal information, as they put the control over information transmitted to the environment into the hands of the user.

In the remainder of this chapter we present input techniques that make use of acceleration or physiological sensors like EMG. Such techniques rely on sensors that are small enough to be carried by the user as handheld devices or to be attached to her body. It is not unreasonable to assume that such sensors will become integrated into everyday objects like rings or items of clothing, removing this annoyance of attaching them altogether.

13.6.1 Acceleration-Based Gesture Recognition

With the advent of Nintendo's new game console, acceleration-based interactions have become very popular. Although most commercial games seem to rely on relatively primitive information, like raw acceleration, more sophisticated gesture recognition is possible. Schlömer and colleagues [38] made use of HMMs to analyze acceleration data. They evaluated their approach with an arbitrary set of five gestures and presented user-dependent recognition rates of up to 93% for this five-class problem. Rehm and colleagues [36] used acceleration-based recognition to capture gestural activity that relates to the cultural background of the user and demonstrated this approach with the Wiimote. Features were calculated on the raw signal. Different classification techniques such as naïve Bayes, nearest neighbor, and multilayer perceptron were compared for different gesture sets like expressivity parameters or German emblems. Results showed that recognition rates are user-dependent and that this approach is feasible with recognition rates for a seven-class problem of German emblems of up to 94%, making use of a standard nearest-neighbour classfier.

In an earlier study, Kela and colleagues [23] developed a similar approach tailored to gestures for controlling a video recorder and making use of a cubelike handheld device equipped with three acceleration sensors, quite like Nintendo's controller. To come up with a realistic gesture set, Kela et al. conducted a participatory design study, which resulted in eight suitable gestures. Gesture analysis was based on HMMs and took the filtered data into account. User-dependent recognition rates reached 99% depending on the number of training samples provided to estimate the model parameters.

Urban and colleagues [42] examined the feasibility of using acceleration sensors for a marshalling task designed to control unmanned aircrafts on a flight desk. The general idea was to allow the marshaller to make use of the same gesture signals employed with manned vehicles. Two problems had to be solved for this 20-class recognition task. On the one hand, Urban et al. evaluated the best placement of the acceleration sensors on the upper and lower arm for robust gesture recognition. On the other hand they showed that time-series classifiers like dynamic time warping for acceleration-based gesture recognition can be an efficient technique.

Strachan et al. [40] faced the problem of reconstructing 3D-movement of the hand from acceleration data. This was no trivial task given the inherent drift of the sensors, which makes the prediction of the exact trajectory difficult. By decomposing gestures in linearly combined motion primitives, the researchers were able to build personalized models of gestures that a user will use in an application. Thus, they integrated subjective idiosyncracies of gestural activity into their recognition system. Whereas this is only a by-product of their approach, the work by Lester et al. [29] was directly tailored to this challenge.

Although most approaches discussed so far focus on the recogntion of discrete gesture classes, Lester and his colleagues [29] exploited the applicability of acceleration-based techniques to identify users by their subjective idiosyncrasies in handling devices. In an ambient intelligence environment, the user will carry a number of devices, which must be coordinated to a certain degree and interact with one another, with the environment, and of course with the user. Enabling the device to identify who is currently carrying it might rid the user of some of the management load. Lester and colleagues used information about the user's specific movement qualities to solve this problem. To this end, they employed a complex coherence function measuring the extent to which two signals are correlated at given frequencies.

The work presented here shows that acceleration-based gesture recognition is feasible and that not only gestures as such can be recognized but also more subtle aspects of gestural activity such as expressivity and other idiosyncratic features, allowing, for instance, the user to be identified.

13.6.2 Gesture Recognition Based on Physiological Input

Another currently not very well explored method of gesture recognition is physiological sensors. These have been used increasingly over recent years to recognize emotional states or at least a user's state of arousal (e.g. [25, 35]). Some sensors, like EMG, measure muscle activity and can thus be adapted to capture certain aspects of gestural movements that might not be easily recognizable by vision- or acceleration-based techniques.

Naik and colleagues [32] first separated the muscle activity from different muscles with a four-channel EMG sensor before attempting to classify specific movements. Making use of independent component analysis and a neural network model, they could distinguish accurately between three types of motion: wrist flexion, finger flexion, and wrist and finger flexion. Depending on the recognition task, this information can be crucial to distinguish gesture classes in sign language, for instance, where finger movements play a crucial role.

Kim et al. [26] allowed a user to radio-control a toy car by different hand gestures, which were recognized from an EMG signal. Four gestures were identified as suitable for this task. Sensors were placed on the lower arm below the wrist. The gesture classification used a combination of naïve Bayes and nearest-neighbor classifiers. The system was evaluated with 30 subjects to find the optimal classifier combination. User-independent recognition rates for this small set of four gestures varied between 87% and 98%, showing convincingly that gesture recognition based on such physiological information is possible.

Whereas Naik et al. are independent of the sensor placement in their approach, more specific gesture recognition tasks need to take into account the exact placing of the sensors in order to read out the correct muscles. Wheeler [44] used EMG sensors to emulate a joystick and a keyboard; depending on the device (i.e., on the movements necessary for it), the number and placement of electrodes was different. In the joystick trial, users had to perform four gestures (up, down, left, right), which were recognized by use of four HMMs, one for each gesture class. Recognition results were accurate for all but the gesture "left," which was recognized in only 30% of cases and otherwise confused with "up." In the more complex keyboard trial, users had to perform 11 gestures (0 to 9, enter) and again one HMM was trained for each gesture class. Recognition rates varied between 70% and 100%, depending on the gesture class.

All approaches show that gesture recognition with EMG is possible, but that it is not easy to achieve robust recognition rates, especially because of problems in placing the sensors. Recognition results depend on the muscles on which the sensors are placed and on the specific gestures realized in an application, making it difficult to come to a general conclusion. A promising solution may be the combination of acceleration-based and EMG-based recognition, as was recently shown by Chen and colleagues [7] for the recognition of Chinese and by Kim and colleagues [27] for the recognition of German sign language.

13.7 CONCLUSIONS

This chapter provided insights into how qualitative aspects of gestural activity can be exploited as an input channel for a variety of contextual variables, such as the emotional state of the user, her personality, and her cultural background. It was shown by evidence from studies on these aspects that a general set of qualitative movement features can be defined, and it was shown how these features can further the recognition of emotion, personality, or cultural background from the user's gestures.

Although the presented approaches are very stimulating and relevant, it remains to be seen how such social-psychological context variables can be integrated into human-centric ambient intelligence. This is because, although the speed and spatial extent of a gesture might give hints of the user's personality profile, these features might also allow infering her cultural background. The fact that the same set of features (or at least subsets of this general set) are applicable for all of the variables presented in this chapter emphasizes that such an integrated account is feasible and also necessary.

REFERENCES

[1] Ball G, Breese J. Relating personality and behavior: Posture and gestures. In: Paiva AM, editor. Affective Interaction. Springer; 2000. p. 196–203.

[2] Bernhardt D, Robinson P. Detecting affect from non-stylised body motions. In: Paiva A, Prada RW, Picard RW, editors. ACII 2007. Springer; 2007. p. 59–70.

[3] Bull PE. Posture and Gesture. Pergamon Press; 1987.

[4] Burgoon JK. Nonverbal signals. In: Knapp ML, Miller GR, editors. Handbook of Interpersonal Communication. SAGE Publications; 1994. p. 229–85.

[5] Caridakis G, Raouzaiou A, Bevacqua E, Mancini M, Karpouzis K, et al. Virtual agent multimodal mimicry of humans. Language Resources and Evaluation 2007;41:367–88.

[6] Castellano G, Villalba SD, Camurri A. Recognising human emotions from body movement and gesture dynamics. In: Paiva A, Prada R, Picard RW, editors. ACII 2007. Springer; 2007. p. 71–82.

[7] Chen X, Zhang X, Zhao Z, Yang J, Lantz V, Wang K. Hand Gesture Recognition Research Based on Surface EMG Sensors and 2D-Accelerometers. In: IEEE International Symposium on Wearable Computers. 2007. p. 11–4.

[8] Crane E, Gross M. Motion capture and emotion: Affect detection in whole body movement. In: Affective Computing and Intelligent Interaction. Springer; 2007. p. 95–101.

[9] Damasio AR. Descartes Irrtum. dtv, 1997.

[10] de Meijer M. The contribution of general features of body movement to the attribution of emotions. J Nonverbal Behav 1989;13(4):247-68.

[11] Efron D. Gesture, Race and Culture. Mouton and Co; 1972.

[12] Ekman P. Basic emotions. In: Dalgleish T, Power M editors. Handbook of Cognition and Emotion. John Wiley; 1999. p. 45-60.

[13] Ekman P, Friesen W. The repertoire of nonverbal behavior: categories, origins, usage and coding. Semiotica 1969;1:49-98.

[14] Ekman P, Rosenberg E, editors. What the Face Reveals: Basic & Applied Studies of Spontaneous Expression Using the Facial Action Coding System (FACS). Oxford University Press; 1998.

[15] Gallaher PE. Individual differences in nonverbal behavior: dimensions of style. J Pers Soc Psychol 1992;63(1):133-45.

[16] Hall ET. The Silent Language. Doubleday; 1959.

[17] Hall ET. The Hidden Dimension. Doubleday; 1966.

[18] Hofstede G. Cultures Consequences: Comparing Values, Behaviors, Institutions, and Organizations Across Nations. Sage Publications; 2001.

[19] Hofstede G, Pedersen PB, Hofstede G. Exploring Culture: Exercises, Stories, and Synthetic Cultures. Intercultural Press; 2002.

[20] Izard CE. Human Emotions; Plenum Press.

[21] Kapur A, Kapur A, Virji-Babul N, Tzanetakis G, Driessen PF. Gesture-based affective computing on motion capture data. In: Tao J, Tan T, Picard RW, editors. Affective Computing and Intelligent Interaction (ACII). Springer; 2005. p. 1-7.

[22] Karpouzis K, Caridakis G, Kessous L, Amir N, Raouzaiou R, Malatesta L. Modeling naturalistic affective states via facial, vocal, and bodily expressions recognition. In: Human Computing. Springer; 2007. p. 91-112.

[23] Kela J, Korpipää P, Mäntyjärvi J, Kallio S, Savino G, Jozzo L. Accelerometer-based gesture control for a design environment. Pers Ubiquitous Computing 2006;10:285-99.

[24] Kendon A. Gesture—Visible Action as Utterance. Cambridge University Press; 2004.

[25] Kim J, André E, Rehm M, Vogt T, Wagner J. Integrating information from speech and physiological signals to achieve emotional sensitivity. In: Proceedings of Interspeech/Eurospeech. 2005. p. 809-12.

[26] Kim J, Mastnik S, André E. Emg-based hand gesture recognition for realtime biosignal interfacing. In: Proceedings of the 13th International Conference on Intelligent User Interfaces. Gran Canaria; 2008. p. 30-9.

[27] Kim J, Wagner J, Rehm M, André E. Bichannel sensor fusion for automatic sign language recognition. In: Automatic Face & Gesture Recognition, 2008. FG '08. 8th IEEE International Conference on, 2008; 2008. p. 1-6.

[28] Labarre W. The cultural basis of emotions and gestures. Journal of Personality 1947;16:49-68.

[29] Lester J, Hannaford B, Borriello G. Are you with me? — Using accelerometers to determine if two devices are carried by the same person. In: Ferscha A, Mattern F, editors. PERVASIVE 2004. Springer; 2004. p. 33-50.

[30] Machotka P. Body movements as communication. Dialogues: Behavioral Science Research 1965;2:33-65.

[31] McNeill D. Hand and mind: What gestures reveal about thought. University of Chicago Press; 1992.

[32] Naik GR, Kumar DK, Singh VP. Proceedings of the HCSNet workshop on Use of vision in human-computer interaction. Canberra, Australia: 2006.

[32a] Palaniswami M. Hand gestures for HCI using ICA of EMG. In: HCSNet Workshop on the Use of Vision in HCI (VisHCI) 2006. p. 67-72.

[33] Pelachaud C. Multimodal expressive embodied conversational agents. In: Proceedings of the 13th Annual ACM International Conference on Multimedia. 2005. p. 683-9.

[34] Picard R. Affective Computing. MIT Press; 1997.

[35] Prendinger H, Dohi H, Wang H, Mayer S, Ishizuka M. Empathic embodied interfaces: Addressing users' affective state. In: André E, et al., editor. Affective Dialogue Systems (ADS-04). Springer; 2004. p. 53-64.

[36] Rehm M, Bee N, André E. Wave like an Egyptian—Acceleration based gesture recognition for culture-specific interactions. In: Proceedings of HCI 2008 Culture, Creativity, Interaction; 2008. p. 13-22.

[37] Rehm M, Nakano Y, André E, Nishida T. Culture specific first meeting encounters between virtual agents. In: Prendinger H, et al., editor. Intelligent Virtual Agents. Springer; 2008.

[38] Schlömer T, Poppinga B, Henze N, Boll S. Gesture recognition with a wii controller. In: Proceedings of the 2nd International Conference on Tangible and Embedded Interaction. p. 11-14.

[39] Shan C, Gong S, McOwan PW. Beyond facial expressions: Learning human emotion from body gestures. In: Proceedings of British Machine Vision Conference (BMVC). University of Warwick; 2007. p. 10-3.

[40] Strachan S, Murray-Smith R, Oakley I, Angeslevä J. Dynamic primitives for gestural interaction. In: Brewster S, Dunlop M, editors. MobileHCI 2004. 2004. p. 325-30.

[41] Ting-Toomey S. Communicating Across Cultures. The Guilford Press; 1999.

[42] Urban M, Bajcsy P, Kooper R, Lementec J-C. Recognition of arm gestures using multiple orientation sensors: Repeatability assessment. In: IEEE Intelligent Transportation Systems Conference. 2004. p. 553-4.

[43] Walbott HG. Bodily expression of emotion. European Journal of Social Psychology 1998;28:879-96.

[44] Watzlawick P, Beavin Bavelas JH, Jackson D-D. Menschliche Kommunikation. Huber; 1969.

[45] Wheeler KR. Device control using gestures sensed from EMG. In: IEEE International Workshop on Soft Computing in Industrial Applications. Binghamton University; 2003. p. 21-6.

[46] Wundt W. Grundriss der Psychologie. Engelmann.

Evaluation of Multimodal Interfaces for Ambient Intelligence

14

Sebastian Möller, Klaus-Peter Engelbrecht, Christine Kühnel, Anja Naumann, Ina Wechsung, and Benjamin Weiss

Quality and Usability Lab, Deutsche Telekom Laboratories, TU Berlin, Berlin, Germany

ABSTRACT

In this chapter, we review assessment and evaluation principles applied to multimodal interfaces for intelligent environments. On the basis of a new taxonomy of quality aspects, quantitative metrics are identified that address different aspects of user and system performance, quality, usability, and acceptability. Example applications are presented for multimodal interfaces to domestic devices, focusing on information presentation—for example, via an embodied conversational agent. It is shown which methods are already available and which ones are still missing to support an efficient development of ambient intelligence systems that are well accepted by their users.

Key words: multimodal interface, ambient intelligence, evaluation, usability.

14.1 INTRODUCTION

Ambient intelligence was defined in [2] as "a digital environment that proactively, but sensibly, supports people in their daily life." The notion of a sensible system emphasizes "intelligence" as a fundamental requirement of such an environment. The idea is to make computing available to people in a nonintrusive way, minimizing explicit interaction. However, sensors of various kinds allow not only a passive, nonintrusive interaction but also an active, intended interaction. Such interactions, using speech or other modalities, require us to consider ambient intelligence systems as (multimodal) dialogue systems. This chapter addresses the evaluation of multimodal interfaces in ambient intelligence, taking smart home systems as an example.

Multimodal dialogue systems have reached a level of maturity that allows widespread application. Examples include information kiosks at airports or train stations, navigation systems, media guides, entertainment and education systems, and intelligent environments [6, 29, 48]. (For an overview of dialogue systems, refer to Chapter 18 in this volume.) Focusing on ambient intelligence systems, multimodality may render the respective interfaces more intuitive and natural because the weaknesses of one modality may be compensated by the strength of another. However, such interfaces also represent a challenge for users, designers, and evaluators. The combination of different input and output modalities does not correspond to the users' prior knowledge, and it is difficult for the system developer to anticipate in which way users will address the system. Unfortunately, methods are missing for quantifying such multimodal interaction behavior, making assessment of system components and evaluation of entire systems a particularly difficult task.

Each system usually passes several assessment and evaluation cycles during its development: Individual components (such as a speech recognizer) are assessed as to whether they provide sufficient performance; initial prototypes are tested in terms of mock-ups or through Wizard-of-Oz simulations; preliminary system versions are evaluated in friendly-user tests; and roll-off systems are evaluated with their first customers. Despite several efforts in the past [11, 17], most evaluations are still individual undertakings: Test protocols and metrics are developed on the spot, with a particular system and user group in focus and with limited budget and time. As a result, we see a multitude of highly interesting—but virtually noncomparable—evaluation exercises that address different quality aspects and rely on different evaluation criteria.

One criterion commonly used by system designers is *performance*: To what degree does the system provide the function it has been built for? From a user's perspective, *quality* is the most important criterion. Quality has been defined as the "result of appraisal of the perceived composition of a unit with respect to its desired composition" [27]. Following this definition, the measurement of quality requires a perception and judgment process by the user. Thus, measurement of quality relies on subjective interaction tests with real or test users.

For spoken dialogue systems, efforts have been made to come up with a standard set of performance and quality metrics. These include interaction parameters describing the performance of system components and the behavior of user and system during interactions [16, 24, 33], as well as questionnaires for collecting quality judgments [16, 22, 26, 33]. For multimodal dialogue systems, standard evaluation metrics are still lacking. One reason for this is that their relevant performance and quality aspects are not understood.

In fact, this lack of understanding of how multimodal interaction works is at least partially due to the lack of agreement on how such interactions are to be evaluated [36]. Although many researchers and practitioners claim to measure "usability," "user satisfaction," or "acceptance," these terms are often used for the same construct, and they are measured using the same metrics. A clear separation of constructs and respective measurement methods will make evaluation results far more useful and will ultimately allow the planning and prediction of such aspects for new systems and services.

As a first step toward a solution, we propose a new taxonomy of performance and quality aspects, including factors influencing the system, the user, and the context of use. It is based on a taxonomy developed for spoken dialogue systems in [32], but considers a broader range of quality aspects and input and output modalities. This new taxonomy will help us to understand and differentiate between general constructs currently used when speaking about assessment or evaluation—"usability," "acceptability," "joy of use," "efficiency," and so forth. It can be used in at least three different ways:

- System developers may search for the interaction performance and quality aspects they are interested in and find the appropriate evaluation metrics; example metrics for each aspect are listed in Sections 14.4 and 14.5.
- The taxonomy could serve as the basis for systematic efforts to collect evaluation data. Examples of such efforts are described in Section 14.6, focusing on the smart-home domain and addressing the validity of the described methods.
- The constructs and influencing factors, once identified, can serve as targets for an automatic or semi-automatic evaluation. Examples for predicting quality aspects on the basis of interaction performance aspects, using data collected through simulations and real experiments, are given, for example, in [12].

The taxonomy consists of three layers:

- *Quality factors* that have an impact on interaction behavior and thus on perceived quality
- *Interaction performance aspects* describing user and system performance and behavior
- *Quality aspects* related to quality perception and judgment

An overall picture of the taxonomy is given in the next section. Sections 14.3, 14.4, and 14.5 provide definitions and available metrics for the quality factors, interaction performance aspects, and quality aspects, respectively. In Section 14.6, we provide an application example of evaluation strategies for multimodal interfaces to domestic devices, focusing principally on the information presentation, for example via an embodied conversational agent (ECA). Finally, Section 14.7 defines the next steps necessary to take full advantage of the approach.

14.2 PERFORMANCE AND QUALITY TAXONOMY

Figure 14.1 shows the three taxonomy layers in detail. The first layer represents quality-influencing factors, as a kind of "input" to a quality production mechanism. These factors can be divided into three groups: those related to the user, those related to the system, and those related to the physical and nonphysical context of use. Quality factors influence perceived quality through the interaction performance aspects in the second layer of the taxonomy. The latter are organized into two cycles: the performance aspects of the user's interaction behavior on the left and those of the system's interaction behavior on the right.

As a result of the interaction described in the second layer, quality "happens" as a multidimensional perceptual event in a particular context of use. We can analyze quality on the level of the interaction (interaction quality), on the level of the inter-action result (e.g., effectiveness and efficiency), on the level of system usability, and finally on the level of system acceptability. Whereas interaction quality is the most interesting to the designer of the system, the aspects in the lower parts of this layer are more relevant to the deployer of the system (e.g., the service provider).

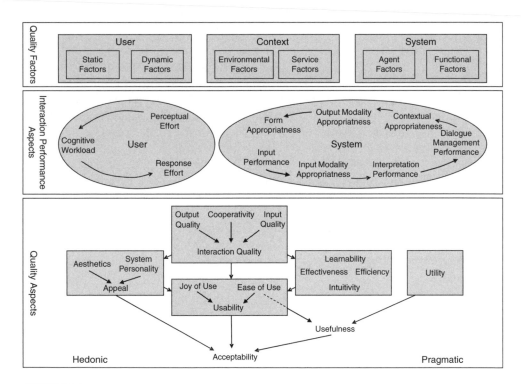

FIGURE 14.1

Taxonomy of quality factors, interaction performance aspects, and quality aspects.

It is obvious from Figure 14.1 that there are relationships between quality factors, interaction performance aspects, and quality aspects. These relationships are mostly not one to one and can vary in their strength depending on the system, user, or context. Inside each layer, however, they are better defined and therefore indicated as far as possible.

The taxonomy is intended to serve as a framework for evaluation, where evaluators may identify possible evaluation targets from a more or less exhaustive list and select corresponding measurement methods. In turn, it is not intended to serve as a precise protocol: Whereas standardized protocols such as those followed by DARPA or Blizzard [3, 40] are very helpful in the development of core technologies, they provide little insight into the appropriateness of those technologies for a system to be developed. Via a framework, developers of ambient intelligence systems are able to tailor evaluation to their individual needs.

Once the constructs and measurement methods have been identified, they may also serve as targets for prediction on the basis of system characteristics and interaction behavior. Models for this purpose have been in use for more than 10 years (e.g., the PARADISE framework for predicting "user satisfaction" on the basis of interaction behavior with spoken dialogue systems [49]), but they lack accuracy because the target constructs and influencing factors have not yet been properly identified. The taxonomy could provide an important step forward: It shows the relationship between influencing factors, interaction performance, and quality perceived by the user, and in this way helps to identify and quantify *meaningful* relationships that are valid for a range of interfaces, domains, and user groups.

In the following sections, we provide definitions and examples of the individual items of the taxonomy. As far as they are available, we also cite metrics for quantifying the items in the evaluation. An application example of some of the constructs and measurement methods is given in Section 14.6.

14.3 QUALITY FACTORS

The quality factors influence the quality aspects through the interaction performance aspects. They include the characteristics of the user, system, and context of use that have an impact on perceived quality.

User factors. All characteristics of the user that influence her interaction behavior and quality judgment. These include static (e.g., age, gender, native language) as well as dynamic characteristics (e.g., motivation, emotional status). *Metrics*: Screening questionnaire at the beginning of an evaluation experiment according to a predefined user classification scheme [21].

System factors. The characteristics of the system as an interaction partner (agent factors) and those related to its functional capabilities (functional factors). Agent factors include the technical characteristics of the individual system modules (speech, gesture, and/or face recognition; multimodal fusion, dialogue management, multimodal fission, etc.) as well as their appearance [33]. Functional factors include the type of task (well- or ill-structured, homogeneous or heterogeneous [5]), the number of available tasks, task complexity, task frequency, and task consequences (particularly important for security-critical systems) [33]. For less-task-directed systems the domain characteristics become more important (e.g., education or entertainment). *Metrics*: Specification documents and task analysis methods, as in [39]. Most agent factors have to be specified by the system developer, whereas aesthetics can be better specified by design experts or experienced salespersons. Functional factors can be best specified by domain experts.

Context factors. The physical environment (home, office, mobile, or public use; space, acoustic, and lighting conditions; transmission channels; potential parallel activities of the user; privacy and security issues) as well as the service factors (e.g. access restrictions, availability of the system, resulting costs). *Metrics*: Specification documents provided by the developers of the system.

14.4 INTERACTION PERFORMANCE ASPECTS

It is during the interaction that the perception and judgment processes forming quality take place. Interaction performance aspects are organized into two cycles, their order reflecting the processing step they are located in.

System interaction performance aspects include

Input performance. This can be quantified, for example, in terms of accuracy or error rate, as is common practice for speech recognizers, gesture recognizers, and facial expression recognizers. In addition, the degree of coverage of the user's behavior (vocabulary, gestures, expressions) as well as the system's real-time performance are indicators of input performance. Concerning special multimodal input such as face detection and person or hand tracking, see [37] for metrics and a corpus to evaluate system components in a comparable way.

Input modality appropriateness. This can be judged on a theoretical basis, for example, with the help of modality properties, as was proposed in [4]. The user's context has to be taken into account when determining appropriateness; for example, spoken input is inappropriate for secret information like a PIN in public spaces.

Interpretation performance. This can be quantified in terms of accuracy when a limited set of underlying semantic concepts is used for meaning description. An example is counting the errors in filling in the correct attribute–value pairs on the basis of an expert-derived correct interpretation. Such measures exist for independent input modalities [24]. However, the performance of the modality fusion component should also be considered by incorporating synchronicity and redundancy in a measure.

Dialogue management performance. This can be defined depending on the function of interest. The dialogue manager's main function is to drive the dialogue to the intended goal and can be assessed only indirectly, in terms of dialogue success. Following this, an important performance factor is the ability of the dialogue manager to cope with errors. This can be measured by the amount of repaired errors and the efficiency with which repair takes place (e.g., number of correction turns per error). On a less pragmatic level, initiative can be assessed by the balance between contributions (e.g., dialogue acts) from each participant. The dialogue manager's ability to correct misunderstandings can, for example, be quantified by counting occurrences of corrected misunderstanding and meta-communication; several metrics for this purpose are listed in [24].

Contextual appropriateness. This can be related to Grice's cooperativity principle [5, 18] and quantified in terms of violations of it—for example, via the contextual appropriateness parameter [16].

Output modality appropriateness. Similar to the input side, output modality appropriateness can be checked on the basis of modality properties [4], taking into account the interrelations between simultaneous modalities. For example, textual information may be presented either visually or auditorily but not simultaneously audiovisually in order to not confuse the user [41].

Form appropriateness. This refers to the surface form of the output provided to the user. For example, form appropriateness of spoken output can be measured via its intelligibility, comprehensibility, or required listening effort. The appropriateness of an embodied conversational agent can be assessed by its ability to convey specific information, including emotions, turn taking backchannels, and so forth. On the user's side, interaction performance can be quantified by the effort required by the user to interact with the system, as well as by the freedom of interaction. Aspects include

Perceptual effort. The effort required to decode system messages and understand and interpret their meaning [51] (e.g., listening or reading effort). *Metrics*: the Borg scale [8].

Cognitive workload. The costs of task performance (e.g., necessary information processing capacity and resources) [47]. An overview of subjective and objective methods for assessing cognitive workload is given in [50].

Response effort. The physical effort required to communicate with the system—for example: that necessary to enter information into a mobile phone. *Metrics*: questionnaires and the like [26].

14.5 QUALITY ASPECTS

So far, we have limited ourselves to influencing factors and performance metrics. However, the ultimate aim of a system developer should be to satisfy the user, or at least to provide acceptable services. According to Hassenzahl and colleagues [20] the user's evaluation of a system is influenced by pragmatic and hedonic quality aspects. These have to be evaluated with the help of real or test users providing judgments on what they perceive. Such judgments can be seen as "direct" quality measurements. In addition, "indirect" quality measurements can be obtained by logging user behavior and relating it to quality. Physiological measures have been used for this purpose [30], as have indices of parallel-task performance [10].

Quality aspects are

Interaction quality. This includes the perceived input and output quality of the system as well as its cooperativity. Input quality relates to perceived system understanding and input comfort; output quality, to perceived system understandability and form appropriateness. Studies have shown that the relationship between, say, perceived system understanding and word accuracy or concept accuracy is weak at best [34]. Cooperativity includes the distribution of initiative between the partners (which may be asymmetric because of different roles and expectations), consideration of background knowledge, and repair and clarification capabilities. Interaction quality as a whole can be quantified in terms of speed/pace, conciseness, smoothness, and naturalness of the interaction. *Metrics*: questionnaire frameworks such as those in [26].

Efficiency-related aspects. These include effectiveness (the accuracy and completeness with which specified users can reach specified goals in particular environments [28]) and efficiency (the effort and resources required in relation to accuracy and completeness [28]), as well as learnability (the speed and facility with which users feel they have been able to master the system [28]) and intuitivity (the extent to which the user is able to interact with a technical system effectively by applying knowledge unconsciously [38]). *Metrics*: questionnaires such as those in [28].

Usability. According to the ISO definition, this is the "extent to which a product can be used by specified users to achieve specified goals with effectiveness, efficiency and satisfaction in a specified context of use" [23]. We consider two aspects of usability: ease of use, influenced by the mentioned consequences of interaction quality, and joy of use. Joy of use depends not only on the quality of the interaction but also on hedonic aspects like the appeal or "personality" of the system. Both ease of use and joy of use may determine user satisfaction, which can be considered a consequence of good usability. *Metrics*: questionnaires, as in [22, 26, 30].

Aesthetics, system personality, and appeal. Aesthetics is the sensory experience the system elicits and the extent to which this experience fits individual goals and spirit [46]. System personality refers to user perception of system characteristics originating from the current combination of agent factors and surface form. Appeal is a result of the aesthetics of the product, its physical factors, and the extent to which it incorporates interesting, novel, and surprising features [20, 44]. *Metrics*: questionnaires [19] or psycho-physiological measures [30].

Utility and usefulness. To judge whether a system is useful, we have to compare the functional requirements of the user with the functions offered. Utility answers the question: Can a specific user carry out his task with the help of the system [7]? Usefulness relates this to usability: How well can a user complete the task, considering not only the effort involved but also the joy experienced [7]? *Metrics*: questionnaires [28].

Acceptability. How readily a user will actually use the system? Acceptability may be represented as a purely economic measure, relating the number of potential users to the quantity of the target group [13].

14.6 APPLICATION EXAMPLES

In this section, we provide examples of how the taxonomy can be used for evaluating multimodal interfaces for ambient intelligence. The systems we use for this purpose are a speech-controlled interface to operate a number of domestic devices in a smart home environment (INSPIRE), and a media recommender developed as an interface to IP-based entertainment services (MediaScout). Although the experiments described here have been carried out at different points in time, and with different systems and system versions, they provide a good use scenario of the taxonomy.

In the following, we first briefly describe the INSPIRE and the MediaScout systems (Section 14.6.1) and the selection of evaluation constructs and corresponding measurement methods (Section 14.6.2). Then we provide a methodological description and some insights from three experimental series addressing the impact of the output metaphor (Section 14.6.3), the quality of an embodied conversational agent (Section 14.6.4), and the use of different questionnaires to capture a multitude of quality aspects of the MediaScout system (Section 14.6.5).

14.6.1 INSPIRE and MediaScout

Our ambient intelligence environment was developed within the framework of the EU-funded IST project INSPIRE ("INfotainment Management with SPeech Interaction via REmote Microphones and Telephone Interface," IST 2001–32746). A user can interact with the INSPIRE system via spoken language to consult an electronic program guide and to operate several home devices, such as the TV or video recorder, the lights, the blinds, the fan, or the answering machine. The system can be accessed at home through a microphone array installed in the house or from remote locations via the telephone (e.g., for controlling the lights or recording a TV show during absence). So far, we tested it in three different environments:

- *Home*: This was implemented at IKA, Ruhr-Universität Bochum, Germany, using a room decorated as a typical living room.
- *Office*: The system could be accessed through a simulated telephone connection with controlled transmission conditions; this environment was also installed at IKA, Ruhr-Universität Bochum.
- *Car*: A simulator was used for this purpose, installed at TNO Human Factors, Soesterberg, The Netherlands.

Feedback from the system is mainly provided by spoken language, but visual feedback on a screen (e.g., listings or a talking head) is available as well. In addition, the user perceives the effect that spoken commands may have on the devices. For example, lights are switched on and off, the TV shows program listings, or the answering machine plays a message.

This feedback supports the personality of the machine interaction partner, as it is perceived by the user. It is reflected by the so-called "metaphor"—that is, the transfer of meaning to the machine interaction partner by the human interaction partner, because of the machine partner's similarity to the human partner in its apparent shape, in its function, and in its use. For the INSPIRE system, several metaphors may be thought of that differ with respect to the output modality and the system voice, including (but not limited to) the following:

- Multiple *intelligent devices*, which the user may directly address individually, instead of addressing a single system that controls all devices, in the home environment. Each of the addressed devices is "intelligent" in that it is able to maintain a spoken interaction with the user on its own, using a distinct voice and communicative behavior and covering a distinct dialogue domain (that of the device).
- A single visible "assistant" or "servant," who operates the devices on behalf of the user and maintains the spoken interaction with him. This assistant may be implemented as an embodied conversational agent or *talking head* displayed on a screen in the home environment.
- An invisible "assistant," who operates the devices on behalf of the user but is immaterial and not localized in the home environment (e.g., a *ghost* somewhere in the room).

All three metaphors (*intelligent devices, talking head,* and *ghost*) were implemented and evaluated in the home environment, whereas only the ghost was available when the system was accessed remotely.

In addition to the INSPIRE system, multimodal access to the television was provided by the MediaScout, a Web-based media recommender and management system developed at Deutsche Telekom Laboratories. Based on a user profile of answers to three questions during initial use, online video libraries and television programs are searched and recommendations are given. The user profile is continuously improved and updated by analyzing the user's selections and ratings. Recommendations are thus more accurate with every use of the system [43]. The application is available on mobile (e.g., PDAs, tablet PCs) as well as fixed devices (e.g., desktop PCs, home entertainment systems). Depending on the device, different modalities such as speech control, motion control, and touch-screen tactile interaction, as well as keyboard and/or mouse interaction, are implemented.

14.6.2 Evaluation Constructs

We now illustrate three different use cases of the taxonomy. In each case, the evaluation methodology was derived by taking into account a limited number of quality factors, interaction performance aspects, and quality aspects defined by the taxonomy. Each use case resulted in a series of experiments, which will be briefly described with a focus on the evaluation methodology, not on the artifact to be evaluated as it serves as an example only. The situation is depicted in Figure. 14.2.

In the first case, we are interested in the impact of quality factors on the output and interaction quality of the INSPIRE system, and on its personality. For this purpose, a first series of experiments was designed to measure the output quality of different system metaphors in three neutralized (listening and viewing only) settings, and then the interaction quality in a realistic interactive setting. Second, we assessed different voice and head combinations of the talking head metaphor. The aim of this second experimental series was to quantify the impact of speech and head performance on perceived output quality as well as to define an appropriate evaluation methodology for a talking head in an increasingly realistic setting. Third, we

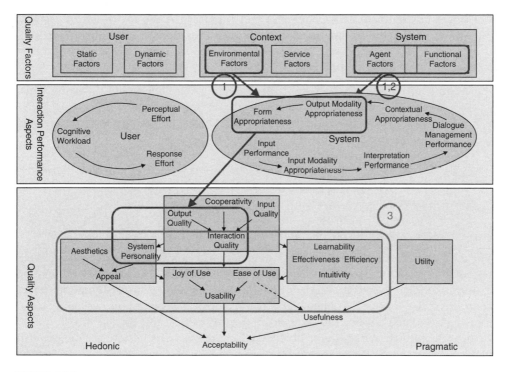

FIGURE 14.2

Use cases of the taxonomy resulting in three experiments. Series 1: Impact of the metaphor (agent factor) and the test environment (environmental and functional factors) on output and interaction quality, and on system personality. Series 2: Impact of voice and head characteristics (agent factors) on output quality and system personality. Series 3: Comparison of several questionnaires for determining quality aspects related to interaction quality, efficiency, appeal, usability, utility, and usefulness of the multimodal MediaScout system.

compared several standardized questionnaires for quantifying quality aspects of the multimodal MediaScout system. The aim was to investigate the extent to which standardized questionnaires developed for unimodal interfaces are useful for evaluating multimodal systems, and thus to provide some guidance for the use of such questionnaires with multimodal ambient intelligence interfaces in the future.

14.6.3 Evaluation of Output Metaphors

In this section, we describe the rationale, the experimental design, and some insights gained from the first study addressing the output metaphor.

Rationale

The interaction metaphors and usage environments would determine how the information output of the INSPIRE system is perceived by its users. Thus, it was necessary to quantify output quality as a function of the metaphor (agent factor) and the usage environment (environmental and functional factor). To get an analytic but still valid insight, we designed three application-oriented listening-only experiments (A1, A2, and A3), each addressing one of the three usage environments (home, office, and car, respectively):

Home environment (A1). Tested aspects were the influence of the system voice and the metaphor (agent factor) and the influence of background noise (environmental factor), as well as differences between the listening-only (A1) and interaction situation (A4).

Office environment (A2). Simulating remote access to the system via telephone. Tested aspects were different transmission channel degradations, user interfaces, and background noise effects (environmental factors).

Car environment (A3). Tested aspects were different transmission channel degradations, system robustness to background engine noise (environmental factors), and the influence of performing a parallel driving task (functional factor).

The use of somehow "neutralized" listening-only tests allowed a relatively large number of test conditions—and consequently factor levels—to be evaluated in one experiment. The use of realistic settings—including additional experimental tasks apart from the quality judgment—ensured that the measurements would be valid for the considered application scenario.

In a second step, we analyzed the interaction quality of the best-performing output metaphor. For this purpose, an interaction experiment (A4) was carried out to investigate the impact of output quality on interaction and usability-related quality aspects, and to better take into account functional factors. This interaction experiment was limited to the home environment and to only one (best-performing) system voice.

Experimental Design

When the INSPIRE system is used to operate home devices, speech output coincides with direct feedback (an action) from the addressed device. For example, the system prompt "I will open the blinds. Please say stop when it is bright enough!" is linked to an opening action of the blinds, which may directly influence perception of the prompt—and thus its quality. This aspect was taken into account in the experimental setup of the home environment, whereas it was irrelevant in the office and car environments (because of the missing device feedback).

During the interaction experiment, A4, all devices were operated by the experimenter replacing the device interface, according to the dialogue system state. During the listening-only experiment, A1, the experimenter manually operated the addressed devices from the control room so that a link between the system prompt and the device action became obvious to the user in both situations. Details of the experimental setup and the test design can be found in [35].

For the listening-only situation (A1–A3), typical prompts of about 5 seconds were generated according to predefined templates, to obtain a comparable degree of complexity. Five natural and one synthesized voice were used in the listening-only experiments, A1–A3, and only the best-performing natural voice in the interaction experiment, A4. The prompts were played back through typical devices (loudspeakers in the home environment, hand-sets and hands-free terminals in the office and car environments) at a defined listening level of 79 dB, with or without background noise (music of 6 dB signal-to-noise ratio in the home environment and car noise in the car environment). To produce a stable metaphor impression in the home environment, experiment A1 was split into three sessions, each corresponding to one metaphor and lasting approximately 15 minutes.

In experiment A3, stimuli were presented in a car simulator. Speech samples were presented via the loudspeaker on the dashboard, and the background engine noise was inserted by loudspeakers positioned outside. To make participants feel they were in a realistic situation, a road scenario with a specific driving task was designed, including sharp curves, a lead car driving with variable speed, road signs, trucks parked along the road, and so forth. Such "road events" were chosen to represent a varying degree of cognitive load for the driver.

The driving task was divided into 24 driving units of approximately 1 minute each. Twelve of these units contained a special road event; the remaining 12, no special event (here the subjects just drove the car on a more or less straight road with minor curves). During a driving unit, one of the 24 speech samples was presented. The samples were distributed to two sessions of approximately 45 minutes, separated by a short pause. The test in the driving simulator was preceded by a 10-minute introduction to familiarize the subjects with the range of conditions to be encountered in the test, as well as with driving in a simulator to prevent motion sickness.

For rendering the listening-only situation realistic, test participants should be stimulated to pay attention to the content of the speech prompt (i.e., what is said), and not only to its surface form (how it is said). To reach this goal, we asked participants to indicate the device (multiple-choice task) and the function (open-answer) addressed by a particular prompt before judging its quality. The procedure was similar to the one proposed in [25] for assessing synthesized speech in telephone applications.

After the identification task, participants had to rate four characteristics of what they heard, on four continuous rating scales capturing overall quality, listening effort, voice pleasantness, and voice adequacy (for the given system). In the car environment (experiment A3), subjects were instructed to drive as they would normally in their own car.

After each driving unit in which a speech sample was presented, the subjects had to stop driving and give ratings to the above-mentioned questions (the stop was insured by introducing a red traffic light). In this environment, questions were presented on a touch screen mounted on the dashboard.

In the interaction experiment, A4, participants had to carry out three interactions with the INSPIRE system. Each interaction corresponded to a specific metaphor and was guided by a scenario explained to the participants before the test. A scenario consisted of a sequence of 9 to 11 tasks that were embedded in a short story. After each interaction, the subject had to fill in a questionnaire with 37 judgments grouped under 7 quality categories (overall impression, reaching the desired goals, communication with the system, system behavior, dialogue, personal impression, usability). This questionnaire was inspired by the SASSI methodology [22] as well as by our own experiments described in [33]; it was very similar to the one recommended in [26]. Further details on the experimental design can be found in [34].

Insights

The experimental results will not be discussed in detail here, but the interested reader is referred to [35].

Among the three quality factors addressed in the experimental series, agent and environmental factors had the most significant influence on quality judgments. The system voice seems to have been the dominant agent factor. In addition, an effect of the system metaphor could be observed but it was not consistent for all voices. This may have been due to similarities in our implementation of the three metaphors (including the lack of auditory-visual synchrony), or our questionnaire may not have been the right method to capture preference. The behavior of test subjects operating the system in a larger home environment (additional experiments were carried out in the Philips HomeLab, Eindhoven, The Netherlands) showed that a considerable advantage of a system that can be addressed from any position in the house is lost when the test subject has to address a screen or device at a fixed location, as was the case for the talking head and intelligent device metaphors. This effect could not be observed in our (small) living-room environment. It pinpoints that participants' behavior might be included as an additional measure of interaction quality.

Among the environmental factors, all user interface, background noise, and transmission channel degradations provoked significant effects. However, changing the test environment as a whole did not clarify where the observed differences in the overall ratings, collected after each experiment, stemmed from: Signal quality may have been an important factor, along with the system functionality displayed to the user (which was reduced in the office and car environments). The functional factors did not show a significant effect on the collected judgments; this may have been due to the quite realistic design of the listening-only test, which seems to be representative of the quality of speech output in an interactive situation as well.

14.6.4 Evaluation of the Quality of an Embodied Conversational Agent

As mentioned, the first series of experiments did not show a preference for the talking head metaphor. The reason for this might be found in the particular implementation of the corresponding ECA, which lacked synchrony of voice and lip movements. As a consequence, we are currently analyzing the relationship between the visual and the acoustic quality of such ECAs concerning the resulting output quality and their impact on both interaction quality and system personality, as indicated in Figure 14.2.

Rationale

In this case, the taxonomy was used to specify the research question even before finding relevant quality aspects and appropriate metrics for assessment. Because the taxonomy shows that there is a potential influence of interaction quality on an ECA's hedonic qualities as well as on its perceived usability, these two relationships between pragmatic and hedonic quality aspects were addressed in this series of experiment.

To examine these relationships, we decided to analyze three different talking heads, each combined with two different speech synthesis systems. The questions addressed in this second series are as follows:

- How important are appearance, animation, voice, and synchrony for overall output quality?
- Which voice is preferred?
- How important is intonation for output quality?
- In a smart-home setting is a human-like head preferred over an artificial head?
- Does the particular combination of voice and head have to fit, or do best head quality and best voice quality always lead to best overall output quality?

The series is currently running at Deutsche Telekom Labs, TU Berlin, and MARCS Auditory Laboratories, University of Western Sydney. It will ultimately consist of four experiments:

1. An evaluation of several ECAs in a neutralized listening-and-watching-only situation (B1). *Tested aspects*: Impact of system voice and head (agent factors) on output quality.
2. A repetition of experiment B1 as Web-based (B2), rendering the test environment uncontrolled. *Tested aspects*: Evaluation methodology—namely, the impact of the test environment.
3. An evaluation of the best-performing ECAs in a simulated, but not fully interactive, setting (B3). *Tested aspects*: Impact of the degree of interactivity on perceived output quality and system personality.
4. An evaluation of the best-performing ECAs in a fully interactive home environment (B4). *Tested aspects*: Interaction quality as a function of system voice and head (agent factors) and its relationship to output quality alone.

So far, only experiment B1 has been fully analyzed and will be described in the following sections. The Web experiment (B2) is a replication of B1 with a reduced duration because of using either the first part (blocked set of stimuli) or the second part (every stimulus randomized) of the original B1. Those stimuli identified as strongly divergent in their speech quality because of the TTS realization of their linguistic content are excluded. As a result of Web experiments, we expect more information about the questionnaires used and—in comparison with B1—whether or not a Web-based experiment will yield any valid results. This will greatly simplify evaluating ECA parameter modifications.

In experiment B3 three aspects are analyzed:

1. *Form appropriateness*, especially with respect to system prompts and how their rating may be influenced by the system output component.
2. *Output quality*, apart from visual, auditory, and overall quality, fit and synchrony are assessed as well as the perceived system personality in terms of likability, naturalness, and how engaging it is.
3. *Interaction quality* itself, with respect to the influence of the output component and the influence of errors intentionally that are introduced (functional factors).

In experiment B4, we will analyze the influence of the environment (realistic living room) compared to experiment B3 (test cabinet). We will address the question of whether or not a visual output component like the head metaphor is preferred in the smart-home environment, and how strong the influence of "interaction quality" on "output quality" is.

Experimental Design

In experiment B1, each head is combined with two different speech synthesis systems, resulting in a 2×3 within-subject design, with the factors "voice" and "head" being manipulated. The three heads are of different appearance as follows:

- The ECA from the Thinking Head (TH) project [45], which is based on a 3D model with the texture created from pictures of the Australian artist STELARC; it moves, smiles, and winks when speaking.
- The Modular Audiovisual Speech SYnthesizer (MASSY) developed by TU Berlin [15].
- A German text-to-audiovisual speech synthesis system based on speaker cloning (Clone) using motion capture [14].

The latter two heads are immobile (apart from a few lower face movements) and show no particular expressions. The speech synthesis systems used are the Modular Architecture for Research on Speech sYnthesis (MARY) [42], based on hidden Markov models, and the Mbrola system [31], based on diphone synthesis. For both speech synthesis systems, a male German voice was used.

Ten sentences were recorded offline as videos for all 2×3 voice–head combinations, resulting in 60 stimuli for experiment B1. They are of variable phrase length, contain both questions and statements, and originate from the smart-home domain. Participants are seated in front of a computer screen in a quiet room and presented with the 60 stimuli. After each stimulus, they are asked first to answer one content-related question and then to rate speech quality, visual quality, and overall quality.

The answer format used is a five-point rating scale, with the descriptions "very good," "good," "undecided," "bad," and "very bad."

Next a set of six stimuli followed by a questionnaire is presented for the voice–head combinations. This questionnaire assesses the overall quality of each combination, and the subject's overall impression, described using 25 semantic-differential items. Every item is rated on a five-point scale, with the poles described by antonyms. These items derive from a questionnaire described in [1].

Finally, example stimuli of all six conditions are simultaneously displayed as frozen images on one screen in random order. The participants can replay the stimuli by clicking on the images and are then asked to order them according to their preference, giving ranks from "1—worst liked" to "6—best liked." Each number can only be given once, resulting in six ranks.

Insights

Experiment B1 is the basis for the remaining three tests. The questionnaires used are evaluated for reliability and completeness. As a first result, we decided to assess synchrony and how well head and voice fit together in the following experiments as well. To reduce the size of experiments B2, B3, and B4, and therefore the number of participants needed, only the two best rated heads are kept.

The results of experiment B1 show that the agent factors "voice" and "head" are perceived and rated separately. As a consequence, both resulting quality aspects (visual and auditory) combine to perceived output quality, whereas the appropriateness of the particular combination is irrelevant. However, this is expected to change with the degree of interaction in experiments B3 and B4.

Assessing the impact of interaction on perceived output quality is the main goal for test B3. Furthermore, most of the participants strongly agree on the rating and ranking of the six combinations. In an interaction scenario, the judgments might be far more diverse. This question will be addressed in experiment B3. First impressions suggest that participants differ in which head is acceptable as a dialogue partner at home. If confirmed, such a result can be incorporated in the presented taxonomy by weighting system personality and output quality accordingly.

14.6.5 Comparison of Questionnaires

A wide range of established usability evaluation methods is currently available, most of them designed for unimodal systems.

Rationale

The aim of this study was to compare the extent to which established and standardized methods originally developed for unimodal systems are appropriate for evaluating multimodal systems. Data from different sources was collected to measure the quality and usability of two multimodal and one unimodal system. Several standardized questionnaires were employed to assess users' opinions. Additionally, log data was collected and then analyzed to determine in which aspects different established questionnaires lead to the same result and where inconsistencies can be found across questionnaires. The log data was used to validate these results.

Experimental Design

The multimodal systems adopted for the test were a PDA (Fujitsu-Siemens Pocket LOOX T830) and a tablet PC (Samsung Q1-Pro 900 Casomii). Both could be operated via voice control and a graphical user interface with touch screen. Additionally, the PDA could be operated via motion control. A unimodal system (a conventional PC with mouse and keyboard) was used as a control condition. The MediaScout system was the same for all devices.

Users performed five types of tasks: seven navigation tasks, six tasks where checkboxes had to be marked or unmarked, four tasks where an option from a drop-down list had to be selected, three tasks where a button had to be pressed, and one task where a phone number had to be entered. The questionnaires used were AttrakDiff [19], the System Usability Scale (SUS) [9], the Software Usability Measurement Inventory (SUMI) [28], and SASSI [22]. SUMI, SASSI, and AttrakDiff were used in their original form, whereas SUS was adapted for voice control by replacing the "system" with "voice control."

All questionnaires except SUS consisted of different subscales assessing different quality aspects (see Table 14.1). Regarding SUMI, an additional global scale could be calculated based on half of the items. For AttrakDiff, the attractiveness scale was assumed to measure overall quality. The authors of SASSI did not mention how to calculate a global scale; thus, the mean of all scales (based on items coded in the same direction) was assumed to be a global measure.

Table 14.1 Subscales of AttrakDiff, SASSI, and SUMI

AttrakDiff	SASSI	SUMI
Attractiveness (ATT)	System response accuracy (ACC)	Affect (AFF)
Hedonic qualities—identity (HQ-I)	Annoyance (ANN)	Control (CON)
Hedonic qualities—stimualtion (HQ-S)	Cognitive demand (CD)	Efficiency (EFF)
Pragmatic qualities (PQ)	Habitability (HAB)	Learnability (LEA)
	Likability (LIK)	Helpfulness (HEL)
	Speed (SPE)	

The order of the questionnaires was randomized. With the help of questionnaires designed or adapted to cover speech-based applications (SASSI and SUS), ratings were collected only for the two multimodal systems (PDA and tablet PC).

Each test session took approximately three hours. Each participant performed all tasks with each system, and was verbally instructed to perform the tasks with a given modality and to repeat them for every modality supported by the specific system used. After that, the tasks were presented again and the participants could freely choose the interaction modality. Finally, they were asked to fill out the questionnaires in order to rate the previously tested system. This procedure was repeated for each of the three systems. To balance fatigue and learning effects, the order of the systems was randomized. After the third system, a final questionnaire on overall impressions and preferences was filled out.

During the experimental session, log data and psycho-physiological data were recorded. Task duration as a measure of efficiency was assessed with the log files and was, for each system, averaged over all tasks. For the results reported here, only data from the test block in which the users could freely choose modalities was analyzed. Since the participants were already familiar with the systems and all modalities, it can be assumed that they used the modality they most preferred. The scales and subscales for each questionnaire were calculated according to the instructions in the respective handbook [9, 19, 22, 28]. All questionnaire items that were negatively poled were recoded so that higher values indicated better ratings.

Insights

We report here some of the findings of the analysis which relate to the questionnaires used in the experiment, as well as to the relationship between questionnaire and performance metrics.

Comparison of questionnaire results

The SUMI ratings were most inconsistent with the results of all other questionnaires. The best system according to SUMI was the PDA, whereas the tablet PC got the highest ratings on the AttrakDiff overall scale (attractiveness) as well as on the SASSI global scale. SUS revealed no significant difference between systems.

Further differences were shown for the subscales: Only on SUMI was the PDA rated best regarding efficiency. The results of the AttrakDiff pragmatic quality scale, which is associated with efficiency and with the speed scale of SASSI, were in sharp contrast to SUMI's results. Both AttrakDiff and SASSI indicated that the tablet PC was most efficient and the PDA least efficient. Furthermore, the SUMI affect scale (on which the PDA was rated best) was inconsistent with similar scales on the other questionnaires. AttrakDiff, for example, implied that the tablet PC had more hedonic qualities than the other systems. The SASSI scales likability and annoyance also pointed to the tablet PC as the system most fun to use. Only for the unimodal system were AttrakDiff and SUMI results consistent.

Considering these results, it remains unclear which system is most usable. It is rather shown that questionnaires designed for unimodal systems are not well suited to multimodal systems, since they seem to measure different constructs. The most coherent questionnaires of our study were AttrakDiff and SASSI.

Comparison of quality and performance metrics

Subjective data (questionnaire ratings) and performance data (task duration) showed concordance only to a limited extent. The questionnaire ratings of SUMI were highly inconsistent with those of the other questionnaires as well as the task duration metric: Both the global scale and the efficiency scale of SUMI correlated positively with task duration. This means that the longer the task duration, the better the SUMI rating for these two aspects, which is implausible especially in light of the other results. In contrast the AttrakDiff pragmatic scale, for example, showed the highest agreement with task duration. Thus, it seems to measure the construct it was developed for. A similar conclusion can be drawn from the SASSI results: Ratings on the speed scale matched the task duration data. Regarding the global scales, all questionnaires except SUMI showed no significant correlation with task duration. According to these results, perceived global usability was hardly affected by system efficiency.

The correlations between quality and performance metrics were in line with the comparison of questionnaire results cited above. Again, AttrakDiff and SASSI were in the best concordance and were not in line with SUMI results. A possible explanation could be that the type of rating scale used in the respective questionnaires was applicable to the MediaScout system. AttrakDiff uses the semantic differential, which seems to be applicable to all systems. Rather than direct questions, it consists of pairs of bipolar adjectives that are not linked to particular system functions. SASSI uses direct questions but is specifically developed for the evaluation of voice control systems and may therefore be more suitable for multimodal systems including voice control than questionnaires developed for GUI-based systems only. For SUMI, we included all questions, although some of them are only appropriate for the evaluation of market-ready interfaces; these inappropriate questions may have affected the SUMI results.

In summary, some of the questionnaires used in this study showed consistent correlations to each other as well as to performance metrics. Others seemed to contradict the metrics, but such findings may have been partly caused by the specific questionnaires used, which might have lacked construct validity for the system assessed here. Our conclusion is that care should be taken in selecting the right method for assessing quality aspects. There is a need for a more reliable, valid, and specific questionnaire addressing multimodal interfaces. In light of the reported results, AttrakDiff provides a proper basis for this purpose. Table 14.2 summarizes the questionnaires used and their ability and appropriateness for assessing different quality aspects of our taxonomy.

Table 14.2 Comparison of Questionnaires and Their Suitability for Assessing Quality Aspects

Subscales	Questionnaire			
	SUS	AttrakDiff	SUMI*	SASSI
Learnability	●	◑ Subscale: PQ	● Subscale: LEA	● Subscale: LIK, HAB
Effectiveness	●	● Subscale: PQ	◑ Subscale: CON, HEL	◑ Subscale: ACC, HAB
Effectivity	●	● Subscale: PQ	● Subscale: EFF	◑ Subscale: SPE, CD
Intuitivity†	○	○	○	○
Aesthetics	○	● Subscale: HQ-S, ATT	◑ Subscale: AFF	○
System Personality†	○	◑ Subscale: HQ-S	○	◑ Subscale: ANN, LIK
Appeal	○	● Subscale: HQ-S, HQ-I	◑ Subscale: AFF, LIK	◑ Subscale: ANN, LIK

● = covered, ◑ = partly covered, ○ = not covered.
*In general, the SUMI questionnaire is not recommended for evaluating multimodal systems.
†Questionnaires assessing intuitivity and system personality are currently under development at Deutsche Telekom Labs.

14.7 CONCLUSIONS AND FUTURE WORK

The presented taxonomy gives empirical results and provides definitions of factors and aspects as well as information about their relationships. On this common ground, comparable evaluation can be performed, its results can be identified and categorized, and metrics for specific purposes (or missing metrics) can be identified. The presented metrics are not exhaustive, however, and many of the established ones have not yet been sufficiently evaluated for their applicability to multimodal systems. In fact, the last example highlights that there is no standard questionnaire that covers all quality aspects of such systems. Because current systems cover a wide range of applications and domains, we anticipate that an open framework will be needed to enable meaningful evaluation for specific contexts.

To make the best possible use of the taxonomy, further evaluation results are needed in order to provide information on how to interpret the proposed metrics. A comparison of individual evaluations on the basis of this taxonomy will help uncover systematic effects of quality factors on quality aspects. With such information, the relevant quality aspects can be identified for a given application, and the relationships between them (as indicated by arrows in Figure 14.1) and the particular influence of quality factors can be weighted accordingly. We foresee a weighted network with quality factors as input and quality aspects as output. Such a network will be very helpful for target-oriented design and optimization of future multimodal dialogue systems.

ACKNOWLEDGMENT

The work described in this chapter has been supported by the Deutsche Forschungsgemeinschaft (DFG), grant MO 1038/6-1. Parts of the experiments have been carried out within the framework of the INSPIRE project (IST-2001-32746) and the ARC and National Health and Medical Research Council Special Initiatives "Thinking Systems" (TS0669874). Contributions from these projects, as well as all support from the respective colleagues, are gratefully acknowledged.

REFERENCES

[1] Adcock A, Van Eck R. Reliability and factor structure of the Attitude Toward Tutoring Agent Scale (ATTAS). Journal of Interactive Learning Research 2005;16(2):195–217.

[2] Augusto JC. Ambient intelligence: Basic concepts and applications. In: Selected Papers from ICSOFT'06. Springer Verlag; 2008. p. 14–24.

[3] Bennett CL, Black AW. The Blizzard challenge 2006. In: Satellite Workshop, INTERSPEECH 2006.

[4] Bernsen NO. Multimodality in language and speech systems—from theory to design support tool. In: Granström B, House D, Karlsson I, editors. Multimodality in Language and Speech Systems. Kluwer Academic Publishers; 2002. p. 93–148.

[5] Bernsen NO, Dybkjær H, Dybkjær L. Designing Interactive Speech Systems—From First Ideas to User Testing. Springer; 1998.

[6] Bernsen NO, Dybkjær L, Kiilerich S. Evaluating conversation with Hans Christian Andersen. In: Proc. LREC 2004. p. 1011–4.

[7] Bevan N. Usability is quality of use. In: Proc. HCII 1995. Elsevier; 1995. p. 349–54.

[8] Borg G. Psychophysical bases of perceived exertion. Med Sci Sports Exerc 14:377–81.

[9] Brooke J. SUS: A "quick and dirty" usability scale. In: Jordan PW, Thomas B, Weerdmeester BA, McClelland BA, editors. Usability Evaluation in Industry. Taylor & Francis; 1996. p. 189–94.

[10] Chateau N, Gros L, Durin V, Macé A. Redrawing the link between customer satisfaction and speech quality. In: Proc. 2nd ISCA/DEGA Tutorial and Research Workshop on Perceptual Quality of Systems. 2006. p. 88–94.

[11] Dybkjær L, Bernsen NO, Minker W. Evaluation and usability of multimodal spoken language dialogue systems. Speech Comm 2004;43:33–54.

[12] Engelbrecht K-P, Kruppa M, Möller S, Quade M. MeMo workbench for semi-automated usability testing. In: Proc. INTERSPEECH 2008. 2008. p. 1662–5.

[13] Eurescom Project. P.807 Deliverable 1. In: Jupiter II—Usability, Performability and Interoperability Trials in Europe. European Institute for Research and Strategic Studies in Telecommunications; 1998.

[14] Fagel S, Bailly G, Elisei F. Intelligibility of natural and 3D-cloned German speech. In: Proc. Audio-Visual Speech Processing Workshop (AVSP 2007). Hilvarenbeek; 2007.

[15] Fagel S, Clemens C. An articulation model for audiovisual speech synthesis – determination, adjustment, evaluation. Speech Comm 2004;44:141–54.

[16] Fraser N. Assessment of interactive systems. In: Gibbon D, Moore R, Winski R, editors. Handbook on Standards and Resources for Spoken Language Systems. Mouton de Gruyter; 1997. p. 564–615.

[17] Gibbon D, Mertins I, Moore RK, editors. Handbook of Multimodal and Spoken Dialogue Systems. Kluwer Academic Publishers;

[18] Grice H. Logic and conversation. In: Cole P, Morgan JL, editors. Syntax and Semantics, Vol. 3: Speech Acts. Academic Press; 1995. p. 41–58.

[19] Hassenzahl M, Burmester M, Koller F. AttrakDiff: Ein Fragebogen zur Messung wahrgenommener hedonischer und pragmatischer Qualität. In: Ziegler J, Szwillus G, editors. Mensch & Computer 2003. Teubner; 2003. p. 187–96.

[20] Hassenzahl M, Platz A, Burmester M, Lehner K. Hedonic and ergonomic quality aspects determine a software's appeal. In: Proc. CHI 2000. Den Haag; 2000. p. 201–8.

[21] Hermann F, Niedermann I, Peissner M, Henke K, Naumann A. Users interact differently: Towards a usability-oriented taxonomy. In: Jacko J, editor. Interaction Design and Usability, Proc. HCII 2007, vol. 1. Springer; 2007. p. 812–7.

[22] Hone KS, Graham R. Towards a tool for the Subjective Assessment of Speech System Interfaces (SASSI). Natural Language Engineering 2000;6(3/4):287–303.

[23] ISO 9241-11. Ergonomic Requirements for Office Work with Visual Display Terminals (VDTs): Part 11: Guidance on Usability. International Organization for Standardization; 1999.

[24] ITU-T Suppl. 24 to P-Series Rec. Parameters Describing the Interaction with Spoken Dialogue Systems. International Telecommunication Union; 2005.

[25] ITU-T Rec. P.85. A Method for Subjective Performance Assessment of the Quality of Speech Voice Output Devices. International Telecommunication Union; 1994.

[26] ITU-T Rec. P.851. Subjective Quality Evaluation of Telephone Services Based on Spoken Dialogue Systems. International Telecommunication Union; 2003.

[27] Jekosch U. Voice and Speech Quality Perception. Assessment and Evaluation. Springer; 2005.

[28] Kirakowski J, Corbett M. SUMI: The Software Usability Measurement Inventory. British Journal of Educational Technology 1993;24(3):210–2.

[29] Lamel L, Bennacef S, Gauvain JL, Dartigues H, Temem JN. User evaluation of the MASK kiosk. Speech Comm 2002;38:131–9.

[30] Mandryk RL, Inkpen K, Calvert TW. Using psycho-physiological techniques to measure user experience with entertainment technologies. Behaviour and Information Technology 2006; 25(2):141–58.

[31] Mbrola Project. *http://tcts.fpms.ac.be/synthesis/mbrola.html*; 2008 [last accessed 05/22/2008].

[32] Möller S. A new taxonomy for the quality of telephone services based on spoken dialogue systems. In: Proc. 3rd SIGdial Workshop on Discourse and Dialogue; 2002. p. 142–53.

[33] Möller S. Quality of Telephone-Based Spoken Dialogue Systems. Springer; 2005.

[34] Möller S. Messung und Vorhersage der Effizienz bei der Interaktion mit Sprachdialogdiensten. In: Fortschritte der Akustik—DAGA 2006. Braunschweig; 2006. p. 463-4.

[35] Möller S, Krebber J, Smeele P. Evaluating the speech output component of a smart-home system. Speech Comm 2005;48:1-27.

[36] Möller S, Ward NG. A framework for model-based evaluation of spoken dialog systems. In: Proc. 9th SIGdial Workshop on Discourse and Dialogue. Association for Computational Linguistics; 2008. p. 182-9.

[37] Mostefa D, Garcia M-N, Choukri K. Evaluation of multimodal components within CHIL: The evaluation packages and results. In: Proc. LREC 2006. 2006. p. 915-8.

[38] Naumann A, Hurtienne J, Israel JH, Mohs C, Kindsmüller MC, Meyer HA, et al. Intuitive use of user interfaces: Defining a vague concept. In: Harris D, editor. Engineering Psychology and Cognitive Ergonomics, Proc. HCII 2007, vol. 13. LNAI 4562. Springer; 2007. p. 128-36.

[39] Nielsen J. Usability Engineering. Academic Press;

[40] Pallett D, Fiscus J, Fisher W, Garofolo J. Benchmark tests for the DARPA spoken language program. In: Proc. DARPA Human Language Technology Workshop; 1993. p. 7-18.

[41] Schnotz W, Bannert M, Seufert T. Towards an integrative view of text and picture comprehension: Visualization effects on the construction of mental models. In: Otero J, Graesser A, Leon JA, editors. The Psychology of Science Text Comprehension. Erlbaum; 2002. p. 385-416.

[42] Schroeder M, Trouvain J. The German text-to-speech synthesis system MARY: A tool for research, development and teaching. International Journal on Speech Technology 2003;6:365-77.

[43] Shani G, Rokach L, Meisles A, Naamani L, Piratla NM, Ben-Shimon D. Establishing user profiles in the MediaScout recommender system. In: Proc. IEEE Symposium on Computational Intelligence and Data Mining (CIDM 2007). p. 470-6.

[44] Stelmaszweska H, Fields B, Blandford A. Conceptualising user hedonic experience. In: Reed DJ, Baxter G, Blythe M, editors. In: Proc. ECCE-12, Living and Working with Technology. EACE; 2004. p. 83-9.

[45] Thinking Systems. Australian Research Council/National Health & Medical Research Council Special Initiative, *http://thinkinghead.edu.au/* [last accessed 05/22/2008].

[46] Vilnai-Yavetz I, Rafaeli A, Schneider Yaacov C. Instrumentality, aesthetics, and symbolism of office design. Environment and Behavior 2005;37(4):533-51.

[47] De Waard D. The Measurement of Drivers' Mental Workload. PhD thesis, University of Gröningen; 1996.

[48] Wahlster W. SmartKom: Foundations of Multimodal Dialogue Systems. Springer; 2006.

[49] Walker MA, Litman DJ, Kamm CA, Abella A. PARADISE: A framework for evaluating spoken dialogue agents. In: Kaufmann M, editor. In: Proc. ACL/EACL 35th Ann. Meeting of the Assoc. for Computational Linguistics; 1997. p. 271-80.

[50] Wickens CD. Engineering Psychology and Human Performance. HarperCollins; 1992.

[51] Zimbardo PG. Psychologie. Springer; 1995.

Smart Environment Applications

New Frontiers in Machine Learning for Predictive User Modeling

15

Ashish Kapoor

Microsoft Research, Redmond, Washington

ABSTRACT

Ambient intelligence often requires sensing and prediction of internal user state. However, reliably recognizing internal user state during interaction with a computer or a smart interface is a challenge, often complicated by sensor noise and drop-out and by the difficulty of obtaining labels for the true states involved. We describe a range of recent advances in machine learning that can help alleviate these problems. Techniques such as semisupervised and active learning specifically address the issue of building predictive user models when the training data is scarce and relatively hard to collect. We discuss these techniques in the context of many different applications that require systems that predict users' affective and cognitive states.

Key words: user modeling, Gaussian process, affect recognition.

15.1 INTRODUCTION

Classification is a key task in many domains, including user modeling, affective computing, and machine perception. Consider, for example, the task of building a predictive model that recognizes the affective and cognitive states of a user. Various kinds of user information can be observed through sensors, such as a video camera, a posture-sensing chair, and other hardware devices or software.

One of the main goals of a pattern recognition system is to associate a class label with different observations, where the labels correspond to affective states such as interest, boredom, and so forth. Similar are activity recognition scenarios, where the aim is to recognize different activities happening in the surroundings using a variety of sensors. For example, with sensors we can obtain observations that describe position information via a global positioning system (GPS), the status of a cellular phone (that is why cell towers are visible), pedometer readings, and the like. Based on these observations, the task in an activity recognition scenario is to identify activities, such as driving to the office, sitting, or walking home. The same analogy can be extended to low-level vision tasks such as object detection. Given an image, detection can be posed as a classification problem where the aim is to identify an object category.

Traditional models of supervised classification aim to learn a decision boundary given a set of observations. However, many scenarios in user modeling far exceed this simplistic model. For example, in many predictive modeling scenarios information from multiple sensors needs to be fused to recover the variable of interest. Similarly, many practical applications in affective computing, activity recognition, and machine vision have the characteristic of having very little training data that is labeled. They usually have much data (e.g., video), but most of it is unlabeled because labeling is tedious, costly, and error-prone. Discriminative modeling techniques such as support vector machines, perceptrons, and logistic regression are popular ways to perform classification tasks; however, it is nontrivial to apply such techniques directly to the scenarios just mentioned.

In this chapter we explore a unified framework that provides a natural extension of supervised classification methods to sensor fusion, semisupervised classification, and active learning. In particular, we discuss advances in machine learning by focusing on Gaussian process (GP) classification, a Bayesian framework for learning discriminative models, and its application to various user-modeling scenarios. One major advantage of viewing different methods in a single Bayesian framework is that we first can use the framework for usually nontrivial model selection tasks. Second, we can now derive new methods for discriminative modeling, such as semisupervised learning and sensor fusion, by exploiting the modularity in the proposed unified framework.

The highly challenging problem addressed in this chapter is motivated by real-world issues in affective computing, activity recognition, and machine perception, and it includes the scenarios described previously. There is often multi-sensory data, most of which is often fairly expensive and cumbersome for labeling. We will center our discussion on four different applications, which we describe below.

The structure of the chapter is organized as follows: Following the description of four real-world problems, we provide a short background on Gaussian process classification. Next, we discuss sensor fusion and semisupervised and active learning, focusing on application of these techniques to real-world user-modeling tasks. We conclude the chapter with a brief discussion of future work.

15.1.1 Multimodal Affect Recognition

Affect recognition is a challenging task that entails combinations of multiple modalities to infer affective states. As a case study, we focus on an affect recognition system described in [9] that aims to recognize affective states such as interest by combining multiple channels. Figure 15.1(a) describes its architecture. Nonverbal behaviors are sensed through a camera, a pressure-sensing chair, a pressure mouse, and a device that measures skin conductance. The camera is equipped with infrared (IR) LEDs for structured lighting to help in real-time tracking of pupils and in extracting other features from the face. Similarly, the data sensed through the chair is used to extract information about postures. Features extracted from the subject's activity on the computer are sent to a multimodal pattern analyzer that combines all of the information to predict the current affective state.

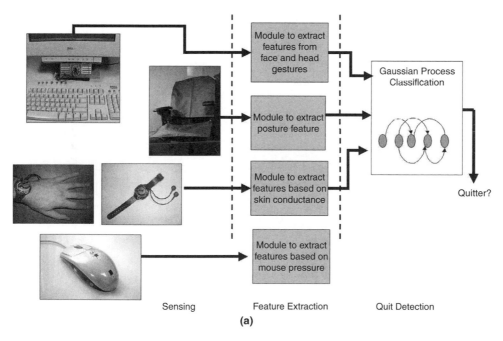

(a)

FIGURE 15.1

Four application scenarios that utilize (a) multimodal affect recognition,

(Continued)

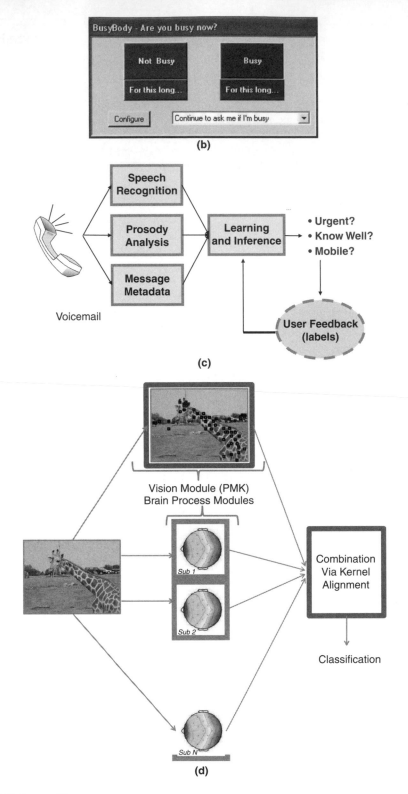

FIGURE 15.1—cont'd

(b) modeling interruptability, (c) voice mails classification, and (d) brain–computer interfaces for visual recognition.

15.1.2 Modeling Interruptability

The goal in this task is to build statistical models that predict the cost of interruptions and that use such predictions to mediate incoming alerts and communications. Methods and opportunities in this area were first presented in [7], which presented a cost–benefit analysis of alerts, weighing the urgency of messages against the cost of interruption as computed by a Bayesian model. In particular, the BusyBody system logs desktop events to build a predictive user model using supervision from the user. Figure 15.1(b) shows a request by BusyBody for input. Recorded events include keyboard and mouse activity, windows in focus, recent sequences of applications and window titles, and high-level statistics about the rates of switching among applications and windows. The system also considers several classes of contextual variables, including the time of day and the day of week, the name of the computer being used, the presence and properties of meetings drawn from an electronic calendar, and wireless signals. It employs a conversation-detection system as well, using a module that detects signals in the human-voice range of the audio spectrum.

15.1.3 Classifying Voice Mails

The aim here is to build a system that can classify voice messages in several ways, including whether the messages are urgent or nonurgent, whether the caller is close or not close to the person being called, and whether the caller is calling from a mobile phone [11]. Given a set of voice messages, a number of features based on prosody and message metadata are extracted. Prosodic features include syllable rate, pause structure, and pitch dynamics, and the metadata features indicate the day and time of the call and the size of the voice mail. Figure 15.1(c) shows the basic pipeline of the system.

15.1.4 Brain–Computer Interfaces for Visual Recognition

In this task, the focus is on the advantages of effectively combining two different processing modes to build better visual categorization models. The idea explores a new form of human involvement in machine learning by directly measuring a user's brain signals so as to provide information to the machine with little conscious effort. This approach is built on the realization that the human brain subconsciously processes different images in different ways, measurable by certain brain-sensing technologies even when the user is not trying to categorize images. The computer vision component is combined with a brain process module that measures EEG data from single or multiple users. This module complements the visual features with activations in the brain as images are presented to multiple subjects. Figure 15.1(d) depicts the overall framework for image categorization.

15.2 A QUICK PRIMER: GAUSSIAN PROCESS CLASSIFICATION

Gaussian process (GP) classification is related to kernel machines, such as support vector machines (SVMs) [3] and regularized least-squares classification (RLSC), and has been well explored in machine learning. In contrast to these methods, GPs provide probabilistic prediction estimates and thus are well suited for sensor fusion, semisupervised classification, and active learning. In this section we briefly review regression and classification with GP priors and describe our model choices.

Intuitively, the assumption behind GP is that similar data points should have the same class assignments/regression values; the similarity between two points $\mathbf{x}_i$ and $\mathbf{x}_j$ is defined via a kernel $k(\mathbf{x}_i, \mathbf{x}_j)$. A kernel matrix $\mathbf{K}$ with $K_{ij} = k(\mathbf{x}_i, \mathbf{x}_j)$ characterizes all pairwise similarities between the data points in $\mathbf{X} = \mathbf{X}_L \cup \mathbf{X}_U$. Examples of kernels include RBF, polynomial, and so forth. Given this smoothness constraint, the information from training data points $\mathbf{X}_L$ with labels $\mathbf{t}_L$ is combined in a probabilistic manner to compute a posterior distribution over a class label t_u of an unlabeled point $\mathbf{x}_u \in \mathbf{X}_U$. Specifically, under a zero-mean Gaussian noise model[1] parameterized with variance σ^2, this posterior distribution takes a very simple form and can be written as a Gaussian: $p(t_u|\mathbf{X}, \mathbf{t}_L) \sim N(\bar{t}_u, \Sigma_u + \sigma^2)$, where

$$\bar{t}_u = \mathbf{k}_L(\mathbf{x}_u)^T (\sigma^2 \mathbf{I} + \mathbf{K}_{LL})^{-1} \mathbf{t}_L$$
$$\Sigma_u = k(\mathbf{x}_u, \mathbf{x}_u) - \mathbf{k}_L(\mathbf{x}_u)^T (\sigma^2 \mathbf{I} + \mathbf{K}_{LL})^{-1} \mathbf{k}_L(\mathbf{x}_u)$$

$\mathbf{k}_L(\mathbf{x}_u)$ is the vector of kernel function evaluations with n labeled training points, and $\mathbf{K}_{LL} = \{k(\mathbf{x}_i, \mathbf{x}_j)\}$ is the training covariance, where $\mathbf{x}_i, \mathbf{x}_j$ are in the training set. The unlabeled point $\mathbf{x}_u$ can be classified according to the sign of $\bar{t}_u$.

One of the main advantages of the GP framework is that, instead of receiving only a label, we get the whole posterior distribution, which, as we will see next, is very useful for sensor fusion and active learning and provides a principled theoretic framework for handling various user-modeling scenarios. The computationally costly operation in GP inference is the inversion of $(\sigma^2 \mathbf{I} + \mathbf{K}_{LL})$, which has a time complexity of $O(n^3)$ for n training examples.

Note that non-Gaussian noise models that use nonlinear squashing functions can also be applied; examples include the logisitic and probit functions. However, since the likelihood is that Gaussian predictions cannot be computed analytically, one has to rely on numerical methods, such as MCMC [28] or approximations of the posterior, such as Laplace and expectation propagation [19].

---

[1]This method is referred to as least-squares classification in the literature (see Section 6.5 of [22]) and often demonstrates performance competitive with other kernel-based techniques.

15.3 SENSOR FUSION

Much recent research has focused on the general problem of combining information from multiple sources. Many feature fusion methods, including boosting [23] and bagging [1], concatenate features extracted from all modalities to form a single representation, and use this to train a classifier. An alternative is to use decision-level fusion [14], with its many possibilities for combining decisions from multiple modalities, including majority vote, sum, product, maximum, and minimum. However, it is difficult to predict which of these fixed rules will perform best. There are also methods that adaptively weigh and fuse the decisions in an expert-critic framework [8, 18, 20, 27]. Unfortunately, they require a large amount of training data.

Gaussian processes provide an elegant solution that enjoys flexibility in feature-level fusion and, similar to decision-level fusion, allows us to fuse arbitrary modalities in a sound manner. Intuitively, the idea is to fuse modalities at the kernel level; assuming that we have similarities (kernels) from different channels, our aim is to combine the kernel matrices such that the resulting kernel is "ideal" for classification [15]. Formally, given the kernels based on k different modalities $\mathbf{K}_1, \ldots, \mathbf{K}_k$, we can seek a linear combination:

$$\mathbf{K} = \sum_{i=1}^{k} \alpha_i \mathbf{K}_i \tag{15.1}$$

The GP framework provides much flexibility and incorporates many alternate parameterizations, including a product of kernels:

$$\mathbf{K} = \prod_{i=1}^{k} \mathbf{K}_i^{\alpha_i} \tag{15.2}$$

The goal in sensor fusion is to find *hyperparameters* $\alpha = \{\alpha_0, \ldots, \alpha_k\}$ that are consistent with the data and that provide maximal discriminative power. GPs provide a principled way to perform such optimization via maximum-likelihood estimation. The idea is to maximize the marginal likelihood or the evidence, which is nothing but the likelihood of the labeled data given the kernel hyperparameters $p(\mathbf{t}_L \mid \mathbf{X})$.

This methodology of tuning the hyperparameters is often called *evidence maximization*, and it has been a favorite tools for model selection. Evidence is a numerical quantity and signifies how well a model fits the given data. By comparing the evidence corresponding to the different models (or the hyperparameters that determine the model), we can choose the model and hyperparameters suitable for the task.

Formally we should choose a set of non-negative hyperparameters α that maximize the evidence: $\hat{\alpha} = \arg\max_\alpha \log[p(\mathbf{t}_L|\mathbf{X}, \alpha)]$. Note that the log evidence $\log(p(\mathbf{t}_L \mid \mathbf{X}, \alpha))$ can be written as a closed-form equation for the Gaussian noise model:

$$\log p(\mathbf{t}_L|\mathbf{X}, \alpha) = -\frac{1}{2}\mathbf{t}_L^T\left(\sigma^2\mathbf{I} + \mathbf{K}_{LL}\right)^{-1}\mathbf{t}_L - \frac{1}{2}\log|\sigma^2\mathbf{I} + \mathbf{K}_{LL}| - Const$$

The evidence maximization procedure entails nonconvex optimization; a convex alternative comprises minimizing a squared Frobenius norm of the difference between $\mathbf{K}$ and an "ideal" kernel $\mathbf{A}$: $\hat{\alpha} = \arg\max_{\alpha}\|\mathbf{K} - \mathbf{A}\|_F^2$. Here, an ideal kernel $\mathbf{A}$ can be defined such that the entry $A_{ij} = 1$ if and only if the ith and the jth examples have the same category label; otherwise, $A_{ij} = 0$. The proposed objective is a convex function, and similar criteria has been proposed in the context of Gaussian processes [21] and geostatistics [2].

Both of the just mentioned objectives can be maximized using nonlinear optimization techniques, such as gradient descent; consequently, we can find the correct parameters without the need for cross-validation to learn an ideal combination of kernels for sensor fusion. Next we describe some applications of this fusion scheme.

15.3.1 Multimodal Sensor Fusion for Affect Recognition

The goal in this application was to build a predictive model that would detect frustration in learners. The evaluation data consisted of sensory observations recorded from 24 middle school students aged 12 to 13. The raw data from the camera, the posture sensor, the skin conductance sensor, and the pressure mouse was first analyzed to extract 14 features that included various statistics of different signals (see [9] for data acquisition details). Out of the 24 children, 10 got frustrated and the rest persevered on the task; thus, the evaluation data set consisted of 24 samples with 10 belonging to one class and 14 to another. The challenge here was to combine the 14 multimodal features to build a good classifier.

To this end the work presented in [9] used a sensor fusion scheme based on Gaussian process classification. Specifically the product of kernels as shown in Equation (15.2) was used, where each individual kernel $\mathbf{K}_l$ was constructed using an RBF kernel with kernel width 1. The sensor fusion procedure thus found optimal hyperparameters α using evidence maximization that scales all modalities appropriately. Table 15.1 compares alternate methods and highlights the advantage of sensor fusion with GP when using a leave-one-out strategy to evaluate classification schemes.

Table 15.1 Multimodal Affect Recognition

Method	Clicked Frustration Button (10 samples)		Persevered on Task/ Clicked Help Button (14 samples)		Accuracy (%)
	Correct	Misses	Correct	Misses	
Random (control)	0	10	14	0	58.3
1-Nearest Neighbor	6	4	10	4	66.67
SVM (RBF Kernel)	6	4	11	3	70.83
Gaussian Process	8	2	11	3	**79.17**

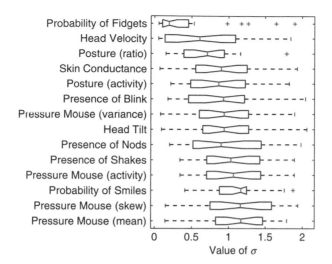

FIGURE 15.2

Finding the most discriminative features: the MATLAB boxplot of kernel hyperparameters, $\sigma_i = \frac{1}{\sqrt{\alpha_i}}$, optimized during the 24 leave-one-out runs. The lines in the middle of the box represent the median, the bounding box represents quartile values, the whiskers show the extent of the values, and the pluses (+) represent statistical outliers. A low value of σ_i corresponds to the high discriminative power of the feature.

Note that the value of optimized hyperparameters $[\alpha_1, \ldots \alpha_k]$ can be used to determine the most discriminative features. Figure 15.2 shows the MATLAB boxplot of the inverse kernel parameters (i.e., $\sigma_i = \frac{1}{\sqrt{\alpha_i}}$) corresponding to the different features obtained during the 24 leave-one-out runs of the algorithm. A low value of the inverse kernel parameter corresponds to high discriminative capability of the feature. From the boxplot we can see that fidgets, velocity of the head, and ratio of postures were the three most discriminative features. However, as mentioned in [9], there were many outliers for the fidgets, which implies that the they can be unreliable, possibly because of sensor failure and individual differences.

15.3.2 Combining Brain–Computer Interfaces with Computer Vision

The EEG data for these experiments was originally used in [24] and the analysis of the sensor fusion was presented in [13]. The EEG signals were originally captured using a Biosemi system at 2 kHz from 32 channels. The electrodes measured the electrical activity on the scalp (typically in the microvolt range) and represent a noisy stream of neural activity occurring in the brain. EEG responses were recorded from 14 users as they viewed the animal, face, and inanimate images. The data set consisted of two groups of images drawn from the three categories. The first group (*group-1*) consisted of 60 images per class shown to each of the subjects only once, whereas the second group (*group-2*) consisted of 20 images per class presented 10 times to each subject in a block-randomized fashion.

The information obtained from the EEG signals was used to compute an RBF kernel. Further, computer vision techniques were used to compute a pyramid match kernel (PMK) [5], which represented a similarity measure between images using SIFT descriptors extracted from the images at salient points. Instead of evidence maximization, these two streams of information were combined using the kernel alignment scheme based on the Frobenius norm. The final kernel was a weighted sum of individual base-level kernels as depicted in Equation (15.1).

It was found that the combined method shows significant gains over individual modalities for a battery of experiments. In particular, for studies with the same data used in the first experimental setup, results suggest that a combined strategy yields superior performance. Figure 15.3 shows that significant gains are obtained by combining the EEG signals with computer vision features. The combination with single presentations outperforms each individual channel, with an accuracy of 86.67% on

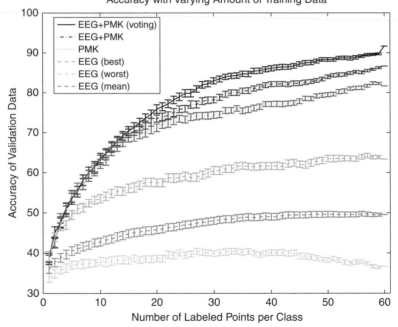

FIGURE 15.3

Performance of different modalities on the test set as the number of labeled examples is varied for a single presentation to the subject. The combined classification based on EEG and PMK significantly outperforms the individual modalities. Presenting the same image multiple times to the subject and voting among the classification outcomes further improves accuracy. The error bars represent standard deviation.

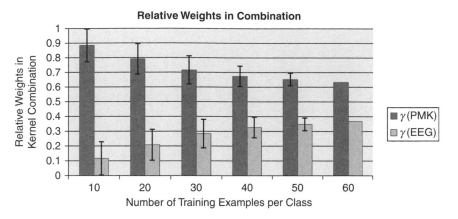

FIGURE 15.4

Comparison of relatives weights of the different modalities as the number of labeled examples per class is varied. The error bars represent represent standard deviation.

the 3-way classification task. This performance further improves to 91.67% when test images are presented multiple times.

Although the vision features consistently outperform the EEG features, the combination performs better than either, suggesting that the EEG signals and the base computer vision analysis complement one another. Furthermore, analysis of the feature weights α_i discovered by the combination algorithm highlights the complementary nature of the information provided by the human and computer vision modalities. Specifically, we look at relative weights defined as $\gamma(PMK) = \frac{\alpha_{PMK}}{\sum_i \alpha_i}$ and $\gamma(EEG) = 1 - \gamma(PMK)$. Figure 15.4 illustrates these relative weights averaged over 100 different runs for various amounts of training data. We can see that the vision modality has higher discriminative power overall, but that the weight of the EEG modality is highly significant and leads to significant gains in accuracy.

15.4 SEMISUPERVISED LEARNING

Often in machine learning problems there are a large number of data points, few of which are labeled. This usually happens because of the expense or difficulty obtaining labels. Given a set of mostly unlabeled data points, the goal in semisupervised learning is to predict their labels using the *complete* set of data points. By looking at both the labeled and the unlabeled data, the learning algorithm can exploit the distribution of data points to learn the classification boundary. Figure 15.5 graphically shows the characteristics of semisupervised classification and highlights its potential advantages.

There have been a number of approaches proposed in recent years for semisupervised learning. The spectrum of approaches spans generative models, support

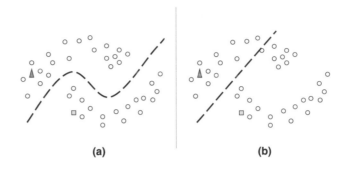

(a)   (b)

FIGURE 15.5

Advantages of (a) semisupervised over and (b) supervised learning methods. Supervised methods look only at labeled data, whereas semisupervised methods learn better classifiers by considering distribution over both labeled and unlabeled data.

vector machines (SVMs), graph-based techniques, co-training, information regularization, and so forth. Here we mostly discuss graph-based semisupervised classification, and we refer readers to [29] for a detailed survey.

Many of the approaches proposed recently are very closely connected and are either implicitly or explicitly based on regularization on graphs [25]. The key idea behind these methods is, again, similarity or kernels; however, the similarity is learned based on the distribution of both labeled and unlabeled data points. Specifically, the smoothness constraint is obtained by creating a graph with the labeled and unlabeled data points as the vertices and with edge weights encoding the similarity between them. The key intuition is that the similarity in the semisupervised kernel is based on the underlying graph structure and characterizes how likely it is that a bit of information will travel from one vertex to another. The idea of quantifying similarities between data points using these *random walks* is captured by the notion of a graph Laplacian.

Formally, given the original kernel $\mathbf{K}$, our goal is to construct a *semisupervised kernel*, $\mathbf{K}_{\text{semi}}$, which accounts for the distribution of both labeled and unlabeled data. This is achieved by first forming an undirected graph over the data points. The data points are the nodes of the graph, and edge weights between them are based on $\mathbf{K}$. Let $\mathbf{G}$ be a diagonal matrix with the diagonal entries $\mathbf{G}_{ii} = \sum_{j,j \neq i} K_{ij}$; then construct the combinatorial Laplacian ($\Delta = \mathbf{G} - \mathbf{K}$) or the normalized Laplacian $\left(\Delta = \mathbf{I} - \mathbf{G}^{-\frac{1}{2}} \mathbf{K} \mathbf{G}^{-\frac{1}{2}}\right)$ of the graph. Both Laplacians are symmetric and positive semi-definite, and we use the pseudo-inverse of either of these matrices to generate a semisupervised kernel $\mathbf{K}_{\text{semi}} = \Delta^{-1}$. Given this semisupervised kernel, the rest of the inference can be applied as described for the supervised case.

15.4.1 Semisupervised Affect Recognition

Data collection for affective studies is challenging; semisupervised techniques can be very useful in these scenarios. To illustrate this, we consider the study presented in [12]. Affective states associated with interest and boredom were elicited through an experiment with children aged 8 to 11 years, and observations corresponding to facial actions, posture, and other contextual variables were recorded, with the goal of building a predictive model of interest. The evaluation data set consisted of labels for level of interest (61 samples of high interest and 75 samples of low interest) in children solving a puzzle on the computer. Each data point was a 19-dimensional real vector summarizing 8 seconds of activity from the face, the posture, and the context.

A normalized Laplacian of the underlying similarity graph was used for the semisupervised classification. Figure 15.6 compares the GP-based semisupervised approach (EP-NL) with other supervised (SVM with RBF kernel) semisupervised (LLGC and SVM with graph kernel) methods for different sizes of the labeled data set. Note that LLGC is equivalent to classification with GPs using a Gaussian noise model. Each point in the graph represents the average error on 20 random splits of the data, where the error bars represent the standard error. The parameters in both SVMs were estimated using leave-one-out. When the number of labeled points was small, both EP-NL and LLGC, which are based on GPs, performed similarly and beat the supervised approaches. These results suggest that semisupervised classification should be beneficial whenever there is lack of labeled data, and further emphasize the use of such techniques in user-modeling scenarios.

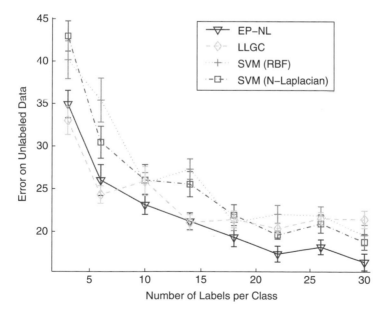

FIGURE 15.6

Performance comparison of the proposed approach with LLGC, SVM using the graph kernel, and supervised SVM (RBF kernel) on the affect data set. The error bars represent the standard error.

15.5 ACTIVE LEARNING

Active learning is another step toward solving the problem of scarce labeled data. Assuming that we have a pool of unlabeled data, $\mathbf{X}_U = \{\mathbf{X}_{n+1}, \ldots, \mathbf{x}_{n+m}\}$. The task in active learning is to find the label for one of these examples that is most useful for the classification task. The goal is to select the sample that would maximize the benefit in terms of the discriminatory capability of the system, consequently utilizing the labeling resources in an efficient manner.

Many heuristics have been used for this. For instance, distance from the classification boundary is popular for SVM-based systems [26]. It can be used for GP classification models very easily just by looking at the magnitude of the posterior mean $\bar{y}_u$. Specifically, we can choose the next point $\mathbf{x}^*$ as $\arg\max_{\mathbf{x}_u \in \mathbf{X}_U} \bar{y}_u$. Freund et al. [4] proposed disagreement among the committee of classifiers as a criterion for active learning. Within the Gaussian process framework, the method of choice has been to look at the expected informativeness of unlabeled data points [16, 17]. All heuristic methods inherently focus on minimizing the misclassification rate.

The Gaussian process framework is easily extended to any of the previously mentioned active learning criteria. However, GP classification provides us with both the posterior mean and the posterior variance for the unknown label t_u. This posterior distribution in turn can be used to compute useful active learning criteria such as misclassification risk, and follows decision-theoretic principles. Moreover, as shown in [11], these risks can be computed for asymmetric cost criteria and can also include labeling cost.

Formally, the active learning scheme selects an unlabeled point according to

$$\mathbf{x}_u^* = \arg\max_{\mathbf{x}_u \in \mathbf{X}_U} VOI(\mathbf{x}_u)$$

Here $VOI(\cdot)$ represents the *value of information* that can be obtained by querying a label for an unlabeled point. All active learning criteria such as uncertainty, information gain, and so forth, can be considered a surrogate function for this value. Gaussian process classification is particularly appealing, as calculation of expected risk is straightforward given the posterior distribution over the labels for $\mathbf{x}_u$. We refer readers to [11] for details of such implementations.

Next, we highlight use of such active learning mechanisms to build a case library that can be used to build good predictive models.

15.5.1 Modeling Interruptability

The original version of BusyBody employed experience sampling to construct personalized models for real-time predictions of the expected cost of interruption [6]. The initial version of the system probed users at random times, constrained to a user-determined overall rate. Recently, an active learning scheme [10] was studied that aimed to probe users based on decision-theoretic criteria. The evaluation focused on data previously collected by BusyBody for two subjects—the first a program manager, the second a developer. The data for each represented two weeks of desk-top activity as well as the busy/not-busy tags collected by the legacy BusyBody system using a random probe policy. The evaluations were performed with hold-out cross-validation, randomly holding out 20% of the data for testing. The system employed the predictive model trained with the data seen *up to* the point being tested. Thus, the performance of the system as it was evolving could be observed and characterized.

A GP classifier using a polynomial kernel of degree 2 was employed as the core machine learning methodology for constructing the predictive model. Two variants of active learning were tested. The first one looked at a moving buffer over a stream of observations to determine the active learning criteria; the other one computed the criteria using just the labeled data. The remaining policies consisted of randomly selecting cases with a probability of 0.5 to query the user and a scheme to select cases on which the predictive user model was most uncertain.

Specifically, the system probed for labels if $0.3 \leq p(t_{new}|\mathbf{x}_{new}) \leq 0.7$. Figure 15.7 shows the gain in utilities over the held-out set as the system saw progressively more labels. The graph highlights the ability of the active learning methodology to provide an efficient means of learning the predictive user model continuously over time.

15.5.2 Classifying Voice Mails

We now explore another study [11] that looked at the selective supervision concepts applied to the voice mail classification challenge. The data set consisted of 207 labeled voice messages received by a single user over a period of 8 months. Annotating a voice mail is tedious, and shorter voice mails can be labeled more quickly than longer ones. Thus, the asymmetric cost criterion was used where the cost of a label scaled with the length of the voice mail. Specifically, it was assumed that the cost of labeling was 0.01 U.S. dollars per second of message length. For Gaussian process classification, the polynomial kernel of degree 2 was used.

The selective-supervision strategy was compared with three other schemes: (1) selecting points randomly, (2) choosing the point where the classification is most uncertain, and (3) choosing a point according to information theoretic criteria [16, 17].

Graphs (a) and (b) in Figure 15.8 compare the different active learning schemes for the task of detecting if the caller was close to the person being called and whether the voice messages originated from a mobile phone. For the studies, results were averaged over 20 runs, where, for each run, one case per class was seeded and the rest of the points were selected according to the different active learning policies. As indicated by the results, active learning can provide significant gains over random sampling in terms of cost and accuracy for classifying messages as close versus distant and mobile versus nonmobile. The criterion for selective supervision provided valuable guidance on labeling efforts under budget constraints.

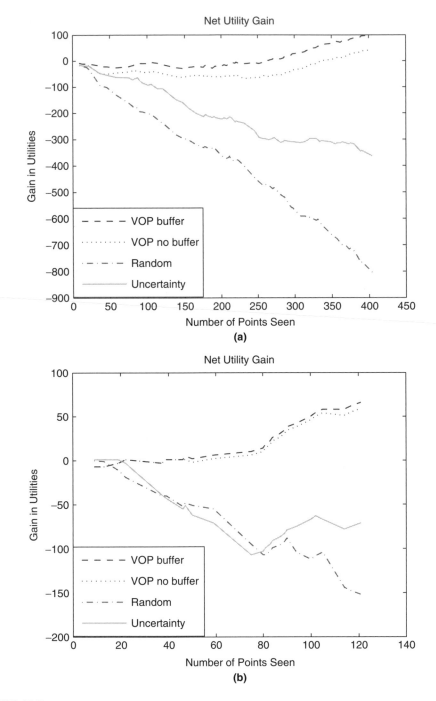

FIGURE 15.7

System net gain in utilities on the test points as the system encounters data instances for (a) the program manager data and (b) the developer data.

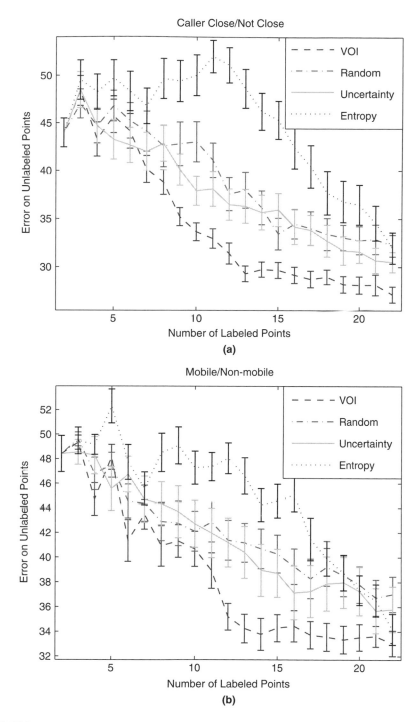

FIGURE 15.8

Comparison of active learning schemes. The graphs show the error on unlabeled points versus the number of labels for classifying voice mails. Figure 15(a) and (b) show performance on the task of classifying Caller Close/Not Close and Mobile/Non-mobile, respectively. VOI criteria can provide good classification performance with significantly lower costs. The results are averaged over 20 runs, and the error bars represent the standard error.

15.6 CONCLUSIONS

The highly challenging problems addressed in this work are motivated by issues in affective computing, user modeling, activity recognition, and machine perception. Specifically, the illustrated schemes can be used in any scenario that needs analysis and machine learning from data obtained from multiple channels and having very few labels and annotations. Many research application scenarios encounter difficulties due to multimodal data or having to annotate an enormous corpus with labels of interest. There are many applications in different domains, such as sensor networks, social networks, and other multimodal scenarios, where the proposed method can be used effectively.

Opportunities exist for future work relating to Gaussian process classification and its extensions and applications to real-world scenarios. Gaussian process classification in general is more flexible than some of its discriminative counterparts. However, for it to achieve a popularity equal to that of other methods, such as SVMs, its computational time needs to be reduced. For sparse GP-based classification methods [16], an interesting direction is to combine them with the extensions proposed in this chapter.

Recently, there has been much interest in structured data. Because many models that handle such data are probabilistic, an interesting question is how to extend the discriminative framework to handle them. The techniques mentioned in this chapter can be mixed and matched to produce novel schemes for handling multimodal channels in conjunction with tackling the problem of labeled data scarcity.

ACKNOWLEDGMENTS

I would like to thank Rosalind W. Picard and Winslow Burleson, who collaborated on my affect recognition work, and Desney Tan and Pradeep Shenoy for collaboration on my BCI work. Further, Yuan (Alan) Qi, Hyungil Ahn, and Rosalind W. Picard worked on semisupervised classification schemes. Lastly, I thank Eric Horvitz for his insights and help with active learning studies on BusyBody and voice mail classification.

REFERENCES

[1] Breiman L. Bagging predictors. Machine Learning 1996;26(2):123–40.

[2] Cressie NAC. Statistics for Spatial Data. Wiley.

[3] Evgeniou T, Pontil M, Poggio T. Regularization networks and support vector machines. Advances in Computational Mathematics 2000;13(1):1–50.

[4] Freund Y, Seung HS, Shamir E, Tishby N. Selective sampling using the query by committee algorithm. Machine Learning 1997;28(2–3).

[5] Grauman K, Darrell T. The pyramid match kernel: Discriminative classification with sets of image features. ICCV; 2005.

[6] Horvitz E, Apacible J, Koch P. Busybody: Creating and fielding personalized models of the cost of interruption. CSCW; 2004.

[7] Horvitz E, Jacobs A, Hovel D. Attention-sensitive alerting. UAI; 1999.

[8] Ivanov Y, Serre T, Bouvrie J. Confidence weighted classifier combination for multi-modal human identification. Technical report, AI memo 2005-035. Massachusetts Institute of Technology, Computer Science and Artificial Intelligence Laboratory.

[9] Kapoor A, Burleson W, Picard RW. Automatic prediction of frustration. IJHCS; 2007.

[10] Kapoor A, Horvitz E. Principles of lifelong learning for predictive user modeling. In: International Conference on User Modeling.

[11] Kapoor A, Horvitz E, Basu S. Selective supervision: Guiding supervised learning with decision-theoretic active learning. IJCAI; 2007.

[12] Kapoor A, Qi YA, Ahn H, Picard RW. Hyperparameter and kernel learning for graph based semi-supervised classification. NIPS; 2005.

[13] Kapoor A, Shenoy P, Tan D. Combining brain computer interfaces with vision for object categorization. CVPR; 2008.

[14] Kittler J, Hatef M, Duin RPW, Matas J. On combining classifiers. Pattern Analysis and Machine Intelligence 20(3):226-39.

[15] Lanckriet G, Cristianini N, Bartlett P, El Ghaoui L, Jordan MI. Learning the kernel matrix with semidefinite programming. JMLR; 2004.

[16] Lawrence N, Seeger M, Herbrich R. Fast sparse Gaussian process method: Informative vector machines. NIPS; 2002.

[17] MacKay D. Information-based objective functions for active data selection. Neural Comput 4(4), 590-604.

[18] Miller DJ, Yan L. Critic-driven ensemble classification. Signal Processing 1999;47(10), 2833-2844.

[19] Minka TP. A Family of Algorithms for Approximate Bayesian Inference. PhD thesis, Massachusetts Institute of Technology, 2001.

[20] Oliver N, Garg A, Horvitz E. Layered representations for learning and inferring office activity from multiple sensory channels. ICMI; 2002.

[21] Platt JC, Burges CJC, Swenson S, Weare C, Zheng A. Learning a Gaussian process prior for automatically generating music playlists. NIPS; 2002.

[22] Rasmusen CE, Williams C. Gaussian Processes for Machine Learning. MIT Press.

[23] Schapire R. A brief introduction to boosting. In: Proceedings of the International Conference on Algorithmic Learning Theory; 1999.

[24] Shenoy P, Tan D. Human-aided computing: Utilizing implicit human processing to classify images. ACM CHI; 2008.

[25] Smola A, Kondor I. Kernels and regularization on graphs. COLT;

[26] Tong S, Koller D. Support vector machine active learning with applications to text classification. ICML; 2000.

[27] Toyama K, Horvitz E. Bayesian modality fusion: Probabilistic integration of multiple vision algorithms for head tracking. ACCV; 2000.

[28] Williams CKI, Barber D. Bayesian classification with Gaussian processes. IEEE Transactions on Pattern Recognition and Machine Intelligence 1998;20(12):1342-51.

[29] Zhu X. Semisupervised learning literature survey. Technical report. University of Wisconsin; 2005.

Games and Entertainment in Ambient Intelligence Environments

16

Anton Nijholt, Dennis Reidsma, and Ronald Poppe

Human Media Interaction, University of Twente, Enschede, The Netherlands

ABSTRACT

In future ambient intelligence (AmI) environments we assume intelligence embedded in the environment and its objects (floors, furniture, mobile robots). These environments support their human inhabitants in their activities and interactions by perceiving them through sensors (proximity sensors, cameras, microphones). Health, recreation, sports, and games are among the needs of inhabitants. The environments can detect and interpret human activity, and can give multimedia feedback to invite, stimulate, guide, advise, and engage.

The purpose of the activity can be to improve physical and mental health (well-being) and improving capabilities related to a profession, recreation, or sports. Fun, just fun, to be achieved from interaction can be another aim of such environments and is the focus of this chapter. We present several examples that span the concept of entertainment in ambient intelligence environments, both within and beyond the (smart) home. In our survey, we identify some main dimensions of ambient entertainment. Next we turn to the design of entertainment applications. We explain in depth which factors are important to consider when designing for entertainment rather than for work.

Key words: ambient intelligence, ambient entertainment, games, experience design, immersion, exertion interfaces, urban games, emergent games.

16.1 INTRODUCTION

Characteristics of games and entertainment, combined with the possibilities offered by ambient intelligence (AmI), allow for the emergence of new entertainment applications that we might describe using the term *ambient entertainment*. In this chapter, we survey the area of computational entertainment against the background of AmI. Instead of introducing a precise definition of the concept, we present a number of examples of novel AmI applications that focus on entertainment, and we discuss several dimensions that are suggestive of the coverage of the concept. This sketches the field of ambient entertainment as we see it. We continue the chapter with a discussion of a set of design considerations that we feel are promising for designing novel ambient intelligence applications that focus on entertainment rather than on work and that can make optimal use of all technical possibilities from AmI in sensor and display technology and the ubiquity of computing devices. The chapter ends with a short conclusion.

16.2 AMBIENT ENTERTAINMENT APPLICATIONS

In this section we discuss a number of ambient entertainment applications. Many games and media applications can take place in an AmI environment but not all of these, we feel, are representative of the concept of ambient entertainment. We will not address traditional PC or console-based gaming that merely uses novel technology for control or that uses novel display technology such as one may find in AmI environments. In this section, several entertainment applications are presented that we see, for varying reasons, as examples of ambient entertainment. This will provide a context for subsequent sections and should give an idea of the coverage of the concept.

16.2.1 **Ubiquitous Devices**

Some ambient entertainment applications rely on the ubiquity of handheld devices such as PDAs and mobile phones. Such devices allow for social gaming experiences with a strong "anytime, anywhere" quality—whenever (potential) players meet, they can play a game together. For example, Suomela et al. [1] described a game in which the camera in mobile phones is used to play a game of "assassin." A player takes pictures of other players without them being aware of it; if successful, the player scores. This game can be played anywhere, at any moment, as long as the players who subscribe to it are present. Importantly, the players are aware of each other as players.

Strömberg et al. [2] presented another mobile multiplayer game where players play together or against each other using their mobile phones on a public display (see Figure 16.1). Here, the players may not know each other and may not even know who of the people sharing the room with them are currently participating. In such a game, players can enter and leave at any time: There is no contract between them to keep playing. The game anonymously connects players, just like certain Web-based casual multiplayer games. However, in contrast to such Web-based games, the players are co-located, interacting with the same display and physically sharing the same environment. This can have a major impact on the presence and connectedness experienced. The kind of drop-in experience referred to above was also discussed by Vogiazou et al. in their paper about CitiTag, another game of "tag" played with mobile devices [3, page 57].

16.2.2 **Exergames**

Another example of entertaining interaction between an instrumented environment and its inhabitants can be found in *exertion interfaces* or *exergames* as exemplified

FIGURE 16.1

Impression of the FirstStrike multiplayer game in a public space, with one common display. Players use their mobile phones to control the game (reprinted from [2], © Springer-Verlag, 2005).

by "Sports over a distance." Exertion interfaces are designed to elicit physical exertion from the user. They may be intended to improve physical skills or to fight health problems such as obesity. Additionally, activities that require bodily exertion from the user may be carried out simply because they are fun, especially in a social context.

One of the best known exertion interfaces is "Sports over a distance" (see Figure 16.2), where players from different sites hit a ball against a wall [4]. The position on the wall and the force with which the ball hits are mediated and made visible to opponents. A player can earn points by breaking tiles on the wall and can profit from weak but not yet broken tiles that are left by her opponent.

A more recent example, "Jogging over a distance" [5], is based on the observation that, although many people enjoy jogging with others for social and motivational reasons, jogging partners might not always live in the same location, and it may be difficult to find a local jogger who runs at the same pace. "Jogging over a distance" allows geographically distant joggers to socialize and motivate one another using spatial audio to convey presence and pace cues, similar to the experience of running side by side.

These exergames are based on augmenting existing physically entertaining activities, such as soccer or jogging, with capabilities made possible by new technological developments, such as the instrumentation of our daily environment with sensor and display technology and ubiquitous networking capabilities.

16.2.3 **Urban Gaming**

The next example of entertainment applications we discuss goes a step up in scale and treats a whole city as a gaming environment. "Can you see me now?" by Benford et al. [6] allows players from anywhere in the world to play online against performers. The online players navigate through a virtual representation of a city. The performers run through the actual city in pursuit of them. The goal for the online players is to avoid getting caught. During play, they can listen to their pursuers

FIGURE 16.2

Two persons at one location playing "Soccer over a distance." The two opponents are visible on the large screen (reprinted from *www.exertioninterfaces.com*).

through the audio from the wearable devices the performers carry with them. Conversely, the performers can track the virtual location of the online players on their handheld devices.

"Uncle Roy all around you," also by Benford et al. [7], is an ambient immersed adventure in which the players themselves play on the real streets of the city. They play out an adventure in search of a mysterious character and are carefully guided through scenarios, locations in the city, and encounters with people (often actors) toward a climax through careful orchestration by a controller team. As the game progresses, players receive instructions and clues through a handheld device, informing them as to what they should do next. The locations and the casual passers-by form the background context against which the adventure is played out.

16.2.4 Dancing in the Streets

The "Dancing in the streets" project of Popat and Palmer [8] is a good example of an entertaining installation embedded in people's daily living space that is *not* a game. It is an outdoor interactive art installation in which light is projected from above onto the ground. The projection space, or rather the movement of people within that space, is observed through infrared cameras. Different cycles of light are projected. Each cycle allows for its own set of possible interactions between the visitor and the projected images. The light patterns as well as the interactions were designed in collaboration with performance artists. The installation is positioned at an unexpected location, outside any particular context traditionally associated with art or interactive systems such as a museum or technology exhibit. Through sensor and display technology embedded in the daily living space, entertaining interaction is elicited between the environment and people casually passing through it.

16.3 DIMENSIONS IN AMBIENT ENTERTAINMENT

The examples just mentioned are different in many ways, yet they share similarities. In this section, we focus on three dimensions that play an important role in ambient entertainment applications: sensors and control, location, and social aspects. For discussions of dimensions in traditional computer gaming, which clearly also apply to ambient entertainment, the reader is referred to Lazzaro [9], Lindley [10], and Lundgren and Björk [11].

16.3.1 Sensors and Control

Many types of sensors are used to provide input for ambient entertainment applications. Dance pads and the Wiimote are well-known examples, but other games also use intuitive controllers. The user can play a toy guitar in Guitar Hero [12]. In "Sports over a distance" [4], pressure sensors are used to determine where the ball hits the wall. The user's location, measured using RFID tags, can also be a means of control.

Computer vision has traditionally been used for various observation tasks. The MIT Kidsroom project [13] detects the location of children in an ambient playground environment. Also, their actions, or rather dance moves, are recognized. In more constrained situations, computer vision has been used to analyze facial expressions and body pose [14]. Analysis of speech can be used to detect affect, as in [15]. Other sensors are also used, such as pressure sensors in chairs [16]. These sensors are all nonobtrusive. Biological signals such as heart rate, blood pressure, and respiration might also be used, but are more obtrusive and thus might be more distracting to the user. The same applies to brain–computer interfaces (BCI), that usually rely on EEG measurements.

For any AmI application, interaction between user and environment is important. From a technical point of view, the manner in which the user can control the environment, or an application therein, has traditionally been a design challenge. We distinguish two main paradigms of control: voluntary (or conscious) versus involuntary (or unconscious). We will explain these terms and present examples of both.

With voluntary control, the user consciously steers the interaction. This requires adaptation from the user to the system at two distinct levels. First, the user requires knowledge of the system's internal functioning. For example, in a multimedia playback system, the user needs to know how songs are organized in order to select the song desired. Second, the control commands need to be known, such as which button to press or which gesture or voice command to use to mute sound. This requires user adaptation to the input device.

Traditional human–computer interfaces typically use the voluntary control paradigm. This paradigm has several advantages, from both user and technological perspectives. Voluntary control is most often unambiguous. Control commands are recognized by the system, which makes the design of interactive applications more straightforward as no feedback dialogues are required. Instead, system dialogues can be designed in such a way that users always know how to perform a certain action. A remote control is a typical example.

Voluntary control is easily suited to novel interaction technologies that still have limited recognition capabilities, such as speech and gestures or BCI. Because the user is still consciously controlling the application and therefore must know the right commands, less variation is to be expected in the command input. However, voluntary control has the drawback that it is cognitively more demanding of the user, as he needs to translate his goals into appropriate commands to steer the interaction.

In contrast, involuntary control does not require adaptation from the user, but can be regarded as intuitive or unconscious. This implies that traditional input devices cannot be used. Instead, sensors measure the behavior of the user or focus on deviations from it. Examples of involuntary control are systems that act on the user's observed mental state. In [17], the level of user frustration is measured and the difficulty of the game is adapted accordingly. A similar idea, described in [18], measures emotional state. These systems do not require the user to act in a specified manner. In other words, users do not need to know the internal functioning of the game or how to steer the interaction. This places the burden of correct recognition on the system.

The voluntary and involuntary paradigms are two extremes of a single dimension. In practice, many applications will be somewhere in between the two. For example, many Nintendo Wii games allow the user to play with the Wiimote as if it were different objects. When playing baseball, the Wiimote becomes the bat. While the user still requires knowledge about how to play the game, he does not actively have to adapt his movements as these are intuitive baseball movements. Also, when the movements are not exactly prescribed by the activity—in contrast to activities such as golf, baseball, or tennis—users often make movements that have an understandable relation to the action they are trying to perform. For example, Höysniemi et al. [19] observed children playing a game in which they had to make a virtual character fly, run, or swim. The children exhibited an intuitive range of behavior trying to control the character (see Figure 16.3). Many of these applications, or

FIGURE 16.3

Children controlling a game character using intuitive movements. A Wizard-of-Oz setting allows the children to choose the movement they find most intuitive (reprinted from [19], © ACM, 2005).

rather games, use this idea of mimicking. In a sense this is voluntary control, but clearly the cognitive burden on the user is less due to the intuitiveness of the commands.

Voluntary and involuntary control are also often used together. While the user consciously controls the interaction, unconscious behavior might be measured and used to adapt the interaction [17, 18]. This could be a way to make the interaction more challenging or responsive, which in turn would result in a higher user engagement.

Ambient intelligence applications in general are increasingly considering involuntary control, as predicted by Weiser [20]. From a technological point of view, this poses challenges, as sensors are required that observe the user's behavior in situations in which that behavior is not constrained. Furthermore, sensors can be obtrusive in voluntary control, as the user is already consciously aware of the interaction. For involuntary control, it is better if the sensors do not take up too much of the users' attention. Nonobtrusive sensors allow for interaction regardless of the location, and make involuntary control possible.

The trend of disappearing interfaces is less visible in ambient entertainment. The main reason is the different nature of entertainment, compared to the more task-focused paradigm of ambient intelligence. Specifically, the interaction itself contributes to entertainment. One example is the e-mail management system described in [21]. Reading and redirecting e-mail is typically not an entertaining task. However, when users can issue commands by making steps on an instrumented floor pad, the interaction becomes more enjoyable.

We end this section by noting that disappearing interfaces—although they offer many interesting possibilities for entertainment applications—are not necessarily better than their more obtrusive counterparts: Sometimes it is specifically the (obtrusive) interaction with the interface that makes an application entertaining.

16.3.2 Location

Although smart homes are a suitable place for ambient entertainment, some applications may reach well beyond them. In this section, we reflect on a number of games introduced in Section 16.2, with a specific focus on how location, or distance between players, can be of key importance. Various techniques can be used to measure player location, such as GPS, computer vision, and RFID tags, but we do not focus on technical aspects.

Here we distinguish a range of ways in which a game can be "location-based," with increasing focus on the actual location. *Games over a distance* are the ambient variant of traditional networked games. These games are characterized by the fact that players are remotely connected. We previously mentioned "Sports over a distance" [22], where two persons play soccer against each other and the game state is transferred between them using a network connection. Similarly, "Jogging over a distance" allows people to run individually but also together in a sense [5]. Partners can talk to each other and their relative locations are revealed by spatially presenting sound as if it were coming from the front or from behind. In this category of location-based games, the user location is of no importance—any suitable running track will do.

In contrast, *geo games* explicitly use the players' environment. Usually, a virtual game map is projected onto a physical area, in which the players can move around. One typical example is Human Pacman [23], where players take on the role of Pacman or Ghost, similar to the traditional console game (see Figure 16.4(a)). Players can chase each other, as their locations are revealed on a PDA. Some geo games take into account both the physical and cognitive challenge [24, 25]. Geo games are characterized by the fact that real-world distances correspond to distances in the game. This motivates players to actively engage in it.

The types of location-based games just discussed do not consider location other than as a sort of map in which movement is possible. In contrast, *urban games* actually focus on the location and its environment. One nice example is the backseat playground described in [26]. A narrative is generated and presented to a listener using earphones. The story makes use of elements from the current environment and landmarks that the listener observes from the backseat of a car. Such a narrative has been found to be more vivid. The urban games discussed earlier, "Uncle Roy all around you" and "Can you see me now," clearly also take the details of the (urban) location into account.

16.3.3 Social Aspects of Gaming

Ambient entertainment, like "normal entertainment," has a strong social aspect. This is important, as humans are intrinsically motivated to engage in social activities.

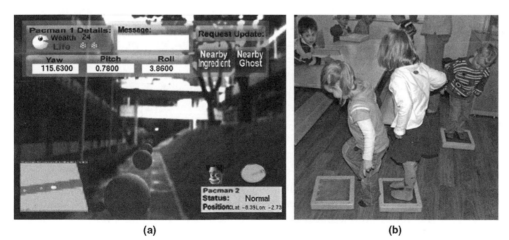

(a)　　　　　　　　　　　　　　　(b)

FIGURE 16.4

(a) Augmented display of the Human Pacman game. The screen shows the real environment with added "pills" and status information (reprinted from [23], © Springer-Verlag, 2004). (b) Children playing with Interactive Tiles and inventing their own games (reprinted from *www.rikwesselink.nl*).

AmI technology presents opportunities for social play at a number of distinct levels. Players can be co-located, where they reside in the same physical location, as in traditional board games. Remote, or mediated, presence is the situation where players are physically apart but some form of communication is available. Traditional networked games are considered mediated, but we focus on examples discussed in the previous section, such as "Sports over a distance" and Human Pacman, which rely on a fixed or mobile network connection.

The important difference between mediated presence and co-location is the ease and richness of communication. In a co-located setting, both verbal and nonverbal communication is possible, without delay. In mediated presence, typically only parts of the social signals are transferred, which in turn affects the perception of presence. The reader is referred to [27] for a more complete overview of the relation between player and location in terms of experience.

Traditional settings with a computer or TV screen do not facilitate interaction between players. The introduction of more public visualization means, such as large screens and touch tables, allows easier perception of others' social signals, including body pose and gaze. Also in mediated presence scenarios, the technology that supports communication increasingly allows users to observe and render social signals over a distance. This gives an increased feeling of presence and immersion. We discuss the role of these factors on player engagement and enjoyment in more detail in Section 16.4.4.

Because AmI technology also allows for integration of daily activities, borders between entertainment and social contacts may become much less obvious. This has implications for both the location where the play occurs and the social relations between players. Ambient entertainment is not limited to the home, as we discussed in the previous section. This gives it a strong "anytime, anywhere" character. Moreover, players and spectators do not necessarily have to be known, but can be strangers. The "Dancing in the streets" examples and the mobile game by Strömberg et al. [2] presented earlier are examples where players might not know each other or even who is participating in the game. While arousal, and consequently enjoyment, is lower when playing against strangers, it is still higher than playing against a computer [28]. We will discuss this type of interaction in more depth in the next section (Section 16.4.1).

The difference between task-based and entertainment applications is also reflected in the role of social interaction. The goal of ambient entertainment is to give the player a fun experience. Performance, for example in terms of score or progress, plays an important role as extrinsic motivation for play, and social interaction might interfere with it. For example, Lindley et al. [29] found that game controllers that afford natural body movement increase the social experience of the players, shown through more social movements and more conversational speech. This observation was made even when these movements interfered with game performance. We elaborate on the relation between social interaction and performance in Section 16.4.3.

16.4 DESIGNING FOR AMBIENT ENTERTAINMENT AND EXPERIENCE

This section presents a number of design concepts that we feel are very promising for achieving novel ambient entertainment applications, especially those that are just for fun.

16.4.1 Emergent Games

Discussions of entertainment technology often focus on games (e.g., console-based and casual) or on media creation and delivery (movies, music libraries, television shows). The "Dancing in the streets" project introduced earlier is a good example of another category of AmI entertainment: emergent games.

Emergent games are not actually predefined by the designer; nor are they explicitly present as a game in the environment. Rather, the environment may simply afford many kinds of playful interaction to its inhabitants. The way the inhabitants react to the offered possibilities may lead to the emergence of game-like interactions between inhabitant and environment, or between inhabitants. This type of "game"— or "play"—may work especially well in heavily instrumented AmI environments because they are already equipped, for other reasons, with many sensors, actuators, and displays that can be harnessed for such playful interactions.

The "Dancing in the streets" project [8] is such an environment. The system is interactive, but there is no concrete task to be solved or goal to be met. Nevertheless, or possibly even because of that, the installation was extremely popular with passers-by. Among the aspects the authors presented as reasons for this popularity is that "... crucially the ways in which the audience could interact with these images were not fully prescribed, but existed within a framework that included potential for significant variability and even surprise within the rules of engagement." The interaction rules were not strictly reactive, but contained elements of chaos and unpredictability ("The butterflies that flocked around participants' feet would fly away out of the projection if they were unable to keep up with the participant's movement. The ghostly feet, whilst following the participants' pathways, would dictate their own routes to a degree."). Also, the authors remark that a large part of the visitors' enjoyment of the system was rooted in the interaction *between the different visitors* that was encouraged:

> *Importantly, the installation was most effective when more than one person was interacting within it. The square space in which the light was projected, and the nature of the projections, encouraged social interaction. One of the images used purple ribbons of light to link everyone standing in the space. As participants moved into the space then the ribbons immediately included them in the web changing the projected geometric shape to accommodate the new body. [8]*

Some of the interactions between the environment and the visitors obtained distinct game-like characteristics.

Another example can be found in work on enhanced playgrounds, such as that of Seitinger et al. [30] and the interactive tiles of Wesselink.[1] These installations partly derive their success from the fact that they do *not* provide games with predesigned rules and winning conditions. Instead, they provide an open-ended environment of objects and interactions around which children construct their own "games" (see Figure 16.4(b)). This relates better to the way play occurs on traditional playgrounds.

Emergent games may adhere to the principle set out in the following quote from Vogiazou et al. [31, page 118]:

> *As Opie and Opie (1969) mention in their book on playground games, play is unrestricted, while games have rules; in the playground there is no need for an umpire, little significance is attached to who wins or loses and it doesn't even seem to matter if a game is not finished.*

Nevertheless, in such interactive applications visitors may use the combination of possible interactions to define their own rules of an ad hoc game, just as children sometimes come up with ad hoc games and rules. This does not necessarily mean that such rules should always be embodied in the application in an explicit way: The possibility to play ad hoc may be one of the highly attractive features of a well-designed emergent game.

Vogiazou et al. [3] look at emergence in game experiences in a slightly different way. They describe a game of tag using mobile devices in which a simple set of rules defined the game play. They looked at the emergence of social behavior between players and of higher-level group strategies from the simple game rules. Also, they observed how a game in a public space and in a social setting is circumscribed not just by the rules or game mechanics, but also potentially by locally established rules (agreements between a group of players) and social and legal rules (imposed by the public setting in which a game is played). In this context they talked about players "bending the game rules" and interpreted "designing for emergence" as "designing for players pushing boundaries."

16.4.2 Rhythm and Temporal Interaction

Rhythmic interaction and temporal co-ordination between user and system may enhance the game experience. In human–human interaction, people typically interact concurrently, in a mutually coordinated manner. Temporal co-ordination in human–human interaction, also called synchrony, relates to a positive evaluation of the conversation partner and of the (effectiveness of the) interaction [32]. To a

---

[1]*www.wesselink.nl.*

certain extent, interactional synchrony has already been shown to have similar effects in interaction with virtual humans or robots [33].

An example that takes a step in the direction of harnessing interactional synchrony for improving the enjoyment and engagement of the user is our Virtual Conductor (see Figure 16.5). In this project, an artificial orchestra conductor was built that not only displays the appropriate conducting behavior for a piece of music, but also interactively leads and corrects an ensemble of human musicians based on audio analysis of the music being played [34, 35]. Among other things, the ensemble's tempo is analyzed and compared to the desired tempo. Based on this, the conductor decides on a response in its conducting behavior, to which the orchestra reacts at that same moment. Conductor and orchestra both need to adapt the timing of their behavior to "external events," that is, events that they do not directly control—here, the behavior of the other. This leads to a mutual feedback loop in the interaction.

In entertainment applications, temporal coordination may be required by the rules of the game, but people also engage in coordinated interaction just because it brings satisfaction and enjoyment [36] (take, for example, dancing, playing music, or certain sports). We investigate how to make entertainment interactions more enjoyable by looking at interaction synchrony. On the one hand, we want to disturb this synchrony in order to introduce new challenges; on the other hand, we want convergence toward coordinated anticipatory multimodal interaction between the human and her artificial partners and their environment [37].

The idea of investigating rhythmic or temporal coordination between a user and an entertainment application is not novel. For example, Weinberg and Driscoll [38] built a robotic drummer that interacts with human musicians rhythmically. Their focus was on musical expressiveness and collaborative music making.

FIGURE 16.5

Interactive Virtual Conductor controlling a real-world ensemble by performing the appropriate movements, adapted based on sound analysis and partiture (reprinted from [35], © ACM, 2008. Image courtesy Stenden Hogeschool/Henk Postma).

Michalowski et al. [39] built a robot that dances rhythmically in response to movements of the user, synchronizing to his rhythm. Tanaka and Suzuki [40] explicitly modeled two-way entrainment for their dancing robot, Qrio, to achieve more user engagement. A core concept in their interaction model is the repetition of sympathy and variations of it:

> We consider that there are two concepts that should be basic units designing the interaction model. One is sympathy between the two (human and robot), and the other is variation to it. Our basic hypothesis is that by the repetition of the sympathy and variation, long-term interaction can be realized. [40, p. 420]

Finally, Tomida et al. [41] attempted to achieve *entertaining interaction* between two humans by eliciting entrainment quite directly. In their MiXer installation, the authors aimed for implicit synchronization between two human users of the system: the "rhythms" of one user are sensed using biosensors (e.g., heart rate, perspiration) and presented to the other user through "biofeedback" (visualization of those rhythms). The other user may then tap a button synchronized to the biofeedback display. The assumption was that an engaging type of entrainment between users will occur in response to this process.

16.4.3 Performance in Play

With respect to the design concept *performance in play* (performance as "dramatic expression," not as "achievement"), we quote Lund et al. [42, p. 6]:

> Often performance is noticed as an extra dimension of a play activity (a shout, a sound effect, a bodily act), but in fact it often becomes the most important activity of the play in itself, and it becomes the one admired and imitated by others. Hence, much of the social gathering around play may be connected with the performance activity. Often the body is the most important instrument in these activities, but also the surroundings can be incorporated and used, such as when children are stumping or shouting in a tunnel to use the feedback from the walls as the echo to make special sound effects, or when a group of children use a specific surface, e.g., a rocking plank or branch to make special jumping and swinging movements. Therefore, development is focused on the surrounding and tools that may enhance the children's possibilities in making performance activities in their play. It should be mentioned that the performance aspects are absent in nearly all cases of so-called "intelligent toys" on the toy market of today.

This suggests that performance in play has a strong physical aspect as well as a strong social aspect. It also suggests that it should be possible to design interactive applications specifically for this. What elements could be used in an interactive application to encourage performance behavior?

In the first place, the interaction should be physically oriented (although [31] described a similar application that uses a 2D virtual environment). Furthermore, it would probably help if the interaction incorporates feedback related to movement intensity and rhythm. Performance in play often has no direct relation to the actual goals of the game. This suggests that one may achieve this by incorporating feedback mechanisms that react to behavior from the player that is not relevant to the game's progress. Reactions can take a form that in turn is not relevant to the progress of the game as such.

A good example of this can be found in the work of Bianchi-Berthouze et al. [12] and Lindley et al. [29]. They described an experiment using the Guitar Hero game controller. Players were given extra points either when they pushed a button on the guitar in response to a certain signal or, for a different group, when they made a flashy rock guitarists' move with the guitar neck (see Figure 16.6). For the second group, the overall response was more embodied and can be described as "performance in play." Players in this group were reported as being significantly more engaged. Such results make performance in play an attractive aspect to consider in the design of ambient entertainment applications.

FIGURE 16.6

Example of expressive movement while playing Guitar Hero in the experiments of Bianchi-Berthouze et al. (reprinted from [12], © Springer-Verlag, 2007).

16.4.4 Immersion and Flow

When modeling game experience, two issues that often arise are flow and immersion [36]. The theory of flow, introduced by Csikszentmihalyi, describes among other things how players' awareness of their body and surroundings reduces when flow draws them into the game:

> *Concentration is so intense that there is no attention left over to think about anything irrelevant, or to worry about problems. Self-consciousness disappears, and the sense of timing becomes distorted. [43, page 71]*

Several elements have been distinguished in Csikszentmihalyi's definition, and it is generally assumed they should be present in a game. Among these, *disappearing concern for the self* relates to the quote above. This feature, as well as the others, can be found as prescriptions in present-day game design literature [44], and they play a role in game experience evaluation.

Immersion has been described as follows.

> *The experience of being transported to an elaborately simulated place is pleasurable in itself, regardless of the fantasy content. We refer to this experience as immersion. Immersion is a metaphorical term derived from the physical experience of being submerged in water. We seek the same feeling from a psychologically immersive experience that we do from a plunge in the ocean or swimming pool: the sensation of being surrounded by a completely other reality, as different as water is from air, that takes over all of our attention, our whole perceptual apparatus. [45, p. 98]*

Some attempts to add to this definition can be found in the literature. For example, in [45] different types of immersion were identified: sensory, challenge-based, and imaginative. Levels of immersion (labeled engagement, engrossment, and total immersion) and how to cross the barriers between them were discussed in [46]. As with the flow theory described above, it seems that an important feature of immersion is the fact that "a completely other reality...takes over all of our attention, our whole perceptual apparatus." See also Jennett et al. [47].

Flow and immersion have proven to be very fruitful concepts in thinking about engagement and enjoyment in games. Both relate, in a sense, to the concept of *presence*: feeling, as a player, "present" in a (virtual/game) world, and feeling others to be present with you. Both concepts are also very "cerebral," in that they assume that flow and immersion cause a lessened awareness from the player of his own body and actual environment. In that respect, Apperley remarked how video game play has often been seen as a rupture in or escape from the everyday. This ignores the fact that the player, as he is playing, is embedded in a local context and a physical body, both placing demands and restrictions on him [48].

Given the previous discussion, we expect that presence, flow, and immersion should be able to work the other way around as well: It should be possible to design ambient entertainment applications in which the player's feeling of presence *within*

FIGURE 16.7

Participants of CHI'06 dancing with the Virtual Dancer. The movements of the Dancer are timed to the beat of the music and selected from a movement repertoire while continuously adapting to the human dancer [49].

her own body and her actual environment is strengthened. Furthermore, it should be possible to do this in such a way that this increased awareness contributes to the entertainment provided by the system. This proposal is a natural extension of real life: People find entertainment in dancing, sports, and many other highly embodied activities.

From the ambient entertainment applications discussed in Section 16.2, we see that urban and location-based games typically induce an increased feeling of presence in the actual environment by making that environment part of the experience. Exertion interfaces typically use an increased feeling of presence in the player's own body to achieve engagement and enjoyment.

We worked on a system for embodied interaction using an interactive Virtual Dancer (see Figure 16.7), who invited visitors to dance with her in a back-and-forth pattern of leading and following [49]. Müller et al. [50] described an interface that allows users the *physical* experience of flying while controlling a flying avatar in a virtual environment, which greatly adds to the users' engagement. Bianchi-Berthouze et al. [12] described how involving expressive body actions in interaction leads to higher engagement (see Section 16.4.3 on performance in play), but this effect depends on the context that causes the body activity. The authors clearly showed that, in one condition of the experiment, higher player engagement was correlated with *less* body activity (as with cerebral flow and immersion, mentioned earlier), but in the other condition higher engagement was significantly correlated with *more* body activity.

16.5 CONCLUSIONS

In this chapter, we surveyed the area of computational entertainment, specifically against the background of ambient intelligence. Examples of entertainment applications that reach well beyond traditional console-based gaming concepts were presented to show the breadth of the field. Novel characteristics of games and entertainment, combined with the possibilities offered by ambient intelligence, allow for the emergence of new entertainment applications that we described as *ambient entertainment.*

Using the example applications as a starting point, we highlighted several dimensions that are suggestive of the coverage of the ambient entertainment concept. Also, we discussed several new design concepts that we feel are relevant for successful development of ambient entertainment applications. Such applications can make optimal use of all technical possibilities from ambient intelligence in sensor and display technology and the ubiquity of computing devices. More important, though, with the aspects discussed in this chapter in mind, we envision interactive applications embedded in our daily living space that aim at fun, just fun.

ACKNOWLEDGMENTS

The authors would like to thank all those who contributed figures to this chapter. This research was supported by the GATE project, funded by The Netherlands Organization for Scientific Research (NWO) and The Netherlands ICT Research and Innovation Authority (ICT Regie).

REFERENCES

[1] Suomela R, Koivisto A. My photos are my bullets—Using camera as the primary means of player-to-player interaction in a mobile multiplayer game. In: Proceedings of the International Conference on Entertainment Computing (ICEC'06). Vol. 4161 in Lecture Notes in Computer Science. Springer Verlag; 2006. p. 250-61.

[2] Strömberg H, Leikas J, Suomela R, Ikonen V, Heinilä J. Multiplayer gaming with mobile phones—Enhancing user experience with a public screen. In: Proceedings of the International Conference on Intelligent Technologies for Interactive Entertainment (INTETAIN'05), Vol. 3814 of Lecture Notes in Computer Science. Springer Verlag; 2005. p. 183-92.

[3] Vogiazou Y, Raijmakers B, Geelhoed E, Reid J, Eisenstadt M. Design for emergence: Experiments with a mixed reality urban playground game. Personal Ubiquitous Computing 2006;11 (1):45-58.

[4] Mueller FF, Agamanolis S. Sports over a distance. Computers in Entertainment 2005;3(3):1-11.

[5] Mueller F, O'Brien S, Thorogood A. Jogging over a distance: Supporting a "jogging together" experience although being apart. In: Extended Abstracts of the SIGCHI Conference on Human Factors in Computing Systems (CHI'07). ACM Press; 2007. p. 2579-84.

[6] Benford S, Crabtree A, Flintham M, Drozd A, Anastasi R, Paxton M, et al. Can you see me now? ACM Transactions on Computer-Human Interaction 2006;13(1):100-33.

[7] Benford S, Crabtree A, Reeves S, Sheridan J, Dix A, Flintham M. The frame of the game: Blurring the boundary between fiction and reality in mobile experiences. In: Proceedings of the SIGCHI Conference on Human Factors in Computing Systems (CHI'06). ACM Press; 2006. p. 427-36.

[8] Popat S, Palmer S. Dancing in the streets: The sensuous manifold as a concept for designing experience. International Journal of Performance Arts and Digital Media 2007;2(3):297-314.

[9] Lazzaro N. Why we play games: 4 keys to more emotion. In: Invited talk at the 2004 Game Developers Conference (GDC'04). *http://www.xeodesign.com/xeodesign_whyweplay games .pdf*; 2004.

[10] Lindley CA. The semiotics of time structure in ludic space as a foundation for analysis and design. International Journal of Computer Game Research 5(1), 2005.

[11] Lundgren S, Björk S. Game mechanics: Describing computer-augmented games in terms of interaction. In: Terms of Interaction—Proceedings of TIDSE'03. Fraunhofer IRB Verlag 2003. p. 45-56.

[12] Bianchi-Berthouze NL, Kim WW, Patel D. Does body movement engage you more in digital game play? And why? In: Paiva A, Prada R, Picard RW, editors. Proceedings of the International Conference on Affective Computing and Intelligent Interaction (ACII'07).Vol. 4738 of Lecture Notes in Computer Science. Springer; 2007. p. 102-13.

[13] Bobick AF, Davis JW. The recognition of human movement using temporal templates. IEEE Trans Pattern Anal Mach Intell 2001;23(3):257-67.

[14] Zeng Z, Pantic M, Roisman GI, Huang TS. A survey of affect recognition methods: Audio, visual, and spontaneous expression. IEEE Trans Pattern Anal Mach Intell 2009;31(1):39-58.

[15] Campbell N. Perception of affect in speech—Towards an automatic processing of paralin-guistic information in spoken conversation. In: Proceedings of the International Conference on Spoken Language Processing (INTERSPEECH'04). ISCA Archive; 2004. p. 881-4.

[16] van den Hoogen WM, de Kort YAW. Exploring behavioral expressions of player experience in digital games. In: Proceedings of the Workshop on Facial and Bodily Expressions for Control and Adaptation of Games (ECAG'08). No. WP08-03 in CTIT Workshop Proceedings Series. Centre for Telematics and Information Technology, University of Twente; 2008. p. 11-20.

[17] Gilleade KM, Dix A. Using frustration in the design of adaptive videogames. In: Proceedings of the International Conference on Advances in Computer Entertainment Technology (ACE'04). ACM Press; 2004. p. 228-32.

[18] Sykes J, Brown S. Affective gaming: Measuring emotion through the gamepad. In: Extended Abstracts of the SIGCHI Conference on Human Factors in Computing Systems (CHI'03). ACM Press; 2003. p. 732-3.

[19] Höysniemi J, Hämäläinen P, Turkki L, Rouvi T. Children's intuitive gestures in vision-based action games. Commun ACM 48(1):44-50.

[20] Weiser M. The computer of the 21st century. Sci Am 1991;265(3):66-75.

[21] Meyers B, Brush AJB, Drucker S, Smith MA, Czerwinski M. Dance your work away: Exploring step user interfaces. In: Extended Abstracts of the SIGCHI Conference on Human Factors in Computing Systems (CHI'06). ACM Press; 2006. p. 387-92.

[22] Mueller F, Agamanolis S, Picard R. Exertion interfaces: Sports over a distance for social bonding and fun. In: Proceedings of the SIGCHI Conference on Human Factors in Computing Systems (CHI'03). ACM Press; 2003. p. 561-8.

[23] Cheok AD, Goh KH, Liu W, Farbiz F, Fong SW, Teo SL. Human Pacman: A mobile, wide-area entertainment system based on physical, social, and ubiquitous computing. Pers Ubiquit Comput 2004;8(2):71-81.

[24] Kiefer P, Matyas S, Schlieder C. Concepts and technologies for pervasive games—A reader for pervasive gaming research, vol. 1. Springer Verlag; 2007 [Chapter: Geogames—Integrating edutainment in location-based games].

[25] Schlieder C, Kiefer P, Matyas S. Geogames—Designing location-based games from classic board games. IEEE Intelligent Systems 2006;21(5):40-6.

[26] Bichard J, Brunnberg L, Combetto M, Gustafsson A, Juhlin O. Backseat playgrounds: Pervasive storytelling in vast location based games. In: Proceedings of the International Conference on Entertainment Computing (ICEC'06). No. 4161 in Lecture Notes in Computer Science. Springer Verlag; 2006. p. 117-22.

[27] de Kort YAW, Ijsselsteijn WA. People, places, and play: Player experience in a socio-spatial context. ACM Computers in Entertainment 6(2):1-11.

[28] Ravaja N, Saari T, Turpeinen M, Laarni J, Salminen M, Kivikangas M. Spatial presence and emotions during video game playing: Does it matter with whom you play? Presence: Teleoperators and Virtual Environments 2006;15(4):381-92.

[29] Lindley SE, Couteur JL, Bianchi-Berthouze NL. Stirring up experience through movement in game play: Effects on engagement and social behaviour. In: Proceedings of the SIGCHI Conference on Human Factors in Computing Systems (CHI'08). ACM Press; 2008. p. 511-4.

[30] Seitinger S, Sylvan E, Zuckerman O, Popovic M, Zuckerman O. A new playground experience: Going digital? In: Extended Abstracts of the SIGCHI Conference on Human Factors in Computing Systems (CHI'06). ACM Press; 2006. p. 303-8.

[31] Vogiazou Y, Eisenstadt M. Designing multiplayer games to facilitate emergent social behaviours online. International Journal of Interactive Technology and Smart Education 2005;2 (2):117-30.

[32] Nagaoka C, Komori M, Yoshikawa S. Embodied synchrony in conversation. In: Nishida T, editor. Conversational Informatics: An Engineering Approach. John Wiley and Sons; 2007. p. 331-51.

[33] Robins B, Dautenhahn K, Nehaniv CL, Mirza NA, François D, Olsson L. Sustaining interaction dynamics and engagement in dyadic childrobot interaction kinesics: Lessons learnt from an exploratory study. In: Proceedings of the 14th IEEE International Workshop on Robot and Human Interactive Communication (RO-MAN'05); 2005. p. 716-22.

[34] Bos P, Reidsma D, Ruttkay ZM, Nijholt A. Interacting with a virtual conductor. In: Proceedings of the International Conference on Entertainment Computing (ICEC'06), No. 4161 in Lecture Notes in Computer Science. Springer Verlag; 2006. p. 25-30.

[35] Reidsma D, Nijholt A, Bos P. Temporal interaction between an artificial orchestra conductor and human musicians. ACM Computers in Entertainment 2008;6(4):1-22.

[36] Nijholt A, van Dijk EMAG, Reidsma D. Design of experience and flow in movement-based interaction. In: Motion in Games (MIG'08). Vol. 5277 of Lecture Notes in Computer Science. Springer Verlag; 2008. p. 166-75.

[37] Nijholt A, Reidsma D, van Welbergen H, op den Akker HJA, Ruttkay ZM. Mutually coordinated anticipatory multimodal interaction. In: Nonverbal Features of Human-Human and Human-Machine Interaction, Vol. 5042 of Lecture Notes in Computer Science. Springer Verlag; 2008. p. 70-89.

[38] Weinberg G, Driscoll S. Robot-human interaction with an anthropomorphic percussionist. In: Proceedings of the SIGCHI Conference on Human Factors in Computing Systems (CHI'06). ACM Press; 2006. p. 1229-32.

[39] Michalowski MP, Sabanovic S, Kozima H. A dancing robot for rhythmic social interaction. In: Proceedings of the ACM/IEEE International Conference on Human-Robot Interaction (HRI'07). ACM Press; 2007. p. 89-96.

[40] Tanaka F, Suzuki H. Dance interaction with QRIO: A case study for non-boring interaction by using an entrainment ensemble model. In: Proceedings of the IEEE International Workshop on Robot and Human Interactive Communication (RO-MAN'04). IEEE Computer Society; 2004. p. 419-24.

[41] Tomida T, Ishihara A, Ueki A, Tomari Y, Fukushima K, Inakage M. MiXer: The communication entertainment content by using "entrainment phenomenon" and "bio-feedback." In: Proceedings of the International Conference on Advances in Computer Entertainment Technology (ACE'07). ACM Press; 2007. p. 286-7.

[42] Lund HH, Jessen C. Playware—Intelligent technology for children's play. Technical Report TR-2005-1. University of Southern Denmark: Maersk McKinney Moller Institute for Production Technology; 2005.

[43] Csikszentmihalyi M. Flow: The Psychology of Optimal Experience. Harper Perennial; 1991.

[44] Sweetser P, Wyeth P. Gameflow: A model for evaluating player enjoyment in games. ACM Computers in Entertainment 3(3):1-24.

[45] Murray JH. Hamlet on the Holodeck: The Future of Narrative in Cyberspace. MIT Press; 1998.

[46] Ermi L, Mäyrä F. Fundamental components of the gameplay experience: Analysing immersion. In: Proceedings of the Conference on Changing Views: Worlds in Play (DiGRA'05). University of Vancouver; p. 14, 2005.

[47] Jennett CI, Cox AL, Cairns P. Being "in the game." In: Proceedings of the Conference on the Philosophy of Computer Games, 2008.

[48] Apperley T. Rhythms of gaming bodies. In: Proceedings of the Australasian Conference on Interactive Entertainment (IE'07). RMIT University; 2007. p. 1-3.

[49] Reidsma D, van Welbergen H, Poppe RW, Bos P, Nijholt A. Towards bi-directional dancing interaction. In: Proceedings of the International Conference on Entertainment Computing (ICEC'06). No. 4161 in Lecture Notes in Computer Science. Springer Verlag; 2006. p. 1-12.

[50] Müller F, Stevens G, Thorogood A, O'Brien S, Wulf V. Sports over a distance. Pers Ubiquit Comput 2007;11(8):633-45, 2005.

Natural and Implicit Information-Seeking Cues in Responsive Technology

17

Maurice Chu and Bo Begole

Palo Alto Research Center, Palo Alto, California

ABSTRACT

Humans move and devise optimal strategies to maximally seek the information they desire. This premise is the guiding framework we adopt to investigate how to design effective information technologies to enhance the shopping experience

415

in retail stores. We discuss our approach, an implicit interaction paradigm that interprets natural behavioral cues, and present a case study of a prototype system we developed called the Responsive Mirror.

Key words: human–computer interfaces, natural interaction, implicit interaction, computer vision, ubiquitous computing, ambient displays.

17.1 INTRODUCTION

Shopping for clothes is an information-seeking activity. Shoppers seek information about availability, cost, size, colors, texture, feel, fit, and style. In contrast to the rapid evolution of online shopping, the shopping experience in a physical retail store has changed little in recent decades. Because of the inherent constraints of physical space, shoppers must expend more energy and time searching for products than when searching online. Often, the full range of a merchant's inventory and product alternatives is not physically apparent. For many products, a shopper can compare only by examining each one sequentially, either because the products are located at different merchants or because the shopper can evaluate only one item at a time, such as when trying on clothes.

Physical retail stores still maintain their value, however, by providing certain kinds of tactile and physical information that cannot be effectively communicated electronically, such as texture, fit, drape, flow, movement, light refraction, and heft. This kind of information is difficult to communicate electronically because it involves human sensing modalities that are not easily quantifiable for electronic transfer and/or are based on personal subjective perception. Although it is possible to simulate the fit and look of clothing on an electronic model, it is ultimately necessary to physically touch the product to gauge an individual's perception of texture, heft, and other factors. For these reasons, shopping for certain classes of products, such as clothing, cannot be wholly supplanted by electronic media.

A number of ubiquitous computing technologies are providing new capabilities to supplement the physical shopping experience. In addition to displaying conventional product information, these technologies can augment a human's assessment of more subjective, perceptual properties by capturing the shopper's experience for use as a memory aid or as an artifact for sharing with friends and family.

In this chapter, we explore shopping as an information-seeking activity. By determining the natural and implicit cues given off by shoppers, we discuss how we can build a system to sense these cues and effectively deliver information in a way that enhances and minimally disrupts the shopping experience. In particular, we present a case study of an interactive system based on natural and implicit cues we call the Responsive Mirror.

17.2 INFORMATION SEEKING AND INDICATIVE CUES

What information do shoppers seek in stores? And what cues do they naturally and implicitly give off that indicate their desire for information? We begin the discussion by imagining and analyzing a simple hypothetical clothes-shopping scenario.

Cindy and her friend Julie walk into a clothing store. Cindy is looking for an outfit for her date tomorrow evening. She walks around the racks, moving throughout the store, glancing around to see if anything catches her eye. She spots a black top with spaghetti straps that she imagines would perfectly match her blue jeans at home. She pulls the top from the rack and takes a closer look.

Cindy calls to Julie to come take a look and asks "What do you think? I think this will match my blue jeans."

Julie smiles and replies as she points to a red top in the next rack, "That's cute, but what about this red top? I think this will make you look sexier for your date."

Cindy considers and agrees. She takes both tops and enters the changing room. She tries on the black top first and comes out to the atrium area to stand in front of a three-way mirror. "Julie, this is top number one."

Julie looks Cindy over and replies, "Okay."

Then Cindy goes back into the changing room and puts on the red top. She comes out, poses in front of the mirror, and says "This is number two. Which do you think is prettier?"

"I think the black one looks more dressy, but the red one is cuter," says her friend.

Cindy looks at the mirror again and turns her body to the side so that she can see her profile. "The red one is a little short and doesn't cover my belly as well. But it's probably better if we go dancing after dinner. I wonder if there's one that's a little longer or maybe a different color." After considering for a while, she goes back into the changing room and changes into the black top again. She says to her friend, "Doesn't this one hang better?"

"Yeah, it does, but the red one is cuter," says her friend.

"I know. Wow, this one is $80! Let me try on the red one again," says Cindy as she walks into the changing room one more time.

17.2.1 Analysis of the Hypothetical Shopping Scenario

Let us analyze the information-seeking behavior in the shopping scenario. Before Cindy goes into the store, she has a goal in mind, which is to buy an outfit appropriate for her date the next evening. The information she seeks is whether there is an outfit in the store that will match her personal tastes for the occasion she has in mind. Assuming she has no knowledge of the existing inventory in the store, and since she has only a limited amount of time to shop, Cindy has devised a strategy to first quickly look over the store's entire inventory and then select a few of the most eligible items.

When she first enters the store, she glances around and walks through different areas to see if anything catches her eye. At this point, she is only performing a quick evaluation of all the clothing in the store to determine which items are worth looking at in detail. Her movement patterns, head motions, and eye gaze are cues about interest and disinterest in items. A slowing of pace or an extended look is a cue that indicates that an item is worth some time to examine in more detail. The direction of gaze and revisits of gaze to the item also indicate level of interest.

When the black top catches her eye, she pulls it out to take a better look. At this point, she is expending significant effort on the top, which indicates more interest in it than in other items in the store. Furthermore, Cindy feels it is worth the effort to get her friend's opinion, so she engages her in evaluating it. Shopping has an important social component, as evidenced by the fact that people shop in groups and ask for feedback often. Feedback requires effort and time, but the fact that it occurs indicates that getting an opinion is important.

After she has sufficiently narrowed down the items that are most eligible, Cindy proceeds to an even more detailed evaluation by going into the fitting room to try on the clothing. This is to see how it will fit on her body, and from the set of viewings with the mirror and comments from Julie, she is evaluating all the criteria that are relevant to satisfying her goal of finding an outfit. The particular motions she makes in front of the mirror, hand gestures, manipulations with the fabric, and conversation with her friend indicate how she is evaluating the clothing. Note that she also focuses on particular characteristics, such as how it covers her belly, which indicates certain features that stand out in her evaluation. Other conventional information like available sizes and colors directly indicate desire for information about inventory, but indirectly indicates some level of satisfaction with the current choices.

This description is not meant to imply that the information-seeking process is linear in the order presented, as it can undergo several iterations in many different permutations.

Our goal is to develop a technology that aids information seeking in retail stores so that the overall experience of the shopper is enhanced without disruption. An example of a disruptive approach was visually imagined in the movie "Minority Report" [1], where the main character is inundated with advertisements and information in an "in-your-face" fashion. It is important that the technology not hinder the usual information-seeking behavior of shoppers by requiring a change of behavior that takes away from their shopping experience. Our idea is to model the information-seeking behavior of shoppers in a store to predict what information they seek and so design an instore technology to deliver information in a manner that is most receptive to shoppers while they are engaged in their usual shopping behavior.

17.2.2 A Framework for Information Seeking

We will adopt an optimization framework for modeling information-seeking behavior during shopping. The shopper's goal is to maximally gather information about the store's inventory of clothing and evaluate all of it. However, given the amount of effort and time it would take to try on every item, shoppers will trade off maximizing information gathering with time and effort expended. An effective strategy to trade off these two concerns is what is known as a "coarse-to-fine" approach, where a quick evaluation of as much inventory as possible is performed followed by detailed evaluation of only the most promising items.

In our framework, we have three phases of information-seeking activity, namely browsing, selection, and decision, which reflect the coarse-to-fine strategy to maximize information gathering while minimizing expenditure of time and effort. These phases should be thought of as filtering stages for clothing, as shown in Figure 17.1, where each item is evaluated and passed to the next phase if it is of interest and worthy of the time and effort needed to evaluate it.

Browsing. The browsing phase is meant to gather maximal breadth of information about the store's inventory in as little time as possible. Browsing typically occurs in the main store area, where the clothing items are displayed on racks and tables. Shoppers tend to walk around the store and quickly glance at items to see what "catches their eye." By only performing coarse evaluation, a shopper is able to obtain a large breadth of item availability in a short amount of time. Items that pass this phase have been deemed worthy of further evaluation.

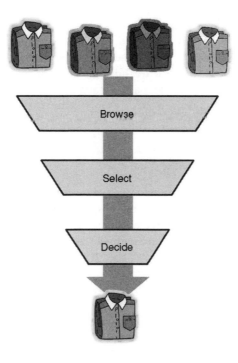

FIGURE 17.1

Phases of information seeking as an efficient clothes-filtering strategy.

Selection. In the selection phase, shoppers evaluate clothing in more detail and hence require more time and effort than needed for the evaluation made during the browsing phase. The shopper's goal is to determine what set of clothing is worthy of further evaluation to make the final decision. Selection typically occurs in the main store area when a shopper stops in the middle of browsing and pulls out clothing to examine it. At this point, shoppers often look at finer details that cannot be easily perceived from afar. They also overlay the clothing on the body to get a quick idea of how it may fit. It is during this phase that the shopper will first ask for feedback from friends or family. If the clothing passes the selection phase, shoppers will carry it with them. If the item does not pass, it is put back onto the rack or table.

Final decision. In the final decision phase, shoppers perform their final evaluation to decide whether to purchase an item. For clothing in particular, this often occurs in the fitting room. Shoppers can be seen trying on the clothing, looking at themselves in various poses in front of the mirror. They also get further feedback. Trying on clothing is time consuming, but the evaluation is necessary for the shopper to make a decision.

In the above, what constitutes *worthiness* of passing to the next phase is dependent on the shopper. For example, some shoppers may find it worthwhile to try on 10 to 20 articles of clothing to find the best one, while others may only find it worthwhile to try on one or two.

The phases are best viewed not as states of the shopper but as states for each clothing item. Some items never pass the browsing phase. Fewer make it to the selection phase. Fewer still make it to the final decision phase. From this point of view, clothing items follow a linear path through these phases in our framework. Also, in our framework the shopper can evaluate the clothing in any order, which allows us to model the iterations between browsing, selecting, and deciding.

17.2.3 Indicative Cues by Phase

People give off indicative cues when involved in an activity. These cues include facial expressions, body movements, gestures, head movements, eye saccades, and many others. Being social animals, we have also developed spoken language to communicate our thoughts to one another, and we have body language to enhance those communications.

In this section, we look at the indicative cues people give off while seeking information during shopping. Some of them are unconscious social signals that Pentland describes as "honest signals" [2]. Because there is a broad set of possible indicative cues we could study and a large body of literature on human interaction in the fields of psychology, sociology, and HCI, for the purposes of this chapter we will limit the discussion to nonvocal cues related to the evaluation of clothing by individual shoppers.

In the following, it is useful to consider the *mechanical* reasons that a particular cue is indicative of a shopper's mental evaluation process. At minimum, a human has nine senses: touch, taste, smell, sight, hearing, thermoception, nociception, equilibrioception, and proprioception. We have dedicated sensory organs for each of these that provide data about the environment. Just like man-made sensors, our sensory organs have limitations due to the physical laws of nature, and so we use our motor capabilities to better position and orient them to maximally obtain the information we seek from the world. For example, saccades and head movements orient our eyes to view objects of interest from different angles. We turn our head to orient the ears to get a better reading of sound waves. And we grab and touch objects to get a feel for their material and functional properties. These mechanical factors are why the location of a person within a store, the items she attends to, and the manipulations she makes with them are indicative.

Browsing. Clothing that is in the browsing phase is generally located in its original position before the shopper enters the store. Some indicative cues that an item may be progressing beyond the browsing phase is when a shopper's gaze dwells on it for some extended period of time beyond a glance. The movement of the shopper through the store is also indicative since she generally cannot see all clothing from one vantage point. Pauses and extended gaze indicate interest in an item, and can be used to gauge transition to the selection phase. Shoppers may also briefly touch items, which indicates that they are interested in either getting a better look at the item or want to feel the fabric.

Selection. In the selection phase, shoppers will generally pull an item off the rack or table to take a closer look. In overlaying the clothing on the body, she is doing a pre-assessment of its potential fit. Other indicators involve asking for feedback from friends or family. The shopper may also examine certain parts of the clothing in detail, which is a cue to particular features that the shopper either likes or dislikes. If the clothing item is taken with the shopper, and it looks like the shopper is going back to browsing, this is a fairly clear indicator that the item has passed the selection phase.

During the selection phase, if the shopper picks up a second item and puts the first back on the rack or table, there is something more appealing about the second item. With information about the features of the first and second items, the shopper has implicitly given a cue about the features she is interested in.

Decision. In the final decision phase, shoppers try on clothing. There are a large number of actions that shoppers make at this stage. The shopper chooses an order for trying on clothing. This could indicate a preference among the selected items. Some clothing is tried on several times, which is also an indicative cue of which clothing she likes best.

As the shopper assesses the clothing in front of a mirror, it is very interesting to note where her eyes are focused and how she turns her body in front of the mirror to get different views of herself. Also, gestures like pulling on the fabric or holding it up in different ways suggest possible modifications that the shopper would like to see.

Side-by-side comparison is often performed when considering a few final items. The shopper is evaluating several criteria to determine which item is the best one to purchase (assuming she has budgeted for only one item).

The cues given off by shoppers are uncertain indicators of the information they are seeking. It is unclear whether prolonged attention corresponds to likability or despicability. The context of the situation can be used to interpret the cues more reliably, but this involves being able to detect context. Another way to combat uncertainty is to use several sources of data at once to collect the user's cues. Perhaps the most promising approach is for devices to learn about a person's particular habits. We are quite good at understanding how our friends and family feel about an item based on observing their interactions with it, and although there may be general patterns over entire populations, some characteristics can only be determined by understanding the individual.

17.3 DESIGNING SYSTEMS FOR NATURAL AND IMPLICIT INTERACTION

It often seems that the world of electronic information is separate from our own; our PCs, handheld computers, and mobile phones provide tiny portals through which we peer into a tiny sliver of the info-sphere. We manipulate information by poking buttons, pushing pucks, touching graphics, and occasionally speaking to devices. Ubiquitous computing takes the philosophy that there should be no distinction between information space and physical reality and that—just as we do not use keyboards to talk to other humans—there should be "natural" ways to interact with computer information. The keyboard and mouse are recent inventions that we train ourselves to use, but our bodies long ago mastered touching, grasping, speaking, moving, gesturing, hearing, and in other ways interacting naturally with the world.

17.3.1 Natural Interaction

What qualifies as "natural" interaction? *Natural* is a subjective term based on the perception and experience of each individual. There are a number of metrics used in the field of human–computer interaction to evaluate the effectiveness of interactive systems: performance speed, number of errors, time on task, perceptions of quality and simplicity, and others. Perhaps the closest metric to the notion of "natural" interaction is ease of learning. A system that is simple to learn will feel natural. The simplicity of learning, however, depends on the skills of the person using the system—someone who has not yet learned to use a mouse will find even the simplest graphical user interface (GUI) difficult to use.

In direct manipulation (originally in contrast to command-line interfaces) users "touch," "move," "select," and in other ways interact with objects that they wish to perform operations on. Objects can be physical or abstract, such as information files and documents, and can be represented visually. Direct manipulation espouses a more natural interaction style than the command-line interfaces that preceded it. Still, direct manipulation interfaces are actually somewhat indirectly controlled through the movement of a mouse on a surface which moves a corresponding pointer on a screen.

An even more direct form of manipulation is present in tangible user interfaces (TUI), such as those created by the Tangible Media Group at MIT beginning in 1996, where the physical space in which information is represented is also what the user interacts with and manipulates [3]. One example of this approach is "Illuminating Clay," a system that allows a landscape designer to manipulate a flexible clay landscape model, which the system laser-scans to calculate heights, contours, water flow, and slopes. These are then projected onto the clay model in near real time. In this case clay, a traditional tool for landscape designers, is used as both the input and output medium, providing direct support for the iterative process of design [4].

Certainly such interfaces are quite "natural" to use; however, most TUI-based applications require some training of users to understand what actions can be performed on the tangible objects and what information will be delivered as a result of those actions.

The oldest medium for exchanging information is speech. Despite ambiguities and imprecision, human language is the richest form in which to express concepts. Computational systems have some ability to recognize human speech, but at lower accuracy than that of human interpretation. To compensate, most speech-based user interfaces require either that the user train the system to her voice or that the system train the user as to the limited vocabulary it can recognize.

Natural interaction is one among a superset of paradigms that has been referred to as reality-based interaction (RBI) [5]. This set covers a broad range of interaction styles "that diverge from the window icon menu pointing device (WIMP) [metaphor] or Direct Manipulation," and includes virtual, mixed, and augmented reality, tangible interaction, ubiquitous computing, context-aware computing, and handheld interaction, as well as perceptual and implicit interaction styles, such as natural interaction. All of these paradigms utilize tacit knowledge in the following four categories: simple physics (gravity, friction, persistence of objects, relative scale); body awareness (proprioception, range of motion, two-handed coordination, whole-body interaction); environment awareness (navigation, depth perception, distance between objects); and social awareness and skills (presence of others, verbal and nonverbal communication). Systems that embody the paradigm of natural interaction leverage a user's knowledge in all four of these categories, as will be demonstrated in our case study.

For the particular activity of shopping, natural interaction will require a system to infer what the shopper is interested in by detecting the natural indicative cues she gives off. This is an important feature in developing a system that can enhance information seeking in stores without taking away from the shopping experience.

17.3.2 Implicit Interaction

In all of the previously mentioned interaction paradigms, the user communicates what she wants the system to do via explicitly designed interactions, a style we will term "explicit interaction." An explicitly designed interaction can generally be described in the form "Doing X" causes the system to "do Y," and the collection of designed interactions encompass the system's interaction model. For example, in modern-day GUIs, "holding down the mouse button on a menu" will cause the system to "show a list of menu options," or "pushing the Save button" will cause the system to "save the file to disk."

In an "implicit interaction" paradigm, systems are designed to learn the user's interaction model rather than the other way around. Developing implicit interaction systems consists of two abilities that are not necessary for explicit interaction systems:

- The ability to infer user goals and intentions and assess the current situation without the use of an explicitly designed interaction model.
- The ability of the system to determine how to respond based on the inferred user interaction model.

Some implicit interaction systems can be very simple. Anti-lock brakes are an example. The driver does not have to learn how to turn on the anti-lock mechanism. Instead, the mechanism monitors the braking situation of the vehicle and automatically activates anti-locking at the appropriate time. Of course, there is explicit input by the driver—stepping on the brake pedal—but activation is implicitly interactive. Another example is the automatic door typically deployed at the entrance of a retail store. This interaction is based on the assumption that when a person is standing near the door, as detected by pressure sensors on the floor or proximity infrared sensors, he intends to open it. It could be argued that this very simple system is an explicit interaction if the pressure or proximity sensor is thought of as an explicitly designed control for opening the door. However, we argue that the automatic door is an implicit interaction system because it was designed based on the usual interaction pattern that people will walk near the door when they wish to open it. The automatic door can only be considered an explicitly designed control if we focus on the implementation. Instead, we distinguish "explicit interaction" from "implicit interaction" from the point of view of the motivations behind the interaction design.

An example of an information technology that encompasses implicit interaction is the recommender system, which infers what products a shopper may be interested in without explicit input. Amazon's "People who bought this also bought the following" is one particularly well-known example. A GUI that allows users to set their preferences for products could have been designed to explicitly capture this information, but users rarely take the time to set these preferences manually. Thus, recommender systems collect user product preferences based on user interactions with system content. In particular, Amazon collects data about the user's buying history as well as what products were viewed in the past to implicitly create a user preference profile.

Section 17.5 will present a case study of a retail system called the Responsive Mirror, which provides information to shoppers while they are standing in front of the mirror in the fitting room.

17.4 CLOTHES SHOPPING SUPPORT TECHNOLOGIES

Technologies that have been deployed in retail clothes shopping stores related to our Responsive Mirror system can be categorized into three groups: fitting room technologies, virtual fittings, and reactive displays.

17.4.1 Fitting Room Technologies

Clothing stores often provide an area for trying on clothes. Generally, there is a private place in which to change clothing, which we refer to as a *changing area*, and an area with a mirror to view the fit, which we refer to as a *fitting area*. In this chapter, we consider these areas separately, although sometimes the fitting and changing areas are the same. We bring up this distinction right away to acknowledge that there are important privacy issues to address regarding cameras where people are disrobing.

The fitting-area mirror is a specific point of customer interaction with products where a shopper makes final decisions on items to purchase. Marketers have recognized this "point of decision" as an opportunity to engage the customer with supplemental information, and a few prototype technologies have been constructed in this domain.

A Prada boutique in New York City offers a sophisticated dressing room designed and constructed by Ideo and IconNicholson [6, 7]. A scanner identifies each garment as the shopper takes it in, and provides additional information about its price and alternate colors and sizes. The fitting room also contains a motion-triggered video camera that records the shopper and plays back the video after a pause.

One of the central components of the system is the Magic Mirror, which allows a shopper trying on clothes to send a video of herself to friends, who can send back comments and vote thumbs up/down. The Magic Mirror can also project a static image of an alternate garment onto the mirror, allowing the shopper to see roughly how it might look on her.

The Magic Mirror has also been deployed in Bloomingdale's. Similar systems have been created and deployed for market evaluation with a number of other retailers [8]. The Gardeur Shop in Essen, Germany, created an RFID-based system that provides product information including price, available sizes and colors, material, and care instructions. Warnaco created a system to show fitting information for women's brassieres. Poggi [8] reports other retailers employing nonsensor technologies in fitting rooms, such as Metropark, Nordstrom, Kira Plastinina, and Macy's.

17.4.2 Virtual Fittings

Some online services, such as Intellifit [9] and MyShape [10], take measurements of a customer's body to suggest clothes that will fit and flatter her shape. These services have been deployed in stores such as Levi's and Charming Shoppes in Ohio, Florida, and Texas. Other Web services such as MyVirtualModel [11], Knicker Picker [12], and 3Dshopping [13] provide a set of predefined body types that allow a shopper to explore an approximation of clothes that fit the type selected. It is also possible to use augmented reality techniques to map an image of a garment onto a captured image of the customer that changes shape in real time as the customer moves in a virtual mirror [14].

In essence, these virtual fitting technologies are comparable to seeing clothing on a personalized mannequin. However, in many cases a customer must actually try the garment on to get the full experience of wearing it. Although sophisticated computer graphics can realistically emulate the drape, folds, and stretch of cloth, Protopsaltou et al. reported that the technology is not completely sufficient and sometimes results in an unexpected fit or color and an unpleasant feel of the fabric [15]. Such technologies also do not cover the full range of ways a person can wear a garment. A buttoned-down shirt, for example, can be worn buttoned or unbuttoned, tight or baggy, tucked or untucked, tied at the bottom, and with sleeves rolled to different lengths. The wide variety of fitting options ultimately requires physically trying on clothes.

17.4.3 Reactive Displays

The ability to change information in reaction to the presence and motion of people has been demonstrated in several systems. Haritaoglu and Flickner described a prototype that uses computer vision to count the people looking at a display and to infer demographic information [16]. Some commercial advertising technologies (Reactrix [17], Freeset Human Locator [18], P.O.P. ShelfAds [19]) detect the presence and motion of people and change the content of the display in reaction. These reactive displays do not display images that mimic the motion of the person looking at the display as the Responsive Mirror does.

17.5 CASE STUDY: RESPONSIVE MIRROR

This section presents the Responsive Mirror. We begin with an overview of the system concept and design considerations, followed by a technical description of the prototype. We conclude the section with impressions and findings from a user study conducted with the prototype.

17.5.1 Concept

To gain insight into the previously described complexities of technology design for physical clothes shopping, we conceptualized a system called the Responsive Mirror, illustrated in Figure 17.3 (see [20] for details of the technology). As a customer

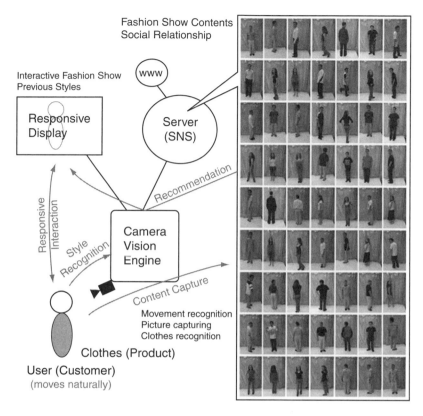

Fashion Show Contents
Social Relationship

Interactive Fashion Show
Previous Styles

www

Responsive
Display

Server
(SNS)

Responsive
Interaction

Recommendation

Style
Recognition

Camera
Vision
Engine

Content Capture

Movement recognition
Picture capturing
Clothes recognition

Clothes (Product)

User (Customer)
(moves naturally)

FIGURE 17.2

Concept diagram of the Responsive Mirror with its social fashion network.

interacts with a conventional mirror, cameras detect her pose as well as the garment being worn. A display on the left of the mirror shows the shopper in a previously tried garment, matching the pose of that image to the pose of the shopper as she moves. This allows the shopper to compare her current garment directly to another item she is considering. The display on the right of the mirror shows images of people wearing similar and different styles (see [21] for details of the similarity computation). These images may come from a store's inventory or may be gathered from an online social fashion network to provide the shopper with information about the people wearing styles similar to and different from the one she is considering.

When a person interacts with a fitting room mirror, she gives off implicit cues about the information she is seeking. When she turns her body, she is observing how the clothes look from different angles. This implicit information-seeking behavior can be detected using sensors, and supplemental information can be provided. Users do not need to be taught how to use the system—they simply behave naturally. This style of implicit interaction is an example of "invisible computing" from the early visions of ubiquitous computing [22]. The following use case scenario illustrates how we imagine the Responsive Mirror would be used.

Kyoko is a 22-year-old woman shopping for blouses in a small clothing store in the Harajuku district of Tokyo, Japan. She browses the rack of recent arrivals for tops in her size, takes a selection into the changing room, and puts them on, one at a time. Each time, she exits the changing room and stands in front of the Responsive Mirror,[1] turning to view the blouse from multiple angles.

There are two electronic displays on either side of the Responsive Mirror. One shows Kyoko wearing each previously tried blouse taken from a camera mounted atop the mirror facing the shopper. As Kyoko turns to view her current blouse from multiple angles, her image in the previous blouse matches her pose, allowing her to directly compare the fit and style.

17.5.2 Privacy Concerns

A common concern that sensor technologies and AmI systems face is how they impact a user's sense of personal privacy. Will users accept a camera or other sensor in a traditionally semi-private space such as a fitting area? What concerns will they have and what measures should the system design incorporate to mitigate them? In the press, privacy concerns are generally not addressed. Reports of the Magic Mirror refer to the camera as "infrared technology," presumably to avoid triggering knee-jerk negative reactions.

People are subjected to video capture on a daily basis, sometimes happily (home movies, videoconferencing, camera-based game controllers) and sometimes without much choice (store surveillance, toll collection, traffic cameras). Such applications have achieved at least some level of tolerance, yet debate continues about the overall effects of sensing technologies on the long-term health of our society. Grudin [23] observed that collecting and distributing such data electronically heightens worry about being susceptible to undesirable uses. The Responsive Mirror design supports the basic framework of feedback and control of image capture outlined by Bellotti and Sellen [24]. Nevertheless, when a camera or other context-sensing technology is introduced into an unexpected situation such as a fitting room, we need to examine the potential impact on privacy.

Palen and Dourish [25], synthesizing the work of Altman on face-to-face interaction [26], discussed the boundaries that people navigate when reacting to situations where there are trade-offs between publicity and privacy in technology-mediated interactions. The Responsive Mirror introduces new capabilities that affect people's expectations under the three boundaries of their framework, described next. Also relevant is the work of Petronio [27], who examined a multitude of publicity/privacy boundaries and their varying permeability. We describe next the potential encroachments across these boundaries that camera technologies create.

---

[1]Small clothing stores in Japan typically have a mirror outside of a small changing room.

Disclosure

People naturally expect a fitting room to be a private place where they can change clothes without being seen. The Responsive Mirror's cameras do not capture images of people in the changing area itself but only in the fitting area outside. Nevertheless, there is still potential for concern regarding capturing the interaction with the mirror. In addition to the awkward poses that a shopper may assume to test the fit of clothing, she naturally expects that she can experiment with styles in which she might not like to be seen for any number of reasons: fit, style, status, expressiveness, and so forth. She may also be troubled if the images will be seen by other people. On the other hand, a shopper interacting with Responsive Mirror may not want the fittings to be completely undisclosed. She may want to show clothes to friends or publish them to a social fashion network.

Identity

The Responsive Mirror presents images of the shopper, as well as others, while she is making decisions about clothing that will become part of her presentation of self. The ability to see images of others provides a way for a person to test the fit of her presentation of self among the presentations of a community. She can examine styles that others are wearing and choose where she wants to fit in. On the other hand, she may not want to be seen as actively positioning herself along such dimensions, perhaps preferring to present a fashionably nonchalant attitude about clothes. Thus, a record of her examination of the images of others can be sensitive.

Temporal

Shoppers today expect an experimental fitting to be transient, not lasting for others to see at another time. In addition to the obvious concern that a shopper might have about recorded images of herself in an embarrassing outfit, images of her in flattering outfits could become problematic as style and tastes change. Although a flattering garment may be an excellent choice at the moment, it could come to represent something contrary to the shopper's future style. This concern can be mitigated by providing the ability to delete regrettable images, but the damage cannot be wholly undone if the images have been stored in an Internet archive. Furthermore, simple deletion is possibly more drastic than desired. The temporal boundary is one that has a varying permeability over time and shoppers might prefer simply that it become more difficult, but not impossible, to see older images.

17.5.3 Social Factors: Reflecting Images of Self and Others

Another under-explored consideration for such technologies is the social aspects of shopping and clothing. Only the Magic Mirror begins to provide support for social interactions by employing mechanisms for synchronous image sharing and voting by remote friends or family. However, synchronous communication with known people is only the tip of the iceberg. What kind of social impressions are shoppers concerned about? How do such systems support exploration of the "language" of clothing?

When buying clothes, shoppers often assess how others will perceive a particular item—that is, the "fashion statement" she is making. Indeed, they often ask companions or store assistants how they look to get this kind of feedback. Although evaluating one's self-image is an important part of clothes-buying decisions, shoppers in a store are provided very little information about what other people are wearing other than what is presented in advertisements. Outside of the store, they find inspiration from others and from the fashion media, some of which contain photographs of nonprofessionals.

Sociologists have long explored the multiple roles that fashion plays in society. In a synthesis of more than 200 sources, Davis [28] examined the social construction of meaning in fashion and how an individual's choices communicate social status, gender, identity, sexuality, and conformity among other subtle characteristics of self. Clothing is undoubtedly used as a form of communication, as declared famously by Lurie [29] and examined in depth by Barnard [30]. Nevertheless, Davis believes it is a code of "low semanticity" because it changes with time and trends and among different groups of individuals.

Although technologies cannot interpret fashion, they can mediate human discourse on the topic. We see this happening today in online social fashion networks, such as ShareYourLook [31] and IQONS [32]. These sites allow members to upload photographs of themselves wearing various outfits. They can categorize, tag, and comment on the images. In this case, the services merely provide scaffolding; the members construct the semantics through tagging and commentary. Providing access to a shopper's social fashion network during a shopping experience provides access to the state of fashion as constructed by the shopper and her online community.

To probe the social aspects of clothes buying, the Responsive Mirror displays images of others wearing outfits of both similar and different styles. The shopper is meant to use the display to determine whether the style she is trying is close to the presentation of self that she wants to project. Figure 17.2 illustrates the social network aspect of the Responsive Mirror concept.

An interesting emerging trend in social networking is the combination of an image similarity service, such as Like.com [33], with a slide show service, such as RockYou [34]. Such services offer product recommendations similar to clothes that appear in a user-supplied photograph. The Responsive Mirror also offers similar and different styles using a matching technology, but it does not make recommendations. Rather, it provides images of similarly and differently dressed people in a social network to illustrate the presentations of self those people are making. Retailers may choose to recommend similar clothing in their inventory, but, because such technologies are fairly well understood, that is not our focus in this research.

Continuing the previous scenario, the following describes Kyoko's experience with images of other people.

The second display shows two sets of people from Kyoko's social network. One set includes people in clothes that are similar in style and color to the outfit Kyoko is currently wearing. The other shows clothes that are dissimilar. As she tries on outfits, Kyoko examines not just how well they fit but also how well they match her self-image. She can see other people wearing similar fashions, which she uses to decide if she thinks of herself as that kind of person. The images and information about people wearing different styles give Kyoko ideas about alternative presentations of self that she may adopt.

After she makes her decision and pays for the garments, the store offers her the option to add images from her Responsive Mirror session to the social fashion network. Kyoko specifies that she would like the items she purchased to be uploaded for anyone to see, but the ones she decided not to purchase can be seen only by "close friends."

The next day, Kyoko receives a text message from her friend Nanami: "Saw your fitting-room photos. Is that the new miumiu look?" Kyoko is pleased to tell Nanami that in fact this was found in a new select shop. "No, this is from a select shop in Harajuku—lots of new collections from selected new brands! I can show you how to get there!"

The purpose of the Responsive Mirror is not to sell items to a targeted user (at least not directly) but to provide opportunities for self-education about fashion by displaying information provided socially. The mirror is no longer just reflecting the shopper's individual social identity. In front of it, she can get hints of other identities from her community (or beyond), and she can expand her own sense of fashion while making product decisions at the store. This capability may benefit retailers as customers become better informed about the fashion trends relevant to their social environment, and it may increase the importance of fashion in their life styles. Moreover, it creates a cycle of customer visitation between a store's online and physical presence. Even before a large-scale network of social content is available, the Responsive Mirror will provide an immediate benefit in allowing shoppers to directly compare options. The system will leverage this immediate benefit to create enough content for the long-term benefits that require a critical mass of users [35].

17.5.4 Responsive Mirror Prototype

The Responsive Mirror prototype consists of a conventional mirror, two cameras, and two electronic displays, as pictured in Figure 17.3. The intent is to install the system outside of the changing room, in the fitting area of a retail store. There is also a database of stored fashion contents, simulating a social network server.

Figure 17.4 shows the system architecture of the Responsive Mirror. A real mirror is at the center, allowing the shopper to view herself as usual. An electronic display to the left shows images from a previous fitting, while a second electronic display to the right shows supplemental information like similar or different clothing and images from the social fashion network. One camera is mounted above the mirror to capture images from its point of view for display and to analyze the clothing worn. A second camera is mounted on the ceiling above where the shopper stands to detect the shopper's body movements.

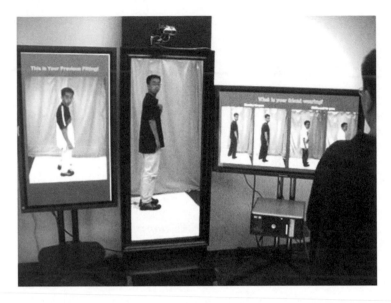

FIGURE 17.3

Responsive Mirror prototype.

17.5.5 Vision System Description

The Responsive Mirror consists of a vision system that analyzes the video captured from the two cameras, as shown in Figure 17.5. The three main parts of the vision system are shopper detection, orientation estimation, and clothes recognition. This is an instance of a multi-camera system that takes advantage of multiple views for different purposes, which we will describe in the following subsections. We built our system using OpenCV [36], an open-source computer vision library with efficient implementations of many commonly used vision algorithms.

Shopper Detection

The first part of the system is detection that a shopper has entered and intends to use the Responsive Mirror. This is accomplished by background subtraction on both cameras to pull out a foreground mask. Because the system will be deployed in controlled indoor settings, we simply take an image of the background from both cameras as our background model. The background may change because of objects within view of the cameras, but there is much literature in background subtraction (e.g., Elgammal et al. [37] and Stauffer et al. [38]) that can handle these situations.

The foreground mask is processed morphologically—in particular, a "closing" operation is performed to close holes within the foreground mask (see Shapiro and Stockman [39] for a reference on morphological processing.). Also, a connected

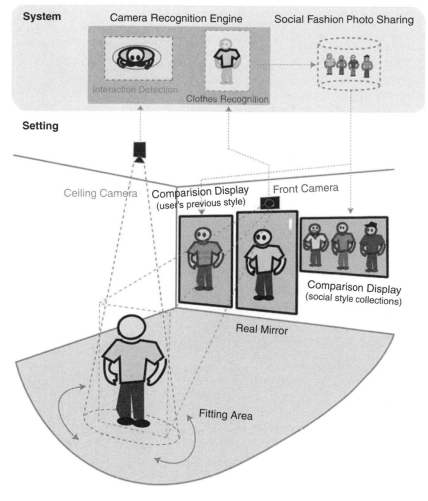

FIGURE 17.4

Responsive Mirror system architecture.

component analysis is performed to discard small noisy artifacts. The result is shown in Figure 17.6, which shows the recovered foreground mask (as white pixels) from the ceiling camera and frontal camera, respectively.

A shopper is considered detected when the number of foreground pixels is greater than a given threshold, which is chosen empirically.

For the shopper detection algorithm to work, there must be no one but the user in the background of either camera's view. The ceiling view is not problematic as it can be adjusted to eliminate others, simply because they do not stand that close to each other when in front of a large mirror. The view from the frontal camera,

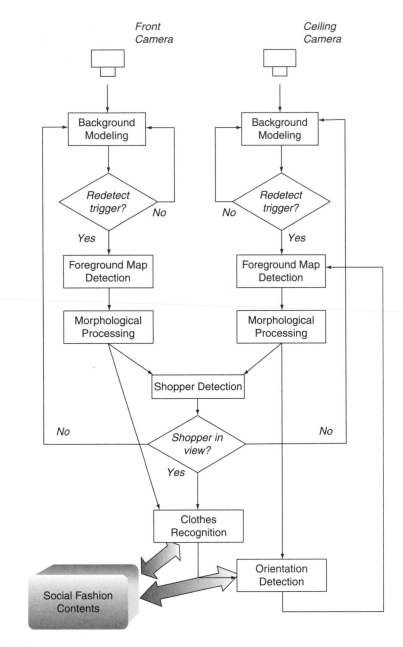

FIGURE 17.5

Responsive Mirror vision system.

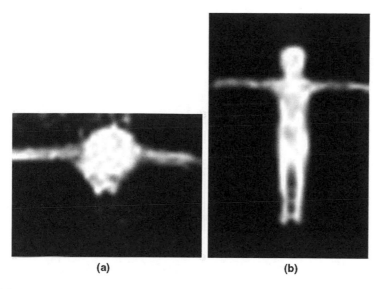

(a)   (b)

FIGURE 17.6

Results of background subtraction: (a) ceiling camera; (b) frontal camera.

however, can be problematic as friends and family will stand behind the user to get a view of how she looks. One solution is to design the space so that others do not stand directly behind the user. A slightly raised platform with perhaps a curtain or wall behind the user would prevent them from leaning into the view of the frontal camera. Also, larger mirrors would allow friends and family to view the user without having to be behind her.

Orientation Estimation

To show an image from a previous session in the orientation in which the user is currently standing, we employ the ceiling camera to estimate and track the orientation in real time. Our approach is to analyze the foreground mask extracted by background subtraction of the ceiling camera image.

We first trace out a contour from the pixels of the foreground mask, then fit an ellipse to it by computing the mean and covariance of the contour pixel locations. (We could have used all pixels from the foreground mask, but the implementation turns out to be faster by tracing out the contour instead.) The minor axis of the ellipse indicates either the front or the back of the shopper. Figure 17.7(a) shows the contour pixel in white overlaid with the computed ellipse. One of the problems of this approach is that, if the user places her arms out to the front as shown in Figure 17.7(b), the computed ellipse's minor axis points along her sides rather than her front and back.

To solve this, we implemented a simple detector to determine whether the foreground mask is convex. We compute the convex hull of the foreground mask, then

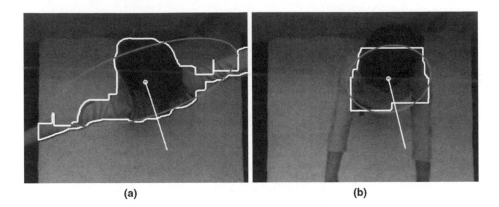

(a)   (b)

FIGURE 17.7

Orientation estimation with arms to sides (a) and arms to the front (b).

compute the ratio of the number of pixels in the foreground mask to the number of pixels in the convex hull. If the ratio is less than a threshold, the foreground mask is considered nonconvex. For a nonconvex foreground mask, we perform a morphological opening operation with a structural element width set to the number of pixels in the typical width of an arm. This results in a contour like the white one shown in Figure 17.7(b).

We are not quite done yet because a flip ambiguity remains. The minor axis gives us two hypotheses about the possible front of the user. We employ the heuristic that people normally face the mirror when they first walk into it, and a nearest-neighbor tracker in angle space to maintain the frontal direction.

Figure 17.8 shows the resulting errors of our orientation estimator. Of the frames we tested, 75% had an error within 15 degrees, shown by the three middle bars around 0, while 97% had an error within 35 degrees.

The output of the orientation estimator is used to tag images taken from the frontal camera. This orientation label can then be used to display the image of an outfit worn previously in the Responsive Mirror by finding the image with the closest orientation tag to the user's current orientation. This implements the self-comparison display on the left of the prototype.

Clothes Recognition

The last part of the visual recognition engine is analysis of the clothing worn by the user to implement the social display on the right of the mirror in our prototype. The key capability we need to develop is a system that can analyze clothing worn by shoppers and return similar and dissimilar clothing items from a database of images. We summarize the approach we take in this section. Further details can be found in [21].

Before we begin, let us consider other methods to identify clothing and their characteristics. One sensing type that could be employed is RFID. Whether a real deployment should use RFID is based on the following trade-offs.

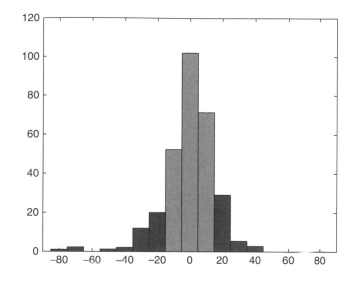

FIGURE 17.8

Distribution of orientation errors from ground truth. Negative values indicate deviations in angle in a counter-clockwise direction.

> *Robustness*. With RFID, clothing can be identified almost perfectly, whereas today's state-of-the-art vision algorithms will produce errors. If this is the only criterion to determine whether to use a vision algorithm or RFID, RFID is the right choice. However, other criteria should be considered.
>
> *Cost*. Today, RFID tags cost a couple of dollars each, but this is still too expensive for tagging every clothing item in a store and in inventory. Also, the cost of RFID readers is on the order of thousands of dollars. On the other hand, once a vision algorithm is developed, there are no extra costs incurred to tag clothing and maintain a database associating RFID identification numbers with each clothing item.
>
> *Untagged existing pictures*. There are many pictures of people in clothing on the Web. With a vision algorithm, these images can become part of the Responsive Mirror system. More generally, advances in vision algorithms for clothes recognition can be applied to other purposes such as identifying material wealth and other characteristics through clothing.

The ultimate answer to whether RFID or a visual recognition algorithm is the better approach will depend on the application. Because there are advantages to visual recognition, we believe it is worth researching its potential.

Subjectivity of Clothing Similarity

How do we begin to quantify subjective notions like clothing similarity? To explore this, we conducted a user study to understand the prominent features of clothing that correlate with similarity and to collect a data set of pairwise similarity relationships. We limited ourselves to men's shirts to simplify the study because there are fewer men's shirt styles than women's tops and dresses.

We collected an image data set of 165 shirts by having 12 people wear shirts from their personal wardrobe in our Responsive Mirror prototype. We then had 65 participants (37 male, 25 female, 3 unknown) perform the following tasks:

- We displayed pairs of shirts from the image data set and asked participants to rate them on a scale from 1 to 5, where 1 meant least similar and 5 meant most similar. Each participant was shown approximately 40 pairs of shirts to rate. The result of this first task was a collection of similarity ratings for pairs of images:

(<img1>, <img2>, <similarity rating>)

- We asked participants to rate how much the following shirt features were correlated with their notion of similarity in clothing on a scale from 1 to 5, where 1 meant not correlated and 5 meant strongly correlated. These features were sleeve length, collar, buttons, color, patterned versus solid, and emblem.

We had users perform the first task to rate similarity as a whole over each pair of shirts. Then they could think back to how they had made their ratings to rate correlation of shirt features with similarity. The subjective ratings of the correlation between shirt feature and similarity from the second task in the user study are summarized in Figure 17.9.

The most prominent factor was sleeve length, followed by collar, buttons, color, pattern, and finally emblem. This makes sense, as some intuitive notions of style, like business shirts, polo shirts, and T-shirts, can be distinguished by sleeve length and collar and buttons. We also split the data between male and female rankings to see if there were any gender differences in the subjective correlation of shirt features and similarity. From this user study, we see no significant gender differences.

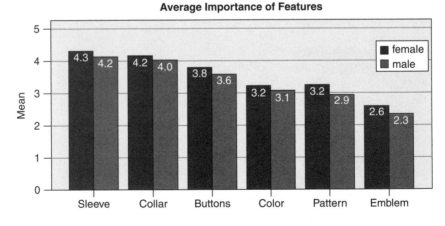

FIGURE 17.9

Subjectve ratings of correlations between shirt feature and similarity.

Clothing Similarity Algorithm

To develop an algorithm that analyzes clothing and outputs similarity ratings, we use the model shown in Figure 17.10. The first part is to develop a feature extractor that analyzes images taken from the frontal camera of the Responsive Mirror and detects the six shirt features. We pass a pair of images through this feature extractor and compute a similarity value for the corresponding features in each image. The similarity values are binary for all features except color, where 1 indicates both shirts either have or do not have the feature. The similarity value for the color is the Bhattacharya distance between the color histograms of the shirt pairs.

These feature similarity values are input to a linear regressor, whose weights can be computed by the labeled data set collected from the user study, so that similarity is computed by the following equation:

$$\text{Similarity} = w_1 \cdot \text{equal}_{\text{sleeve}} + w_2 \cdot \text{equal}_{\text{collar}} + w_3 \cdot \text{equal}_{\text{buttons}} +$$
$$w_4 \cdot \text{colorHistDist} + w_5 \cdot \text{equal}_{\text{pattern}} + w_6 \cdot \text{equal}_{\text{emblem}}$$

In the following, we briefly describe the different parts of the feature extraction and refer the reader to [21] for more details.

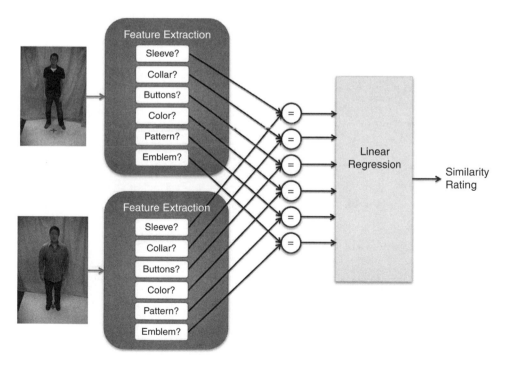

FIGURE 17.10

Clothing similarity measure.

Feature Extraction—Shirt Parts Segmentation

The first part of our feature extraction algorithm segments the parts of the shirt that correspond to sleeve, collar, button, and emblem. Because we computed foreground masks, we simply segment them by using heuristic ratios. Figure 17.11 shows several areas that we will use in the rest of the feature extraction components.

Feature Extraction—Sleeve Length Detection

To detect sleeve length, we look for skin-colored pixels in the arm areas, depicted as vertical boxes around the arm in Figure 17.11. Because skin color can vary from person to person, we first model it by extracting the main color from the face area, depicted by the boxes around the face in Figure 17.12. Then we detect and count the skin-colored pixels in the arm area. By learning a decision stump on the number of skin color pixels, we get about 89% accuracy in our data set. The 10% error is due to shirts that have nearly skin-like color.

Feature Extraction—Collar Detection

To detect collars, we consider several features from the collar area: number of Harris corner points, variance of y-coordinates, distance from neck to shoulder (Figure 17.13), number of skin pixels (Figure 17.14), and sum of the Harris measure (Figure 17.15). The intuition is that collared shirts have more corners than noncollared, (e.g., T-shirts). By training a linear SVM on the above features, we obtain

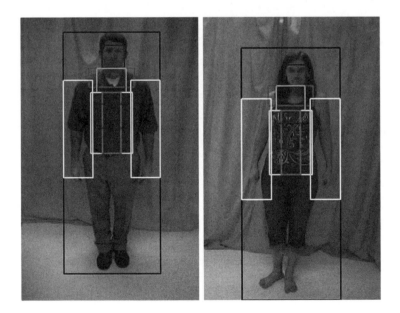

FIGURE 17.11

Shirt parts segmentation.

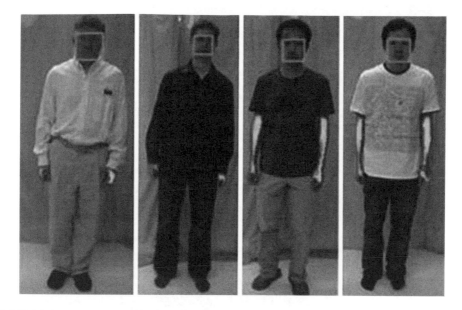

FIGURE 17.12

Sleeve length detection.

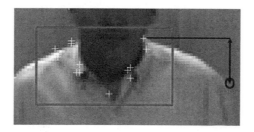

FIGURE 17.13

Features from collar area for collar detection.

FIGURE 17.14

Skin-colored pixels in the collar area.

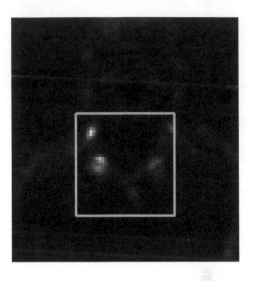

FIGURE 17.15

Harris measure in the collar area (cyan square).

79% accuracy, with the most discriminative feature being the number of Harris corner points. The least discriminative feature is the skin area. Errors in classification are primarily due to shape differences in the collar and variable lighting conditions from shadows.

Feature Extraction—Button Detection

Detecting buttons is very difficult with our cameras because of low resolution and the fact that buttons are often the same color as the shirt. As a substitute for button detection, we detect the placket, the fold in the front of buttoned shirts, by preprocessing the image with the Canny edge detector and extracting the following features: total number of vertical edges in the placket area (shown as the long vertical box in Figure 17.16), number of vertical edges in the upper placket area, number of vertical edges in the lower placket area, vertical variance of vertical edges in the upper area, and vertical variance of vertical edges in the lower area. The idea is that a shirt with a placket has more vertical edges. Collecting the above features and training a linear SVM result in 84% accuracy. The number of vertical edges in the upper placket area is the most discriminative feature. Errors are primarily due to the failure to detect vertical edges from the placket area because of the low resolution of the camera.

Feature Extraction—Pattern Detection

We detect whether shirts are solid-colored or patterned (e.g., stripes or checkerboard) by considering several image features in the torso area (the vertical boxed area around the torso in Figure 17.11): number of Harris corner points, spatial

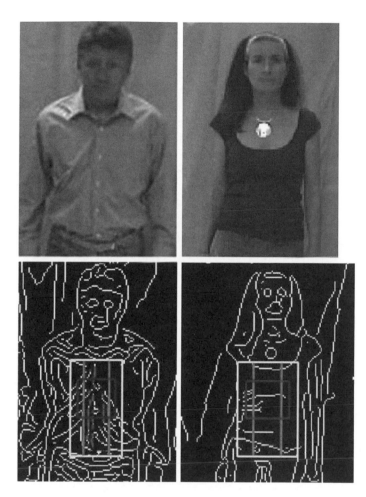

FIGURE 17.16

Placket detection.

variance of the Harris corner points, number of Canny edge points, spatial variance of the Canny edge points, and entropy of the color histogram. The intuition is that patterned shirts have more color complexity than solid ones. Collecting the above features and training a linear SVM results in 88% accuracy. The number of Canny edge points is the most discriminative feature.

Feature Extraction—Emblem Detection

Finally, we consider the following features to build an emblem detector. In particular, we focused only on centered emblems, as we noticed that many T-shirts have them. The image features we consider were from the torso area (shown in Figure 17.11). We also make a further distinction between the inner torso area, (the small box in the middle of the shirt in Figure 17.11) from the outer torso area. Features include average distance from the Harris corner points to the center, average distance from the Canny edge points to the center, difference in the number of Harris corner points between the inner and outer torso, difference in the number of Canny edge points between the inner and outer torso, difference in the entropy of color in the inner and outer torso, and Bhattacharya distance between color histograms within the inner and outer torso. The intuition is that a shirt with a center emblem has more color complexity than one without. Using these features to train a linear SVM results in 99% accuracy. The difference in the number of Harris corner points is the most discriminative.

This completes the description of the various shirt feature detectors that feed into the linear regression model to generate a similarity rating. By employing this algorithm, we can implement the right-side display in the Responsive Mirror prototype to show clothing similar and dissimilar to the clothing being worn.

17.5.6 Design Evaluation

Our prototype has been designed to test assumptions about the usefulness of the new capabilities and to draw out lessons for future design. First, will shoppers benefit from being able to directly compare their clothing alternatives in a physical shopping experience? Second, will shoppers find value from images of other people wearing similar and different clothes? We also want to learn which, if either, capability shoppers prefer, what uses they make of it, and what other capabilities they desire.

In addition, we are interested in the range of behaviors shoppers use to interact with a mirror in a fitting room. We believe that shoppers use more than four basic orientations in our initial design, but we do not know what other poses are common or what other actions people take to test the fit of clothing. Because it is difficult to arrange for field observations in an actual store's fitting room, we observed people's behavior using our prototype in the lab.

Method

We recruited 12 male participants in the age range of 28 to 52 years old. We evaluated only male participants and developed our prototype's vision system to handle only men's shirts because we felt that the lesser variation in men's styles than women's styles would be easier for an initial evaluation. However, we acknowledge that men are potentially an insignificant subpopulation of the main user population (i.e., women), but testing on this demographic allowed faster iteration of the technology–design cycle.

The experiment consisted of three conditions:

- *Mirror*. A conventional mirror alone.
- *Previous outfit*. A conventional mirror with a display on the left showing an image of the shopper from the most recent previous fitting. The orientation in the image matches the orientation in real time.

- *Other people*. A conventional mirror with a display on the right showing four images of other people: two of people wearing a shirt that the system classified as "similar" to the shirt the participant was wearing and two of "different" shirts. We did not inform participants of the algorithm used to determine similarity.

For each condition, participants tried on six different shirts: three collared polo shirts and three crew neck shirts with a mix of colors. The price of the shirt was removed. There were three sets of six shirts with a comparable mix of colors and patterns across sets. The order of conditions and shirt sets was counter-balanced using a Latin-square three-by-three design.

Task and Procedure

Participants were told to imagine themselves in a scenario where they would need to decide which, if any, of the six shirts they would buy. To eliminate price as a factor in their decision, participants were told to imagine that they could afford as many shirts as they wanted and to consider price to be reasonable in all cases. For each shirt, the participant stood approximately 250 cm (8.2 ft) from a full-length mirror (165 cm [65 in] high by 73 cm [29.5 in] wide). Participants were asked to view the shirt from multiple angles in a natural way.

After trying all six shirts per condition, the participants were asked to fill out a questionnaire measuring how appealing they found the shirt and how likely they were to buy it on a five-point scale. They were also asked questions about the condition they had just experienced. After all three conditions were complete, the participants filled out a questionnaire with questions spanning the conditions and potential privacy issues.

Results

To examine whether the display conditions affected participants' perception of the appeal of the shirts or their desire to purchase any of them, we conducted two repeated-measures ANOVAs (analysis of variance [40]) with display condition as the within-subject variable and appeal and purchase as dependent variables in turn. Neither the ratings of the desire to purchase nor the appeal of the shirts were significantly different among conditions (respectively, $F[2, 110] = .42$, $p = .66$; and $F[2, 110] = .32$, $p = .73$).

We asked participants to rank their preference for the three conditions plus a configuration using all three components (which they did not experience). To test whether participants ranked these four configurations differently, we performed a Friedman test on the ranked values within subjects. There was a significant difference in the rankings ($2 = 9.10$, $p = .03$), where the preference (from strongest to weakest) were Previous Outfit plus Other People ($M = 1.92$) > Previous Outfit ($M = 2.00$) > Other People ($M = 2.83$) > Plain Mirror ($M = 3.25$).

Finally, we asked participants how much the Previous Outfit and Other People conditions enhanced their shopping experience. Participants rated Previous Outfit ($M = 3.00$, $SD = .85$, where 5 = Extremely Helpful and 1 = Not Helpful at All) as having enhanced their experience more than Other People (M = 2.50, SD = .52), which was in line with the ranked measures. A paired-samples t-test showed the ratings to be significantly different between the conditions (t[11] = −2.57, p = .03).

These results indicate that although participants considered the displays somewhat helpful, their use did not change perceptions of the shirts or decisions to buy. As one might expect, participants' comments indicated that the quality of the shirt itself was the determining factor, not the method used to assess it. Although the Responsive Mirror's information was considered somewhat helpful, retailers using this technology should not expect an immediate change in purchasing decisions or sales. However, as we discuss later, retailers may reap longer-term benefit from increased customer satisfaction with the shopping experience.

Fitting Room Behavior

Participants exhibited a variety of individual behaviors when examining the clothing. Some moved very little in front of the mirror while others moved a great deal. As we had instructed them, the majority turned to look at themselves from one or more sides. In addition, we observed the movements in the following list. We asked participants to explain the reasons for the motions which are included in the list. We present this list to guide other designers of fitting room technologies, as it is difficult to obtain such data via in-situ observation.

- Arms raised straight out from sides of the body to view how the sleeve looks hanging below the arm and how wide the torso of the shirt is.
- Arms raised straight forward from body to feel the stretch of the fabric across the back.
- Arms folded across the chest to feel the stretch of the fabric.
- Arms raised straight above the body to feel and view the stretch of the shirt below the sleeves.
- Body twisted to feel and view the stretch across the torso.
- Sports movements such as a golf swing to feel the shirt through the entire movement.
- Shirt bottom of an untucked shirt rolled up to simulate how it would look tucked in.
- Inside and outside of emblems touched to check the texture.

We observed each individual using a subset of these poses, usually following an individualized routine or test suite. The range of behaviors suggests that the system needs a more general pose-matching capability than the Responsive Mirror's current system of detecting and matching rotational orientation. Our research is investigating appropriate pose-matching algorithms.

User Suggestions for Enhancement

We asked participants to provide suggestions for other features they would like to see in such a system. The most common was an ability to see all of the previous shirts during a fitting session, not just the most recent, which was the limitation of the prototype. Participants wanted to be able to specify which image to show. Three said that their typical strategy is to compare just two shirts at a time.[2]

Three participants wanted control of the orientation of images of previous outfits, not necessarily having it rotate with them. In particular, they wanted to be able to see the back without having to face away from the display. Another suggestion was to put another mirror in the rear of the room to reflect the shopper's back. Some conventional fitting rooms do this already.

Two participants suggested capturing images in more poses, such as the various arms stretches and other movements we observed. One claimed half-jokingly that he sometimes simulates sports poses such as golf and tennis swings.

Some participants suggested maintaining a record of their past visits. A few expressed some desire to upload images of their entire wardrobe. They expressed varying willingness to actually photograph their wardrobe to this end.

Another common suggestion was to use a more sophisticated matching algorithm for detecting similar clothing. The system's use of color matching was not adequate. Participants mentioned the following factors (in order of frequency): collar versus crew neck, presence and number of buttons (polo versus full placket), pattern present or not, general pattern complexity (e.g., thin plaid versus wide stripes), T-shirt emblem size and placement, sleeve length, and tuck required (e.g., work shirt) versus tuck optional (casual shirt). Participants also suggested being able to sort and view shirts along these dimensions.

Use of Images of Other People

We asked participants to describe ways they would use the images of other people. Generally, they saw these images as being analogous to alternate product recommendations as seen at online merchants. We instructed them that the shirts might or might not be available in the store, and they responded that it would still cause them to look for similar items. They saw the presentation of *similar* shirts as being potentially useful if there was one better than the one they were trying on. They saw the presentation of *different* shirts as potentially providing ideas for completely different looks in cases where they didn't like the shirt they were trying.

A few participants suggested that they would be primarily interested in images of specific people who they thought generally dressed well, not necessarily anyone in their social network. They imagined being able to specify who in their social network they want to see.

One participant said that it was interesting to see the clothes people in a certain age range were wearing, to determine if the one he was trying on was appropriate. This comment suggests that the images of others would provide a representation of "appropriate" clothing within various social demographics.

We had expected more use of the images of other people for social comparison than participants reported. Instead, our participants saw them as product promotions. Displays in stores are typically used to promote products, and participants

---

[2]Note that at the time of this study, we had implemented a simple clothing similarity matching algorithm based on color only. The findings reported here were used to design the clothing similarity algorithm described in section 17.5.5.

expected a similar purpose for the images our system displayed. A contributing factor is likely that the demographic of our experiment (male, technology industry) was not strongly interested in other people's clothing. Or it may be that images from a social network are not widely useful and may only have value to a small segment of shoppers, such as those who are involved in social fashion networks. We will probe the usefulness of social images with a different demographic in future research.

Results from Privacy-Related Questions

Regarding the issues of disclosure, we asked participants how much it would bother them if someone from the same or opposite gender and specific social group (family, friends, co-workers, and strangers) viewed images of them captured by the system. They specified their response on a five-point scale (5 = bothers me a great deal, 1 = doesn't bother me at all). The responses were not significantly different according to the gender of who would see the image, so we calculated the mean for each social group across gender. The means were Family = 1.08 (SD = .19), Friends = 1.50 (SD = .71), Stranger = 2.08 (SD = 1.06), and Co-worker = 2.25 (SD = 1.14). We performed a repeated-measures ANOVA and found a significant difference among social groups ($F[3,33] = 5.76$, $p = .003$). Post hoc contrasts revealed that Family is not significantly different from Friends and that Co-workers is not significantly different from Strangers. However, Family and Friends is significantly different from Co-workers and Strangers ($p = .01$). The frequency distributions for all groups have a mode of 1 (doesn't bother me at all) except Co-workers, which is bimodal with modes at 1 (doesn't bother me at all) and 3 (bothers me somewhat).

We asked participants how much it would bother them on the same five-point scale if other people saw images of them wearing a shirt that looks good versus a shirt that looks bad. Participants rated their level of concern significantly higher for bad shirts (M = 3.0) versus good shirts (M = 1.42) ($p = .001$).

As for personal and group identity, we asked participants how often (5 = always, often, sometimes, seldom, never = 1) they think of someone else who might like the clothes they are trying on. The mean response was 2.67 (SD = 0.98). Then we asked how often they think about how similar the clothes were to what people they know and don't know are wearing. The mean for people they know was 2.92 (SD = 0.9) and for people they don't know 2.33 (SD = 0.98) with no significant difference between them. Participants responded with a mean of 3.6 (SD = 1.07) to the question of how often they consciously consider how others will perceive them in the clothes they are trying.

On issues of temporality, we asked participants if, should their tastes change in the future, they would want to remove images of themselves wearing a contrary style. On a five-point scale (5 = Definitely, 1 = Definitely Not), participants responded with a mean of 3.08 (SD = 1.16) (closest to Possibly). We asked them at what period of time would they consider removing images of themselves they had allowed others to see. The highest number of responses was for three months (five participants) and the distribution of the remaining responses was spread across times within one year (five participants) and never (two participants). These responses can guide the points in time at which to remind users of the existence of past images.

17.6 LESSONS FOR AMBIENT INTELLIGENCE DESIGNS OF NATURAL AND IMPLICIT INTERACTION

One limitation of this study is that it used participants of only one gender (male). Thus, it is not clear to what extent the same phenomena would be observed with participants of the other gender (female), particularly regarding questions of privacy and social effects. The design and evaluation of this prototype elicited a mix of application-specific and generic design guidelines for ubiquitous computing systems.

Technologies are increasingly entering our physical environments, including retail shopping. In addition to the practical issues of deploying pervasive technology in physical spaces (power, placement, lighting, etc.) designers of applications in this domain need to consider the information goals of shoppers as well as their social concerns. Our experience with the Responsive Mirror uncovered some unexpected issues in the design of user experience in this domain.

Users immediately understood the implicit interaction with the visual estimation of their orientation to the mirror and were able to focus on the evaluation of the clothes rather than on explicitly controlling the information display. Having learned the system, however, some participants wanted more control over what they could display: more clothes from previous sessions, clothes from their personal wardrobe, specific people within or beyond their social network, different styles, and so forth. On the other hand, some participants preferred a strategy of comparing only two shirts at a time. Designers must take care not to lose the benefit of natural and implicit interaction by introducing explicit interface controls that may be useful only occasionally.

Designers of implicitly controlled systems such as the Responsive Mirror face a greater challenge than designers of gesture recognition systems. Gesture recognition is an explicit interaction because a fixed set of hand gestures have been explicitly designed to be differentiable by a computer. To truly develop an implicit interaction system, a prototype to observe user interaction is a requirement to account for natural individual behavior variations.

Although it may generally be true that algorithms must be more complex to handle the variations of individual behavior, systems can be designed to naturally elicit certain behaviors that can simplify algorithms. For example, when people are in front of a mirror, they tend to center themselves to get the best view. The narrower the mirror, the more constrained the set of positions for users to see themselves. This means algorithms can take advantage of people's natural behavior to position and orient their sensory organs to maximize information gain.

Several aspects of our prototype were more limited than the design goals: The interaction with the camera should be more fluid, the displays should carry more detail, and there should be more social network content. Nevertheless, a critical lesson from our exploration is that these factors are not divided into easily separable layers like hardware versus software or content versus functionality. System capabilities are interrelated; the user experience is augmented by interaction with visual recognition that retrieves content from the social network, "invisibly" targeting the shopper's information needs and objectives in a physical retail store. Designs of such systems need to consider how elements of the design propagate throughout the entire system.

Designers of pervasive technology must be aware of the ways information systems such as these are affected by our notions of personal privacy. We already see that the increasing volumes of social content creation, sharing, and retrieving are modifying societal norms. Designers of retail systems should shape the system to provide benefits that balance, or potentially outweigh, the risks to privacy in terms of disclosure, identity, and temporal boundaries. Our experience indicates that some users are receptive to a system that bundles the capture of potentially sensitive images with the consumption of images from others as well as with contributions to a social community.

Our results uncovered another challenge in displaying information in this domain: Users have come to expect product pitches. Participants did not separate the idea of images of other people from in-store product recommendations. This effect may be a result of years of experience seeing advertisements in stores and online. Therefore, the perception of new technologies must deal with preconceptions in order to properly communicate information. A retail store has traditionally been a hermetically sealed information environment where the merchant controls what is shown, so shoppers may naturally expect that all information directly serves the merchant's goals. Of course, merchants benefit most when they satisfy customers' goals, and it will be in their interest to connect customers with relevant external information. The challenge for designers is to avoid triggering cynical suspicions.

Finally, people have a wide variety of preferences, as exhibited from the breadth of user feedback about the Responsive Mirror prototype. The ultimate goal for designing natural and implicit interaction systems is to accomodate each person on an individual basis rather than most people in an aggregate sense. The challenges are immense and worth pursuing.

ACKNOWLEDGMENTS

The authors would like to thank Takashi Matsumoto, Wei Zhang, Juan Liu, and Nick Yee for their contributions to the Responsive Mirror system.

REFERENCES

[1] Minority report. *http://www.imdb.com/title/tt0181689/* [Last accessed Dec. 22, 2008].

[2] Pentland A. Honest Signals: How They Shape Our World. MIT Press; 2008.

[3] Ishii H, Ullmer B. Tangible bits: Towards seamless interfaces between people, bits, and atoms. In: Proceedings of the Conference on Human Factors in Computing Systems (CHI '97). ACM Press; 1997. p. 234–41.

[4] Piper B, Ratti C, Ishii H. Illuminating clay: A 3-D tangible interface for landscape analysis. In: Proceedings of Conference on Human Factors in Computing Systems (CHI '02). ACM Press; 2002.

[5] Jacob RJ, Girouard A, Hirshfield LM, Horn MS, Shaer O, Solovey ET, et al. Reality-based interaction: A framework for post-WIMP interfaces. In: Proceeding of the Twenty-Sixth Annual SIGCHI Conference on Human Factors in Computing Systems (CHI '08). ACM Press; 2008. p. 201–10.

[6] Iconnicholson magic mirror. *http://www.iconnicholson.com/* [Last accessed Dec. 22, 2008].

[7] Brown J. Prada gets personal, Business Week. *http://www.businessweek.com/magazine/content/02_11/b3774612.htm* [Last accessed Dec. 22, 2008].

[8] Poggi J. Dressing rooms of the future, Forbes.com. *http://www.forbes.com/2008/07/22/style-shopping-retailer-forbeslife-cx_jp_0722style* [Last accessed Dec. 20, 2008].

[9] Intellifit. *http://www.intellifit.com/* [Last accessed Dec. 22, 2008].

[10] Myshape. *http://www.myshape.com/* [Last accessed Dec. 22, 2008].

[11] My virtual model. *http://www.mvm.com/* [Last accessed Dec. 22, 2008].

[12] Knickerpicker.com. *http://www.knickerpicker.com/* [Last accessed Dec. 22, 2008].

[13] 3dshopping.com. *http://www.3dshopping.com* [Last accessed Dec. 22, 2008].

[14] Ehara J, Saito H. Texture overlay onto deformable surface for virtual clothing. In: Proceedings of the 2005 International Conference on Augmented Tele-Existence (ICAT '05). ACM Press; 2005. p. 172–9.

[15] Protopsaltou D, Luible C, Arevalo M, Magnenat-Thalmann N. A body and garment creation method for an Internet based virtual fitting room. In: Proceedings of Computer Graphics International 2002 Conference. Springer Verlag; 2002. p. 105–22.

[16] Haritaoglu I, Flickner M. Attentive billboards. In: Proceedings of the 11th International Conference on Image Analysis and Processing. IEEE Press; 2001. p. 162–7.

[17] Reactrix. *http://en.wikipedia.org/wiki/Reactrix_Systems,_Inc* [Last accessed Dec. 22, 2008].

[18] Freeset Human Locator. *http://www.freeset.com/* [Last accessed Dec. 22, 2008].

[19] P.O.P. shelfAds. *http://www.popbroadcasting.com/main/intilashelf.html* [Last accessed Dec. 22, 2008].

[20] Zhang W, Matsumoto T, Liu J, Chu M, Begole B. An intelligent fitting room using multi-camera perception. In: Proceedings of 2008 Conference on Intelligent User Interfaces (IUI 2008). ACM Press; 2008. p. 60–9.

[21] Zhang W, Begole B, Chu M, Liu J, Yee N. Real-time clothes comparison based on multi-view vision. In: Proceedings of ACM/IEEE International Conference on Distributed Smart Cameras (ICDSC-08); 2008.

[22] Weiser M. The computer for the 21st century. Sci Am 1991;265:94–104.

[23] Grudin J. Desituating action: Digital representation of context. Human-Computer Interaction 2001;16(2–4):269–86.

[24] Bellotti V, Sellen A. Design for privacy in ubiquitous computing environments. In: Proceedings of the European Conference on Computer-Supported Cooperative Work (ECSCW). Kluwer Academic Publishers; 1993. p. 77–92.

[25] Palen L, Dourish P. Unpacking "privacy" for a networked world. In: Proceedings of the SIGCHI Conference on Human Factors in Computing Systems (CHI '03). ACM Press; 2003. p. 129–36.

[26] Altman I. The Environment and Social Behavior: Privacy, Personal Space, Territory and Crowding. Brooks/Cole; 1975.

[27] Petronio S. Boundaries of Privacy: Dialectics of Disclosure. State University of New York Press; 2002.

[28] Davis F. Fashion, Culture and Identity. University Of Chicago Press; 1994.

[29] Lurie A. The Language of Clothes. Random House; 1981.

[30] Barnard M. Fashion as Communication. 2nd ed. Routledge; 2002.

[31] Shareyourlook. *http://www.killerstartups.com/Social-Networking/shareyourlook-com-a-social-network* [Last accessed Dec. 22, 2008].

[32] IQONS. *http://www.iqons.com/* [Last accessed Dec. 22, 2008].

[33] Like.com. *http://www.like.com* [Last accessed Dec. 22, 2008].

[34] Rockyou. *http://www.rockyou.com/* [Last accessed Dec. 22, 2008].

[35] Ehrlich SF. Strategies for encouraging successful adoption of office communication systems. ACM Transactions on Information Systems 1987;5(4):340–57.

[36] Bradski G, Kaehler A. Learning OpenCV: Computer Vision with the OpenCV Library. 1st ed. O'Reilly Media; 2008.

[37] Elgammal A, Duraiswami R, Harwood D, Davis LS. Background and foreground modeling using nonparametric kernel density estimation for visual surveillance. In: Proceedings of the IEEE; 2002. p. 1151–63.

[38] Stauffer C, Grimson W. Adaptive background mixture models for real-time tracking. In: Proceedings of Computer Vision and Patter Recognition Conference (CVPR 1999); 1999. p. 246–52.

[39] Shapiro L, Stockman G. Computer Vision. Prentice Hall; 2001.

[40] Ferguson G, Takane Y. Statistical Analysis in Psychology and Education. 6th ed. McGraw-Hill Ryerson Limited; 2005.

CHAPTER

Spoken Dialogue Systems for Intelligent Environments

18

W. Minker, T. Heinroth, P.-M. Strauss, and D. Zaykovskiy

Ulm University, Institute of Information Technology, Ulm/Donau, Germany

ABSTRACT

An intelligent environment is a physical space augmented with computation, communication, and digital content. In this chapter, we will discuss how spoken dialogue system technologies, critical for user-friendly human–computer interaction, can be deployed in intelligent environments. The presented theories, paradigms, and approaches will be illustrated with recent projects and research, including a client–server approach to large-vocabulary speech recognition for mobile devices, a distributed information access system for cellular phones, a spoken dialogue guidance system for pedestrians, and a proactive dialogue companion for restaurant selection.

Key words: Speech, mobile devices, information access, spoken dialogue system.

18.1 INTRODUCTION

Smart devices that control and automate various tasks now populate everyday environments (e.g., home, office, car) which for this reason are progressively becoming *intelligent environments*.

Smart devices are also used by nonexperts and should therefore be easy to use and nonintrusive, and should exploit the most natural communication means. Spoken dialogue is a key factor in a user-friendly and consistent interaction in intelligent environments. Providing easy access to the technical possibilities of these environments, spoken dialogue systems (SDSs) have become an increasingly important interface between humans and computers.

The SDS technologies that are particularly important for intelligent environments include robust natural language processing (recognition and understanding), adaptive and proactive dialogue modeling, multimodality, intelligent planning, monitoring and plan adaptation, embedded agents, reasoning, inferencing, flexible end-device technology, and networking. Some of these will be addressed throughout this chapter. We will present in detail systems operating in potential application environments at home, at work, and on the move.

International research projects have long been concerned with spoken dialogue interaction. We describe some here.

- In SmartKom (1999–2003), promoted by the BMBF, concepts were tested for the development of new forms of human–computer interaction [1]. The aim was the exploration and development of a self-declared, user-adapted interface for interaction between humans and devices using dialogue. The advantages of speech dialogue communication were combined with those of graphical user interfaces and gestics-mimics.
- The INVITE project developed tools for an innovative information and knowledge exchange to realize remote workstations.
- The EMBASSI project explored the homogeneous multimodal remote control of all electronic appliances of everyday life to minimize the complexity of user interfaces and operating instructions.
- The digital pocket-sized assistant, developed by the MAP project, offers new technical mobile solutions through integration of multimodal interactive functions, new assistance systems, agent technologies, and multimedia.
- In Smart Web (2004–2007), methods and technologies were researched and implemented in the fields of intelligent user interfaces, semantic Web, and information extraction [2]. The semantic Web is based on a textual description of digital documents with standardized vocabularies, which have machine-readable semantics. We observe a transition from a "web of reference structures" to a "web of content structures." This opens new dimensions in the fields of Internet services, information retrieval, mobile computing, e-commerce, and e-work.
- The EU-project SENECA (Speech Control Modules for Entertainment, Navigation and Communication Equipment in Cars) integrates and enhances speech

recognition technology in cars [3]. The dialogue interface enables users to access a large number of entertainment, navigation, and communication services for the mobile application environment. SENECA applies noise compensation technologies, speech recognition, and dialogue management. Its prototypes have been evaluated in user tests.

■ The aim of the ATRACO project, supported by a grant from EU ICT/FET Proactivc2, is the realization of trusted ambient ecologies [4]. These comprise interactive appliances, collaborative devices, and context-aware artifacts, as well as models, services, and software components. A context-aware artifact, appliance, or device uses sensors to perceive its context of operation and applies an ontology to interpret it. It also uses internal trust models and fuzzy decision-making mechanisms to adapt to context changes. Finally, it employs adaptive dialogue models to communicate its state and interact with users.

18.2 INTELLIGENT ENVIRONMENTS

An intelligent environment (IE) is a location equipped with actuators, sensors, devices, and services that are networked with each other and the Internet. In such environments the availability of a large variety of complex technical functionalities and devices requires an increasingly complex human–computer interaction. Requirements are, in particular, access to information services, standard communication devices, integrated planning, and problem-solving applications. There are three main classes of IEs: home, office, and on the move.

Under some specific conditions, notably in on-the-move scenarios, the complexity of human–computer interaction is a major concern. People walking or driving through, say a city center are nearly always equipped with a mobile phone. We presume that in the future such a mobile device will serve, from a user's point of view, as the core of an on-the-move IE. Currently, only a few mobile phones support Web browsing, and the mobile user has to pay a high price for his information retrieval: Large HTML files have to be transmitted over costly GPRS or UMTS connections between the phone and the Web server. And in most cases, this information is not suitable for small screens, which implies low usability.

In this chapter we present an information retrieval system that fits the conditions in an on-the-move scenario.

18.2.1 System Architecture

Undeniably, multimodal SDSs, especially in mobile scenarios, have already shown their potential in improved safety and user friendliness in human–computer interfaces. An additional enhancement may consist of rendering these interfaces more intelligent. In particular, there appears to be a specific need for an integrated solution that is aware of the inter-dependencies between the user's actions, state, and goals. In other words, the knowledge to be gained from environmental and situational contexts should be incorporated into the human–computer interaction. For example, a calendar manager integrated with a route calculator may suggest suitable appointments according to the traveling times between locations. Or the search request for the closest restaurant can be refined based on cuisine preferences implicitly noticed in a previous dialogue.

We argue that the human–computer interface needs to be supported with enhanced task-oriented, context-aware knowledge representation and reasoning capabilities. This support should allow isolated services to be integrated into a system that acts as the user's uniform assistant. To substantiate this claim, we aim to develop an architecture that exhibits high user friendliness, provides environment- and context-aware services, consumes few computational resources, and has low operational costs.

The architecture we propose is shown in Figure 18.1. The core of the system is the application server (AS), which acts as an intermediate point enabling the integration of its services and providing a uniform view of its functionalities. The idea is that the client appliance accesses a wanted service not directly but via the AS. The AS enables the actual information retrieval by maintaining concurrent knowledge contexts, signaling inferences and choice points that may initiate further dialogue between the user and the system.

From the perspective of the AS, dialogue management (DM) negotiates a shared knowledge context with the user. This signifies that the DM is responsible for keeping the user and system synchronized when this shared context changes. Synchronization is achieved by communicating the changes. Changes originate from the AS only if it infers new information and they originate from the DM if the user specifies new information or retracts previously specified information, such as parameter values, constraints, and choices between alternatives.

Based on user request and so far collected knowledge, the AS activates the corresponding service, obtains information, and sends the result in a context-optimized and compressed form to the user. Since the information sent to the client represents the essence of the data initially provided by the particular service, transmission costs are reduced and, at the same time, the usability of the service is increased.

18.2.2 The Role of Spoken Dialogue

Being the most natural way of communication between humans, speech is also an increasingly important means of interaction between humans and computer systems integrated into intelligent environments. The speech modality for information input and output successfully augments and often replaces standard user interfaces, contributing to overall usability and friendliness of technical and information systems.

Spoken dialogue is particularly important in the context of mobile applications, where consistent interaction is complicated by the limitations of end-user devices. Factors such as small screens, simplified and shortened keyboards, and tiny buttons make the speech modality highly desired in human–computer interfaces for mobile scenarios.

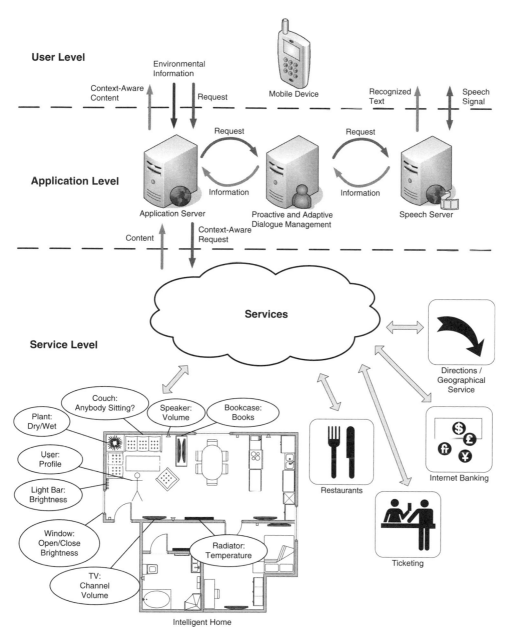

FIGURE 18.1

Architectures of speech-enabled information systems.

The substantial effort made in automatic speech recognition (ASR) throughout the last decades has resulted in effective and reliable speech recognition systems. Modern general-purpose ASR systems use statistical algorithms to convert the audio signal into machine-readable input. Such systems can be structurally decomposed into front-end and back-end (Figure 18.2). In the front-end the process of feature extraction takes place; the back-end searches for the most probable word sequence based on acoustic and language models.

Since we are mostly concerned with mobile scenarios, where end-user devices provide a certain connectivity, we classify mobile-oriented ASR systems according to the location of the front-end and back-end. This allows us to distinguish three principal system structures:

- *client-based*, or embedded ASR, where both front-end and back-end are implemented on the terminal
- *server-based*, or network speech recognition (NSR), where speech is transmitted over the communication channel and the recognition is performed on the powerful remote server
- *client–server*, or distributed speech recognition (DSR), where the features are calculated on the terminal and classification is on the server side

Each approach has its individual strengths and weaknesses, which may influence the overall performance of the system. Therefore, the appropriate implementation depends on the application and the terminal's properties. Some small recognition tasks can be performed directly on client devices [5, 6]. However, for complex large-vocabulary speech recognition, the computing resources available on current mobile devices are not sufficient. In this case remote speech recognition, which uses powerful servers for classification, is recommended [7].

In the following we consider two possible architectures implementing remote speech recognition: NSR and DSR. We analyze the problems associated with each architecture in detail and provide recommendations for practical realization of the corresponding approach.

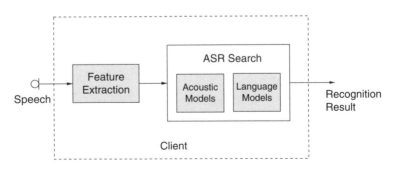

FIGURE 18.2

Terminal-based ASR—embedded speech recognition.

Network Speech Recognition

We have adopted the NSR architecture for implementing the pedestrian navigation system to be presented in Section 18.3.1. The main idea behind this is shown in Figure 18.3. We use Voice-over-IP software to call a speech server. Referring to the overall architecture presented in Figure 18.1, the *user level* consists of a PDA, a mobile phone providing Internet access, and a GPS receiver. Skype is running on the PDA to access the speech server but it is also possible to use any other Voice-over-IP client.

Figure 18.4 shows the design of the system at the *user* and the *application levels* in detail. We use a speech server to process the dialogue flow hosted by TellMe [8] and an application server to translate geo-coordinates into a grid of sectors zoning the test route. This is necessary to bridge the gap between the output of the GPS receiver and the spoken directions.

One benefit of this system design is that it is easy to implement and fast in place, especially for evaluation purposes. It is also very flexible because different speech servers and Voice-over-IP clients may be used. It is not necessary to have any kind of speech recognizer or synthesizer running on the client device. A disadvantage is the bandwidth required to run the system: A UMTS flat rate was required for system evaluation.

Distributed Speech Recognition

As mentioned previously, speech recognition in a DSR architecture is distributed between the client and the server. Here one part of an ASR system, feature extraction, resides on the client while the ASR search is conducted on the remote server (Figure 18.5).

Even though both DSR and NSR make use of the server-based back-end, there are substantial differences in these two schemes.

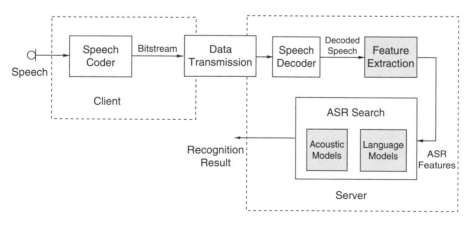

FIGURE 18.3

Server-based ASR—network speech recognition.

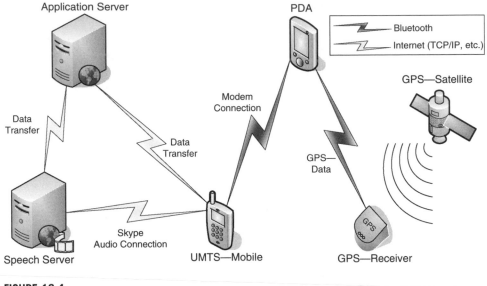

FIGURE 18.4

User and application level in detail.

In the NSR case the features are extracted from the resynthesized speech signal. Since lossy speech codecs are optimized for the best perceptual quality and not for the highest recognition accuracy, the coding and decoding of speech reduces recognition quality [9, 10]. This effect becomes much stronger in the case of transmission

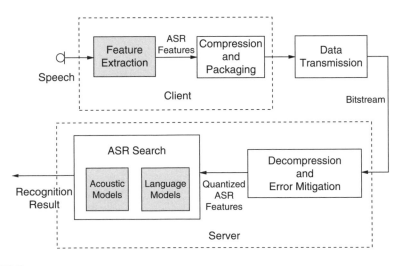

FIGURE 18.5

Client–server ASR—distributed speech recognition.

errors, where data loss needs to be compensated. Since in DSR we are not constrained to the error mitigation algorithm of the speech codec, better error-handling methods in terms of word error rate (WER) can be developed.

Another factor favoring DSR is the lower bit rate required. For the ASR search, high-quality speech is not required but rather some set of characteristic parameters. Therefore, the generated traffic is lower with respect to NSR.

Finally, since the feature extraction is performed at the client side, the sampling rates may be increased to cover the full bandwidth of the speech signal.

ETSI DSR front-end standards

The successful deployment of the DSR technology is only possible in practice if both the front-end and the DSR back-end assume the same standardized procedure for feature extraction and compression. Four standards have been developed under the auspices of the European Telecommunications Standards Institute (ETSI) (see Table 18.1).

The first standard, ES 201 108 [11], was published by ETSI in April 2000. It specifies the widely used Mel-cepstrum–based feature extraction algorithm together with compression and transmission error mitigation algorithms. ES 201 108 is our target version of the DSR front-end to be ported into Java ME. This front-end operates at a 4.8-kbit/s bit rate and will be considered in more detail later.

To improve the performance of the DSR system in noisy environments a noise-robust version of the front-end has been developed. This advanced front-end (AFE) [12] version was published as ETSI standard document ES 202 050 in February 2002.

In 2003 both standards were enriched to the extended versions ES 202 211 [13] and ES 202 212 [14], allowing for the cost of additional 0.8-kbit/s reconstruction of the intelligible speech signal out of the feature stream.

Publicly available C implementations exist for all four standards. Moreover, for the extended advanced front-end there is a standardized C realization TS 126 243 [15] using only fixed-point arithmetic.

A Java ME implementation of the DSR front-end

Considering the mobile phone as a target device, we had to fathom the possibilities for application development on it. The most widespread technology in this field is Java Micro Edition (Java ME, formerly known as J2ME). The second most widespread, the Symbian technology, is not common on consumer mobile phones. Thus

Table 18.1 Overview of ETSI Standards for DSR Front-Ends

Speech Reconstruction	Noise Robustness	
	Basic	Advanced
No	FE ES 201 108	AFE ES 202 050
Yes	xFE ES 202 211	xAFE ES 202 212

with nearly every new device being shipped with Java, it seemed to be the most attractive choice. To cope with the conditions on mobile devices—low memory and processing power—we chose to implement the ETSI basic front-end standard, ES 201 108, abandoning noise reduction [16]. The front-end performs feature extraction and feature compression using vector quantization (VQ).

Most mobile phones are shipped with low-cost processors lacking a floating-point unit (FPU). Floating-point operations on such devices are feasible in Java; however, they perform poorly since floating-point arithmetic is software-emulated. Accordingly, we implemented two front-end versions, one based on floating-point arithmetic for exhausting the possibilities on FPU devices and another based on fixed-point arithmetic. The latter emulates real numbers by using integer variables, which speeds up processing by a factor of up to 4 (Sony Ericsson W810i).

Moreover, our front-end can be run in single-threading as well as multi-threading mode: The feature extraction and the vector quantization modules can be launched either sequentially or in parallel. The first alternative requires more memory (5.6 kByte/s), since the extracted features have to be buffered before the VQ is launched, which can be crucial regarding larger utterances. The multi-threading version, however, is able to compress the extracted features on the fly, and thus only a small, constant buffer is needed (< 1 kByte). Multi-threaded processing results in slightly slower processing times compared to single-threading mode (on average, a 12% increase).

As can be seen from the results of our performance assessments in Table 18.2, several devices on the market are already capable of performing front-end processing with Java in real time, such as the Nokia 6630 and the Nokia N70. For performance comparison, we ported the ES 201 108 front-end to Symbian C to compare

Table 18.2 Time Required for Feature Extraction (FE only) and Compression (FE+VQ) related to Utterance Duration

| Cellular Phone | FE Only | | FE+VQ | | | |
| | | | Single-Threaded | | Multi-Threaded | |
	Float	Fixed	Float	Fixed	Float	Fixed
Nokia 6630, N70	1.3	0.7	1.8	0.9	2.0	1.4
Nokia E70	1.3	0.9	1.8	1.2	1.9	1.3
Nokia 7370	1.2	2.7	1.6	3.7	1.7	3.8
Nokia 7390	0.9	1.6	1.3	2.2	1.4	2.3
Nokia 6136, 6280, 6234	1.1	2.2	1.5	3.0	1.5	3.1
Siemens CX65, CX75	3.1	2.1	4.4	2.7	5.0	3.8
Sony-Ericsson W810i	7.9	2.0	12.5	2.9	13.4	3.1

Java and C on the same device. In Symbian C, our Nokia E70 test device processed feature extraction by a real-time factor of 0.6, compared to 1.3 in the Java implementation (FE only, floating-point). This means that Symbian C approaches need to be taken into consideration. Further developments in this direction can be found in [17].

Today the main stumbling block for broad use of our Java front-end architecture is the neglectful implementation of the recording functionality by device manufacturers. Although defined in the Java specification JSR 135 (MMAPI), so far only a few manufacturers follow the standards defined by the Java Community Process. For instance, virtually all Sony Ericsson devices capture data compressed by the adaptive multirate (AMR) codec, which is worthless for speech recognition. According to our investigations, only devices shipped with implementations of MMAPI on Sun and Symbian currently follow the standard and enable capture of uncompressed voice data. We expect other device manufacturers to further enhance their implementations in the near future.

18.2.3 **Proactiveness**

An important characteristic of systems operating in intelligent environments is proactiveness. This can be defined as the way the dialogue system takes the initiative to control a situation instead of waiting to respond to something after it happens. A system should operate independently and anticipatorily, always with an eye on its goals. Proactive behavior is achieved by full contextual awareness. Constantly observing the situation and the relevant context enables the system to instantly detect any problem. If a problem comes up, the system should try to find a solution and initiate the necessary actions.

As an example of a system in which proactive behavior would be of great benefit, the following scenario is considered: A user has an early meeting the next morning that is a one-hour drive away from home. He or she sets the alarm clock to get up early enough to get ready and comfortably reach the meeting place in time. The envisaged intelligent system operating in this environment monitors, among other things, traffic flow and weather conditions. If it detects any obstacles on the way, such as a traffic jam, it resets the alarm to an earlier time according to the potential delay. This way, the user can still reach the meeting on time in spite of the longer journey.

Besides the strong reasoning and problem-solving capabilities that constitute the intelligence of the system (e.g. the functionality to detect potential problems) proactive behavior requires a thorough model of the context and the ongoing dialogue to allow access to all necessary information. Along with modeling the usual context comprising semantic, linguistic, perceptual, and social aspects as well as processing state [18], special attention has to be paid to the dialogue history, which stores the entire conversation up to the current point.

The dialogue history allows for references back to something mentioned earlier in the dialogue and also enables optimistic strategies for grounding. As it allows backtracking for, say, hastily integrated propositions, an optimistic grounding strategy can be deployed to integrate propositions at an earlier point in the dialogue, before it has been fully grounded. While the difference this makes in two-party interactions is not so prominent, it is especially relevant for systems involving more than one user. In fact, this way a system becomes more flexible in terms of the number of users. An example of a proactive system operating in a multi-party environment is given in Section 18.3.3.

18.3 INFORMATION ACCESS IN INTELLIGENT ENVIRONMENTS

Besides hardware and software compatibility, privacy, and social acceptance, *information access* is a key aspect of IEs. Two main types of information access can be recognized:

- Environment-centred information access (computer–computer interaction)
- User-centered information access (human–computer interaction)

On the one hand, the environment itself has to gain access to as many information sources as possible to become intelligent. Since the number of entities within the environment could be from one to several thousands, this access might not be easy to achieve. By definition the IE should have the user as its center and because of this another problem arises: All data must also be user centered. The project ATRACO, mentioned in Section 18.1, focuses on this kind of information access.

On the other hand, when we talk about information access in IEs we refer to human–computer interaction. As mentioned, the user is the center of the environment so he may explicitly ask for any kind of information. If it is not possible for him to do this in an easy and natural way, he may not accept the environment.

In the following we focus on the second type of information access: human–computer interaction. The remaining three sections present applications that may be used within IEs. Section 18.3.1 presents an intelligent pedestrian navigation system; Section 18.3.2, a journey-planning system; and Section 18.3.3, a proactive speech dialogue system to help users choose the appropriate restaurant.

18.3.1 Pedestrian Navigation System

The system presented here is an example of an on-the-move IE application [19]. We may think of on-the-move IE as a bubble surrounding the user [20]. The user is guided by this bubble along her route. We assume pedestrians prefer not to carry a large and fragile display that would present information as in a paper-based map. For pedestrians a rather common strategy is just to ask for directions. Here, speech is well suited for short directions, but long and complex instructions can sometimes be cognitively demanding if expressed using speech. Being accompanied by an intelligent bubble acting like a human local guide would be optimal.

We have developed a speech-based prototype named ArriGator[1] that acts as a specialized navigation application within an on-the-move IE by providing an always-online (i.e., connected to the speech server) voice interface for the user. The evaluation of this system is presented at the end of this section and should give hints as to whether pedestrians would appreciate such a virtual guide featuring voice entry and audio response.

System Description

Corresponding to Figure 18.1, at the *user level* ArriGator runs on a voice-over-IP client. At the *application level* we use a speech server and an application server to provide information about the surroundings. At the *service level* the system accesses a database providing geographical information, especially about landmarks [21]; orientation is mainly achieved using landmarks, photos of which may be obtained to serve as an additional source of information. A simplified map showing an overview of the entire route (but not the current position) is available on the client. To provide sufficient bandwidth for the voice transfer via Skype [22], the client has to be connected to an UMTS network.

Every five seconds when the system is running, the client sends the current geographical position to the application server. The AS's main task is to translate the client's positioning information into a representation that is understood by the speech server. The area around the test route and the route itself have been divided into geographical sectors. This enables the application server to transmit information on which sector the user enters rather than actual geo-positions. Finally, the speech server executes the VoiceXML dialogue and maintains communication with the user (via the Skype protocol) [23]. The entire system has been developed for the English language.

When a user enters a sector, he is provided with suitable directions by the speech dialogue. However, at any time he is allowed to ask for further information using several predefined commands:

- Information about something (e.g., "Information church")
- A repeat of the last direction (e.g., "Repeat")
- Further directions (e.g., "Next direction")
- The name of the street the user should take (e.g., "Tell me the street name," "Street name")
- Still the right way? (e.g., "Right way")
- Possible commands (e.g., "Help me please")

If the user wishes to obtain more information about a landmark, relevant photos are displayed on the PDA along with a detailed description. Furthermore, he may ask the server to repeat information at any time. He can also listen to all further route directions and may ask for streets he needs to take to his destination. If the user is

---

[1]ArriGator = *Arri*val+Navi*Gator. Arigatou* is Japanese for *Thanks.*

embarrassed to talk to a computer in public he does not have to. ArriGator's landmark-enriched directions are sufficiently detailed for him to reach the destination without speaking a single word. The following dialogue shows a possible interaction with the system.

> S: Turn to your right. You should have the small church on your right hand. Follow the small street uphill!
> U: Tell me the streetname.
> S: Take the street called Sankt-Leonard-Strasse. Repeat or Back?
> U: Back.
> S: When you see the Kronen beer factory in front of you. Turn to your right.
> U: Give me information about the Kronen beer factory.
> S: Take a look at the picture on the PDA. The Kronen beer factory is a small brewery with a parking place in front of it. They serve excellent beer! Repeat or back?
> U: Back.

Evaluation

We have performed test runs with 18 subjects. Their evaluations addressing ArriGator's usefulness, ease of handling, and operator convenience gave insights about the system's usability. We have tried to determine if a speech dialogue system with only restricted visual support can provide guidance to a pedestrian who is unfamiliar with the surrounding area. Each of the 18 subjects was asked to complete the test run at first go. After completion he or she filled in a questionnaire with several questions concerning ArriGator's usefulness and usability. To provide user profiles the subjects answered some general questions regarding, for example, their English skills and how familiar they are with navigation systems and mobile devices, as well as with the surroundings of the test area.

The test route, about 1.15 miles long, went through a suburb of a German city. To complete it subjects needed between 25 and 40 minutes. We have chosen the test area for two reasons: The suburb was characterized by small houses, causing less degradation of satellite positioning than tall buildings, and an area-wide UMTS network was available.

The subjects were German native speakers but had at least high school knowledge of English. We therefore chose a simple structured command vocabulary to implement the dialogue. The subject group consisted of ten males and eight females, with ages ranging between 20 and 71. All subjects were rather unfamiliar with mobile devices, navigation systems, and the area where the test run took place.

At the beginning of the run each subject was handed a short instruction manual to carry with her or him. It described all available commands. Additionally, an instructor gave a short introduction to the ArriGator system. In total only 5 out of the 18 subjects had problems finding the route right away. However, with the request for additional information all but one were able to continue and reach their destination. Figure 18.6 shows the number of subjects who used a particular voice command on the left side of the column pairs and the total number of commands used on the right side.

The most frequently used commands were "Repeat!" and "Streetname!" Fifteen out of 18 subjects used the repeat command, meaning that only three subjects were able to understand everything at first go. We assume that many difficulties in understanding were caused by problems with the English language. It is also possible that some subjects wanted to hear explanations or directions again because of memory constraints. The command "Repeat!" was called for 94 times, so during each test run we had 5 calls on average. "Streetname!" was called for 101 times. Fourteen subjects made their navigation decisions at least in part according to the name of the street. The subjects used the command 6 times on average. About 59 times two-thirds of the subjects asked if they were still on the right route. Even though ArriGator automatically interferes if the user deviates from the predefined path, the users wanted to reassure themselves with such confirmations. Half of the subjects called the command "Next direction!" for a total of 34 times to get the next directions in advance.

Less than one-third of the subjects asked twice on average for additional information about a landmark. We assume that in most cases it was obvious which landmark the system referred to and so there was no need to ask for further information. As

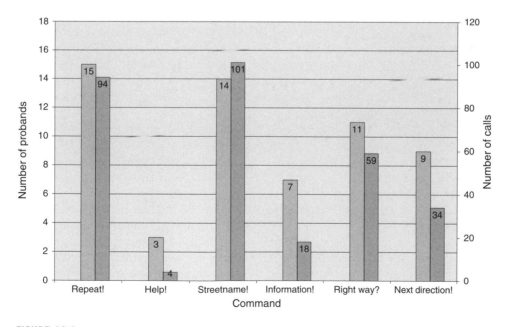

FIGURE 18.6

Number of subjects using a command and total number of used commands.

mentioned previously, the subjects were allowed to take the short manual with them, which led to less frequent use of the command "Help me please!" Only three subjects used ArriGator's integrated help.

After the subjects filled in their personal information, they were invited to give their impressions of the prototype. Figure 18.7 presents an overview of the results. The overall usability of ArriGator was judged as "good." In particular, the understandability of the dialogue, the directions' quality, and the usefulness of the landmarks were rated between "excellent" and "good" on average. The subjects indicated that the landmarks made wayfinding much easier for them. These results seem to confirm our intuition that speech is the most useful modality in our experiment. In fact, the landmark photos were rarely used, so their usefulness was judged "average." The simplified map was used by only two subjects. One tried to continue the route with the help of this map after a total loss of the GPS signal and rated it "bad." Another navigated with the map and received the GPS signal as well. He rated the map "good."

Two-third of the subjects would be inclined to use a voice-driven system in their everyday life. Finally, all subjects stated the need of metric information, not provided by ArriGator, to get an idea of a particular distance. Compared to the voice features, ArriGator's visual output was considered unimportant.

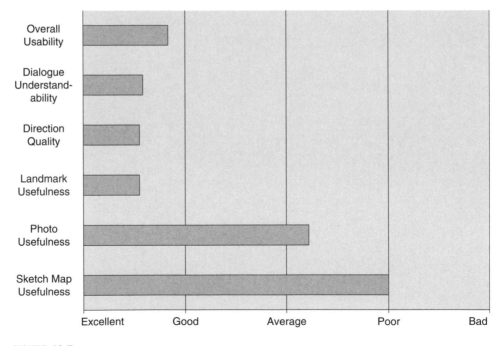

FIGURE 18.7

Average ratings of the evaluation concerning overall usability of the prototype.

Several possible improvements for ArriGator can be derived from the experiments. Some subjects mentioned that it would be helpful to indicate street names along with the directions. This seems to be confirmed by the high number of "Street name!" commands shown in Figure 18.7. It would be useful to provide the street name if it is visible to the user; otherwise, it might be of no help or even confusing. Providing distance in meters should be optional, since it requires enhanced technical features.

It may be argued that a system providing detailed, landmark-enriched directions needs no visual support. However, in a crowded city center this is debatable. The suburb where the evaluations were carried out is a rather open area, and landmarks are easy to recognize because there are not many of them. Overall the subject feedback was very positive. Some subjects tried to have a natural and conversational interaction with ArriGator, for example responding with "Thank you" after being given directions. However, the current prototype is not able to support a real conversation. The present evaluation shows that pedestrians are willing to be directed and accompanied by our vision of a virtual local guide and that such an application would perfectly fit into an on-the-move IE.

18.3.2 Journey-Planning System

As another example of speech-enabled distributed information access, we present a public transport journey-planning system for cellular phones [24]. The Internet portal "Elektronische Fahrplan Auskunft Baden-Württemberg für Busse und Bahnen" (an Electronic Information System for Regional Public Transportation)[2] was used as a data provider.

The system architecture follows the paradigm presented in Section 18.2. The client application, which runs on a Java-equipped cellular phone, gathers from the user information regarding time and date of the journey and departure and destination points. That information is transmitted to an application server, which retrieves the required route from the portal. The server then sends the plan of the journey back to the client, where it is presented in a user-friendly way. The user interface on the client side is shown in Figure 18.8. The system virtually provides the functionality of the EFA-BW Internet portal and optimizes the user interface for use on a mobile phone.

The system traffic generated between the client device and the application server for one request amounts to 2–3 kB, in contrast to the 60–80 kB produced when directly requesting the portal.

Inquiries can be made for journeys between any two transport stops in Germany. To enter the departure and destination points for the cities Ulm and Neu-Ulm the user can use both keypad and voice. We have developed a DSR system for the recognition of 279 bus stops.

The server side of the DSR system is based on the Sphinx4 recognizer [25] with adequately trained acoustic models. For an error-free transmission channel we obtained a recognition accuracy of about 99%. For the DSR client we used our Java

---

[2]www.efa-bw.de

FIGURE 18.8

User interface on the Nokia E70 cellular phone.

ME implementation of the ETSI front-end [11], processing speech signals sampled at 8 kHz.

Utterances of up to three seconds can be captured, which is sufficient for all bus stop names. The total request-round-trip time—that is, the time necessary for feature extraction, feature compression, packaging, data transmission over the GPRS channel, error mitigation, recognition, and result transmission—is approximately eight seconds (in the multi-threaded fixed-point version of the front-end).

To assess the usability of the system we have performed some subjective tests. Using the Nokia E70 mobile phone, subjects had to enter a bus station name using keypad and speech, and then provide a score (see Table 18.3).

Each of the ten subjects, ranging in age from 25 to 45, evaluated five randomly chosen bus stop names. The tests were performed under normal office background noise conditions. The subjects included males and females as well as native and non-native German speakers. All subjects were experienced cellular phone users.

The results of the tests are shown in Figure 18.9. As we observe, in more than one-half of the cases the speech input modality received score 2, meaning it was considered to be *much more convenient*. The resulting mean opinion score was

Table 18.3 Scores for the Mean Opinion Test of Speech Usability	
Score	**Versus Keypad**
2	**Much more convenient**
1	**More convenient** than keypad
0	**Same convenience**
−1	**Less convenient** than keypad
−2	**Much less convenient** than keypad

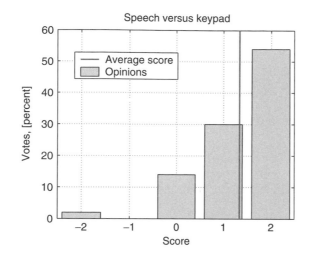

FIGURE 18.9

Historgram of received usability scores.

1.34, lying between *more convenient* and *much more convenient*. The average time required for manually typing the stop name amounted to 24.7 seconds, compared to 8 seconds in the case of speech recognition.

For three seconds of speech the total generated traffic amounted to 4800 Bytes and 7800 Bytes for transmission with two and one feature vector pairs per packet, respectively. Currently this implies a cost of 5 to 10 cents.

18.3.3 Independent Dialogue Partner

As a final example of a speech-based dialogue application, we present a system that acts as an independent dialogue partner in a conversation with two human users. The scenario is restaurant selection, set in an office environment. The system silently observes the conversation between the dialogue partners, thereby capturing the relevant conversational context and detecting whether the current discourse falls within the specified domain, at which point it becomes active. It then "listens" attentively to the conversation. While the human users discuss an appropriate restaurant, the system models the conversation and stores all relevant data in a dialogue history. When required by the conversational situation it takes the initiative and becomes meaningfully involved in the interaction.

One of the dialogue partners is the system's main interaction partner. Besides proactive interaction, the system reacts to this partner's direct interaction requests. Interaction requests can be posed verbally (addressing the system directly) or visually (looking at the system) through gaze direction tracking.

The following dialogue is a short interaction example.

U2: Look at this weather, isn't it beautiful!

U1: Absolutely. Why don't we leave it for today? I'm getting hungry anyway.

U2: Do you want to go eat something? I feel like a huge pizza!

U1: Sounds great! Let's go somewhere where we can sit outside. [**looks at computer**] Is there anything over in the park maybe?

S: Unfortunately not. However, Pizzeria Napoli is close to here and has a patio. Would you like to see the menu?

U1: Yes, please.

[**Menu pops up on the screen.**] . . .

During the conversation, the system assists the partners in finding a suitable restaurant by performing database queries based on their preferences and the dialogue context. The system is displayed in the form of an avatar (as seen in Figure 18.10(b)), which moves its lips and produces synthesized speech output. A restaurant menu, city map, or local bus schedule are presented on the screen when suitable. At the end of the conversation, the system removes itself when it is no longer needed, that is, the task is completed.

In the following, particular system characteristics are described in more detail.

Proactive system interaction. Proactive behavior is characteristic of an independent dialogue partner. The system should be able to take the initiative for interaction instead of relying on a user request. It has to know where the conversation stands and what is important or reasonable to say. At the same time, the system should remove itself when it is no longer needed, i.e. when the task is completed or the users have permanently switched to a different topic without concluding their restaurant search.

Proactive interaction requires complete understanding of the conversational and situational context at any point in the conversation. Only then can the

(a)   (b)

FIGURE 18.10

(a) Scene from the data recordings performed with this system. (b) The system avatar users see on the screen.

system make meaningful contributions. Extensive context modeling and a thorough dialogue history are deployed for this reason. Refer to the subsection Proactive Dialogue Modeling for more information on dialogue history.

Levels of attentiveness. The dialogue system is "always-on." It is not turned on when needed but constantly runs in the background, becoming active when necessary. In the current state, the system does not deploy a memory of different interactions. Thus, every interaction cycle starts fresh, without knowledge of past interactions. The system's activity cycle is depicted in Figure 18.11. The different levels of attentiveness are defined as follows:

Inactive. While the human users talk about anything but the specified domain, the system does not need to pay full attention. It "overhears" the conversation and waits for key words to detect the point at which the conversation topic changes to the one specified. In the previous example dialogue the system is in inactive mode until it hears "hungry" uttered by U1 in the second utterance.

Active. As soon as the system recognizes certain key words, it assumes that the conversation has entered the specified domain and switches over to pay full attention. From that point on, it "listens" closely to the conversation, analyzing the complete utterances, extracting the users' preferences and building up a dialogue history to store all relevant information.

Interactive. When necessary (i.e., after a certain interaction trigger), the system becomes involved in the conversation through interaction, task and problem solving, and presentation of results. After the task has been carried out or the

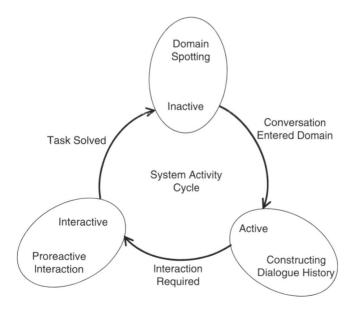

FIGURE 18.11

System activity cycle.

dialogue has permanently moved to a different topic, the system switches back to inactive mode.

Proactive Dialogue Modeling

The dialogue modeling in our system enables proactive interaction in multi-party environments. For this, we deploy the *information state update approach* (e.g., [26–28]), modified to handle our special needs. Dialogue can be described as a sequence of events (i.e., utterances) that act on the current dialogue state (*information state*). That is, each event modifies or updates the current state of the dialogue according to the event's contents. The process of organizing this information—integrating incoming information into the information state at each dialogue step, updating the data according to the input and the current dialogue state, and finally determining an appropriate next move—is the task of the dialogue manager.

A simplified version of the information state deployed in our system is depicted in Figure 18.12. It is, as usual, divided into two parts. The private part contains the dialogue partner's private information, such as goals and how to further proceed in the dialogue. The shared part models the information shared among all dialogue participants—in other words, the current topic (i.e., the question under discussion (QUD)), the preferences accumulated in the dialogue so far (the task model (TASK)), the result set of the latest database query (RES), the speaker and addressees, as well as the dialogue moves of the latest utterance and the dialogue history.

Dialogue history. The dialogue history deserves special attention in our setup. Usually, it starts following the conversation from the point of the first interaction of the system or a request to it. In our system, however, to enable proactive behavior and interaction with previous knowledge, the dialogue history starts

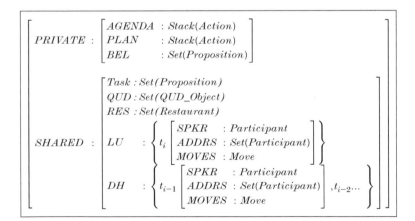

FIGURE 18.12

Example information state at time t_i of the dialogue.

at the point in the conversation when the users begins to speak about the specified domain and the system is not yet interacting. This way, the system can proactively interact and present a solution at any desirable point.

Grounding strategy for multi-party dialogues. One of the difficulties in multi-party dialogue modeling lies in differentiating between addressees in general, and potential or obligated responders. Because it is difficult to anticipate the actual responders, the system needs a way to be less dependent on the grounding performed by each individual addressee (which in real dialogue is not likely to happen) and at the same time enable it. In our system, we deploy an optimistic grounding strategy (similar to the *cautiously optimistic* strategy in [28]) that facilitates the handling of multi-party dialogues to a large extent. The dialogue history allows backtracking for, say, hastily integrated propositions. Thus, an optimistic grounding strategy can be adopted to integrate a proposition in the dialogue without waiting for all addressees to respond to it. This further renders a system more flexible in terms of the number of users.

Usability Evaluation

To assess the usability of our system as an independent dialogue partner, we have performed an evaluation using an extensive *Wizard-of-Oz* setup [29] for data recordings. The evaluation was conducted on dialogues from the PIT Corpus [30] that were recorded partly with and without the avatar shown on the screen. Besides the overall impression, this enabled evaluating the effect the avatar has on usability. Fourteen dialogues with the avatar were compared to eleven dialogues without avatar.

For evaluation, a questionnaire was filled out by the participants in the data recordings after interaction with the system. A short version of the SASSI questionnaire by Hone and Graham [31] was used. SASSI was developed for multidimensional analysis of dialogue systems in particular and is composed of 34 statements rated on a 7-point Likert scale. Example statements are "The interaction with the system is fast" and "The system didn't always do what I wanted." The higher the rating, the more positive it is. Our shortened version of the questionnaire, SASSISV, contains 16 of these items specifying the same six subscales as determined by the original. SASSISV shows high correlation with the original version in all subscales of the questionnaire.

As shown in Figure 18.13, the outcome was very positive, indicating good acceptance by users. It can also be seen that use of an avatar made a considerable difference.

18.4 CONCLUSIONS

In this chapter we presented an overview of our current research in human-computer interaction through spoken dialogue systems. A specific focus was on their deployment in intelligent environments.

We discussed the use of appropriate system architectures that allow us to integrate the technology in everyday—even small and computationally less powerful—

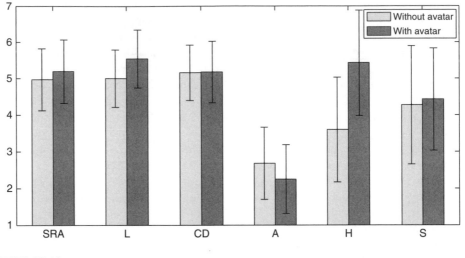

FIGURE 18.13

System usability evaluation, including standard deviation, using SASSISV. The scales are system response accuracy (SRA), likability (L), cognitive demand (CD), annoyance (A), habitability (H), and speed (S). The higher the ratings the better they are (except for annoyance).

devices. This seems to be essential to make these interfaces accessible for a large public and to increase their usability and acceptability. The capability to flexibly integrate information from various sources and to negotiate solutions between the sources and the user is another feature that we consider important for managing the rising complexity of current and future technical systems. Intelligent proactive dialogue behavior in particular contributes to this endeavor because it guarantees that the user is informed in the right way at the right time.

ACKNOWLEDGMENTS

The research leading to these results has received funding from the European Community's Seventh Framework Programme (FP7/2007-2013) under grant agreement no. 216837 and from the Transregional Collaborative Research Centre SFB/TRR 62 "Companion-Technology for Cognitive Technical Systems" funded by the German Research Foundation (DFG).

REFERENCES

[1] Berton A, Bühler D, Minker W. SmartKom: Foundations of multimodal dialogue systems. In: Cognitive Technologies. Springer Verlag; 2006. p. 523–41.

[2] Wahlster W. SmartWeb: Mobile applications of the semantic Web. In: Proceedings of Informatik 2004. 2004.

[3] Minker W, Haiber U, Heisterkamp P, Scheible S. Spoken multimodal human-computer dialogue in mobile environments. In: Text, Speech and Language Technology, vol. 28. Springer; 2005. p. 287–310.

[4] Goumopoulos C, Kameas A, Hagras H, Callaghan V, Gardner M, Minker W, et al. ATRACO: Adaptive and trusted ambient ecologies. In: Proceedings of the Workshop on Pervasive Adaptation at SASO. Venice (Italy): 2008.

[5] Köhler T, Fugen C, Stüker S, Waibel A. Rapid porting of ASR-systems to mobile devices. In: Proceedings of the 9th European Conference on Speech Communication and Technology, Lisbon, Portugal: 2005. p. 233–6.

[6] Hagen A, Pellom B, Connors DA. Analysis and design of architecture systems for speech recognition on modern handheld computing devices. In: Proceedings of the 1st IEEE/ACM/IFIP International Conference on Hardware/Software Codesign and System Synthesis. Newport Beach, USA: 2003. p. 65–70.

[7] Rose RC, Partharathy S. A tutorial on ASR for wireless mobile devices. In: Tutorial in 7th International Conference on Spoken Language Processing. Denver, Colorado, USA: *http://www.ece.mcgill.ca/~rrose1/icslp02_tutorial/icslp02_denver.pdf*; 2002.

[8] TellMe.Studio. *https://studio.tellme.com*.

[9] Huerta JM. Speech recognition in mobile environments. Ph.D. thesis. Carnegie Mellon University; 2000.

[10] Yoma N, Molina C, Silva J, Busso C. Modeling, estimating, and compensating low-bit rate coding distortion in speech recognition. IEEE Transactions on Audio, Speech and Language Processing 2006;14(1):246–55.

[11] ETSI. Standard ES/201/108, Speech Processing, Transmission and Quality Aspects (STQ); Distributed Speech Recognition; Front-End Feature Extraction Algorithm; Compression Algorithm. 2003.

[12] ETSI. Standard ES/202/050, Speech Processing, Transmission and Quality Aspects (STQ); Distributed Speech Recognition; Advanced Front-End Feature Extraction Algorithm; Compression Algorithm. 2002.

[13] ETSI. Standard ES/202/211, Distributed Speech Recognition; Extended Front-end Feature Extraction Algorithm; Compression Algorithm, Back-End Speech Reconstruction Algorithm. 2003.

[14] ETSI. Standard ES/202/212, Distributed Speech Recognition; Extended Advanced Front-end Feature Extraction Algorithm; Compression Algorithm, Back-End Speech Reconstruction Algorithm. 2003.

[15] ETSI. Technical Specification TS/126/243, Digital Cellular Telecommunications System (Phase 2+); Universal Mobile Telecommunications System (UMTS); ANSI C Code for the Fixed-Point Distributed Speech Recognition Extended Advanced Front-End. 2004.

[16] Zaykovskiy D, Schmitt A. Java to Micro Edition front-end for distributed speech recognition systems. In: Proceedings of the 2007 IEEE International Symposium on Ubiquitous Computing and Intelligence (UCI'07). Niagara Falls, Canada: 2007. p. 353–7.

[17] Zaykovskiy D, Schmitt A. Java vs. Symbian: A comparison of software-based DSR implementations on mobile phones. In: Proceedings of the 4th IET International Conference on Intelligent Environments. Seattle, WA: 2008. p. 1–6.

[18] Bunt H. Context representation for dialogue management. Lecture Notes in Artificial Intelligence 1999;1668:77–90.

[19] Heinroth T, Bühler D. Arrigator—evaluation of a speech-based pedestrian navigation system. In: Proceedings of the 4th IET International Conference on Intelligent Environments. Seattle, WA: 2008.

[20] Beslay L, Hakala H. European Visions for the Knowledge Age. Cheshire Henbury; *http://cybersecurity.jrc.es/docs/digitalterritorybubbles.pdf*; 2005 [Chapter 6].

[21] May A, Ross T, Bayer S, Tarkiainen M. Pedestrian navigation aids: Information requirements and design implications. Personal and Ubiquitous Computing 2003;7:331–8.

[22] Skype. *http://www.skype.com/intl/de/*.

[23] Oshry M, Auburn R, Baggia P. Voice Extensible Markup Language (voiceXML) Version 2.1. W3C – Voice Browser Working Group; *http://www.w3.org/TR/voicexml21/*; 2007.

[24] Zaykovskiy D, Schmitt A, Lutz M. New use of mobile phones: Towards multimodal information access systems. In: Proceedings of the 3rd IET International Conference on Intelligent Environments. Ulm, Germany: 2007.

[25] Walker W, Lamere P, Kwok P, Raj B, Singh R, Gouvea E, et al. Sphinx-4: A flexible open source framework for speech recognition. Technical report TR-2004-139. Sun Microsystems Laboratories; 2004.

[26] Ginzburg J. Interrogatives: Questions, facts and dialogue. In: Lappin S, editor. The Handbook of Contemporary Semantic Theory. Blackwell; 1996. p. 385–422.

[27] Matheson C, Poesio M, Traum D. Modelling grounding and discourse obligations using update rules. In: Proceedings of the First Conference of the North American Chapter of the Association for Computational Linguistics. Morgan Kaufmann; 2000. p. 1–8.

[28] Larsson S. Issue-Based Dialogue Management. Ph.D. thesis. Göteborg University; 2002.

[29] Strauss P-M, Hoffmann H, Minker W, Neumann H, Palm G, Scherer S, et al. Wizard-of-Oz data collection for perception and interaction in multi-user environments. In: Proceedings of the 5th International Language Resources and Evaluation (LREC'06) Conference. Genoa, Italy: 2006. p. 2014–7.

[30] Strauss P-M, Hoffmann H, Minker W, Neumann H, Palm G, Scherer S, et al. The PIT corpus of German multi-party dialogues. In: Proceedings of the 6th International Language Resources and Evaluation (LREC'08) Conference. Marrakech, Morocco: 2008. p. 2442–5.

[31] Hone KS, Graham R. Towards a tool for the subjective assessment of speech system interfaces (SASSI). Natural Language English 2000;6(3–4):287–303.

Deploying Context-Aware Health Technology at Home: Human-Centric Challenges

19

Stephen S. Intille, Pallavi Kaushik, and Randy Rockinson

House_n Consortium, Massachusetts Institute of Technology, Cambridge, Massachusetts

ABSTRACT

Recent work has demonstrated that sensors placed in the home environment can be used to develop algorithms that infer context, such as activities of daily living. Context-aware applications can then be created that may help people stay healthy, active, and safe in their homes as they age. Although automatic detection of context from home sensors is an active research area, some critical aspects of the "human-centric" side of creating and deploying these home health systems related to sensor installation, algorithm training, and error recovery have been largely ignored by the research community. Using an example of a medication adherence system, and motivated by some pilot experiments in which we had subjects self-install sensors in a home, we set out twelve questions that we encourage context-aware application developers (as well as machine learning researchers providing the context detection algorithms) to ask themselves as they go forward with their research. We argue that these human-centric questions directly impact not only important aspects of human–computer interface design but also the appropriateness of the selection of specific context detection algorithms.

Key words: health, technology, sensors, installation, home, ubiquitous, computing, interfaces, pervasive, context.

19.1 INTRODUCTION

The medical systems in many industrialized countries around the world face an impending crisis: how to pay for the care of an aging population. The U.S. Census Bureau, for example, estimates that, from 2010 to 2030, the percentage of the U.S. population age 65 and older will rise from 13% to 19% [1]. Other countries, such as Japan, will have even older populations, with over 30% of the population age 65 or older by 2033 [2]. This growth, and the rising cost of medical procedures, will place an enormous strain on governments and health providers in the coming years. New ways to lower the cost of the rising number of people needing chronic care are needed.

Home sensor technology may create a new opportunity to reduce costs by helping people stay healthy and in their homes longer as they age. An interest has therefore emerged in using home sensors for health promotion. One way to do this is by telemonitoring, where devices such as Internet-enabled scales, blood pressure monitors, and blood glucose monitors typically found in clinics are used at home to monitor conditions such as diabetes, congestive heart failure, and self-reported affective state [3]. Another way, and the focus of this chapter, is through general-purpose sensors in the home that collect data that is then used to infer information about everyday home behaviors. This type of context detection system enables entirely new types of *context-aware* [4] health applications to be envisioned. These include monitoring the elderly and sending data to physicians [5], providing "peace of mind" communication between elders and family caregivers [6–8], promoting social connectedness in new ways [9, 10], helping with medication adherence [11], detecting onset of cognitive decline [12], detecting falls or instability [13], and even helping people change behaviors that may impact their overall sense of well-being, such as television watching [14]. Sensors being used in such prototype systems range from video cameras to audio to small wireless motion or RFID-based object-usage sensors and multimodal combinations of sensor input. A key challenge is creating algorithms that can reliably infer patterns of behavior from the sensor data.

As of this writing, automatic detection of home activity from sensor data to support context-aware home health technology is an active area of research. In this chapter, we set out twelve "human-centric" questions that are nearly always ignored in the literature but are critical to the success of real-world deployment of home health systems. The questions relate to the issue of who will install, set up, and maintain the context detection system when placed in a home.

We argue that our human-centric questions directly impact not only important aspects of the health system's interface design but the appropriateness of the context detection algorithms as well. Papers on context detection algorithms typically report results in terms of algorithm recognition performance. Rarely do they discuss the implications of these results in practical terms. Even if a system is 95% accurate in detecting an activity (which would be considered a good result), the key question may actually be "What are the user's options the remaining 5% of the time, when the algorithm fails?"

With most algorithms that have been proposed, the implicit assumption is that to fix the system the user must provide more training data. However, for home activity detection, it is usually not clear how an end user, especially a nontechnical end user, is to provide such data. In practice, how does a designer create a system that makes it easy for an elderly person to provide 5, 10, or 100 more labeled examples of "cooking" or "toileting" or "watching television" so that an algorithm using, say, support vector machines can relearn a model and improve its context detection? Moreover, how can such a system be affordably installed in the home in the first place, and if the context detection algorithms require initial training data, where does this data come from? We discuss these questions and others that we plan to use to frame our future research. We hope that others find them useful to consider as well.

19.2 THE OPPORTUNITY: CONTEXT-AWARE HOME HEALTH APPLICATIONS

Developments in ubiquitous computing for health and well-being have largely been in three separate areas: monitoring, compensation, and prevention. The most powerful health applications may ultimately combine all three areas, creating what have been called *embedded assessment* applications [15]. While such applications offer great promise, they also require that sensors be distributed in the home setting, sometimes in complex ways. Many also require sophisticated context inference algorithms if the envisioned concepts are to be fully realized beyond laboratory prototypes.

19.2.1 Medical Monitoring

Medical-monitoring health technologies generally fall into two categories. Some systems *detect or allow for user-triggered alerts of a crisis*, such as a heart attack or a fall. Most systems that are already commercially available are of this type because it is relatively easy to create wearable sensors or notification systems that can detect such events from single, specially designed sensors.

More difficult is to *detect crises before they occur by detecting changes in patterns of behavior*, and systems of this type are generally still in the prototype stages of development. For instance, a context-aware system that detects changes in the activities of daily living over hours, days, or months might be able to detect the onset of a health condition such as depression [16]. Data on changes in everyday behaviors might be sent to medical providers, family caregivers, or the end users themselves for health assessment [17]. Numerous research efforts exist to develop sensor-enabled systems for the home that detect activities of daily living for this purpose (e.g. [7, 17–24]), and some projects aim to detect specific conditions, such as changes in gait (e.g., [25]). Other efforts focus on detecting patterns of activities using wearable sensors worn both in and outside the home [26]. In some cases, data is collected by altering devices that people already use, such as computer games, to track changes in performance [27]. Commercial systems are currently limited to a small number of sensors per dwelling—typically motion sensors that do not track activities of particular interest but only variations from baseline movement throughout a home (e.g., QuietCare from Living Independently Group).

Few clinical trials or even pilot medical trials have been conducted with in-home context-aware monitoring systems to date, largely because it is still very difficult to deploy the enabling sensor technologies affordably on a sufficiently large scale. Most large studies use only single, relatively simple technologies, such as home blood pressure monitors (e.g., [28]) or a small number of sensors combined with occupancy sensing (e.g., [29, 30]).

19.2.2 Compensation

In addition to or instead of monitoring, a context-driven health technology might help someone compensate for cognitive and physical decline [6] or maintain independence in and outside the home [26]. For example, home activity detection with targeted just-in-time information [31] could reorient a user after he is interrupted during an everyday task such as cooking [6]. Or it might be used to help a user compensate for memory loss by prompting her to take medications regularly [32, 33]. Ubiquitous computing systems have also been proposed to help people remain socially engaged by compensating for impaired recall of names and faces [34], providing visual feedback on social activity to elders and their caregivers [35], and forging connections between people with common interests in social settings [36].

19.2.3 Prevention

In addition to monitoring and prevention, home context detection systems could be used to build systems for "just-in-time" information delivery intended to encourage healthy behaviors that might either lower the probability of serious illness for those at risk or help prevent worsening of an illness [31]. Behavior change is motivated through the delivery of information at key times in the decision-making process: points of decision, behavior, and consequence [37]. The promise is in creating systems that would, like an effective personal trainer, provide tailored messages at teachable moments—the place and time when a person is most receptive to information—to motivate behavior, belief, or attitude change. Ubiquitous computing technologies that simplify data collection and provide summary information may lead to more informed decision making—for example, encouraging physical activity [38].

19.2.4 Embedded Assessment

Monitoring systems are generally perceived with skepticism by people who have lived comfortably in their homes for many years without them. They are also typically difficult to install and maintain. These may be some of the reasons that few monitoring systems have been proposed in the literature for those who consider themselves healthy. One way for people to use monitoring preemptively may be to embed assessment into preventive and compensatory applications that have more compelling and immediate value to the end user.

In *embedded assessment* applications, as described by Morris et al. [15], implicit or passive monitoring is integrated into the activities and tools of daily life (e.g., how people use objects or behave in their home). These systems monitor health status by tracking the degree and quality of assistance (in the form of hints, prompts, encouragement, and adaptive system adjustments) required by the user for particular activities. They search for meaningful patterns that can inform self-directed wellness strategies or medical care.

An embedded assessment system allows a user to go about his life, but gathers information from sensors either embedded in, attached to, or observing objects that he uses regularly. Unlike monitoring-only applications, when embedded assessment applications involve compensation and prevention components and the context detection technologies go awry, the end user is likely to not only notice but also be required to take some action. Moreover, to enable the applications in the first place, the sensors will usually need to be distributed in the home, and the context algorithms will probably need to be tailored to the activity of that particular user and his environment.

The practical issues related to sensor installation and algorithm training for such context-driven health applications have been largely ignored in the literature up to now. In the next section, we use observations from testing one of our own prototype context-aware health systems to highlight some of the potential user-centric design pitfalls.

19.3 CASE STUDY: CONTEXT-AWARE MEDICATION ADHERENCE

Poor adherence to medication and lifestyle guidance is a major challenge facing the health care community in industrialized countries. In the United States alone, the annual cost of nonadherence is estimated to be over $100 billion [1]. Despite extensive research into interventions for improving adherence (such as providing reminders over the telephone), systematic reviews have found that even the most successful solutions are complex, labor-intensive, and not consistently effective [2]. A system embedded in the home might use knowledge of usage of household objects and movement of an occupant to infer especially convenient times to present medication reminders, thereby providing value without becoming burdensome over time.

19.3.1 Prototype System

We built a pilot system to explore the use of context sensing to identify opportune moments for delivering context-sensitive medical reminders. A study participant was asked to follow an intentionally complex regimen of simulated medical tasks while living in an instrumented apartment [42] for ten days. This regimen consisted of four medication tasks and four other health-related tasks: exercise, disinfecting hands, caring for a wound, and testing blood glucose. Via a mobile computing device that he was asked to carry, the participant received context-sensitive reminders that were automatically time-shifted based on sensor data readings so as to minimize potential disruption to his everyday activities.

Data was obtained from small, wireless stick-on object usage sensors [40] and limb movement sensors [41], as well as from built-in sensors measuring appliance and electrical use [42]. The sensor data was used to change how reminders were presented based on the user's activity, proximity to areas of the home, and changes in ambulatory state (see [43] for details on system design and operation). If the system detected that the volunteer completed a medication adherence task prior to presenting a reminder for the task, no reminder was given.

19.3.2 Evaluation

The pilot system was evaluated by having a 50-year-old male (with an advanced but nontechnical degree) in good physical and cognitive health live in the instrumented home, where the system was fully functional, for ten days. During that time he received both timed and context-sensitive reminders and was given no information that differentiated the two conditions. As in most reported work, researchers installed the sensors needed by the system, and the system training and context detection modules were "black boxes" that were critical to, but independent from, the user interface. What quickly became clear during a post-study interview was that, even in this relatively simple system, where context detection was based primarily on proximity to objects or regions of the home, our design ignored an important relationship between the user's behavior, his reaction to the interface, and the system's context detection modules.

19.3.3 **Human-Centric Design Oversights**

Our first observation was that *the context detection system could not operate independently of the user's mental model of what the context system was doing.* As he experienced more reminders, the participant tried to understand how they were being triggered. He assumed, incorrectly in many cases, that they were "context sensitive." This phrase was introduced by the participant, not the research team. The participant was confused, for example, about reminders for bedtime tasks when he was still in the living room watching TV, and he described these as "absurd." He said he often questioned whether time of day alone was triggering the reminder, but he thought that the system would be more advanced than this. (In fact, 50% of the time it was triggering reminders based only on time of day.) Without being instructed or encouraged to do so, the participant was building a mental model of how the system behaved, and his model did not map well to its actual behavior. The problem was especially pronounced when an activity was not detected properly.

The participant felt particularly annoyed because he assumed that the system should have been better than it sometimes was at understanding what he was doing. The participant further admitted to changing his behavior in order to "fool" the system into doing a better job, but since he didn't understand how the system worked, this behavior was counterproductive. If users do not have an understanding of how the system works or why it makes errors, they are likely to create their own erroneous mental models and change behavior accordingly. These changes in behavior may further erode system performance. The problem is exacerbated because, as some have forewarned [44], in a ubiquitous computing system in the home it is difficult for the user to know where the system begins and ends and what is and is not influencing its behavior.

Also clear from the short pilot was that the system must *allow the user the opportunity to suggest activity detection strategies.* Our participant created a "cheat sheet" for himself with personalized notes about when he would complete the different tasks relative to time of day and his typical activities, and it was noteworthy that he tied reminders to specific behaviors that he knew he would be doing, such as *Lights & (turning down) shades* or *Take J's call.* In effect, he created his own activity-based reminders and, when interviewed, proactively suggested how the context detection could be improved by linking certain reminders with specific activities that he knew that he would routinely do, such as opening and closing the blinds and turning on and off the radio or TV. Conversely, he identified specific behaviors that would be associated with situations when he would not be receptive to reminders, such as when he was in the bathroom, washing hands, or at the door leaving the house. The ability to "attach" customized reminders to activities performed in the home seems to be useful—and perhaps required—from a user's perspective.

Our short pilot test with a single person in a real home for ten days clearly indicated that any future version of the system would need redesign. In particular, the pilot suggested that the black-box context modules should be replaced with interface components that allow nontechnical end users to draw on insights about their own domestic patterns—to have the system work in line with their mental models of how it *should* work. Furthermore, the system needs to allow adaptation over time. Finally, given that the test suggested the end user needed the ability to "train" the system in some way, it became more apparent that the user would also need to understand something about the sensor system itself, such as where sensors are installed, what each one does, and what the inference algorithms are capable of.

In hindsight, the behavior of the participant was not surprising. Personal health–tracking tools, as opposed to monitoring systems, make it more likely that the end user will become cognizant of the context detection system's performance (or lack of it), because real-time feedback makes it easy to detect an error. Unfortunately, there is little discussion in the literature of how one might design context-aware ubiquitous computing applications so as to permit end users to correct context detection subsystems in real time. Even the application developers themselves, let alone the target users, can have difficulty understanding how to include statistical learning algorithms in the systems they are building, and they need better tools to do so [45].

One might argue that the pitfalls we encountered were to be expected, and that the importance of avoiding them has been well documented. Some have warned against designing a system where the user cannot recover from mistakes—the user's or the system's [46]. Others have warned about the challenges of inference in the presence of ambiguity, the lack of a system administrator in home applications, and the difficulty of understanding precisely the boundaries of "the system" in a ubiquitous computing application in the home [44]. Yet designing a full-fledged home health sensing system using advanced context inference technology is a complex endeavor. Building a prototype may require not only writing inference and user interface algorithms but also building or modifying sensor systems. Finally, testing the system in a real home setting can be time consuming and logistically complex, even for a small pilot [47].

Thus, it is understandable that our earlier work and that of others oversimplify the problem by compartmentalizing sensor installation and context inferencing from the remainder of the system design. In fact, the human-centric component relating to installation, setup, and long-term maintenance of real-world home-based context-aware systems has been nearly completely ignored in the research literature (with a few notable exceptions, to be discussed).

A context detection system usually consists of these components:

- Sensors that are installed in an environment, often carefully placed on objects of interest.
- Software that collects and processes sensor data to infer activity and context. The accuracy of the algorithms is greatly influenced by sensor placement.
- A set of training data that is used by the inference software. Training data usually consists of a set of example sensor traces for known contexts of interest. It is fed into the inference software in order to customize recognition so that it will work despite differences between individuals and environments.

In published studies where algorithms infer context from sensor data, researchers are usually directly involved in each of these steps, tweaking procedures and algorithms to overcome many of the practical challenges that arise when conducting in-home trials of health systems. Is it desirable, as typical in reported work, to propose and discuss the algorithms used to detect context without explicitly addressing how they support adequate solutions for the practical issues of installation, training, and system maintenance? Based on our own experiences testing prototype context-aware systems in the home, we increasingly think not.

19.4 DETECTING CONTEXT: TWELVE QUESTIONS TO GUIDE RESEARCH

In the remainder of this chapter, we lay out twelve questions that we ignored or did not sufficiently address in the design of our medication adherence prototype. Others building home health care systems have generally ignored them as well. We will use these questions to guide our future research, and we hope that other context-aware developers of human-centric interfaces for the home will be influenced by considering this heuristic human-centric checklist.

The questions can be clustered into three categories relating to sensor installation, activity model training, and activity model maintenance. In short, how does the user of the context-aware system—without any help from a researcher—install, customize, and fix a new embedded health system? Do the answers impact the selection and operation of the context detection algorithms?

19.4.1 Sensor Installation ("Install It")

The first major issue we should consider in our (re)design of a medication adherence system is how to practically install the sensors required to run it.

Question 1: What Type of Sensors Will Be Used?

The type of sensors used clearly has a big impact on system acceptability. Most prior work, however, does not explicitly address the reason for choosing a particular sensor type and the impact of that choice on installation cost and complexity. General-purpose sensors such as cameras and microphones offer the advantage that relatively few are needed to cover a home. Unfortunately, robust automatic behavior inference from these devices in home settings, with complex lighting and acoustical properties, is still an unsolved problem. These sensors also tend to be viewed with skepticism by end users, who are typically not interested in being "monitored" by cameras, which they regard as invasive.

In response, there has been an increasing interest in ultra-dense sensing [48], where simpler sensors are scattered throughout environments, attached to or embedded in objects that people use. Although more sensors are typically required, the ultra-dense sensing approach has been used in some promising activity detection work, and it may be more practical for real-world deployment than cameras given privacy concerns. It is already conceivable that by using RFID tags it might be possible to tag hundreds of objects for less than a few hundred dollars [49], allowing a system to detect when a user wearing a special bracelet is touching them. And work is ongoing to create other types of sensors that may enable affordable ultra-dense sensing using powerline positioning [50], modified sensor power strips [51], miniature low-cost accelerometers attached to objects [40], and acoustical sensing on pipes [52]. We assume in this chapter that ultra-dense sensing has been selected to support the next generation of our medication adherence system.

Question 2: Are the Sensors Professionally Installed or Self-Installed in the Home?

With one notable exception, research papers on context-aware home health systems explicitly or implicitly assume that the sensors used will be installed by experts. This is an important assumption that affects the practicality of any ideas proposed. Suppose we want to commercialize a medication reminder system that requires professional installation. Not only does the user need to purchase the sensors, but installation must be paid for—an expense that can very well be more than that for the technology itself. Moreover, the user must then have a stranger come to her home to install sensors throughout the environment—an awkward and inconvenient barrier to adoption.

Assume that we deem the cost of expert installation acceptable. An installer will expertly select where and how sensors must be placed because presumably he is trained in the details of the how the sensors and algorithms work. This "optimal" sensor placement and testing increases the likelihood that the application will perform as desired—for a while. However, professional installation obviates the need for the system designer to ensure that the end user actually understands some of the limitations of the sensor system. This may create additional problems when the user needs to train and fix the system, as we discuss shortly.

The only prior work we have identified where end-user installation is explicitly addressed is by Beckmann et al. [53], who report five broad design principles uncovered by observing users self-installing sensor mockups in homes. These principles are

- Make appropriate use of user conceptual models for familiar technologies.
- Balance installation usability with domestic concerns.
- Avoid use of cameras, microphones, and highly directional sensors if possible.
- Detect incorrect installation of sensors and provide value for partial installations.
- Educate the user about data collection, storage, and transmission.

These guidelines, our own experiences with the medication reminder system and other home deployments, and other recommended principles for deploying ubiquitous computing in homes [44, 46] all suggest that the more the end user is removed from an understanding of low-level sensor installation and behavior, the more challenges may be encountered once the installer leaves the home and the system ceases to behave as the user expects it to.

Preferable to expert installation might be to allow a user of a medication adherence system to purchase the inexpensive hardware herself and self-install it for free. The system would need to be designed so that the nontechnical end user understands what the sensors do and can make decisions about where they should be installed. The implication of this self-installation procedure, however, is that the algorithm designer would no longer be able to count on having particular sensors, perfect sensor placement, or exhaustive coverage in the environment.

Question 3: What Is the Cost of (end-user) Installation?

End users must perceive the opportunity presented by the system to improve their daily lives as greater than the demands and inadequacies of the technology [54]. The costs of installation, in time, money, and inconvenience, must be factored in. In addition to financial costs of the sensors and of an installer, if one is needed, careful attention must also be paid to the cost of installation in *time*. This may be especially critical for a system using ultra-dense sensing. If user installation of each sensor takes three to five minutes, a dense object-sensing system that needs 100+ sensors to reliably infer context will take the user between six and ten hours. The designer must determine if incurring this start-up time is reasonable given the benefits that the application provides. The design of the sensors themselves becomes important. It may be possible, for example, to simplify the design so that sensors can be attached in just a few seconds versus just a few minutes (see [40] for an example). In our experience, even attaching relatively simple RFID tags to objects when used with a wrist reader [55] requires at least one to two minutes of thought and testing by well-trained researchers to achieve optimal performance.

We therefore believe it unlikely that a system will meet the time/cost criterion unless it allows for *incremental* sensor installation while providing some end-user value immediately upon the installation of the first set of sensors. Nearly all published work assumes the entire sensor system is installed at one time, and trained at one time, and does not change after that. Could algorithms support a user-centric interface where the user can clearly see the benefit of each additional minute of time devoted to additional sensor installation or adjustment?

Question 4: Where Do Sensors Need to Go?

In published work on activity detection in homes, this question is rarely explicitly discussed. Usually the implicit answer is "wherever they need to go so the researcher can maximize system performance." That is fine for research prototypes used in pilot studies, but to allow self-installation of a system and to make real-world, large-scale deployment practical, the end user must be provided with rules about where and why sensors must be attached in certain locations or to specific objects. This is not a simple endeavor.

Consider the medication adherence system. The researchers know that the more objects that have sensors on them, the better the system will work. Yet it is difficult to quantify how much any particular sensor will impact system performance. We have, in fact, asked volunteers in our instrumented apartment to do this, and have found that, much like the participant testing our medication adherence system, they construct (incorrect) mental models about what the system will find useful. Even when very clearly told to install sensors on *as many objects as possible*, a user's reasoning tends to be as follows: "Whether or not I'm using the television remote has nothing to do with taking my medications (and installing these sensors is taking a lot of time), so I don't need to put a sensor on that device." This is false from the system's point of view, however, because television-viewing detection can be used to determine if it is a convenient time for a reminder.

The challenge is even greater. In one application we built and tested (a home-based language-learning tool), we found that impressions of the ultra-dense sensing system and the necessity of sensors on certain objects *changed* as the system was used [56]. Once again, allowing *incremental* sensor installation seems important to practical deployment success. Users are likely to change where and how they believe sensors should be located as they gain experience using the applications that the context detection subsystems support. Unfortunately, even though specific criteria for sensor location will have a dramatic impact on context detection results, they are treated as an afterthought in published work.

Question 5: How Are Sensors Selected, Positioned, and Labeled?

Assume a location for a sensor has been chosen. The end-user must now select a sensor, position it, and label it so that it can be used by the context detection system.

Selection

First consider selection. Even within the same class of sensor system (e.g., RFIDs), the user may still have decisions to make each time a sensor is installed. RFID tags come in different sizes and shapes (e.g., buttons, stickers) that impact range and how well they can be affixed to objects. Some sensors may be placed on objects that get wet or go in the microwave; others may not. As designers know, too much choice, especially when its implications are poorly understood, can be debilitating for the user.

More critically, there is an important trade-off between speed of installation and sensor selection and labeling. The designer of the system needs to decide if some sensors will be prelabeled to possibly simplify installation. For instance, the user could be provided with a kit of prelabeled sensors for common objects such as appliances. This would eliminate the need to label sensors during installation, but would perhaps increase the complexity and cost of sensor kit manufacture and assembly. In effect, the design of the kit can enforce use of certain sensors and perhaps reduce complexity, but the trade-off is that it may be difficult to create a kit appropriate for all home types and sizes.

Positioning

Systems that use cameras and computer vision processing may require experts to place equipment in ways such that secularities and highly variable light sources (e.g., windows) are not in camera views. Likewise, sensors requiring careful positioning may introduce installation challenges for end users [53]. With ultra-dense object sensing, once the target object for a sensor has been chosen, it can still be challenging to affix the sensor, especially if it is orientation dependent. With large objects, such as a sofa, it may not be clear if one or more sensors are needed and how to place them. With small objects, aesthetic or usability concerns may cause a user to second-guess the need for the sensor in the first place.

We have found that even using a clearly marked arrow on the sensor to indicate primary orientation can be confusing for users (i.e., we ask them to align the arrow with the direction in which the object is moved most forcefully). In some of our deployments, we used two-axis motion sensors because we had access to them, and, if researchers install these sensors, they are perfectly adequate. However, it is clear that the lack of a sensor in the third dimension adds substantial, unwanted complexity to end-user self-installation. Next-generation sensors should be redesigned.

Labeling

The context detection system will require that each sensor have a unique ID. This is achieved by sensor labeling, a semantic association of each sensor with an object or space. Sensor labeling may be simple (e.g., sensor ID #345 is labeled "Telephone"). However, more complicated labeling may be required by the system, such as associating object, location, or related activities information with a sensor (e.g., sensor ID #180 is attached to a "Toaster oven" and is located in the "Kitchen," Camera #1 has a view of half of the "Living room," or sensor ID #189 is attached to a table used for working, not dining). One question is where these labels come from, because entering them during installation will increase installation time and complexity substantially. The more labels per sensor, the more costly and complicated the installation. Sensors must be labeled not only so that the context detection algorithms can use the information to improve their performance, but also so that the system can ultimately communicate with the end user about system state. For example, suppose the system needs to alert the user that the battery powering sensor #345 is low. How will it do so? With hundreds of sensors in the environment, the user may have no easy way of remembering where sensor #345 is located, and the system may need to guide her to it.

The system designer must therefore consider when and how sensor-labeling information will be gathered. Important considerations are (1) at what point during installation or system use should information be associated with each sensor; (2) the method or interface to be used to associate the information; and (3) who should be responsible for associating the sensor with the corresponding labels. No matter what technique is adopted, the installation labeling quality and level of detail may impact both the system's usability and its recognition accuracy.

19.4.2 Activity Model Training ("Customize It")

Context detection algorithms require more than the selection, placement, and labeling of sensors. Assuming these are adequate (keeping in mind they probably need to be *incremental*), the system designer also must consider how to train the algorithms, if such training is required.

Based on work on home activity detection in the literature, options for creating context detection systems can be roughly sorted as follows:

- Labeled training examples are used by supervised learning algorithms to automatically construct or improve models of activities (e.g., [18, 57–61]).
- Large amounts of data are used to uncover patterns of activity that are subsequently labeled (e.g., [62]).
- Experts (i.e., knowledge engineers) construct rules or probabilistic networks for recognizing activities. These models are adjusted by the experts or automatically based on particular home settings.
- Rules and/or statistical relationships are automatically generated from existing data sources, such as "how-to" material on the Internet (e.g., [19, 63]).
- End users construct rules for recognizing activities, without explicit generation of training examples.

The first approach has generated the most amount of attention in the literature recently, because, irrespective of concerns about how the training data is acquired and how the system will be maintained over time, the algorithms can obtain good recognition performance on test data sets for some types of activities. To do this, they need labeled training examples of users performing the target activities in environments where the sensor system has been installed. Our work, including prototype deployments such as the medication adherence system, has led us to question how practical this approach may be once systems move beyond laboratory testing. An alternative is to use rule-based algorithms, where prespecified rules are customized so that they work in the particular environment of interest. In either case, obtaining useful prior information to train or tune the algorithms introduces human-centric design challenges, especially in the home environment where activities are highly varied and personalized and disruption is not readily tolerated.

Question 6: What Type of Training Data Do the Activity Models Require?

The complexity of obtaining labeled activity data is, in part, determined by the precision required in labeling. Typically when researchers label activities of interest, they (painstakingly) label their start and end points using video of people performing them in an environment with a functional sensor system fully installed. This is in contrast to the simpler, but less informative, procedure of marking that an activity "is occurring." Alternatively, participants are given technology, such as a mobile device, that signals when they should start and stop performing target activities. This eliminates the need for offline data annotation, but makes it far less likely that the data acquired represents the real-world complexity of how people actually do things in their homes when they are not being told exactly what to do when. Neither method is conducive to end-user annotation of data to bootstrap a context awareness system.

Some temporally complex activities, such as cooking, also create labeling dilemmas—even for researchers who tend to spend an unusual amount of time thinking about activity ontologies. If a user is cooking pasta sauce, and it takes many hours, is the entire span of time labeled as cooking or only the time when he interacts with cooking-related objects? Or are two different activities defined to correspond roughly to "background cooking" and "active cooking"? Although researchers can pick and choose the label detail needed, research papers do not discuss how this example data will be obtained in real-world deployments with users who are not inclined to understand subtle distinctions among activity labels. The hope appears to be that further research will lead to reliable person-independent and household-independent activity recognition models. Yet, as we discuss later, even in that situation, we find it difficult to envision a system where the end user is ultimately not required to provide some type of labeled example data to extend or maintain it.

If end users must acquire this data on their own, it is likely that one of three approaches will be required:

Diary. End users or experts record when activities are happening, creating labeled instances of target activities synchronized with sensor readings. Time diaries unfortunately rely on people remembering to periodically log their activities, a task often forgotten or error prone [64].

Experience sampling. End users carry a device that prompts via beep or vibration [65], possibly in a context-sensitive way [66], for information about what activities are occurring and possibly when they start and stop. These labels are synchronized with sensor readings. The user can specify how long the current activity has been ongoing, which may provide the activity start point but without a high degree of precision. This method may be made more tolerable for the end user by the use of speech recognition [67].

Labeling by demonstration. The system indicates to the end user that she should play-act or demonstrate a particular activity, manipulating objects and possibly indicating the passage of time. This approach seems easy for some activities (e.g., *making tea, ironing*) but may be difficult for those that are harder to define (e.g., *socializing*) or those that take place over long periods of time with high variability in objects used (e.g., *cooking dinner*).

In systems with rules that can be constructed manually by experts or end users, other techniques for specifying activity models may be feasible, such as developing graphical user interfaces to facilitate end-user programming of system behavior [68]. Unsupervised approaches have yet to be tested with large numbers of home activities, but they would still require an end user to somehow label the clusters of activities that the system detects.

We are aware of no papers whose authors have obtained good activity recognition results from real home environments where *end users*, without the help of an expert, have gathered their own training data, created rule-based models, or self-labeled clusters of activity uncovered by unsupervised learning algorithms. Even more challenging would be to prove that a system could detect activities reliably when the sensor system was not only trained but also installed by the end user.

A related question is whether person-specific or home-specific training data is required. In some problem domains where statistical machine learning is used, such as speech recognition, large corpora of data are obtained and used to train person-independent models. In the home setting, however, the environment—the people in it and the layout and location of objects—has a dramatic impact on behavior. It is not clear that such massive corpora can be obtained, given the logistical challenge of instrumenting homes. Even if they can be, it is uncertain if they can generate person-independent models that would work well in practice. In all likelihood, at least some person- or household-specific data will need to be obtained upon installation of the sensor system. Performance of the best automatic speech dictation systems, for instance, still improves with user-specific customization.

It is often difficult to assess in the literature how generalizable home activity recognition results are beyond a particular individual. In many cases, the test data was acquired from either the same person or the same environment. Person/household-specific training is performed or the same home and sensor system used with multiple people. The latter is unlikely to capture the high amount of environment-to-environment variability we expect.

Question 7: How Many Examples Are Needed?

Another challenge when creating data sets of home behaviors is the infrequency with which many activities are performed. For example, how many months or years would it take an algorithm to learn the "spring cleaning" activity, which usually happens once or twice a year? Could an automated system reliably detect an occupant in medical distress given how infrequently this behavior is likely to be observed for a given individual? It is difficult to quantify the minimal number of examples required by the inference algorithms to achieve adequate recognition performance, especially because most testing to date has been on relatively small data sets that may not fully reflect the complexity with which people do household activities. Most algorithms work better with more examples and minimally need tens of them to work moderately well. The more variability that exists in the environment (e.g., errors, complexity of the context being recognized, number of sensors deployed), the more information the algorithm needs to reliably recognize context from the sensor streams.

What is clear from talking with potential end users, however, is that they expect the algorithm to learn and generalize as they do. That is, a single example should be good enough to learn a concept. Our participant in the medication adherence study had clear ideas about behavioral triggers the system could use to detect specific points in his day. A system that required him to provide tens of examples of those activities (when he felt he could easily specify the rules) would not have been well received.

There is a great deal of diversity in home activity related to how often events occur and for how long. For example, brushing teeth may occur for less than two minutes less than twice a day. An activity such as ironing may occur only once a week and take place in different rooms for different lengths of time. Cooking a particular type of meal may take place bimonthly. Other activities, such as snacking, are highly variable and can be intertwined with other activities, some performed rarely (ironing, for instance). In practice, we found accurately labeling activities in real homes to be quite challenging—even for the researcher—because of multitasking and activity interleaving [69]. Recognition of activities with multiple goals [60] or interleaved activities [57, 70] is likely to require even larger numbers of training examples.

After working on systems that require training data that is difficult even for a researcher to obtain, and after deploying systems in the home where user expectations of what is reasonable differ substantially from what the statistical learning algorithms need them to do, we have been left wondering how to reconcile these user-centric and algorithm-centric expectations. Even without the additional variability and lack of control that end-user installation of the sensor system would introduce, acquisition of adequate training data appears to be a substantial barrier to deployment of health systems that rely on home activity recognition.

19.4.3 Activity Model Maintenance ("Fix It")

Even if, for the sake of argument, a user has self-installed and self-trained a home activity recognition system, an additional hurdle to adoption persists. Our pilot of the medication adherence system made clear that the end user needs to feel in control of the technology. User control has long been recognized as important in the design of user-friendly desktop applications [71], but achieving control (or at least a sense of it) in a ubiquitous computing system dependent on automatic context recognition is challenging when system behavior is based on models of activity that have been learned from training examples. As pattern recognition researchers know, the models the system learns are, even for an expert, often difficult to interpret.

This is problematic because, although results in the literature treat activity recognition as a static, train-once–run-forever problem, the reality is that any system that relies on context detection will need to empower the end user to *incrementally install sensors* and *dynamically adjust the system* to respond to changing conditions.

Question 8: Who Will Maintain the System as Activities Change, the Environment Changes, and Sensors Break?

Researchers proposing activity recognition systems for the home need to acknowledge that the system is targeting a dynamic, not static, situation. First, activities will change. For example, schedules change when a child attends school versus when she is on summer vacation. Such a change might substantially influence the type, duration, and complexity of activities observed in the home—how dinner is eaten, for example. It is unlikely that a context detection application developer will anticipate all the ways in which domestic ubiquitous technology will need to adapt to changes in user behavior and environments, or that at the time of system installation an expert can help the system obtain realistic examples of all behaviors that adequately reflect the diversity of conditions under which they will be performed.

Second, the environment will change. Suppose that a context-aware system has learned a user's patterns of behavior in his kitchen, but then a new food processor is purchased and used extensively. Even such a seemingly trivial change, impossible to predict in advance, could detrimentally impact the performance of a context detection system based on labeled training data. The system may need a sensor on the food processor and new models to be trained for the cooking activities. Finally, sensors will break, become dislodged, or require battery replacement. As others have pointed out, in real-world deployments there is no system administrator who will perform regular maintenance [44].

Even if a system is professionally installed, for changes in activities, environment, or sensor functional status, it seems unreasonable, costly, and invasive to call in a technician to fix it. A far preferable option is to design the system from the outset so that end users will be able, on their own, to maintain its effective operation. Consider cost alone. With a health-monitoring system as a safety backup to prevent an illness the user may feel she is highly unlikely to contract, each time the system requires a repair or upgrade that incurs a $100 to $200 maintenance visit, the user will be increasingly likely to stop using it altogether. There is a disincentive to keep the system running optimally.

A far superior option is for the end user to fix the system herself. This is an additional argument for end-user sensor installation and training. One downside to professional installation is that the end user is not involved in where and how sensors are placed. Users of professionally installed systems may be fearful of replacing sensors or acquiring new training data themselves, even if they have the knowledge to do so. Conversely, users of self-installed systems will have gradually acquired the expertise and confidence needed to keep the system running for the long term. The hands-on nature of end-user sensor installation creates an opportunity for the user to become comfortable with the technology being introduced into the home. Not only might the practice give users a chance to handle and inspect the sensors, but the task of installing sensors may provide them with a feeling of "ownership" of the entire system.

The promise of home health technology is that it may lead to low-cost solutions to help people stay healthy. If the systems cannot be self-installed and maintained, however, this potential may never be realized. Today, commercial sensor-based elder-monitoring and home security systems that require personalized design, installation, service, and maintenance have estimated annual costs of over $7500 [72]. This financial commitment dramatically limits adoption of the innovative services ubiquitous computing health technology researchers propose. Somehow, the system needs to provide immediate feedback and value, even during the installation process, so that the user will care that it is operating properly [56].

Question 9: How Does the User Know What Is Broken?

An insidious problem not yet addressed in the literature is how to inform the end user (or, for that matter, the expert) about what part of a context-aware system has broken down. Is the problem a broken sensor? A misplaced sensor? A bad activity example? Or is it something new in the environment? A missing sensor? Or simply a lack of sufficient training examples?

The literature provides no guidance for developers. Most statistical learning algorithms create models that are difficult to interpret by hand, let alone automatically. Models that often work well in practice, such as support vector machines, provide little information that can be used by the system to explain a result to a user. A valid criticism is that the models are "opaque and cannot be used to help understand the nature of the solution" [73]. More research on statistical models with an explanatory component is required. Even those that produce models that are somewhat easier to understand and sometimes considered interpretable, such as decision trees, in practice become unwieldy when paired with recognition in large, complex domains such as the home, and they typically generate models that an end user has difficulty understanding.

If the system cannot identify malfunctions for the user, it is exceedingly unlikely the user will be able to fix the problem. Further, if the developer does not provide the user with a model of the system's behavior, the user will develop a model of her own—correctly or, more likely than not, incorrectly, as did our participant using the medication adherence system. This may be the strongest argument for driving context detection system development from the user-centric point of view: A user who does not understand what the system is doing will make something up and begin changing behavior accordingly, in some cases possibly to the further detriment of overall system performance. One system we constructed, a language-learning tool that teaches users foreign words when they move objects with attached sensors, was designed explicitly so that interaction with the application itself creates opportunities for the end user to detect sensor problems [56]. A sensor system that supports language learning might also be appropriate for a context-aware health system.

Question 10: Can the User Make Instantaneous, Nonoscillating Fixes?

Our participant in the medication adherence system wanted to fix the system—immediately—without having to provide tens of examples of an activity. Not only did he have to be able to fix the system, however, he needed a fix that would not negatively impact what he may have fixed before. Example-based statistical learning algorithms do not have this property. In fact, as researchers working with the algorithms know, a new example can frustratingly undo prior good performance. This is unacceptable behavior from the user-centric point of view, but the research literature has yet to address it.

Question 11: What Will Keep the User's Mental Model in Line with the Algorithmic Model?

As discussed previously, engaging the user in the installation, training, and maintenance of a system (and making the behavior of the system sufficiently simple for this to be possible) will help keep the user's mental model of the system's expected behavior consistent with its actual behavior. In systems making health recommendations, lack of understanding of system behavior is likely to make the user dubious and distrustful of the information being presented [39], as we found with the pilot user of our medication adherence system. The system must build trust, not erode it, the longer it is used. An oscillating, unpredictable system will rapidly erode that trust.

Question 12: How Does a User Add a New Activity to Recognize?

Over time, users will want or need to add a new activity to be recognized by the system. What should be a basic requirement has been simply overlooked by the literature. No one knows the behavioral patterns observed in a specific home more intimately than the individuals who live and interact there on a daily basis. If a user understands what the sensors do at some basic level and grasps how activity recognition works well enough to keep the system running long term, adding a new activity (that does not corrupt the system's current working behavior) should not be difficult. In practice, however, achieving this will require innovation in activity recognition algorithms that have been proposed.

19.5 CONCLUSIONS

The twelve questions set out in this chapter were motivated by promising new context-aware health applications for embedded assessment in the home proposed by ubiquitous-computing and health technology researchers. If successful, these technologies may use automatic detection of context to help people live healthier, happier lives by monitoring for the onset of health conditions, helping them cope with chronic conditions, and providing just-in-time information that may help them stay healthy and fit as they age. While pilot projects have been described in the literature that show how sensor data can be used to infer information about everyday activities and how it can be applied to the design of user interfaces for health and wellness, they generally have not addressed the practical—and significant—barriers that must be overcome to make it possible to install, set up, and maintain such systems in actual home environments.

Overcoming these barriers is a significant challenge. In fact, we believe that developers of context detection algorithms for the home would benefit by shifting from an algorithmic to a user-centric point of view. System designers may need to think anew about the problem from installation up. How can the system be made sufficiently simple so that an end user can *incrementally* install the sensors? And how can the end user provide whatever models or training data the system requires to bootstrap itself? Once the system is working, how can the user adjust its performance without requiring any outside expertise? We encourage developers of the next generation of ubiquitous-computing home health technologies to adopt a user-centric versus an algorithmic perspective and to take up the challenge of creating systems designed for real-world deployment.

A cynic might argue that there is no way to achieve these goals, that it is not possible to produce home health technologies that rely on sophisticated, automatic context detection but which a nontechnical layperson can install, train, and maintain. Can we make such a technology so easy to master, so user-centric, that someone who is not technically inclined can benefit from it? If we cannot, we may still develop intellectually interesting context detection systems usable by a small percentage of the population, but perhaps we will have solved the wrong problem.

ACKNOWLEDGMENTS

This work was funded, in part, by National Science Foundation grant #0313065, Intel Corporation, and the MIT House_n Consortium.

The authors would like to thank Margaret Morris, Jennifer Beaudin, Jason Nawyn, and Fahd Albinali for their work on related research projects and many thoughtful discussions. Emmanuel Munguia Tapia and Kent Larson contributed to the design and deployment of tools used in this research. Finally, we would like to thank our research participant in the medication adherence study.

REFERENCES

[1] U.S. Census Bureau. U.S. Population Projections. 2008.

[2] National Institute of Population and Social Security Research. Population Projections for Japan: 2001–2050. 2002.

[3] Paré G, Jaana M, Sicotte C. Systematic review of home telemonitoring for chronic diseases: The evidence base. J Am Med Inform Assoc 2007;14:269–77.

[4] Abowd GD, Mynatt ED. Charting past, present, and future research in ubiquitous computing. ACM Transactions on Computer-Human Interaction 2000;7:29–58.

[5] Stern DJ. Behavioral telemonitoring: The next frontier of senior care management. Caring 27:26–9.

[6] Mynatt BD, Rogers WA. Developing technology to support the functional independence of older adults. Aging International 2002;27(Winter):24–41.

[7] Barger T, Brown D, Alwan M. Health status monitoring through analysis of behavioral patterns. In: Proceedings of the 8th Congress of the Italian Association for Artificial Intelligence (AI*IA) on Ambient Intelligence. Springer-Verlag; 2003. p. 22–7.

[8] Rowan J, Mynatt ED. Digital Family Portrait field trial: Support for aging in place. In: Proceedings of the SIGCHI Conference on Human Factors in Computing System. ACM Press; 2005. p. 521–30.

[9] Oulasvirta A, Raento M, Tiitta S. Context contacts: Re-designing Smartphone's contact book to support mobile awareness and collaboration. In: Proceedings of the 7th International Conference on Human–Computer Interaction with Mobile Devices and Services (MobileHCI'05). ACM Press; 2005. p. 167–74.

[10] Nagel KS, Hudson JM, Abowd G. Predictors of availability in home-life context mediated communication. In: Proceedings of Computer Supported Cooperative Work (CSCW). ACM Press; 2004. p. 497–506.

[11] Vurgun S, Philipose M, Pavel M. A statistical reasoning system for medication prompting. In: Proceedings of UbiComp 2007: Ubiquitous Computing. Springer; 2007.

[12] Davis KBL, Burgio L. Measuring problem behaviors in dementia: Developing a methodological agenda. Advances in Nursing Sciences 1997;20:40–55.

[13] Sixsmith A, Johnson N. A smart sensor to detect falls of the elderly. IEEE Pervasive Computing 2004;3:42–7.

[14] Nawyn J, Intille SS, Larson K. Embedding behavior modification strategies into consumer electronic devices. In: Proceedings of UbiComp 2006. Springer-Verlag; 2006. p. 297–314.

[15] Morris M, Intille SS, Beaudin JS. Embedded assessment: Over-coming barriers to early detection with pervasive computing. In: Proceedings of Pervasive 2005. Springer-Verlag; 2005. p. 333–46.

[16] Kaye J. Home-based technologies: A new paradigm for conducting dementia prevention trials. Alzheimer's and Dementia 2007;4:S60–6.

[17] Mynatt ED, Essa I, Rogers W. Increasing the opportunities for aging in place. In: Proceedings of the Conference on Universal Usability. 2000. p. 65–71.

[18] Munguia Tapia E, Intille SS, Larson K. Activity recognition in the home setting using simple and ubiquitous sensors. In: Proceedings of Pervasive 2004. Springer-Verlag; 2004. p. 158–75.

[19] Philipose M, Fishkin KP, Fox D, Kautz H, Patterson D, Perkowitz M. Guide: Towards understanding daily life via auto-identification and statistical analysis. In: Ubihealth 2003: The 2nd International Workshop on Ubiquitous Computing for Pervasive Healthcare Applications. 2003.

[20] Wilson D, Atkeson C. Automatic health monitoring using anonymous, binary sensors. In: CHI Workshop on Keeping Elders Connected, 2004. 2004.

[21] Matsouoka K. Smart house understanding human behaviors: Who did what, where, and when. In: Proceedings of the 8th World Multi-Conference on Systems, Cybernetics, and Informatics. 2004. p. 181–5.

[22] Haigh KZ, Kiff LM, Myers J, Guralnik V, Krichbaum K, Phelps J, et al. The Independent Life-Style AssistantTM (I.L.S.A.): Lessons Learned. Technical report. Honeywell Laboratories; 2003.

[23] Korhonen I, Paavilainen P, Sárelá A. Application of ubiquitous computing technologies for support of independent living of the elderly in real life settings. In: UbiHealth 2003: The 2nd International Workshop on Ubiquitous Computing for Pervasive Healthcare Applications. 2003.

[24] Mihailidis A, Carmichael B, Boger J, Fernie G. An intelligent environment to support aging-in-place, safety, and independence of older adults with dementia. In: UbiHealth 2003: The 2nd International Workshop on Ubiquitous Computing for Pervasive Healthcare Applications. 2003.

[25] Dockstader SL, Berg MJ, Tekalp AM. Stochastic kinematic modeling and feature extraction for gait analysis. IEEE Trans Image Process 2003;12:962–76.

[26] Patterson DJ, Liao L, Fox D, Kautz H. Inferring high-level behavior from low-level sensors. In: Proceedings of Ubicomp 2003. Springer-Verlag; 2003. p. 73–89.

[27] Jimison HB, Pavel M, Pauel J, McKanna J. Home monitoring of computer interactions for the early detection of cognitive decline. In: Proceedings of the IEEE Engineering in Medicine and Biology Conference. 2004. p. 4533–6.

[28] Madsen LB, Kirkegaard P, Pedersen EB. Blood pressure control during telemonitoring of home blood pressure: A randomized controlled trial during 6 months. Blood Press 2008;17:78–86.

[29] Alwan M, Dalal S, Mack D, Kell S, Turner B, Leachtenauer J, et al. Impact of monitoring technology in assisted living: Outcome pilot. IEEE Trans Inf Technol Biomed 2006;10:192–8.

[30] Virone G, Alwan M, Dalal S, Kell SW, Turner B, Stankovic JA, et al. Behavioral patterns of older adults in assisted living. IEEE Trans Inf Technol Biomed 2008;12:387–98.

[31] Intille SS. A new research challenge: Persuasive technology to motivate healthy aging. IEEE Trans Inf Technol Biomed 2004;8:235–7.

[32] Pollack ME, Brown L, Colbry D, McCarthy CE, Orosz C, Peintner B, et al. Autominder: An intelligent cognitive orthotic system for people with memory impairment. Robotics and Autonomous Systems 2003;44:273–82.

[33] Floerkemeier C, Siegemund F. Improving the effectiveness of medical treatment with pervasive computing technologies. In: UbiHealth 2003: The 2nd International Workshop on Ubiquitous Computing for Pervasive Healthcare Applications. 2003.

[34] Morris M, Lundell J, Dishman E. Ubiquitous computing for mild cognitive impairment: A prototype for embedded assessment and rehearsal. Gerontologist 2003;43(403).

[35] Morris M, Lundell J, Dishman E. Computing for social connectedness. In: Proceedings of CHI. 2004. p. 1151.

[36] Morris ME. Social networks as health feedback displays. IEEE Internet Computing 2005;9:29–37.

[37] Fogg BJ. Persuasive technologies. Communications of the ACM 1999;42:27–9.

[38] Consolvo S, Everitt K, Smith I, Landay JA. Design requirements for technologies that encourage physical activity. In: Proceedings of the SIGCHI Conference on Human Factors in Computing Systems. ACM Press; 2006. p. 457–66.

[39] Fogg BJ, Tseng H. The elements of computer credibility. In: Proceedings of the CHI 99 Conference on Human Factors in Computing Systems. 1999. p. 80–7.

[40] Tapia EM, Intille SS, Larson K. Portable wireless sensors for object usage sensing in the home: Challenges and practicalities. In: Proceedings of the European Ambient Intelligence Conference 2007. Springer-Verlag; 2007. p. 19–37.

[41] Munguia Tapia E, Intille SS, Lopez L, Larson K. The design of a portable kit of wireless sensors for naturalistic data collection, In: Fishkin KP, Schiele B, Nixon P, Quigley A, editors. Proceedings of Pervasive 2006. LNCS, Vol. 3968. Springer-Verlag; 2006. p. 117–34.

[42] Intille SS, Larson K, Munguia Tapia E, Beaudin J, Kaushik P, Nawyn J, et al. Using a live-in laboratory for ubiquitous computing research. In: Proceedings of Pervasive 2006. Springer-Verlag; 2006. p. 349–65.

[43] Kaushik P, Intille SS, Larsen K. User-adaptive reminders for home-based medical tasks. A case study. Methods Inf Med 2008;47:203–7.

[44] Edwards WK, Grinter RE. At home with ubiquitous computing: Seven challenges. In: Proceedings of the Conference on Ubiquitous Computing. 2001. p. 256–72.

[45] Patel K, Fogarty J, Landay JA, Harrison B. Examining difficulties software developers encounter in the adoption of statistical machine learning. In: Proceedings of the Association for the Advancement of Artificial Intelligence. AAAI Press; 2008. p. 1563–6.

[46] Bellotti VM, Back MJ, Edwards WK, Grinter RE, Lopes CV, Henderson A. Making sense of sensing systems: Five questions for designers and researchers. In: ACM Conference on Human Factors in Computing Systems. ACM Press; 2002. p. 415–22.

[47] Kismel J, Lundell J. Exploring the nuances of Murphy's Law—long-term deployments of pervasive technology into the homes of older adults. Interactions 2007;14:38–41.

[48] Philipose M. Large-scale human activity recognition using ultra-dense sensing. In: Proceedings of the U.S. Frontiers of Engineering Symposium Presentations 35.

[49] Smith JR, Fishkin KP, Jiang B, Mamishev A, Philipose M, Rea AD, et al. RFID-based techniques for human activity detection. In: Communications of the ACM Special Issue: RFID: Tagging the World. 2005. p. 39–44.

[50] Patel S, Truong K, Abowd G. PowerLine positioning: A practical sub-room-level indoor location system for domestic use. In: Proceedings of UbiComp 2006. Springer-Verlag; 2006. p. 441–58.

[51] Lifton J, Feldmeier M, Ono Y, Lewis C, Paradiso JA. A platform for ubiquitous sensor deployment in occupational and domestic environments. In: Proceedings of the International Conference on Information Processing in Sensor Networks (IPSN). 2007. p. 119–27.

[52] Fogarty J, Au C, Hudson SE. Sensing from the basement: A feasibility study of unobtrusive and low-cost home activity recognition. In: Proceedings of the Nineteenth Annual ACM Symposium on User Interface Software and Technology (UIST'06). 2006. p. 91–100.

[53] Beckmann C, Consolvo S, LaMarca A. Some assembly required: Supporting end-user sensor installation in domestic ubiquitous computing environments. In: Proceedings of UbiComp 2004. Springer-Verlag; 2004. p. 107–24.

[54] Rodden T, Crabtree A, Hemmings T, Koleva B, Humble J, Åkesson KP, et al. Between the dazzle of a new building and its eventual corpse: Assembling the ubiquitous home. In: Proceedings of the 2004 Conference on Designing Interactive Systems: Processes, Practices, Methods, and Techniques. ACM Press; 2004. p. 71–80.

[55] Fishkin KP, Philipose M, Rea A. Hands-on RFID: Wireless wearables for detecting use of objects. In: Proceedings of the Ninth IEEE International Symposium on Wearable Computers. IEEE Press; 2005. p. 38–41.

[56] Beaudin JS, Intille SS, Munguia Tapia E, Rockinson R, Morris M. Context-sensitive microlearning of foreign language vocabulary on a mobile device. In: Proceedings of the European Ambient Intelligence Conference 2007. Springer-Verlag; 2007. p. 55–72.

[57] Wu T-Y, Lian C-C, Hsu JY J. Joint recognition of multiple concurrent activities using factorial conditional random fields. In: Proceedings of the AAAI Workshop on Plan, Activity, and Intent Recognition. 2007.

[58] Aipperspach R, Cohen E, Canny J. Modeling human behavior from simple sensors in the home. In: Proceedings of Pervasive. Springer-Verlag; 2006. p. 337–48.

[59] Wilson DH, Atkeson C. Simultaneous tracking and activity recognition (STAR) using many anonymous, binary sensors. In: Proceedings of Pervasive. Springer-Verlag; 2005. p. 62–79.

[60] Hao Hu D, Pan SJ, Zheng VW, Liu NN, Yang Q. Real world activity recognition with multiple goals. In: Proceedings of the 10th International Conference on Ubiquitous Computing. ACM Press; 2008. p. 30–9.

[61] Philipose M, Fishkin KP, Perkowitz M, Patterson DJ, Fox D, Kautz H. Inferring activities from interactions with objects. IEEE Pervasive Computing 2004;3:50-7.

[62] Huynh TA, Fritz M, Schiele B. Discovery of activity patterns using topic models. In: Proceedings of the 10th International Conference on Ubiquitous Computing. ACM Press; 2008. p. 10-9.

[63] Perkowitz M, Philipose M, Patterson DJ, Fishkin K. Mining models of human activities from the Web. In: Proceedings of The Thirteenth International World Wide Web Conference (WWW'04). ACM Press; 2004. p. 573-82.

[64] Whitley BE. Principles of Research in Behavioral Science. 2nd ed. McGraw-Hill; 2002.

[65] Barrett LF, Barrett DJ. An introduction to computerized experience sampling in psychology. Social Science Computer Review 2001;19:175-85.

[66] Intille SS, Rondoni J, Kukla C, Anacona I, Bao L. A context-aware experience sampling tool. In: Proceedings of CHI'03, Extended Abstracts on Human Factors in Computing Systems. ACM Press; 2003. p. 972-3.

[67] van Kasteren T, Noulas A, Englebienne G, Kröse B. Accurate activity recognition in a home setting. In: Proceedings of the 10th International Conference on Ubiquitous Computing. ACM Press; 2008. p. 1-9.

[68] Sohn T, Dey A. iCAP: An informal tool for interactive prototyping of context-aware applications. In: Proceedings of CHI'03, Extended Abstracts on Human Factors in Computing Systems. ACM Press; 2003. p. 974-5.

[69] Logan B, Healey J, Philipose M, Munguia Tapia E, Intille S. A long-term evaluation of sensing modalities for activity recognition. In: Proceedings of the International Conference on Ubiquitous Computing. Springer-Verlag; 2007. p. 483-500.

[70] Modayil J, Bai T, Kautz H. Improving the recognition of interleaved activities. In: Proceedings of the 10th International Conference on Ubiquitous Computing. ACM Press; 2008. p. 40-3.

[71] Nielsen J. Heuristic evaluation. In: Nielsen J, Mack RL, editors. Usability Inspection Methods. John Wiley & Sons; 1994. p. 25-61.

[72] Scheschareg R. Delivering advanced home healthcare products and services through the home installer and integrator channel. In: Proceedings of the Healthcare Unbound Conference. 2006.

[73] Witten IH, Frank E. Data Mining: Practical Machine Learning Tools and Techniques with Java Implementations. Morgan Kaufmann; 1999.

Epilogue: Challenges and Outlook

This book explored the multidisciplinary area of human-centric interfaces for ambient intelligence, which focuses on the concepts and technologies that provide services by understanding user needs and intentions through a network of interconnected sensors in a smart environment. By offering a collection of related work in visual interfaces, speech and dialogue management systems, and multimodal interfaces and applications, the book aimed to provide a perspective on the academic research and industrial development now being carried out.

Like ambient intelligence (AmI), human-centric interfaces offer a variety of interdisciplinary topics for development. Besides interface design based on the modalities discussed here, topics from related disciplines demand further investigation—handling privacy concerns; adaptation to user availability, preferences, or limitations, knowledge accumulation and user behavior modeling, modes of communication between users in a social network setting, and the study of behavior change caused by the technology.

Human-centric interface technology presents social implications that must be carefully addressed in order to make AmI systems widely accepted by users. For example, if cameras are used to track user activity, it is essential to guarantee that there is no unauthorized use of the image data captured.

A number of challenges need to be addressed in the design and deployment of interface systems for ambient intelligence. One is the lack of standards and validation tools that can offer uniformity in system implementation. A number of projects co-funded by the European Commission are addressing this need by developing a middleware that allows developers to interconnect heterogeneous physical devices in their applications by means of easy-to-use Web interfaces.

Another area of development is the enhancement of core technologies to make systems more usable under real-world conditions. One example, in vision and visual interfaces, is the need for real-time techniques that can register and interpret user activities and natural gesture–based intentions. Robustness in natural environments and ease of setup and operation are among the basic requirements for systems and processing algorithms.

Such techniques also need to pay close attention to user preferences regarding privacy and modes of visual communication with the outside world. An important aspect of technology development for human-centric interfaces is the implication that user preferences can have for applications that place the user in a social networking context through communication links. Figure 1 illustrates the relationship between human-centric interface technology and user acceptance in developing applications. Systems that are aware of and responsive to users and context may

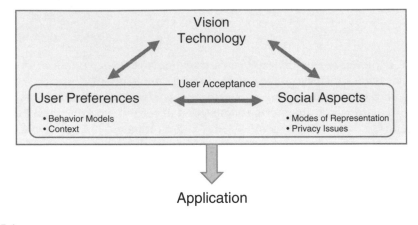

FIGURE 1

Influence of user preferences and social aspects on technology design.

need different kinds of processing algorithms when the privacy settings change, when the user changes the mode of availability to the outside world, or when the system detects a change of context. It is thus of paramount practical importance for system and algorithm designers to consider user acceptance in their development cycle.

Related to the processing of data acquired by the user interface module is how such information can direct the visualization module to the modes of availability, and how the data is rendered to the user or to the outside world. Creating an interface layer between these two modules is an objective of future development. This layer can be employed to register user preferences and availability and thus to determine the visualization module's action. It can also use observation history to evaluate the confidence of the current observation reported by the processing module. Figure 2 illustrates the various components of these modules.

Regarding speech processing and dialogue management, besides improvement in the technological state of the art, new evaluation methods are needed. This is so because automatic speech recognition is very much influenced by a number of factors for which performance metrics are hard to define, such as speaker accent, false starts, vocabulary sets, speaking styles, acoustic conditions, and noise. As speech recognition is the basis of a speech-based system, the performance of this module is critical because it impacts the operation of the system as a whole.

The goal of spoken language understanding is to extract semantic and pragmatic information from a speaker's utterances. Though straightforward for humans most of the time, this is a difficult task for a speech understanding system, which must deal with the classical problems related to natural language processing—resolution of anaphora, ellipsis, and ambiguity, among others. In addition, the errors made by the speech recognition module can cause insertion, deletion, or substitution of words in the recognized sentence, making it wrongly formed or grammatically

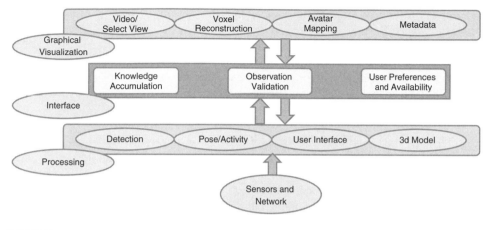

FIGURE 2

Interfacing between the processing and graphical visualization modules.

incorrect. Because of the complexity of the problem, satisfactory results are nowadays obtained if the understanding system is employed in simple domains.

In a speech-based system, the dialogue manager decides the next action to be taken by the computer in carrying out a particular task. A typical action is querying a database for information requested by the user. Other actions include prompting the user for additional data necessary to complete the query and confirming words provided by the speech recognition module. The overall goal is to make the interaction with the computer as natural and friendly as possible. This requires extensive expertise and effort from the designer to make the interaction acceptable, given that many users reject these systems because of their limitations. The list of current topics for enhancing dialogue management includes handling user emotions, user simulation, and user modeling.

The speech synthesizer, the final module of a speech-based system, produces the computer's voice for communicating with the user. A number of speech synthesis techniques can be employed to carry out this task (e.g., parametric, concatenative, formant-based, and articulatory synthesis). For many applications, the one most often employed is text-to-speech (TTS) synthesis, which transforms into voice any sentence in text format created by a natural language generation module. The list of topics of current interest includes adapting the synthesized output to different environments and user needs, and enhancing the naturalness of the generated voice, especially including emotional features, to make it more pleasant to the ear.

Visual and audio stimuli are valuable means of interaction between a smart environment and its users. Any technology that can facilitate this interaction is worth considering. Some methods are popular and appear convenient to most users; others may be challenged by different target users' preferences and needs. So far, the most common interaction options based on vision and image processing focus on the analysis of body posture, gaze, and facial expressions. These features facilitate the understanding of important dimensions like action, behavior, intention, and mood.

Research on sound (e.g., speech recognition and dialogue understanding) has also been conducted intensively for many years. Advances in this area have enlightened the development of new systems that can sustain spoken interaction, understand the context based on the sounds that emanate from such interaction, and take into account the emotions perceived from human speech.

While video and audio interactions are predominant, there are other options to consider. One, tactile interaction, is feasible in a number of ways. Users can choose options on a screen, for example, or they can use a joystick, a digital pen, or other device to express their choices (e.g., a joystick can be used not only in computer games but also to guide a robot wheelchair). Alternatively, wearable and handheld devices (which are very popular in virtual reality contexts) can be used to give commands to the computer (think of the Wii mote, where the user's movements are registered by the console). Biometric information can also be used by humans and computers to interact—for example, voice, iris, and fingerprint interpretation for identification purposes.

The integration of different subsets of these interaction modes is an important challenge ahead. While progress has been made in the last decade on integrating some elements (typically vision and sound), there is still much to be achieved in terms of integration efficacy. Sensor fusion is currently a popular topic. The problem of aligning inputs from different sensing devices acquired independently remains a formidable task.

A need exists for a flexible set of options from which the user can choose the best one in a particular situation. Besides a user-selectable mode of availability, the list of options should include a way for the user to decide how to interact with the system and which interaction media to use.

As for future smart environment applications, it is conceivable that, for many of them, a combination of interfacing mechanisms will be involved not only to offer a variety of services in the same environment but also to allow users to express their feedback and preferences to the system in a natural way. This requires methods to obtain implicit input from users as they perform their daily routines.

In smart environment applications, the output of the interface system and the processing module feeds into a high-level reasoning module, which further interprets the user's state relative to the knowledge base and the contextual information, and into a graphical visualization module, which produces the desired type and rendering of information to the user or to others. Interface layers between the data acquisition/processing unit and the high-level reasoning and visualization modules need to be developed. These interface layers can also provide a real-time instruction and feedback path to the sensing and interfacing module for better processing of the acquired data.

If smart environment applications are going to be adopted by the world to the extent so eloquently portrayed by Weiser's metaphor of the "disappearing computer," their interfaces must be human-centric. The technology deployed in homes and public spaces will not become "transparent" if the user has to go to a great deal of effort to interact with a system in order to obtain a benefit from it. Consider a common source of consumer complaint: having to read a lengthy manual to understand how to use a domestic appliance. Users feel disappointed when they can only use a few basic features of an expensive gadget they have purchased. Analogously, only through a concrete and comprehensive study of the fundamental principles of user satisfaction will the field of ambient intelligence flourish. Human-centric interfaces will be instrumental in its success.

We hope this book achieved its objective of introducing to its readers the exciting area of human-centric interfaces and thus stimulating new ideas, approaches, and techniques in the development of ambient intelligence applications. Moreover, we hope that the material covered, and the multidisciplinary nature of many potential applications, will encourage cooperation among academia and industry—a crucial factor in achieving the potential of this technology in the years to come.

Hamid Aghajan,
Ramón López-Cózar Delgado,
and Juan Carlos Augusto

Index

Note: Page numbers followed by *f* indicate figures; *t* indicate tables.

511